Fodor's 93
Scotland

D1316519

Fodor's Travel Publications, Inc.
New York • Toronto • London • Sydney • Auckland

Fodor's Scotland

Editor: Caroline V. Haberfeld
Area Editor: Gilbert Summers
Contributors: Dave Albury, Anita Guerrini, John Hutchinson, Beth Ingpen, Moira MacDonald, Marcy Pritchard
Creative Director: Fabrizio La Rocca
Cartographers: David Lindroth, Mapping Specialists
Illustrator: Karl Tanner
Cover Photograph: Catherine Karnow

Design: Vignelli Associates

Special Sales

Fodor's Travel Publications are available at special discounts for bulk purchases (100 copies or more) for sales promotions or premiums. Special editions, including personalized covers, excerpts of existing guides, and corporate imprints, can be created in large quantities for special needs. For more information write to Special Marketing, Fodor's Travel Publications, 201 East 50th Street, New York, NY 10022. Inquiries from Canada should be sent to Random House of Canada, Ltd., Marketing Department, 1265 Aerowood Drive, Mississauga, Ontario L4W 1B9. Inquiries from the United Kingdom should be sent to Fodor's Travel Publications, 20 Vauxhall Bridge Road, London, England SW1V 2SA.

MANUFACTURED IN THE UNITED STATES OF AMERICA
10 9 8 7 6 5 4 3 2 1

Contents

Maps

Contents

Foreword

While every care has been taken to ensure the accuracy of the information in this guide, the passage of time will always bring change, and consequently, the publisher cannot accept responsibility for errors that may occur.

All prices and opening times quoted here are based on information supplied to us at press time. Hours and admission fees may change, however, and the prudent traveler will avoid inconvenience by calling ahead.

Fodor's wants to hear about your travel experiences, both pleasant and unpleasant. When a hotel or restaurant fails to live up to its billing, let us know and we will investigate the complaint and revise our entries where the facts warrant it.

Send your letters to the editors of Fodor's Travel Publications, 201 E. 50th Street, New York, NY 10022.

Highlights'93 and Fodor's Choice

Highlights '93

Tourism Developments Scottish tourism is big business. The most recent figures available indicate that it is worth £1.4 billion to the Scottish economy annually. Small wonder that the network of tourist information centers in Scotland (almost 200 in 1993) probably offers the best service of any European country. The U.S. market is important enough to the Scottish Tourist Board for it to continue to expand its educational program for U.S.-based travel agents. Originally written by Edinburgh University, the course offers an opportunity to become a SCOTS—specialist counselor on tourism in Scotland. With 1,250 agents intended to be in post by 1993, you are never far from a SCOTS agent. So, when you inquire about a Scottish vacation, make certain that you are dealing with a SCOTS—it is a sure way to get the best advice from someone who knows Scotland and has undergone extensive training.

Transportation As the 1990s roll on, it seems to be even easier to reach Scotland. If you insist on flying to London, England, first (and, the Scots would say, spend too much while in the expensive south), you can get to Scotland by any one of a number of airlines whose fares remain pretty competitive; there are, for instance, some bargains to be had on the Dan Air services to Inverness. If you wisely choose to fly directly to Glasgow, however, then you will find Glasgow Airport busily upgrading in 1993 to give international passengers even better service. (The airport increased its space for passengers by 70% in 1992.) Eventually, the airport will have the capacity to handle about 10 million passengers each year. With Loch Lomond and the Highlands only half an hour away by car, downtown Glasgow about the same distance, and Edinburgh barely an hour farther, the "Gateway Glasgow" option is an excellent choice for visitors who wish to maximize their time in Scotland.

Accommodations The Scottish Tourist Board was the first tourism authority in the United Kingdom to launch an inspection scheme for accommodations, which includes an assessment of an establishment's quality as well as its facilities. (After all, you might like to know that a hotel has a night porter, but it is actually more useful to know if he is helpful or bad tempered!) This inspection scheme has been so successful that more than a thousand establishments are now checked annually (or graded and classified, as the board calls it).

The facilities are rated by crown symbols. The more crowns, the better equipped the facility. But the important point is the grade. New for 1993 is the introduction of a "Deluxe" grade. That is the top award and means that you can expect something very special. The other grades, in order of excellence, are "Highly Commended" (very good), "Commended" (good), and "Approved" (OK, but nothing startling). Remember that you are probably better off in a De-Luxe or Highly Commended one-crown establishment than in an Approved three-crown establishment. So far, only a handful of businesses have won the De-Luxe award, notably the Caledonian Hotel in Edinburgh.

Another shortcut to the best of Scotland's accommodations is to choose a hotel that is a member of Scotland's Commended Country Hotels and Inns (tel. 0349/64040). This is an association of independently owned hotels that pride themselves in offering the sought-after combination of value for your money with a high standard of comfort. All are participants in the Scottish Tourist Board's quality evaluation scheme described above, and many of them are set in very scenic rural locations.

On the budget front, the number of bed-and-breakfasts with private facilities continues to increase, often at prices that cannot be matched by hotels. Many of them offer evening meals or, if not, usually have a selection of menus from local eating places and will happily give advice. Very often, they will serve tea and home-baked biscuits later in the evening as a kind of snack-supper. Remember to check out the grading of these places, as described above. They may have only one or two crowns, but the best of them will be at least Commended, if not higher.

Events and Attractions This is not a particularly good anniversary year for Scotland, though 1993 is the 150th anniversary of the death of Charles Macintosh (1766–1843). He invented the garment that bears his name, updated versions of which should be in every traveler's luggage, just in case. (It is unlikely that the tourism authorities would want to be reminded of this fact!)

This year will see the continued expansion of Stirling's summer program of historical theater. Already proving very popular, the setting of Stirling Castle and the Old Town below comes alive with the reenactment of historic incidents from Scotland's history; the use of professional actors in a variety of locations throughout the town is a memorable experience. Stirling Castle was the chief seat of the Stewart monarchs of Scotland. This is also the first full season of the Scottish Wool Centre at Aberfoyle, southern gateway to the beautiful Trossachs area, only a few minutes from Stirling. This major development portrays the wool and textile industry in Scotland from its domestic origins to the present day. It is also typical of the new kind of sophisticated visitor center now springing up in Scotland. It presents "The Story of Scottish Wool" in a 150-seat covered arena. There is also a cashmere kids' farm and "hands-on" opportunities to try carding, spinning, and weaving, as well as demonstrations of sheep shearing and working sheepdogs. A children's adventure playground, shop, and restaurant complete the entertainment.

Fodor's Choice

No two people will agree on what makes a perfect vacation, but it can be fun and helpful to know what others think. We hope you'll have a chance to experience some of Fodor's Choices yourself while visiting Scotland. For detailed information on individual entries, see the relevant sections of this guidebook.

Sights to Remember

Edinburgh Castle at night, illuminated by floodlights

The view of Princes Street in Edinburgh from Calton Hill

The view of Loch Lomond from the top of Duncryne Hill, Gartocharn (Central Highlands)

The Cuillin Hills seen from Sligachan, Isle of Skye (Northern Highlands)

Scott's view of the Eildon Hills (Borders)

The Falls of Clyde at New Lanark (Glasgow)

The heather in full bloom in Glen Shee (Central Highlands) or in Deeside (Aberdeen)

Times to Remember

The train ride from Fort William to Mallaig (Argyll)

Meeting "King James IV of Scotland" in the Great Hall of Stirling Castle during the summer theater program in Stirling (Central Highlands)

Hearing the one o'clock gun on Princes Street in Edinburgh

Having an entire sandy beach to oneself on Harris in the Outer Hebrides (Northern Highlands)

Tasting Lagavulin single-malt whiskey in a pub on the island of Islay (Argyll and the Isles)

Watching a herd of red deer graze by the roadside at Glen Muck, near Ballater (Aberdeen)

Buildings and Monuments

Castle Campbell, Ochil Hills, near Stirling (Central Highlands)

The facade of Marischal College, Aberdeen

The Black House at Arnol, the Isle of Lewis in the Outer Hebrides (Northern Highlands)

The Georgian House, Edinburgh

Traquair House, near Walkerburn (Borders)

The Standing Stones of Callanish, Lewis (Northern Highlands)

Mellerstain House (Borders)

Torosay House, Isle of Mull (Argyll and the Isles)

Blair Castle (Central Highlands)

Scenic Drives

The road west of Aberdeen into Royal Deeside, on either bank of the River Dee (Aberdeen)

The east bank of Loch Ness, from Fort Augustus to Inverness via Dores (Around the Great Glen)

The route between Brig o' Turk and Aberfoyle in the Trossachs (Central Highlands)

The Drumbeg road, north of Lochinver (Northern Highlands)

Parks and Gardens

The rock garden at the Royal Botanic Gardens in Edinburgh

The rhododendron gardens at Brodick Castle, Isle of Arran (Glasgow)

The wooded vistas of Castle Kennedy Gardens (Southwest)

The Japanese pond at Kildrummy Castle Gardens (Aberdeen)

Crathes Castle Gardens, Deeside (Aberdeen)

Logan Botanic Gardens (Southwest)

Hotels

The Caledonian, Edinburgh (*Very Expensive*)

Cameron House, Balloch, Central Highlands (*Expensive–Very Expensive*)

Auchterarder House, Auchterarder, Central Highlands (*Expensive*)

Roman Camp Hotel, Callander, Central Highlands (*Moderate–Expensive*)

Cringletie House, Peebles, Borders (*Moderate*)

The Holly Tree, Kentallen, Argyll (*Moderate*)

Restaurants

The Ubiquitous Chip, Glasgow (*Very Expensive*)

Auchterarder House, Auchterarder, Central Highlands (*Expensive*)

The Cellar, Anstruther, Fife (*Expensive*)

The Old Monastery, Buckie, Aberdeen (*Expensive*)

Broughton's, Blair Drummond, Central Highlands (*Moderate*)

The Kalpna, Edinburgh (*Inexpensive–Moderate*)

Museums and Visitor Centers

Fife Folk Museum, Ceres (Fife)

Auchendrain Farming Museum (Argyll)

Scottish Museum of Woollen Textiles, Walkerburn (Borders)

Kirkcaldy Museum and Art Gallery (Fife)

Paisley Museum (Glasgow)

Scottish Fisheries Museum (Fife)

Highland Folk Museum, Kingussie, near Aviemore (Around the Great Glen)

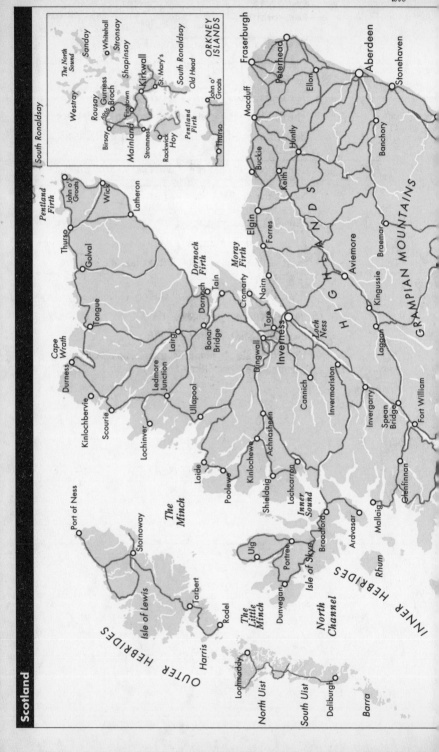

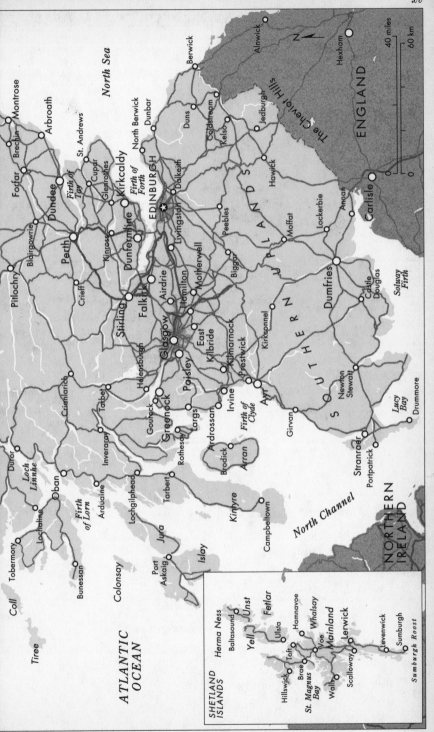

ICELAND

⊛ Reykjavik

NORWAY
Bergen○

SCOTLAND

NORTHERN
IRELAND

⊛ Edinburgh

*North
Sea*

Skagerrat

⊛ Belfast

IRELAND   *Irish
Sea*   GREAT

Dublin ⊛   BRITAIN

DENMARK

WALES   ENGLAND

Hamburg○

HOLLAND
Amsterdam⊛
The Hague○   ⊛
Rotterdam○

Cardiff ⊛

London ⊛

*ATLANTIC
OCEAN*

English Channel

Brussels ⊛
BELGIUM   Bonn○
Paris ⊛   Frankfurt●
LUXEMBOURG

GERM

FRANCE   Zürich○   Munich○
Bern ⊛   Salzburg○
SWITZERLAND
LIECHTENSTEIN

Lyon○
Milan○   Venice

PORTUGAL

⊛ Madrid

Nice○
Marseille○   Monaco
Florence○

ANDORRA

⊛ Lisbon

SPAIN

○ Barcelona   *Corsica*

Seville○   ○Granada   *Balearic
Islands*   *Sardinia*

Tyrrhenian

Gibraltar○   *Mediterranean Sea*

MOROCCO   ALGERIA

0   400 miles

0   600 km

TUNISIA

World Time Zones

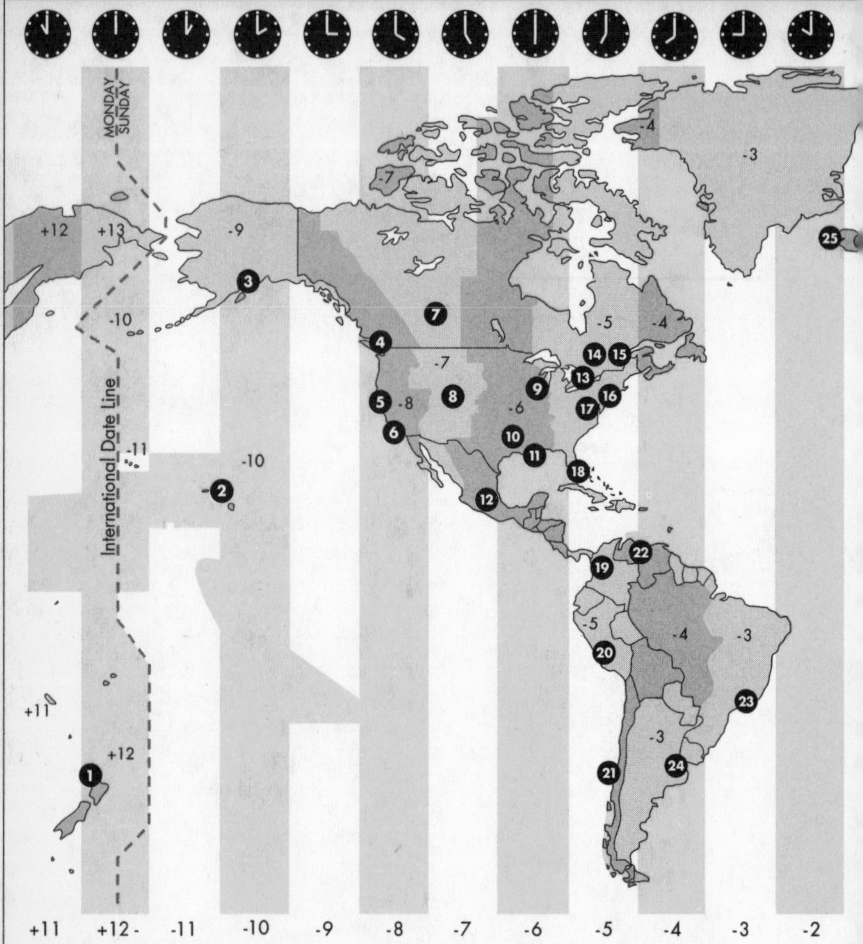

MONDAY
SUNDAY

+12 +13

International Date Line

-9

-10

-11

-10

+11

+12

-4

-3

-5 -4

-7

-8 -6

-5

-4 -3

-5

-4

-3

-3

25

| +11 | +12 - | -11 | -10 | -9 | -8 | -7 | -6 | -5 | -4 | -3 | -2 |

Numbers below vertical bands relate each zone to Greenwich Mean Time (0 hrs.).
Local times frequently differ from these general indications,
as indicated by light-face numbers on map.

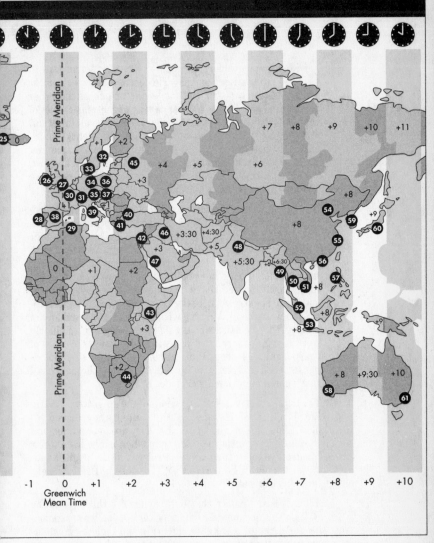

Introduction

On some old recordings of Scottish songs still in circulation you may run across *Roamin' in the Gloamin'* or *I Love a Lassie* or one of the other comic ditties of Harry Lauder, a star of the music halls of the 1920s. With his garish kilt, short crooked walking stick, rich rolling "R"s and *pawky* (cheerfully impudent) humor, chiefly based on the alleged meanness of the Scots, he impressed the Scottish character on the world. But his was, needless to say, a false impression and one the Scots have been trying to stamp out ever since.

How, then, do you characterize the Scots? Temperamentally, they are a mass of contradictions. They have been likened, not to a Scotch egg, but to a soft-boiled egg: a dour hard shell, a mushy middle. The Scots laugh and weep with almost Latin facility, but to strangers they are reserved, noncommittal, in no hurry to make an impression. Historically, fortitude and resilience have been their hallmarks, and there are streaks of both resignation and pitiless ferocity in their makeup, warring with sentimentality and love of family. Very Scottish was the instant reaction of an elderly woman of Edinburgh 200 years ago, when news arrived of the defeat in Mysore in India and of the Scottish soldiers being fettered in irons, two by two: "God help the puir chiel that's chained tae oor Davie."

The Scots are in general suspicious of the go-getter. "Whizz kid" is a term of contempt. But they are by no means plodders, though it is true to say that they are determined and thorough, respecting success only when it has been a few hundred years in the making. Praise of some bright ambitious youngster is quenched with the sneer: "Him? Ah kent (knew) his faither."

Yet this is the nation that built commerce throughout the British Empire, opened wild territories, and was responsible for much of mankind's scientific and technological advancement, a nation boastful about things it is not too good at and shamefacedly modest about genuine achievements. Consider the following extract from a handout about the Edinburgh School of Medicine: "If one excepts a few discoveries such as that of 'fixed air' by Black, of the diverse functions of the nerve-roots by Bell, of the anaesthetic properties of chloroform by Simpson, of the invention of certain powerful drugs by Christison and of the importance of antiseptic procedures by Lister, the influence of Edinburgh medicine has been of a steady constructive rather than a revolutionary type."

Among things that strike most newcomers to Scotland are the generosity of the Scots; their obsession with respectability; their satisfaction with themselves and their desire to stay as they are; and, above all, their passionate love of Scotland. An obstinate refusal to go along with English ideas has led to accusations that the nation has a head-in-the-sand attitude toward progress. But the Scots have their own ideas of progress, and they jealously guard the institutions that remain unique to them.

When it comes to education, Scotland has a proud record. The nation boasted four universities—St. Andrews, Aberdeen, Glasgow, and Edinburgh—when England had only two: Oxford and Cambridge. The *lad o' pairts* (man of talents)—the poor child of a feckless father and a fiercely self-sacrificing mother, sternly tutored by the village *dominie* (schoolmaster) and turned loose at the age of 13 with so firm a base of learning that he rose to the very top of his profession—this type of lad is a phenomenon of Scottish social history. The sacrifices that boys made as a matter of course to further their education are an old Scottish tradition. "Meal Monday," the long midsemester holiday at a Scottish university, is a survivor of the long weekend that once enabled students to return to their distant homes—on foot—and replenish the sack of "meal" (oatmeal) that was their only subsistence.

I t is a British cliché that an English education teaches you to think and a Scottish education stuffs your head with information. The average Scot does appear to be better informed than his English neighbor and to discuss facts rather than ideas. Scots pride themselves on their international outlook and on being better linguists than the English. The Scots get on well with foreigners, and they offer strangers a kindly welcome and a civility not often found in the modern world.

Just as the Scots have their own traditions in education, so is their legal system distinct from England's. In England the police both investigate crime and prosecute suspects. In Scotland there is a public prosecutor directly responsible to the Lord Advocate (equivalent to England's Attorney General), who is himself accountable to Parliament.

For the most part, however, you will notice few practical differences except in terminology. The barrister in England becomes an advocate in Scotland. Law-office nameplates designate their occupants "S.S.C." (Solicitor to the Supreme Court) or "W.S." (Writer to the Signet); cases for prosecution go before the "procurator fiscal" and are tried by the "sheriff" or "sheriff-substitute." The terms are different in England, and procedures are slightly different, too, for Scotland is one of the few countries that still bases its legal system on the old Roman law.

Crimes with picturesque names from ancient times remain on the statute book: *hamesucken*, for example, means assaulting a person in his home. In criminal cases Scotland adds to "Guilty" and "Not Guilty" a third verdict: "Not Proven." This, say the cynics, signifies "Don't do it again."

The Presbyterian Church of Scotland—the "Kirk"—is entirely independent of the Church of England. Until the 20th century it was a power in the land and did much to shape Scottish character. There are still those who can remember when the minister visited houses like an inquisitor and put members of the families through their catechism, punishing or reprimanding those who were not word-perfect. On Sunday morning the elders patrolled the streets, ordering people into church and rebuking those who sat at home in their gardens.

Religion in Scotland, as elsewhere, has lost much of its grip. But the Kirk remains influential in rural districts, where Kirk officials are pillars of local society. Ministers and their wives are seen in all their somber glory in Edinburgh in springtime, when the General Assembly of the Kirk takes place, and, for a week or more, Scottish newspapers devote several column-inches daily to the deliberations.

The Episcopalian Church of Scotland has bishops, as its name implies (unlike the Kirk, where the ministers are all equal), and a more colorful ritual. Considered genteel, Episcopalianism in Scotland has been described rather sourly by the Scottish novelist Lewis Grassie Gibbon as "more a matter of social status than theological conviction . . . , a grateful bourgeois acknowledgment of anglicisation."

Of the various nonconformist offshoots of the established Kirk, the Free Kirk of Scotland is the largest. It remains faithful to the monolithic unity of its forefathers, promoting the grim discipline that John Knox promoted long ago. The Free Kirk is strong in parts of the Outer Hebrides—Lewis, Harris, and North Uist. On Sunday in these areas no buses run, all the shops are shut, and there is a general atmosphere of a people cowering under the wrath of God. Among the fishing communities, especially those of the Northeast from Buckie to Peterhead, evangelical movements, such as the Close Brethren and Jehovah's Witnesses, have made impressive inroads.

Other than religion, Scotland on the whole is mercifully free of the class consciousness and social elitism that so often amuse or disgust foreign residents in England. But its turbulent history has left Scotland a legacy of sectarian bigotry comparable to that of Northern Ireland. Scotland's large minority population of Roman Catholics is still to some extent underprivileged. Catholics tend to stick together, Protestants to mix only with Protestants. Even the two most famous soccer teams in Scotland—Rangers and Celtic—are notorious for their sectarian bias.

A word, finally, is needed on the vexed subject of nomenclature. A "scotchman" is a nautical device for "scotching," or clamping, a running rope. It is not a native of Scotland. Though you may find some rather more conservative people refer to themselves as "Scotchmen" and consider themselves "Scotch," most prefer "Scot" or "Scotsman" and call themselves "Scottish" or "Scots."

There are exceptions to this rule. Certain internationally known Scottish products are "Scotch." There is Scotch whiskey, Scotch wool, Scotch tweed, Scotch mist (persistent drizzling rain). A Scotch snap is a short accented note followed by a longer one—a phrase that is characteristic of Scottish music, though certainly not unique to it. A snack food of a hard-boiled egg wrapped in sausage is a Scotch egg.

You may include the Scots in the broader term British, but they dislike the word *Brits*, and nothing infuriates them more than being called English. Nonetheless, there are a lot of Anglo-Scots, that is, people of Scottish birth who live in England or are the offspring of marriages between Scottish and English people. The term Anglo-Scots is not to be confused with Sassenachs, the Gaelic word for Saxon, which is applied facetiously or disdainfully to all the English. But at the same time, English people who live in Scotland remain English to their dying day, and their children after them. Similarly, the designation of North Britain for Scotland, which crept in during Victorian times, has now crept out again. It survives only in the names of a few North British hotels. Scots feel that it denies their national identity, and there are some who, on receiving a letter with "N.B." or "North Britain" in the address, will cross it out and return the envelope to the sender.

1 Essential Information

Before You Go

Government Tourist Offices

In the U.S.: 40 W. 57th St., New York, NY 10019, tel. 212/581–4700; 875 N. Michigan Ave., Chicago, IL 60611, tel. 312/787–0490; World Trade Center, Suite 450, 350 S. Figueroa St., Los Angeles, CA 90071, tel. 213/628–3525; 2305 Cedar Springs Rd., Suite 210, Dallas, TX 75201–1814, tel. 214/720–4040.

In Canada: 94 Cumberland St., Toronto, Ontario M5R 3N3, tel. 416/925–6326.

In the U.K.: Scottish Tourist Board, 23 Ravelston Terr., Edinburgh EH4 3EU, tel. 031/332–2433; London office: 19 Cockspur St. London SWIY 5BL, tel. 071/930–8661/2/3.

Tour Groups

No longer standing in England's shadow, Scotland has built a solid reputation as a tourist destination in its own right. And tour operators have responded by dedicating entire packages to the exploration of its bonnie banks, romantic Highlands, and hidden treasures. Creative itineraries hit the traditional tourist spots, such as Edinburgh, Glasgow, and St. Andrews, as well as out-of-the-way places like the Orkney and Shetland Islands. If group travel is not your style, consider an independent package. You can divide your time between Edinburgh and London, create a customized tour using a combination of rail and rental car travel, or design your own fly/drive itinerary, staying in Scottish guest houses and hotels along the way.

When evaluating any tour, be sure to find out exactly what expenses are included (particularly tips, taxes, service charges, side trips, additional meals, and entertainment); ratings of all hotels on the itinerary and the facilities they offer; cancellation policies for both you and the tour operator; and, if you are traveling alone, the cost of a single supplement.

Listed below is a sampling of operators and packages to give you an idea of what is available. For additional resources, contact your travel agent or the British Tourist Authority. Most tour operators request that bookings be made through a travel agent—there is no additional charge for doing so.

General-Interest Tours
Trafalgar Tours (21 E. 26th St., New York, NY 10010, tel. 800/854–0103 or 212/689–8977) offers a seven-day introduction to Scotland, as well as a nine-day "CostSaver" tour that utilizes tourist-class hotels. Sixteen other tours include two to four days in Scotland.

At the upper end of the price spectrum, **Abercrombie & Kent** (1420 Kensington Rd., Oak Brook, IL 60521–2106, tel. 800/323–7308 or 708/954–2944) has an eight-day "Scottish Sampler," which takes a circle route from Glasgow across the Highlands and down to Edinburgh. Accommodations are in country-house hotels. A six-day luxury rail journey aboard the *Royal Scotsman* is also available. **Caravan Tours** (401 N. Michigan Ave., Suite 3325, Chicago, IL 60611, tel. 800/CARAVAN or 312/321–9800) takes a more leisurely pace, hitting the Scottish highlights in 10 days. **Delta Dream Vacations** (tel. 800/872–7786) does it in 13 days and includes highlights of Britain.

Maupintour (Box 807, Lawrence, KS 66044, tel. 800/255–4266 or 913/843–1211) spends 16 days touring Scotland's lochs, glens, and bonnie banks. An eight-day jaunt takes in the famous Edinburgh Festival and the Military Tattoo, then it's off to London for two theater performances.

For a quick overview of Great Britain, **CIE Tours International** (108 Ridgedale Ave., Morristown, NJ 07960, tel. 800/CIE–TOUR or 201/292–3438) shows you the best of England and Scotland—from London to the Trossachs in 11 or 17 days.

American Express Vacations (300 Pinnacle Way, Norcross, GA 30093, tel. 800/241–1700 or 800/421–5785 in Georgia), **Olson-Travelworld** (Box 10066, Manhattan Beach, CA 90226, tel. 800/421–2255 or 310/546–8400, in Calif. 800/421–5785), **TWA Getaway Vacations** (tel. 800/GET–AWAY) and **American Airlines Fly AAway Vacations** (tel. 800/321–2121 or 817/355–1234) have a wide selection of escorted tours covering the highlights of Scotland, England, Ireland, and Wales in various combinations.

Package Deals for Independent Travelers

British Airways (tel. 800/AIR–WAYS) combines three nights in London with three nights in Edinburgh, including round-trip air transportation between London and Edinburgh, airport transfers, and city sightseeing. The airline also offers special rates at hotels in Edinburgh, Dornoch, Inverness, Oban, Glasgow, and Fort William.

CIE Tours International (*see* General-Interest Tours, *above*) and **Aer Lingus** (tel. 800/223–6537) both offer self-drive packages that include accommodations at hotels or Scottish town and country homes, a rental car with unlimited mileage, and full breakfast daily.

Continental's Grand Destinations (tel. 800/634–5555) also lets you design your own self-drive itinerary, choosing from an extensive menu of countryside hotels and car rental options.

American Express Vacations (*see* General-Interest Tours, *above*) gives you three or more nights in Edinburgh, including daily breakfast and city sightseeing.

For those traveling on a tight timetable, **American Airlines Fly AAway Vacations** (*see* General-Interest Tours, *above*) offers one night in "Cultural Glasgow" or four days in "Historic Scotland." A seven-day package gives golfers a chance to tee off at St. Andrews; optional extensions to Gleneagles, Royal Dornoch, and Nairn are also available.

When to Go

The Scottish climate has been much maligned (sometimes with justification). You can be unlucky: You may spend a summer week in Scotland and experience nothing but low clouds and drizzling rain. But, on the other hand, you may enjoy month-long spells of calm Mediterranean-like weather even in early spring and late fall.

Generally speaking, Scotland is three or four degrees cooler than southern England. The east is drier and colder than the west; Edinburgh's rainfall, for example, is comparable to

Rome's, while rainfall in Glasgow is more like that in Vancouver—yet the cities are only 44 miles apart and both are at sea level.

All visitors comment on the long summer evenings, which grow longer still as you travel north. Dawn in Orkney and Shetland in June is at around 1 AM, no more than an hour or so after sunset. The other side of this coin, though, are the very short winter days.

Scotland has few thunderstorms and little fog, except for local sea mists near coasts. But there are often variable winds that reach gale force even in summer (which at least blow away the hordes of gnats and midges, the curse of the western Highlands).

Climate What follows are average daily maximum and minimum temperatures for major cities in Scotland.

Aberdeen	Jan.	43F	6C	May	54F	12C	Sept.	59F	15C
		36	2		43	6		49	9
	Feb.	43F	6C	June	61F	16C	Oct.	54F	12C
		36	2		49	9		43	6
	Mar.	47F	8C	July	63F	17C	Nov.	47F	8C
		36	2		52	11		40	4
	Apr.	49F	9C	Aug.	63F	17C	Dec.	45F	7C
		40	4		52	11		36	2

Edinburgh	Jan.	43F	6C	May	58F	14C	Sept.	61F	16C
		34	1		43	6		49	9
	Feb.	43F	6C	June	63F	17C	Oct.	54F	12C
		34	1		49	9		45	7
	Mar.	47F	8C	July	65F	18C	Nov.	49F	9C
		36	2		52	11		40	4
	Apr.	52F	11C	Aug.	65F	18C	Dec.	45F	7C
		40	4		52	11		36	2

Glasgow	Jan.	41F	5C	May	59F	15C	Sept.	61F	16C
		34	1		43	6		49	9
	Feb.	45F	7C	June	65F	18C	Oct.	56F	13C
		34	1		49	9		43	6
	Mar.	49F	9C	July	67F	19C	Nov.	49F	9C
		36	2		52	11		38	3
	Apr.	54F	12C	Aug.	67F	19C	Dec.	45F	7C
		40	4		52	11		36	2

Highlands	Jan.	43F	6C	May	58F	14C	Sept.	61F	16C
		32	0		43	6		49	9
	Feb.	45F	7C	June	63F	17C	Oct.	56F	13C
		34	1		49	9		43	6
	Mar.	49F	9C	July	65F	18C	Nov.	49F	9C
		36	2		52	11		38	3
	Apr.	52F	11C	Aug.	65F	18C	Dec.	45F	7C
		40	4		52	11		34	1

Orkney Islands	Jan.	43F	6C	May	54F	12C	Sept.	58F	14C
		36	2		43	6		49	9
	Feb.	43F	6C	June	58F	14C	Oct.	52F	11C
		36	2		47	8		45	7
	Mar.	45F	7C	July	61F	16C	Nov.	47F	8C
		38	3		50	10		41	5
	Apr.	49F	9C	Aug.	61F	16C	Dec.	45F	7C
		40	4		50	10		38	3

Current weather information for more than 750 cities around the world may be obtained by calling **WeatherTrak** information service at 900/370–8728 (cost: 95¢ per minute). A taped message will tell you to dial the three-digit access code for the destination in which you're interested. The code is either the area code (in the United States) or the first three letters of the foreign city. For a list of all access codes, send a stamped, self-addressed envelope to Cities, 9B Terrace Way, Greensboro, NC 27403. For more information, call 800/247–3282.

A similar service operated by **American Express** can be accessed by dialing 900/WEATHER (tel. 900/932–8437). As well as supplying a three-day weather forecast for 600 cities worldwide, this service provides international travel information and time and day. Cost is 75¢ per minute.

Festivals and Seasonal Events

The **Scottish Tourist Board** (Box 15, Edinburgh EH1 1UY) will send you a free booklet of *Events in Scotland* for the coming year (it is usually available in November). Below, we note the principal activities for each month without specifying precise dates because most of them change every year.

January **Burns Night dinners** and other entertainments are held on January 25 in memory of Robert Burns in Glasgow, Ayr, Dumfries, Edinburgh, and many other towns and villages.

May **Glasgow Mayfest** (Festival Dir., 18 Albion St., Glasgow G1 1LH, tel. 041/552–8000) is a citywide international festival of theater, dance, music, and street events. It is Glasgow's answer to the Edinburgh Festival.
The **Perth Festival of the Arts** (tel. 0738/21672) offers orchestral and choral concerts, drama, opera, recitals, and ballet throughout Perth, Tayside.

July The **British Open Championship** (Royal and Ancient Golf Club, St. Andrews, Fife KY16 9JD, tel. 0334/72112) is played at a different course each year.

August The **Edinburgh International Festival** (held from mid-August through early September) is the world's largest festival of the arts. Festivities include the nighttime **Edinburgh Military Tattoo.** Information is available from the Edinburgh Festival Society (21 Market St., Edinburgh EH1 1BW, tel. 031/226–4001).

September The **Braemar Royal Highland Gathering** (Princess Royal and Duke of Fife Memorial Park, Braemar, Grampian, tel. 03397/55377) hosts kilted clansmen from all over Scotland.

What to Pack

Clothing Lightweight clothing is usually adequate in summer, but add a jacket, sweater, or cardigan for evenings. A waterproof coat or parka is essential. In Scotland casual clothes are *de rigueur*, and you will find very few hotels or restaurants that insist on jackets and ties for men in the evenings. If you expect to attend some gala occasion (a premier at the Edinburgh Festival, for example), men should have a tuxedo, women an evening dress. Many visitors to Scotland appear to think it necessary to adopt a Scottish costume. It is not. Scots themselves do not wear tartan ties or Balmoral "bunnets," and only an enthusiastic minority prefer the kilt for everyday wear.

Drip-dry and crease-resistant fabrics are a good bet. If you are touring, it is almost impossible to get any laundering or cleaning done, except in the most prestigious hotels.

The golden rule is to travel light; generally, try not to take more than you can carry yourself. Not only are porters more or less wholly extinct these days (and where you can find them they're very expensive anyway), the less luggage you take, the easier checking in and out of hotels becomes.

Carry-on Luggage Passengers aboard major U.S. carriers are usually limited to two carry-on bags. For a bag you wish to store under the seat, the maximum dimensions are 9″ x 14″ x 22″, a total of 45″. For bags that can be hung in a closet or on a luggage rack, the maximum dimensions are 4″ x 23″ x 45″, a total of 72″. For bags you wish to store in an overhead bin, the maximum dimensions are 10″ x 14″ x 36″, a total of 60″. Your two carry-ons must each fit one of these sets of dimensions, and any item that exceeds the specified dimensions will generally be rejected as a carry-on and handled as checked baggage. Keep in mind that an airline can adapt these rules to circumstances, so on an especially crowded flight don't be surprised if you are only allowed one carry-on bag.

In addition to the two carry-ons, travelers may also bring aboard a handbag (pocketbook or purse); an overcoat or wrap; an umbrella; a camera; a reasonable amount of reading material; an infant bag; and crutches, a cane, braces, or other prosthetic devices upon which the passenger is dependent. Infant-child safety seats can also be brought aboard if parents have purchased a ticket for the child or if there is space in the cabin. Note that these regulations are for U.S. airlines only. Foreign airlines generally allow one piece of carry-on luggage in tourist class, in addition to handbags and bags filled with duty-free goods. Passengers in first and business class are also allowed to carry on one garment bag. It is best to check with your airline ahead of time to find out what its exact rules are regarding carry-on luggage.

Checked Luggage U.S. airlines allow passengers to check in two suitcases whose total dimensions (length + width + height) do not exceed 62″ and whose weight does not exceed 70 pounds.

Rules governing foreign airlines vary from airline to airline, so check with your travel agent or the airline itself before you go. All the airlines allow passengers to check in two bags. In general, expect the weight restriction on the two bags to be not more than 70 lbs. each, and the size restriction on each bag to be not more than 62" for its total dimensions.

Labeling Luggage Before you go, itemize the contents of each bag in case you need to file an insurance claim. Be certain to put your home or business address on each piece of luggage, including carry-on bags.

If your luggage is lost or stolen and later recovered, the airline will deliver the luggage to your home free of charge.

Taking Money Abroad

Traveler's checks and major U.S. credit cards—particularly American Express—are accepted in larger cities and resorts. In smaller towns and rural areas, you may need cash. You won't get as good an exchange rate at home as abroad, but it's wise to change a small amount of money into pounds before you go; lines at airport currency-exchange booths can be very long. If your local bank can't change your currency, you can exchange money through **Thomas Cook Currency Services.** To find the office nearest you, contact the main office at 29 Broadway, New York, NY 10006 (tel. 212/757–6915).

For safety and convenience, it's always best to take traveler's checks. The most recognized traveler's checks are American Express, Barclay's, Thomas Cook, and those issued through major commercial banks, such as Citibank and Bank of America. Some banks will issue the checks free to established customers, but most charge a 1% commission fee. Buy part of the traveler's checks in small denominations to cash toward the end of your trip. This will save you from having to cash a large check and ending up with more foreign money than you need. (Hold on to your receipts after exchanging your traveler's checks; it's easier to convert foreign currency back into dollars if you have the receipts.) Remember to take the addresses of offices where you can get refunds for lost or stolen traveler's checks. *The American Express Traveler's Companion,* a directory of offices to contact worldwide in case of loss or theft of American Express traveler's checks, is available at most travel service locations. In Scotland, the number to call is 0800/521–313.

Getting Money from Home

There are at least three ways to get money from home:

(1) Have it sent through a large commercial bank with a branch in the town where you're staying. The only drawback is that you must have an account with the bank; if not, you'll have to go through your own bank and the process will be slower and more expensive.

(2) Have it sent through American Express. If you are a cardholder, you can cash a personal check or a counter check at an American Express office for up to $1,000 ($2,500 for gold cardholders) in cash or traveler's checks. There is a 1% commission on traveler's checks. American Express also provides another service, which you don't have to be a cardholder to use: the American Express MoneyGram. You will have to call home and have someone go to an American Express office or Money-Gram agent and fill out the necessary form. The amount sent must be in increments of $50 and must be paid for with cash, MasterCard or Visa, or the Optima card. The American Express MoneyGram agent authorizes the transfer of funds to an American Express office in the town where you're staying. You'll need to show identification when picking up the money. You will also need to know the transaction reference number, so be sure to get it from the person at home who placed the or-

der. In most cases, the money will be available in 15 minutes. Fees vary according to the money sent. For sending $300, the fee is $35; for $1,000, $70; for $5,000, $170. For the American Express MoneyGram location nearest your home and the locations of offices in Scotland, call 800/543–4080.

(3) Have it sent through Western Union (tel. 800/325–6000). If you have a MasterCard or Visa, you can have money sent for any amount up to your credit limit. If not, have someone take cash or a certified cashier's check to a Western Union office. The money will be delivered in two business days to a Bank of Scotland. Fees vary with the amount of money being sent. For $1,000 the standard fee is $47, plus an additional $10 for a phone transaction, and another $25 for sending it to Europe ($82 total).

Cash Machines Virtually all U.S. banks belong to a network of ATMs (automated teller machines), which dispense cash 24 hours a day in cities throughout the country. There are some eight major networks in the United States, the largest of which are Cirrus, owned by MasterCard, and Plus, affiliated with Visa. Some banks belong to more than one network. To receive a card for one of these systems you must apply for it. Cards issued by Visa and MasterCard also may be used in the ATMs, but the fees are usually higher than the fees on bank cards. There is also a daily interest charge on credit card "loans," even if monthly bills are paid on time. Each network has a toll-free number you can call to locate machines in a given city. The Cirrus number is 800/4–CIRRUS; the Plus number is 800/THE–PLUS. Check with your bank for information on fees and on the amount of cash you can withdraw on any given day. Express Cash allows American Express cardholders to withdraw up to $1,000 in a seven-day period (21 days overseas) from their personal checking accounts at ATMs worldwide. Gold-card members can receive up to $2,500 in a seven-day period (21 days overseas). Express Cash is not a cash advance service; only money already in the linked checking account can be withdrawn. Every transaction carries a 2% fee with a minimum charge of $2 and a maximum of $6. Apply for a PIN (personal identification number) and link your accounts at least 2–3 weeks before departure. Call 800/CASH–NOW to receive an application or to locate the nearest Express Cash machine.

Scottish Currency

Britain's currency is the pound sterling, which is divided into 100 pence (100p). Notes are issued to the values of £50, £20, £10, and £5 (also £1 in Scotland). Coins are issued to the values of £1, 50p, 20p, 10p, 5p, 2p, and 1p. Scottish coins are the same as English ones, but Scottish notes are issued by three banks: the Bank of Scotland, the Royal Bank of Scotland, and the Clydesdale Bank. They have the same face values as English notes, and English notes are interchangeable with them in Scotland. Scottish £1 notes are no longer legal tender outside Scotland. English banks and post offices will exchange them for you, but fewer and fewer English shops are accepting them.

Except on public holidays, banks are open weekdays 9:30–3:30, some days to 4:45. Some close for an hour at lunchtime. All are closed on Saturday and Sunday. The larger travel agents, the more expensive hotels, the biggest multiple stores, and the independent *bureaux de change* in the cities will change money for you and cash checks. But it is best to compare the rates they offer and the commissions they charge: They do vary. Banks offer the best deal. The major airports operate 24-hour banking services seven days a week.

At press time, the exchange rate for the pound sterling was £1.80 to the dollar.

What It Will Cost

This is about the hardest travel question to answer in advance. A trip to Britain can cost as little (above a basic minimum) or as much (with virtually no limit) as you choose. Budgeting is much simplified if you take a package tour. As an indication: A packaged five-day stay in Edinburgh, including hotel, meals except lunch (but with lunch included on two full-day sightseeing trips), and visits to leading sights and the theater, costs anywhere from £250 to £600, depending upon the hotel category. A good-quality package six-day bus tour can be had for about £350–£600 (again depending on the quality of the hotel).

Sample Costs   For dining and lodging costs, *see* each chapter under that heading.

A man's haircut will cost £4 and up; a woman's anywhere from £10 to £20. It costs about £1.50 to have a shirt laundered, from £3 to dry-clean a dress, and from £3.50 to dry-clean a man's suit. A local newspaper will cost you about 30p and a national daily, 40p. A pint of beer is around £1.20, and a serving of whiskey, about the same. A cup of coffee will run from 50p to £1, depending on where you drink it; a ham sandwich, £1.50; lunch in a pub, £2.50 and up (plus your drink).

A theater seat will cost from £4.50 to £15 or £20 in Edinburgh and Glasgow, less elsewhere. Nightclubs will take all they can get from you—even the membership fees are variable.

Sales Tax   The British sales tax, VAT (Value Added Tax), was increased in March 1991 from 15% to 17.5%. The tax is almost always included in quoted prices in shops, hotels, and restaurants. Where it is quoted separately, the idea—as in the United States—is to make the quoted price look more attractive. *See* Shopping, later in this section, for the ways to recover VAT when you leave the country.

Passports and Visas

Americans   U.S. citizens need a valid passport to enter Scotland. Visas are not required for a stay of up to six months. Travelers may be asked to show onward/return tickets. For more information, contact the **British Embassy,** 3100 Massachusetts Ave. NW, Washington, DC 20008, tel. 202/462–1340.

To obtain a new passport, apply in person; renewals can be obtained in person or by mail. First-time applicants should apply to one of the 13 U.S. Passport Agency offices at least five weeks in advance of their departure date. In addition, local county courthouses, many state and probate courts, and some post offices accept passport applications. Necessary documents include: (1) a completed passport application (Form DSP–11); (2) proof of citizenship (a certified birth certificate issued by the Hall of Records in your state of birth or naturalization papers);

(3) proof of identity (an unexpired driver's license or a state, military, or student ID card with your photograph and signature); (4) two recent, identical, 2-inch-square photographs (black-and-white or color head shot with a white or off-white background); and (5) a $65 application fee for a 10-year passport (those under 18 pay $40 for a five-year passport). Passports are mailed to you in about 10–15 working days. You may pay with a check, cash, or money order. If you are paying in cash, you must have exact change; no change is given. To renew your passport by mail, you'll need to send a completed Form DSP-82; two recent, identical passport photographs; your current passport (less than 12 years old and issued after your 16th birthday); and a check or money order for $55.

If your passport is lost or stolen abroad, report it immediately to the nearest U.S. embassy or consulate and to local police authorities. If you can provide the consular officer with the information contained in the passport, he or she will most likely be able to issue you a new passport. For this reason, it is a good idea to keep a copy of the data page of your passport in a separate place, or leave the passport number, date, and place of issuance with a relative or friend in the United States.

Canadians Canadians must have a valid passport to enter Scotland. Travelers may be required to show onward/return tickets. Canadians under 27 years of age are entitled to a Working Holiday visa, valid for up to six months. For further information, contact your nearest consulate. To acquire a passport, send a completed application (available at any post office or passport office) to the Bureau of Passports, Suite 215, West Tower, Complexe Guy Favreau, 200 Boulevard René-Lévesque Ouest, Montréal, Québec H2Z 1X4. Include $25, two photographs, a guarantor, and proof of Canadian citizenship. Applications can be made in person at regional passport offices in many locations, including Edmonton, Halifax, Montréal, Toronto, Vancouver, and Winnipeg. Passports are valid for five years and are nonrenewable.

Customs and Duties

On Arrival Entering the United Kingdom, a traveler 17 or over can take in (1) 200 cigarettes or 100 cigarillos or 50 cigars or 250 grams of tobacco; (2) one liter of alcohol over 22% volume or two liters of alcohol under 22% volume or two liters of fortified or sparkling wine; (3) two liters of still table wine; (4) 60 ml of perfume and 250 ml of toilet water; (5) other goods to a value of £32 but no more than 50 liters of beer or 25 mechanical lighters.

On Departure You may bring home duty-free up to $400 worth of foreign
U.S. Customs goods, as long as you have been out of the country for at least 48 hours and you haven't claimed that exemption in the past 30 days. Each member of the family is entitled to the same exemption, regardless of age, and exemptions may be pooled. For the next $1,000 worth of goods, a flat 10% rate is assessed; above $1,400, duties vary with the merchandise. Included in the allowances for travelers 21 or older are one liter of alcohol, 100 cigars (non-Cuban), and 200 cigarettes. Only one bottle of perfume trademarked in the United States may be imported. There is no duty on antiques or works of art over 100 years old. Anything exceeding these limits will be taxed at the port of entry and may be taxed additionally in the traveler's home state.

Gifts valued at under $50 may be mailed duty-free to friends or relatives at home, but you may not send more than one package per day to a single addressee, packages may not include perfumes costing more than $5, tobacco, or liquor.

Canadian Customs Exemptions for returning Canadians range from $20 to $300, depending on length of stay out of the country. For the $300 exemption, you must have been out of the country for one week. In any given year, you are only allowed one $300 exemption. You may bring in duty-free up to 50 cigars, 200 cigarettes, 2.2 pounds of tobacco, and 40 ounces of liquor, provided these are declared in writing to customs on arrival and accompany you in hand or checked-through baggage. Personal gifts should be mailed labeled "Unsolicited Gift—Value under $40." Obtain a copy of the Canadian Customs brochure *I Declare* for further details.

Traveling with Film

If your camera is new, shoot and develop a few rolls of film before leaving home. Pack some lens tissue and an extra battery for your built-in light meter. Invest about $10 in a skylight filter: It will protect the lens and reduce haze.

Film doesn't like hot weather, so if you're driving in summer, don't store film in the glove compartment or on the shelf under the rear window. Put it behind the front seat on the floor, on the side opposite the exhaust pipe.

On a plane trip, never pack unprocessed film in check-in luggage; if your bags get X-rayed, say good-bye to your pictures. Always carry undeveloped film with you through security and ask to have it inspected by hand. (It helps to keep your film in a plastic bag, ready for quick inspection.) Inspectors at American airports are required by law to honor requests for hand inspection. The newer airport scanning machines used in all U.S. airports are safe for anything from five to 500 scans, depending on the speed of your film. The effects are cumulative; you can put the same roll of film through several scans without worry. After five scans, though, you're asking for trouble.

If your film gets fogged and you want an explanation, send it to the **National Association of Photographic Manufacturers** (550 Mamaroneck Ave., Harrison, NY 10528). They will try to determine what went wrong. The service is free.

Language

"Much," said Doctor Johnson, "much may be made of a Scotchman *if he be caught young*." This quote sums up—even today—the attitude of some English people to the Scots language. They simply assume that their English is superior. Since they speak the language of Parliament and much of the media, their arrogance is understandable. The Scots have for long been made to feel uncomfortable about their mother tongue and have only themselves to blame, being actively encouraged—at school, for example—to ape the dialect of the Thames Valley ("Standard English") in order to "get on" in life. The Scots language (that is, Lowland Scots, not Gaelic) was a northern form of Middle English and in its day was the language of court and literature. It borrowed from Scandinavian, Dutch, French, and Gaelic. After a series of historical body blows—such as the decamping of the Scottish Court to England after 1603 and the printing of the King James Bible in English, but not in Scots—it declined as a literary or official language. It survives, in various forms, virtually as an underground language spoken at home, in shops, on the playground, the farm, or quayside among ordinary folk, especially in its heartland, in northeast Scotland. (There they describe Scots who use the brayed diphthongs of the English Thames Valley as speaking with a *bool in the mou*—marble in the mouth!) Plenty of Scots speak English with only an accent and virtually all will "modulate" either unconsciously or out of politeness into understandable English when conversing with a nondialect speaker. As for Gaelic, that belongs to a different Celtic culture and, though threatened, hangs on in spite of the Highlands depopulation.

Staying Healthy

There are no serious health risks associated with travel to Scotland. If you have a health problem that may require purchasing prescription drugs while in the country, have your doctor at home write a prescription using the drug's generic name. Brand names vary widely from country to country. To avoid problems clearing customs, diabetics carrying needles and syringes should have a letter from their physician confirming their need for insulin injections.

The **International Association for Medical Assistance to Travelers** (IAMAT) is a worldwide association offering a list of approved doctors whose training meets very high standards. For a list of physicians and clinics that are part of this network, contact IAMAT, 417 Center St., Lewiston, NY 14092, tel. 716/754–4883. **In Canada:** 40 Regal Rd., Guelph, Ontario N1K 1B5, tel. 519/836–0102. **In Europe:** 57 Voirets, 1212 Grand-Lancy, Geneva, Switzerland. Membership is free.

Inoculations are not needed for visitors going to Scotland.

Insurance

Travelers may seek insurance coverage in four areas: health and accident, lost luggage, trip cancellation, and flight. Your first step is to review your existing health and home-owner policies; some health insurance plans cover health expenses incurred while traveling, some major medical plans cover emergency transportation, and some home-owner policies cover the theft of luggage (*see below*).

Health and Accident Several companies offer coverage designed to supplement existing health insurance for travelers:

Carefree Travel Insurance (Box 310, 120 Mineola Blvd., Mineola, NY 11501, tel. 516/294–0220 or 800/323–3149) provides coverage for emergency medical evacuation and accidental death and dismemberment. It also offers 24-hour medical phone advice.

International SOS Assistance (Box 11568, Philadelphia, PA 19116, tel. 215/244–1500 or 800/523–8930), a medical assistance company, provides emergency evacuation services, worldwide medical referrals, and optional medical insurance.

Travel Assistance International (1133 15th St. NW, Suite 400, Washington, DC 20005, tel. 202/331–1609 or 800/821–2828) provides emergency evacuation services, 24-hour medical referrals, and medical insurance.

Travel Guard International, underwritten by Transamerica Occidental Life Companies (1145 Clark St., Stevens Point, WI 54481, tel. 715/345–0505 or 800/782–5151), offers reimbursement for medical expenses, with no deductibles or daily limits, and emergency evacuation services.

Wallach and Company, Inc. (Box 480, Middleburg, VA 22117, tel. 703/687–3166 or 800/237–6615) offers comprehensive medical coverage, including emergency evacuation services worldwide.

Lost Luggage On international flights, airlines are responsible for lost or damaged property of up to $9.07 per pound (or $20 per kilo) for checked baggage, and up to $400 per passenger for unchecked baggage. If you're carrying valuables, either take them with you on the plane or purchase additional insurance for lost luggage. Some airlines will issue extra luggage insurance when you check in, but many do not. Insurance for lost, damaged, or stolen luggage is available through travel agents or directly through various insurance companies. Luggage-loss coverage is usually part of a comprehensive travel insurance package that includes personal accident, trip cancellation, and sometimes default and bankruptcy. Two companies that issue luggage insurance are **Tele-Trip** (Box 31685, 3201 Farnam St., Omaha, NE 68131–0618, tel. 800/228–9792), a subsidiary of Mutual of Omaha, and **The Traveler** (Ticket and Travel Dept., 1 Tower Sq., Hartford, CT 06183–5040, tel. 203/277–0111 or 800/243–3174). Tele-Trip operates sales booths at airports and also issues insurance through travel agents. Rates vary according to the length of the trip. The Traveler will insure checked or hand luggage at $500–$2,000 valuation per person, for a maximum of 180 days. Rates for one to five days for $500 valuation are $10; for 180 days, $85. Other companies with comprehensive policies include **Access America, Inc.,** a subsidiary of Blue Cross–Blue Shield (Box 11188, Richmond, VA 23230, tel. 800/334–7525 or 800/284–8300); **Near Services** (450 Prairie Ave., Suite 101, Calumet City, IL 60409, tel. 708/868–6700 or 800/654–6700); **Travel Guard International** and **Carefree Travel Insurance** (*see* Health and Accident, *above*).

Trip-Cancellation and Flight Consider purchasing trip-cancellation insurance if you are traveling on a promotional or discounted ticket that does not allow changes or cancellations. You are then covered if an emergency causes you to cancel or postpone your trip. Trip-cancellation insurance is usually included in combination travel insurance packages available from most tour operators, travel agents, and insurance agents.

Flight insurance, which covers passengers in the case of death or dismemberment, is often included in the price of a ticket when paid for with American Express, MasterCard, or other major credit cards.

Renting and Leasing Cars

Car Rental If you're flying to Scotland and plan to spend some time first in Edinburgh, save money by arranging to pick up your car in the city the day you depart; otherwise, arrange to pick up and return your car at the airport. Weigh the added expense of renting a car from a major company with offices in town. If you're arriving and departing from different airports, look for a one-way car rental with no return fees. If you're traveling to more than one country, make sure your rental contract permits you to take the car across borders and that the insurance policy covers you in every country you visit. Remember, however, that Britain drives on the left, and the rest of Europe on the right. Therefore, you may want to leave your hire car in Britain and pick up a left-side drive when you cross the Channel.

Be prepared to pay more for a car with automatic transmission. Since they are not as readily available as those with manual transmissions, reserve them in advance. Rental rates vary widely, depending on the size and model, number of days you use the car, insurance coverage, and whether special drop-off fees are imposed. In most cases, rates quoted include unlimited free mileage and standard liability protection. Not included are Collision Damage Waiver (CDW), which eliminates your deductible payment should you have an accident; personal accident insurance; gasoline; and European Value Added Tax (VAT). The VAT in Great Britain is 17.5%.

Driver's licenses issued in the United States and Canada are valid in Great Britain. You might also take out an International Driving Permit before you leave to smooth out difficulties if you have an accident or as an additional piece of identification. Permits are available for a small fee through local offices of the **American Automobile Association** (AAA) and the **Canadian Automobile Association** (CAA), or from their main offices: **AAA** (1000 AAA Dr., Heathrow, FL 32746, tel. 800/336–4357); **CAA** (2 Carlton St., Toronto, Ontario M5B 1K4, tel. 416/964–3002).

It's best to arrange car rental before you leave. You won't save money by waiting until you arrive in Britain, and you may find that the type of car you want is not available at the last minute. Rental companies usually charge according to the exchange rate of the dollar at the time the car is returned or when the credit card payment is processed. To help you hedge against the falling dollar, these companies guarantee advertised rates if you pay in advance: **Budget Rent-a-Car** (3350 Boyington St., Carrollton, TX 75006, tel. 800/527–0700); **Connex Travel International** (23 N. Division St., Peekskill, NY 10566, tel. 800/333–3949).

Other budget rental companies serving Britain include **Europe by Car** (1 Rockefeller Plaza, New York, NY 10020, tel. 212/245–1713; 800/223–1516; in CA, 800/252–9401); **Auto Europe** (Box 1097, Sharps Wharf, Camden, ME 04843, tel. 207/236–8235 or 800/223–5555 in U.S. or Canada); **Foremost Euro-Car** (5430 Van Nuys Blvd., Suite 306 Van Nuys, CA 91401–5680, tel. 800/272–3299); and **Kemwel** (106 Calvert St., Harrison, NY 10528, tel. 800/678–0678). Other companies include **Avis** (tel. 800/331–1212); **Hertz** (tel. 800/654–3131); and **National** or **Europcar** (tel. 800/227–7368).

Leasing For trips of 21 days or more, you may save money by leasing a car. With the leasing arrangement, you are technically buying a car and then selling it back to the manufacturer after you've used it. You receive a factory-new car, tax free, with international registration and extensive insurance coverage. Rates vary with the make and model of car and length of time used. Before you go, compare long-term rental rates with leasing rates. Remember to add taxes and insurance costs to the car rentals, something you don't have to worry about with leasing.

Companies that offer leasing arrangements include **Kemwel, Europe by Car,** and **Auto Europe,** all listed above.

Rail Passes

If you plan to travel a lot in Britain, you may consider purchasing a **BritRail Pass,** which gives unlimited travel over the entire British Rail network.

A variety of passes are offered. The adult first-class pass costs $319 for eight days, $479 for 15 days, $599 for 22 days, and $689 for one month. The adult second-class pass costs $209 for eight days, $319 for 15 days, $399 for 22 days, and $465 for one month. Travelers over 60 can obtain a **Senior Citizen Pass,** which entitles the bearer to unlimited first-class travel. It costs $289 for eight days, $429 for 15 days, $539 for 22 days, and $619 for one month. The senior citizen second-class pass costs $189 for eight days, $289 for 15 days, $359 for 22 days, and $419 for one month. Young people (ages 16–25) can purchase the **BritRail Youth Pass,** which allows unlimited second-class travel. It costs $169 for eight days, $255 for 15 days, $319 for 22 days, and $375 for one month.

You must purchase the BritRail Pass before you leave home. It is available from most travel agents throughout the world or from the BritRail Travel International office (1500 Broadway, New York, NY 10036; tel. 212/575–2667 or 800/677–8585).

Student and Youth Travel

The **International Student Identity Card** (ISIC) entitles students to special fares on local transportation, rail passes, intra-European student charter flights, and discounts at museums, theaters, sports events, and many other attractions. If purchased in the United States, the $14 cost of the ISIC card also includes $3,000 in emergency medical coverage, plus hospital coverage of $100 a day for up to 60 days. Apply to the **Council on International Educational Exchange** (CIEE) (205 E. 42nd St., New York, NY 10017, tel. 212/661–1414). In Canada, the ISIC is available for $13 (Canadian) from **Travel Cuts** (187 College St., Toronto, Ontario M5T 1P7, tel. 416/979–2406). In the United Kingdom, students enrolled in university programs can purchase the ISIC at any student union or student travel company upon presentation of a valid university ID. Travelers (students and nonstudents) under age 26 can apply for a **Youth International Educational Exchange Card** (YIEE) issued by the Federation of International Youth Travel Organizations (FIYTO, 81 Islands Brugge, DK–2300 Copenhagen S, Denmark). It provides similar services and benefits as the ISIC card. The YIEE card is available in the United States from CIEE (address above) or from ISE (Europa House, 802 W. Oregon St., Urbana, IL 61801, tel. 217/344–5863). In Canada contact the **Canadian Hostelling Association** (CHA) (1600 James Naismith Dr., Suite 608, Gloucester, Ontario K1B 5N4, tel. 613/748–5638).

An **International Youth Hostel Federation** (IYHF) membership card is the key to inexpensive dormitory-style accommodations at more than 5,000 hostel locations in 70 countries around the world. Hostels provide separate sleeping quarters for men and women at rates ranging from $7 to $20 a night per person, and many have family accommodations. Youth Hostel memberships, which are valid for 12 months from the time of purchase, are available in the United States through **American Youth Hostels** (AYH, Box 37613, Washington, DC 20013, tel. 202/783–6161), in Canada through the **Canadian Hostelling Association** (address above), and in the United Kingdom through the **Scottish Youth Hostel Association** (7 Glebe Crescent, Stirling FK8 2JA, Scotland, tel. 0786/51181). By joining one of the national (American, Canadian, or British) youth hostel associations, members automatically become part of the International Youth Hostel Federation and are entitled to special reductions on rail and bus travel around the world. Handbooks listing these special concessions are available from the associations. The cost for a first-year membership is $25 for adults 18 to 54. Renewal thereafter is $20. For youths (17 and under) the rate is $10, and for senior citizens (55 and older) the rate is $15. Family membership is available for $35.

Economical bicycle tours for small groups of adventurous, energetic students are a popular AYH student travel service. For information on these and other AYH activities and publications, contact the AYH at the address above.

Council Travel, a CIEE subsidiary, is the foremost U.S. student travel agency, specializing in low-cost charters and serving as the exclusive U.S. agent for many student airfare bargains and tours. CIEE's 72-page *Student Travel Catalog* and *Council Charter* brochures are available free from any Council Travel office in the United States (enclose $1 postage if ordering by mail). In addition to CIEE headquarters (205 E. 42nd St., New York, NY 10017) and a branch office (35 W. 8th St., New York, NY 10009), there are Council Travel offices in Arizona (Tempe); California (Berkeley, La Jolla, Long Beach, Los Angeles, San Diego, San Francisco, Sherman Oaks); Colorado (Boulder); Connecticut (New Haven); Washington, DC; Georgia (Atlanta); Illinois (Chicago, Evanston); Louisiana (New Orleans); Massachusetts (Amherst, Boston, Cambridge); Michigan (Ann Arbor); Minnesota (Minneapolis); North Carolina (Durham); Ohio (Columbus); Oregon (Portland); Rhode Island (Providence); Texas (Austin, Dallas); Washington (Seattle); and Wisconsin (Milwaukee).

Students who would like to work abroad should contact CIEE's **Work Abroad Department** (205 E. 42nd St., New York, NY 10017, tel. 212/661–1414, ext. 1130). The council arranges paid and voluntary work experiences overseas for up to six months. CIEE also sponsors study programs in Europe, Latin America, Asia, and Australia and produces several books of interest to the student traveler. These include *Work, Study, Travel Abroad: The Whole World Handbook* ($12.95 plus $1.50 book-rate postage or $3 first-class postage); *Volunteer! The Comprehensive Guide to Voluntary Service in the U.S. and Abroad* ($8.95 plus $1.50 book-rate postage or $3 first-class postage); and *The Teenager's Guide to Travel, Study, and Adventure Abroad* ($11.95 plus $1.50 book-rate postage or $3 first-class postage.) The Information Center at the **Institute of International Education** (IIE) (809 UN Plaza, New York, NY 10017, tel. 212/883–8200) has reference books, foreign-university catalogs, study-abroad brochures, and other materials that may be consulted free. IIE administers a variety of grant and study programs offered by U.S. and foreign organizations and publishes a well-known annual series of study-abroad guides. The Information Center is open weekdays 10–4; it's closed on holidays.

In Scotland
Accommodations
During vacation periods (mid-March to mid-April, July to September, and Christmas) many universities and colleges throughout Britain open their halls of residence to visitors. Campus accommodations—usually single study-bedrooms with access to lounges, libraries, and sports facilities—include breakfast and generally cost about $30 per night. Locations vary from city centers to bucolic lakeside parks. For information contact the **British Universities Accommodation Consortium** (BUAC, Box 585, University Park, Nottingham NG7 2RD, England, tel. 0602/504–571), or the **Higher Education Accommodation Consortium** (HEAC, 36 Collegiate Crescent, Sheffield S10 2BP, England, tel. 0742/683–759).

For information on YMCA accommodations, write to **YMCA Britain** (National Council of YMCAs, 640 Forest Rd., Walthamstow, London E17 3DZ, England).

Camping is another economical option for young travelers. Ask the British Tourist Authority for its booklet *Camping and Caravan Parks in Britain*, or contact the **Forestry Commission** (231 Corstorphine Rd., Edinburgh EH12 7AT, Scotland, tel. 031/334–0066) and request a copy of the free leaflet *Forestry Commission Camping and Caravan Sites*. If you are planning a bicycle camping trip and need technical advice or information on route planning, **The Camping and Caravanning Club** (11 Lower Grosvenor Pl., London SW1W 0EY, England) may be of help.

Getting Around
If you plan to do a lot of rail travel within Great Britain, the **BritRail Youthpass**, available to young people ages 16–25 and sold only outside Britain, offers excellent value. Ask the British Travel Authority (BTA) for information about prices and for a list of participating travel agents.

Full-time students aged 17 and older qualify for a **Student Coach Card** from National Express, offering one-third off all long-distance coach fares throughout Britain. The card, valid for a full year, can be purchased from any National Express agent in Britain. Nonstudents ages 16–23 are eligible for the Young Person's Coach Card, offering the same discount.

Young travelers interested in exploring Scotland by bus should consider one of the Scottish Youth Hostel Association's special holiday packs, offering unlimited coach travel and overnight vouchers for SYHA accommodations. Information is available at any Scottish hostel, or through the **SYHA National Office** (7 Glebe Crescent, Stirling FK8 2JA, Scotland, tel. 0786/51181).

Traveling with Children

Publications
Family Travel Times is a newsletter published 10 times a year by TWYCH (Travel With Your Children, 45 W. 18th St., 7th-floor tower, New York, NY 10011, tel. 212/206–0688). A one-year subscription costs $35 and includes access to back issues. The organization also offers a free phone-in service with advice and information on specific destinations. *Great Vacations with Your Kids,* by Dorothy Jordan and Marjorie Cohen, offers complete advice on planning your trip with children, from toddlers

to teens. If unavailable in bookstores, it can be ordered for $12.95 from E. P. Dutton, 375 Hudson St., New York, NY 10014, tel. 212/366–2000.

Innocents Abroad: Traveling with Kids in Europe, by Valerie Wolf Deutsch and Laura Sutherland, is a new guide to child- and teen-friendly activities, food, and transportation in Britain and on the continent, with individual sections on each country. If unavailable in bookstores, send $14.95 to New American Library, Penguin USA, 375 Hudson St., New York, NY 10014, tel. 212/366–2000.

Kids and Teens in Flight, a useful brochure about children flying alone, is available from the U.S. Department of Transportation. To order a free copy, call 202/366–2220.

Traveling With Children—And Enjoying It offers tips on how to cut costs, keep kids busy, eat out, reduce jet lag, and pack properly. Available in bookstores or from the Globe Dequot Press, Box Q, Chester, CT 06412, tel. 203/526–9571.

Getting There   All children, including infants, must have a valid passport for foreign travel. Family passports are no longer issued. On international flights, children under 2 not occupying a seat pay 10% of the adult fare. Various discounts apply to children ages 2 to 12, so check with your airline when making reservations. Regulations about infant travel on airplanes are in the process of changing. Until they do, however, if you want to be sure your infant is secure, you must bring your own infant car seat and buy a separate ticket. Check with the airline in advance to be sure your seat meets the required standard. If possible, reserve a seat behind one of the plane's bulkheads, where there's usually more legroom and enough space to fit a bassinet (which is available from the airlines). The booklet *Child/Infant Safety Seats Acceptable for Use in Aircraft* is available from the Federal Aviation Administration (APA–200, 800 Independence Ave. SW, Washington, DC 20591, tel. 202/267–3479). If you opt to hold your baby on your lap, do so with the infant outside the seat belt rather than inside it so he or she doesn't get crushed in case of a sudden stop.

When reserving tickets, also ask about special children's meals or snacks. The February 1990 and 1992 issues of *Family Travel Times* include TWYCH's *Airline Guide,* which contains a rundown of the children's services offered by 46 different airlines.

Getting Around   Children ages 5 to 15 can get a **BritRail Youth Pass** at half the adult fare (*see* Rail Passes, *above*).

Hotels   Although there is no general policy regarding hotel rates for children in Scotland, **Milton Hotels** allow children under 14 to stay for free in their parents' room. Many also have adjoining family rooms. **Embassy Hotels** allow up to two children under 16 to stay free when sharing their parents' room and offer a 25% discount for children occupying their own rooms. For further information and reservations contact **Scots-American Travel** (26 Rugen Dr., Harrington Park, NJ 07640, tel. 201/768–5505).

Home Exchange   Exchanging homes is a surprisingly inexpensive way to enjoy a vacation abroad, especially if you plan a lengthy visit. The largest home-exchange company, **Intervac U.S. International Home Exchange Service** (Box 590504, San Francisco, CA 94159, tel. 415/435–3497 or 800/756–4663), publishes three directories a year. The $45 membership entitles you to one listing and all three directories (there is an additional charge for postage). Photos of your property cost an additional $11, and listing a second home costs $10. **Loan-a-Home** (2 Park La., Apt. 6E, Mount Vernon, NY 10552, tel. 914/664–7640), which publishes two directories (in December and June) and two supplements (in March and September) each year, is popular with professors on sabbatical, businesspeople on temporary assignments, and retired people on extended vacations. There is no annual membership fee or charge for listing your home, but one directory and a supplement cost $35. All four books cost $45.

Cottage Rentals   **Villas International** (605 Market St., Suite 510, San Francisco, CA 94105, tel. 415/281–0910 or 800/221–2260) offers a range of rental properties in Scotland, from simple cottages in the Highlands to lochside farmhouses and castles.

Farmhouse and Crofting Holidays   A popular option for families with children is a farmhouse holiday, combining the freedom of bed-and-breakfast accommodations with the hospitality of Scottish family life. Information is available from the BTA or from **Scottish Farmhouse Holidays** (5 Drumtenant, Ladybank, Fife, KY7 7UG, Scotland, tel. 0337/30451). Another organization that offers authentic farming experiences (and, incidentally, helps farmers to stay in business in the present economic climate) is the Farm Holiday Bureau (National Agricultural Centre, Stoneleigh, Warwickshire, England CV8 2LZ, tel. 0203/696909). It can supply a "Heart of Scotland" farm and country holiday brochure.

Baby-Sitting Services   The concierge at your hotel or guest house should be able to recommend a local baby-sitting service or agency.

Camps and Activity Centers   For information about activity centers and summer camps offering organized recreational programs for families and unaccompanied children, contact the BTA or send an International Reply Coupon to the **British Activity Holiday Association** (Norton Terr., Llandrindod Wells, Powys, LD1 6AE, Wales, tel. 0597/3902).

Hints for Disabled Travelers

The following organizations in the United States provide advice and services:

The Information Center for Individuals with Disabilities (Fort Point Pl., 1st floor, 27–43 Wormwood St., Boston, MA 02210, tel. 617/727–5540) offers useful problem-solving assistance, including lists of travel agents who specialize in tours for the disabled.

Moss Rehabilitation Hospital Travel Information Service (1200 West Tabor Rd., Philadelphia, PA 19141–3099, tel. 215/456–9600; TDD 215/456–9602) for a small fee provides information on tourist sights, transportation, and accommodations in destinations around the world. It also provides toll-free telephone numbers for airlines with special lines for the hard of hearing.

Travel Industry and Disabled Exchange (TIDE, 5435 Donna Ave., Tarzana, CA 91356, tel. 818/368–5648) publishes a quarterly newsletter and a directory of travel agencies and tours catering specifically to the disabled. The annual membership fee is $15.

Mobility International USA (Box 3551, Eugene, OR 97403, tel. 503/343–1284–voice and TDD) is an internationally affiliated organization. For a $20 annual fee, it coordinates exchange programs for disabled people around the world and offers information on accommodations and organized study programs.

The **Society for the Advancement of Travel for the Handicapped** (347 5th Ave., Suite 610, New York, NY 10016, tel. 212/447–7284, fax 212/725–8253) provides access information and lists of tour operators specializing in travel for the disabled. The annual membership costs $45, or $25 for students and senior citizens. Send $1 and a stamped, self-addressed envelope for information on a specific destination.

Publications *The Itinerary* (Box 2012, Bayonne, NJ 07002, tel. 201/858–3400) is a bimonthly travel magazine for the disabled. Call for a subscription ($10 for one year, $20 for two); it's not available in bookstores.

Twin Peaks Press (Box 129, Vancouver, WA 98666, tel. 206/694–2462 or 800/637–2256 for orders only) specializes in books for the disabled. *Travel for the Disabled* offers helpful hints, as well as a comprehensive list of guidebooks and facilities geared to the disabled. *The Directory of Travel Agencies for the Disabled* lists more than 350 agencies throughout the world. Twin Peaks also offers a "Traveling Nurse's Network," which provides registered nurses to accompany and assist disabled travelers.

In Scotland Facilities for the disabled in Scotland, like those in the rest of Great Britain, are better than average. Many hotels offer facilities for wheelchair users, and special carriages are beginning to appear on intercity and long-distance trains. However, since much of Scotland's beauty is found in hidden hills and corners "off the beaten track," renting a car is probably a better option.

The **Holiday Care Service** (2 Old Bank Chambers, Station Rd., Horley, Surrey RH6 9HW, England, tel. 0293/774–535) is a registered charity that provides free information and advice on holidays for people with special needs. Information is available on accommodations, transportation, and package holidays offered by both commercial operators and voluntary associations. **The Scottish Tourist Board** (23 Ravelston Terr., Edinburgh EH4 3EU, Scotland, tel. 031/332–2433) also publishes a variety of brochures offering information on accommodations and transportation for people with disabilities. Another source of useful information for disabled visitors to Scotland is the **Scottish Council on Disability** (18/19 Claremont Crescent, Edinburgh EH7 4QD, tel. 031/556–3882). The **National Trust for Scotland** (5 Charlotte Sq., Edinburgh EH2 4DU, tel. 031/226–5922) publishes an annual book indicating which historic houses and monuments have provisions for handicapped visitors.

Getting Around **Hertz** (tel. 800/654–3131) can provide hand controls for indivi-
by Car duals with lower-limb disability at its rental offices in Glasgow and Edinburgh.

Getting Around With advance notification, British Rail staff will provide assist-
by Rail ance to disabled passengers. For further information about special provisions and fare concessions, contact **RADAR** (25 Mortimer St., London W1N 8AB) or inquire at any British Rail area office.

Hints for Older Travelers

The American Association of Retired Persons (AARP, 601 E St. NW, Washington, DC 20049, tel. 202/434–2277) has two programs for independent travelers: (1) the **Purchase Privilege Program,** which offers discounts on hotels, airfare, car rentals, RV rentals, and sightseeing; and (2) the **AARP Motoring Plan,** provided by Amoco, which furnishes emergency road-service aid and trip-routing information for an annual fee of $33.95 per person or couple. The AARP also arranges group tours through **AARP Travel Experience from American Express** (400 Pinnacle Way, Suite 450, Norcross, GA 30071, tel. 800/927–0111). AARP members must be 50 years old or older; annual dues are $5 per person or couple.

If you're allowed to use an AARP or other senior-citizen identification card to obtain a reduced hotel rate, mention it at the time you make your reservation, rather than when you check out. At participating restaurants, show your card to the maître d' before you're seated, as discounts may be limited to certain menus, days, or hours. When renting a car, be sure to ask about special promotional rates that may offer greater savings than what is available with your discount ID.

Elderhostel (75 Federal St., 3rd floor, Boston, MA 02110–1941, tel. 617/426–7788) is an innovative, educational program for people 60 and older. Participants live in dorms on some 1,600 campuses around the world. Mornings are devoted to lectures and seminars; afternoons to sightseeing and field trips. Fees for two- to three-week international trips—including room, board, tuition, and round-trip transportation—range from $1,800 to $4,500.

National Council of Senior Citizens (1331 F St., NW, Washington, DC 20004, tel. 202/347–8800) is a nonprofit advocacy group with some 5,000 local clubs across the United States. Annual membership is $12 per person or couple. Members receive a monthly newspaper with travel information and an ID card for reduced-rate hotels and car rentals.

Mature Outlook (6001 N. Clark St., Chicago, IL 60660, tel. 800/336–6330), a subsidiary of Sears, Roebuck & Co., is a travel club for people over 50 that provides hotel and motel discounts and publishes a bimonthly newsletter. Annual membership is $9.95. Instant membership is available at Sears stores and participating Holiday Inns.

Saga International Holidays (120 Boylston St., Boston, MA 02116, tel. 800/343–0273) specializes in group travel for people over 60. A selection of variously priced tours allows you to choose the package that meets your needs.

Publications *The International Health Guide for Senior Citizen Travelers,* by W. Robert Lange, MD, is available for $4.95 plus $1.50 for shipping, from Pilot Books (103 Cooper St., Babylon, NY 11702, tel. 515/422–2225).

In Scotland Scotland offers a wide variety of discounts and travel bargains for senior citizens (men over 65 and women 60 and over). The **Senior Citizen Railcard,** available in all major British Rail stations, offers one-third off all rail fares. Seniors over 60 get one-third off all National Express coach fares. For discounted admission to hundreds of museums, historic buildings, and attractions throughout Britain, senior citizens need show only their passport as proof of age. Reduced-rate tickets to theater and ballet are also available.

Accommodations Many hotels advertise off-season discounts for senior citizens, and some offer year-round savings. **Stakis Hotels and Inns** (tel. in Scotland 03552/49235) offer a 10% discount to all guests over 60 staying a minimum of two nights, and **Scottish Highland Hotels** (tel. in Scotland 041/332–6538) have a special year-round "Golden Times" package offering one-third off regular rates. Budget-minded seniors may also consider overnight accommodations at a university or college residence hall (*see* **BUAC** under Student and Youth Travel, *above*).

Arriving and Departing

Visitors have a choice of three types of flights: nonstop—no changes, no stops; direct—no changes, but one or more stops; and connecting—two or more planes, one or more stops.

From North America by Plane

Since the air routes between North America and Great Britain are heavily traveled, you'll have many airlines and fares to choose from. But fares change with stunning rapidity, so consult your travel agent on which bargains are currently available.

Airlines Airlines serving Edinburgh, Glasgow, and other major cities in Britain include **American Airlines** (tel. 800/433–7300); **British Airways** (tel. 800/247–9297); **Delta** (tel. 800/241–4141); **Northwest Airlines** (tel. 800/447–4747); and **TWA** (tel. 800/892–4141).

Flying Time The flight to Glasgow from New York is about 6½ hours, from Chicago 7½ hours, and from Los Angeles 10 hours.

Enjoying the Flight If you're lucky enough to be able to sleep on a plane, it makes sense to fly at night. Many experienced travelers, however, prefer to take a morning flight to Scotland and arrive in the evening, just in time for a good night's sleep. Because the air on a plane is dry, it helps, while flying, to drink a lot of nonalcoholic beverages; drinking alcohol contributes to jet lag, as does eating heavy meals on board. Feet swell at high altitudes, so it's a good idea to remove your shoes at the beginning of your flight. Sleepers usually prefer window seats to curl up against; those who like to move about the cabin ask for aisle seats. Bulkhead seats (located in the front row of each cabin) have more legroom, but seat trays are attached rather awkwardly to the arms of the seat rather than to the back of the seat ahead. Generally bulkhead seats are reserved for the disabled, the elderly, or parents traveling with babies.

Discount Flights The major airlines offer a range of tickets that can increase the price of any given seat by more than 300%, depending on the day of purchase. As a rule, the further in advance you buy the ticket, the less expensive it is and the greater the penalty (up to 100%) for canceling. Check with airlines for details. The best buy is not necessarily an APEX (advance purchase) ticket on one of the major airlines, because these tickets carry certain restrictions: They must be bought in advance (usually 21 days), they restrict your travel, usually with a minimum stay of seven days and a maximum of 90, and they also penalize you for changes—voluntary or not—in your travel plans. . . can work around these drawbacks (and most travele they are among the best-value fares available.

Travelers willing to put up with some restrictions and inc veniences, in exchange for a substantially reduced airfare, may be interested in flying as an air courier. A person who agrees to be a courier must accompany shipments between designated points. There are two sources of information on courier deals: 1) A telephone directory lists courier companies by the cities to which they fly. Send $5 and a self-addressed, stamped, business-size envelope to Pacific Data Sales Publishing, 2554 Lincoln Blvd., Suite 275–I, Marina Del Rey, CA 90291. 2) For *A Simple Guide to Courier Travel*, send $15.95 (includes postage and handling) to Box 2394, Lake Oswego, OR 97035. For more information, call 800/344–9375.

Charter flights offer the lowest fares but often depart only on certain days and seldom on time. Though you may be able to arrive at one city and return from another, you may lose all or most of your money if you cancel your trip. Don't sign up for a charter flight unless you've checked with a travel agency about the reputation of the packager. It's particularly important to know the packager's policy concerning refunds should a flight be canceled; some travel agents recommend that travelers purchase trip-cancellation insurance if they plan to book charter flights. One of the most popular charter operators to Europe is **Council Charter** (205 E. 42nd St., New York, NY 10017, tel. 212/661–0311 or 800/800–8222), a division of the Council on International Educational Exchange (CIEE). Other companies advertise in Sunday travel sections of newspapers.

Somewhat more expensive—but up to 50% below the cost of APEX fares—are tickets purchased through consolidators, companies that buy blocks of tickets on scheduled airlines and sell them at wholesale prices. Tickets are subject to availability, so passengers must generally have flexible travel schedules. Here again, you may lose all or most of your money if you change plans, but at least you will be on a regularly scheduled flight with less risk of cancellation than on a charter. As an added precaution, you may want to purchase trip-cancellation insurance. Once you've made your reservation, call the airline to confirm it. Among the best-known consolidators are **UniTravel** (Box 12485, St. Louis, MO 63132, tel. 314/569–2501 or 800/325–2222) and **Access International** (101 W. 31st St., Suite 1104, New York, NY 10001, tel. 212/465–0707 or 800/825–3633). Others advertise in Sunday newspaper travel sections.

Another option is to join a travel club that offers special discounts to its members. Several such organizations are **Discount Travel International** (114 Forrest Ave., Narberth, PA 19072, tel. 215/668–7184 or 800/334–9294); **Moment's Notice** (425 Madison Ave., New York, NY 10017, tel. 212/486–0500); **Travelers Advantage** (CUC Travel Service, 49 Music Square West, Nashville, TN 37203, tel. 800/548–1116); and **Worldwide Discount Travel Club** (1674 Meridian Ave., Miami Beach, FL 33139, tel. 305/534–2082). These cut-rate tickets should be compared with APEX tickets on the major airlines.

Smoking If cigarette smoke bothers you, ask for a seat far from the smoking section. It is best to request a nonsmoking seat at the time that you book your ticket. If a U.S. airline representative tells you there are no seats available in the nonsmoking section, insist on one: Department of Transportation regulations require U.S. flag carriers to find seats for all nonsmokers on the day of the flight, provided they meet check-in time restrictions.

From North America by Ship

The *Queen Elizabeth 2* (*QE 2*) is the only cruise ship that makes regular transatlantic crossings. Other cruise ships that sail from European ports in the summer and North American ports in the winter make transatlantic repositioning crossings as one season ends and another begins. Some sail straight across, often at reduced rates to passengers. Others have several ports of call before heading for the open sea. Arrangements can be made to cruise one way and fly the other. Since itineraries can change at the last minute, contact the cruise line for the latest information.

Cunard Line (555 5th Ave., New York, NY 10017, tel. 800/221–4770) operates four ships that make transatlantic crossings. The *QE 2* makes regular crossings April through December, between Southampton, England, and Baltimore, Boston, and New York City. Arrangements for the *QE 2* can include one-way airfare. Cunard Line also offers fly-cruise packages and pre- and post-land packages. Check the travel pages of your Sunday newspaper for other cruise ships that sail to Britain.

From England by Plane

There is a "bus-service" of flights from London to Scotland. **British Airways** and **British Midland** operate from London Heathrow to Edinburgh and Glasgow. Between them they operate some 17 flights to Edinburgh and 18 to Glasgow each weekday. **Loganair, Brymon Airlines, Dan Air,** and **Air U.K.** also connect Scotland with English airports, including London Gatwick.

From England by Train

There are two main rail routes from the south to Scotland. The first is the west coast main line, which runs from London Euston to Glasgow Central via Rugby, Crewe, Preston, and Carlisle. These frequent and reliable services cover the 400 miles to central Scotland in just over five hours. The standard service is of one train per hour, and some have portions for Edinburgh that are detached at Carstairs. For daytime travel to the Scottish Highlands, the *Clansman* is a very useful train, taking you direct to Stirling and Aviemore and terminating at Inverness. The train also carries an excellent restaurant car. The *Royal Highlander* sleeper services run overnight from London Euston to Perth, Stirling, Aviemore, Fort William, and Inverness. All the trains contain new air-conditioned and sound-proof sleeping carriages. Family compartments are available. These services allow you to leave London in the late evening and arrive refreshed at your destination early the following morning. They obviously offer a restful way of getting into the heart of the Scottish Highlands.

The second route is the east coast main line from London King's Cross to Edinburgh via Newcastle and Durham, crossing into Scotland at Berwick on Tweed. This line is the quickest way of reaching the Scottish capital. Between 8 in the morning and 6 in the evening there are 15 trains to Edinburgh, three of which run through to Aberdeen. Limited-stop expresses like the *Flying Scotsman* take around four hours for the 393-mile London–Edinburgh journey. Connecting services from Edinburgh to most other parts of Scotland are much better than from Glasgow. For travel to Glasgow Queen Street there is a half-hourly service, with the fast trains taking only 45 minutes. Travelers bound for the Western Highlands and Islands—Mallaig, Oban, and Fort William—will find it easier to travel via Edinburgh to Glasgow Queen Street because this cuts out the need to cross between stations in Glasgow. Reservations on all sleeper services are essential.

Trains from elsewhere in England are good: There is regular service from Birmingham, Manchester, Liverpool, Bristol, Southampton, and Penzance to Glasgow and Edinburgh. For travelers entering Britain via Harwich (ships from Holland, Germany, and Denmark), there is the *European,* which runs through to Glasgow via North London and Birmingham. For faster connections catch the new train, the *Rinelander,* and change at Peterborough for the east coast main line to Edinburgh.

From England by Bus

Buses (or coaches, as the long-distance and touring buses are usually called) provide the cheapest method of transport between England and Scotland. About 20 coach companies operate services between English cities, especially London, and Scottish towns and cities, especially Glasgow and Edinburgh. The best-known operators are **Scottish Citylink Coaches** and **Caledonian Express.** Journey time between London and Glasgow or Edinburgh is 8 to 8½ hours, and the coaches run day and night. Most are quite comfortable; some offer catering facilities and videos on board. Fares on the long-distance coaches are approximately one-third of the rail fares for comparable trips.

The main London terminal is Victoria Coach Station, but some Scottish companies use Gloucester Road Coach Station in west London, near the Penta Hotel. Many people travel to Scotland by coach; in summer a reservation three or four days ahead is advisable. Scottish Bus Group timetables are obtainable from the group's offices at 114–116 George Street, Edinburgh EH2 4LX, or in London from Scottish Citylink Coaches (298 Regent St., London W1R 6LE, tel. 071/636–9373 or 071/636–9374) or from the Coach Travel Center (13 Regent St., London SW1Y 4LR, tel. 071/730–0202). Travel centers and travel agents also have details, and some travel agents sell tickets.

Staying in Scotland

Getting Around

By Plane   Although a small country, Scotland nonetheless has a significant internal air network. **British Airways**, the principal carrier, has fly/drive packages to Orkney and Shetland of four to 14 days from all main U.K. airports. British Airways' *Highland Rover* airpass (cost: £213) allows eight flights between mainland and/or island airports over eight to 21 days. **Loganair** is another important carrier within Scotland.

By Train Scotland has a good rail network extending all the way to Thurso and Wick, the most northerly stations in the British Isles. Lowland services are generally reliable and fast. They radiate mostly from Glasgow and Edinburgh, between which there is a half-hourly shuttle taking some 45 minutes. (For information about Edinburgh's and Glasgow's train stations, *see* chapters 3 and 4, respectively.)

Although many routes in Scotland run through extremely attractive countryside, several are outstanding. The best are from Glasgow to Oban via Loch Lomond; to Fort William and Mallaig via Rannoch (ferry connection to Skye); from Edinburgh to Inverness via the Forth Bridge and Perth; from Inverness to Kyle of Lochalsh and to Wick; and from Inverness to Aberdeen. One word of caution: There are very few trains in the Highlands on Sundays.

Some lines in Scotland—all suburban services and lines north and west of Inverness—are one class only (standard). Long-distance services carry buffet and refreshment cars.

Train fares vary according to the type of ticket purchased as well as class. The fare system is complex. Always go to the Information Office/Travel Center first and ask about the cheapest way to travel and if there are any special offers. Ask about *InterCity Saver* and about the *Family Railcard* if children are with you. It is important to remember that these days, on overcrowded intercity trains, a ticket does *not* guarantee you a seat. Seat reservations must be made and paid for separately. A charge of £1 *per train* will be made. So if you have to change trains, you will need to book a seat on each train and will be charged £2. You will be offered a choice of sitting facing toward or away from the engine, in a smoking or nonsmoking compartment.

A luxury private train, the *Royal Scotsman,* does scenic tours, partly under steam power. Gourmet banquets are served en route. Book with **Abercrombie & Kent** (Sloane Square House, Holbein Pl., London SW1W 8NS, tel. 071/730–9600; in the U.S.: 1420 Kensington Rd., Oak Brook, IL 60521, tel 800/323–7308 or 312/954–2944); cost is from $1,800 (three days) to $4,500 (six days). **British Rail** offers occasional pullman rail cruises, partly steam-hauled, on the *Orcadian* and *West Highlander* (window seat guaranteed, overnights in sleeper or hotel); from London the fare ranges from £295 to £340, according to season. Details are available from the London (Euston) Travel Center; you can book through **InterCity Scottish Land Cruises** (104 Birmingham Rd., Lichfield, Staffs WS14 9BW, tel. 0543/254076).

The *Freedom of Scotland Rover* ticket, which offers unlimited travel north of Berwick on Tweed and Carlisle, costs £69 (seven days) or £105 (15 days). It's available from most Scottish stations and certain English ones.

By Bus There is a very extensive bus network throughout the country. City bus services are comprehensive, though service in country districts is less comprehensive. Express service links main cities and towns, connecting, for example, Glasgow and Edinburgh to Inverness, Aberdeen, Perth, Skye, Ayr, Dumfries, and Carlisle. From Inverness there are routes to Aberdeen,

Wick, Thurso, and Fort William. These express services are very fast, and the fares are quite reasonable.

Full details of all these services can be had from most bus stations or the **Travel Center** (Buchanan Street Bus Station, Glasgow G2 3NP, tel. 041/332–7133); **S.M.T.** (St. Andrew Bus Station, Edinburgh EH1 3DU, tel. 031/556–8464); and **Edinburgh and Scotland Travel Centre,** (3 Princes St., Edinburgh EH2 2QP, tel. 031/557–1700).

For town, suburban, or short-distance journeys you normally buy your ticket on the bus, from a paybox or the driver. Sometimes the exact fare is demanded (no change will be given). For longer journeys—for example, Glasgow–Inverness—it is usual to reserve and pay at the bus station booking office.

By Ferry With so many islands, plus the great Firth of Clyde waterway, ferry services in Scotland are of paramount importance. Most of these are now vehicle ferries, although a number of the smaller ones are passenger only. All vehicle ferries carry foot passengers.

The main operator is **Caledonian MacBrayne Ltd.** (The Ferry Terminal, Gourock PA19 1QP, tel. 0475/33755), a state-owned company, known generally as Calmac. Their services extend from the Firth of Clyde, where they operate an extremely extensive network, right up to the northwest of Scotland and all of the Hebrides. Calmac offers a *Car Rover* runabout ticket, which is ideal for touring holidays in the islands, as well as an island-hopping scheme called *Island Hopscotch.* **Western Ferries** (16 Woodside Crescent, Glasgow G3 7UT, tel. 041/332–9766) operates the Dunoon–Gourock route on the Clyde, as well as a run from Islay (Port Askaig) to Jura.

The Orkney Islands are linked to the mainland by car ferry from Scrabster (near Thurso) to Stromness (on the main island of Orkney, called Mainland). This ferry is operated by **P & O Ferries** (Jamieson's Quay, Box 5, Aberdeen AB9 8DL, tel. 0224/572615). The ferry runs daily with an extra service from Aberdeen to Lerwick; there are five sailings weekly in each direction. The main ferries on this route, the *St. Clair* and the *St. Sunniva,* have cabin accommodations. This service is operated by P & O as well.

By Car If you are already a member of a motoring organization, there may be reciprocal membership benefits available between your auto club and the Automobile Association (AA) in Britain, including breakdown assistance. Check with your club; it will also be able to advise you about procedures, insurance, and necessary documentation. If your auto club doesn't have such arrangements, both the AA (Fanum House, Basingstoke, Hants, RQ212EA, tel. 0256/20123) and the **Royal Automobile Club** (RAC House, Bartlett St., Box 10, Croydon, Surrey CR2 6XW, tel. 081/686–2525) offer associate membership for overseas visitors with all the benefits of membership. The AA and the RAC have large touring departments that offer a wealth of detailed information about motoring in Britain.

Types of Roads There's now a very good network of superhighways (motorways) and divided highways (dual carriageways) throughout most of Britain, though in the remoter areas of Scotland where the motorway has not penetrated, travel is noticeably slower. Motorways shown with the prefix "M" are mainly two or three lanes in each direction, without any right-hand turns. If you'll be covering longer distances, these are the roads to use, though inevitably you'll see less of the countryside. Service areas are situated about an hour's (or less) travel time apart. Dual carriageways, usually shown on a map as a thick red line (often with a black line in the center) and the prefix "A" followed by a number perhaps with a bracket "T" (for example, A304[T]), are similar to motorways, except that right turns are sometimes permitted and you'll find both traffic lights and traffic circles on them.

The vast network of other main roads, which the map shows as either single red "A" roads, or narrower brown "B" roads, also numbered, are for the most part the old coach and turnpike roads built for horses and carriages in the last century or earlier. Travel along these roads is much slower because passing is more difficult, and your trip may take twice the time it would take along a motorway. On the other hand, you'll see much more of Scotland.

Minor roads (shown as yellow or white on maps, unlettered and unnumbered) are the ancient lanes and byways of Britain, roads that are not only living history but a superb way of discovering the real Scotland. You have to drive along them slowly and carefully—sometimes there isn't even room for two vehicles to pass, and you must reverse into a passing place if you meet an oncoming car or tractor.

Rules of the Road The most noticeable difference for the visitor is that when in Britain, you drive on the left. This takes a bit of getting used to, but it doesn't take very long, particularly if you're driving a British car where the steering and mirrors will be adjusted for U.K. conditions. You should be particularly careful, if you have picked up your car at the airport, to give yourself time to adjust to driving on the left—especially if you have jet lag.

One of the most complicated questions facing visitors to Britain is that of speed limits. In urban areas, except for certain freeways, it is generally 30 miles per hour, but it is 40 mph on some main roads, as indicated by circular red signs. In rural areas the official limit is 60 mph on ordinary roads and 70 mph on motorways—and traffic police can be hard on speeders, especially in urban areas. In other respects procedures are similar to those in the United States.

Gasoline Expect to pay a good deal more for gasoline than in the United States, though costs have been remarkably stable in recent years, at about £2 a gallon (45p a liter) for 4-star—though it can be up to 10p a gallon higher in remote rural locations. Remember, too, that the British Imperial gallon is about 20% more in volume than the U.S. gallon. What you may find confusing is that although service stations advertise prices by the gallon (mainly for the benefit of the conservative British who continue to resist metrification), pumps actually measure in liters. A British gallon is approximately 4.5 liters. Most British people solve the conundrum by buying gas by the tankful or several pounds' worth.

Most gas stations stock 4-star (97 octane), unleaded and super unleaded, plus diesel. Service stations are located at regular intervals on motorways and are usually open 24 hours a day, though stations elsewhere usually close from 9 PM to 7 AM, and in country areas many close at 6 PM and all day on Sundays.

Telephones

The public telephone system in Britain is generally reliable. Public telephone boxes use coins or convenient phone cards, which can be purchased from many shops (newsagents, etc.) and post offices. With the ongoing modernization program for telephone exchanges, the services available are always improving.

Mail

Postal Rates Airmail letters to the United States and Canada cost 39p; postcards 33p; aerograms 34p. Letters and postcards to Europe under 20 grams cost 28p (24p to other European Community member countries). Within the U.K. first-class letters cost 24p, second-class letters and postcards 18p.

Receiving Mail If you're uncertain where you'll be staying, you can arrange to have your mail sent to American Express. The service is free to cardholders; all others pay a small fee. You can also collect letters at Edinburgh's main post office.

Tipping

Some restaurants and most hotels add a service charge of 10%–15% to the bill. In this case you are not expected to tip. If no service charge is indicated, add 10% to your total bill, but always check first. Taxi drivers should also get 10%. You are not expected to tip theater or movie theater ushers, elevator operators, or bartenders in pubs. Hairdressers and barbers should receive 10%–15%.

Opening and Closing Times

Banks Banks are open weekdays 9:30–4:30. Some have extended hours on Thursday evenings, and a few are open on Saturday mornings.

Shops Usual business hours are Monday–Saturday 9–5:30. Outside the main centers, most shops observe an early closing day once a week, often Wednesday or Thursday. They close at 1 PM and do not reopen until the following morning. In small villages, many also close for lunch. In large cities department stores stay open for late-night shopping (usually until 7:30 or 8) one day a week. Apart from some newsstands and small food stores, almost all shops are closed on Sunday.

Shopping

The best buys in Britain in general are antiques, craft items, woolen goods, china, men's shoes, books, confectionery, and toys. In Scotland, many visitors go for tweeds, designer knitwear, Shetland and Fair Isle woolens, tartan rugs and materials, Edinburgh crystal, Caithness glass, Celtic silver, and pebble jewelry. The Scottish Highlands bristle with old *bothies* (farm buildings) that have been turned into small craft workshops where visitors are welcome—but not pressured—to buy attractive handmade items of bone, silver, wood, pottery, leather, and glass. Handmade chocolates, often with whisky or Drambuie fillings, and the traditional "petticoat tail" shortbread in tin boxes are popular; so, too, at a more mundane level, are boiled sweets in jars from particular localities—Berwick cockles, Jethart snails, Edinburgh rock, and similar crunchy items. Dundee cake, a rich fruit mixture with almonds on top, and Dundee marmalades and heather honeys are among the other eatables that visitors take home from Scotland.

Dining

Scottish restaurants are noted for helpful attention and modest prices, but not, in most places, for an exotic or imaginative cuisine. In all districts you will find restaurants that have risen, or are beginning to rise, above the old dull stereotyped level—but they are still in the minority.

City Scots usually take their midday meals in a pub, wine bar, bistro, or department store restaurant (which may be nonalcoholic and nonsmoking). When traveling, the Scot generally eats inexpensively and quickly at a country pub or village tea room. Places like Glasgow, Edinburgh, and Aberdeen, of course, offer restaurants of cosmopolitan character and various price levels. The more notable ones tend to open only in the evening. Most smaller towns and many villages have at least one restaurant where—certainly if a local is in charge—the service is a reminder of a Highland tradition that ensured that no stranger could travel through the country without receiving a welcome.

In a country so involved in the tourism industry, "all day" meal places are becoming quite widespread. The normal lunch period, however, is 12:30–2:30. A few places offer "high tea"—one hot dish and masses of cakes, bread and butter, and jam, served with tea only, around 5:30–6:40.

You will come across restaurants that offer "A Taste of Scotland" menu, which means you'll find oddly named traditional dishes that are often cooked and served in traditional pots and pans. The Taste of Scotland scheme, initiated by the Scottish Tourist Board, has helped—almost by accident—to preserve some of the Scots language, especially the names for a variety of traditional dishes.

Lodging

Scotland was the first part of the United Kingdom to run a national "Classification and Grading Scheme" to take some of the guesswork out of booking accommodations. When you are considering a hotel, guest house, or bed-and-breakfast, make sure that you pay close attention to its classification and its grading. The classification part is easy. The number of crowns from zero to five tells you the range of the establishment's facilities. Zero crowns (confusingly described as "Listed") is basic; five crowns luxury. The grading part is actually more important. It purports to assess the quality of the place objectively. Very roughly, the ordinary is "Approved," the good "Commended," and the very good "Highly Commended." Thus a two-crown "Highly Commended" is probably better value all around than a four-crown "Approved." The awards are part of the accommodations listing in the *Where to Stay* guides distributed at most tourist information centers. Not all establishments participate, but the scheme is becoming popular. In many small towns and villages there are excellent-value inns and hotels offering reasonable comfort (central heating, rooms with bath or shower and telephone and television) at competitive prices. But rural Scotland is bed-and-breakfast land, and, because Scottish breakfasts are usually nothing if not hearty, these are a pretty good value. Indeed, for anyone planning to tour Scotland, they can be hard to beat, especially since most offer genuinely warm hospitality, as well as home cooking and comforts. The Scottish Tourist Board's *Scotland—Hotels and Guest Houses* (£6.30 by mail) and *Where to Stay Bed and Breakfast* (£4.60) together give details of more than 4,000 bed-and-breakfasts.

Hotels in the larger cities are generally also good. Glasgow and Edinburgh boast a number of very superior hotels, as well as an extensive range of good hotels in all other price categories. Both have active and helpful accommodations offices should you arrive without reservations.

Bookings are generally easy to make since, in recent years, even in the height of the season—July and August—only some 80% of all available accommodations have been booked. So if you are touring around, you are not likely to be stranded unless you arrive in Edinburgh at Festival time or some place where a big Highland Gathering or golf tournament is in progress. Your choice of accommodations will then be extremely limited. Try, if possible, to make reservations in advance, either through a travel agent at home or in England, or from one of the many Scottish Tourist Board booklets listing accommodations when you arrive in Scotland and have decided what your itinerary will be. Telephone booking should be confirmed by letter, and country hotels expect you to turn up by about 6 PM. You can also make reservations through local Information Centres (*see* the individual city or regional chapters), making use of their "Book-a-Bed-Ahead" services.

Credit Cards

The following credit-card abbreviations have been used: AE, American Express; D, Discover; DC, Diners Club; MC, MasterCard; V, Visa. It's a good idea to call ahead to check current credit-card policies.

2 Portraits of Scotland

Scotland at a Glance: A Chronology

c 3000 BC Neolithic migration from Mediterranean: "chambered cairn" people in north, "beaker people" in southeast

c 300 BC Iron Age: infusion of Celtic peoples from the south and from Ireland; "Gallic forts," "brochs" built

AD 79–89 Julius Agricola, Roman governor of Britain, invades Scotland; Scots tribes defeated at Mons Graupius (Grampians): "they make a desert and call it peace." Roman forts built at Inchtuthil and Ardoch

142 Emperor Antoninus Pius orders Antonine Wall built between the Firths of Forth and Clyde

185 Antonine Wall abandoned

367 Massive invasion of Britain by Picts, Scots, Saxons, Franks

400–1000 Era of the Four Peoples: redhaired Picts in the north, Gaelic-speaking Scots and Britons in the west and south, Germanic Angles in the east. Origins of Arthur legend (Arthur's Seat, Ben Arthur). Picts, with bloodline through mothers, eventually dominate 392 Ninian's mission to Picts: first Christian chapel at Whitehorn

563 Columba establishes monastery at Iona

780–1065 Scandinavian invasions; Hebrides remain Norse until 1263, Orkney and Shetland until 1472

1005–1034 Malcolm II unifies Scotland and (temporarily) repels the English

1040 Malcolm's heir, Duncan, is slain by his rival, Macbeth, whose wife has a claim to the throne

The House of Canmore

1057 Malcolm III, known as "Canmore" ("Big Head"), murders Macbeth and assumes the throne

1093 Death of Malcolm's queen, St. Margaret, founder of modern Edinburgh

1124–1153 David I, "soir sanct" (sore saint), builds the abbeys of Jedburgh (1118), Kelso (1128), Melrose (1136), and Dryburgh (1150) and brings Norman culture to Scotland

1290 The first of many attempts to unite Scotland peacefully with England fails when the Scots queen Margaret, "the Maid of Norway," dies on the way to her wedding to Edward, son of Edward I of England. The Scots naively ask Edward I (subsequently known as "the hammer of the Scots") to arbitrate between the remaining 13 claimants to the throne. Edward's choice, John Balliol, is known as "toom tabard" (empty coat)

1295 Under continued threat from England, Scotland signs its first treaty of the "auld alliance" with France. Wine trade flourishes

1297 Revolt. William Wallace, immortalized by Burns, leads the Scots against the English

1305 Wallace captured by the English and executed

1306–29 Reign of Robert Bruce (Robert I). Defeats Edward II at Bannockburn, 1314; Treaty of Northampton, 1328, recognizes Scottish sovereignty

1368 Edinburgh Castle rebuilt

The House of Stewart

1371 Robert II, son of Robert Bruce's daughter Marjorie and Walter the Steward, is crowned. Struggle (dramatized in Scott's novels) between the crown and the barony ensues for the next century, punctuated by sporadic warfare with England

1411 Founding of University of St. Andrews, modeled on Paris

1451 University of Glasgow founded

1488–1515 Reign of James IV. The Renaissance reaches Scotland. The "Golden Age" of Scots poetry includes Robert Henryson, William Dunbar, Gavin Douglas, and the king himself

1495 University of Aberdeen founded

1507 Andrew Myllar and Walter Chapman set up first Scots printing press in Edinburgh

1513 At war against the English, James is slain at Flodden

1542 Henry VIII defeats James V at Solway Moss; the dying James, hearing of the birth of his daughter, Mary, declared: "It came with a lass [Marjorie Bruce] and it will pass with a lass"

1542–67 Reign of Mary Queen of Scots. Romantic, Catholic, and with an excellent claim to the English throne, Mary proved to be no match for her barons, John Knox, or her cousin Elizabeth of England

1560 Mary returns to Scotland from her childhood in France, at the same time that Catholicism is abolished in favor of Knox's Calvinism

1565 Mary marries Lord Darnley, a Catholic

1567 Darnley is murdered at Kirk o' Field; Mary marries one of the conspirators, the earl of Bothwell. Driven from Scotland, she appeals to Elizabeth, who imprisons her. Mary's son, James (1566–1625), is crowned James VI of Scotland

1582 University of Edinburgh is founded

1587 Elizabeth orders the execution of Mary

1603 Elizabeth dies without issue; James VI is crowned James I of England. Parliaments remain separate for another century

1638 National Covenant challenges Charles I's personal rule

1639–41 Crisis. The Scots and then the English Parliaments revolt against Charles I

1643 Solemn League and Covenant establishes Presbyterianism as the Church of Scotland ("the Kirk"). Civil War in England

1649 Charles I beheaded. Cromwell made Protector

1650–52 Cromwell roots out Scots royalists

1658　First Edinburgh–London coach: the journey took two weeks

1660　Restoration of Charles II. Episcopalianism reestablished in Scotland; Covenanters persecuted

1688–89　Glorious Revolution; James VII and II, a Catholic, deposed in favor of his daughter Mary and her husband, William of Orange. Supporters of James ("Jacobites") defeated at Killiecrankie. Presbyterianism reestablished

1692　Highlanders who refuse oath to William and Mary massacred at Glencoe

1698–1700　Attempted Scottish colony at Darien fails

1707　Union of English and Scots Parliaments under Queen Anne; deprived of French wine trade, Scots turn to whiskey

The House of Hanover

1714　Queen Anne dies; George I of Hanover, descended from a daughter of James VI and I, crowned

1715　First Jacobite Rebellion. Earl of Mar defeated

1730–90　Scottish Enlightenment. The Edinburgh Medical School is the best in Europe; David Hume (1711–1776) and Adam Smith (1723–1790) redefine philosophy and economics. In the arts, Allan Ramsay the elder (1686–1758) and Robert Burns (1759–1796) refine Scottish poetry; Allan Ramsay the younger (1713–1784) and Henry Raeburn (1756–1823) rank among the finest painters of the era. Edinburgh's New Town, begun in the 1770s by the brothers Adam, provides a fitting setting

1745–46　Last Jacobite Rebellion. Bonnie Prince Charlie, grandson of James VII and II, is defeated at Culloden; wearing of the kilt is forbidden until 1782. James Watt (1736–1819) of Glasgow is granted a patent for his steam engine

1771　Birth of Walter Scott, Romantic novelist

1778　First cotton mill, at Rothesay

1788　Death of Bonnie Prince Charlie

1790　Forth and Clyde Canal opened

1800–1850　Highland Clearances: overpopulation, increased rents, and conversion of farms to sheep pasture led to mass migration, sometimes forced, to North America and elsewhere. Meanwhile, the lowlands industrialize; Catholic Irish immigrate to factories of southwest

1828　Execution of Burke and Hare, who sold their murder victims to an Edinburgh anatomist, a lucrative trade

1832　Parliamentary Reform Act expands the franchise, redistributes seats

1837　Victoria accedes to the British throne

1842　Edinburgh–Glasgow railroad opened

1846　Edinburgh–London railroad opened

1848　Queen Victoria buys estate at Balmoral as her Scottish residence. Andrew Carnegie emigrates from Dunfermline to Pittsburgh

1884–85 Gladstone's Reform Act establishes manhood suffrage. Office of Secretary for Scotland authorized

1886 Scottish Home Rule Association founded

1901 Death of Queen Victoria

The House of Windsor

1928 Equal Franchise Act gives the vote to women. Scottish Office established as governmental department in Edinburgh. Scottish National Party founded

1931 Depression hits industrialized Scotland severely

1945 Two Scottish Nationalists elected to Parliament

1959 Finnart Oil Terminal, Chapelcross Nuclear Power Station, and Dounreay Fast Breeder Reactor opened

1964 Forth Road Bridge opened

1970 British Petroleum strikes oil in the North Sea; revives economy of northeast

1973 Britain becomes a member of the European Economic Community ("Common Market")

1974 Eleven Scottish Nationalist MPs elected. Old counties reorganized and renamed new regions

1979 Referendum on "devolution" of a separate Scotland: 33% for, 31% against; 36% don't vote

1981 Europe's largest oil terminal opens at Sullom Voe, Shetland

1988 Revival of Scots nationalism under banner of "Scotland in Europe," anticipating 1992 economic union

1992 Increasing attention focused on Scotland's dissatisfaction with rule from London, England. Poll shows 50% of Scots want independence

The Story of Scotland

By Gordon
Donaldson

*Professor
Emeritus Gordon
Donaldson of
Edinburgh
University is Her
Majesty's
Historiographer
Royal in Scotland
and the author of
more than 30
books, mainly on
Scottish history.*

Scotland almost defies classification. It is no longer an independent country and it has no legislative organ of its own, for the United Kingdom Parliament at Westminster legislates for it. Yet it has a distinct executive, with a Secretary of State and a number of ministers; its own legal system and its own law courts, different and separate from those of England (the British House of Lords, however, is the final court of appeal in civil cases). There is a Church of Scotland whose government is Presbyterian and totally separate from the Episcopalian Church of England. The local government system is now constructed not (as in England) of counties, but mainly of regions, each containing a number of districts, and one still finds "burghs" (not boroughs) and "provosts" (not mayors). Scottish sheriffs are salaried judges and therefore different from the sheriffs of either England or the United States. Scotland has its own banks and banknotes.

It is arguable whether there is a Scottish nation. The Scots of today are descended from Scandinavians, Irish, English, Welsh, French, and Flemings, who immigrated in earlier centuries and obliterated traces of more primitive inhabitants. The whole of Britain has a Celtic fringe, which in the south consists of Wales and Cornwall and in Scotland consists of the central and west Highlands. A new factor entered in the 19th century with a massive immigration from Ireland, which has left conspicuous features, not least a very large Roman Catholic element.

If there is no Scottish race, it is equally true that there is no Scottish language. The speech of the earliest known inhabitants has long vanished, leaving two tongues, which arrived about 500 BC. A people from Ireland calling themselves "Scots" settled in Argyll and brought with them the Gaelic language of Ireland, which used to be known in Scotland, quite accurately, as "Irish." The fact that the name is sometimes pronounced "Gallic" must not mislead the unwary into thinking that there is anything French about it. From the European continent came the Angles or English, who settled in northeastern England and southeastern Scotland, introducing what became the speech of England and most of Scotland. The area where Irish or Gaelic was spoken shrank steadily until it was confined to the western fringe of the mainland and some of the Hebrides. The Scandinavian tongue, which was brought by immigrants from Norway—some of them "vikings"—to Orkney and Shetland, has left many traces in the speech of the people there. French was spoken by the Norman immigrants of the 12th century (who introduced many familiar Scottish surnames, such as Bruce, Cumming, Fraser, Hay,

Somerville, Colville, Mowat, Menzies, and Stewart), but it hardly extended much beyond the aristocracy and probably died out in the 14th century.

The Lowlands must be considered to include the Orkney and Shetland islands and to continue along a coastal plain stretching from Caithness down nearly the entire eastern seaboard, extending various distances inland, and finally crossing the country from the Firth of Forth to the River Clyde. The southern uplands, that is, the hills between the Forth–Clyde line and the Border, while not Lowland in a physical sense, are racially and linguistically part of the Lowlands. Thus the Highlands lie to the west rather than to the north of the Lowlands and include the mountainous center of Scotland and the entire west coast. There is a Highland town south of Berwick in England: Campbeltown in Kintyre.

The fertile Lowlands were suitable for arable farming, although also with good grazing on hill slopes, while the Highlands lent themselves to a mainly pastoral economy in the glens or valleys, which ran through the barren wastes of the mountains. In later times it was chiefly in the Lowlands that industries developed. The eastern, Lowland areas have a fairly dry and temperate climate; in the central Highlands there are severe winters, whereas the western seaboard has in general mild conditions, usually kind to both plant and animal life, but the area is apt to be lashed by tempests of wind and rain. Few activities are more dispiriting than farming in the west Highlands, but there was little else to provide a livelihood. The Highlands could hardly ever have been economically viable without outside subsidies. For centuries these took the shape of raids by Highlanders on their Lowland neighbors, who despised and hated the westerners. It was said that after God created the first Highlander (out of a piece of horse manure),

Quoth God to the Highlander, "What will you now?"
"I will down to the Lowland, Lord, and there steal a cow."

The tourist's image of the Scot is of a bagpipe-playing figure in what is called "Highland dress" and sometimes miscalled "Scottish national dress." In fact, if anyone arrayed in Highland dress had turned up in the Lowlands three or four hundred years ago, he would probably have been shot on sight.

The many peoples who inhabited early Scotland were gradually brought under the rule of a single king. The lands north of the Forth and Clyde were united in 844 in the kingdom of Alba—in or about 1018 the king of Alba established control over the country between those rivers and the present border. In 1266 the western isles were ceded by Norway, and in 1468-69 Orkney and Shetland, too, came under Scottish rule.

The geography of the country presented so many obstacles to communications that, until a relatively late date, order could not be maintained everywhere, especially in the Highlands and the Borders. It is noticeable that the cathedrals for the dioceses that covered the Highlands were in towns situated in or near the Lowlands—Dunblane, Dunkeld, Elgin, Dornoch, and Fortrose. Similarly, the sheriffs who were supposed to administer justice in the Highlands sat in Dingwall, Inverness, Banff, and Perth. They were safer there! Highland chiefs often allied with the English against their own kings. It was not until after James VI became king of England in 1603 that joint Anglo-Scottish action could be taken against disorderly Borderers who sought refuge across the frontier and against disorderly Highlanders who sought refuge in Ireland.

There were strong local loyalties, arising partly from the fact that even in the Lowlands one fertile and populous area was often separated from another. Thus the Tweed valley was cut off by bleak hills from Edinburgh and its hinterland, while Angus and Kincardinshire were isolated from Aberdeenshire by mountains thrusting eastward to the sea near Stonehaven. Then there were elements in Scottish society that made the task of government difficult. The head of a great family was acknowledged as the leader of his own blood relations, of collateral branches of the family descended from a common ancestor, of tenants and vassals whose links with him sprang from land tenure and not from blood, of men who contracted to serve him, and of men who simply happened to share his surname. Very much the same kind of social organization existed throughout the whole country in the Middle Ages.

In the Highlands, the practice of accepting the leadership of a chief persisted until well into the 18th century. The "clan" has somehow captured the imagination of those who have no idea what a clan was. The historic Highland clan did not consist of people with the same surname, and indeed until the 18th century few Highlanders had surnames at all. The Highland clan comprised people associated for much the same reasons as the Lowland groupings just described. The modern clan, composed on the basis of surnames, has little historical foundation. It may be added that nearly all the clan tartans were devised by manufacturers in the 19th or 20th century and are simply big business.

While the government of Scotland involved many internal problems, the country was fortunate to escape the kind of competition for the throne that led to the Wars of the Roses in England: The succession in the house of Stuart proved so stable that for three centuries (1371–1649) the crown passed from father to child without deviation. This did mean, however, that at a time when almost everything depended on the ability of the monarch in person, the throne was frequently occupied by minors and government was weak.

The great external problem was relations with England. In the 12th and 13th centuries the ruling families of the two countries frequently intermarried and peace generally prevailed, but at the end of the 13th century there was a disputed succession in Scotland that gave Edward I of England an opportunity to attempt conquest. The Scots resisted, at first unsuccessfully under William Wallace (who was victorious at Stirling in 1297, but defeated at Falkirk in 1298) and then successfully under Robert the Bruce (who defeated the English at Bannockburn in 1314). In 1320 the Scottish nobles put their seals to a Declaration of Independence, dated at Arbroath, in which they declared: "As long as a hundred of us remain alive, we will never be subject to the English king; because it is not for riches, or honors, or glory that we fight, but for liberty alone, which no worthy man loses save with his life." But war went on intermittently for more than another two centuries, with many Scottish defeats like Flodden (1513) and Pinkie (1547). Yet the Scots succeeded in preserving their independence against their mighty neighbor.

As a result of the marriage in 1503 of James IV, king of Scots, to Margaret Tudor, daughter of Henry VII of England, their great-grandson, James VI, became king James I of England in 1603 on the death of Elizabeth, the last of the Tudors. Scotland and England were still distinct kingdoms, each with its own parliament and its own administration. Such an arrangement could work only if there were no conflicts of interest or if the Crown was more powerful than the parliaments. In the middle of the century, as a result of the civil war occasioned by the unpopular policies of Charles I, the union broke down, for after the execution of the king, the English declared a republic while the Scots proclaimed their allegiance to Charles II; the result was the conquest of Scotland by the armies of Oliver Cromwell. In 1660, when the monarchy was restored, there were again two kingdoms, separate but under the same king.

The next crisis arose in the 1690s, after James VII (of Scotland) and II (of England) had been deposed in favor of William of Orange. This revolution increased the powers of the two parliaments and made friction more likely. The Scottish parliament adopted independent economic policies that threatened to lead to separate foreign policies. It became clear that either the existing union might have to be dissolved (which would probably have led to war) or the countries would have to be more closely united. It was the latter course that prevailed, when the two parliaments agreed on May 1, 1707, that the kingdom of Scotland and the kingdom of England alike should come to an end and be replaced by a United Kingdom of Great Britain, with one parliament.

William of Orange was followed by Anne and then by the house of Hanover, beginning with George I (1714), but James (VII and II) left a son, "the Old Pretender," and had two grandsons, the elder of them Charles Edward, "Bonnie Prince Charlie," and the claims of this line were supported by the Jacobites, who raised two serious rebellions, in 1715 and 1745. The "Fifteen" was a dull affair led by dull men and ended in an indecisive battle at Sheriffmuir. But the "Forty-Five" was a dashing affair led by the glamorous Prince Charlie and supported mainly by gallant Highlanders. They gained a brilliant victory at Prestonpans and made a spectacular dash into the heart of England before suffering a disastrous defeat at Culloden (1746).

The union preserved Scots law and the existing Scottish church system, which had characteristics rooted in a long history. In simple terms, whereas in England the more extreme reformers, the Puritans, failed, in Scotland they succeeded. In the course of opposition to Charles I, the Scots adopted a manifesto called the National Covenant (1638), from which developed the concept of a "covenanted nation," or Chosen People, comparable to the Jews. After parliament finally decided in 1690 that the Church was to be Presbyterian, there were many divisions within it, especially the Disruption of 1843, which founded the Free Church, and although there have been many reunions, some small dissenting Presbyterian churches still exist, especially in the west Highlands.

Perhaps the ecclesiastical disputes were related to the fact that the Scots were not only argumentative, but sufficiently well educated to grasp the finer points that were at issue. From its earliest days the reformed church had stressed the need for education, and already in the 17th century it was normal for a parish in Lowland Scotland to have a school, although the Highlands were not adequately served until later. One looks in vain in Scottish literature for the "ignorant yokel" so familiar in English literature, and for generations Scotland was far ahead of England in its educational standards. Scots like to boast that they had five universities when England had only two, and it was claimed that higher education and a successful career were always open to a "lad o' pairts" (a boy with the ability to make his way in the world).

In the Middle Ages Scotland was not alone in being constantly under threat from England. France also faced English aggression, and it was natural that France and Scotland should form "The Auld Alliance," first formulated in 1295 and continuing to the reformation and even after it. In the 16th century it was agreed that the two peoples should have joint nationality. There was thus a strong Continental influence on Scottish law, universities, and architecture, and French words found their way into Scottish speech. Scotland, although more physically remote, was a less insular, more Continental country than England, where the law in particular followed its own unique development. Apart from the French connection, Scotland had close ties with the Low Countries, Denmark, and the Baltic, so that she was not isolated in a distant northern backwater but drew cultural inspiration from the mainstream of European civilization.

Partly because resources at home were limited and the ambitious saw better prospects abroad, already in the Middle Ages Scots were to be found all over Europe as merchants, soldiers, and scholars. With the development of colonization, new fields opened up, and Scots peopled lands overseas in numbers far out of proportion to the population of their own country. There are some common misconceptions about the causes. Many inhabitants of the American continent are convinced that their ancestors were Jacobites who had to flee after Culloden. It is true that a small number of rebels were deported to America as their punishment, but there is little evidence of voluntary flight. Others see the Highland Clearances as a main reason for emigration; in the Highlands, as elsewhere, the population had so increased as to outstrip subsistence by about 1800, and people were trying to live on tiny holdings, precariously dependent on the potato crop, which sometimes failed. Some landlords decided to turn their estates over to sheep farming and to develop fishing, which meant displacing tenants. However, few of those tenants went overseas immediately, and the population of the Highlands actually increased during that period. Curiously, it was only after tenants gained protection against arbitrary eviction in 1886 that the Highland population fell disastrously.

Whatever the causes, there was not a part of the world in which Scots were not to be found, and they gained a reputation for success. An observer in 1888 remarked that "from Canada to Ceylon, from Dunedin to Bombay, for every Englishman that you meet who has worked himself up to wealth from small beginnings without external aid, you find ten Scotchmen. . . . Wherever abroad you come across a Scotchman, you invariably find him prosperous and respected." It was put more briefly: "You never find a foolish Scot abroad; all the fools stay at home."

Thomas Edison; Samuel Morse; Edgar Allan Poe; Washington Irving; Robert E. Lee; Presidents Jefferson, Monroe, Jackson, Grant, and Polk; Patrick Henry; and James McNeil Whistler all claimed Scottish ancestry. Allan Pinkerton of the detective agency was born in Glasgow; John Paul Jones, founder of the U.S. Navy, came from the Solway shore. Samuel Wilson, whose parents sailed to America from Greenock on the Clyde, has been officially recognized as the original Uncle Sam.

The Scottish John Macdonald and Alexander Mackenzie were Canada's first and second prime ministers. That country's Fraser and Mackenzie rivers are named for Scottish pioneers, as is her leading university, McGill.

Some pioneers carried royal blood to the New World, if the genealogists are to be believed. Jimmy Carter, through his alleged descent from King Henry III, must be linked with the Stuarts; the Irish Kennedys' Scottish cousins went back to Robert the Bruce, as did those of Thomas Jefferson, James Monroe, and James Buchanan; while Ulysses S. Grant claimed descent from an earlier king, David I, and Theodore Roosevelt boasted three clan chieftains—a Stuart, a Drummond, and a Douglas—in his ancestry.

Perhaps the most famous American Scot was Andrew Carnegie, steel baron and multimillionaire, who started work as a bobbin boy in a Pittsburgh mill. When he was a baby in Dunfermline (Fife), his parents sold everything they had to raise the fare for the passage to New York.

While it was often the enterprising, rather than the economically depressed, who emigrated, periods of slump usually saw heavy emigration: During the 1920s, when Scotland's heavy industries felt the full blast of depression, nearly 400,000 people left the country, and its population fell for the first time.

Although the Union of 1707 gave Scotland and England a single parliament, there was at first little to stimulate the Scots to an interest in British politics. The Liberal party had a majority of Scottish seats at almost every election between 1832 and 1914, and sometimes the Scottish Liberal vote ensured a Liberal government in London for which the majority of the English had not voted. In the past few decades the Labour party began to take the place of the Liberals in Scottish attachment, with the result that, in a reversal of the earlier situation, the Scots have had Conservative governments sitting in Westminster for which they did not vote. (On the other hand, it should be remembered that out of nine successive prime ministers between 1892 and 1924, six were Scots.)

For over a century now there have been intermittent demands for legislative devolution, and Home Rule was proposed several times before 1914. In recent years anxiety over the poor state of the Scottish economy has led to renewed agitation for Home Rule, though its cause usually makes a poor showing at general elections, and in a referendum on the subject in 1979, Home Rule did not raise the required 40% of the votes needed. However, an election in Govan, a Glasgow constituency was won overwhelmingly by a Scottish Nationalist candidate at the end of 1988, since when the cause of Scotland for the Scots has been firmly back on the agenda.

Robert Burns, Scotland's Eternal Laureate

By Holly Hughes

Holly Hughes has written books on Dickens and Eliot and is a contributing editor to Literary Cavalcade *magazine.*

Before I ever visited Scotland, I had only a foggy sort of notion of who Robert Burns was. Then I traveled to Edinburgh one summer for the arts festival and discovered Burns everywhere. His rakish dark eyes and bold features peered skeptically from portraits and monuments and even biscuit tins; phrases from his poems popped up in advertising jingles and newspaper headlines and in the names of tea shops and bed-and-breakfasts.

On subsequent trips, I discovered that Scotland's map is covered with places that claim an association with Burns—not just his own homes (and there are plenty, for he was constantly on the move, leaving behind him a trail of debts and lovelorn lasses), but pubs where he drank, landscapes he praised, cemeteries where his lovers and enemies were buried—it's almost like the proliferation of historic homes in the eastern United States that claim "Washington slept here."

Ayrshire is officially Burns country, beginning with the thatched cottage in Alloway, near Ayr, where Burns was born in 1759, and ending with Dumfries, where Burns was buried in St. Michael's churchyard in 1796 (the very same day his youngest son, Maxwell, was born). Tarbolton was the village where young Burns enjoyed many a late evening drinking with the Bachelor's Club and where he fell in love with Mary Campbell, the subject of some of his finest love lyrics ("Ye banks and braes and streams around/ The castle o' Montgomery!/ Green be your woods, and fair your flowers,/ Your waters never drumlie./ There Simmer first unfald her robes,/ And there the langest tarry;/ For there I took the last fareweel/ O' my sweet Highland Mary"). At the Burns farm in Mossgiel, visitors can see the field where he ploughed up the "Wee, sleekit, cowrin, tim'rous beastie" eulogized in "To A Mouse." Kilmarnock, with its Burns monument and museum, was where his first book of poetry, *Poems Chiefly in the Scottish Dialect*, was printed in 1786. Mauchline was where Burns and his wife, Jean Armour, married and had their first home together, and its churchyard's graves are covered with names familiar from his poems. Moffat, Lochlea, Kirkoswald, and many other Ayrshire towns all boast some kind of Burns connection, often of a purely imaginative provenance: Grey Mare's Tail, near Moffat in Galloway, is simply a magnificent cascade that has been named after the tail of Tam O'Shanter's horse,

Meg, who was pursued by a horde of witches in one of Burns's most famous comic ballads.

Even the Highlands boasts Burns associations, quoting his song "My heart's in the Highlands" ("Wherever I wander, wherever I rove/ The hills of the Highlands forever I love"). Burns traveled there in 1787, following what was probably a fairly typical tourist's itinerary. He began in Stirling, where he visited the battlefield of Bannockburn, then up the north road to Inverness, with side trips to Culloden Moor and to Cawdor, with its Macbeth associations. From there he went east along the Moray Firth, down to Peterhead, and along the coast to Aberdeen, Dundee, and Perth, where there were side trips to Scone Palace and to Ossian's grave at Crieff.

Wherever you go throughout Scotland, it's easy to believe that Robert Burns must be as important a poet as Shakespeare or Milton or Keats or any of those English scribblers. Burns didn't just spring out of nowhere, of course. He was one of the many fruits of the Scottish Enlightenment, that glorious era of the 18th century when Scotland, seeking its own identity after being swallowed up in a political union with England, suddenly produced an astonishing crop of scientists, philosophers, and writers. Scotland's literary history up to that point could boast only of the 15th century's so-called Scottish Chaucerians, William Dunbar and Robert Henryson, and Gavin Douglas, who translated the *Aeneid* into Scots in 1513. The earliest lights of the 18th-century Scottish literary renaissance had to prove themselves by writing in English and hobnobbing in London, as did Edinburgh-born James Thomson, who published the first book of the immensely popular poem *The Seasons* in 1726, and James Boswell, whose *Journal of a Tour of the Hebrides*, documenting his travels with the sage Samuel Johnson, appeared in 1785. In midcentury, two somewhat more homegrown talents, Allan Ramsay and Robert Fergusson, brought forth some rather good poetry written in a literary mixture of Scots (the dialect of the Lowlands) and English, and Invernesshire's James Macpherson published several volumes of Gaelic epic poems supposedly written by Ossian, the son of the ancient Scottish hero Fingal, which Macpherson said he had simply translated into modern English. This turned into a scandal, however, when Macpherson, encouraged by his success, kept "discovering" more lost poems to translate and couldn't even produce authentic manuscripts for them.

Although this hoax tarnished Scotland's reputation in London, Edinburgh was still a flourishing cultural capital in 1786 when the first edition of Robert Burns's poetry appeared. Intellectuals and wealthy patrons of the arts in Edinburgh were quick to seize upon this Ayrshire farmer's son, praising his portraits of rural Scotland and extolling the vigor and grace of his use of Scots dialect, much the same way as music critics in the early 1960s rushed to praise the Beatles as natural untutored geniuses. And like the Beatles, Burns came equipped with dashing good looks, a way with the ladies, dangerously radical political views, and a taste for hard liquor. Though not conventionally handsome, with his stocky build, thick features, and thin dark hair, he managed to cut quite a figure at fashionable Edinburgh soirees during the year and a half, from 1786 through 1788, after the phenomenal success of his first volume. Perhaps it helped that everyone, expecting to meet a clownish Ayrshire farmer with clods of mud still sticking to his boots, found instead a literate, intelligent fellow in a genteel dark jacket, light-colored waistcoat, and modestly ruffled linen shirt.

Yet while Edinburgh's elite pursued this new prodigy, Burns himself seemed uncomfortable with all this lionizing, asserting himself with a forthright honesty that all too often bordered on rudeness. He became increasingly restless as his stay in the capital dragged on (and his debts piled up and his love affairs grew more entangled), and one senses in his letters a note of relief once he cut himself free and returned to Ayrshire and to the uncertain prospect of life as a farmer and, after the failure of his crops, as an excise collector. Centuries later, this is the image of Burns his fans treasure most: riding about the countryside, singing to himself as he molded random bits of song into polished poems, or hunkering down with a congenial group of local wits at a country pub.

Neither of Scotland's other two great literary figures, Sir Walter Scott (1771–1832) and Robert Louis Stevenson (1850–94), have remained as firmly lodged in the hearts of their countrymen as Burns has. Scott, who celebrated Scotland in both poetry (*The Lay of the Last Minstrel, Marmion,* and *The Lady of the Lake*) and novels (*Ivanhoe, The Heart of Midlothian,* and *Waverly*) was enormously popular throughout the 19th century, and his career was longer and his output greater than Burns's. Stevenson, although born in Edinburgh, was never associated as closely with Scotland as Burns and Scott were, since frail health, poverty, and a roaming spirit conspired to make him live abroad from the age of 23 on. Except for a handful of Scottish historical novels—*The Master of Ballantrae, Kidnapped, David Balfour,* and *Weir of Hermiston*—Stevenson's best-known works (*Dr. Jekyll and Mr. Hyde, Treasure Island*) are not even set in Scotland.

As an English major whose professors never bothered to teach me about Burns, after my travels I became curious to reread his poetry, and I discovered that it really is wonderful. And looking back at my old school anthologies, I see that, with the exception of "To A Mouse," almost every one had a different selection of Burns's poems to include, which is a clue to just how many good things he really wrote. Of course, Robert Burns has never really faded from the general public's literary consciousness. For instance, just about every song that we associate with Scotland turns out to have lyrics by Burns: "My Love Is Like a Red, Red Rose," "Auld Lang Syne," "Flow Gently, Sweet Afton," "Green Grow the Rushes," "My Heart's in the Highlands," "The Banks O' Doon." *Bartlett's Quotations* devotes several pages to Burns, listing such well-known phrases as "the best-laid schemes of mice and men," "man's inhumanity to man," "to see ourselves as others see us," "death's untimely frost," "a man's a man for all that," "nursing her wrath to keep it warm," and "nae man can tether time or tide."

I suppose the main barrier for modern readers is the unfamiliar Scots dialect that peppers Burns's poems, but it is nowhere near as incomprehensible as, say, Chaucer's Middle English. And if you read the verses out loud—the best way to enjoy those lilting stanzas anyway—many of the oddly spelled Scots words are perfectly easy to understand. After all, Burns was not writing in some kind of primitive, substandard rural slang. He was following a very specific literary style, following the precedent of Allan Ramsay and Robert Fergusson. Despite his rural upbringing, Burns had enough education to write perfectly standard English English, as shown by all his personal correspondence and a good number of his poems (though, tellingly, these are usually not his most successful verses). Burns himself, teetering precariously between social classes, probably shifted in conversation from correct English—which he would have spoken at dinner parties thrown by his wealthy Edinburgh patrons—to broad Scots dialect, which would have been useful when he took his farm produce to market or set about wooing local peasant girls. (Scots was the everyday speech of Lowland Scotland, as opposed to the Highlands' Gaelic dialect, and therefore it is also sometimes called Lowlands, or Lallans.) In his poems, he inserted dialect where any good poet uses his or her most unusual vocabulary—as intensifying adjectives, line endings, and rhymes. The result is an extraordinarily effective poetic language, with a wide range of emotion and humor.

There are other reasons, though, apart from the quality of his verse, why Robert Burns has become enshrined as Scotland's national bard and why his birthday, January 25, is still celebrated with formal dinners (called Burns Suppers) around the globe. Burns's personality somehow speaks to us across the ages, corny as that may sound. People who knew him wrote invariably of his personal magnetism—his dark, flashing eyes; his lively wit; his zest for living—and what has survived of his correspondence suggests that he must have been one of those people you can't help being fond of. He also embodies something that is very near and dear to the Scottish national character: He had a wonderful common touch. He felt at home with ordinary village life; loved bawdiness and roistering; and was deeply suspicious of authority, especially as it was vested in the Scottish kirk, with all its dour piety. Instinctively he was a hardy partisan of individual liberty, though his political convictions were inconsistent—he also nursed a sentimental fondness for Scottish royalty, especially the romantic figure of Mary Queen of Scots. Sentimentality, indeed, was curiously mixed with cynicism in his emotional makeup. Burns was capable of writing both achingly romantic love poetry and bawdy verses about lust; while poems such as "The Cotter's Saturday Night" mawkishly extol the virtues of humble poverty, in other poems Burns is just as likely to lament how hard it is to eke out a living, as in the poignant last stanza of "To A Mouse": "Still thou are blest, compar'd wi' me;/ The present only toucheth thee,/ But och! I backward cast my e'e,/ On prospects drear!/ An' forward, tho' I canna see,/ I guess an' fear!"

Burns's myth, in truth, has been distorted a bit to make him even more glamorous to 20th-century fans. For example, popular imagination wants to believe that Burns drank himself to death. There's no question that Burns enjoyed a good carouse as well as the next Scotsman—after all, this is the man who wrote, in "Scotch Drink," "O whisky! soul o' plays and pranks!/ Accept a bardie's gratefu' thanks!/ When wanting thee, what tuneless cranks/ Are my poor verses!" Contemporary accounts, however, confirm that he was only a social drinker. His death was most probably a result of bacterial endocarditis, brought on by rheumatic fever, although he didn't help matters any by going out one night to a local tavern, getting roaring drunk, and passing out in the January cold on his way home. Never really robust, he had been subject to periods of weakness and depression ever since he was a teenager working long, hard days on his father's Ayrshire farm.

Another indelible part of the Burns myth is the image of him as a great womanizer, seducing well-born ladies, making peasant girls swoon wherever he went, and scattering bastard bairns around the countryside. It's true that his first children with Jean Armour were born out of wedlock, and one of his finest poems is written to the illegitimate child he fathered on Elizabeth Paton ("Welcome! my bonie, sweet, wee dochter,/ Tho' ye come here a wee unsought for,/ And tho' your comin' I hae fought for,/ Baith kirk and queir;/ Yet, by my faith, ye're no unwrought for,/ Thast I shall swear!"). But Burns was no mere rake—he was usually romantically in love with whatever girl he was chasing, and when it came down to it, he was a loyal (if not entirely faithful) husband to Jean. She herself seemed calmly resigned to his ardent nature, saying philosophically, "Our Robbie should ha' had twa wives."

3 Scotland: The Home of Golf

Golfing throughout the Country

*By John
Hutchinson*

*John Hutchinson
worked for many
years with the
Scottish Tourist
Board and is an
expert on the
history and lore of
golf in Scotland.*

There are more than 400 golf courses in Scotland and only 5 million local residents, so the country has probably the highest concentration of courses to people anywhere in the world. Some of these courses are world famous as venues for major championships, and any golfer coming to Scotland will probably want to play the "famous names" sometime in his career. Telling your friends in the clubhouse back home that you got a birdie at the Road Hole on the Old Course in St. Andrews, where Lyle, Faldo, and Jacklin have played, somehow carries more weight in terms of prestige than an excellent round at an obscure but delightful little course that no one has ever heard of.

So, by all means, play the championship courses and get your prestige, but remember they are championship courses and, therefore, they are difficult; you may enjoy the actual game itself much more at an easier, if less well-known, location. Remember, too, that everyone else wants to play them, so booking can be more of a problem, particularly on peak days during the summer. Do book early, or, if you are staying in a hotel attached to a course, get them to book for you. And then having satisfied your pride, look around for some of the easier, quieter courses nearby.

Look at the main golfing areas of Scotland to see what choice there is; but first, it's important to know a little of the history of the game in Scotland. There has always been considerable debate as to who invented golf. Like many other games that involve hitting a ball with a stick, golf evolved during the Middle Ages and gradually took on its present form, particularly in the Low Countries and in Scotland.

There is no doubt, however, that its development into one of the most popular games in the world stems from Scotland. The first written reference to golf, variously spelled as "gowf" or "goff," was as long ago as 1457, when James II of Scotland declared that both golf and football should be "utterly cryit doune and nocht usit" because they were distracting his subjects from their archery practice.

Mary Queen of Scots, it seems, was fond of golf. When in Edinburgh, she played on Leith Links and on Bruntsfield Links, perhaps the oldest course in the world where the game is still played. When in Fye, she played at Falkland near the palace and St. Andrew itself.

Golf must surely rank as one of Scotland's earliest cultural exports. In 1603, when James VI of Scotland also became James I of England, he moved his court to London. With him went his golf-loving friends, and they set up a course on Blackheath Common, then on the outskirts of London.

Golf clubs as we know them today first began in the middle of the 18th century. The earliest written evidence of the existence of a club is of the Honourable Company of Edinburgh Golfers, now residing at Muirfield, in 1744, and of the Royal and Ancient at St. Andrews in 1754. From then on, clubs sprang up all over Scotland: Royal Aberdeen (1780), Crail Golfing Society (1786), Dunbar (1794), and the Royal Perth Golfing Society (1824).

By the early years of the 19th century, golf clubs had been set up in England, and the game had begun to be carried all over the world by enthusiastic Scots. With them, these Scottish golf missionaries took their knowledge not only of golf, but of golf courses. Scotland is fortunate in that large parts of its coastline are natural golf courses, and the origins of bunkers and the word "links" are to be found in the sand dunes of the Scottish shore. But other countries were not so fortunate. The natural terrain did not exist, and courses had to be designed and created. This undoubted art developed into another profitable Scottish golf export. Willie Park of Musselburgh (who laid out Sunningdale), James Braid, and C. K. Hutchison (whose crowning glory is at Gleneagles Hotel), are some of the best known of the golf architects.

Golf has always had a peculiar classlessness in Scotland. It is a game for everyone, and for centuries towns and cities in Scotland have had their own golf courses for the enjoyment of the citizens. The snobbishness and exclusivity of golf clubs in some parts of the world have few echoes here.

Many of the important changes in the design and construction of balls and clubs were pioneered by the professional players who lived and worked around these town courses and who made the balls and clubs themselves. The original balls, called "featheries," were leather bags stuffed with boiled feathers. When, in 1848, the gutta percha ball, called a *guttie*, was introduced, there was considerable friction, particularly in St. Andrews, between the makers of the two rival types of ball. The gutta percha proved superior and was in general use until the invention of the rubber-core ball in 1901.

Clubs were traditionally made of wood: shafts of ash, later hickory, and heads of thorn or some other hard wood like apple or pear. Heads were spliced then bound to the shaft with twine. Players generally managed with far fewer clubs than today. About 1628 the marquis of Montrose, a great golf enthusiast, had a set of clubs made for him in St. Andrews that illustrate the range of clubs used in Stuart times: "Bonker clubis, a irone club, and twa play clubs."

Caddies—the word comes from the French *cadet*, a young boy, and was used, particularly in Edinburgh, for anyone who ran messages—carried the players' clubs around, usually under the arm. Golf carts did not come into fashion in Britain until the 1950s.

The technology of golf may change, but its addictive qualities are timeless. Toward the end of the 18th century, an Edinburgh golfer called Alexander McKellar regularly played golf all day and refused to stop even when it grew dark. One night his wife carried his dinner and nightcap on Bruntsfield Links where he was playing in an attempt to shame him into changing his ways. She failed.

The addiction continues.

Where to Play

Scotland's courses are well spread throughout the country in all areas but the far northern Highlands and some of the islands. So finding a holiday golf course is never a problem. The country's main golfing areas are outlined below. Some suggestions are also given for the things nongolfers could do in an area. For more information region by region, *see* Sports and Fitness in Chapters 4 through 13.

The Stewartry Starting at the very southern border, the first of these areas is a delightful part of Scotland set in the rich farmlands around Dumfries, a golfing holiday area since Victorian times.

Powfoot and Southerness are excellent links courses with magnificent views over the Solway Firth, while inland, Dumfries and Moffat have long-established courses that provide excellent golf in a clean invigorating environment. There are also several fine 9-hole courses in the area.

Ayrshire and the Clyde Coast Lying just an hour to the south of Glasgow either by car or by train, Ayrshire and the Clyde Coast has been a holiday area for Glaswegians for generations. Few people need an introduction to the famous names of Turnberry, Royal Troon, Prestwick, or Western Gailes, all excellent links courses along this coast. In addition, there are at least 20 courses in the area within an hour's drive. Remember, too, that at major locations, such as Turnberry, Troon, and Ayr, there are several different courses to play from the same base.

East Lothian The sand dunes that stretch eastward from Edinburgh along the southern shore of the Firth of Forth made an ideal location for some of the earliest golf courses in the world. Muirfield is perhaps the most famous course in the area, but around it are over a dozen more, at Gullane, North Berwick, Dunbar, and Aberlady and, nearer Edinburgh, at Longniddry, Prestonpans, and Musselburgh. All are links courses, many with views to the island of the Firth of Forth and northward to Fife, and if you weary of the East Lothian courses, just 20 or so miles away there are nearly 30 more within the city of Edinburgh.

Fife Few would dispute the claim of St. Andrews to be the Home of Golf, holding as it does the Royal and Ancient, the organization that governs the sport worldwide. Golf has been played in the area since the very beginning, and to play in Fife is for most golfers a cherished ambition. St. Andrews itself has a wide range of full 18-hole courses in addition to the famous Old Course, and along the shores of the Firth of Forth is a string of ancient villages, each with its harbor, ancient red-roofed buildings, and golf course. In all, there are about 30 in the area.

Perthshire The first island golfing area to be considered is included because of the variety of really excellent courses developed specifically for holiday golf and for visitors, rather than for large numbers of local club members. Gleneagles Hotel is, of course, the most famous of these golf resort hotels. Its facilities are considered outstanding when compared with anywhere in the world. But other courses in the area, set on the edges of beautiful Highland scenery, will delight any golfer. Crieff, Taymouth, and other courses are in the mountains; Blairgowrie and Perth are set amid the rich farmlands nearer the sea.

Angus East of Perthshire, north of the city of Dundee, is a string of excellent courses along the shores of the North Sea and inland into the foothills of the Grampian Mountains. The most famous course in Angus is probably Carnoustie, one of several British Open Championship venues in Scotland, but there are many more along the same stretch of coast from Dundee northward as far as Stonehaven. Golfers who excel in windy conditions will particularly enjoy the breezes blowing eastward from the sea. Inland Edzell, Forfar, Brechin, and Kirriemuir all have courses nestling in the farmlands of Strathmore.

Aberdeenshire The city of Aberdeen, Scotland's third largest, is particularly known for its sparkling granite buildings and the amazing displays of roses each summer. It also offers a good range of courses for the golfer. Aberdeen itself has four major courses, and to the north, as far as Fraserburgh and Peterhead, there are five others, including the popular Cruden Bay. Royal Deeside has three, and in the rich farmlands to the north are three more with at least six 9-hole courses as well.

Speyside Set on the main A road an hour south of Inverness amid the Cairngorm Mountains, the valley of the River Spey is one of Scotland's most attractive all-year sports centers, with winter skiing and in summer, sailing and canoeing, pony-trekking, fishing, and some excellent golf. The main courses in the area are Newtonmore, Grantown on Spey, and Boat of Garten, all fine inland courses with wonderful views of the surrounding mountains and challenging golf provided by the springy turf and the heather. For a change of pace, the Moray Firth courses, with their seaside attractions, are only an hour's drive away.

Moray Coast No one can say that the Lowlands of Scotland have a monopoly of Scotland's fine seaside golf courses. The Moray Coast, stretching eastward from Inverness, has some spectacular sand dunes, and these have been adapted to create stimulating and exciting links courses.

The two courses at Nairn have long been known to golfers famous and unknown. Charlie Chaplin regularly played there. But in addition there are a dozen courses looking out over the sea from Inverness as far along as Banff and Macduff and several inland amid the fertile Moray farmland.

Dornoch Firth North of Inverness, the east coast is deeply indented with firths along whose shores are to be found some excellent and relatively unknown golf courses. Royal Dornoch has recently been "discovered" by international golf writers, but knowledgeable golfers have been making the northern pilgrimage for well over a hundred years. There are half a dozen excellent links courses around Dornoch and inland, another Victorian golfing holiday center, Strathpeffer, preserves much of the atmosphere these gentlemen of a past age set out to achieve.

Courses Around the Country

Most courses welcome visitors with the minimum of formalities and often at surprisingly low cost. (Out of season, a few clubs still use the "honest box," in which you drop your fees!) Admittedly, there are at least a few clubs that have always been noted for their exclusive air, and there are newer golf courses emerging as part of exclusive leisure complexes. These are exceptions to the long tradition of recreation for all. Golf in Scotland is usually a very democratic game, played by ordinary folk as well as the rich and leisured. Here is a selection of clubs that welcome visitors. Just two short pieces of advice (particularly for North Americans): 1) in Scotland the game is usually played slightly faster than we are used to, so please don't hang about if others are waiting, and 2) caddy carts are hand-pulled carts for your clubs, not the electric golf carts that are more familiar to U.S. golfers and rarely available in Scotland.

Balgownie, Royal Aberdeen Golf Club. This old, established club (1780) is the archetypal Scottish links course: long and testing over uneven ground with the frequently added hazard of a sea breeze. Prickly gorse is inclined to close in and form an additional hurdle. The course is tucked behind the rough, grassy sand dunes, and there are surprisingly few views of the sea. One historical note: In 1783, this club originated the five-minute-search rule for a lost ball. *Tel. 0224/702221. 18 holes. Yardage: 6,372. Par 70. Fees: £20/round, £25 daily. Weekend restrictions, letter of introduction required. Advance reservations. Facilities: practice area, catering.*

Ballater. This club has a holiday atmosphere and a course laid out along the river flats of the River Dee. Originally opened in 1906, the club makes maximum use of the fine setting between river and woods and is ideal for a relaxing round of vacation golf. The variety of shops and pleasant walks in nearby Ballater make this a good place for nongolfing partners. *Tel. 03398/55567 or 03398/55658. 18 holes. Yardage: 5,638. Par 67. Fees: On application. Visitors welcome weekdays. Advance reservations. Facilities: practice area, caddy carts, catering.*

Banff, Duff House Royal Gold Club. Although it is within moments of the sea, this club is a curious blend of a coastal course with a parkland setting. The course, which is only minutes from Banff center, lies within the parkland grounds of Duff House, an Adam mansion that was donated to the town. The club has inherited the ancient traditions of seaside play (golf records here go back to the 17th century). Mature trees and gentle slopes create a pleasant playing atmosphere. *Tel. 0261/812062. 18 holes. Yardage: 6,161. Par 69. Fees: weekdays £9/round, £12 daily; weekends £12/round, £15 daily. Advance reservations. Facilities: practice area, caddy carts, catering.*

Boat of Garten. Possibly one of the greatest "undiscovered" courses in Scotland, Boat of Garten was designed by famous golf architect James Braid. Each of the 18 holes is individual: Some cut through birchwood and heathery rough, most have long views to the Cairngorms and a strong Highland ambience. An unusual feature is the preserved steam railway that runs along part of the course. The occasional puffing locomotive can hardly be considered a hazard. *Tel. 047983/282. 18 holes. Yardage: 5,720. Par 68. Fees: weekday £12/round, weekend £15/round, £60 weekly. Starting sheet used on weekends. Advance reservations. Facilities: caddies, caddy carts, catering.*

Callander. Another course well worth seeking out, Callander was designed by Tom Morris and has a scenic upland feel. Pine and birchwoods and hilly fairways offer fine views, and the tricky moorland layout demands accurate hitting off the tee. *Tel. 0877/30090. 18 holes. Yardage: 5,125. Par 66. Fees: weekday £10/round, £19 daily; weekend £14/round, £19 daily; £52 weekly. Facilities: practice area, caddies, caddy carts, catering.*

Carnoustie. Home in former days of the British Open Championship, the extensive coastal links around Carnoustie have been played for generations. Carnoustie was also once a training ground for golf coaches, many of whom went to the United States. The choice municipal course here is therefore full of historical snippets and local color, as well as being tough and full of interest. *Tel. 0241/53789. 18 holes. Yardage 6,936. Par 74. Fees: £30/round, £85 3 days, £120 5 days. Visitors welcome except*

Sat. morning, Sun. before 11:30 AM. Advance reservations. Facilities: caddies, caddy carts (May–Oct.), catering.

Cruden Bay. Another east-coast Lowland course sheltered behind the extensive sand hills, this one offers a typical Scottish golf experience. Runnels and valleys, among other hazards, on the challenging fairways ensure plenty of excitement, and some of the holes are rated among the finest anywhere in Scotland. Like Gleneagles and Turnberry, this course owes its origins to an association with the grand railway hotels that were built in the heyday of steam. Unlike the other two, however, Cruden Bay's railway hotel and the railway itself have gone, though the course has only gotten better. *Tel. 0779/812285. 18 holes. Yardage: 6,370. Par 71. Fees: weekdays, £16 daily; weekends, £22 daily, £55 weekly; £85 for 2 weeks. Visitors welcome weekdays, restricted weekends. Advance reservations. Facilities: practice area, caddy carts, catering.*

Dornoch. This course, which was laid out by Tom Morris in 1886 on a sort of coastal shelf behind the shore, has matured to become one of the world's finest. Its location in the north of Scotland, though less than an hour's drive from Inverness Airport, means that it is far from overrun even in peak season. It may not have the fame of a Gleneagles or a St. Andrews, but if time permits, Dornoch is a memorable golfing experience. The little town of Dornoch, behind the course, is both sleepy and charming. *Tel. 0862/810219. 18 holes. Yardage 6,533. Par 72. Fees: on application. Advance reservations. Facilities: practice area, caddies, caddy carts, catering.*

Dunbar. This ancient golfing site by the sea even has a lighthouse at the 9th hole. It's a good choice for a typical east-coast Lowland course within easy reach of Edinburgh. *Tel. 0368/62317. 18 holes. Yardage: 6,441. Par 71. Fees: weekdays, £18 daily; weekends, £30 daily. Visitors welcome after 9:30 AM except Thurs. Advance reservations. Facilities: practice area, caddies (by reservation), catering.*

Fraserburgh. A northeast town with extensive links and dunes that seem to have grown up around the course rather than the other way around. Be prepared for a hill climb and a tough finish. *Tel. 0346/28287. 18 holes (4 additional for warmup). Yardage: 6,216. Par 70. Fees: weekdays, £7 daily; weekends, £10 daily; £35 weekly. Facilities: practice area, catering.*

Girvan. An old established course with play along a narrow coastal strip and a more lush inland section beside the Water of Girvan—the neighborhood river that constitutes a particular hazard at the 15th, unless you are a big hitter. This is quite a scenic course, with good views of the Clyde estuary. *Tel. 0465/4272. 18 holes. Yardage: 5,078. Par 65. Fees: weekdays, £5/round, £8 daily; weekends, £6.60/round, £10 daily. Visitors welcome weekdays. Facilities: caddy carts, catering.*

Killin. A splendidly scenic course, typically Highland, with a roaring river, woodland birdsong, and backdrop of high green hills. There are a few surprises, including two blind shots to reach the green at the 4th. The village of Killin is very attractive, almost alpine in feel, especially in spring when the hilltops may still be white. *Tel. 05672/312. 9 holes. Yardage: 2,410. Par 65. Fees: weekdays, £6.50/round; weekends, £8.50/round. Facilities: caddy carts, catering.*

Ladybank. Fife is famous for its choice of coastal courses, but this one offers an interesting contrast: Though laid out on fairly level ground, the firwoods, birches, and heathery rough give it a Highland flavor among the gentle Lowland fields. Qualifying rounds of the British Open are played here when the main championship is played at St. Andrews. *Tel. 0337/30814. 18 holes. Yardage: 6,617. Par 72. Fees: Nov.–Apr., £13/round, £19 daily; May and Oct., £16/round, £23 daily; June–Sept., £20/round, £27 daily. Visitors welcome except Sat. Advance reservations. Facilities: practice area, caddy carts, catering.*

Leven. Another fine Fife course used as a British Open qualifier, this one also feels like the more famous St. Andrews, with hummocky terrain and a tang of salt in the air. The 1st and 18th share the same fairway. *Tel. 0333/28859. 18 holes. Yardage: 6,426. Par 71. Fees: weekdays, £16/round, £22.50 daily; weekends, £20/round, £30 daily. Visitors welcome except Sat. Advance reservations. Facilities: catering.*

Lossiemouth, Moray Golf Club. Discover the mild airs of the "Moray Riviera," as Tom Morris did in 1889 when he was inspired by the lie of the natural links. There are two courses plus a 6-hole minicourse. There is lots of atmosphere here, with golfing memorabilia in the clubhouse, as well as the tale of the British prime minister, Lord Asquith, who took a holiday in this out of the way spot, yet still managed to be attacked by a crowd of militant suffragettes at the 17th. All other hazards on these testing courses are entirely natural. *Tel. 0343/2018. 18 holes each (6 separate). Yardage: 6,643, 6,258. Par 72, 71. Fees: on application. Facilities: practice area, caddy carts, catering.*

Machrihanish, by Campbeltown. This is a western course that many enthusiasts discuss in hushed tones—a kind of out-of-the-way golfers' Shangri-La. It was laid out in 1876 by Tom Morris on the links around the sandy Machrihanish Bay. The drive of the 1st tee is across the beach to reach the green—an intimidating start to a memorable series of very individual holes. If you are short on time, consider flying from Glasgow to nearby Campbeltown, the last town on the long peninsula of Kintyre. *Tel. 058681/277. 18 holes. Yardage: 6,228. Par 70. Fees: weekdays, £15 daily; weekends, £16 daily; £60 weekly, £100 for 2 weeks. Advance reservations. Facilities: practice area, caddy carts, catering.*

Nairn. Widely regarded in golfing circles as a truly great course, Nairn dates from 1887 and is the regular home of Scotland's Northern Open. Huge greens, aggressive gorse, a beach hazard for five of the holes, a steady prevailing wind, and distracting views across the Moray Firth to the northern hills make play here a memorable experience. *Tel. 0667/53208. 18 holes. Yardage: 6,483. Par 71. Fees: weekdays, £18/round, £25 daily; weekends, £22/round, £30 daily. Advance reservations. Facilities: practice area, caddy, caddy carts, catering.*

Rosemount, Blairgowrie Golf Club. Well known to native golfers looking for an exciting challenge, Rosemount's 18 are laid out in the firwoods, which certainly bring a wild air to the scene. You may encounter a browsing roe deer if you stray too far. There are also, however, wide fairways and at least some large greens. *Tel. 0250/2622. 18 holes. Yardage: 6,556. Par 72. Fees: on application. Visitors welcome Mon., Tues., Thurs. Facilities: practice area, caddies, caddy carts, catering.*

4 Edinburgh and the Lothians

Introduction

By Gilbert
Summers

Gilbert Summers,
author of most of
this book, is a
native Scot who
writes frequently
about Scotland,
tourism, and
leisure activities.

The first-time visitor to Scotland may be surprised that the
country still has a capital city at all, thinking perhaps that the
seat of government was drained of all its resources and power
after the union with England in 1707. Far from it. The Union of
Parliaments brought with it a set of political partnerships—
such as separate legal, ecclesiastical, and educational systems—that Edinburgh, as former seat of the Scottish parliament, assimilated and integrated with its own surviving institutions. In the trying decades after the union, many influential
Scots, both in Edinburgh and beyond, went through an identity
crisis, but out of the 18th-century difficulties grew the Scottish
Enlightenment, during which great strides were made by educated Scots in medicine, economics, and science. By the mid-
18th century, it had become the custom for wealthy Scottish
landowners to spend the winter in town houses in the Old Town
of Edinburgh, huddled between the high castle rock and the
Royal Palace below. In the tall crowded buildings—called, in
Scots, *tenements*—of old Edinburgh, all mixed and mingled together. The well-to-do tended to have their rooms in the middle
of these blocks, while the "lower orders" occupied dwellings on
the top floors and ground floors. Such an overcrowded arrangement bred plenty of unsavory and odorous hazards (more on
this later), but it also bred ideas. Uniquely cross-fertilized in
the coffeehouses and taverns, by the *mercat* (Scots for market)
cross, or on the twisting stairs, intellectual notions flourished
among a people deprived of their identity in a political sense,
yet determined to remain Scottish. One result was a campaign
to expand and beautify the city, to give it a look worthy of its
nickname, Athens of the North. Thus was the New Town of
Edinburgh built, with broad streets and gracious buildings
creating a harmony that even today's throbbing traffic cannot
obscure.

Edinburgh today is the second-most-important financial center
in the United Kingdom. Its residents now come from all over
Britain—not least of all because the city regularly ranks near
the top of surveys that measure "quality of life," and New Town
apartments in fashionable streets sell for considerable amounts
of money. In some senses the city is showy and materialistic,
but the legacy of Thatcherism appears to be at odds with older
intellectual values. Edinburgh still supports several learned
societies, many of which have their roots in the Scottish Enlightenment: The Royal Society of Edinburgh, for example, established in 1783 "for the advancement of learning and useful
knowledge," is still an important forum for interdisciplinary
activities, both in Edinburgh and in Scotland as a whole, pub-
lishing scientific papers, holding academic symposia and meetings, and administering research fellowships in many Scottish
universities. Hand in hand with the city's academic and scientific life is a rich cultural life, with the Edinburgh International
Festival attracting lovers of all the arts.

Thousands of years ago, an eastward-grinding glacier encountered the tough basalt plug or core of an ancient volcano. It
swept around the core, scouring steep cliffs and leaving a trail
of material like the tail of a comet. This material formed a
ramp, gently leading down from the rocky summit. On this
"crag and tail" would grow the city of Edinburgh. The lands
that rolled down to the sea were for centuries open country, be-

tween Castle Rock and the tiny community clustered by the shore that grew into Leith, Edinburgh's seaport. By the 12th century Edinburgh had become a walled town, still perched on the hill. Its shape was becoming clearer: like a fish with its head at the castle, backbone running down the ridge, with "ribs" leading briefly off on either side. The backbone gradually became the continuous thoroughfare now known as the Royal Mile, and the ribs became the "closes" (alleyways), some still surviving, which were the scene of many historic incidents. By the early 15th century Edinburgh had become the undisputed capital of Scotland. The bitter defeat of Scotland at Flodden in 1513 (when Scotland aligned itself with France against England) caused a new defensive wall to be built there, and, though the castle escaped, the city was burned by the English earl of Hertford under the orders of King Henry VIII of England. By the time that Mary, Queen of Scots, returned already widowed from France, in 1561, the guest house of the Abbey of Holyrood had grown to become the Palace of Holyroodhouse. Mary's legacy to the city included the destruction of most of Edinburgh Castle, held by her supporters after she was forced to flee her homeland. The castle fell in ruins in 1573, after a siege of six years.

Many buildings erected in the 17th century still stand today—including John Knox House, Huntly House, and a new Parliament House. The Union of Parliaments in 1707 meant that the Scots Parliament would no longer ride in grand procession down the canyonlike thoroughfare of the Royal Mile. The castle had one more warlike role to play, however, when it held out against the Jacobite forces of Prince Charles Edward Stuart as he passed through the city on his way south in 1745. Unsuccessful in his assault of the castle, the Bonnie Prince contented himself with a grand ball at the Palace of Holyroodhouse.

By the end of the 18th century the grand New Town was taking shape, though it never was taken as far as the sea at Leith, which had been the original intention. Victorian suburbs added to the gradual sprawl. Despite the expansion, the guardian castle remained the focal point. Princes Street—a master stroke in city planning—was built up only on one side, allowing magnificent views of the great rock on which the fortress stands. The result for today's visitor is a skyline of sheer drama and an aura of grandeur. Edinburgh Castle watches over the city, frowning down on Princes Street, now the main downtown shopping area, as if disapproving its modern razzmatazz. Its ramparts still echo with gunfire each day when the traditional one o'clock gun booms out over the city, startling unwary shoppers. To the east, the top of New Town's Calton Hill is cluttered with sturdy, neoclassical structures, somewhat like an abandoned set for a Greek tragedy.

These theatrical elements give a unique identity to downtown, but turn a corner, say, off George Street (parallel to Princes Street), and you will see, not an endless cityscape, but blue sea and a patchwork of fields. This is the county of Fife, beyond the inlet of the North Sea called the Firth of Forth—a reminder, like the Highlands to the northwest glimpsed from Edinburgh's highest points, that the rest of Scotland lies within easy reach.

Essential Information

Important Addresses and Numbers

Tourist Information Visitors arriving in Edinburgh can get expert advice on what to see and do, where to go, and what's going on throughout Scotland at the **Edinburgh and Scotland Travel Centre,** adjacent to Waverley Station. Follow the TIC signs in the station and throughout the city. In addition to free information and literature, its comprehensive range of services also includes an accommodations service (Book-A-Bed-Ahead), route planning, a Scottish bookshop, and currency exchange. Visitors can also buy National Trust, Historic Scotland, and Great British Heritage passes here. *3 Princes St., tel. 031/557–1700. Open May, June, Sept., Mon.–Sat. 8:30–8, Sun. 11–8; July, Aug, Mon.–Sat. 8:30 AM–9 PM, Sun. 11–9; Nov.–Mar., weekdays 9–6, Sat. 10–5; Oct. and Apr., weekdays 9–6, Sat. 9–5.*

Complete information is also available at the tourist-information desk at **Edinburgh Airport.** *Tel. 031/333–1000. Open Apr.–Oct., Mon.–Sun. 9:30–9:30; Nov.–Mar., Mon.–Fri. 9–6, Sat. 9:30–1, Sun. 10:30–2:30.*

The List, a publication available from city-center bookshops and newsagents, and *What's On in Edinburgh,* from the Tourist Centre, both list information about all types of events, from movies and theater to sports. *The Scotsman,* a national newspaper published in Edinburgh, is good for both national and international news coverage, as well as for reviews and notices of upcoming events in Edinburgh and elsewhere in Scotland.

Consulate **American Consulate General** (3 Regent Terr., tel. 031/556–8315).

Emergencies For **police, ambulance,** or **fire,** dial 999. No coins are needed for emergency calls made from pay phones.

Hospitals **Edinburgh Royal Infirmary** (51 Lauriston Pl., tel. 031/229–2477) is south of the city center—down George IV Bridge and then to the right. **Western General Hospital** (Crewe Rd., tel. 031/332–2525) is northwest of the city center, beyond the Royal Botanic Garden and Inverleith Park.

Where to Change Money Most city-center banks have a **bureau de change** (usual banking hours are Mon.–Fri. 9:30–4:45.) The bureau de change at the **Clydesdale Bank** (Tourist Centre, Waverley Market) is open on Sunday from May to September. There are also bureaux de change at **Waverley Rail Station, Edinburgh Airport,** and **Frasers** department store (west end of Princes Street during shopping hours, Mon.–Sat. 9–5:30).

Late-Night Pharmacies You can find out which pharmacy is open late on a given night by looking at the notice posted on every pharmacy-shop door. A pharmacy—or "dispensing chemist"—is easily identified by its sign, showing a green cross on a white background.

Boots (48 Shandwick Pl., west end of Princes St., tel. 031/225–6757) is open Monday through Saturday 8:45 AM–9 PM and Sunday 10–5.

Travel Agencies **American Express** (139 Princes St., tel. 031/225–7881) is near Frasers department store, at the west end of Princes Street.

Thomas Cook (79a Princes St., tel. 031/220–4039) is near Littlewoods department store, in the middle of Princes Street.

Lost and Found To retrieve lost property, try the **Lothian and Borders Police Headquarters** (Fettes Ave., tel. 031/311–3131).

Post Offices The **Head Post Office** is at 2 Waterloo Place, at the east end of Princes Street (tel. 031/550–8232. Open Mon.–Thurs. 9 AM–5:30 PM, Fri. 9:30–5:30, Sat. 9:30 AM–12:30 PM). Main post offices in the city center are at 40 Frederick Street, 33 Forrest Road, and 7 Hope Street. Many newsagents also sell stamps.

Arriving and Departing by Plane

Airports and Airlines Edinburgh is in the embarrassing position of being a capital city without its own international airport. **Glasgow Airport** (tel. 041/887–1111, ext. 4552), 50 miles west of Edinburgh, is now the major point of entry into Edinburgh for transatlantic flights (*see* Arriving and Departing in Chapter 4). **Edinburgh Airport** (tel. 031/333–1000), 7 miles west of the city, has airlinks throughout the United Kingdom—London Heathrow/Gatwick/Stanstead, Birmingham, Guernsey, Jersey, Manchester, Leeds/Bradford, Norwich, Southampton, East Midlands, Humberside, and Belfast in Northern Ireland—as well as with a number of European cities, including Amsterdam, Dublin, Brussels, Cologne, Dusseldorf, Hanover, Paris, and Zurich. There are flights to Edinburgh Airport virtually every hour from London's Gatwick and Heathrow airports; it's usually faster and less complicated to fly through Gatwick, which has excellent rail service from London's Victoria Station. Airlines serving Edinburgh include **British Airways, British Midland, Air UK, Dan Air, Loganair, Maui Airlines, Sabena, Aer Lingus, Manx Airlines,** and **Air France.**

Transatlantic passengers flying direct to Scotland on charter flights also use **Prestwick Airport** (tel. 0292/79822, ext. 5090 or 5091), on the Clyde coast (*see* Arriving and Departing in Chapter 4).

Between Edinburgh Airport and City Center There are no rail links to center city, despite the fact that the airport sits between two main lines. By bus or car you can usually make it to Edinburgh in a comfortable half hour, unless you hit the morning or evening rush hours (7:30–9 AM and 4–6 PM).

By Bus Two companies, **Lothian Regional Transport** (tel. 031/220–4111) and **Guide Friday** (tel. 031/556–2244), run buses between Edinburgh Airport's main terminal building and Waverley Bridge, in center city and within easy reach of several hotels. The buses run every 15 minutes during the day (9–5) and less frequently (roughly every 45 minutes) during off-peak hours and on weekends. The trip takes about 30 minutes (about 45 minutes during rush hour). Single fare for Lothian Regional Transport is £2.50, for Guide Friday, £2.70.

By Taxi These are readily available outside the terminal. The trip takes 20–30 minutes to center city, 15 minutes longer during morning and evening rush hours. The fare is £12. Note that because of a local regulation, airport taxis picking up fares from the terminal are not the typical black cabs, although these do take fares going to the airport.

By Rental Car   There is a good choice of self-drive/car rental companies operating from the terminal building. The cost is from £25 a day, depending on the firm. If you choose to plunge yourself into
Edinburgh's traffic system, take care on the first couple of traffic circles (called "roundabouts") you encounter on the way into
town from the airport—even the most experienced drivers find
them challenging. By car the airport is about 7 miles west of
Princes Street downtown and is clearly marked from A8. The
usual route to downtown is via the suburb of Corstorphine. The
following rental firms have booths at the airport: **Avis** (tel. 031/
333–1866 or 800/331–1212), **Eurodollar** (tel. 031/333–2588),
Guy Salmon (tel. 031/333–5100), **Hertz** (tel. 031/333–1019 or
800/654–3131), and **Swan National** (tel. 031/333–1922).

By Limousine   The following Edinburgh firms provide chauffeur-driven limousines to meet flights at Edinburgh Airport: **A1 Chauffeur** (8
Merchiston Mews, tel. 031/229–8666; cost, about £32), **Scothire
Chauffeur Drive** (46 Ladywell Ave., tel. 031/334– 9017; cost,
£25), and **Sleigh Ltd.** (6 Devon Pl., tel. 031/337–3171; cost,
about £40).

Between Glasgow   Scottish Citylink Coaches (tel. 041/332–9191) buses leave Glas-
Airport and   gow Airport every half hour for Buchanan Bus Station in
Edinburgh   downtown Glasgow (a 20-minute trip) and then continue to St.
By Bus and Train   Andrew Bus Station in downtown Edinburgh. The trip takes
one hour and 40 minutes, including the stop in Glasgow, and
costs about £4. A somewhat more pleasant option is to take a
cab from Glasgow Airport to Glasgow's Queen Street Train
Station (15 minutes, £7) and then take the train to Waverley
Station in Edinburgh. Trains leave about every 30 minutes; the
trip takes 50 minutes and costs £5. Another, less expensive alternative—best for those with little luggage—is to take the 20-
minute bus ride from Glasgow Airport to Glasgow's Buchanan
Bus Station, walk five minutes to the Queen Street train station, and take the train to Edinburgh.

By Taxi   Taxis to downtown Edinburgh take about 70 minutes and cost
about £40.

**Between Prestwick   Prestwick Railway Station, on the main Glasgow–Ayr line, is
Airport and   half a mile from the airport, and a regular courtesy bus is avail-
Edinburgh   able for transfer. Take the train to Glasgow's Central Station;
from there, take a bus or taxi for a short ride to Queen Street
Station, where you can get a train to Waverley Station in Edinburgh (departures every half hour). Taxis are also available at
the airport for the short trip to Prestwick Railway Station, for
about £2.50. By car, take A77 from the airport toward Glasgow, joining M8 eastbound near downtown Glasgow.

Arriving and Departing by Car, Train, and Bus

By Car   Downtown Edinburgh usually means Princes Street, which
runs east–west. Drivers from the east coast will come in on A1,
Meadowbank Stadium serving as a landmark. The highway bypasses the suburbs of Musselburgh and Tranent; therefore, any
bottlenecks will occur close to downtown. From the Borders
the approach to Princes Street is by A7/A68 through Newington, an area offering a wide choice of accommodations. From
Newington the east end of Princes Street is reached by North
Bridge and South Bridge streets. Approaching from the southwest, drivers will join the west end of Princes Street (Lothian
Road), via A701 and A702, and those coming west from Glas-

gow or Stirling will meet Princes Street from M8 or M9, respectively. A slightly more complicated approach is via M90—from Forth Road Bridge/Perth/east coast; the key road for getting downtown is Queensferry Road, which joins Charlotte Square close to the west end of Princes Street.

By Train Edinburgh's main train station, **Waverley,** is downtown, below Waverley Bridge and around the corner from the unmistakable spire of the Scott Monument. The station has recorded summaries of services to King's Cross Station in London—information is available over the telephone for weekday service (tel. 031/557–3000), Saturday service (tel. 031/557–2737), and Sunday service (tel. 031/557–1616). For information on all other destinations or for other inquiries, call 031/556–2451. King's Cross Station can be reached by dialing 071/278–2477. Travel time from Edinburgh to London by train is as little as four hours for the fastest services.

Edinburgh's other main station is **Haymarket,** about four minutes (by rail) west of Waverley. All Glasgow and other western and northern services stop here. Haymarket can be slightly more convenient for visitors staying in hotels beyond the west end of Princes Street.

By Bus **Scottish Citylink Coaches** (Bus Station, St. Andrew Sq., tel. 031/556–8464; recorded timetable, tel. 031/556–8414) and **Caledonian Express** (Walnut Grove, Perth, tel. 0738/33481) provide bus service to and from London. The main terminal, St. Andrew Square Station, is only a couple of minutes (on foot) north of Waverley rail station, immediately east of St. Andrew Square. Long-distance coaches can be booked in advance from the booking office in the terminal. Edinburgh is approximately eight hours by bus from London.

Getting Around

By Car Driving in Edinburgh has its quirks and pitfalls, but competent drivers should not be intimidated. Newcomers should note that all traffic moving down Hanover Street is routed up the Mound—you cannot turn on to Princes Street from Hanover Street. Look out for a few other minor traps of the same nature. Metered parking in center city is scarce and expensive, and the local traffic wardens are alert. When parking, note that illegally parked cars are now routinely wheel-clamped and towed away. Getting your car back will be expensive. After 6 PM, however, the parking situation improves considerably, and you may manage to find a space quite near your hotel, even downtown. But if you park on a yellow line or in a resident's parking bay, be prepared to move your car by 8 AM the following morning, when the rush hour gets under way. If your car is in a metered space at that hour, you must either move the car or start feeding the meter.

Princes Street is usually considered the city center. The street runs east–west; motorists using the A1 east-coast road enter the city from the east end of Princes Street. Edinburgh now has a complete bypass, so it is possible to reach key points to the west, such as the airport or the Forth Road Bridge (gateway to the north), from many parts of the outskirts and from East Lothian without getting tangled up in downtown traffic.

By Train Edinburgh has no suburban rail system at present.

By Bus **Lothian Regional Transport,** operating dark-red-and-white buses, is the main operator within Edinburgh. The **Edinburgh Freedom Ticket,** allowing unlimited one-day travel on the city's buses, can be purchased in advance. More expensive is the **Tourist Card,** available in units of two to 13 days, which gives unlimited access to buses and includes vouchers for savings on tours. *Waverley Bridge, tel. 031/220–4111. Open Mon.–Sat. 8 AM–7 PM, Sun. 9–4:15; also 14 Queen St., tel. 031/554–4494. Open Mon.–Sat. 9–5.*

S.M.T. (St. Andrew Sq., tel. 031/556–8464), operating green buses, provides much of the service into Edinburgh and offers day tours around and beyond the city. You will also see other bus companies, including **Lowland Scottish** and **Fife Scottish,** which generally operate routes into and out of Edinburgh to other parts of Scotland.

By Taxi Taxi stands can be found throughout the downtown area; the following locations are the most convenient: the west end of Princes Street, South St. David Street and North St. Andrew Street (both just off St. Andrew Sq.), Waverley Market, Waterloo Place, and Lauriston Place. Alternatively, hail any taxi in an area that displays an illuminated "For Hire" sign.

Maps Several excellent city maps are available at bookshops. Local tourist-information centers can also supply good tourist maps. The *Bartholomew Edinburgh Plan,* with a scale of approximately 4 inches to 1 mile, by the once-independent and long-established Edinburgh cartographic company John Bartholomew and Sons Ltd., is particularly recommended.

Guided Tours

Some of the tour companies listed below offer orientation/general-interest tours, as well as special-interest and theme tours. The travel trade in Scotland is a fairly intimate network—if one agent or company cannot meet your request, it will most likely know someone who can.

Orientation **Scottish Tourist Guides** (25 Regent Terr., tel. 031/557–4111), endorsed by the Scottish Tourist Board, offers knowledgeable guides appropriate for an individual or a group. The tours are wide ranging and flexible.

Lothian Regional Transport's Edinburgh Classic Tour provides a worthwhile introduction to the Old Town and the New Town. The tour doesn't offer the most in-depth commentary, but it is useful for orienting new visitors to the city. The ticket is quite a bargain because it is valid on any other Lothian bus (except Airlink and night buses) for the remainder of the day. There are frequent departures from Waverley Bridge (outside the rail station) and other points around the city. Open-top buses operate in suitable weather. This is a flexible, show-up-and-hop-on service, meaning that you can get off the bus at any attractions you may want to see more closely. Allow an hour for the complete tour. You can buy tickets from the Lothian Regional Transport office on Waverley Bridge or at the Tourist Centre on Waverley Market (*see* Getting Around, *above*), or you can buy them from the driver. *Cost: £3.50 adults, £1.50 children.*

Scotline Tours' City Tour offers a comprehensive introduction to the city, as well as visits to Edinburgh Castle, the High Kirk of St. Giles, and the Palace of Holyroodhouse. (Note that the fees quoted below include admission to the castle and palace on the morning tour but not on the afternoon tour.) Allow at least 3½ hours for the entire tour. Scotline also offers a range of day tours to points beyond the city. *87 High St., tel. 031/557–0162. Call 8 AM–11 PM for reservations. Cost: £14 adults, £7 children.*

Guide Friday, Ltd., also offers an orientation tour. It runs less frequently than Lothian Regional Transport's equivalent, but you may enjoy riding through the streets of Edinburgh on one of Guide Friday's cheerful open-top, double-decker buses. The commentaries provided tend to be more colorful than accurate. The minimum tour time is 70 minutes. *Reception Centre, Waverley Station, tel. 031/556–2244. Cost: £4.50 adults, £1 children 5–12, £3.50 senior citizens.*

The Cadies Scottish Guides, fully qualified members of the Scottish Tourist Guides Association, have since 1983 steadily built a reputation for combining entertainment and historical accuracy in their lively, enthusiastic, and varied walking tours through the Old Town. *1 Upper Bow, Royal Mile, tel. 031/ 225–6745. Cost: £4 adults, £3 children.*

Special-Interest **Scottish Tourist Guides** (*see* Orientation Tours, *above*) will design tours tailored to your interests; it also offers a special Nightlife Tour. **The Cadies** (*see above*) operates a number of theme tours in addition to its historical jaunts through Old Town. These specialized tours tend toward the ghostly and mysterious—for which the Old Town alleyways make an atmospheric backdrop—and feature costumed guides and other theatrical characters en route.

Robin's Edinburgh Tours, run by an Edinburgh native, offers a number of tours built around specific themes, such as Georgian Edinburgh, Robert Burns in Edinburgh, and Holyrood Royal Park, as well as a range of talks and slide shows. *66 Willowbrae Rd., tel. 031/661–0125. Cost: £4.*

Tours from Both **Lothian Regional Transport** and **Scotline Tours** (*see* Orien-
Edinburgh tation Tours, *above*) offer day trips to destinations such as St. Andrews and Fife or the Trossachs and Loch Lomond.

Personal Guides **Scottish Tourist Guides** (tel. 031/557–4111) can supply guides (in 19 languages) who are fully qualified and will meet clients at any point of entry into the United Kingdom or Scotland.

Exploring Edinburgh

Orientation

Edinburgh falls both historically and geographically into two parts—the Old Town and the New Town—so it is logical to divide central Edinburgh into two corresponding tours. Much of the historical interest is concentrated in the Old Town, which bears a great measure of symbolic weight as the "heart of Scotland's capital." The Old Town is for lovers of atmosphere and history. The New Town, by contrast, is for those visitors who appreciate the unique architectural heritage of Edinburgh's Enlightenment. If you belong in both categories, don't worry—the Old and the New Towns are only yards apart. For visitors with more time, a wider Edinburgh lies beyond (*see* Off the Beaten Track and Shopping, *below*). Remember that Edinburgh, as cities go, is compact, and much of the interesting city-center environment can be covered on foot.

Edinburgh Castle dominates the city center. It is the essence of Scotland's capital and the nation's martial past. More practically, it serves as an important landmark for visitors and a natural focus or starting point for excursions on foot.

Until the 18th century the city grew upward, in a confined area along the rocky slope east of the castle. Then the city fathers decided, during the Scottish Enlightenment, to encourage a breaking out from this cramped site. Their plan resulted in the building of another Edinburgh, a little to the north, between the castle and the Firth of Forth. Great swaths of this "New Town," with its elegant squares, classical facades, wide streets, and harmonious proportions, are still intact and inhabited today. Old and New towns are separated by Princes Street Gardens (and the railway). These formerly private gardens were created from the marshy hollow that was originally part of the Castle Rock's northerly defenses. Princes Street, conceived as an exclusive residential street, with an open outlook southward and upward to the castle, has been greatly altered by the needs of commerce and shopping, though its beauty survives.

Time and progress (of a sort) have swept away some of the narrow "closes" (alleyways) and tall tenements of the Old Town, but enough remain for the visitor to imagine the original shape of Scotland's capital, which stretched from the guardian fortress on the crag to the royal residence, the Palace of Holyroodhouse. The Old and the New are the essence of Edinburgh, even if, away from this central core, Victorian expansion and urban sprawl have greatly increased the city's dimensions. The following tours bring out the contrasts between the two facets of the city. The first samples the flavor of the Old Town, with a leisurely stroll down the Royal Mile; the second takes in the best of New Town architecture.

Highlights for First-time Visitors

Edinburgh Castle (*see* Tour 1)
Forth Road and Rail Bridges (*see* Tour 3 in Excursions from Edinburgh)
Georgian House (*see* Tour 2)
National Gallery of Scotland (*see* Tour 2)
Palace of Holyroodhouse (*see* Tour 1)
Princes Street (*see* Tour 2)
Rosslyn Chapel (*see* Tour 4 in Excursions from Edinburgh)
Royal Mile (*see* Tour 1)
Scottish National Portrait Gallery (*see* Tour 2)

Tour 1: The Old Town

Numbers in the margin correspond to points of interest on the Edinburgh map.

❶ Probably every visitor to the city tours **Edinburgh Castle,** which is more than can be said for many of the city's residents. Its popularity as an attraction is due not only to the castle's symbolic value as the center of Scotland, but to the outstanding views offered from its battlements. Parts of the castle complex

Edinburgh

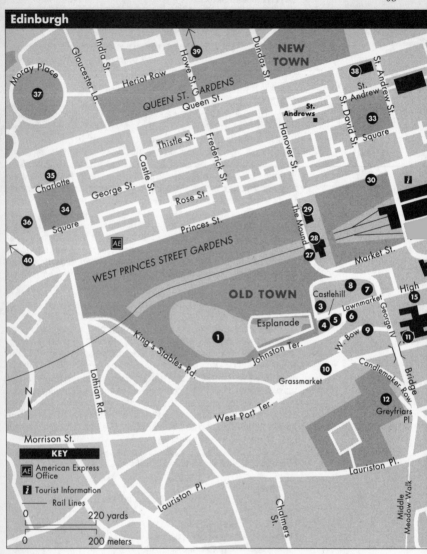

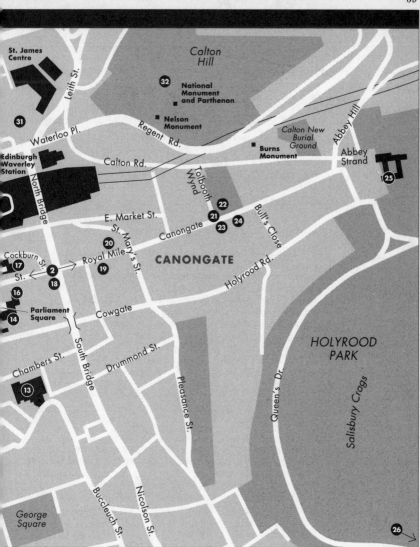

St. James Centre

Leith St.

National Monument and Parthenon

Calton Hill

Nelson Monument

Regent Rd.

Calton New Burial Ground

Abbey Hill

Burns Monument

Waterloo Pl.

Edinburgh Waverley Station

Calton Rd.

Abbey Strand

North Bridge

Tolbooth Wynd

E. Market St.

Canongate

Bull's Close

CANONGATE

St. Mary's St.

Cockburn St.

Royal Mile

Holyrood Rd.

Parliament Square

Cowgate

HOLYROOD PARK

Chambers St.

South Bridge

Drummond St.

Queen's Dr.

Salisbury Crags

Pleasance St.

George Square

Buccleuch St.

Nicolson St.

Scottish National
Gallery of Modern
Art, **40**

Scottish National
Portrait Gallery, **38**

Tolbooth Kirk, **5**

Tron Kirk, **18**

Upper Bow, **6**

Victoria Street, **9**

West Register
House, **36**

are currently under renovation, and work is expected to continue well into 1993.

Recent archaeological investigations have established that the rock was inhabited as far back as AD 1000, in the latter part of the Bronze Age. There have been fortifications here since the mysterious people called the Picts first used it as a stronghold in the 3rd and 4th centuries BC. The Picts were dislodged by Saxon invaders from northern England in BC 452, and for the next 1,300 years the site saw countless battles and skirmishes.

The castle has been held by Scots and Englishmen, Catholics and Protestants, soldiers and royalty; during the Napoleonic Wars it even contained French prisoners of war, whose carvings can still be seen on the vaults under the great hall. In the 16th century, Mary, Queen of Scots, gave birth in the castle to the future James VI of Scotland, who was also to rule England, as James I. Until 1573 the castle defended Mary as rightful Catholic queen of Scotland; it was her last stronghold and was virtually destroyed by English artillery.

The oldest surviving building in the complex—in fact, in the entire city—is the tiny 11th-century **St. Margaret's Chapel,** named in honor of Saxon Queen Margaret, who had persuaded her husband, King Malcolm, to move his court from Dunfermline to Edinburgh because the latter's environs—the Lothians—were occupied by Saxon settlers with whom she felt more at home, or so the story goes. (Dunfermline was surrounded by Celts.) The chapel was the only building spared when the castle was razed in 1314 by Scots, having won it back from their English foes. Also worth seeing are the **crown room,** which contains the **regalia of Scotland**—the crown, scepter, and sword that once graced the Scottish monarch; the **old parliament hall**; and **Queen Mary's apartments,** where she gave birth to James. The **great hall** features an extensive collection of arms and armor and has an impressive vaulted, beamed ceiling.

There are several military features of interest, including the **Scottish National War Memorial,** the **Scottish United Services Museum,** and the famous 15th-century Belgian-made cannon *Mons Meg,* which is so huge that 100 men, five carpenters, and a large number of oxen were needed to heave it into position. This enormous piece of artillery has been silent since 1682, when it exploded while firing a salute for the duke of York; it now stands in an ancient hall behind the Half-Moon Battery, the curving ramparts that give Edinburgh Castle its distinctive appearance from miles away. Contrary to what you may hear from locals, it is not *Mons Meg* but the battery's time gun that goes off with a bang every weekday at 1, frightening visitors and reminding Edinburghers to check their watches.

The **Esplanade,** the huge forecourt of the castle, was built in the 18th century as a parade ground, using earth from the foundation of the Royal Exchange to widen and level the area. Although it now serves as the castle parking lot, it comes alive with color each year during the festival, when it is used for the Tattoo, a magnificent military display and pageant. *Edinburgh Castle, tel. 031/244–3101. Admission: £3.40 adults, £1.70 children and senior citizens, £8.50 family ticket. Open Apr.–Sept., daily 9:30–5:15; Oct.–Mar., daily 9:30–4:15.*

2 The **Royal Mile** starts immediately below the Esplanade. It runs roughly west to east, from the castle to the Palace of Holyroodhouse (*see below*), and changes its name as it progresses, from Castlehill to Lawnmarket, High Street, and Canongate. On your stroll downhill from the castle you will need, first, imagination, to re-create the former life of the city; and second, sharp eyes, to spot the numerous details, such as historic plaques and ornamentation that make the excursion more than simply a parade of buildings. Note on Castlehill, for example, the little fountain recalling the burning of hundreds of witches here between 1479 and 1722. Notice also the cannonball imbedded in the west gable of **Cannonball House.** Legend says it was fired from the castle during the Jacobite rebellion in 1745 led by Bonnie Prince Charlie, the most romantic of the Stuart pretenders to the British throne. Most authorities agree on a more prosaic explanation, however, saying it was a height marker for Edinburgh's first piped water-supply system, installed in 1681.

3 On the left of Castlehill the **Camera Obscura** in **Outlook Tower** offers armchair views of the city. This 17th-century building was significantly altered in the 1850s with the installation of the present system of lenses, which, on a clear day, project an image of the city onto a white, concave table. *Castlehill, tel. 031/226–3709. Admission: £2.75 adults, £1.40 children, £2 student, £1.65 senior citizens, £7 family ticket. Open Apr.–Oct., weekdays 9:30–6, weekends 10–6; Nov.–Mar., weekdays 9:30–6, weekends 10–5.*

4 Opposite, the **Scotch Whisky Heritage Centre** reveals the mysterious process that turns malted barley and spring water into one of Scotland's most important exports. Although the process of making whiskey is not in itself packed with drama, the center manages an imaginative presentation using models and tableaux viewed while riding in low-speed barrel-cars. At one point visitors find themselves inside a huge vat surrounded by bubbling sounds and malty smells. A gift shop offers a variety of malt whiskies. *358 Castlehill, tel. 031/220–0441. Admission: £3.20 adults, £1.75 children, £2 senior citizens, £2.70 students, £8.50 family ticket. Open June–Sept., daily 9–6:30; Oct.–May, daily 10–5.*

5 Farther down on the left the Gothic **Tolbooth Kirk,** built in 1842–44 for the General Assembly of the Church of Scotland (*kirk* means *church*), boasts the tallest spire in the city—240 feet.

6 Continuing down to the intersection at the end of Castlehill, look for the **Upper Bow** on the right, immediately east of where Johnston Terrace joins the Lawnmarket. This was once the main route westward from town and castle. Before Victoria Street was built, in the late-19th century, Upper Bow led down into a narrow dark thoroughfare canyoned with tenements. All traffic struggled up and down this steep slope from the Grassmarket, which joins the now-truncated West Bow at its lower end. Walk a few yards down Upper Bow to look over the parapet into Victoria Street before resuming your stroll down the Royal Mile.

From **Lawnmarket** you can start your discovery of the **Old Town closes,** alleyways that are like ribs leading off the Royal Mile backbone.

Time Out There are a number of atmospheric pubs and restaurants in this
section of the Royal Mile. Try the **Jolly Judge** (James Ct.), a
friendly pub where bright firelight cheers the gloom of dark-
wood beams. You'll also find good beer at the **Ensign Ewart,** in a
more conspicuous spot opposite the Lawnmarket traffic circle.

❼ The narrow six-story tenement known as **Gladstone's Land,**
just beside the Assembly Hall on the left, is a survivor from the
17th century, demonstrating typical architectural features, including an arcaded ground floor and an entrance at second-floor
level (livestock sometimes inhabited the ground floor). It is
furnished in the style of a 17th-century merchant's house.
*Lawnmarket, tel. 031/226-5856. Admission: £2.20 adults,
£1.10 children, students, and senior citizens. Open Apr.–Oct.,
Mon.–Sat. 10–5, Sun. 2–5.*

❽ Close by Gladstone's Land, down yet another close, is **Lady
Stair's House,** a good example of 17th-century urban architecture. Built in 1622, it evokes Scotland's literary past with exhibits on Sir Walter Scott, Robert Louis Stevenson, and Robert
Burns. *Off Lawnmarket, tel. 031/225-2424, ext. 6593. Admission free. Open June–Sept., Mon.–Sat. 10–6, Sun. during festival 2–5; Oct.–May, Mon.–Sat. 10–5.*

At this point practically every close provides an introduction to
one or more of Edinburgh's past "worthies." In 1598 a royal
banquet was held by King James VI at Baillie MacMorran's
House, down Riddle's Close, to the right off Lawnmarket. A
little farther down, also on the right, you'll find Brodie's Close
and Deacon Brodie's Tavern. The Brodie in question was the in-
famous Deacon William Brodie. *Chambers Dictionary*—published in Edinburgh with an entirely appropriate Scots bias—
defines a deacon as a "master of an incorporated company." In
Brodie's case the company was the Guild of Wrights, or cabinetmakers. Cabinetmakers knew their way around keys and
locks, and Deacon Brodie used this knowledge to his own benefit for many years without being caught. Pillar of society by day
and philanderer by night, Brodie was eventually found out in
1788 and hanged in the Tolbooth. Robert Louis Stevenson and
W. E. Henley wrote a play about Deacon Brodie, and he was
later the inspiration for Stevenson's *Doctor Jekyll and Mr.
Hyde.*

For a worthwhile shopping diversion, turn right down George
❾ IV Bridge, then down **Victoria Street** to the right, a 19th-centu-
ry improvement—or intrusion—on the shape of the Old Town.
Its shops offer antiques, old prints, and high-quality giftware.
Some of the shops in this quarter are quite specialized: one offers fashion for tall women and another sells only handmade
❿ brushes. Down in the **Grassmarket,** which for centuries was, as
its name suggests, an agricultural market, the shopping continues, though here the expensive designer wares seem a little
out of place, especially when viewed alongside the panhandlers
who often gather here in argumentative huddles.

Sections of the Old Town wall can be approximately traced on
the north (castle) side by a series of steps that runs steeply up
from Grassmarket to Johnston Terrace above. By far the best-
preserved section of the wall, however, is to be found by crossing to the south side and climbing the steps of the lane called
The Vennel. Here you can see a section of the 16th-century
Flodden Wall, which comes in from the east and turns south-

ward at Telfer's Wall, a 17th-century extension. From here there are outstanding views northward to the castle. Frame the scene in the viewfinder of your camera, using the high wall as a foreground, and you'll feel as if you've gone back at least three centuries.

On your way back across Grassmarket to the Royal Mile, note the cobbled cross set in the ground and railed off. This is the site of the town gallows. Among those hanged here were many 17th-century Covenanters (*see below*). Judges were known to issue the death sentence for these religious reformers with the words, "Let them glorify God in the Grassmarket."

Another famous incident that took place in the vicinity was the Porteous Riot of 1736. One of two smugglers from Fife, condemned to death, managed to escape from the authorities because of a heroic diversion instigated by his partner. Smuggling was an activity with which the public sympathized in those days, and Captain Porteous of the town guard, in charge of the remaining prisoner's execution, was a brutal and unpopular figure. As usual, a crowd gathered in the Grassmarket to watch the hanging. After the grim deed was done, stones and other missiles were thrown at the hangman and guard—as was the custom on these occasions—whereupon Porteous ordered his men to fire at the crowd. Nine were killed. Porteous was arrested, tried, and found guilty of murder, but was in due course pardoned, through the effort of well-connected friends. Thereafter the townsfolk took matters into their own hands, breaking into the Tolbooth where Porteous was held and hanging him at a quarter to midnight from a dyer's pole at the east end of the Grassmarket. You can find his gravestone in Greyfriar's churchyard (*see below*) and a genteel 1855 painting of the incident by James Drummond in the Scottish National Gallery on the Mound (*see* Tour 2: The New Town, *below*). Sir Walter Scott took a few liberties with the incident in his novel *The Heart of Midlothian*.

To visit another of Edinburgh's historic churches, walk from the Grassmarket back along Victoria Street to George IV
⑪ Bridge, where you'll see the **National Library of Scotland** straight ahead. *Tel. 031/226–4531. Admission to exhibitions free. Open Mon., Tues., Thurs., Fri. 9:30–8:30, Wed. 10–8:30, Sat. 9:30–1.*

⑫ A little farther down, to the right, is the **Kirk of the Greyfriars,** built on the site of a medieval monastery. Here, in 1638, the National Covenant was signed, declaring the independence of the Presbyterian Church in Scotland from government control. The covenant plunged Scotland into decades of civil war. At the corner of George IV Bridge and Candlemaker Row, near the Greyfriars church, stands one of the most-photographed sculptures in Scotland, *Greyfriars Bobby.* This famous West Highland terrier kept vigil beside his master's grave in the churchyard for 14 years, leaving only for a short time each day to be fed at a nearby pub after the one-o'clock salute from the castle. *Greyfriars Pl., tel. 031/225–1900. Admission free. Open Easter–Sept., weekdays 10–6, Sat. 10–noon.*

Time Out **Lilligs** (30 Victoria St.) is an establishment popular with students that offers everything from coffee and cake in the afternoon to full-scale evening meals. It's a relaxed and friendly place where you won't be hurried through your meal.

Before returning to Lawnmarket, you might detour down Chambers Street, which leads off from George IV Bridge. **⑬** Here, in a lavish Victorian building, the **Royal Museum of Scotland** displays a broad collection drawn from natural history, archaeology, and scientific and industrial history. The great Main Hall, with its soaring roof, is architecturally interesting in its own right. *Chambers St., tel. 031/225-7534. Admission free. Open Mon.–Sat. 10–5, Sun. 2–5.*

Return to High Street via George IV Bridge, and, near Parliament Square, look on the right for a heart set in cobbles. This marks the site of the vanished **Tolbooth,** the center of city life from the 15th century until the building's demolition in 1817. This ancient civic edifice, formerly housing the Scottish parliament and used as a prison from 1640 onward, inspired Scott's novel *The Heart of Midlothian.* Nearly every city and town in Scotland once had a tolbooth. Originally a customs house where tolls were gathered, the name came to mean "town hall" and later "prison" because detention cells were located in the basement.

⑭ **Parliament House**—the seat of Scottish government until 1707, when the crowns of Scotland and England were united—is partially hidden by the bulk of St. Giles's. It's now the home of the Supreme Law Courts of Scotland. Parliament Hall inside is remarkable for its hammer beam roof and its display of portraits by major Scottish artists. *Parliament Sq., tel. 031/225-2595, ext. 223. Admission free. Open Tues.–Fri. 10–4.*

⑮ The **High Kirk of St. Giles,** originally the city's parish church, became a cathedral in 1633 and is now often called **St. Giles's Cathedral.** There has been a church on the site since AD 854, although most of the present structure dates from 1829. The spire, however, was completed in 1495; the choir is mostly 15th-century, and four of the interior columns date from the early 12th century. The **Chapel of the Order of the Thistle,** bearing the belligerent national motto NEMO ME IMPUNE LACESSIT ("No one provokes me with impunity"), was added in 1911. *High St., tel. 031/225-4363. Kirk admission free. Thistle Chapel admission: 30p. Open Mon.–Sat. 9–5 (until 7 in summer), Sun. 2–5.*

Another landmark in Old Town life can be seen just outside Par- **⑯** liament House. The **Mercat Cross** ("mercat" means "market"), a focus of public attention for centuries, is still the site of royal proclamations. The cross itself is modern, but part of its shaft is as old as the city.

Time Out **Le Sept** (7 Old Fishmarket Close) does a brisk business at lunchtime.

⑰ Across High Street from St. Giles's are the **City Chambers,** now the seat of local authority. Designed by John Adam in 1753, the building brings a flavor of the New Town's neoclassicism to the Old Town's severity. The chambers were originally known as the Royal Exchange and intended to be a place where merchants and lawyers could conduct business. Note that the building drops 12 stories to Cockburn Street on its north side.

⑱ Farther down on the right is the **Tron Kirk.** A "tron" is a weigh
beam used in public weigh houses, and the church was named
after a salt tron that used to stand nearby. The kirk itself was
built after 1635, when St. Giles's became an Episcopal cathedral for a brief time. In this church in 1693 a minister offered an
often-quoted prayer for the local government: "Lord, hae mer-
cy on aa [every] fool and idiot, and particularly on the Magis-
trates of Edinburgh." The Tron Kirk was closed in 1952, and
rumors periodically surface suggesting it may be turned into a
visitor center.

On the right, two blocks below the North Bridge–South Bridge
⑲ junction, is the **Museum of Childhood,** a celebration of toys that
even adults will enjoy. *42 High St., tel. 031/225–2424. Admission free. Open June–Sept., Mon.–Sat. 10–6, Sun. during festival 2–5; Oct.–May, Mon.–Sat. 10–5.*

⑳ Opposite is **John Knox House.** It is not certain that Scotland's
severe religious reformer (1514–72) lived here, but mementos
of his life are on view inside. This distinctive dwelling offers a
glimpse of what Old Town life was like in the 16th century. The
projecting upper stories were once commonplace along the
Royal Mile, darkening and further closing in the already narrow passage. Perhaps dating from as early as 1490, the building
survived devastation by the invading English forces under the
earl of Hertford in the episode known as the "rough wooing."
Look for the initials of former owner James Mossman and his
wife, carved into the stonework on the "marriage lintel."
Mossman was goldsmith to Mary, Queen of Scots, and was
hanged in 1573 for his allegiance to her. *45 High St., tel. 031/
556–9579. Admission: £1.20 adults, 50p children, £1 senior citizens. Open Mon.–Sat. 10–5.*

Beyond this point you would once have passed out of the safety
of the town walls. A plaque outside the **Netherbow Theatre** de-
picts the **Netherbow Port,** a gate that once stood on the site.
Look for the brass studs in the street cobbles that mark its location.

Below is the **Canongate,** named for the canons who once ran the
abbey at Holyrood, now the site of Holyrood Palace. In Scots,
"gate" means "street." Canongate itself was originally an independent "burgh," another Scottish term used to refer to a community with trading rights granted by the monarch. This
㉑ explains the presence of the handsome **Canongate Tolbooth,** on
the left, where the town council once met. Now the tolbooth is a
museum dedicated to the ordinary folk of Edinburgh. Called
"The People's Story," this museum is a reminder that the capital's history is not altogether bound up with monarchs, aristo-
crats, and politicians. Its exhibits focus on the lives of ordinary
people from the 18th century to today; special displays include
a reconstruction of a cooper's workshop and a 1940s kitchen.
*Canongate Tolbooth, tel. 031/225–2424, ext. 6638. Admission
free. Open June–Sept., Mon.–Sat. 10–6, Sun. during festival
2–5; Oct.–May, Mon.–Sat. 10–5.*

㉒ Opposite the tolbooth is **Acheson House** (c. 1633), once a fine
town mansion, which, like so much of the property in the
Canongate, fell on hard times. It has now been restored, as has
Moray House, which dates from 1628, a little farther up the
street.

㉓ In the graveyard of **Canongate Kirk** are buried some notable Scots, including Adam Smith, author of *The Wealth of Nations* (1776), who once lived in 17th-century Panmure House nearby. Here you can also visit the grave of the undervalued Scots poet Robert Fergusson. The fact that Fergusson's grave is even marked is due to the efforts of the much more famous Robert Burns. On a visit to the city Burns was dismayed to find the grave had no headstone, so he commissioned an architect—by the name of Robert Burn—to design one. (Burn reportedly took two years to complete the commission, so Burns, in turn, took two years to pay.) Burn also designed the Nelson Monument, the tall column on Calton Hill to the north, which you can see from the churchyard.

Before you leave the cemetery, look for the monument to Robert Burns himself, also on Calton Hill and visible from the churchyard; it is the circular temple below Regent Road (*see* Tour 2: The New Town, *below*). Devotees of Burns will want to visit one other grave. Against the eastern wall of the churchyard is a bronze sculpture of the head of Mrs. Agnes McLehose, "Clarinda" of the copious correspondence Burns engaged in while confined to his lodgings with an injured leg in 1788. Burns and Mrs. McLehose—an attractive and talented woman who had been abandoned by her husband—exchanged passionate letters for some six weeks that year, Burns signing his name "Sylvander"; Mrs. McLehose, "Clarinda." The missives were dispatched across town by a postal service that delivered them for a penny an hour. The curiously literary affair ended when Burns left Edinburgh to take up a farm tenancy and marry Jean Armour.

㉔ Opposite the churchyard is gable-fronted **Huntly House** (1570), now a museum of local history. The exhibits include collections of Scottish pottery and Edinburgh silver and glass. *142 Canongate, tel. 031/225–2424, ext. 6689. Admission free. Open June–Sept., Mon.–Sat. 10–6, Sun. during festival 2–5; Oct.–May, Mon.–Sat. 10–5.*

Time Out You can get a good cup of tea and a sticky cake (a quintessentially Scottish indulgence) from **Clarinda's** (69 Canongate) or the **Abbey Strand Tearoom** (The Sanctuary, Abbey Strand), near the palace gates.

㉕ Facing you at the end of Canongate are the elaborate wrought-iron gates of the **Palace of Holyroodhouse,** official residence of the queen when she is in Scotland.

The palace came into existence originally as a guest house for the Abbey of Holyrood, which was founded in 1128 by Scottish king David I, after a vision of the cross (*rood* means *cross*) saved his life on a hunting trip. According to the legend David was attacked and unhorsed by a wounded stag when hunting in the—then royal—forest. As the stag bent to finish him off, a crucifix appeared between its antlers. The king clasped the crucifix and the animal fled. David gave the land for the abbey to Augustinian friars in gratitude to God and commanded them to build the Abbey of Holyrood—the Church of the Holy Cross.

Before you enter the gates, look for the brass letters "SSS" set into the road at the beginning of Abbey Strand (the continuation of the Royal Mile beyond the traffic circle). The letters stand for "sanctuary" and recall the days when the former abbey was literally a place of retreat. The abbey served as a refuge for debtors for some 350 years, until 1880, when the government stopped imprisoning people for debt. The houses in the Abbey Strand area served as lodgings for the debtors (and criminals) who sought refuge here. Curiously, the area of sanctuary extended across the former royal hunting forest, now Holyrood Park, so debtors could get some fresh air without fear of being caught by their creditors. Oddest of all, however, was the agreement that after debtors checked in at Holyrood they were able to go anywhere in the city on Sunday. This made for great entertainment on Sunday evening as midnight approached: the debtors raced back to Holyrood before the stroke of 12, often hotly pursued by their creditors. The poet Thomas de Quincey and the comte d'Artois, brother of the deposed King Louis XVIII of France, were only two of the more exotic of Holyrood's denizens.

Throughout its history the palace has been the setting for high drama, including at least one notorious murder, a spectacular funeral, several major fires, and centuries of the colorful lifestyles of larger-than-life, power-hungry personalities. The murder occurred in 1566, when Mary, Queen of Scots, was dining with her favorite, David Rizzio, who was hated at court for his social climbing. Mary's second husband, Lord Darnley, burst into the chamber with his henchmen, dragged Rizzio into an antechamber, and stabbed him more than 50 times. (Darnley himself was murdered in Edinburgh the next year, to make way for the queen's marriage to her lover, Bothwell.) Only 22 years before these shocking events, the palace had been severely damaged by an invading English army, which set fire to the building; only the great tower (on the left as you look at the front facade) survived.

After the Union of the Crowns in 1603, when the Scottish Royal Court packed its bags and decamped for England, the building fell into decline. In 1650 the palace burned again, this time by accident, and the great tower's massive walls once more resisted the flames. Oliver Cromwell, the Protestant Lord Protector of England, who had conquered Scotland, ordered the palace rebuilt after the 1650 fire, but the work was poorly carried out and lasted only until the restoration of the monarchy, after Cromwell's death. When Charles II ascended the British throne in 1660, he ordered Holyrood rebuilt in the architectural style of the French "Sun King," Louis XIV, and that is the palace that visitors see today.

In 1661 Holyroodhouse was the scene of one of the most bizarre funerals in history. The marquis of Montrose, a Scottish royalist general, had been executed by Cromwell for high treason, and his limbs and head were displayed around the country. Following the restoration of the Stuart monarchy, Montrose's body was put together for a final farewell ceremony. One of his legs was brought from Aberdeen; his head from a spike in London; his other leg and his arms from, respectively, Glasgow, Stirling, and Perth; and the rest of his remains from the local gallows. The body lay in state in Holyrood for four months, after which the coffin was paraded through the streets, borne aloft by 14 earls, and buried in the Kirk of St. Giles.

In 1688 an anti-Catholic faction ran riot within the palace, and in 1745 the palace was occupied by Prince Charles Edward Stuart, during the last Jacobite campaign. After the 1822 visit of

King George IV, in more peaceable times, the palace sank into decline once again. However, Queen Victoria and her grandson King George V renewed interest in the palace, and the buildings were once more refurbished and made suitable for royal residence.

When the royal family is not in residence, you can go inside for a conducted tour. The highlights include the **King James Tower**, the oldest surviving section, which contains the rooms of Mary, Queen of Scots, on the second floor, and Lord Darnley's rooms below. Though much has been altered, there are fine fireplaces, paneling, plasterwork, tapestries, and 18th-century furniture throughout the structure. Along the front of the palace, between the two main towers, are the duchess of Hamilton's room and the Adam-style dining room. Next to it are the Grand Stairs, adorned with broadswords.

Along the southern side of the palace are the Throne Room and other drawing rooms now used mainly for social and ceremonial occasions. Among the rooms at the back of the palace is the King's Bedchamber. Another notable attraction is the **Picture Gallery**, which has a huge collection of portraits of Scottish monarchs (some of the royal figures honored here are actually purely fictional, and the likenesses of others are purely imaginary). All the portraits were painted by a Dutch artist, Jacob de Witt, who, in 1684, signed a contract with the Queen's Cashkeeper Hugh Wallace that bound De Witt to deliver 110 pictures within two years, for which he received an annual stipend of £120. Surely one of the most desperate scenes in the palace's history is that of the Dutch artist feverishly turning out potboiler portraits at the rate of one a week for two years. *Tel. 031/556–7371. Admission: £2.50 adults, £1.30 children, £2 senior citizens, £6.50 family ticket. Open Apr.–Oct., Mon.–Sat. 9:30–5:15, Sun. 10:30–4:30; Nov.–Mar., Mon.–Sat. 9:30–3:45; closed during royal and state visits. (Because of renovations, the palace will be closed to visitors Nov. 1992–mid-Feb. 1993.)*

Behind the palace lie the open grounds and looming crags of **Holyrood Park**, which enclose Edinburgh's minimountain, ❷❻ **Arthur's Seat** (822 ft.). The park was the hunting ground of early Scottish kings. The views of the city and the surrounding area from the top of Arthur's Seat are breathtaking. A steep stroll to **Salisbury Crags,** the long wavering line of cliffs visible from the palace grounds, is also rewarding. Photographers, in particular, appreciate the unusual views, both of Holyrood itself and of the photogenic series of monuments on Calton Hill to the northwest.

Across from the south gates of the palace is an **interpretation center** operated jointly by the Scottish Wildlife Trust and Historic Scotland. *Holyrood Park Rd., tel. 031/312–7765. Call ahead for admission and opening and closing information.*

Tour 2: The New Town

The Old Town has almost 1,000 years of history echoing along its narrow streets, but the New Town has only a brief 200 years. At the dawn of the so-called Scottish Enlightenment, in the 18th century, the city fathers busied themselves with various schemes to improve the capital. By that time Edinburgh's unsanitary ambience—created primarily by the crowded conditions in which most people lived—was becoming notorious. The well-known Scots fiddle tune "The Flooers (flowers) of Edinburgh" was only one of many ironic references to the capital's unpleasant atmosphere, which so embarrassed the Scot James Boswell, biographer and companion of the English lexicographer Dr. Samuel Johnson. In his *Journal of a Tour of the Hebrides,* Boswell recalled that on retrieving the newly arrived Johnson from his grubby inn in the Canongate, "I could not prevent his being assailed by the evening effluvia of Edinburgh. . . . Walking the streets at night was pretty perilous and a good deal odoriferous. . . ."

To help remedy this sorry state of affairs, in 1767 the city's Lord Provost (Scots for mayor), James Drummond, urged the town council to hold a civic competition to design a new district for Edinburgh. The winner was an unknown young architect named James Craig. His plan was for a grid of three main east–west streets, balanced at either end by two grand squares. These streets survive today, though some of the buildings that line them were altered by later development. Princes Street is the southernmost, with Queen Street to the north and George Street as the axis, punctuated by St. Andrew and Charlotte squares. A look at the map will show you the district's symmetry, unusual in Britain. Even Princes Street Gardens are balanced by Queen Street Gardens to the north.

27 Start your walk on **The Mound,** the sloping street that joins Old and New towns. The Mound originated in the need for a dry-shod crossing of the muddy quagmire that was left behind when Nor' Loch, the body of water below the castle, was drained (the railway now cuts through this area). The work is said to have been started by a local tailor, George Boyd, who tired of struggling through the mud en route from his New Town house to his Old Town shop. The building of a ramp was under way by 1781, and by the time of its completion, in 1830, "Geordie Boyd's mud brig" (bridge), as the street was first known, had been built up with an estimated two million cartloads of earth dug from the foundations of the New Town.

Two galleries immediately east of this great linking ramp are the work of W. H. Playfair (1789–1857), an architect whose neoclassical buildings contributed greatly to Edinburgh's title, **28** the Athens of the North. The **National Gallery of Scotland,** immediately east of the Mound, has a wide selection of paintings, from the Renaissance to the Post-Impressionist period, with works by Velásquez, El Greco, Rembrandt, Turner, Degas, Monet, and Van Gogh, among others, as well as a fine collection of Scottish art. The rooms of the gallery are attractively decorated, and it is a pleasure to browse. *The Mound, tel. 031/556–8921. Admission free. Open Mon.–Sat. 10–5 (extended during festival), Sun. 2–5.*

29 The other gallery, The **Royal Scottish Academy,** its imposing, columned facade overlooking Princes Street, holds an annual exhibition of students' work. *Princes St., tel. 031/225–6671. Admission: £1.20 adults, 50p children and concessions, £3 season ticket. Open late-Apr.–July, Mon.–Sat. 10–6, Sun. 2–5.*

The north side of **Princes Street** is now one long sequence of chain stores whose unappealing modern fronts can be seen in almost any large British town. Luckily the other side of the street is occupied by well-kept gardens, which act as a wide

30 green moat to the castle on its rock. Walk east until you reach the unmistakable 200-foot-high Gothic spire of the **Scott Monument,** built in 1844 in honor of Scotland's most famous author, Sir Walter Scott (1771–1832), author of *Ivanhoe, Waverley,* and many other novels and poems. Note the marble statue of Scott and his favorite dog. The monument has recently been under renovation. The building of the monument on this favored site on Princes Street was possible only after a special Act of Consent was passed because the original citizens of Princes Street had fought long legal battles to keep the south side of the street free from buildings. On the death of Sir Walter Scott, however, public sentiment demanded a grand acknowledgment of the work of the then wildly popular writer. After much delay the committee supervising the construction of a suitable memorial announced a competition for its design. (If in doubt about how to procede with any civic development, the burghers of Edinburgh usually hold a competition.) After the Gothic skyrocket that you now see was chosen, the committee was somewhat dismayed to learn that the design, submitted under a pseudonym, turned out to be not the work of a prestigious architect, but rather that of a carpenter and self-taught draughtsman, George Meikle Kemp. A well-traveled man, Kemp incorporated elements of France's Rheims Cathedral into his design for the Scott Monument. By a strange coincidence, some years before, the then still-struggling artisan, walking on the road to Galashiels, had accepted a ride offered by a gentleman in a coach. Only later, on alighting, did Kemp find out he had journeyed with Sir Walter himself. As a final twist in Kemp's odd story, he drowned in mysterious circumstances in a local canal before his masterwork was completed. *Princes St., tel. 031/225-2424. At press time, still closed for renovation.*

Just opposite is **Jenners**—Edinburgh's equivalent of London's Harrod's department store. Jenners is noteworthy not only for its high-quality wares and good restaurants, but also because of the building's interesting architectural detail—baroque on the outside, with a mock-Jacobean central well inside. By way of a contrast, Edinburgh's high-tech shopping district is just beyond, on the other side of the road in the **Waverley Market.** Apart from a selection of Scottish woolens and tweeds, nothing differentiates this shopping development from any other modern shopping mall of the indoor-plant, tinkling-waterfall variety. There is another mall—the **St. James Centre**—farther on, beyond Register House.

31 **Register House,** opposite the main post office, marks the end of Princes Street. This was Scotland's first custom-built archives depository and was partly funded by the sale of estates forfeited by Jacobite landowners, following their last rebellion in Britain (1745–46). Work on the building, designed by Robert Adam, Scotland's most famous neoclassical architect, started in 1774. The statue in front is of the duke of Wellington. *Princes St., tel. 031/556-6585. Admission free. Open weekdays, legal collection 9:30-4:30, historical collection 9-4:45, general exhibitions 10-4.*

Time Out Immediately west of Register House is the **Café Royal** (17 W. Register St.), one of the city's most interesting pubs. It has good beer and lots of character, with ornate tiles and stained glass contributing to the atmosphere.

---

32 The monuments on **Calton Hill,** growing ever more noticeable ahead as you walk east along Princes Street, can be reached by first continuing along Waterloo Place, the eastern extension of Princes Street. There is some fine neoclassically inspired architecture on this street, all designed as a piece by Archibald Elliott. The Regent Bridge or, more precisely, the **Regent Arch**—a simple, triumphal, Corinthian-column conceit on top of the bridge, was intended as a war memorial. The road then continues in a single sweep through the **Calton Burial Ground** to the screen walling at the base of Calton Hill. On the left you'll see steps that lead to the hilltop. Drivers—or walkers who don't feel up to the steep climb—can take the road farther on to the left, which loops up the hill at a more leisurely pace.

Beyond the photogenic collection of columns and temples, the views from Calton Hill range over the Lomond Hills of Fife, in the north, to the Pentland Hills, in the southwest, behind the spire of St. Giles's. This was Robert Louis Stevenson's favorite view of his beloved city.

The architectural styles represented on Calton Hill include the Gothic—the Old Observatory, for example—and the neoclassical. Under the latter heading fall William Playfair's monument to his talented uncle, the philosopher and mathematician John Playfair, as well as his cruciform **New Observatory.** The piece that commands the most attention, however, is the so-called **National Monument,** often referred to as "Edinburgh's [or Scotland's] Disgrace." Intended to copy Athens's Parthenon, this monument for the dead of the Napoleonic Wars was started in 1822 to the specifications of a design by the ubiquitous Playfair. In 1830, however, only 12 columns later, money ran out, and the columned facade became a monument to high aspirations and poor fund-raising. On the opposite side of the road, in the Calton Burial Ground, is a monument to Abraham Lincoln and the Scottish American dead of the Civil War. (An impressive American monument to the Scottish soldiers of World War I stands in West Princes Street Gardens, among various memorials of Scottish and foreign alliances.) The tallest monument on Calton Hill is the 100-foot-high **Nelson Monument,** completed in 1814 in honor of Britain's naval hero. *Tel. 031/225–2424, ext. 6689. Admission Nelson Monument: 60p. Open Apr.–Sept., Mon.–Sat. 10–6; Oct.–Mar., Mon.–Sat. 10–3.*

After leaving Calton Hill you may wish to continue east along Regent Road, perhaps as far as the **Robert Burns Monument,** to admire the views westward of the castle and of the facade of the former Royal High School (directly above you). Make your way **33** to **St. Andrew Square** by cutting through the St. James Centre shopping mall, across Leith Street, and then through the Bus Station.

On St. Andrew Square, immediately south of the bus station, is the headquarters of the **Royal Bank of Scotland;** take a look inside at the lavish decor of the central banking hall. In the distance, at the other end of George Street, on Charlotte Square, you can see the copper dome of the former St. George's Church. In Craig's symmetrical plan for the New Town, a matching church was intended for the bank's site, but Sir Lawrence Dundas, a wealthy and influential baronet, somehow managed to acquire the space for his town house. The grand mansion was later converted into the bank. The church originally intended for the site, St. Andrew's, is a little farther down George Street on the right.

Walk west along George Street, with its variety of shops, noting on the way the statue of King George IV, at the intersection of George and Hanover streets. George IV visited Scotland in 1822; he was the first British monarch to do so since King Charles II, in the 17th century. By the 19th century Scotland was perceived at Westminster, distant English seat of Parliament, as being almost civilized enough for a monarch to visit in safety. The city fathers needed a good public-relations manager for the occasion and appointed the popular Sir Walter Scott, who stage-managed the entire circus. It was a wonderful opportunity for everyone to dress up, and it gave the tartan industry a great boost. (For a leisurely and dignified passage across Hanover, Frederick, and Castle streets, you may be dependent on the politeness of the local drivers, sometimes an unreliable commodity.)

Time Out Hanover Street, the first cross-street west of St. David Street, offers a choice of good eating places. Try **La Lanterna** (83 Hanover St.), situated in a wood-panel basement, for value, cheerful service, and no-nonsense Italian home cooking.

The ubiquitous Sir Walter turns up again farther down the street. It was at a grand dinner in the Assembly Rooms (between Hanover and Frederick streets on the left) that Scott acknowledged having written the *Waverley* novels (the name of the author had hitherto been a secret.) You'll meet Scott once again, in the form of a plaque just downhill to your right, at 39 Castle Street, where he lived from 1797 on.

By now you will have appreciated the views at each intersection northward over the Firth of Forth to Fife. This was another deliberate element in the grand New Town scheme. Much has been altered in this part of town, however, since it was first developed. Remember that the New Town was conceived as a residential quarter—shopping and services were to be confined to narrow Thistle and Rose streets, north and south of George Street. By the first part of the 19th century most of Princes Street was overtaken by commerce—and today the stores there are mainly dull British retail chains. George Street, similarly, now houses slightly more upscale shops, as well as the inevitable banks and finance houses.

34 The essence of the New Town spirit survives in **Charlotte Square,** at the western end of George Street. Note the palatial facade of the square's north side, designed by Robert Adam—it is considered one of Europe's finest pieces of civic architec-
35 ture. Here you will find the **Georgian House,** which the National Trust for Scotland has furnished in period style to show the elegant domestic arrangements of an affluent family of the late-18th century. The hallway was designed to accommodate sedan chairs, in which 18th-century grandees were carried through the streets. *7 Charlotte Sq., tel. 031/225–2160. Admission: £2.40 adults, £1.20 children and senior citizens. Open Apr.–Oct., Mon.–Sat. 10–4:30, Sun. 2–4:30.*

Also in the square, the former St. George's Church, mentioned above as part of the New Town Plan, now fulfills a different

③⑥ role, as **West Register House,** an extension of the original Register House. *Charlotte Sq. Admission free. Open weekdays, exhibitions 10–4, research room 9–4:45.*

Time Out Try **Bianco's** (9–11 Hope St.), close to the Georgian House, for coffee and croissants. You never have to wait in line; the atmosphere is relaxed; the seats are comfortable; and the coffee, by Edinburgh standards, is very good.

To explore further in the New Town, choose your own route northward, down to the wide and elegant streets centering on ③⑦ **Moray Place,** a fine example of an 1820s development, with imposing porticoes and a central, secluded garden. The area remains primarily residential, in contrast to the area around Princes Street. The gardens in the center of the square are still for residents only.

③⑧ A neo-Gothic building on Queen Street houses the **Scottish National Portrait Gallery** and the Queen Street premises of the **Royal Museum of Scotland.** The gallery contains a magnificent Gainsborough and portraits by the Scottish artists Ramsay and Raeburn. In the museum, don't miss the 16th-century Celtic harps and the Lewis chessmen—mysterious, grim-face chess pieces carved from walrus ivory in the Middle Ages. *Gallery and museum, Queen St., tel. 031/225–7534. Admission free. Open Mon.–Sat. 10–5, Sun. 2–5.*

③⑨ Another attraction within reach of the New Town is the **Royal Botanic Garden.** Walk down Dundas Street, the continuation of Hanover Street, and turn left across the bridge over the Water of Leith, Edinburgh's small-scale river. These 70-acre gardens offer the largest rhododendron and azalea collection in Britain; peat, rock, and woodland gardens; a magnificent herbaceous border; an arboretum; and capacious greenhouses. There is also a convenient cafeteria on the premises. *Inverleith Row, tel. 031/552–7171. Admission free (voluntary donation for greenhouses). Open Mar.–Oct., Mon.–Sat. 9–one hour before sunset, Sun. 11–one hour before sunset; Nov.–Feb., Mon.–Sat. 9–sunset, Sun. 11–sunset. Greenhouses close daily at 5.*

④⓪ The **Scottish National Gallery of Modern Art,** also close to the New Town, occupies a former school building on Belford Road and features paintings and sculpture, including works by Picasso, Braque, Matisse, and Derain. *Belford Rd., tel. 031/556–8921. Admission free. Open Mon.–Sat. 10–5, Sun. 2–5 (extended during the festival).*

Edinburgh for Free

Brass Rubbing Centre (*see* What to See and Do with Children)
Festival Fringe street events (during the three-week-long Edinburgh Festival)
Huntly House (*see* Tour 1)
Lady Stair's House (*see* Tour 1)
Museum of Childhood (*see* Tour 1)
New Town Conservation Centre displays an exhibition on the restoration of buildings in the New Town. *13a Dundas St., tel. 031/557–5222. Open Mon.–Fri. 9–1 and 2–5.*
Princes Street Gardens (*see* Tour 2)
Royal Botanic Garden (*see* Tour 2)
Royal Museum of Scotland (*see* Tour 1)

Scottish National Gallery of Modern Art (*see* Tour 2)
Scottish National Portrait Gallery (*see* Tour 2)
Scottish Record Office. On display in West Register House is an exhibition on 800 years of Scottish history (*see* Tour 2).

What to See and Do with Children

Edinburgh emphasizes its history and architecture to such a great degree that children's facilities have to be hunted down. The Tourist Centre above Waverley Market offers up-to-date listings of facilities and activities for children.

Leisure Centers and Activities
The **Brass Rubbing Centre,** near John Knox House on the Royal Mile, provides all the materials children (and adults) need to create do-it-yourself replicas from original Pictish stones and markers, rare Scottish brasses, and medieval church brasses. No experience is needed for this pastime, which children find quite absorbing. *Trinity Apse, Chalmers Close, tel. 031/556–4364. Admission free but a charge (40p–£10.50) is made for every rubbing. Open June–Sept., Mon.–Sat. 10–6 (Sun. during festival 2–5); Oct.–May, Mon.–Sat. 10–5.*

Dalkeith Park is the nearest boisterous woodland-adventure playground (offering some cause for anxiety for the nervous parent). The more sedate will enjoy the woodland walks and 18th-century bridge. It is not suitable for toddlers. *Dalkeith Park, east end of Dalkeith High St., Dalkeith (10 mi south of Edinburgh; regular bus service from St. Andrew Sq. Bus Station), tel. 031/663–5684. Admission: £1 for adult-and-child ticket. Open Easter–Oct., daily 11–6, Nov., weekends 11–6.*

Hillend Ski Centre operates a ski school throughout the year that offers group and individual tuition on an artificial surface. All equipment can be rented, although there is nothing available for children under six years. *Biggar Rd., (south of the city), tel. 031/445–4433. Charge for chair lift: £1.45 adults, 65p children and senior citizens. Open Apr.–Sept., Mon.–Fri. 9:30–9; Oct.–Mar., daily 9:30–10.*

Little Marco's Leisure Centre is an indoor play area with slides, mazes, climbing frames, and other paraphernalia for energetic toddlers, plus cartoons for the tired out. *51–59 Grove St., tel. 031/228–2341. Admission: £1.50 for 1½ hours of supervised play (£3 for over 3s). Open weekdays 9:30–7, weekends 9:30–8.*

Kennedy's Fun Centre, *3 Windsor Pl., Portobello, tel. 031/669–1075. Cost: £1.50 per child (must be under 10 and accompanied by an adult). Open sessions: Fri. 1–3, Sat. 9:30–11:30 (call for details of other open sessions).*

Museums
The **Museum of Childhood** (*see* Tour 1, *above*) appeals to both adults and children. The museum offers a collection of childhood memorabilia, vintage toys, and dolls, as well as a reconstructed schoolroom, street scene, fancy-dress party, and nursery. This often (cheerfully) noisy museum was the first in the world to be devoted solely to the history of childhood.

Zoos
Edinburgh Butterfly and Insect World is a breath of the tropics—a sticky and humid, indoor, walk-through, junglelike experience filled, not unexpectedly, with brightly colored butterflies and other creepy-crawlies. *Melville Nurseries, near Dalkeith, tel. 031/663–4932. Admission: £2.85 adults, £1.60*

children, £2.20 senior citizens and students, £8.20 family tick-
et. Open Apr.–Oct., daily 10–5:30.

Edinburgh Zoo offers traditional zoo delights plus animal
contact and handling sessions in the main season, as well as
its ever-popular Penguin Parade (held daily in summer).
Corstorphine Rd., beside Post House Hotel (4 mi west of city),
tel. 031/334–9171. Admission: £4.30 adults, £2.30 children and
senior citizens, £12 family ticket. Open Mon.–Sat. 9–6 (or
dusk if earlier), Sun. 9:30–6 (or dusk).

Off the Beaten Track

Not all of Edinburgh's points of interest are confined within
Old and New towns—nor do they all require a day-long excursion. There are many places within easy reach that make for rewarding exploration if you have a spare morning or afternoon.

Duddingston. Tucked behind Arthur's Seat—you could walk
from Princes Street via Holyrood Park—this little community
(formerly of brewers and weavers) has an interesting church
with a Norman doorway and a watchtower that was built to
keep body snatchers out of the graveyard. The church overlooks Duddingston Loch, popular with birdwatchers, and moments away is an old-style pub called the Sheep's Heid Inn,
which offers a variety of beers and the oldest skittle-alley in
Scotland. *LRT Bus 42/46.*

Cramond. This compact settlement on the coast west of the city
is the place to watch summer sunsets over the Firth of Forth,
with the Cramond Inn nearby offering refreshment. The River
Almond joins the main estuary here. Its banks, once the site of
mills and works, now offer pleasant leafy walks and plenty to
interest the industrial archaeologist. *LRT Bus 41 (18 in eve-*
ning and on Sun.).

Swanston. In the shadow of the Pentland Hills, this conservation village is in sight of, but a world apart from, the southern
suburbs and bypass road. There are picturesque white-washed
cottages and walks into the hills. Information boards explain
the Robert Louis Stevenson connection—his family had a summer cottage here. *LRT Bus 4 to Fairmilehead, then walk along*
the footpath leading west along the edge of the golf course.

Leith. Edinburgh's ancient seaport has been revitalized in recent years, with the restoration of those fine commercial buildings that survived an earlier, and insensitive, redevelopment
phase. It is worth exploring the lowest reaches of the Water of
Leith, an area where pubs and restaurants now proliferate.
LRT Buses 7, 10, 11, or 16.

Colinton. Here you can sample the flavor of a leafy Edinburgh
suburb on the banks of the Water of Leith. Tall trees shelter a
riverside walkway that leads to (and beyond) Colinton's Parish
Church, another site associated with Robert Louis Stevenson
(his grandfather was the local minister). *LRT Bus 45, then look*
for signs to Colinton Dell.

The Pentlands. This unmistakable range of hills immediately
south of the city has the longest artificial ski slope in Britain, at
Hillend, and an all-year chair lift offering magnificent views
(even to nonskiers). There are several other access points along
the A702 running parallel to the hills—the best is Flotterstone

(where there is a car park; pub; and easy, quiet road-walking).
*LRT Bus 4 to Hillend, or 101/101/102 to Flotterstone (Eastern
Scottish Buses offer limited service).*

Shopping

To make the most of shopping in Edinburgh you will need at
least two days, in part because the town's most interesting
shops are distributed among several districts. In Edinburgh's
downtown are the High-Street-type chain stores, lined up
shoulder to shoulder and offering identical goods. But within a
few yards, down some of the side streets, you'll find shops offering more exclusive wares, such as designer clothing; unique
craft items; 18th-century silverware; and wild-caught Scottish
salmon, smoked.

As the capital city and an important tourist center, Edinburgh
features a cross section of Scottish specialties, such as tartans
and tweeds, rather than products peculiar to the Edinburgh
area. Once you venture into Edinburgh's "villages"—perhaps
Stockbridge, Bruntsfield, Morningside, or even the Old Town
itself—you will find many unusual stores specializing in single
items, such as brushes, antique clocks, and designer knitwear
using the finest Scottish wool and cashmere. In many cases the
goods sold in these stores are unavailable elsewhere in Scotland.

If you are interested in antiques, Edinburgh should be a pro-
ductive hunting ground. Scotland has a strong tradition of distinctive furniture makers, silversmiths, and artists, and top-
quality examples of their work can still be found, at a price.
Most reputable dealers are able to arrange transport abroad
for your purchases if you buy something too bulky to fit into
your luggage. Antiques dealers tend to cluster together, so it
may be easier to concentrate on one area—St. Stephen Street,
Bruntsfield Place, Causewayside, or Dundas Street, for example—if you are short of time. Suggestions for particular shops
are made below.

In most shops the prices quoted include the 17½% value-added
tax (VAT), if applicable. For certain goods the VAT is not included in the price but will be added to the bill. In any case VAT
may be reclaimed once you're home, and most shops that are
accustomed to handling foreign customers will supply the necessary forms. Keep your receipt as proof of purchase—refunds
will be refused without it.

Shopping hours are generally 9 to 5 or 5:30; many shops stay
open until 7 or 8 on Thursday evening. Some of the more specialized shops, such as antiques dealers, may have shorter
opening hours. Laws passed in Scotland (not in England) several years ago allow stores to open their doors on Sunday; though
this practice has by no means been universally embraced by
Scottish shopkeepers, you will find shops with Sunday hours,
especially in the main tourist season.

Shopping Districts

Princes Street Although it is world renowned as a shopping street, Princes
Street in New Town may disappoint many visitors because of
its plethora of anonymous modern architecture, chain stores,

and fast-food outlets. It is, however, one of the best spots to shop for tartans, tweeds, and knitwear—especially if your time is limited—and the view upward toward the castle is still magnificent.

Holding their ground amid the general banality at ground level are a few gems, the most noteworthy being **Jenners,** Edinburgh's last surviving independent department store (4 Princes St., opposite the Scott Monument). Claiming to be the world's oldest department store (established in 1838), Jenners is housed in a handsome Victorian (and later) building, graced outside with caryatids, which emphasize the importance of women to the business. Although you can buy almost anything here, the store does specialize in china and glassware and in upmarket tweeds and tartans. Its Food Hall features Scottish products—shortbreads and Dundee cakes, honeys and marmalades, many available in attractive gift packs—as well as a range of high-quality groceries. (The Food Hall may remind you, in miniature, of Harrods Food Hall, in London.) Jenners is a must-visit, not least for the spectacle of its galleries rising from the main shopping hall. **The Scotch House** (60 Princes St.) is popular with overseas visitors for its top-quality (if topprice) clothing and accessories.

Rose Street, one block north of Princes Street, has many smaller specialty shops; part of the street is a traffic-free pedestrian zone, so it's a pleasant place to browse. **Alistir Tait** (116a Rose St.) offers a collection of high-quality antique and fine jewelery, silver, clocks, and crystal. If you plan on doing a lot of hiking or camping in the Highlands or the Islands once you leave Edinburgh, you may want to look over the selection of outdoor clothing, boots, jackets, and heavy- and lightweight gear at **Graham Tiso** (115–123 Rose St.).

George Street   Parallel to Princes Street, George Street retains much more of its attractive Georgian and Victorian architecture (though some facades are literally that, with entirely new office blocks built directly behind). The shops here tend to be fairly upscale. London names, such as **Laura Ashley, Liberty,** and **Waterstones** bookshop, are prominent, though some of the older independent stores continue to hold their own. Try **Waterstons** (57 George St., not to be confused with the above bookshop) not only for stationery but for an excellent selection of small gift items. **Grays** (89 George St.) is a long-established ironmonger and hardware store that believes in old-fashion service. The jeweler **Hamilton and Inches** (87 George St.), established in 1866, is a silver- and goldsmith, worth visiting not only for its modern and antique gift possibilities, but also for its late-Georgian interior, designed by David Bryce in 1834—all gilded columns and elaborate plasterwork.

The streets crossing George Street—Hanover, Frederick, and Castle—are also worth exploring. **Dundas Street,** the northern extension of Hanover Street, beyond Queen Street Gardens, features several antiques shops. On **Howe Street** (beyond Frederick Street) **Rowland's** delicatessen will tempt you with excellent cheeses (try the Lanark Blue—a local specialty). **Thistle Street,** originally George Street's "back lane," or service area, has several boutiques and more antiques shops, including **Joseph Bonnar,** a specialist in antique jewelry. **South St. Andrew Street,** at the east end of George Street, is home to the oldest hatters in Scotland, **Cunningham and Co.,** founded in 1817; this is the place to go for a genuine Scottish tammie or a length of tweed or cashmere.

The Royal Mile   As may be expected, many of the shops along the Royal Mile in the Old Town sell what may be politely or euphemistically described as tourist-ware. Careful exploration, however, will reveal some worthwhile establishments. For example, **Aika** (248 Canongate) specializes in hand-knit garments in natural fibers (wool, cotton, angora, alpaca, mohair, silk, and linen). **Geoffrey (Tailor) Highland Crafts** (57–59 High St.) can clothe you in full Highland dress, with kilts made in its own workshops.

In addition to offering a good selection of whiskies, tartans, and tweeds, shops on the Royal Mile cater to some highly specialized interests and hobbies. For example, one store offers a large selection of playing cards, and another is devoted to doll houses and doll furniture.

Victoria Street/   Close to the castle end of the Royal Mile, just off George IV
West Bow/   Bridge, the specialty shops of Victoria Street are contained
Grassmarket   within a small area. If you aren't overwhelmed by the choices here, follow the tiny West Bow to Grassmarket for more of the same. For an original, easy-to-pack souvenir try the range of antique-print maps, watercolors, and drawings at **John Nelson** (22 Victoria St.). More unusual is **Robert Cresser's** brush shop (40 Victoria St.), featuring brushes of all kinds, every one handmade. On the topic of unusual presents and souvenirs, **Mr. Wood's Fossils** (in the Grassmarket) can provide you with a small prehistoric (and Scottish) shark encased in rock. This shop offers fossils to suit every budget. Diagonally opposite is **Bill Baber's Sheepish Looks** (66 Grassmarket), one of the most imaginative of the many Scottish knitwear designers and a long way from the conservative pastel "woollies" stocked by some of the large mill shops. Some of Baber's knitwear is lined; you'll find warm, subtly colored cardigans here that double as stylish jackets. **Eric Davidson** (4 Victoria St.) has extensive antique-furniture showrooms, with paintings, bronzes, and porcelain also stocked. Back up Victoria Street again try **Byzantium** (9A Victoria St., tel. 031/225–1768) for an eclectic mix of antiques, crafts, clothes—and an excellent coffee shop on the top level. For those investigating their Scottish ancestry, **Clan Connections** (30A Victoria St.) offers a selection of clan- (Highland) and family- (Lowland) related items, including crests and ties.

Bruntsfield   Bruntsfield, just beyond Tollcross at the top of Lothian Road, is an old, respectable part of Edinburgh, a little distance from the main tourist haunts and worth discovering for that reason alone. The area merges with Morningside, and you could plan a pleasant shopping walk from Tollcross to Morningside or in the reverse direction. The area is dotted with small family businesses, and prices for many goods are better than those you'll find on Princes Street. For example, **Alex Gibb** (120 Bruntsfield Pl., tel. 031/229–3523), established in 1820, offers a good selection of handbags and briefcases. Nearby, **Alistir Tait** (188 Bruntsfield Pl., tel. 031/229–9585) is a qualified gemologist offering an enticing range of antique jewelry. **Fabulous Fakes** (170 Bruntsfield Pl., tel. 031/228–1893) is also owned by Alistir Tait, but here, as the name suggests, costume jewelry glitters—by famous names, such as Butler and Wilson and Monty Don.

On Bruntsfield Road below Bruntsfield Links you'll find a cluster of antiques shops. **Bruntsfield Clocks** (7 Bruntsfield Pl., tel. 031/229–4720) has an unusually knowledgeable staff.

Stockbridge North of Princes Street, on the way to the Botanic Gardens, this is an oddball shopping area of some charm, particularly on St. Stephen Street. Look for **Hand in Hand** (3 North West Circus Pl.) for beautiful antique textiles; there are also several antique furniture shops. To get to Stockbridge, walk down Frederick Street and Howe Street north away from Princes Street, then turn left onto North West Circus Place. St. Stephen Street is farther down the hill, before the road reaches the bridge. Stockbridge "High Street" is beyond the bridge.

Stafford Street/ This is a small, upscale shopping area in a Georgian setting.
William Street Studio One (10–16 Stafford St., tel. 031/226–5812) has a well-established and comprehensive inventory of gift articles. June Johnston (60 Thistle St.) will take care of ladies' shoe and accessory needs, and Something Simple (10 William St.) or The Extra Inch (No. 16; for European size 38 and over) could complete the new outfit. To get to this neighborhood, walk to the west end of Princes Street and along its continuation, Shandwick Place, then turn into Stafford Street. William Street crosses Stafford halfway down.

Department Stores In contrast to other major cities, Edinburgh has few true department stores. Shops tend to specialize. However, in the city center you will find not only **Jenners** (*see* Princes Street, *above*) but also **Frasers,** at the other (west) end of Princes Street, and the ubiquitous **John Lewis,** in the St. James Centre. Unlike Jenners, the two latter stores are not local, independently owned firms, and the goods are similar to those stocked in other, United Kingdom–wide branches. However, John Lewis recently expanded to stock a huge selection of household goods and is worth investigating for perfume, gloves, handbags, and haberdashery items. The store is famous for its slogan "Never knowingly undersold," and its prices are certainly competitive. Frasers is more clothes oriented, stocking designer names you will see all over the United Kingdom, but its own brand goods are worth a look for quality at a reasonable price. The High Street multiples, **Marks and Spencer, Littlewoods, British Home Stores,** and so on, are also represented on Princes Street. However, even given the competition, if you plan a morning or a whole day wandering from department to department, trying on beautiful clothes, buying crystal or china, or stocking up on Scottish food specialties, with a break for lunch at an in-store restaurant, then Jenners is the store to choose.

Arcades and Shopping Centers

Like most large towns Edinburgh has succumbed to the fashion for "under one roof" shopping. If you dislike a breath of fresh air (or a wonderful view) between shops—or if it's raining—try **Waverley Market** (Princes St.), which offers three floors of shops and a fast-food area. The **St. James Centre,** at the same end of Princes Street, has just undergone extensive refurbishment. **Cameron Toll** shopping center, on the south side of the city, likewise caters to local residents, with food stores and High Street brand names.

Clothing Boutiques

Edinburgh is home to several top-quality designers (although, it must be said, probably not as many as are found in Glasgow, the country's fashion center) some of whom make a point of using Scottish materials in their creations. In addition to those already mentioned (Bill Baber, Aika), try **Betty Davies** (51A George St., tel. 031/226–3434) for unique dresses, jackets, and suits. Harris tweed is also available here by the yard—take home a length for a new skirt or for some handsome cushions.

If you are shopping for children, especially those who fit the tousled-tomboy mold, try **Baggins** (12 Deanhaugh St., Stockbridge, tel. 031/315–2011) for practical, reasonably priced clothes made from natural fibers. All the clothes here are made to the owner's design in the shop-cum-workshop. Some of the sportswear is made in adult sizes.

Scottish Specialties

A few examples on the theme of Scottish gifts include tartans and tweeds, knitwear, cakes and shortbread, whiskey, salmon, crystal, river pearls, and Celtic-inspired jewelry. In short, there is a good choice of high-quality giftware, all available in Edinburgh. (With such a choice, you may wonder why so many so-called gift shops sell so little of interest, among the kilted grotesquerie of plastic dollies and T-shirts with banal slogans.)

If you want to identify a particular tartan, several of the shops in Princes Street will be pleased to assist. The **Clan Tartan Centre** (70–74 Bangor Rd., Leith, tel. 031/553–5100) has extensive displays of various aspects of tartanry. For craftware, use as your quality guide the **Royal Mile Living Craft Centre** (12 High St.). Here, crafts are made on the premises, and you can talk to the craftspeople as they work. The range of items available includes hand-woven tartan, kilts, bagpipes, silver, pottery, Aran knitwear, and other crafts; there is also the Taste of Scotland coffee shop. **Edinburgh Crystal** makes fine glassware that is stocked by many large stores and gift shops in the city center, but you can also visit its premises (visitor center, restaurant, and shop) at Penicuik, just south of the city (Eastfield, Penicuik, tel. 0968/72244). The complex is open Monday through Saturday from 9 to 5 and Sunday from 11 to 5. Tours are given Monday through Friday 9–3:30.

Bookstores

As a university city and cultural center, Edinburgh is well endowed with excellent bookshops, some of the most central being **James Thin, The Edinburgh Bookshop** (57 George St., tel. 031/225–4495; and 53 South Bridge, tel. 031/556–6743), **Waterstones** (83 George St., tel. 031/225–3436, and 13/14 Princes St., tel. 031/556–3034). All stock a wide range of guides and books giving information about every aspect of Edinburgh life, and all have extended opening hours (until 10 PM on certain nights), including Sunday.

Sports and Fitness

Edinburgh has shared in the fitness boom of the past decade, as can be noted in **Holyrood Park**. At almost any time of day or night joggers run the circuit around Arthur's Seat. The **Royal Commonwealth Pool** (nearby on Dalkeith Rd., tel. 031/667–7211) is the largest swimming pool in the city; the complex includes a fitness center and a cafeteria. **Meadowbank Stadium,** northeast of the city center (tel. 031/661–5351) has facilities for over 30 different track and indoor sports.

Some of the larger Edinburgh hotels have their own **fitness centers.** Examples include the **Calton Highland** (North Bridge; swimming pool, snooker, squash, gymnasium, massage), **Capital** (Clermiston Rd.; pool, gymnasium), **Edinburgh Sheraton** (Lothian Rd.; pool, gymnasium), **Swallow Royal Scot** (Glasgow Rd.; pool, gymnasium), **Forth Bridges Moat House** (South Queensferry; pool, gymnasium, snooker, squash). (*See* Lodging, *below.*) Most facilities are free to guests, although there may be a charge for snooker and squash. The facilities are generally open to nonguests only through private membership.

Bicycling Edinburgh is a fairly compact, if hilly, city, and **bicycling** is a good way of getting around, though careful route planning may be needed to avoid traffic. The East Lothian countryside, with its miles of twisting roads and light traffic, is within cycling distance of the city. Cycles may be hired from **Sandy Gilchrist Cycles** (1 Cadzow Pl., tel. 031/652–1760), **Secondhand Bike Shop** (31–33 Iona St., Leith, tel. 031/553–1130), and **Central Cycle Hire** (13 Lochrin Pl., tel. 031/228–6333). Rates in summer are about £20–£30 per week for a three-speed, £30–£40 for a ten-speed, and £37–£50 for a mountain bike. The Secondhand Bike Shop runs a sell-and-buy-back scheme for longer periods (say, more than two weeks), which can save you money.

Golf Golf courses abound—there are about 20 courses within or close to the city (not including the easily accessible East Lothian courses), many of which welcome visitors. The Tourist Centre will provide local details, and the Scottish Tourist Board offers a free leaflet on golf in Scotland, available from the Edinburgh and Scotland Travel Centre (*see* Important Addresses and Numbers in Essential Information, *above*).

The following courses are open to visitors:

Braids (3 miles south of Edinburgh, tel. 031/447–6666). Course 1: 18 holes, 5,731 yards, SSS 68. Course 2: 18 holes, 4,832 yards, SSS 63.
Carrick Knowe (5 miles west of Edinburgh, tel. 031/337–1096). 18 holes, 6,229 yards, SSS 70.
Craigentinny (3 miles east of Edinburgh, tel. 031/554–7501). 18 holes, 5,418 yards, SSS 68.
Liberton (Kingston Grange, 297 Gilmerton Rd., tel. 031/664–8580). 18 holes, 5,229 yards, SSS 66.
Lothianburn (Biggar Rd., tel. 031/445–2206). 18 holes, 5,750 yards, SSS 69.
Portobello (Stanley St., tel. 031/669–4361). 9 holes, 2,410 yards, SSS 32.
Silverknowes (Silverknowes Parkway, tel. 031/336–3843). 18 holes, 6,210 yards, SSS 70.

Swanston (Swanston Rd., tel. 031/445–2239). 18 holes, 4,825 yards, SSS 64.

Torphin Hill (Torphin Rd., tel. 031/441–1100). 18 holes, 5,025 yards, SSS 66.

Skiing At Hillend on the southern edge of the city is the longest artificial ski slope in the United Kingdom—go either to ski (equipment can be hired on the spot) or to ride the chair lift for fine city views. *Biggar Rd., tel. 031/445–4433. Charge for chair lift: £1.45 adults, 65p children and senior citizens. Open Apr.–Sept., weekdays 9:30–9; Oct.–Mar., daily 9:30 AM–10 PM.*

Soccer and Rugby The **Heart of Midlothian Football Club** (soccer) is based at Tynecastle and its rival club **Hibernian** at Easter Road, and Murrayfield Stadium is the venue for international rugby matches. Crowds of good-humored rugby fans from Ireland and Wales add greatly to the atmosphere in the streets of Edinburgh during the early spring, when Scotland plays its international matches at Murrayfield.

Dining

Edinburgh is a sophisticated city, and its restaurants offer an interesting, diverse mix of traditional and exotic cuisines, from Scottish to ethnic. Indeed, the city is now home to the first Philippine restaurant in Scotland, if not in all Great Britain, as well as to restaurants featuring the cuisines of the Soviet Union, Mexico, Thailand, and Greece.

Be sure, particularly at festival time, to make reservations well in advance. Also, be warned that there is an element of "it'd be fun to open a restaurant" about Edinburgh's eating scene, and some restaurants come and go in a few months.

Another important fact to note about dining in Edinburgh is that it is possible to eat well without spending a fortune. Even those restaurants that are ranked in the Very Expensive category could be squeezed into the top of the Expensive range, depending on how one picks and chooses from the menu. A service charge of 10% may be added to your bill, though this practice is not adhered to uniformly. If no charge has been added and you are satisfied with the service, a 10% tip is appropriate.

Dining hours in Edinburgh are much the same as in the rest of Great Britain, with the main rush at lunchtime, from 1 to 2, and at dinner, from 8 to 9.

Highly recommended restaurants are indicated by a star ★.

Category	Cost*
Very Expensive	over £25
Expensive	£15–£20
Moderate	£10–£15
Inexpensive	under £10

per person, excluding VAT, tax, service, and drinks

Very Expensive

L'Auberge. A number of Edinburgh restaurants take the best Scottish food and prepare it French style, but L'Auberge is French through and through. The decor is elegant and mellow, with gray velvet chairs, peach tablecloths, and soft lights; the dining room is separated by a partition adorned with two enormous mirrors. A large number of tables are set for two—the French are so romantic here in the heart of reserved Edinburgh. The menu is all in French with only a cursory translation; owner-manager Monsieur Daniel wants to have the pleasure of explaining the recipes to you in detail, so you must ask. The menu changes frequently, but you may be able to choose, for example, the terrine of seafood, the guinea fowl with mushrooms and claret sauce, or venison with Armagnac. The impressive wine list is French (unsurprisingly) and includes—unusual in Edinburgh—excellent dessert wines. The duke and duchess of York number among the upscale clientele. *58 St. Mary St., tel. 031/556–5888. Reservations advised. Jacket and tie advised. AE, DC, MC, V. Closed Christmas Day, Dec. 26, New Year's Day.*

The Grill. Set in the Edwardian splendour of the newly renovated Balmoral Hotel, the Grill has established itself at the top end of Edinburgh's dining scene. The room has a luxurious ambience created by a green marble floor, Chinese lacquer wall panels, an abundance of silver and crystal, and an Oriental theme. The seating is particularly comfortable, and the tables are widely spaced, which makes it a great place for a private conversation or romantic dinner. The service is formal but relaxed, with no pressure to finish up. As its name suggests, the restaurant specializes in grills, which you can see being cooked on the open grill, but there is also an extensive à la carte menu. *Princes St., tel. 031/556–2414. Reservations required. Jacket and tie required. AE, DC, MC, V.*

Pompadour. Insulated by arched windows and red drapes from the bustle of west-end Princes Street, the Pompadour aims to impress—almost to the point of intimidation. The decor, with its subtle plasterwork and rich murals, is inspired by the court of Louis XV, as may be expected in a restaurant named after the king's mistress, Madame de Pompadour. The cuisine is also classic French, with top-quality Scottish produce completing the happiest of alliances. The extensive well-chosen wine list complements such dishes as rosette of salmon with scallops; roasted angler fish with leeks and woodland mushrooms; and chicken with herbs in a pastry shell, served with a sauce of red wine, shallots, and marrow. With chef Tony Binks in control and an utterly professional, dedicated staff, this is the place to go if you want a festive night out. It's more relaxed and informal at lunchtime. *Caledonian Hotel, Princes St., tel. 031/225–2433. Reservations advised. Jacket and tie required. AE, DC, MC, V. No weekend lunch.*

Expensive

Beehive Inn. One of the oldest restaurants in the city, the Beehive snuggles in the Grassmarket, under the majestic shadow of the castle. Some 400 years ago the restaurant was a coaching inn—if its walls could speak, what a story they'd tell. Outside its doors stood the main set of gallows, where over the centuries numerous executions were held. The restaurant lies hidden

Edinburgh Dining and Lodging

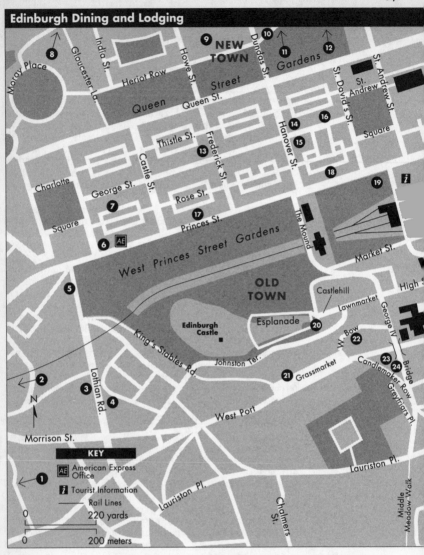

Dining

Beehive Inn, **21**
Buntoms Thai Restaurant, **12**
The Grill, **19**
Henderson's Salad Bowl, **15**
Kalpna, **29**
Kelly's, **28**
Kweilin, **10**
La Lanterna, **14**

L'Alliance, **23**
Lancers, **8**
L'Auberge, **27**
Lilligs, **23**
Martins, **7**
Merchants, **24**
Old Orleans, **4**
Pompadour, **18**
Vitos, **13**
Waterloo Place, **25**
The Witchery by the Castle, **20**

Xian City Seafood Restaurant, **26**

Lodging

Balmoral Hotel, **19**
Caledonian, **5**
Edinburgh Sheraton, **3**
George Intercontinental, **16**
Grosvenor Hotel-- Stakis, **2**

Howard Hotel, **11**
Mount Royal Hotel, **17**
Norton House, **1**
Roxburghe, **6**
Royal Terrace, **31**
Sibbet House, **9**
Teviotdale House, **30**
Thrums Private Hotel, **22**

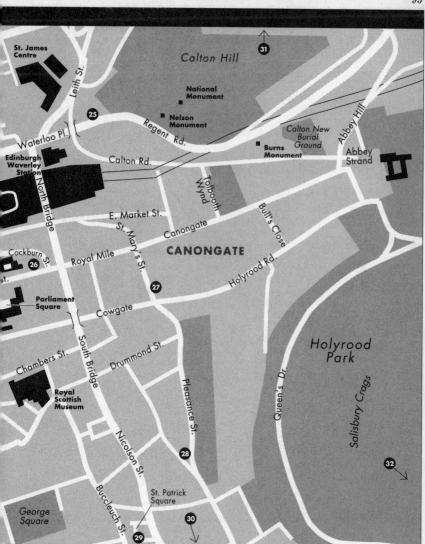

upstairs behind a heavy paneled door. As you pass through this door, pause to think of those who have passed this way before you: This is the original door of Calton Gaol's cell for condemned prisoners. The room you enter bears no resemblance to the gloomy box that greeted those poor wretches; here you will find subtle lighting and subdued decor. The menu features steaks and fish, and, if your taste embraces both, there is the Salmon-Bagger Steak: charcoal-grilled Aberdeen Angus loin stuffed with Scottish salmon. Crowned heads of Europe have dined here, as have many other renowned personalities. *18/20 Grassmarket, tel. 031/225-7171. Reservations advised on weekends. Dress: casual. AE, MC, DC, V.*

Kelly's. This Scottish restaurant with a French influence is slightly off the beaten track on the south side of the city, but is still only a short taxi ride or 20-minute walk from the center. The entrance to this former bakery, difficult to spot in a line of residential properties, leads into a pine-furnished, peach-tinted dining room with only nine or 10 tables. The ambience is intimate, ideal for a quiet discussion over an unhurried meal. Among the fine choices here are smoked Scottish salmon with mushrooms in Pernod sauce and Border lamb cutlets with a Grand-Marnier-and-rosemary glaze. *46 W. Richmond St., tel. 031/668-3847. Reservations advised. Jacket and tie advised. AE, MC, V. Lunch during festival only. Closed Sun., Mon.*

★ **Martins.** Don't be put off by the look of this restaurant on the outside. It's tucked away in a little back street and has a typically forbidding northern facade. All's well inside, though, and the food is tops. The decor is low-key but elegant, with plain white tables, pastel colors, gentle candlelight, and fresh flowers. Organically grown local products, both animal and vegetable, are prominent on the menu, which has a strong hint of Scotland yet could not be further from a haggis-and-whiskey theme. The best Scotch beef, salmon, venison, fish, and west-coast shellfish appear in various forms—poached, baked, roasted, and in casseroles—usually with inventive sauces. Starters may include rabbit liver and mushrooms with wild-mushroom sauce or terrine of rabbit and chicory with orange. There's also a far-famed cheese board. This is the place for serious eating in an unstuffy atmosphere, and lunches are an excellent value. The wine list is serious but affordable and includes an excellent choice of half-bottles. Smoking is not permitted. *70 Rose St., North La., tel. 031/225-3106. Reservations advised. Dress: casual but neat. AE, DC, MC, V. No Sat. lunch. Closed Sun., Mon., 2 weeks at Christmas and New Year's.*

Merchants. On a street running below George IV Bridge and only moments from the Grassmarket and looming Edinburgh Castle, Merchants is competent and reliable—almost sober, in fact, which is not to say dull. The decor is gently understated, with pinewood flooring, crisp white tablecloths, cane chairs, and exposed beams. The light jazz music playing in the background is definitely not intrusive, although Pierre the parrot has been known to squawk along with it from time to time. A sophisticated menu, in French and English, has such adventurous moments as veal in dill and coriander; lamb chops with raspberry-and-mint sauce; and herb roulade filled with prawns and avocado mousse, with orange-and-tarragon vinaigrette. *17 Merchant St., tel. 031/225-4009. Reservations advised. Dress: casual but neat. AE, DC, MC, V. Closed Sun., Christmas Day, Dec. 26, New Year's Day, Jan. 2.*

Vitos. Like La Laterna (*see below*), this is a basement restaurant, but here you'll find a whitewashed wine cellar, with vaulted ceiling, arches, and nooks and crannies for intimate meals. Close to George Street, it's ideal for discreet, private dining—the tables are widely spaced. The vaguely rustic Italian decor complements the genuinely Italian cuisine (there's a southern Italian owner and northern Italian chef, so all regions are featured on the menu). Dishes include king prawns in a sauce of tomato, cream, and brandy and veal stuffed with cheese and ham. The separate bar area is a good place for a quiet drink before dinner. *53A Frederick St., tel. 031/225–5052. Reservations advised. Jacket and tie advised. AE, DC, MC, V.*

★ **Waterloo Place.** This excellent restaurant has as its chef Andrew Radford (formerly of the *Royal Scot* luxury train, which was noted for its gourmet meals, and Handsels Restaurant) whose stated aim is to serve high-quality food at affordable prices, which he achieves with ease. The surroundings reflect the same theme: a Georgian building with simple decor that lets the architecture speak for itself. The menu uses the freshest ingredients combined in original (and successful) ways: Pigeon in any form is recommended, as is the shellfish. The vegetables are especially good—crisp spring cabbage stir-fried with Chinese mushrooms, for example—as are the puddings, particularly the sorbets and ice creams (the mango coconut is mouth-watering). The menu changes daily, always the sign of a top-quality restaurant. *29 Waterloo Place, tel. 031/557–0007. Reservations strongly advised. Dress: smart casual. AE, MC, V. Closed Sat. lunch, Sun. all day.*

The Witchery by the Castle. As the name indicates, a somewhat eerie ambience—complete with flickering candlelight—reigns here. There are, in fact, supposed to be three ghosts in the place, one of whom haunts the refrigerator! The lugubrious, cavernous interior is festooned with cauldrons and broomsticks and decorated with cabalistic insignia. The inspiration for this spooky haunt derives from the fact that some 300 years ago hundreds of witches were executed on the Castlehill, barely a few dozen yards from where you will be seated. There's nothing spooky about the food, however, with fine venison Marie Stuart, grilled Loch Fyne oysters, Magic Mushrooms stuffed with bread crumbs and garlic mayonnaise, and Auld Reekie fillet steak among the specialties. *352 Castlehill, Royal Mile, tel. 031/225–5613. Reservations advised. Dress: casual. AE, DC, MC, V.*

Moderate

Buntoms Thai Restaurant. A room in the Linden Hotel was recently converted into this authentic-looking Thai restaurant by the addition of genuine Thai wall coverings and antiques. You can leave Georgian New Town at the door and be transported halfway around the world with such savory delights as hot-and-sour squid and mushroom salad, seafood cooked with broccoli in oyster sauce, or spiced chicken fried with cashew nuts and onions (one of this restaurant's best offerings). Don't come here if you're on a tight schedule—each dish is prepared fresh, but it's definitely worth the wait, and you'll want to savor each bite. *Linden Hotel, 9–13 Nelson St., tel. 031/557–4344. Reservations advised. Dress: casual. MC, V.*

Kweilin. This pleasant family-run restaurant in Edinburgh's sedate New Town is popular with the city's Chinese community, as well as with tourists. The decor is traditional Chinese, with several large paintings depicting scenes from the Kwangsi province, of which Kweilin is the capital. There are always several suggested menus for two, three, or four diners, which are recommended; but you can, of course, select your own combinations of dishes. The fixed-menu offerings are a good value, starting at £10 per person and going up to £16 a head for the "Menu Executif." *19–21 Dundas St., tel. 031/557–1875. Reservations advised. Dress: casual. MC, V.*

La Laterna. This inconspicuous basement-level trattoria serves wholesome and straightforward pastas—among them tagliatelle carbonara and risotta Milanese—and other Italian dishes, all in the best of humor. The dish of the day is usually a good value. The family who runs the business can afford to be cheerful—their straightforward approach is popular and packs in the customers. The decor is pine-walled and postcard-pinned. Seats are comfortable, though tables are set close. The restaurant is well located in center city, two minutes from Princes Street. *83 Hanover St., tel. 031/226–3090. Reservations advised. Dress: casual. MC, V. Closed Sun.*

L'Alliance. Despite its obviously French name, l'Alliance has shaken off its Gallic chains and become Edinburgh's leading pan-European restaurant. There is at least one dish on the menu from every country in the European Community: You'll find *camarones fritos en massa* (deep-fried squid) from Portugal, for example; or *Frell am Riesleck*, which is trout cooked according to a recipe from Luxembourg (pan-fried and served in a sauce made with Riesling, paprika, tarragon, and cream); or a Belgian casserole of squab, bacon, and vegetables in white wine. If you can't decide which cuisine you're in the mood for, this restaurant is the perfect choice. It's advisable to take a taxi, since this spot is a little hard to find, although it's not far from the city center. L'Alliance is at the end of a short cul-de-sac, under one of the arches of the George IV Bridge; the building was actually built into the arch, which accounts for the curve of the restaurant's high ceiling. The interior walls are made of stark whitewashed stone; the wall at the back of the restaurant is decorated with a three-dimensional representation of a "typical" European house and courtyard. *7 Merchant St., tel. 031/225–2002. Reservations advised. Dress: casual. AE, MC, V.*

Lancers. This intimate Indian restaurant, decorated with rosewood tables and chairs, is located in the Stockbridge area of Edinburgh, just a short taxi ride from city center. It's on a fairly busy road, but external distractions are blocked out by window blinds, which add to the sense of intimacy. The feel of this place is a little like that of an officers' mess in Bengal, which is entirely appropriate, since it was named after the famed Bengal Lancers, who fought with such distinction alongside the British army in every quarter of the globe. As a simple introduction to Bengali cuisine, you could try the vegetarian (or nonvegetarian) *thali* (a sampler tray including rice, lentils, curries, etc.); those already initiated to the delights of this cuisine can pick and choose among varieties of *pasandas, kurmas, tikkas,* and *bhundas. 5 Hamilton Pl., tel. 031/332–3444 or 031/332–9551. Reservations advised. Dress: casual but neat. MC, V.*

Old Orleans. A first in Edinburgh: Cajun and mesquite cooking, served with real Southern panache, plus Mexican and U.S. dishes including red snapper and alligator. Choose the spare ribs and you are thoughtfully provided with a large bib and finger bowl of hot water. Decor is typical New Orleans: trellise and metalwork, brass instruments, and music and travel-related items; the music is blues and jazz. There is also a large, mirrored, American-style bar. *30 Grindlay St., tel. 031/229–1511. Reservations advised. Dress: casual. AE, MC, V.*

Inexpensive–Moderate

★ **Kalpna.** This vegetarian Indian restaurant is on the city's south side, close to the university. Don't be put off by the unremarkable facade among an ordinary row of shops or by the low-key decor enlivened by Indian prints and fabric pictures: The food is unlike anything you are likely to encounter elsewhere in the city. If you can't decide what you want to eat, order an Anapurna Thali curry, with coconut, peas, fresh coriander, and a touch of garlic; vegetables in a reduced cream sauce spiced with nutmeg; or melt-in-the-mouth halva, as you work your way around the tray of side dishes. Kalpna tends to fill up as the evening progresses, so book ahead if you want to eat after 8. At lunchtime and in the early evening (except perhaps at festival time) you can sometimes just drop in. *2/3 St. Patricks Sq., tel. 031/667–9890. Reservations advised for dinner. Dress: casual. MC, V. Closed Sun., Christmas Day, Dec. 26, New Year's Day.*
Xian City Seafood Restaurant. Named after the fabled home of Chinese warriors, the Xian City specializes in Cantonese fare and provides a wealth of choices: The menu runs to five pages, offering a selection of duck, chicken, beef, pork, and vegetarian creations, in addition to the seafood dishes that head the list. The walls are adorned with back-lit Chinese scenes, and a large fish tank stands proudly in the middle of the restaurant, dividing it into two pleasant, comfortably sized dining rooms. Fixed-menu dinners are priced at around £12.50 per person for five courses. *217 High St., Royal Mile, tel. 031/225–2999. Reservations advised. Dress: casual. MC, V.*

Inexpensive

Henderson's Salad Bowl. This was Edinburgh's original vegetarian restaurant, long before that cuisine became fashionable. If you haven't summoned the courage to try an authentic haggis while in Scotland, come here to sample a vegetarian version. *94 Hanover St., tel. 031/225–2131. Reservations not required. Dress: casual. AE, DC, MC, V. Closed Sun. except during festival.*
Lilligs. Halfway along the curve of Victoria Street, a sign and a metal staircase in a hallway awash with posters and leaflets indicates that Lilligs lies above. Stone-walled—like a cellar, only one floor up—Lilligs has a menu that is hard to categorize: Mexican bean pie is next to mussels baked in garlic; mushrooms meunière can be a main course after poached squid. But you can expect it all to be good—the standard of cooking here is well above average for this type of café-restaurant. Eclectic is too grand a word for the informal, definitely-no-neckties place—though the description does apply to the selection of background music. Lilligs stays open until 1 every morning, later than many other Edinburgh restaurants. *30 Victoria St., tel. 031/225–7635. Reservations accepted but not usually necessary. Dress: casual. AE, DC, MC, V.*

Lodging

Edinburgh offers a variety of accommodations, many in traditional Georgian properties, some even in the New Town, only a few minutes from downtown. There are also a number of upscale hotels in the downtown area, each with an international flavor. If you are planning to stay in the area during the festival, be sure to reserve several months in advance.

Highly recommended lodgings are indicated by a star ★.

Category	Cost*
Very Expensive	over £120
Expensive	£100–£120
Moderate	£80–£100
Inexpensive	under £80

All prices are for two people sharing a double room, including service, breakfast, and VAT.

Very Expensive

★ **Balmoral Hotel.** If £23 million guarantees the premier position among Edinburgh's hotels, then the Balmoral's recent expenditure on total refurbishment will be justified. The attention to detail in the elegant rooms and the sheer élan that has re-created the Edwardian heyday of this former grand railroad hotel all contribute to making the Balmoral a very special place to stay. Staying here, below the impressive clocktower marking the east end of Princes Street, gives a strong sense of being at the center of Edinburgh life. The hotel's main restaurant is the plush and stylish Grill Room. *Princes St., EH2 2EQ, tel. 031/556-2414. 167 bedrooms, 22 suites. Facilities: restaurant (reservations advised; jacket and tie preferred), bar, wine bar, patisserie, health club. AE, DC, MC, V.*

★ **Caledonian.** A conspicuous block of red sandstone beyond the west end of Princes Street Gardens, "the Caley" was built as the flagship hotel of the Caledonian Railway. A train-station clock and other echoes of the age when steam was king are still on view within the portals of this impressive establishment, but the rail station that once stood nearby was gone long ago. Recently modernized and refurbished at vast expense, the hotel's imposing Victorian decor has been faithfully preserved and has lost none of its original dignity and elegance. The public areas feature marbled green columns and an ornate stairwell with a burnished-metalwork balustrade. Rooms are exceptionally large and well appointed, and the generous width of the corridors reminds guests that this establishment was designed in a more sumptuous age. *Princes St., EH1 2AB, tel. 031/225-2433, fax 031/225-6632. 238 rooms with bath. Facilities: restaurant, bar, garden, in-house movies. AE, DC, MC, V.*

Edinburgh Sheraton. This hotel, built in 1985, looks out (from the back, at least) over Edinburgh Castle; the lounge bar and restaurant share the same historic view as the best guest rooms. The finely proportioned exterior was designed to complement the Georgian style prevalent throughout the city. All rooms are well above average size and are furnished with modern light-wood fittings and pastel fabrics. Prices vary with the view (castle, city, or parking lot). The restaurant is notable for its success in capturing the rich colors of Scotland with its tweedy and pearly shades, without resorting to tartan-draped cliché; it has also developed a strong reputation among local residents for its food. The hotel staff is helpful and friendly, and the service is excellent. This may be the Edinburgh representative of an international chain, but the comfortable chairs and sofas in the endless marble and pastel-shaded public areas and lounge fill with locals after work and in the evenings after a concert in the Usher Hall across the street. In short, the Sheraton is very much a part of Edinburgh's social life. *1 Festival Sq., EH3 9SR, tel. 031/229–9131, fax 031/228–4510. 263 rooms with bath. Facilities: restaurant, bar, in-house movies, health club, pool, sauna. AE, DC, MC, V.*

Expensive

George Intercontinental. Part of this hotel served as an insurance-company office during the 19th century; the splendidly ornate business hall remains intact as the Carvery Restaurant, the less expensive of the two dining rooms. The hotel's modern extension, added a few years ago, is carefully blended with the original structure (1881), and the George retains a more intimate feeling than you'd expect from a rather large hotel. The central location, only yards from the financial center of St. Andrew Square, has only one disadvantage: difficult parking. The George's impressive reception area has elegant marble floors and fluted columns. Guest rooms are light, airy, and immaculate, with reproduction-antique furnishings; sizes range from adequate to spacious, and the desks are unusually large. The best rooms are at the back of the hotel, high up and looking north over the New Town roofs to the Firth of Forth and to Fife beyond. However, even rooms overlooking George Street southward are quiet and have bird's-eye views of the 18th-century surroundings. The public areas are particularly welcoming and, in addition to the discreetly lighted, lush-blue bar, there are sofa-filled nooks where coffee or something stronger can be enjoyed in privacy. The pricey French-style Le Chambertin restaurant has excellent food, and its sommelier is one of only two members of the Guild of Master Sommeliers in Scotland. *19–21 George St., EH2 2PB, tel. 031/225–1251, fax 031/226–5644. 195 rooms with bath. Facilities: 2 restaurants, bar, minibars and tea- and coffee-making facilities in rooms. AE, DC, MC, V.*

★ **Grosvenor Hotel–Stakis.** This attractive, comfortable hotel in the West End is distinguished by an elegant Victorian facade. Once a part of the original row of terrace houses, the Grosvenor comprises several converted houses. Just a short walk from the West End's shopping district, the hotel is convenient to the Haymarket railway station. Guests are pampered as soon as they enter the large reception area, which is furnished with ample Chesterfield armchairs. Baskets of fresh fruit are provided in all guest rooms, all of which have recently been refurbished and are appointed with pleasant fixtures. The single rooms are fairly small. *Grosvenor St., EH12 5EA, tel. 031/226–6001. 136 rooms with bath. Facilities: 2 restaurants, bar. AE, DC, MC, V.*

Howard Hotel. The Howard, close to Drummond Place, is a

good example of a New Town building, elegant and superbly proportioned. It is small enough to offer personal attention. Some of the bedrooms are spacious and well equipped, and some overlook the garden. *32 Great King St., EH3 6QH, tel. 031/557-3500. 25 rooms with bath. Facilities: restaurant, garden. AE, DC, MC, V.*

★ **Royal Terrace.** Over 150 years ago, the renowned Edinburgh architect Playfair designed the street called Royal Terrace as a tribute to King George IV. Most of the impressive Georgian homes on this block were owned by merchants, and the upper floors command a view across the Firth of Forth to Fife. From this vantage point the residents could watch for their ships as they sailed into the port of Leith, and, because many of these merchants were involved in the whiskey trade, the road was eventually nicknamed "Whisky Row." The Royal Terrace Hotel consists of a half dozen of these original merchant houses, combined to create one of the most luxurious lodgings in the city. The exterior is unassuming, giving no hint of the sybaritic interior. That this is a hotel devoted to comfort, however, becomes immediately apparent as one enters the reception area, which is deeply carpeted and adorned with a massive pair of chandeliers and an eclectic collection of objets d'art, such as Indian carvings supporting delicate Chinese vases. All rooms are furnished to an equally high standard and even include telephones in the marble bathrooms. The best rooms—commanding the view across the city to the Forth—are on the top floors at the front. *18 Royal Terr., EH7 5AQ. 97 rooms with bath. Facilities: restaurant; bar; health club with whirlpool, pool, steam room, and sauna; in-house movies; patio; gardens. AE, DC, MC, V.*

Moderate

Mount Royal Hotel. Perched above the ground-floor shops on Princes Street and overlooking Edinburgh Castle and the Princes Street Gardens, the reception and other public areas of this modern building have recently been redecorated to great effect. Improvements to the bedrooms are also now complete (the best views are from the rooms at the front of the hotel). The entrance to the Mount Royal is almost hidden between two of the city's major stores (Jenners and Marks and Spencer) and could easily be overlooked at first. The friendly staff more than makes up for any minor shortcomings in the decor. *52 Princes St., EH2 2DQ, tel. 031/225-7161. 159 rooms with bath. Facilities: restaurant. AE, DC, MC, V.*

Norton House. This magnificent 1861 manor house was once the home of the Usher brewing family and still has the feeling of a private country home. Situated on idyllic grounds on the outskirts of Edinburgh, the Norton House provides a lovely alternative to downtown lodgings, yet is easily accessible from center city. The elegant reception area is graced by marble pillars, and there is a striking wooden staircase leading to the upper floors. The airy guest rooms are decorated with modern furniture and delicate pastel shades. Guests can choose between two restaurants—the elegant main dining room inside, which offers decent Continental food, or the Conservatory, with its fine views of the gardens. *Ingliston, EH28 8LX, tel. 031/333-1275. 46 rooms with bath. Facilities: 2 restaurants, bar, tea- and coffee-making facilities in rooms; parking, courtesy bus to airport and train stations. AE, DC, MC, V.*

Roxburghe. As you sit in a deep leather armchair, the ticking of an antique clock in the background, and look out over the trees of Charlotte Square, it is easy to forget you are half a minute from Princes Street and in the heart of Edinburgh's financial center. The furniture, which includes many antique pieces, has the sheen of generations of polish. In the rooms, Adam fireplaces and ornate plasterwork (depending on the bedroom) complement the hotel's harmonious Georgian architecture. This country-house-come-to-town moves nearer modern times with its busy bar and informal ground-floor restaurant, the Buttery, but becomes positively overdone in its excessively draped, green-and-red main dining room downstairs. (The food, unlike the decor, is forgettable.) Not as expensive as the Sheraton or the Caledonian, the Roxburghe is hard to beat for a convenient location, though it can be a little noisy. *38 Charlotte Sq., EH2 4HG, tel. 031/225–3921, fax 031/220–2518. 75 rooms with bath. Facilities: restaurant, bar, coffee shop, tea- and coffee-making facilities in rooms. AE, DC, MC, V.*

Inexpensive

★ **Sibbet House.** The late-18th-century Georgian elegance of this small terraced townhouse in Edinburgh's New Town has been enhanced by careful attention to drapery, decor, and period antique furniture. Prices are reasonable, and breakfasts are traditionally Scottish and sustaining, to say the least. You must eat out in the evenings, but all kinds of restaurants are only a few minutes' stroll away. This establishment also offers a facility that few others can match—the host plays the bagpipes (but only on request). The ambience of a family home may be an overused phrase, but it fits Sibbet House. *26 Northumberland St., EH3 6LS, tel. 031/556–1078, fax 031/557–4356. MC.*

Teviotdale House. This is a small, family-run and owned hotel in Edinburgh's genteel south side. The hosts, the Covilles, are friendly, and the house is a warm retreat on a tree-lined street away from center-city bustle but within easy reach of it (a 20-minute walk from Charlotte Sq.). Individually decorated rooms, innovative and appetizing home cooking, and access to the host's collection of German wines make this a pleasant, reasonable budget alternative to center-city hotels. The establishment is entirely nonsmoking. *53 Grange Loan, EH9 2ER, tel. 031/667–4376. 7 rooms; 5 with bath, 2 with shared bath. AE, MC, V.*

Thrums Private Hotel. There is a pleasing mix of the modern and traditional in this detached Victorian house. It is small, cozy, and quiet, yet surprisingly close to downtown Edinburgh. *14 Minto St., EH9 1RQ, tel. 031/667–5545. 14 rooms, 12 with bath. Facilities: garden. Closed Christmas Day, New Year's Day. No credit cards.*

The Arts and Nightlife

The Arts

Edinburgh is world renowned for its flagship arts event, the **Edinburgh International Festival,** and there is no escaping a sense of theater if you visit the city from August to early September. The annual festival has attracted all sorts of international performers since its inception in 1947. Even more obvious to the casual stroller during this time is the refreshingly irreverent Edinburgh Festival Fringe, unruly child of the official festival, which spills out of halls and theaters and onto the streets all over town. At other times throughout the year professional and amateur groups alike offer a range of cultural options appropriate to a capital city, even if the publicity that emanates from Edinburgh's rival, Glasgow, would want you to believe otherwise. *The List,* available from newsagents throughout the city, and *What's On in Edinburgh,* available from the Tourist Centre (*see* Important Addresses and Numbers in Essential Information, *above*) carry the most up-to-date details about cultural events. *The Scotsman,* an Edinburgh daily, also carries reviews on its arts pages on Monday and Wednesday. Tickets are generally available from the relevant box office in advance; in some cases, from certain designated travel agents; or at the door, although concerts by national orchestras often sell out long before the day of the performance.

The **Edinburgh International Festival** (1993 dates: Aug. 15–Sept. 4), the premier arts event of the year, has for more than 40 years attracted performing artists of international caliber to a celebration of music, dance, and drama. *Advance information, programs, tickets, and reservations available from the Edinburgh Festival Office, 21 Market St., Edinburgh EH1 1BW, tel. 031/226–4001.*

The **Edinburgh Festival Fringe** offers many theatrical and musical events, some by amateur groups (you have been warned) and is more of a grab bag than the official festival. The Fringe offers a vast choice of diversions (a condition of Edinburgh's artistic life found only during the three- or four-week festival season). During festival time it's possible to arrange your own entertainment program from morning to midnight and beyond, if you do not feel overwhelmed by the variety available. *Information, programs, and tickets available from Edinburgh Festival Fringe, 180 High St., Edinburgh EH1 1QS, tel. 031/226–5257 or 031/226–5259.*

Every two years during the **Edinburgh Book Festival** (1993: Aug. 14–25), the gardens in the center of Charlotte Square host an under-canvas celebration of literature, with guest speakers, discussions, demonstrations, and an opportunity to rub shoulders with best-selling authors. *Tel. 031/225–1915.*

The **Edinburgh Film Festival** (1993: August 14–29) is yet another aspect of this busy summer festival logjam. *Advance information and programs available from the Edinburgh Film Festival, at the Filmhouse, 88 Lothian Rd., Edinburgh EH3 9BZ, tel. 031/228–4051. Box office, tel. 031/228–2688.*

The **Edinburgh Military Tattoo** (1993: Aug. 6–28) may not be art, but it is certainly entertainment. It is sometimes confused with the festival itself, partly because the dates overlap. This celebration of martial music and skills is set on the castle esplanade, and the dramatic backdrop augments the spectacle. Dress warmly for late-evening performances. Even if it rains the show most definitely goes on. *Tickets and information available from Edinburgh Military Tattoo, 22 Market St., tel. 031/225–1188.*

Away from the August-to-September festival overkill, the **Edinburgh Folk Festival** usually takes place around Easter each year. This 10-day event blends performances by Scottish and international folk artists of the highest caliber.

Traditional Theater Edinburgh's two main theaters are the **Royal Lyceum** (Grindlay St., tel. 031/229–9697) and the **King's** (Leven St., tel. 031/229–1201), both of which offer contemporary and traditional dramatic works. The King's also offers ballet from time to time and in general has the more varied bill of fare, including light-entertainment shows and Christmas pantomimes.

The **Playhouse** (Greenside Pl., tel. 031/557–2692) is visited in season by the Scottish Opera and also has a Christmas pantomime. At Musselburgh, on the eastern outskirts of Edinburgh, the **Brunton Theatre** (Brunton Hall, High St., Musselburgh, tel. 031/665–2240) offers a regular program of performances. At the **Church Hill Theatre** (Morningside Rd., tel. 031/447–7597), local dramatic societies mount productions of a high standard.

Modern Theater The **Traverse Theatre** (Cambridge St., tel. 031/228–1404) has developed a solid reputation as a venue for stimulating new work—though it has toned down its previously avant-garde approach a little in an effort to secure sponsorship. However, it is well worth investigating. It has just moved to new, custom-built premises ideal for new plays.

The **Netherbow Arts Centre** (43 High St., tel. 031/556–9579) includes modern plays in its program of music, drama, and cabaret, as does the **Theatre Workshop** (34 Hamilton Pl., tel. 031/225–7942).

Music The **Usher Hall** (Lothian Rd., tel. 031/228–1155) is Edinburgh's grandest concert hall, venue for the Scottish National Orchestra during its winter season. More intimate in scale and used generally for smaller recitals and chamber music is the **Queen's Hall** (Nicolson St., tel. 031/668–2019). You can find popular artists at the **Playhouse,** but it also serves as an opera venue (*see* above). Apart from performances given at the Playhouse by the occasional visiting opera company, Edinburgh has been a desert for opera lovers; however, plans are now on course to convert the Empire Theatre on the south side of the city into an opera house. Ask the Tourist Information Centre for up-to-date details.

For jazz enthusiasts the main focus of entertainment is the **International Jazz Festival,** held in August each year, but throughout the year live jazz can also be found in the city. Consult *The List* for information.

Dance Edinburgh has no ballet or modern-dance companies of its own, but visiting companies perform from time to time at the King's Theatre or Royal Lyceum (*see above*).

Film Apart from cinema chains, Edinburgh has the excellent **Filmhouse** (88 Lothian Rd., tel. 031/228–6382; box office, 031/228–2688), which is the best venue for modern, foreign-language, offbeat, or simply less-commercial films. A copy of its diverse monthly program is available from the box office and at a variety of other locations throughout the city (at the Tourist Centre, for example, or in theater foyers).

Of the other cinemas, the family-owned and run **Dominion** (Newbattle Terrace, tel. 031/447–2660) is by far the most pleasant to visit—it is small and friendly and has a bar and restaurant offering light meals. The choice of films is as good as that of the larger movie houses.

Nightlife

Edinburgh's nightlife is quite varied and includes both discos and Scottish musical evenings or *ceilidhs* (pronounced *kay*-lees) for the older set. The City Information Centre above Waverley Market (*see* Important Addresses and Numbers in Essential Information, *above*) can supply information on various categories of nightlife, especially on spots offering dinner-dances. Jazz and folk music in general are wide ranging, though pub and hotel venues change. *The List* gives much information on the music scene. In quiet-living Edinburgh, there are no nightclubs of the cabaret-and-striptease variety.

Casinos **Berkeley Casino Club** (2 Rutland Pl., tel. 031/228–4446) is a private club that offers free membership on 48 hours' notice.

Public casinos include **Casino Martell** (7 Newington Rd., tel. 031/667–7763) and **Royal Chimes Casino** (3 Royal Terr., tel. 031/556–1055).

Stakis Regency Casino (14 Picardy Pl., tel. 031/557–3585) makes membership available after a 48-hour waiting period. It also features a restaurant.

Discos Many Edinburgh discos offer reduced admission and/or less expensive drinks for early revelers.

Blue Oyster Club (96A Rose St. La. North, tel. 031/226–6458) is a very popular gay club with a wide range of music. Open Thursday 10:30 PM–4 AM, Friday 11 PM–4 AM, Saturday 10:30 PM–6 AM.
Buster Browns (25–27 Market St., tel. 031/226–4224) offers mainstream chart sounds Friday and Sunday 10:30 PM–3 AM, Saturday 10:30 PM–4 AM.
Century 2000 (31 Lothian Rd., tel. 031/229–7670) is one of Edinburgh's busiest and biggest discos, open for dance night Friday and party night Saturday 10 PM–4 AM.
Madison's (Greenside Pl., tel. 031/557–3807) specializes in rock music. Open Friday and Saturday 10 PM–4 AM.
Millionaires (Niddry St.) attracts hardened clubbers (and drinkers) with its late license. It's open Friday and Saturday, 10 PM–6 AM, Monday–Thursday 11 PM–4 AM.
The Network (West Tollcross, tel. 031/228–3252) is a venue offering different clubs and types of music on each night throughout the week. Open Monday–Wednesday and Friday–Sunday 10:30 PM–4 AM, Thursday 10:30 PM–2 AM.
The Rave Cave (69 Cowgate) specializes in Techno and rave. Open Friday and Saturday 11 PM–4 AM.
Red Hot Pepper Club (3 Semple St., tel. 031/229–7733), open Thursday–Saturday, play mainstream music Friday and Saturday 10 PM–4 AM, Thursday 10 PM–3 AM.
The Solution (12 Shandwick Pl., tel. 031/220–4167), with a restaurant, cocktail bars, cabaret, and live music, provides a good night out for the over-25s. Open daily 8:30 PM–4 AM.

Folk Clubs There are always folk performers in various pubs throughout the city. Edinburgh Folk Club (Osborne Hotel, York Pl., tel. 031/339–4083) features folk music every Wednesday at 8:15 PM.

Scottish Evenings and Ceilidhs Several hotels feature traditional Scottish-music evenings, including the Carlton Highland Hotel (North Bridge, tel. 031/556–7277) and George Hotel (George St., tel. 031/225–1251). Contact the individual hotels for information.

Other well-established Scottish entertainments include **Jamie's Scottish Evening** (King James Hotel, Leith St., tel. 031/556–0111). At events sponsored by **Jacobean Banquets** (Dalhousie Ct., Cockpen, Bonnyrigg, tel. 031/663–5155) the emphasis is on musical entertainment, rather than food. Guests are expected to eat their meal in true Jacobean style—with their fingers or with a dagger!

Excursions from Edinburgh

Tour 3: West Lothian and the Forth Valley

Numbers in the margin correspond to points of interest on the West Lothian and the Forth Valley map.

The Lothians is the collective name given to the swath of countryside surrounding Edinburgh. This driving tour of West Lothian explores the Forth Valley west of Edinburgh, as well as some of the territory north of the River Forth. In a round-trip of about 70 miles, it is possible to see plenty of the central belt of Scotland and to skirt the edge of the Central Highlands. The river Forth snakes across a widening flood-plain on its descent from the Highlands, and by the time it reaches the western extremities of Edinburgh, it has already passed below the mighty Forth bridges and become a broad estuary.

This is the route to take if your interests incline toward castles and stately homes because they sprout thickly on both sides of the Forth. Note that it is possible to visit some of the places included in this excursion by train: Dalmeny, Linlithgow, and Dunfermline all have rail stations. Bus services link most areas as well, but working out a detailed itinerary by bus would be best left to your travel agent or guide.

41 Leave Edinburgh by Queensferry Road—the A90—and follow signs for the Forth Bridge. Beyond the city boundary at **Cramond** (*see* Off the Beaten Track, *above*) take the slip road, B924, for South Queensferry, watching for signs to **Dalmeny House,** the first of the stately homes clustered on the western edge of Edinburgh. Home of the earl and countess of Rosebery, this 1815 Tudor Gothic pile displays among its sumptuous contents the best of the family's famous collection of 18th-century French furniture. (Much of this collection was formerly displayed at Mentmore, the country seat 40 miles north of London, which belonged to the present earl's grandfather, Baron Mayer de Rothschild.) Highlights include the library; the drawing room, with its tapestries and highly wrought French furniture; the Napoleon Room; and the Vincennes and Sevres porcelain collections. *B924, by South Queensferry (7 mi west of Edinburgh), tel. 031/331–1888. Admission: £3 adults, £1.50 children, £2.50 students and senior citizens. Open May–Sept., Sun.–Thur. 2–5:30.*

42 Follow the B924 for the descent to South Queensferry and views of the **Forth bridges.** The **Forth Rail Bridge,** which looms over the former Forth ferry port, was opened in 1890 and is 2,765 yards long, except on a hot summer's day when it expands by about another yard! Its neighbor is the 1,993-yard-long **Forth Road Bridge,** opened in 1964.

West Lothian and the Forth Valley

108

The B924 continues westward under the approaches to the suspension bridge and then blends into the A904. On turning **43** right, you'll see signs for **Hopetoun House.** These palatial premises, home of the marquesses of Linlithgow, are considered to be among the Adam family's finest designs. The pile was started in 1699 to the original plans of Sir William Bruce, then enlarged between 1721 and 1754 by William Adam and his son Robert. There is a notable painting collection, and the house has decorative work of the highest order, plus all the paraphernalia to amuse visitors: nature trail, restaurant, stables, museum, garden center. Much of the wealth that created this sumptuous building came from the family's mining interests. Scotland's miners were among the least privileged members of the nation's workers, living as serfs or bonded slaves till 1799 and even after in conditions of deprivation, which for generations placed them apart from the rest of society. *West of South Queensferry, tel. 031/331–2451. Admission: £3.30 adults, £1.60 children, £2.80 students and senior citizens. Open Easter–Sept., daily 10–5.*

44 On this Forth Valley castle trail you can also visit the **House of the Binns,** signed from the A904. Here the 17th-century General Tam Dalyell transformed a fortified stronghold into a gracious mansion. The present exterior dates from around 1810 and shows a remodeling into a kind of mock fort with crenellated battlements and turrets. Inside there are magnificent plaster ceilings in Elizabethan style. *Off A904, 4 mi west of Linlithgow, tel. 050683/4255. Admission: £2.80 adults, £1.40 children, students, and senior citizens. Open Easter (Sat.–Mon.) and May–Sept., Sat.–Thurs. 2–5 (last tour 4:30).*

For a look at a more austere flavor fortress, follow signs off the **45** A904 to **Blackness.** The castle here stands like a grounded gray hulk on the very edge of the Forth. A curious 15th-century structure, it has had a varied career as a strategic fortress, state prison, powder magazine, and youth hostel. There is a tradition that an underground passage leads from the base of one of the turrets at the House of the Binns to this odd seagoing castle. The countryside is gently green and cultivated, and open views extend across the blue Forth to the distant ramparts of the Ochil Hills (seen in close-up later on the route). *B903, 4 mi northeast of Linlithgow, tel. 031/244–3101. Admission: £1 adults, 50p children. Open Apr.–Sept., Mon.–Sat. 9:30–6, Sun. 2–6; Oct.–Mar., Mon.–Wed. and Sat. 9:30–4, Thurs. 9:30–noon, Sun. 2–4.*

From Blackness, take the B903 to its junction with the A904. Turn left for Linlithgow on the A803.

Time Out The **Four Marys** (67 High St., Linlithgow) specializes in uncomplicated wholesome pub lunches.

On the edge of Linlithgow Loch stands the splendid ruin of **46** **Linlithgow Palace,** birthplace of Mary, Queen of Scots (1542). Burned, perhaps by accident, by Hanoverian troops during the last Jacobite rebellion in 1746, this impressive shell stands on a site of great antiquity, though nothing for certain survived an earlier fire in 1424. The palace gatehouse is from the early 16th century, and the central courtyard's elaborate fountain dates from around 1535, but the halls and great rooms are cold stone echoing husks. *South shore of Linlithgow Loch, tel. 031/244–*

3101. Admission: £1.50 adults, 80p children, £4 family ticket. Open Apr.–Sept., Mon.–Sat. 9:30–6, Sun. 2–6; Oct.–Mar., Mon.–Sat. 9:30–4, Sun. 2–4.

At this point it's best to join the M9, which will speed you westward. From the M9 you will begin to gain tempting glimpses of the Highland hills to the northwest and the long humped wall of the Ochil Hills, across the river-plain to the north. The **River Carron,** which flows under the M9, gave its name to the *carronade,* a kind of cannon manufactured in Falkirk, a few minutes to the southwest. On your right you'll notice the apocalyptic complex of Grangemouth Refinery (impressive by night), which you may also smell if the wind is right (or wrong!). The refinery processes North Sea crude, but was originally sited here because of the now extinct oil-shale extraction industry of West Lothian, pioneered by a Scot, James "Paraffin" Young. This short section may not be the most scenic in Scotland, but it has certainly played its role in the nation's industrial history.

Follow Kincardine Bridge signs off the motorway, cross the Forth and take the A977 north from Kincardine, formerly a trading port and distillery center. It also used to be a crossing point for cattle. In the old droving days before railways, cattle were fattened in the Highlands, then walked south to market. There was a major cattle market, or *tryst* (Scots for *meeting place*) at Falkirk. The cattle crossed the Forth by ferry here, taking precedence over passengers on every second trip!

Take the A985 to Alloa, get on the A908 (signed Tillicoultry) for a short stretch, and then pick up the B908 (signed Alva). At this point you'll be leaving the industrial northern shore of the Forth behind. The scarp face of the **Ochil Hills** looms unmistakably ahead, an old fault line, bearing up the harder volcanic rocks in contrast to the softer coal measures through which you have just traveled. The steep Ochils provided grazing land and water power for Scotland's second largest textile area. Some mills still survive in the so-called Hillfoots towns on the scarp edge east of Stirling. You can explore this region by following the A91 eastward at **Alva.** This is an area often overlooked by visitors who are preoccupied with the Trossachs farther to the west. Several walkers' routes run into the narrow chinks of glens here. Behind Alva is **Alva Glen** (park near the converted Strude Mill, at the top and eastern end of the little town). A little farther east is the **Ochil Hills Woodland Park,** which provides access to Silver Glen. The **Mill Glen** behind Tillicoultry (pronounced tilly-*coot*-ree) and its giant quarry, fine waterfalls, and interesting plants is another option for energetic explorers. The tourist information center at Tillicoultry can provide further information, as well as a *Mill Trail* brochure, which can lead you to a variety of mill shops offering bargain woolen and tweed goods.

The main road, squeezed between the gentle River Devon and the steep slopes above, continues to **Dollar.** This *douce* (Scots for *well-mannered* and *gentle*) and tidy town below the slopes lies at the mouth of Dollar Glen. At first sight, the tilting slopes seem an unlikely terrain for wheeled vehicles. By following signs for **Castle Campbell,** however, you will find a road that angles sharply up the east side of the wooded defile. The narrow road ends in a car park from which it's only a short walk to Castle Campbell, high on a great sloping mound in the center of the glen. With the green woods below, bracken hills above, and a view that on a clear day stretches right across the Forth Valley to the tip of Tinto Hill near Lanark, this is certainly the most atmospheric fortress within easy reach of Edinburgh. Formerly known as Castle Gloom, Castle Campbell stands out among Scottish castles for the sheer drama of its setting. The sturdy square of the tower house survives from the 15th century, when this site was first fortified by the earl of Argyll. Other buildings and enclosures were subsequently added, but the sheer lack of space on this rocky eminence ensured that there were never any drastic changes. The castle is associated with the earls of Argyll, as well as with with John Knox, the fiery religious reformer, who preached here. It also played a role in the religious wars of the 17th centruy, having been captured by Oliver Cromwell in 1654 and garrisoned with English troops. *Dollar Glen, 1 mi north of Dollar, tel. 031/244–3101. Admission: £1.50 adults, 80p children. Open Apr.–Sept., Mon.–Sat. 9:30–6, Sun. 2–6; Oct.–Mar., Mon.–Wed. and Sat. 9:30–4, Thurs. 9:30–noon, Sun. 2–4.*

From the castle, retrace your route to the main road. Just a few minutes from Dollar, turn right onto a minor road (signed Rumbling Bridge). Then turn right onto the A823. Follow A823 through Powmill (signs for Dunfermline); then go right, following the signs for Saline (a pleasant if undistinguished village), and take an unclassified road due south to join the A907. Turn right, and then within a mile go left on the B9037, which leads down to **Culross.** On the muddy shores of the Forth, this is one of the most remarkable little towns in all Scotland. It once had a thriving industry and export trade in coal and salt (the coal was used in the salt-panning process). It also had, curiously, a trade monopoly in the manufacture of baking *girdles* (griddles). But as local coal became exhausted, the impetus of the Industrial Revolution passed it by and other parts of the Forth Valley prospered. Culross became a backwater town, and the merchants' houses of the 17th and 18th centuries were never replaced by Victorian developments or modern architecture. In the 1930s, the very new and then very poor National Trust for Scotland started to buy up the decaying properties. With the help of a variety of other agencies, these buildings were conserved and brought to life, and Culross is now a vigorous community, even if it has the air of a film set. With its mercat cross, cobbled streets, tolbooth, and narrow wynds, Culross is a living museum of a 17th-century town. Several properties are open to view, including the "Palace" or town house (1597) of Sir George Bruce, one of the settlement's successful coalmasters. *7½ mi west of Dunfermline, tel. 031/226–5922. Admission £1 adults, 50p children. Open Easter and May–Sept. daily 11–1 and 2–5.*

Take the B9037 east to join the A994, which leads to **Dunfermline,** once the world center for the production of damask linen (the Dunfermline District Museum on Viewfield Terrace, tel. 0383/721–814, tells the full story), but perhaps better known as the birthplace of millionaire philanthropist Andrew Carnegie. Undoubtedly Dunfermline's most famous son, Carnegie endowed the town with a library, health and fitness center, spacious park, and, naturally, a Carnegie Hall, still the focus of culture and entertainment. The 1835 weaver's cottage in which Carnegie was born is now the **Andrew Carnegie Birthplace Museum.** Don't be misled by the cottage's exterior. Inside it opens into a larger hall, where documents, photographs, and artifacts tell Carnegie's fascinating life story. You will learn such obscure details as the fact that Carnegie was only the third man in the United States to be able to translate Morse code by ear as it came down the wire! *Moodie St., tel. 0383/724–302. Admission free. Open Apr.–Oct., Mon.–Sat. 11–5, Sun. 2–5; Nov.– Mar., daily 2–4.*

㊿ Also of note in the town are the **Dunfermline Abbey and Palace** complex. The abbey was founded by Queen Margaret, the English wife of the Scots King Malcolm Canmore (1057–93). Some Norman work can be seen in the present church, where Robert the Bruce lies buried. The palace grew from the abbey guest house and was the birthplace of Charles I. Dunfermline was the seat of the Royal Court of Scotland until the end of the 11th century, and its central role in Scottish affairs is explored by means of display panels dotted around the draughty but hallowed buildings. *Monastery St., tel. 031/244–3101. Admission: £1.20 adults, 60p children. Open Apr.–Sept., Mon.–Sat. 9:30–5, Sun. 2–5; Oct.–Mar., Mon.–Wed., Fri., and Sat. 9:30–4, Thurs. 9:30–noon, Sun. 2–4.*

From Dunfermline, follow Edinburgh signs to the A823 and return via the Forth Road Bridge (toll: 40p).

Tour 4: Midlothian and East Lothian

Numbers in the margin correspond to points of interest on the Midlothian and East Lothian map.

This car tour covers the rest of the Lothians to the south and southeast of Edinburgh. The area south of Edinburgh, known as Midlothian, was until recently often overlooked. Only in the past few years has the region begun to overcome its industrial legacy of mills and coal mining, now almost entirely gone. In spite of the finest stone carving in Scotland (at Rosslyn Chapel), associations with Sir Walter Scott, outstanding castles, and miles of varied rolling countryside, for years Midlothian remained off the beaten tourist path. Perhaps a little in awe of sophisticated Edinburgh to the north and the well-manicured charm of the stockbroker belt of nearby upmarket East Lothian, Midlothian remained quietly preoccupied with its own workaday little towns and dormitory suburbs. Now Midlothian has decided it is at least as interesting as are several other parts of Scotland that are fervently marketing themselves as tourism destinations. Judge for yourself in this tour.

As for East Lothian, it started with the advantage of golf courses of world-rank, most notably Muirfield, plus a scattering of stately homes and interesting hotels. Red pantiled and decidedly middle class, East Lothian is an area of glowing grainfields in summer and quite a few discreetly polite, "strictly private" signs at the end of driveways. It nevertheless has plenty of interest for the visitor, including photogenic villages, active fishing harbors, and vistas of pastoral Lowland Scotland, a world away (but much less than an hour by car) from bustling Edinburgh.

The tour described here can certainly be driven in one day, although it could be split into two separate excursions if you want to budget more time for some individual sights. Public transport is available to many of the venues described. Inquire at the St. Andrew Square bus station for bus services. Train service is available to Dunbar and North Berwick. (For more information, *see* Getting Around by Bus and Getting Around by Train, *above*.)

Leave Edinburgh via the A701 (Liberton Road). At the not-very-picturesque community of Bilston, look for signs left for **⑤ Rosslyn Chapel** (signed Roslin B7006). Conceived by Sir William Sinclair and dedicated to St. Matthew in 1450, the chapel is famous for the quality and variety of the stone carving inside. Human figures, animals, and plants are all included, covering almost every square inch of stonework. The chapel is perhaps best known for the Apprentice Pillar, a fluted column festooned with four separate spirals of highly wrought foliage. Associated with this breathtaking craftsmanship is the (apocryphal) tale of the apprentice who carved it in his master's absence. When the master mason returned, he was so incensed with the high quality of the workmanship that, in a fit of jealous rage, he killed the apprentice with his mallet. The chapel was actually never finished. The original design called for a cruciform structure, but only the choir and parts of the east transept walls were completed. *Roslin, off A703, 7 ½ mi south of Edinburgh, tel. 031/440–2159. Admission: £2 adults, £1.50 senior citizens, 75p children. Open Apr.–Oct., Mon.–Sat. 10–5, Sun. noon–4:45.*

From Roslin return to the A703 for **Penicuik,** which is primarily a bedroom community for people who work in Edinburgh, although its own—typically Scottish—town square is worth seeing. There are fine views of the Pentland Hills beyond the town, **⑤ but its chief attraction for the tourist is the Edinburgh Crystal Visitor Centre.** You may have seen this distinctive style of glassware in Edinburgh's upscale shops. Guided tours reveal the stages involved in the manufacture of cut-crystal. A large factory store is attached to the center. *Eastfield, Penicuik, 10 mi south of Edinburgh, tel. 0968/75128. Admission to center free. Cost of tours: £1 adults, 50p children. Center, restaurant, and shop open Mon.–Sat. 9–5, Sun. 11–5. Tours Mon.–Fri. 9–3:30.*

Time Out The **Old Bakehouse Tearoom** (tel. 0968/60564) at West Linton, southwest of Penicuik on the A702, serves home-cooked fare in quaint, wood-beamed rooms. The waitresses' costumes—neat white pinafores and old-fashioned dresses—add to the pleasantly low-tech atmosphere. This is a good spot for lunch or afternoon tea.

After pausing to admire the Pentland Hills arching along the skyline to the southwest, follow the B7059 and the A701 to Leadburn and then Howgate. Get onto the A6094 for a few minutes, then turn right onto the B6372 and continue past Temple, an attractive village on the edge of the Moorfoot Hills, toward Gorebridge.

At the junction of B6372 with A7, just before Gorebridge, you have a choice. If your interests tend toward social history, turn **⑤ left and drive two miles to reach the Scottish Mining Museum at Newtongrange.** Here, in the buildings of a now-closed colliery, you can learn something about the history of Scotland's coal miners. You can visit various buildings in the complex and view the giant winding engine, as well as the ranks of rusty, coal-dusty boilers that supplied the steam to turn it. The mine's for-

Midlothian and East Lothian

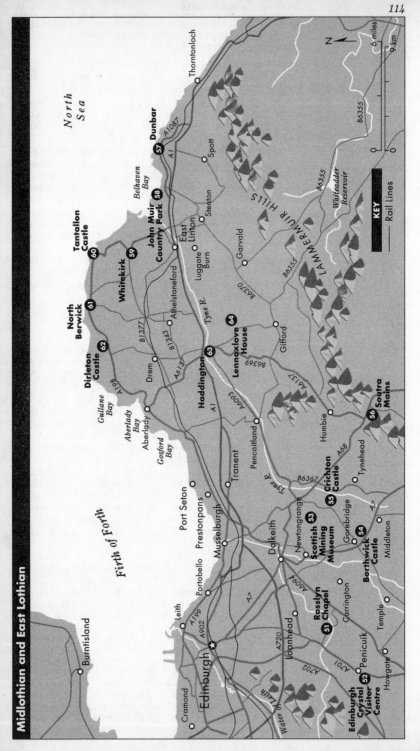

North Sea

Firth of Forth

LAMMERMUIR HILLS

KEY
— Rail Lines

Edinburgh

Dunbar **57**
John Muir Country Park **58**
Whitekirk **59**
Tantallon Castle **60**
North Berwick **61**
Dirleton Castle **62**
Haddington **63**
Lennoxlove House **64**
Soutra Mains **56**
Crichton Castle **55**
Borthwick Castle **54**
Scottish Mining Museum **53**
Edinburgh Crystal Visitor Centre **52**
Rosslyn Chapel **51**

Burntisland
Cramond
Leith
Portobello
Port Seton
Prestonpans
Musselburgh
Dalkeith
Newtongrange
Gorebridge
Loanhead
Penicuik
Howgate
Temple
Middleton
Carrington
Tynehead
Humbie
Pencaitland
Tranent
Aberlady
Gullane Bay
Aberlady Bay
Gosford Bay
Drem
Athelstaneford
Belhaven Bay
East Linton
Luggate Burn
Stenton
Spott
Garvald
Gifford
Thorntonloch
Whiteadder Reservoir

Tyne R.

Water of Leith

A1
A7
A68
A720
A199
A902
A701
A702
A6094
A198
A6137
B1377
B1343
A6093
B6369
B6368
A6137
B6367
B6370
B6355
A1087

miles
km
N

mer offices now relate, by means of realistic tableaux, the power that the mining company had over the lives of the individual workers in a frighteningly autocratic system that survived well into the 1930s. The mining company owned the houses, shops, and even the pub. Newtongrange was in fact the largest planned mining village in Scotland. The scenery is no more attractive than you would expect around a former mining community, though the green Pentland Hills are still in view in the distance. *Tel. 031/663–7519. Admission free. Open Apr.–Sept., Mon.–Sat. 9:30–7, Sun. 2–7; Oct.–Mar., 9:30–4, Sun. 2–4.*

If you turn right at the Gorebridge junction (A7/B6372), a few moments' travel takes you a world away from gloomy thoughts of worker exploitation by the mine-owning aristocracy. Follow the A7 south to a sign for **Borthwick.** Take a left onto an unclassified road off A7, and a few minutes later, in green countryside with scattered woods and lush hedgerows, you can see **54** **Borthwick Castle.** Dating from the 15th century and still occupied (it is now a hotel), this stark, tall twin-towered fortress is associated with Mary, Queen of Scots. She came here on a kind of honeymoon with her ill-starred third husband, the earl of Bothwell. Their already dubious bliss was interrupted by Mary's political opponents, often referred to as the Lords of the Congregation, a confederacy of powerful nobles who were against the queen's latest liaison and who instead favored the crowning of her young son James. Rather insensitively, they laid siege to the castle while the newlyweds were there. The history books relate that Mary subsequently escaped "disguised as a man." (Under the warlike circumstances, you may think this was a risky strategy.) She was not free for long, however. It was only a short time before she was defeated in battle and imprisoned. She languished in prison for 21 years before Queen Elizabeth of England signed her death warrant (1587). Bothwell's fate was equally gloomy: He died insane in a Danish prison.

55 From Borthwick, you can reach the next destination—**Crichton Castle**—by taking a peaceful walk through the woods (there are signposts along the way) or by doubling back by car to the B6372 and turning right onto the A68. Crichton Castle is just beyond the village of Pathhead (you'll see signs on A68). This was a Bothwell family castle. Queen Mary attended the wedding here of Bothwell's sister, Lady Janet Hepburn, to Mary's natural brother, Lord John Stewart. Of particular interest in the extensive ruin is the curious arcaded range with its diamond faceted stonework. This particular geometric pattern cut into the stone is unique in Scotland and is thought to have been inspired by Renaissance styles on the Continent, particularly Italy. The oldest part of the work is the 14th-century keep (square tower). Like Borthwick Castle, Crichton is set in attractive, rolling Lowland scenery, interrupted here and there with patches of woodland. *B6367, 7 mi southeast of Dalkeith, tel. 031/244–3101. Admission: £1.20 adults, 60p children. Open Apr.–Sept., Mon.–Sat. 9:30–6, Sun. 2–6; Oct.–Mar., Sat. 9:30–4, Sun. 2–4.*

If the attractive setting of Crichton has beguiled you, you may want to end this section of the tour to explore the countryside and then return to Edinburgh via the A68 and Dalkeith. To continue the tour into East Lothian, follow the A68 south, away from Edinburgh, to the very edge of the Lammermuir Hills.

⑤⑥ Just beyond the junction with the A6137 you'll come to a spot called **Soutra Mains.** There's a small car park here, from which you can enjoy glorious unobstructed views extending northward over the whole of the Lothian plain to Arthur's Seat, Edinburgh Castle, and the Firth of Forth and southward to the Pentland Hills.

Make your way back to the A6137, turn right onto the B6355, and head east for the junction with the B6370, which leads to Dunbar.

Time Out The **Goblin Ha' Hotel** (tel. 062081/244) in Gifford, a peaceful backwater town on the B6355, on the very edge of the Lammermuir hills, offers a wholesome afternoon tea that is very popular with day-trippers from Edinburgh. Gifford itself, with its 18th-century kirk and mercat cross, is a good example of a tweedily respectable, well-scrubbed, red-pantile-roofed East Lothian village.

⑤⑦ In the days before tour companies started offering package deals to the Mediterranean, **Dunbar** was a popular holiday resort. Now a bit faded, the town is of interest primarily because of a number of spacious Georgian-style properties, characterized by the astragals, or fan-shaped windows, above the doors; the symmetry of the house fronts; and the parapeted roof lines. Though not the popular seaside playground it once was, Dunbar does still have an attractive beach and a picturesque harbor, as well as opportunities for golf and sailing.

⑤⑧ West of Dunbar, on the way back to Edinburgh, the A1087 leads to the sandy reaches of **Belhaven Bay,** signposted from the main road, and to the **John Muir Country Park,** which takes in the estuary of the River Tyne winding down from the Moorfoot Hills. The country park offers varied coastal scenery: rocky shoreline, golden sands, and the mixed woodlands of Tyninghame, teeming with wildlife. Dunbar-born John Muir (whose family emigrated to the United States when he was a child) founded the U.S. national parks system. Only recently has the work of this early conservationist been acknowledged in his native Scotland.

⑤⑨ From the park, drive north on the A198 (a right turn off the A1), to reach **Whitekirk.** The unmistakable red sandstone church, with Norman tower, stands on a site occupied since the 6th century. It was a place of pilgrimage in medieval times because of its healing well. Behind the kirk, in a field, stands a tithe barn. Tithe barns originated in the practice of giving to the church a proportion of local produce, which then required storage space. At one end of the structure is a 16th-century tower house, which at one point in its history accommodated visiting pilgrims. The large three-story barn was added to the tower house in the 17th century. *St. Mary's Parish Church, A198. Admission free. Open early morning to late evening.*

⑥⓪ Only minutes farther on, grim and battered **Tantallon Castle** rises on a cliff beyond the flat fields. This substantial ruin defends a headland with the sea on three sides. The red sandstone is pitted and eaten by time and sea-spray, with the earliest surviving stonework dating from the late-14th century. The fortress was besieged in 1529 by the cannons of King James V. (Rather inconveniently, the besieging forces ran out of gunpowder.) Cannons were used again, to deadlier effect, in a later siege during the Civil War in 1651. Twelve days of battering with the heavy guns of Cromwell's General Monk greatly damaged the flanking towers. However, much of the curtain wall of this former Douglas stronghold survives. *A198, 3 mi east of North Berwick, tel. 031/244–3101. Admission: £1.50 adults, 80p children. Open Apr.–Sept., Mon.–Sat. 9:30–6, Sun. 2–6; Oct.–Mar., Mon.–Tues. and Sat. 9:30–4, Wed. and Thurs. noon–4., Sun. 2–4.*

61 The seaside resort of **North Berwick,** a few minutes west on the A198, is a pleasant little place that manages to retain a small-town personality even when it's thronged with city visitors on warm summer Sunday afternoons. Munching on ice cream, the city folk stroll on the beach and in the narrow streets or gape at the sailing craft in the small harbor.

Sandy shores run westward toward **Yellowcraigs,** where you can walk among the trees or along a stretch of roadless coast, **62** signed from the village of Dirleton, just off the A198. **Dirleton Castle** is a 12th-century castle surrounded by a high outer wall. Within the wall you'll find a 17th-century bowling green, set in the shade of yew trees and surrounded by a herbaceous flower border that comes ablaze with color in high summer. Dirleton Castle was once occupied by King Edward I of England, in 1298, as part of his campaign for the continued subjugation of the unruly Scots. *A198, 8 mi west of North Berwick, tel. 031/244–3101. Admission: £1.50 adults, 80p children. Open Apr.–Sept., Mon.–Sat. 9:30–6, Sun. 2–6; Oct.–Mar., Mon.–Sat. 9:30–4, Sun. 2–4.*

Very noticeable along this coastline are the golf courses of East Lothian on every available links space. Next to Dirleton is **Gullane,** which is respectable and clad mostly in expensive golfing sweaters. **Muirfield,** venue for the Open Championship, is nearby, as is **Greywalls,** now a hotel, but originally a private house designed by Sir Edwin Lutyens. Away from the golf, Gullane's beach, well within driving distance of the city, offers opportunities for restful summer evening strolls.

From Aberlady take the A6137 south to the former county **63** town of **Haddington,** one of the best-preserved medieval street plans in the country. Among the many buildings of architectural or historical interest is the Town House, which was designed by William Adam in 1748 and enlarged in 1830. A wall plaque at the Sidegate recalls the great heights of floods from the River Tyne. Beyond is the medieval Nungate footbridge, with the Church of St. Mary a little way upstream.

Just to the south of Haddington, by way of the B6369, is **64** **Lennoxlove House,** which displays items associated with Mary, Queen of Scots. A turreted country house, part of it dating from the 15th century, Lennoxlove is a cheerful mix of family life and Scottish history. Housed in the beautifully decorated rooms are collections of portraits, furniture, and porcelain. *B6369, 1 mi south of Haddington, tel. 062/082–3720. Admission: £2.50 adults, £1.25 children. Open Easter weekend and May–Sept., Wed., Sat., and Sun. 2–5.*

Return to the A1 and head west back to Edinburgh. From Haddington it's about 15 miles back to center city.

5 Glasgow

Introduction

*By John
Hutchinson*

In the days when Britain still had an empire, Glasgow proudly called itself the Second City of the Empire. The people of Glasgow were justifiably proud of their city, since it was there that Britain's great steamships (including the 80,000-ton *Queen Elizabeth*) were built. The term *Clydebuilt* (from Glasgow's River Clyde) became synonymous with good workmanship and lasting quality. It was also the Glaswegians who built the railway engines that opened up the Canadian prairies, the South African veldt, the Australian plains, and the Indian subcontinent. Glasgow provided the machinery and the men to run them. Scots engineers were to be found wherever there were engines (and so it was perhaps no coincidence that even Captain Kirk on the Starship *Enterprise* had to say, "Beam me up, Scottie" to his engineer).

In the past two decades Glasgow has weathered the problems of an industrial city in decline, but thanks to the natives' innate adaptability, optimism, and cosmopolitanism, Glasgow has once again emerged as a dynamic, prosperous international city in the 1990s.

Scholars have argued for years about what the name Glasgow means (pronounce it to rhyme with *toe* and put the stress on the first syllable) but, generally, "dear green place" is the interpretation that finds most favor today. Most suitable it is, too, for a city that, despite industrialization, has more city parks than anywhere else in Britain, and even the famous River Clyde is now clean enough for trout and salmon.

Glasgow first came into prominence in Scottish history somewhere around 1,400 years ago, and typically for this rambunctious city it was all to do with an argument between a husband and his wife. One of the local chieftains suspected, with some justification, that his wife had been having an affair, so he crept up on the suspect, one of his knights, and took from him a ring that she had rather foolishly given her lover—foolishly, because it had originally been given to her by her husband. The furious husband flung the ring into the River Clyde, then told his wife the next day that he wanted her to wear it that evening. The lady was distraught and called on the local holy man, Mungo, to help. Clearly a useful man to have in a tricky situation, Mungo sent a monk out fishing, and the first bite the monk had was a salmon with the ring in its mouth. Whether the lady learned her lesson or called on Mungo's services regularly after that, history does not relate.

Mungo features in two other legends: one of a pet bird that he nursed back to life and another, of a bush or tree, the branches of which he used to relight a fire. Tree, bird, and the salmon with a ring in its mouth are all to be found on the city of Glasgow's coat of arms, together with a bell that Mungo brought from Rome. Mungo is now the city's patron saint. His tomb is to be found in the mighty medieval cathedral that bears his name.

Glasgow led a fairly quiet existence in the Middle Ages. Its cathedral was the center of religious life and, although the city was made a Royal Burgh in 1175 by King William the Lion, its population was never more than a few thousand. What changed Glasgow irrevocably and laid the foundations for its immense prosperity was the Union of the Crowns between Scotland and England in 1707. This allowed Scotland to trade with the essentially English colonies in America, and with their expansion Glasgow prospered. In came cotton, tobacco, and rum; out went various Scottish manufactured goods and clothing. The key to it all in the early days was tobacco, and the prosperous merchants were known as the Tobacco Lords. It was they who ran the city, and their wealth laid the foundation stone for the manufacturing industries of the 19th century.

As Glasgow prospered, so her population grew. The "dear green place" became built over. The original medieval city around the cathedral and the High Street expanded westward. The 18th-century Merchant City, today the subject of a great deal of refurbishment, lies just to the south and west of George Square, and the houses of the merchants are even farther westward, along the gridiron pattern of Glasgow's streets up the hill toward Blytheswood Square.

But the city is not known as an 18th-century city; that honor is left to its sister city, Edinburgh, in the east. Rather, Glasgow is known as the greatest Victorian city in Europe. The population grew from 80,000 in 1801 to over 700,000 in 1901, and with this enormous growth there developed also a sense of exuberance and confidence, which is reflected in its public buildings. The City Chambers, built in 1888, are an extravaganza of marble and red sandstone, a clear symbol of the Victorian merchants' hopes for the future.

Yet, always at the forefront of change, Glasgow boasts, side by side with the overtly Victorian, an architectural vision of the future in the work of Charles Rennie Mackintosh. The Glasgow School of Art, the Willow tearoom, and the churches and school buildings he designed point clearly to the clarity and simplicity of 20th-century lines.

Today, Glasgow has taken the best of the past and adapted it for the needs of the present day. The "dear green places" still remain in the city-center parks, to be enjoyed by citizens and visitors alike; the medieval cathedral stands proud, as it has done for 800 years; the Merchant City is revived and thriving; the Victorian splendor has been cleaned of its grime and will look good for many years to come; and the cultural legacy of museums and performing arts lives on stronger than ever. To crown it all, Glasgow was home to the Garden Festival in 1988 and was European City of Culture in 1990, a fitting tribute to the renaissance of this ancient and dynamic city.

Essential Information

Important Addresses and Numbers

Tourist Information
The **Greater Glasgow Tourist Board** (tel. 041/204–4400) offers an excellent all-around tourist-information service from its headquarters at 35 St. Vincent Place, which is just around the corner from George Square and Queen Street Station. There is also an accommodations-booking service; bureau de change; theater- and travel-ticket service; and books, maps, and souvenirs. The office is open Monday–Saturday 9 AM–6 PM and, in summer Monday–Saturday 9 AM–8 PM and Sunday 10 AM–6 PM. The tourist board's branch office at the airport is open daily 8–8.

What's On information is provided through the Greater Glasgow Tourist Board's own publications, as well as through *What's On Across Scotland* magazine, *The List*, and the *Glasgow Herald* newspaper.

Consulate **Canadian Consulate** (151 St. Vincent St., tel. 041/221–4415).

Emergencies For fire, police, or ambulance, dial 999 from any telephone. No coins are needed for emergency calls from public phone booths.

Hospitals Twenty-four-hour accident and emergency services are provided at **Glasgow Royal Infirmary** (Castle St., tel. 041/552–3535). The hospital is by the cathedral. Facilities are also available at **Glasgow Western Infirmary** (Dumbarton Rd., tel. 041/339–8822), near the university.

Dentists Most dentists will treat visitors by appointment. A full list can be found in the Yellow Pages telephone directory. Emergency dental treatment can be obtained from the **Glasgow Dental Hospital** (378 Sauchiehall St., tel. 041/332–7020).

Late-night Pharmacies in Glasgow operate on a rotating basis for late-
Pharmacies night opening (hours are posted in storefront windows), but **R. H. Brown** (693 Great Western Rd., tel. 041/339–0012) is open daily 9–9.

Post Office The **head post office** is at 1–5 George Square (tel. 041/248–2882); there are many smaller post offices around the city.

Arriving and Departing by Plane

Airports and **Glasgow Airport** is about 10 miles west of the city center on the
Airlines M8 to Greenock.

Glasgow Airport offers internal Scottish and British services, European and transatlantic scheduled services, and vacation-charter traffic. It is a modern airport and has greatly expanded its services in the past few years. Most major European carriers fly into Glasgow, offering frequent and convenient connections to Amsterdam, Berlin, Brussels, Copenhagen, Dusseldorf, Frankfurt, Hanover, Munich, Paris, and Stavanger. There are frequent shuttle services from London, as well as regular flights from Birmingham, Bristol, East Midlands, Leeds/Bradford, and Manchester. There are also flights from Wales (Cardiff) and Ireland (Belfast, Carrickfinn, Dublin, and Londonderry).

Local Scottish connections can be made to Aberdeen, Barra, Benbecula, Campbeltown, Edinburgh, Inverness, Islay, Kirkwall, Shetland, Stornoway, and Tiree. There is an airport information desk (tel. 041/887–1111) and a tourist information desk and accommodations-booking service (tel 041/848–4440).

Airlines operating through Glasgow Airport to Europe and the rest of the United Kingdom include **British Airways** (tel. 0345/222–111), **British Midland** (tel. 041/889–0660), **Air UK** (tel. 0345/666777), **Loganair** (tel. 041/889–3181), **Manx** (tel. 041/221–0162), **Aer Lingus** (tel. 041/248–4121), **Air France** (tel. 0345/581393), **Icelandair** (tel. 081/568–9144), **Lufthansa** (tel. 041/221–7132), **Sabena** (tel. 0345/056341), and **SAS** (tel. 0345/090900).

Scheduled services to and from North America are provided by **American Airlines** (tel. 0800/0101–51), **Air Canada** (tel. 0800/

181–313), **British Airways** (tel. 041/887–1111), and **Northwest Airlines** (tel. 041/848–4794).

Between the Airport and Center City Though there is a railway station (Paisley Gilmour St.) about 2 miles from Glasgow airport, most people travel the short distance to the city center by road. Journey time is about 20 minutes, but it can be longer at rush hour.

By Bus Express buses run from Glasgow Airport to the Central railway station (tel. 041/204–2844) and to the Anderston Cross and Buchanan Street bus stations (tel. 041/248–7432, 041/332–7133, or 041/332–9191). There is service every 30 minutes throughout the day. The fare is about £2. Buses also connect with the hourly service to Edinburgh city center.

By Taxi Metered taxis are available at the terminal building. The fare should be about £10.

By Rental Car All the usual rental companies, including **Avis** (tel. 041/221–2827), **Hertz** (tel. 041/887–2451), **Budget** (tel. 041/887–0501), **Europcar** (tel. 041/423–5661, and **Swan** (tel. 041/887–7915), have offices within the terminal building. Costs vary according to the size of the cars, but average about £20–£30 per day.

The drive from Glasgow Airport into the city center is normally quite easy even for visitors who are used to driving on the right. The M8 motorway runs beside the airport (junction 29) and takes you straight into Glasgow city center (and offers excellent views of the city and the River Clyde). Thereafter Glasgow's streets follow a grid pattern, at least in the city center, but a map is useful and can be supplied by the rental company. A driver's license from your own country is normally acceptable, but if you are under 25 or over 70, check your insurance policy to be sure that no other documentation is needed.

By Limousine Most of the companies that provide chauffeur-driven cars and tours will also do limousine airport transfers. Companies that are currently members of the Greater Glasgow Tourist Board are **Broom** (tel. 041/638–6588, **Charter** (tel. 041/942–4228), **Eastwood** (tel. 041/644–5496), **Kingston** (tel. 041/554–6066), **Little's** (tel. 041/883–2111), **Rosewood** (tel. 041/885–1111), and **Windsor** (tel. 0505/31777 or 0836/766085).

Arriving and Departing by Car, Train, and Bus

By Car Visitors who come to Glasgow from England and the south of Scotland will probably approach the city from the M6, M74, and A74. The city center is clearly marked from these roads. From Edinburgh the M8 again leads straight to the city center and is the motorway that cuts straight across the city center and into which all other roads feed. From the north either the A82 from Fort William or the A/M80 from Stirling also feed into the M8 in Glasgow city center. From then on, you only have to know your exit. Exit 16 serves the north of the city center, 17/18 leads to the northwest and Great Western Road, with 18/19 the exit for the hotels of Sauchiehall Street, the Scottish Exhibition Centre, and around the Anderston Centre.

By Train Glasgow has two main rail stations: **Central** and **Queen Street.** Central is the arrival and departure point for trains from London Euston (journey time is approximately 5 hours), which come via Birmingham, Crewe, and Carlisle in England, as well as from other cities in the northwest of England and towns and ports in the southwest of Scotland. These include Kilmarnock, Dumfries, Ardrossan (for the island of Arran), Gourock (for Dunoon), Wemyss Bay (for the island of Rothesay), and Stranraer (for Ireland). Queen Street Station has Edinburgh connections (journey time 45 minutes) and onward on the east coast route to Aberdeen or south via Edinburgh to Newcastle, York, and London Kings Cross. Other services from Queen Street go to Stirling, Perth, and Dundee; northward to Inverness, Kyle of Lochalsh, Wick, and Thurso; along the Clyde to Dumbarton and Balloch (for Loch Lomond); and on the scenic West Highland line to Oban, Fort William, and Mallaig. Oban and Mallaig have island ferry connections. The passenger-information line (tel. 041/204–2844) for both Central and Queen Street stations operates 24 hours.

A regular bus service links Queen Street and Central stations. Both of these are close to stations on the Glasgow Underground (subway). At Queen Street go to Buchanan Street, and at Central go to St. Enoch. Black city taxis are available at both stations.

By Bus Glasgow also has two bus stations: Buchanan Street (tel. 041/ 332–7133 or 041/332–9191), which serves a wide variety of towns and cities in Scotland, Wales, and England, including London (journey time from London is approximately 8 hours) and Anderston Cross (tel. 041/248–7432), which also serves Scottish destinations. Both bus stations have services to Glasgow Airport and Edinburgh. Buchanan Street is close to the underground station of the same name and Queen Street station. Anderston Cross is close to many of the new hotels in the southwestern part of the city center north of the Clyde.

Getting Around

Glasgow city center—the area defined by the M8 motorway to the north and west, the River Clyde to the south, and Glasgow Cathedral to the east—is relatively compact, and visitors who are staying in this area should make some of their excursions on foot. Glaswegians themselves walk a good deal and the streets are designed for pedestrians (some are pedestrians-only). Walking has the additional benefit of allowing you to look above street level to admire the extraordinary degree of architectural decoration that the Victorians put on their buildings. The streets are relatively safe even at night (though be sensible), and good street maps are available from bookstores and the excellent tourist-information center (*see* Important Addresses and Numbers, *above*). Suggested walks are given below. Most of the streets follow a grid plan; if you get lost, though, just ask a local—they are famous for being friendly.

To go farther afield, to the West End (the university, the Transport Museum, Kelvingrove Museum and Art Gallery, or the Hunterian Museum) or to the south (for example, the Burrell Collection), some form of transportation is required.

By Subway As befits the Second City of the Empire, Glasgow is the only city in the United Kingdom beside London that has a subway, or underground, as it's called here. It was built at the end of the last century and takes the simple form of two circular routes, one going clockwise and the other counterclockwise. All trains will eventually bring you back to where you started, and the complete circle takes 24 minutes. This extremely simple and effective system operated relatively unchanged in ancient carriages (cars) until the 1970s when it was entirely modernized. The tunnels are relatively small, so the trains themselves are tiny (by London standards) and this, together with the affection in which the system is held and the bright orange paintwork of the trains, gives it the nickname the Clockwork Orange.

Flat fares and day tickets are available. Trains run regularly Monday to Saturday, with a limited Sunday service, and connect the city center with the West End (for the university) and the city south of the River Clyde. Look for the orange "U" signs marking the 15 stations. Further information is available from the Strathclyde Passenger Transport Executive Travel Centre, St Enoch Square (tel. 041/226–4826).

By Car As has been suggested, a car is not necessary in the city center and, indeed, as with all city centers, it presents a problem with parking, though most of the newer hotels have their own parking lots. If you are staying a short distance from the city center or have a rental car anyway, getting through the city is easy. Simply use the motorway. But if you want to come into the city center, perhaps to go to the theater, then Strathclyde PTE offers a number of park-and-ride schemes at underground stations (Kelvinbridge, Bridge St., and Shields Rd.) that will bring you into the city center in a few minutes. The West End museums and galleries have their own car parks, as does the Burrell, so there are no problems there. Remember, illegal parking in the city center causes hazards and traffic jams. Parking wardens are constantly on patrol, and you will be fined if you park illegally. Multistory parking garages are open 24 hours a day at the following locations: Anderston Centre, George Street, Waterloo Place, Mitchell Street, Cambridge Street, and Buchanan Street.

By Train In addition to the underground, the Glasgow area has an extensive network of suburban railway services. They are still called the "Blue Trains" by local people, even though most of them are now orange. Look for signs to LOW LEVEL TRAINS at Queen Street and Central stations. Suburban and Scotrail trains run westward north of the Clyde to Clydebank, Dumbarton (for the castle), Balloch (for Loch Lomond), and Helensburgh (for the Hill House) and westward south of the Clyde to Paisley, Port Glasgow, Greenock, Gourock (for ferry to Dunoon), Wemyss Bay (for ferry to Rothesay—and a superb cast-iron walkway to the pier), Largs (for ferry to Cumbrae), Ardrossan (for ferry to Arran), and Ayr (for Burns Country).

To the south of the city, trains run to the Burrell Collection in Pollok Park (station: Pollokshaws West), to Kilmarnock, Neilston, East Kilbride, Hamilton (for Chatelherault), Motherwell, Lanark (for New Lanark), and Shotts. North and east trains run to Coatbridge and Airdrie, Cumbernauld, Croy, Bishopbriggs, Bearsden, and Milngavie (pronounced *mulguy*).

For further information on all these services and a free map, call Strathclyde PTE (tel. 041/226–4826) or Scotrail (tel. 041/204–2844). Details are also available from the tourist board.

By Bus The many different bus companies cooperate with the underground and Scotrail to produce the Family Day Tripper Ticket, which is an excellent way to get around the whole area from Loch Lomond to Ayrshire. Tickets are a good value and are available from the PTE and at main railway and bus stations and post offices.

By Taxi Metered taxis (usually black and of the London type) can be found at taxi ranks all over the city center. Most are radio controlled, so they can be called very easily. Some have also been specially adapted to take wheelchairs. In the street, a taxi can be hailed if it is displaying its illuminated FOR HIRE sign. Taxi firms also arrange tours of the city. They vary from one to three hours, usually at a fixed price. They can be booked in advance, and you can be picked up and dropped off where you like. Contact the **Taxi Owners Association** (tel. 041/332–7070) or the **Taxi Cab Association** (tel. 041/332–6666).

By Limousine The chauffeur-driven limousine companies listed under airport transfers (*see* Arriving and Departing by Plane, *above*) will also provide tours of the city center and beyond.

Guided Tours

Orientation Glasgow has a compact city center, so walking tours and short taxi or bus tours will soon give you a flavor of the place. Its superb location also makes it an ideal base from which to enjoy day tours of the Scottish countryside. Burns Country, the gardens of Galloway, the islands of the Clyde, Loch Lomond, the Trossachs, and Argyll are only about an hour or so from the city center, as is Edinburgh. Most city bus tours last about two hours and cover the city center, the West End, and the Burrell Collection.

Discovering Glasgow tours by single-decker bus leave daily from the west side of George Square. The Greater Glasgow Tourist Board (*see* Important Addresses and Numbers, *above*), can give further information and arrange reservations. **Strathclyde** buses (the orange ones) also follow a similar route from George Square. (Tickets may be purchased on the bus, or call 041/226–4826 for information.) Both companies also run day tours from the city to some of the places mentioned above, and details of longer tours northward to the Highlands and Islands can be obtained from the tourist board.

Special-Interest **The Scottish Tourist Guides Association** (tel. 041/776–1052) can tailor a tour to suit you. Standard fixed fees apply. For tours of whiskey distilleries, *see* Sightseeing Checklists, *below*.

Classique Sun Saloon Luxury Coaches (tel. 041/889–4050) operates restored buses from the '50s, '60s, and '70s on tours to the north and west.

Boat Tours There are cruises on the Clyde daily, starting from the Broomielaw, the traditional departure pier for over 100 years for vacationers on the river. Services are operated by **Clyde Marine** (tel. 041/221–8702) and depart hourly. You can book through the tourist board or call Clyde Marine directly. For a longer cruise, no one who loves the nostalgia of old ships should miss the *Waverley* (tel. 041/221–8152), the world's last oceangoing paddle steamer, which sails down the Clyde to Largs, Dunoon, Rothesay, and elsewhere during the day in summer and offers evening cruises. You can make reservations through the tourist board or call direct. Cruises are also available on Loch Lomond and to the islands in the Firth of Clyde; details are available from the tourist board.

Helicopter Tours **Clyde Helicopters** (tel. 041/226–4261) swoop over downtown Glasgow and the immediate environs, taking off from the helipad at the Scottish Exhibition Centre. Trips normally last 15 to 30 minutes. Call for more information.

Personal Guides and Walking Tours In each case your first contact should be the tourist board, where you can find out about special walks on a given day. The **Scottish Tourist Guides Association** (tel. 041/776–1052) also offers an all-around service.

Exploring Glasgow

Orientation

At the heart of Glasgow is its commercial prosperity laid over a sleepy medieval burgh, so it is fitting that the first walking tour of the city should include the ancient cathedral; the oldest house in Glasgow; the High Street; and the center of medieval activity, the Merchant City, which developed as Glasgow prospered. Included, too, is the river on which Glasgow's trade across the Atlantic developed. The river is always at the center of the city, cutting it in half and offering often surprising views across to the buildings on the other side. In this central part of the city are some of the best examples of the confidence and exuberance in architecture that so characterized the Glasgow of 100 years ago and that today are experiencing a renaissance and a newfound appreciation.

The second tour goes westward and encompasses that other side of Glasgow, often forgotten in the old, and now no longer justified, image as a grimy city of heavy industry. Glasgow has had a university since 1451, making it the third-oldest in Scotland after St. Andrews and Aberdeen, and at least 130 years ahead of the University of Edinburgh. It has thrived as a center of educational excellence, particularly in the sciences. The university buildings are set in parkland, reminding the visitor that Glasgow is a city with more green space per citizen than any other in Europe. It is also a city of museums and art galleries, having benefited from the generosity of industrial and commercial philanthropists and from the deep-seated desire of the city fathers to place Glasgow at the forefront of British cities.

The first walk is relatively flat and almost entirely on city streets. There is much to see, but be careful about crossing roads. Use pedestrian crossings at traffic lights and remember to check which way traffic is moving. Not only do they drive on the left, but many of the streets are one way, so traffic may actually be coming from the right. The second walk is away from the city center and is partly through parkland. It is quieter and less bustling, and there are some gentle slopes to walk up.

Highlights for First-time Visitors

Burrell Collection and Pollok House (*see* Off the Beaten Track)
City Chambers (*see* Tour 1)
Glasgow Cathedral (*see* Tour 1)
Glasgow School of Art (*see* Tour 2)
Hunterian Art Gallery (*see* Tour 2)
Kelvingrove Museum and Art Gallery (*see* Tour 2)
Merchant City (*see* Tour 1)

Museum of Transport (*see* Tour 2)
People's Palace (*see* Tour 1)
Tenement House (*see* Tour 2)

Tour 1: Medieval Glasgow and the Merchant City

Numbers in the margin correspond to points of interest on the Glasgow map.

① **George Square,** the focal point of Glasgow's business district, is the natural starting point for any walking tour. It's in the very heart of Glasgow and convenient to the Buchanan Street bus and underground stations and parking lot, as well as to the Queen Street railway station. The tourist information center of the Greater Glasgow Tourist Board is also close by on St. Vincent Place. The square itself is lined with an impressive array of statues of worthies from days gone by: Queen Victoria; Scotland's national poet Robert Burns; the inventor and developer of the steam engine, James Watt; and Prime Minister William Gladstone. And towering above them all is Scotland's champion, Sir Walter Scott.

② The magnificent Italian Renaissance-style **City Chambers** on the east side of the square was opened by Queen Victoria in 1888. Among the outstanding features of the interior are the vaulted ceiling of the entrance hall, marble and alabaster staircases, and the banqueting hall, as well as a number of the smaller suites, each furnished in different woods. *George Sq., tel. 041/227–4017. Free guided tours weekdays at 10:30 and 2:30.*

Leave George Square by the northeast corner and head eastward through a not particularly pretty part of the city along Cathedral Street, past the University of Strathclyde. Turn left **③** at High Street, then go up the hill to **Glasgow Cathedral,** an unusual double church, one above the other. Dedicated to St. Mungo, Glasgow's patron saint, the cathedral was begun in the 12th century and completed about 300 years later. It was spared the ravages of the Reformation, which destroyed so many of Scotland's medieval churches, because the trade guilds of Glasgow regarded it as their own church and defended it. In the lower church is the splendid crypt of St. Mungo, who is sometimes also called St. Kentigern. (*Kentigern* means "chief word," while *Mungo* is perhaps a nickname meaning "dear name.") The site of the tomb has been revered since the 6th century, when St. Mungo founded a church there. *Cathedral St., tel. 031/244–3101. Admission free. Open Apr.–Sept., Mon.–Sat. 9:30–7, Sun. 2–7; Oct.–Mar., Mon.–Sat. 9:30–4, Sun. 2–4.*

The Cathedral Square area has been considerably smartened up over the past few years, as have some of the statues in it. One fascinating if macabre place just off the square is the **④** **Necropolis,** an ancient burying ground with some extraordinarily elaborate Victorian graves, watched over by a statue of John Knox. *Behind Glasgow Cathedral, tel. 041/649–0331. Check for opening times.*

⑤ Opposite the cathedral, across Castle Street, is **Provand's Lordship,** Glasgow's oldest house. It was built in 1471 by Bishop Andrew Muirhead as the manse of the Hospital of St. Nicholas. Mary, Queen of Scots, is said to have stayed here. After her day, however, the house fell into decline and was used alter-

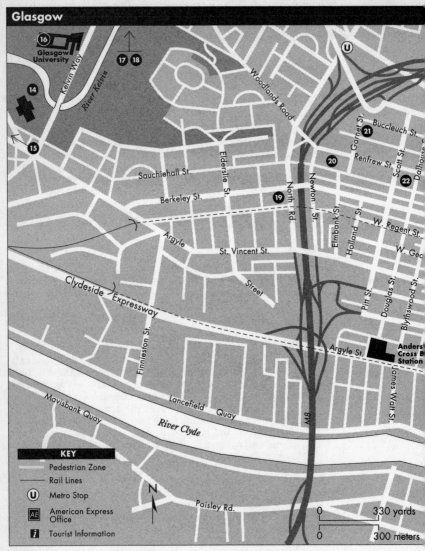

Glasgow

KEY
- Pedestrian Zone
- Rail Lines
- Ⓤ Metro Stop
- AE American Express Office
- ℹ Tourist Information

0 — 330 yards
0 — 300 meters

N

The Barras, **7**
Botanic Gardens, **18**
City Chambers, **2**
George Square, **1**
Glasgow Green, **8**
Glasgow School of Art, **22**
Glasgow Cross, **6**
Glasgow Cathedral, **3**
Hunterian Art Gallery, **17**

Hunterian Museum, **16**
Hutcheson's Hall, **10**
Kelvingrove, **14**
Mitchell Library, **19**
Museum of Transport, **15**
Necropolis, **4**
People's Palace, **9**
Provand's Lordship, **5**

Regimental Museum of the Royal Highland Fusiliers, **20**
Royal Exchange, **12**
Scottish Stock Exchange, **13**
Tenement House, **21**
Virginia Court, **11**

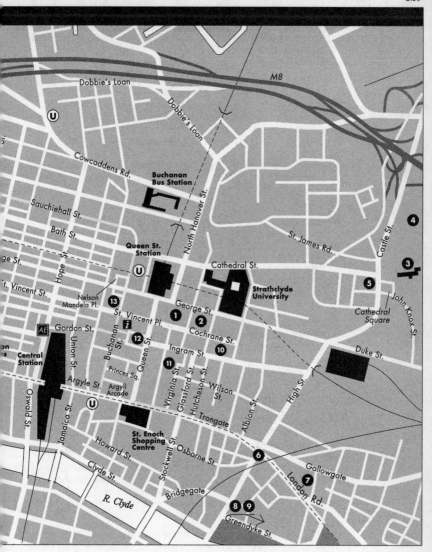

nately as a sweet shop, a soft-drink factory, the home of the
city hangman, and a junk shop. It was eventually rescued by
the city and turned into a museum. Exhibits show the house as
it might have looked in its heyday. *Castle St., tel. 041/552–
8819. Admission free. Open Mon.–Sat. 10–5, Sun. noon–6.*

Retrace your steps down Castle Street and High Street. Look
for the Greek goddess Pallas on top of the former bank building,
⑥ before reaching the **Tolbooth Steeple** at **Glasgow Cross.** This
was the very center of the medieval city. The mercat cross,
topped by a unicorn, marked the spot where merchants met,
where the market was held, and where criminals were executed. Here, too, was the *tron*, or weighbeam, used to check
merchants' weights, installed in 1491. The Tolbooth Steeple itself dates from 1626 and served as the civic center and place
where travelers entering the city paid tolls.

Continue east along London Road about a quarter of a mile and
⑦ you'll come to **The Barras** ("barrows" or pushcarts), Scotland's
largest indoor market, a mecca for those addicted to searching
through piles of junk for bargains. Open only on weekends, this
is probably the nearest Scotland gets to a flea market. The atmosphere is always good humored, and you can find just about
anything here, in any condition, from very old model railroads
to almost-new cheese rolls. *Tel. 041/552–7258. Admission free.
Open weekends 9–5.*

⑧ Just down Greendyke Street from London Road is **Glasgow
Green** by the River Clyde. Glasgow's oldest park has a long
history as a favorite spot for public recreation and political demonstrations. Note the Nelson Column, erected long before
London's; the Arch, now the finish line for the thousands of
runners of the Glasgow Half Marathon; and the Templeton
Business Centre, designed late the last century in the style of
the Doge's Palace in Venice. The most significant building in
⑨ the park is the **People's Palace,** an impressive Victorian red
sandstone building that houses an intriguing museum dedicated to the city's social history; included among the exhibits is
one devoted to the ordinary folk of Glasgow, called "The People's Story." Behind the museum are the well-restored Winter
Gardens, a relatively sheltered spot favored by visitors who
want to escape the often-chilly winds whistling across the
green. *Tel. 041/554–0223. Admission free. Open Mon.–Sat.
10–5, Sun. noon–6.*

Return to the Tolbooth Steeple and walk westward along
Trongate. This is where the powerful "tobacco barons" who
traded with the Americas presided. On the right, down Albion
Street, are the offices of Glasgow's daily papers, the *Glasgow
Herald* and the *Evening Times.* Farther down on the left, at
New Wynd, is the Tron Steeple, all that remains of a church
burned down in 1793 when a joke by the local chapter of the
Hell-Fire Club got out of hand. The rebuilt church has now
been converted into the Tron Theatre.

Turn right into Hutcheson Street, and you'll find yourself in
Glasgow's **"Merchant City."** You can enjoy the architecture of
this area, although you may be diverted by the designer boutiques springing up in this part of town. The City and County
Buildings on your right at the top were built in 1842 to house
civil servants; note the impressive arrangement of bays and
Corinthian columns. At the end of the street, just south of

⑩ George Square, look for **Hutcheson's Hall,** a visitor center, shop, and regional office for the National Trust for Scotland. This elegant, neoclassical building was designed by David Hamilton in 1802. The hall was originally a hospice founded by two brothers, George and Thomas Hutcheson; you can see their statues in niches in the facade. *158 Ingram St., tel. 041/552–8391. Admission free. Open weekdays 9–5, Sat. 10–4. Shop open Mon.–Sat. 10–4.*

Turn west into Ingram Street and note particularly the extensive restoration work that has been done in this area; a number of fine buildings have recently emerged from the grime. There are a great number of specialty shops in the area and, for those who want to rest weary feet, plenty of cafés and restaurants.

Turn left down Glassford Street to see the **Trades House** on the right, which has a facade built in 1791 to designs by Robert Adam. Then turn right along Wilson Street to reach Virginia Street, another favorite haunt of Glasgow's tobacco merchants. **⑪** At No. 33, a former tobacco exchange survives. Nearby, **Virginia Court,** somewhat faded now, also echoes those far-off days. Peer through the bars of the gates and note the wagon-wheel ruts still visible in the roadway. Nearby is a good range of antiques shops, notably the Virginia Galleries.

Walk northward up Virginia Street back to Ingram Street. To the left you'll have a good view down to the elegant **Royal Exchange Square** and the **Royal Exchange** itself. Designed by **⑫** David Hamilton and finished in 1829, the Exchange was a meeting place for merchants and traders but was transformed in the 1950s into **Stirling's Library.** It incorporates the mansion built in 1780 by William Cunninghame, one of the wealthiest of the tobacco lords. Royal Exchange Square leads, for pedestrians, westward to the pedestrian-zone shopping area of Buchanan Street. The Princes Square shopping area on the east side has a particularly good selection of specialty shops; farther south across Argyle Street is the massive new St. Enoch Centre, a huge glass-and-metal monument to consumerism. Of more modest proportions is the elegant Argyll Arcade at the foot of Buchanan Street, built in 1827.

Looking to the west on Argyle Street, you'll see the large railway bridge supporting the tracks going into **Central Station,** known as the "Heilanman's Umbrella," because it was the point of meeting for so many Highlanders who had moved to Glasgow in search of better economic opportunities. Pause to look at the lovely iron arcading of **Gardner's Warehouse** at 1855 Jamaica Street before turning north. As you make your way up Union Street, note the extraordinary architecture of Nos. 84–100, the so-called **Egyptian Halls,** designed and built in 1871 by Alexander "Greek" Thomson. At the junction with Gordon Street look left to the restored frontage of Central Station and right to the **Ca' d'Oro** building, dating from 1872 and restored after a fire in 1987.

From here continue north to St. Vincent Place and then to Nelson Mandela Place, also called St. George's Place. If you want **⑬** to see today's commercial life, visit the **Scottish Stock Exchange** on Buchanan Street, worthwhile for the exterior alone: It was built in 1877 in an ornate "French Venetian" style. *7 Nelson Mandela Pl., tel. 041/221–7060, ext. 25424/25434. Admission free. Visitors gallery open weekdays 9–6:30.*

Pause briefly at the handsome **Merchants' House** on the corner of West George Street and George Square (now the home of Glasgow's Chamber of Commerce) to look at the golden sailing ship against the sky, a reminder of the importance of trade to Glasgow's prosperity. *W. side of George Sq., tel. 041/221–8272. Admission free. Hall and anterooms may be seen by arrangement. Open May–Sept., Mon.–Fri. 2–4.*

Tour 2: The West End

This walk could really start in any one of several locations and need not form a continuous circuit. Included are a number of museums and galleries, each of which could take up an enjoyable day in itself, so you could think of this as the basis of several walks. You can use the suggested route here to acquaint yourself with the rich legacy of education, culture, art, and parkland that is to be found in Glasgow's West End.

A good place to start is at the city's main art gallery and muse-⓯ um, **Kelvingrove**—looking like a combination of cathedral and castle—in Kelvingrove Park, west of the M8 beltway, at the junction of Sauchiehall and Argyle streets (note that Sauchiehall is pronounced *socky-hall*). There are parking facilities, and plenty of buses go there from downtown. The building is a magnificently ornamented red sandstone edifice dating from the early part of this century. There has always been debate as to which facade is the front and which is the back. However you enter, Kelvingrove houses what is claimed to be Britain's finest civic collection of British and Continental paintings, with 17th-century Dutch art, a selection from the French Barbizon school, French Impressionism, Scottish art from the 17th century to the present, silver, ceramics, European armor, even Egyptian archaeological finds. *Tel. 041/357–3929. Admission free. Open weekdays 10–5, Sat. 10–10, Sun. noon–6.*

Across Argyle Street in the Old Kelvin Hall exhibition center is ⓯ the **Museum of Transport**. Here Glasgow's history of locomotive building is dramatically displayed with full-size exhibits. The collection of Clyde-built ship models is world famous. Anyone who remembers Britain in the 1950s will be able to wallow in nostalgia at the re-created street scene from that era. *Kelvin Hall, 1 Bunhouse Rd., tel. 041/357–3929. Admission free. Open weekdays 10–5, Sat. 10–10, Sun. noon–6.*

Kelvingrove Park takes its name from the River Kelvin, which flows through it. Lord Kelvin, the scientist who pioneered a great deal of work in electricity, is remembered by a statue in the park. The city purchased the land for the park in 1852, and, apart from the abundance of statues of prominent Glaswegians, the park is graced by a massive fountain commemorating a Lord Provost of Glasgow from the 1850s, a duck pond, a play area, a small open-air theater, and lots of exotic trees. It can be a charming retreat from the noise and bustle of the city.

As you walk up Kelvin Way through the trees, the skyline to your left is dominated by the Gilbert Scott building, the University of Glasgow's main edifice. Built just over a century ago, the building is a good example of the Gothic Revival style. Leave Kelvingrove Park and turn left up University Avenue, past the Memorial Gates, which were erected in 1951 to celebrate the university's 500th birthday. On either side of the road here are two important galleries, both maintained by the uni-

versity. They house the collections of William Hunter, an 18th-
century Glasgow doctor who assembled a staggering quantity
of extremely valuable material. On the south side of University
Avenue, in the Victorian part of the university in the park, is
16 the **Hunterian Museum,** the city's oldest (1807), which displays
Hunter's hoards of coins, manuscripts, scientific instruments,
and archaeological artifacts in a striking Victorian building.
*Glasgow University, tel. 041/330–4221. Admission free. Open
weekdays 9:30–5, Sat. 9:30–1.*

17 Even more interesting is the **Hunterian Art Gallery,** in an unremarkable building from the 1970s across the road. The gallery
houses the doctor's collection of paintings, together with prints
and drawings by Reynolds, Rodin, Rembrandt, and Tintoretto,
as well as a major collection of paintings by James McNeill
Whistler, who had a great affection for the city that bought one
of his earliest paintings. Also in the gallery is a replica of
Charles Rennie Mackintosh's town house, which used to stand
nearby. The rooms are all furnished with Mackintosh's distinctive Art Nouveau chairs, tables, beds, and cupboards, while
the walls are decorated in the equally distinctive style devised
by him and his wife, Margaret. *Glasgow University, Hillhead
St., tel. 041/330–5431. Admission to gallery free; Mackintosh
House 50p weekdays and Sat. morning. Open weekdays
9:30–5, Sat. 9:30–1. Mackintosh House closed weekdays
12:30–1:30.*

At this point you can either make a small detour to the Botanic
Gardens and return along the banks of the River Kelvin to
Kelvingrove Park or you go directly through some of Glasgow's elegant 19th-century districts to the extreme northwest
of the downtown area, where the rest of the tour resumes.

18 The walk from the university to the **Botanic Gardens** is unfortunately not very exciting, but it's worth the effort. Continue
along University Avenue and turn right at Byres Road, going
as far as Great Western Road and the Grosvenor Hotel. The
gardens are across the busy Great Western Road. Begun by the
Royal Botanical Institute of Glasgow in 1842, the displays here
include an herb garden, a wide range of tropical plants, and a
world-famous collection of orchids. The most spectacular building in the complex is the **Kibble Palace,** built in 1873; it was originally the conservatory of a Victorian eccentric named John
Kibble. Its domed, interlinked, almost spaceshiplike greenhouses have a unique collection of tree ferns, palm trees, and
plants from temperate climates, together with appropriately
exotic Victorian statues. Elsewhere on the grounds are more
conventional greenhouses, as well as well-maintained lawns
and colorful flower beds. *Great Western Rd., tel. 041/334–2422.
Admission free. Gardens open daily 7–dusk; Kibble Palace
open daily, noon–4:45.*

After leaving the Botanic Gardens, cross the River Kelvin on
St. Margaret Drive just past the BBC Scotland building. Turn
right, then right again down the steps to the Kelvin Walkway
on the north bank of the river. (Farther upstream the Kelvin
Walkway connects with the West Highland Way, an official
long-distance footpath leading to Fort William, approximately
100 miles away.) The walkway headed downstream back toward the city center first crosses a footbridge, then passes old
mill buildings and goes under Belmont Street and the Great
Western Road at Kelvinbridge before passing Kelvinbridge

underground station and going under the Gibson Street bridge and back into Kelvingrove Park.

At this point, you can choose to take one of the paths up the hill and explore the stately Victorian crescents and streets of the park area or you can take the lower road past the fountain and head directly back to Sauchiehall Street. Whichever way you choose, you should end up, having walked eastward, at the point where Sauchiehall Street crosses the M8 motorway. Down North Street to your right (southward) you'll see the front of **Mitchell Library,** the largest public reference library in Europe; it houses over a million volumes, including what is claimed to be the largest collection on Robert Burns in the world. The library's founder, Stephen Mitchell, who died in 1874 (the same year the library was founded), is commemorated by a bust in the entrance hall. Minerva, goddess of wisdom, looks down from the library's dome, encouraging the library's users and frowning at the drivers thundering along the motorway just in front of her. The western facade (at the back) is particularly beautiful. *North St., tel. 041/221–7030. Admission free. Open weekdays 9:30–9, Sat. 9:30–5.*

Cross the M8 motorway, past the so-called bridge to nowhere— a modern monument to the follies of urban redevelopment and now itself being redeveloped—and continue down Sauchiehall Street to the **Regimental Museum of the Royal Highland Fusiliers,** which displays the history of this famous regiment and the men who served in it. Exhibits include medals, badges, and uniforms. *518 Sauchiehall St., tel. 041/332–0961. Admission free. Open Mon.–Thurs. 9–4:30, Fri. 9–4.*

Turn up Garnet Street and go right to the top, then down to Buccleuch (pronounced buck-*loo*) Street. Turn left to reach the **Tenement House,** a very special find tucked away from normal tourist routes. This is an ordinary, simple city-center apartment that was occupied from 1911 to 1965 by the same lady, Miss Agnes Toward, who never seemed to throw anything away. What is left is a fascinating time capsule, painstakingly preserved with her everyday furniture and belongings. The red sandstone tenement building itself dates from 1892. *145 Buccleuch St., tel. 041/333–0183. Admission: £1.20 adults, 60p children. Open early Jan.–Mar. and early Nov.–mid-Dec., weekends 2–4. Apr.–Oct., daily noon–5.*

Coming out of the Tenement House, turn east and go back along Buccleuch Street as far as Scott Street. Turn south on Scott Street, noticing the mural that reflects the name of the area, Garnethill, then onto Renfrew Street to reach Charles Rennie Mackintosh's masterpiece, the **Glasgow School of Art.** The building—exterior and interior, structure, furnishings, and decoration—forms a unified whole, reflecting the inventive genius of this man, who was only 28 years old when he won the competition for the design of the building. Architects and designers from all over the world come to admire it, but because it is a working school of art, general visitor access is sometimes limited. Conducted tours are available, and there is always the chance that you can have a quick look inside. It's best to call ahead for more information. *167 Renfrew St., tel. 041/332–9797.*

Time Out The **Willow Tearoom** (above a jeweler's shop at 217 Sauchiehall St.) is restored to its original archetypal Art Nouveau design by Charles Rennie Mackintosh, right down to the decorated tables and chairs. The building was designed by Mackintosh in 1903 for Miss Kate Cranston, who ran a chain of tearooms. The tree motifs are echoed in the street address, since *sauchie* is an old Scots word for *willow*.

To return to the city center you can either continue down Sauchiehall Street or turn south down Blythswood Street, noting the elegant Blythswood Square (1823–29).

Glasgow for Free

Most of Glasgow's museums, churches, galleries, and all the parks are free. Street entertainment and free open-air concerts are not very common, but during the specific festivals, such as Mayfest (May) and Streetbiz (August), the city streets take on a livelier appearance and become free attractions for visitors. Major shopping areas, such as Princes Square and the St. Enoch Centre, also have entertainments, as do some of the art galleries, cafés, and restaurants.

What to See and Do with Children

Many of Glasgow's attractions are also suitable for children, in small doses. The tourist board (*see* Important Addresses and Numbers in Essential Information, *above*) can provide detailed information and can tell you about swimming pools and sports centers. Most of Glasgow's parks have tennis, lawn-bowling, and putting facilities. In addition, the following attractions are available at individual parks: boating, dry ski slope, windsurfing, croquet, trampolines, and table tennis. Check with the Parks Department (tel. 041/227–5064 or 041/227–5066) for details.

Eastwood Butterfly Kingdom, set in lovely Rouken Glen Park not far from the city center, offers a touch of the exotic, with free-flying butterflies and moths in a tropical setting. There is also a tearoom and gift shop. *Rouken Glen Park, tel. 041/620–2084.*

Glasgow Zoo, situated on a wooded hillside above the North Calder Water, is a modern open-plan collection with a fine tiger house and a large number of deer, camels, rhinos, and other exotic animals. Inside, the zoo specializes in pythons, boas, and other reptiles; the reptile breeding house is a particularly popular attraction. The zoo is at Calder Park in Uddingston, 6 miles from Glasgow city center, at the end of London Road and near the M74. There is ample parking. *Tel. 041/771–1185. Admission: £2 adults, £1 children. Open Sept.–June, daily 10-5; July–Aug., daily 10–6.*

Haggs Castle, an ancient house of the Maxwell family, has been given over entirely to children. Adults are tolerated if they behave themselves. Many of the rooms are designed to illustrate what life was like for children in days gone by; during school holidays the museum runs an extensive interactive program aimed at helping children experience history firsthand. *100 St. Andrews Dr., tel. 041/427–2725. Admission free. Open Mon.–Sat. 10–5, Sun. noon–6.*

The **Museum of Education** is of great interest to children (even though some profess to hate it). Located in Scotland Street

School, one of Charles Rennie Mackintosh's elegant buildings (1906), the museum's classrooms are fitted out in the styles of different historical periods, and the staff is dressed in appropriate costume. *225 Scotland St., tel. 041/429–1202. Admission free. Open Mon.–Sat. 10–5, Sun 2–5.*

People's Palace (*see* Tour 1)

Tenement House (*see* Tour 2)

Victoria Park has a pleasant boating lake and an arboretum, as well as a remarkable Fossil Grove, where the fossilized stumps of trees said to be over 330 million years old have been preserved. (Glasgow has obviously been laying out excellent parks for a long time.) *Victoria Park Drive N, off Airthrey Ave., tel. 041/959–2128. Admission free. Open Mon.–Sat. 8– dusk, Sun. 10–dusk; Fossil Grove open by appointment.*

Off the Beaten Track

Pollok Country Park **Pollok Country Park** provides a peaceful green oasis off Paisley Road, just 3 miles southwest of the city center. (You can get there by taxi or car, by city bus, or by a train from Glasgow Central Station to Pollokshaws West Station.) The key attraction here is the **Burrell Collection,** Scotland's finest art collection. A new, custom-built, airy, and elegant building houses treasures of all descriptions, from ancient Egyptian, Greek, and Roman artifacts to Chinese ceramics, bronzes, and jade to medieval tapestries, stained glass, Rodin sculptures, and exquisite French Impressionist paintings—all from the magpie collection of an eccentric millionaire, Sir William Burrell. The building was designed with large glass walls so that the items on display relate to their surroundings: art and nature in perfect harmony. *Tel. 041/649–7151. Admission free. Open Mon., Tues. and Thurs.–Sat. 10–5; Wed. 10–10; Sun. noon–6.*

Also located in Pollok Country Park is **Pollok House,** which dates from the mid-1700s and contains the Stirling Maxwell Collection of paintings, including works by El Greco, Murillo, Goya, Signorelli, and William Blake. Fine 18th- and early 19th-century furniture, silver, glass, and porcelain are also on display. The house has fine gardens and looks over the White Cart River and Pollok Park, where, amid mature trees and abundant wildlife, the City of Glasgow's own highland cattle peacefully graze. *Tel. 041/632–0274. Admission free. Open Mon., Tues., Thurs, Fri. 10–5, Wed. 10–10, Sun. noon–6.*

Together, Pollok Park, Pollok House, and the Burrell Collection represent one of the greatest examples of generosity to a city anywhere in Britain. The park and the house were given to the city in 1966 by Mrs. Anne Maxwell Macdonald, and the Burrell Collection was presented to the city by Sir William and Lady Burrell in 1944.

Paisley Once a distinct burgh in its own right, Paisley is now part of the Greater Glasgow suburban area. If your taste runs toward the urban rather than the rural, this town offers plenty of gritty character, largely because of vestiges of its industrial heritage. Paisley can be easily reached by taxi, car, or bus. Trains also run regularly from Glasgow Central to Paisley Gilmour Street Station. Town trail leaflets are available from the tourist information center.

Paisley's industrial prosperity came from textiles and, in particular, from the woolen Paisley shawl. The internationally recognized Paisley pattern is based on the shape of a palm shoot, an ancient Babylonian fertility symbol brought to Britain by way of Kashmir. The full story of the pattern and of the innovative weaving techniques introduced in Paisley is told in the **Paisley Museum and Art Gallery,** which has a world-famous shawl collection. *High St., tel. 041/889–3151. Admission free. Open Mon.–Sat. 10–5; closed public holidays.*

The life of the workers in the textile industry is brought to life in **Sma' Shot Cottages,** re-creations of millworkers' houses. *11/ 17 George Pl., tel. 041/814–2513. Admission free. Open May– Sept., Wed. and Sat. 1–5 or by appointment.*

The name of Coats, one of the world's largest manufacturers of cotton thread, is recalled in the impressive red sandstone **Coats Memorial Baptist Church,** as well as in **Coats Observatory,** with its 100-year-old weather-recording apparatus and telescopes. Thanks to the recent installation of a satellite receiver, it is now one of the best observatories in the country. *Oakshaw St., tel. 041/889–2013. Admission free. Open Mon., Tues., Thurs. 2–8; Wed., Fri., Sat. 10–5.*

Paisley's 12th-century Cluniac **Abbey** dominates the town center. Almost completely destroyed in 1307 and then rebuilt after the Battle of Bannockburn, the abbey is traditionally associated with Walter Fitzallan, the High Steward of Scotland, who gave his name to the Stewart monarchs of Scotland. Outstanding features include the fine stone-vaulted roof and stained glass of the choir. Paisley Abbey is today a busy parish church. *Tel. 041/889–7654. Admission free; group visits by arrangement. Open Mon.–Sat. 10–12:30 and 1:30–3:30.*

Shopping

The old image of industrial Glasgow has changed considerably in recent times as the city has strenuously shrugged off its poor-cousin-to-Edinburgh label. This is evidenced by the many stores, individual shops, and malls that have enhanced Glasgow's style without sacrificing its undoubted character.

Department Stores

The three main department stores are **Arnott's, Debenham's,** and **Frasers;** other High Street names—**Littlewoods, British Home Stores,** and **Marks and Spencer**—are also represented. Frasers is the store most worth visiting, not only for its exceptional interior and display (*see* Buchanan Street, *below*), but also for its variety of designer names and helpful, friendly staff.

Shopping Districts

Argyle Street/ St. Enoch Square Start at St. Enoch Square (which is also the main underground station); it houses the St. Enoch Shopping Centre. Walking out of the square, you will see **Arnott's** department store immediately on the left. Heading east toward the main pedestrian area of Argyle Street, you will find all the usual High Street chain stores. The recently much-improved **Debenham's** department store may be of particular interest (it can also be entered from the St. Enoch Centre). The pedestrian zone on Argyle Street is invariably overcrowded, especially on Saturday, and is certainly not for the impatient shopper. An interesting diversion off Argyle Street is the **Argyll Arcade,** which is the largest collection of jewelers under one roof in Scotland. This L-shape arcade, built in 1904, houses several locally based jewelers and a few shops specializing in antique jewelry. To be recommended are **Bercotts** (56 Argyll Arcade) and the arcade branch of **Laing the Jeweller** (48 Argyll Arcade) for handmade and contemporary designs, while **Mr. Harold** (33 Argyll Arcade) has a good collection of antique and reproduction designs. Because these shops are privately owned, it is not unheard of to get a cash discount (try asking, you may be lucky). The other end of the Argyll Arcade leads to Buchanan Street.

St. Enoch Square/Argyle Street can be reached on the underground system and directly by the internal rail system. Many buses run along either part of Argyle Street or streets nearby.

Buchanan Street This is probably Glasgow's premier shopping street and is almost totally pedestrianized. Immediately opposite the exit of the Argyll Arcade is **Frasers** (45 Buchanan St.), Glasgow's largest and most interesting department store. Frasers is a Glasgow institution, and its wares reflect much of Glasgow's new and traditional images, leading European designer clothes and fabrics combining with home-produced articles, such as tweeds, tartans, glass, and ceramics. The magnificent interior is itself worth a visit, set off by the grand staircase rising to various floors and balconies. Other shops to look out for in Buchanan Street include **R. G. Lawrie Ltd** (110 Buchanan St.), which specializes in highland outfitting, Scottish gifts, woolens, and cashmere, and **Pitlochry Knitwear Company** (130 Buchanan St.), less traditional and perhaps a little more fashionable, which sells high-quality pure-wool suits and a good selection of knitwear for men, women, and children. You will find excellent outerwear at **Graham Tiso** (129 Buchanan St.). Household names like Laura Ashley, Liberty, Jaeger, and Roland Cartier are found here as well. Buchanan Street also sports the entrances to the excellent **Princes Square** development. Elegant and stylish, this houses many of the finest specialty stores.

Running perpendicular to Buchanan Street, about halfway along to the left, is Gordon Street. Along this street, toward Central Station, you will find **Waterstones** bookstore and one or two other smaller shops of interest, including **Catherine Shaw** (24 Gordon St.), where there is an excellent range of specially designed and unique Charles Rennie Mackintosh–style clocks and jewelry.

For another shop worthy of mention, follow Buchanan Street to St. Vincent Street, turn to your left, and you will find **Graham's** tobacconist (71 St. Vincent St.). This shop has a tremendous variety of tobaccos and pipes. Much of Glasgow's wealth was generated by the Tobacco Lords during the 17th and 18th centuries; at Graham's you will experience a little of that colorful history.

Buchanan Street runs perpendicular to Argyle Street. At one end are Buchanan Street underground and Scotrail Queen Street stations.

Merchant City   This area on the edge of the city center is a recent upscale development consisting of some new buildings and old warehouses converted into living space. It is home to many of Glasgow's young and upwardly mobile. Shopping here is expensive, but the area is certainly worth visiting for those who are seeking the young Glasgow style.

Visit **The Warehouse** (61–65 Glassford St.) or **Blondes** (18 Wilson St.) if you are looking for something exclusive to wear. For younger people, **Miki** (Garth St.) has an excellent selection of designer outfits for children and teenagers. Top off the outfit with a creation from **The Hat Shop** (Wilson St.), where there are some really unusual concoctions. Also worth a visit are **In House** (24–26 Wilson St.) and **Casa Fina** (2 Wilson St.), for stylish and modern furniture and giftware. Wander around **Stockwell China Bazaar** (67–77 Glassford St.) for a huge array of fine china and earthenware, glass, and ornaments.

While in this area you will also find the **National Trust for Scotland's** shop (Hutcheson's Hall, 158 Ingram St.). Many items for sale are designed exclusively for National Trust properties and are often handmade.

The Merchant City is a small area incorporating only three or four shopping streets and leads to Candleriggs, where you may notice some contrast in style. There are a covered market and a number of stalls in the street, where you may experience a taste of the Glasgow "patter" and you may even find a bargain.

The Merchant City is close to Scotrail's High Street station or can be easily reached by walking eastward from Scotrail's Argyle Street station.

The Barras   This is Glasgow's famous weekend street market and should certainly not be missed during your visit. Apart from the excellent opportunity to pick up a bargain while you browse among the stalls, you will enjoy the lively and colorful surroundings. Stalls sell antique (and not-so-antique) furniture, bric-a-brac, student-designed jewelry and textiles—you name it, it's here. The Barras is approximately 80 years old and is made up of nine markets—the largest indoor market in Europe. It prides itself on selling everything "from a needle to an anchor."

You can reach the Barras by walking from Scotrail's Argyle Street station, or take any of the various buses to Glasgow Cross at the foot of the Gallowgate.

West Regent Street/   For antiques connoisseurs and art lovers, a walk along West Re-
Blythswood Square   gent Street is highly recommended. Your first stop should be the **Victorian Village** (57 West Regent St.), a complex of small antiques shops. Of particular interest among the jewelry, coins, and bric-a-brac are stores specializing in antiquarian books, army memorabilia, clothing, and sporting items. Farther along West Regent Street are various galleries and antiques shops, some specializing in Scottish antiques and paintings. **Cyril Gerber** (148 West Regent St.), specialists in 20th-century British paintings, will export, as will most galleries. The **Compass Gallery** usually has interesting exhibitions on view.

In this area you are not far from **Glasgow School of Art** (167 Renfrew St.), and apart from the famous Charles Rennie Mackintosh building itself, there is a shop selling various books, cards, jewelry, and ceramics. There are also guided tours during the summer months. Students often sell their work, if you are lucky enough to be visiting during the degree shows in June.

West Regent Street can be reached by walking from Renfield Street (parallel to Buchanan Street); most buses from the West End coming into town travel along this street or one running parallel to it. Renfrew Street can be reached by walking to the right along Pitt Street at the end of West Regent Street.

The West End/ This part of the city is dominated by the university, and the
Byres Road shops cater to local and student needs. One place of interest is **De Courcey's** antiques and crafts arcade (5–21 Cresswell La.). There are quite a few shops to visit, and a variety of goods, including paintings and jewelry, are regularly auctioned here. De Courcey's is in one of the cobblestone lanes to the rear of Byres Road.

Byres Road is reached on the underground system: Get off at Hillhead station. By bus from the city center, numbers 44 and 59 pass by the university and cross over Byres Road (get off at the first stop on Highburgh Road and walk back).

Arcades and Shopping Centers

As in many other major cities and towns, various centers can be found in and around the city. **St. Enoch's Shopping Centre** is relatively new and is Europe's largest glass-roof shopping center (eye-catching if not especially pleasing). It houses various stores, but most could be found elsewhere. There is, however, an indoor ice-skating rink where equipment can be rented, an interesting diversion during a day's shopping. Other centres include Sauchiehall Street Centre and The Forge Shopping Centre at Parkhead, which both offer a variety of shopping. By far the best complex, however, is **Princes Square** (48 Buchanan St.), high-quality shops in an art-nouveau setting, with cafés and restaurants. The **Whisky Shop** here is a must-visit; on display is one of the most extensive selections of Scottish whiskey to be found anywhere, both in full and miniature sizes. On the top floor of the center is the **Jean Pain Gallery,** which has a selection of limited-edition prints from around Scotland.

Specialty Stores

Clothing Glasgow has a very fashion-conscious image in Scotland, and a variety of both local and international fashion houses can be visited. The Merchant City area, with the stores already mentioned in that section, is popular with young people. At Princes Square the traditional **Hunters** is alongside famous design names like **Katherine Hamnett.** The West End has a number of shops where you may find items of local design: **Panache** (266 Woodlands Rd.) offers designer knitwear in luxury yarns, such as angora, silk, and mohair; **Solo Fashions** (181 Hyndland Rd.) has Continental fashions for all occasions. Worth a special mention is **Strawberry Fields** (517 Great Western Rd.), housing a colorful array of children's wear. At **Riah Harvey** (198 Kilmarnock Rd.), on the south side of the city, there is a good selection of fashion for women 5'2" and under. **Romika** (14 Royal Exchange Sq.), back in the city center, offers shoes, umbrellas, and some unusual accessories.

Gifts All the usual Scottish-theme gifts can be found in various locations in Glasgow. Gift items here tend to be a little more interesting and of a higher quality than those found in other, more tourist-oriented areas of the country.

MacDonald MacKay Ltd (105 Hope St.) makes and sells Highland dress and accessories, ladies' kilts, and skirts made to measure and offers an export service. **Wm M Houston** (216 Argyle St.), featuring Scottish gifts and clan memorabilia, is worth a visit; it specializes in large sizes for men.

Glasgow has a definite place in the history of art and design, being most famous for its association with Charles Rennie Mackintosh. For high-quality giftware in his style, **Catherine Shaw** (24 Gordon St. and in the Argyll Arcade) offers a unique selection. Also, try **MacKintosh and Company Ltd.** (Glasgow Style Gallery, 487 Great Western Rd.) for copies of Art Nouveau glass, furniture, and fabrics in the Glasgow style.

Glasgow Environs

Ayr Ayr has a good mixture of traditional and new shops. Queen's Court, Sandgate, combines small crafts and gift shops. The **Diamond Factory** (27 Queen's Ct.) is a jewelry workshop where visitors are invited to view craftsmen at work. All jewelry is designed and made on the premises. Ask about rings that can be engraved with a family crest and about seal engraving. The store will export your purchases if you do not have time to wait for completion of the work. At **New Courtyard Craft Supplies** you'll find various crafts materials, mainly wools and silks. The **Mill Shop, Begg of Ayr** (Viewfield Rd.) has a good selection of scarves, stoles, plaids, and travel rugs that are handmade on the premises. **Acanthus** (11–15 Old Bridge St.), specialists in china and crystal, will export any purchase worldwide.

Troon This small coastal town north of Ayr is famous for its international golf course, Royal Troon. Many Glaswegians frequent **Regalia** (44–48 Church St.) for its unusual collection of designer outfits. **Valance** (39 Ayr St.) is a traditional confectionery; try the specially boxed handmade fudge and shortbread.

Both Ayr and Troon can be reached easily from Glasgow by train from Central Station; trains run every half hour during the week.

Sports and Fitness

Bicycling and Jogging The tourist board (*see* Important Addresses and Numbers in Essential Information, *above*) can provide a list of the many parks and gardens in Glasgow with facilities for these sports; many of the parks also have tennis courts and/or bowling greens.

Fishing With loch, river, and sea fishing available, the area is a mecca for fishermen. Details of fishing permits and locations are available from the tourist board.

Golf Seven courses are operated within Greater Glasgow by the local authorities, where bookings are relatively inexpensive and can be made with ease, especially during the week. A comprehensive list of contacts, facilities, and charges is available from the Greater Glasgow Tourist Board.

Alexandra Park (tel. 041/554–4887). 9 holes, 2,281 yards.
King's Park (Croftfoot, tel. 041/637–1066). 9 holes, 2,103 yards, SSS 32.
Knightswood (Lincoln Ave., tel. 041/959–2131). 9 holes, 2,717 yards, SSS 33.
Lethamhill (Cumbernauld Rd., tel. 041/770–6220). 18 holes, 6,081 yards, SSS 69.
Linn Park (Simshill Rd., tel. 041/637–5871). 18 holes, 4,814 yards, SSS 64.
Littlehill (Auchinairn Rd., tel. 041/772–1916). 18 holes, 6,199 yards, SSS 69.
Ruchill (Brassey St., tel. 041/946–9728). 9 holes, 2,208 yards, SSS 32.

Health and Fitness Clubs There are some 40 clubs throughout the city. Most include a swimming pool and gymnasium, and some have squash, karate, horseback riding, shooting, badminton, or sailing facilities. See the brochure available from the tourist board for details. The larger hotels in the city also offer a variety of sports and leisure facilities, usually free of charge, to their guests. Currently, the following hotels have at least a pool and gym: **Moat House** (tel. 041/204–0733), **Holiday Inn** (tel. 041/226–5577), **Dury's Pond** (tel. 041/334–8161), and **Swallow** (tel. 041/427–3146).

Soccer The city has been sports-mad, especially for football (soccer), for over 100 years, and the rivalry between its two main clubs, Rangers and Celtic, is legendary. Rangers wear blue, are predominantly Protestant, and play at Ibrox to the west of the city; the Celtic team wear green, are predominantly Roman Catholic, and play in the east. Matches are played usually on a Saturday in winter, and Glasgow has in total nine different teams playing in the Scottish Leagues. Admission prices start at about £5. Do not go looking for the family-day-out atmosphere of many American football games; soccer remains a man's game played in relatively primitive surroundings, though Ibrox is an exception to this.

Sailing and Water Sports The Firth of Clyde and Loch Lomond both offer water-sports facilities with full equipment rental. Details are available from the tourist board.

Dining

The restaurants of Glasgow have diversified over the past several years; as a result, this is one of the cities in Scotland where you'll find Chinese, Italian, and Indian food in addition to the usual French and Scottish offerings. Some of the shopping-arcade cafés provide acceptable alternatives for lunch and afternoon tea. Pubs are also good bets for cheap bar lunches.

Highly recommended restaurants are indicated by a star ★.

Category	Cost*
Very Expensive	over £25
Expensive	£15–£25

Moderate	£10–£15
Inexpensive	under £10

*per person, including appetizer, main course, dessert, and VAT

★ **Rogano.** The striking art-deco design of this restaurant is enough to recommend it—the bonus is that the food, at the lively downstairs diner, at the main restaurant on the ground floor, and at the oyster bar near the entrance, is excellent. Specialties include venison liver pâté and fresh seafood superbly prepared. Vegetarians are also provided for. It's a great favorite with Glaswegians, so be sure to reserve ahead. *11 Exchange Sq., tel. 041/248–4055. Reservations required. Jacket and tie required. AE, DC, MC, V. Closed Sun. and national holidays. Very Expensive.*

★ **The Ubiquitous Chip.** Set in a converted courtyard inside a Victorian mews (once used for stables) and abundantly decorated with plants, this is one of the most interesting locales in which to relax over a meal. The menu, which leans heavily toward traditional Scottish fare, changes daily. Specialties depend on what is available fresh at top quality, but will usually include fish and seafood, roe-deer steaks, and lamb. An ample wine list complements the fine cuisine. *12 Ashton La., tel. 041/334–5007. Reservations advised. Dress: casual. AE, DC, MC, V. Pub open 11–11; wine shop open noon–10. Very Expensive.*

★ **Buttery.** Located in a former Masonic temple, the Buttery is close to the Ring Street expressway tangle. The food here is down-to-earth, with excellent lamb and seafood at the fore. The service is friendly and the ambience relaxed. *652 Argyle St., tel. 041/221–8188. Reservations required. Dress: informal. AE, DC, MC, V. Closed Sat. lunch and Sun. Expensive.*

The Ho Wong. Genuine Chinese watercolors adorn the wood-panel walls of this peaceful restaurant. This isn't the place to go if you want fast food: The seating is comfortable and patrons are encourged to relax and enjoy the experience. The menu offers a selection of Cantonese- and Peking-style food. For the really adventurous there are such specialties as the Imperial State Banquet. *82 York St., tel. 041/221–3550. Reservations advised. Dress: informal. AE, MC, V. Closed Sun. Expensive.*

Colonial. In this traditional dining room you will find a wide range of Indian cuisine, especially the hotter and spicier dishes from the southern regions of the country. Goanese fish and prawns, *Sali Boti* (a selection of dishes using sun-dried fruits, spices, and cream), and recipes using wine and cognac are specialties. *25 High St., tel. 041/552–1923. Reservations advised. Jacket and tie advised. AE, DC, MC, V. Moderate.*

De Quinceys. This is principally a wine bar, but it serves a superb buffet lunch, featuring a choice of salads, plus afternoon tea and coffee with luscious pastries and cakes. In the evening the tempo changes, and De Quinceys becomes a lively cocktail bar offering beers as well, including many popular Continental brews. One of the main attractions of the place is the decor: ceramic walls and a high, tile ceiling, dating from the 1890s. It is worth dropping in after a round of sightseeing to have a quick snack and admire the stylish surroundings. *71 Renfield St., tel. 041/333–9725 or 041/333–0633. Reservations not required. Dress: casual. AE, MC, V. Moderate.*

Change at Jamaica. This restaurant, just south of the river and under a railway bridge, has a clean modern, design. The menu

Glasgow Dining and Lodging

Dining
Buttery, **8**
Change at Jamaica, **13**
Colonial, **19**
De Quinceys, **12**
The Ho Wong, **10**
Koh-I-Noor, **6**
Rogano, **17**
The Ubiquitous Chip, **2**

Lodging
Babbity Bowster's, **18**
Central Hotel, **11**
The Crest, **9**
Forte Crest, **7**
Kirklee Hotel, **4**
Marie Stuart, **14**
One Devonshire Gardens, **1**

Queen's Park Hotel, **16**
The Stakis Grosvenor, **3**
Tinto Firs, **15**
The White House, **5**

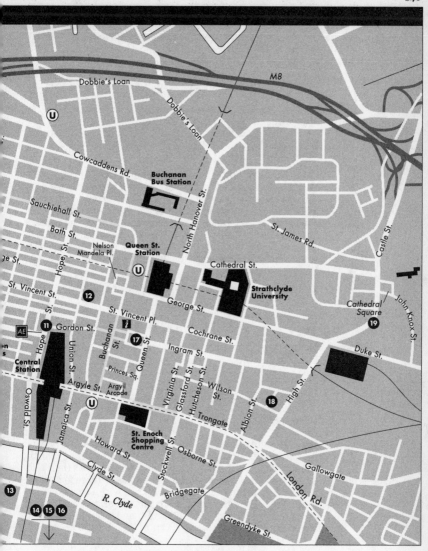

is long and varied, offering a little of everything. A late-night haven, Change at Jamaica usually doesn't close until around 5 AM. *11–17 Clyde Pl., tel. 041/429–4422. Reservations not required. Dress: informal. AE, DC, MC, V. Inexpensive.*

Koh-I-Noor. This excellent Indian restaurant has a special gourmet buffet dinner every Monday evening from 7 to 9. At £9 per person, this all-you-can-eat offer has to be one of the best deals in the city. *235 North St., Charing Cross, tel. 041/221–1555 or 204–1444. Reservations advised. Dress: informal. No Sun. dinner. No credit cards. Inexpensive.*

Lodging

Glasgow is now better equipped with hotels of all categories than it has ever been. The city has become a major business destination in the past several years, with the Scottish Conference and Exhibition Centre serving as the focal point. There are now some big city-center hotels of both expensive and moderate character and some good and reasonable small hotels and guest houses in the suburbs (in most cases, transportation into town is quick and dependable). All the larger hotels have restaurants open to nonguests.

Highly recommended lodgings are indicated by a star ★.

Category	Cost*
Very Expensive	over £120
Expensive	£100–£120
Moderate	£80–£100
Inexpensive	under £80

All prices are for two people sharing a double room, including service, breakfast, and VAT.

★ **One Devonshire Gardens.** This fine town mansion offers luxury accommodations. Elegance is the theme, from the sophisticated drawing room to the sumptuous bedrooms with their rich drapery and traditional furnishings, including three four-poster beds. The restaurant is equally stylish, with a new menu for each meal. Specialties include salmon with orange and ginger sauce, chicken livers with almonds, and magnificent fillet steaks. *1 Devonshire Gardens, G12 0UX, tel. 041/339–2001. 8 apartments with bath. Restaurant reservations advised. Dress in restaurant: Jacket and tie required. AE, DC, MC, V. Very Expensive.*

The Stakis Grosvenor. This hotel has a stunningly beautiful Victorian facade, which is best seen at night, when it is spectacularly floodlit. The guest rooms vary from standard to the honeymoon suite, which is outfitted with a four-poster bed. There are two excellent restaurants, the Terrace and the Steakhouse, plus a choice of several bars. Set away from downtown, the Stakis Grosvenor is convenient to the Burrell Collection and the Botanic Gardens. *Grosvenor Terr., Great Western Rd., G12 0TA, tel. 041/339–8811. 93 rooms with bath. Facilities: 2 restaurants, bars. AE, DC, V. Very Expensive.*

The Crest. Centrally located on Argyle Street, this hotel is very convenient to a number of Glasgow's major shopping districts. There is a fine restaurant and lounge areas, and all the rooms are well decorated and restful. *377 Argyle St., G2 8LL, tel. 041/ 248–2355. 120 rooms with bath. Facilities: restaurant, bar, tea served in lobby lounge. AE, DC, MC, V. Expensive.*

★ **Forte Crest.** Well positioned in the center of the city, the Forte Crest is generally rated as one of the best of Glasgow's hotels. One cannot expect the personal attention that one would get in smaller hotels, but the service is very professional and friendly. *Bothwell St., G2 7EN, tel. 041/248–2656. 254 rooms with bath. Facilities: restaurant, lounge, bar. AE, DC, MC, V. Expensive.*

★ **Kirklee Hotel.** Located in a quiet district of Glasgow near the university, this hotel is small and cozy. Its owners take pride in being friendly and helpful and in keeping the hotel spotless and comfortable. *11 Kensington Gate, G12 9LG, tel. 041/334–5555. 11 rooms with bath. No credit cards. Expensive.*

Tinto Firs. This modern hotel on the parklike south side of Glasgow is more country-house than city style. The lounge/cocktail bar has dark-wood paneling and rattan chairs; the bedrooms have stunning wall coverings and matching fabric furnishings. *470 Kilmarnock Rd., G43 2BB, tel. 041/637–2353. 27 rooms with bath. Facilities: garden, in-house movies. AE, DC, MC, V. Expensive.*

The White House. This is an unusual hotel insofar as it has no dining room, though it does offer food prepared by a chef who won a bronze medal in the 1989 Culinary Olympics. In the evening, a chauffeur-driven car is available to drive you to one of the three restaurants in the city with which the hotel has made special arrangements for feeding its guests (the award-winning chef reigns over the kitchen of one of these establishments). All accommodations at the White House are in self-contained suites, and guests can either cook their own food in the fully appointed kitchen or have food delivered to their suites. *11–13 Clevedon Crescent, G12 0PA, tel. 041/339–9375, fax 041/337–1430. 26 suites, 6 mews cottages, all fully equipped. Facilities: restaurant, bar. AE, DC, MC, V. Expensive.*

Central Hotel. A typical Victorian railroad hotel, there are thick carpets, mobcapped chambermaids, and ample rooms from another era here. Public areas feature brass chandeliers and plenty of greenery. The **Entresol** restaurant serves breakfast, lunch, and dinner. *Gordon St., G1 3SF, tel. 041/221–9680. 229 rooms, 170 with bath. Facilities: bar, in-house movies. AE, DC, MC, V. Moderate.*

Babbity Bowster's. If you want to combine lively atmosphere with historical detail, you can take a room in this small, intimate hotel in a restored 18th-century town house (designed by Robert Adam). In addition to a gallery on the first floor that features many works by Glaswegian artists, the hotel offers a bar, restaurant, and café. *16–18 Blackfriars St., G1 1PJ, tel. 041/552–5055. 6 rooms with bath. Facilities: restaurant, bar, café. AE, DC, V. Inexpensive.*

Marie Stuart. Well-equipped rooms and excellent service highlight this hotel. The bar is lively and popular, and the staff is friendly. *46 Queen Mary Ave., G42 8DT, tel. 041/424–3939. 31 rooms, 9 with bath. No credit cards. Inexpensive.*

Queen's Park Hotel. There's a good all-around standard of comfort and service here. Meal hours are flexible, a plus for late-nighters or late sleepers. *10 Balvicar Dr., G42 8QT, tel. 041/ 423–1123. 30 rooms, 18 with bath. No credit cards. Inexpensive.*

The Arts and Nightlife

Glasgow was the 1990 European City of Culture, the first British city to be so designated. Given that the previous European Cities of Culture were Athens, Florence, Amsterdam, Berlin, and Paris, it's clear just how strong Glasgow's international reputation is when it comes to cultural events. That reputation has grown from the strong base developed by the city authorities in the 19th century and has continued in the remarkable renaissance the city has enjoyed in the past 10 years.

The Arts

Theater Glasgow is better endowed with functioning theaters than is Edinburgh. One of the most exciting in Britain is the **Citizen's Theatre** (119 Gorbals St., tel. 041/429–0022), where productions of often hair-raising originality are the order of the day. The **King's Theatre** (Bath St., tel. 041/227–5511) stages drama, light entertainment, variety shows, musicals, and amateur productions. The **Mitchell** (Mitchell Library, North St., tel. 041/227–5511) limits itself mostly to amateur productions, but hosts lectures and meetings as well. The **Pavilion** (tel. 041/332–1846) offers family variety entertainment along with rock and pop concerts. The **Royal Scottish Academy of Music and Drama** (100 Renfrew St., tel. 041/332–5057) stages a variety of international and student performances. The **Tramway** (tel. 041/227–5511), the city's old museum of transport, is now an exciting venue for opera, drama, and dance. Finally, the **Tron** (63 Trongate, tel. 041/552–4267) houses Scottish and international theater.

Tickets for performances can be purchased at theater box offices.

Concerts Glasgow's **Royal Concert Hall** (2 Sauchiehall St., tel. 041/332–3123) was opened for the City of Culture celebrations in 1990. It has 2,500 seats and is the permanent home of the Scottish National Orchestra, which performs a winter series of concerts and a summer proms series. Other concert halls include **City Halls** (Candleriggs, tel. 041/227–5511); the **Henry Wood Hall** (Claremont St., tel. 041/332–3868), a former church now used for classical concerts; and the **Scottish Exhibition and Conference Centre** (tel. 041/248–3000), which is a regular venue for pop concerts.

Film The **Glasgow Film Theatre** (Rose St., tel. 041/332–6535) is an independent public cinema screening popular reruns and classic revivals from all over the world. The **Cannon Film Complex** on Sauchiehall Street (tel. 041/332–9513) and the **Odeon Film Centre** on Renfield Street (tel. 041/332–8701) both show all the latest releases. For details of programs, consult the daily newspapers.

Opera and Ballet Glasgow is home to the Scottish Opera and Scottish Ballet, both of which perform at the **Theatre Royal** (tel. 041/332–9000). Visiting dance companies from many countries perform here also.

Nightlife

Glasgow is famous for its nightlife, but, rather than give particulars here, with names and venues changing rapidly, we suggest you consult the tourist board (*see* Important Addresses and Numbers in Essential Information, *above*) for up-to-date information. There are literally hundreds of pubs and wine bars in this city that is famous for its drinking and conviviality. Many have folk or jazz bands on certain nights. *The List* or a daily newspaper will give you details.

Short Excursions from Glasgow

Glasgow is well placed as a touring base for excursions northward to the Highlands or south to the fertile farmlands of Ayrshire and the Clyde Valley. Here are two one-day itineraries you could do by car or, in a modified form, by public transportation. You will find details of places to visit in the north covered in the Central Highlands section of this book.

Tour 1: Ayrshire and the Clyde Coast

Numbers in the margin correspond to points of interest on the Glasgow Excursions: Ayrshire and the Clyde Valley map.

Robert Burns is Scotland's national and well-loved poet. His birthday is celebrated with speeches and dinners, drinking and dancing (Burns Suppers) on January 25, in a way in which few other countries celebrate a poet. He was born in Alloway, just an hour or so to the south of Glasgow, and the towns and villages where he lived and loved make an interesting day out from the city.

Ideally, you need a car, but if not, you can go by bus or train (*see* Getting Around in Essential Information, *above*, for excursion-ticket details) Take the bus or train to Largs for Cumbrae; Ardrossan for Arran; Ayr and Kilmarnock for the Burns Heritage Trail; and Troon, Prestwick, and Ayr to play golf. Bus companies also operate one-day guided excursions to this area. The Scottish Tourist Guides Association provides guides.

If you travel by car, begin your trip from Glasgow city center westbound on the M8, signposted for Glasgow Airport and Greenock. The road is a fast motorway (freeway) or dual carriageway (divided highway) right down the southern shore of the River Clyde. You will pass the Erskine Bridge and look

㉓ across to **Dumbarton** and its Rock, a nostalgic farewell point for emigrants leaving Glasgow. Note, too, how narrow the river is here and remember that the *Queen Elizabeth 2* and the other *Queens* and great ocean liners sailed these waters from the place of their birth.

Join the A78 and follow it from Greenock to Gourock and around the coast past the Cloch lighthouse. The views north and west to Loch Long, the Holy Loch, and the Argyll Forest Park are outstanding on a clear day—and may make you want to abandon your plans and take the ferry across the estuary to Dunoon. Head south, having resisted the temptation, to the old

㉔ Victorian village of **Wemyss Bay,** where the station and espe-

Glasgow Excursions: Ayrshire and the Clyde Valley

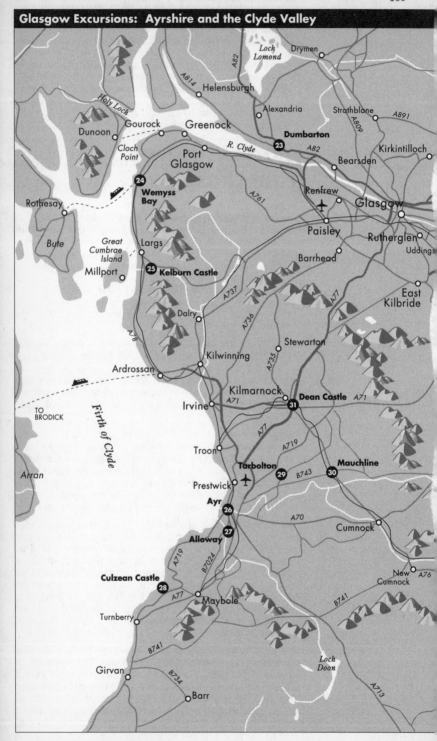

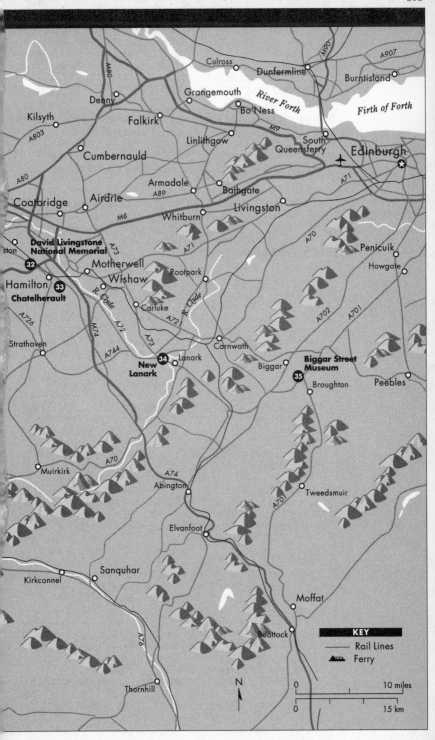

Culross
Dunfermline
Burntisland
Grangemouth
River Forth
Bo'Ness
Firth of Forth
Denny
Kilsyth
Falkirk
Linlithgow
South
Queensferry
Edinburgh
A907
M90
A803
M80
M9
Cumbernauld
Armadale
Bathgate
Livingston
A80
A89
A71
Coatbridge
Airdrie
Whitburn
M8
David Livingstone
National Memorial
A73
A71
A70
Penicuik
ston
32
Motherwell
Rootpark
Howgate
Hamilton
33
Wishaw
Chatelherault
R. Clyde
Carluke
R. Clyde
A702
A701
Strathaven
A726
M74
A72
A72
Carnwath
Biggar Street
Museum
A744
A73
New
Lanark
34
Lanark
Biggar
35
Broughton
Peebles
Muirkirk
A70
A74
Abington
A701
Tweedsmuir
Elvanfoot
Sanquhar
Kirkconnel
Moffat
A76
Beattock
KEY
Thornhill
N
— Rail Lines
Ferry
0   10 miles
0   15 km

cially the covered walkway between platform and steamer pier, with its exuberant wrought ironwork, are a reminder of the grandeur and style of the Victorian era and the generations of visitors who used trains and ferries for their summer holidays. South of Wemyss Bay, the island of Arran, another Victorian holiday favorite, comes into view and then the island of Great Cumbrae (a weighty name for a tiny island) and its ferryport, Largs.

㉕ South of the town is **Kelburn Castle and Country Park,** the historic estate of the earl of Glasgow. There are walks and trails through the mature woodlands, showing off the trees and shrubs from all over the world. The visitor center explains it all, and the adventure center and commando-assault course will wear out overexcited children. (They tell a tale here of rescuing an elderly lady from halfway around the assault course, who commented "Well, I did think it was rather a *hard* nature trail." Make sure you read the signposts.) *Fairlie, Ayrshire KA2Q ORE, tel. 0475/568685. Admission: £3.00 adults, £1.50 children. Open Easter–Sept., daily 10–6; grounds only, Oct.– Easter, daily 11–5.*

Follow the A78 ever southward through Ardrossan to Irvine (pronounced not like the place in California, but as *Irvin*) where the Magnum Leisure Centre, Sea World Exhibition, and Scottish Maritime Museum are all of interest. Robert Burns puts in an appearance at Irvine. He came here to learn to dress flax (the raw material for linen), and the heckling (flax-dressing) shed where he worked and the house where he lived are museums. The Irvine Burns Club is possibly the oldest in the world.

Continue on A78 past Troon and Prestwick, two holy places for golfers, particularly since the first British Open was played at Prestwick. You can easily see why golf is so popular here. The whole coast seems one endless golf course. Go past Prestwick **㉖** airport to reach **Ayr,** a peaceful and elegant town with an air of prosperity and some good shops. Burns was baptized in the Auld Kirk (Old Church) in the town and wrote a humorous poem about the Twa Brigs (two bridges) that cross the river nearby. He described Ayr as a town unsurpassed "for honest men and bonny lasses." The Tam o' Shanter Museum has plenty of Burns relics and reminders of one of his most famous poems, **㉗** "Tam o' Shanter." The poet was born at **Alloway** on the B7024 about 2 miles south of town. The thatched whitewashed cottage (and adjacent museum), which his father built, is a shrine to Burns's memory. Just to the south is a whole cluster of places associated with Burns: the Old Kirk of Alloway (where the witches were holding their meeting in "Tam o' Shanter"); the Brig o' Doon (to where the disturbed witches chased Tam in the same poem); the Burns Memorial and Gardens, which overlook it; and, around the corner, the Land o' Burns Centre, which tells the story of Burns's life.

Time Out   Ayr has a number of attractive cafés and hotels. Try the **Tudor Restaurant** (tel. 0292/261404) or the **Honey Pot** (tel. 0292/ 263239), both in Burns Statue Square. The **Land o' Burns Centre** in Alloway (Mill Rd.) also serves food and drinks in an attractive setting.

If you have time, continue south from Ayr and Alloway to
28 **Culzean Castle and Country Park.** This magnificent mansion
was built by Robert Adam on a dramatic clifftop setting. It
stands just off the A719, and you could easily spend a whole day
there walking around the classically elegant rooms, the gardens, and the estate. The people of Scotland made a gift of a flat
in the castle to President Eisenhower. The Eisenhower Presentation is another feature to see inside. *Tel. 06556/274. Admission: county park, £5 car; castle: £3 adult, £1.50 children.
Open Apr.–Oct., daily 10:30–5:30.*

You'll return to Ayr, then turn eastward on the A758, the
Mauchline Road, but before you get there, turn left on a little
29 road to **Tarbolton,** where you will find the **Bachelors' Club,** a
17th-century house where Burns learned to dance, founded a
debating and literary society, and became a Freemason. *Admission: approximately £1 adult. Open summer daily in afternoon.*

30 **Mauchline** also has strong connections with the poet. There is a
Burns House here; four of his daughters are buried in the
churchyard; and Poosie Nansie's pub, where he used to drink, is
still in use today. The village is also famous for making curling
stones.

Head north on A76 to Kilmarnock, an industrial town, home of
Johnny Walker whiskey, where again Burns enthusiasts will
enjoy the Burns Museum and the Dick Institute. If you are
31 looking for something different by now, go to **Dean Castle and
Country Park** off Glasgow Road to enjoy a 14th-century castle
with a wonderful collection of medieval arms and armor. Burns
also inevitably gets a mention. Glasgow is only half an hour
away on the fast A71.

Tour 2: The Clyde Valley

The River Clyde is (or certainly was) famous for its shipbuilding and heavy industries, yet its upper reaches flow through
some of Scotland's most fertile farmlands, which concentrate
on growing tomatoes. It is an interesting area, with ancient
castles as well as industrial and social museums that tell the
story of manufacturing and mining prosperity.

Take A724 out of Glasgow south of the river through Ruther-
glen toward Hamilton. It is not a very pretty road, but in Blan-
32 tyre look for signs to the **David Livingstone National Memorial,**
a park area around the tiny (tenement) apartment where the
great explorer of Africa was born in 1813. Displays tell of his
journeys, of his meeting with Stanley ("Doctor Livingstone, I
presume"), of Africa, and of the industrial heritage of the area.
Close by at Uddingston is Bothwell Castle, dating from the
13th century. Its walls are well preserved and stand above the
River Clyde. *Tel. 0698/823140. Admission: £1.70 adults, 85p
children, £1 senior citizens. Open all year Mon.–Sat. 10–6,
Sun. 2–6.*

The Hamilton Mausoleum, in Strathclyde Country Park near
the industrial town of Hamilton, was built in the 1840s as an extraordinary monument to the lavish eccentricities of the dukes
33 of Hamilton. Also nearby is **Chatelherault** (pronounced *shat-
lerro*), a unique one-room-deep facade, part shooting lodge,
part glorified dog kennel, designed by William Adam, also for

the dukes of Hamilton. Within Chatelherault is an exhibition describing life on the estate in all its former glory.

Time Out For a cup of tea and some homemade baked goods, stop at the **Hamilton Old Parish Church,** built by William Adam, Robert's father, in 1734. The church is open in the morning and contains an ancient cross, a Covenanters Memorial, and fine embroideries.

From Hamilton, take the A72 to **Lanark,** past the ruins of medieval Craignethan Castle, past lots of greenhouses for tomatoes, as well as plant nurseries and gnarled old orchards running down to the Clyde. Lanark is a pleasant agricultural town. Nearby, down a long winding hill, is **New Lanark,** one of the world's most important industrial heritage sites—though in this wooded river valley, the ambience is hardly industrial. Here in 1785 a "model" village was set up to house the workers employed in cotton mills, which were powered by the fast-flowing waters of the Clyde. After many changes of fortune the mills eventually closed, but the site has been saved and has a new lease on life with renovated housing. One of the mills has been converted into an interpretation center, which tells the story of this brave social experiment. Upstream, the Clyde flows through some of the very finest river scenery anywhere in Lowland Scotland, with woods and spectacular waterfalls.

A72 continues south of Lanark to join A702 near Biggar. The **Biggar Street Museum** offers a fascinating portrayal of life in the town; the old gasworks—which is actually much more interesting than it sounds—is preserved and there is a puppet theater. By the time you get to Biggar, you are near the headwaters of the Clyde, on the moors in the center of southern Scotland. The Clyde flows west toward Glasgow and the Atlantic Ocean, while the Tweed, only a few miles away, flows eastward toward the North Sea. There are fine views around Biggar: to Culter Fell and to the Border Hills in the south.

Time Out In Biggar High Street, try the **Elphinstone Hotel** (tel. 0899/20044) or a café called **La Venue**. Outside Biggar, the **Shieldhill House Hotel,** near the curiously named village of Quothquan, is excellent (tel. 0899/20035), as is the **Tinto Hotel** at Symington (tel. 08993/454). In Lanark, try the **Cartland Bridge Hotel,** on the Carluke–Hamilton road.

At the end of a full day of touring you can return to Glasgow the quick way by joining the M74 from the A744 west of Lanark (the Strathaven road) or take a more scenic route through Strathaven (pronounced *stra*-ven) itself, A726 to East Kilbride, and enter Glasgow from south of the river.

6 The Borders and the Southwest

Dumfries and Galloway

Introduction

By Gilbert
Summers

If you are coming to Scotland from any point south of the border in England, then the Borders is the first region of Scotland you will encounter. Let it be said straightaway that although the border has no checkpoints or customs outposts, the Scottish tourist authorities firmly promulgate the message to visitors that it is indeed Scottish land they are on once they cross the border. All the idiosyncracies that distinguish Scotland—from the myriad names for beer, to the seemingly unpredictable Monday local holidays—start as soon as one reaches the first Scottish signs by the main roads north.

Although most visitors inevitably pass this way, the Borders and especially Galloway to the west are unfortunately overlooked. So strong is the tartan-ribboned call of the Highlands that many visitors rush past, pause for breath at Edinburgh, then plunge northward, thus missing a scenic portion of upland Scotland. This area never possessed the high romance of the Gaelic-speaking clans in the Highlands to the north, but it did have (and still has) powerful Border families, whose ancestry is soaked in the bloodshed that occurred along this once very real frontier between Scotland and her more powerful and opportunist neighbor to the south.

Both the Borders and the Dumfries and Galloway regions feature as broad a selection of stately homes and fortified castles as you will encounter in Scotland (with the possible exception of Grampian). Galloway, the area west of Dumfries, has the advantage of a coastline facing south, made even more appealing by the North Atlantic Drift (Scotland's part of the Gulf Stream), which bathes the coastal lands with warmer water. The results have yielded Galloway a number of resplendent gardens, some featuring exotic yet delicate flora. Small wonder then that an important outstation of Edinburgh's Royal Botanic Garden is off to the far west. Logan Botanic Gardens is noted for its interesting tree ferns and cabbage palms, which grow in abundance here like nowhere else in Scotland.

Galloway is indeed one of Scotland's best-kept secrets. Though today a little off the beaten track, the region played its part in Scotland's story. Caerlaverock, Threave, Cardoness, and Castle Kennedy are symbols of Scots-English struggles and wars between kings and unruly barons. The principal abbeys, Lincluden, Dundrennan, Luce, and Sweetheart, have also known moments of turbulent history. With its coastal farmlands giving way to woodlands, high moors, and some craggy hills, Galloway may not be the Highlands, but it gives a convincing impression to those seeking the authentic Scotland.

The Borders folk have a strong character and great pride in the region's heritage as Scotland's main woolen-goods manufacturing area. To this day the residents possess a marked determination to defend their towns and communities. The changing times, however, have thankfully allowed them to reposition their priorities: Instead of guarding against southern raiders, they now concentrate on maintaining a fiercely competitive rugby team for the popular intertown rugby matches. The Borders are a stronghold of this European counterpart to American football.

Border communities are also reestablishing their identities through the curious affairs known as the Common Ridings. Long ago it was essential that each town be able to defend its area, and over the centuries this need has become formalized in mounted gatherings to "ride the boundaries." The observance of the tradition lapsed in certain places but has been revived. Leaders and attendants are solemnly elected each year, and Borderers who now live away from home make a point of attending their own event. Thus the Common Ridings in Hawick, Selkirk, and Melrose, for example, are certainly not staged as tourist promotions. You can watch and are welcome to enjoy the excitement of clattering hooves and banners proudly displayed, but this is essentially a time for the native Borderers. The Common Ridings possess as much, if not more, authenticity and historic significance as the concocted Highland Games, so often taken to be the essence of Scotland. The little town of Selkirk, in fact, claims its Common Riding to be the largest mounted gathering anywhere in Europe.

Essential Information

Important Addresses and Numbers

Tourist Information The main tourist-information centers in the area are open all year. They are the **Dumfries and Galloway Tourist Board Information Centre** (Whitesands, Dumfries, tel. 0387/53862) and the **Scottish Borders Tourist Board Tourist Information Centre** (Murray's Green, Jedburgh, tel. 0835/63435). Seasonal information centers are located at Castle Douglas, Coldstream, Dalbeattie, Eyemouth, Galashiels, Gatehouse-of-Fleet, Gretna, Hawick, Kelso, Kirkcudbright, Langholm, Melrose, Moffat, Newton Stewart, Peebles, Sanquhar, Selkirk, and Stranraer.

Emergencies For **police, fire** or **ambulance,** dial 999 from any telephone. No coins are needed for emergency calls from public telephone booths.

Late-Night Pharmacies All towns in the region have at least one pharmacy. Pharmacies are not found in rural areas, where general practitioners often dispense medicines. The police will provide assistance in locating a pharmacist in an emergency.

Arriving and Departing by Plane

Airports and Airlines The nearest Scottish airports are at **Edinburgh, Glasgow,** and **Prestwick.** *See* Chapters 3 and 4 for details.

Arriving and Departing by Car, Train, and Bus

By Car Route A68, in the east, makes an attractive border crossing from England into Scotland. (The A1 along the east coast is not recommended north of the border because of the high volume of traffic.) However, the main route into both the Borders and Galloway from the south is the M6, which deteriorates into the less well-maintained A74 north of the Border (it is currently being upgraded). The A7 through Hawick makes an attractive although slow alternative to the A74.

By Train Visitors can use the Intercity services from **London Euston,** in England, to **Glasgow;** these trains stop at **Carlisle,** just south of

the border. There are also direct trains to **Lockerbie** and
Dumfries. On the east coast some Intercity services stop at
Berwick-Upon-Tweed, just south of the border. The Borders
are not well served by rail. For more information, call Glas-
gow's Central Station (tel. 041/204–2844). (*See also* Getting
Around, *below.*)

By Bus   From the south the main bus services use the M6 or A1, with
appropriate feeder services into the hinterland; contact
Citylink (tel. 041/332–9191). There are also bus links from
Edinburgh and Glasgow. Contact **Lowland Scottish** (tel. 0896/
2237) or **Western Scottish** (tel. 0563/22551, 0387/53496, or 0776/
4484).

Getting Around

By Car   A solid network of rural roads allows you to avoid the A1 in the
eastern borders, as well as the A75, which runs along the Solway coast east to west, linking **Dumfries** and **Stranraer.** Both
roads carry heavy traffic, partly because of the poor rail connections.

By Train   Train travel is not very practical in the Borders. In fact the
Scottish Borders Rail Link is nothing of the kind: it's actually a
bus service linking **Hawick, Selkirk,** and **Galashiels** with Intercity services at **Carlisle.** In Galloway there are connecting
trains from Carlisle to **Stranraer,** which also has a direct link to
Ayr and Glasgow. Once again, so-called Station Link coaches
(not trains) provide express service between Dumfries station
and Stranraer, and a bus link operates within Dumfries between the rail and bus stations. (Both the Borders and Galloway suffered badly in the short-sighted contraction of Britain's
rail network in the 1960s.) Contact **British Rail** (tel. 0228/
44711) for further details.

By Bus   Bus service in the area includes **Citylink** (tel. 041/332–9191)
long-distance coaches that call at main towns along the A75, including **Annan, Dumfries, Castle Douglas, Kirkcudbright, Twyn-
holm, Gatehouse-of-Fleet, Creetown, Newton Stewart,** and
Glenluce. Lowland Scottish (tel. 0896/2237) offers Reiver Rover
and Waverley Wanderer flexible tickets, which provide considerable savings.

Guided Tours

Orientation   The bus companies mentioned above also run a variety of orientation tours in the area. In addition, tours are run by **R K Arm-
strong Coaches** (Black Park Rd., Castle Douglas, tel. 0556/
3391), **Galloway Heritage Tours** (26 Georgetown Rd., Dumfries,
tel. 0387/62724), and **Nelson's Coaches** (107 South Drumlanrig
St., Thornhill, tel. 0848/30376).

Special-Interest   The area is primarily covered through Edinburgh- or Glasgow-
based companies (*see* Chapters 3 and 4 for details). The following local companies offer chauffeur-driven tours tailored to customers' requirements: **Ramtrad Holidays** (54 Edinburgh Rd.,
Peebles, tel. 0721/20845) and **Jas French** (Coldingham, tel.
08907/71283).

Exploring the Borders and the Southwest

Orientation

If you are coming by car from the south, you can choose from a number of routes into Scotland. Starting from the east, the A1, which is located north of the English city of **Newcastle,** brings you to the border in about an hour. The A1 has the added attraction of Berwick-Upon-Tweed, on the English side of the border. Moving west, the A697, which leaves the A1 beside **Alnwick** (in England) and crosses the border at **Coldstream,** is a leisurely back-road option with an attractive view of the countryside. The A68 offers probably the most scenic route to Scotland: after climbing to **Carter Bar,** it reveals a view of the rolling blue Border hills and windy skies before dropping into the ancient town of **Jedburgh,** with its ruined abbey.

The fast M6 becomes the A74 (currently being upgraded) as soon as it arrives in Scotland. The M6 gives car-borne visitors the choice of the leisurely A7 northeastward toward Edinburgh or the A75 and other parallel routes westward into Galloway and to the ferry ports of **Stranraer** and **Cairnryan.** If you choose to get off one of these main arteries and explore some back roads on your way west, you may occasionally be delayed by a herd of cows on their way to the milking parlor, but this is often far more pleasant than tussling with heavy-goods vehicles rushing to make the Irish ferries.

Highlights for First-time Visitors

Abbotsford (*see* Tour 1)
Caerlaverock Castle (*see* Tour 2)
Castle Kennedy Gardens (*see* Tour 2)
Dryburgh Abbey (*see* Tour 1)
Floors Castle (*see* Tour 1)
Glen Trool Forest Park (*see* Tour 2)
Jedburgh Abbey (*see* Tour 1)
Logan Botanic Gardens (*see* Tour 2)
Scott's View (*see* Tour 1)
Smailholm Tower (*see* Tour 1)
Threave Gardens (*see* Tour 2)

Tour 1: The Borders—Towns, Towers, and Countryside

Numbers in the margin correspond to points of interest on the Borders map.

❶ The town of **Jedburgh** (*-burgh* is always pronounced *burra* in Scots, never *burg*) on the A68 makes a good starting point for a circle through the best sights of the Borders—a route that also encompasses all four of the great ruined abbeys. The monks in these long-abandoned religious foundations were the first to work the fleeces of their sheep flocks, hence laying the foundation for what is still the area's main industry. It should be noted that this route will certainly take more than one day. To travel it in a leisurely way and spend time at some of the grand man-

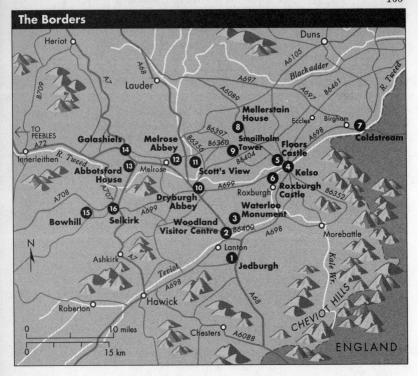

sions noted, one could easily allow three days, although the total driving distance is not great. In the Borders there are several points of interest located quite close to one another.

Jedburgh was for centuries the first major Scottish target of invading English armies. In more peaceful times it developed textile mills, most of which have since perished. The large landscaped area around the town's tourist-information center was once a mill but now provides an encampment for the modern armies of tourists. The past still clings to this little town, however. The ruined abbey dominates the skyline and is compulsory visiting for anyone interested in acquiring a feeling of the former role of the border abbeys.

Still impressive, though it is now only a roofless shell, **Jedburgh Abbey** was destroyed by the English earl of Hertford's forces in 1544–45, during the destructive time known as "the Rough Wooing." This was the English King Henry VIII's armed attempt to persuade the Scots that it was a good idea to unite the kingdoms by the marriage of his young son to the infant Mary, Queen of Scots. (The Scots disagreed and sent Mary to France instead.) The full story is explained in vivid detail at the Jedburgh Abbey Visitor Centre, which provides information on interpreting the ruins. Only ground patterns and foundations remain of the once-powerful religious complex. *High St., tel. 031/244–3101. Admission: £1.70 adults, 90p children and senior citizens. Open Apr.–Sept., Mon.–Sat. 9:30–6, Sun. 2–6; Oct.–Mar., Mon.–Sat., 9:30–4, Sun. 2–4.*

There is much else to see in Jedburgh, including the **Mary, Queen of Scots, House.** This *bastel* (from the French *bastille*) was the fortified town house in which, some say, Mary stayed before embarking on her famous 20-mile ride to visit her wounded lover, the earl of Bothwell, at **Hermitage Castle** (*see* Off the Beaten Track, *below*). An interpretative center in the building relates the tale. *Queen St., tel. 0835/63331. Admission: £1 adults, 55p children, students, and senior citizens. Open Easter–mid-Nov., daily 10–5.*

Just a few miles to the north along the A68 you'll encounter signs for the **Woodland Visitor Centre,** where you can learn about the role that the Borders estates—major landholdings with woodland and tenanted farms—played in shaping the Borders landscapes. The center is on the estate of the marquis of Lothian and conveys the life of a Borders estate through a custom-built interpretative center, which contains audiovisuals and displays on the theme of timber and woodland management. *Monteviot, at the junction of A68 and B64000, tel. 08353/306. Admission: £1.50 adults, 75p children. Open Easter–Oct., daily 10:30–5:30.*

You can then navigate eastward on the A698, keeping the **Waterloo Monument** on your left. This pencil-thin tower is another reminder of the whims and power of the landowning gentry: An earlier marquis of Lothian built the monument in 1815, with the help of his tenants, in celebration of the victory of Wellington at Waterloo. If you have time, you can walk to the tower from the Woodland Centre. *Off B6400, 5 mi north of Jedburgh.*

Kelso, about 5 miles to the northeast, is one of the most attractive Borders burghs. Often described as having a Continental flavor—some visitors think it resembles a Belgian market town—the town has a broad, paved square and accurate examples of Scots town architecture. **Kelso Abbey** is the least intact ruin of the four great Border abbeys—just a gaunt fragment of what was once the largest of the group. Tall and slim with little rounded turrets, it must have looked reassuringly fortresslike when the Benedictines from Picardy moved in, in 1128. The Tweed crossing at Kelso was important to both sides in the Border wars, however, and the abbey was much knocked about by armies advancing to or retreating from each other's countries. The last monks and the townsfolk who had taken refuge with them died leaping from the turrets onto the English spikes and spears in 1545, after which the structure was reduced to its present fragmentary—but highly atmospheric—state. *Bridge St., tel. 031/244–3101. Admission free. Open Apr.–Sept., Mon.–Sat. 9:30–6, Sun. 2–6; Oct.–Mar., Mon.–Sat., 9:30–4, Sun. 2–4.*

Just 2 miles northwest of Kelso, on the bank of the **River Tweed,** stands the palatial mansion of **Floors Castle.** Ancestral home of the duke of Roxburghe, the castle was built by William Adam in 1721 and modified with mock-Tudor touches by William Playfair in the 1840s. A holly tree in the deer park marks the place where King James II was killed in 1460 by a cannon that "brak in the shooting." *A6089, tel. 0573/223333. Admission: £3 adults, £1.50 children, £2.40 senior citizens, £8 family ticket. Open mid-Apr.–late Sept., Sun.–Thurs. 10:30–5:30; July and Aug., open daily, 10:30–5:30; Oct., Sun. and Wed. 10:30–4:30. Check locally for variations.*

Do not confuse the comparatively youthful Floors Castle with **Roxburgh Castle,** nearby, off the A699. Only traces of rubble and earthworks remain of this ancient pile. The modern-day village of **Roxburgh** is young. The original Roxburgh, one of the oldest burghs in Scotland, has virtually disappeared, though its name lives on not only in the duke's title, but in the name of the old county of Roxburghshire.

Follow the A698 eastward about five miles along the north bank of the Tweed to **Coldstream,** perched on the English border. This stretch of the Tweed is lined with dignified houses and gardens, the best known of which is **The Hirsel,** the estate of former British prime minister Sir Alec Douglas Home (Lord Home of The Hirsel). A complex of farmyard buildings now serves as a craft center and museum, and there are interesting walks in the extensive grounds. It's a favorite spot for bird-watchers, and superb rhododendrons bloom here in late spring. (The house itself is not open to the public.) *A697, immediately west of Coldstream, tel. 0890/2834. Open daily during daylight hours.*

Three miles above Coldstream the England-Scotland border extends down from the hills and runs beside the Tweed for the rest of its journey to the sea. Coldstream itself, once, like Gretna, a marriage place for runaway couples from the south (a plaque on the former bridge tollhouse recalls this fact), is celebrated in military history. In 1659, General Monck raised a regiment of foot guards here on behalf of his exiled monarch Charles II; known as the Coldstream Guards, the successors to this regiment have become an elite corps in the British army. The **Coldstream Museum,** situated in the guards' former headquarters, recalls the founding of the regiment. *Market Square, Coldstream, tel. 0890/2630. Admission: 50p adults, 25p children. Open Easter–Oct., Mon.–Sat. 10–1 and 2–5, Sun. 2–5.*

If you are spending a lot of time in the area, you could tour even farther east, certainly as far as **Berwick-Upon-Tweed** and **Manderston House** (*see* Off the Beaten Track, *below*). Otherwise circle westward on any of a number of minor routes west of the A697 to reach **Mellerstain House,** 7 miles northwest of Kelso. Devotees of ornate country houses are well served in the Borders. Begun in the 1720s, Mellerstain was finished in the 1770s by Robert Adam and is considered to be one of his finest creations. Sumptuous plasterwork covers almost all interior surfaces, and there are outstanding examples of 18th-century furnishings. The beautiful terraced gardens are as renowned as the house. *Off A6089, tel. 057-381/225. Open Easter and May–Sept., Sun.–Fri. 12:30–5.*

West of Mellerstain is the B6397, and a short way west of that sits a characteristic Borders structure that certainly contrasts with the luxury of Mellerstain House. **Smailholm Tower** stands gaunt and uncompromising on top of a barren, rocky ridge. Built solely for defense, this 16th-century Border *peel* (small fortified towers common to this region) offers memorable views. If you let your imagination wander in this windy spot, you can almost see the flapping pennants and rising dust of an advancing raiding party and hear the anxious securing of doors and bolts. Sir Walter Scott found this an inspiring spot. His grandfather lived at nearby Sandyknowe Farm (not open to the public), and the young Scott visited the tower often during his childhood. *Off B6404. Admission: £1 adults, 50p children and* *senior citizens. Open Apr.–Sept., Mon.–Sat. 9:30–6, Sun. 2–6; Oct.–Mar., Mon.–Sat., 9:30–4, Sun. 2–4.*

⑩ Sir Walter's final resting place, **Dryburgh Abbey,** is another five miles to the southwest. Situated on gentle parkland in a loop of the Tweed, Dryburgh is certainly the most peaceful and secluded of the abbeys on this excursion. The abbey suffered from English raids until, like Melrose, it was abandoned in 1544. The style is Transitional, a mingling of rounded Romanesque and pointed Early English. The side chapel, where the Haig and Scott families lie buried, is lofty and pillared, detached from the main buildings. *Off A68. Admission: £1.70 adults, 90p children and senior citizens. Open Apr.–Sept., Mon.–Sat. 9:30–6, Sun. 2–6; Oct.–Mar., Mon.–Sat., 9:30–4, Sun. 2–4.*

There is no escaping Sir Walter in this part of the country: Four
⑪ miles from Dryburgh is **Scott's View,** possibly the most photographed rural view in the south of Scotland. (Perhaps the only view that is more often used to summon a particular interpretation of Scotland is Eilean Donan Castle, far to the north.) You arrive at this peerless vista by taking the B6356 north from Dryburgh. A poignant tale is told of the horses of Scott's funeral cortege: On their way to Dryburgh Abbey they stopped here out of habit as they had so often in the past. The sinuous curve of the River Tweed, the gentle landscape unfolding to the triple peaks of the **Eildons,** then rolling out into shadows beyond, is certainly worth seeking—and costs nothing to enjoy.

Next cross the main A68 to reach Melrose, another five miles to
⑫ the west. **Melrose Abbey,** last of the four Borders abbeys in the tour, is in the center of this handsome community. It is still impressive: a red sandstone shell with slender windows in the Perpendicular style and some delicate tracery and carved capitals, carefully maintained. Among the carvings high on the roof is one of a bagpipe-playing pig, a figure you are not likely to encounter elsewhere in your travels. "If thou would'st view fair Melrose aright, go visit it in the pale moonlight," wrote Scott in *The Lay of the Last Minstrel,* and so many of his fans took the advice literally that a sleepless custodian begged him to rewrite the lines. *Main Square, Melrose, tel. 031/244–3101. Admission: £1.70 adults, 90p children and senior citizens. Open Apr.–Sept., Mon.–Sat. 9:30–6, Sun. 2–6; Oct.–Mar., Mon.–Sat., 9:30–4, Sun. 2–4.*

Next to the abbey is the National Trust for Scotland's **Priorwood Gardens,** which specializes in flowers for drying. There is also an orchard adjacent to the gardens with a variety of old apple species. *Admission by donation. Open Apr., Nov., and Dec., Mon.–Sat. 10–5:30; May–Oct., Mon.–Sat. 10–5:50, Sun. 2–5:30.*

Also in the main square—which is really a triangle—is the renovated **Melrose Station,** the only surviving station of the old **Waverley Route,** which until 1969 ran between Edinburgh and Carlisle. (The first main line in Britain to be abandoned, the Waverley Route was discontinued amid much public protest.) Built in Jacobean style and long considered one of the most handsome small-town stations in Scotland, the Melrose Station was saved and its exterior restored. It is now used as offices, with a restaurant on the ground floor (*see* Time Out, *below*).

Time Out The **Melrose Station Restaurant** (tel. 089–682/2546) offers light lunches as well as complete evening meals.

Also in the center of Melrose at the **Ormiston Institute** is the Trimontium Exhibition, which reveals the fact that the largest Roman settlement in Scotland was at Newstead nearby and displays artifacts discovered there. *Admission: £1 adult, 50p children. Open Mar.–Oct., daily 10–12:30 and 2–4:30.*

⓭ Two miles west of Melrose stands one of the Borders' most visited attractions, **Abbotsford House,** home of Sir Walter Scott. In 1811, already an established writer, Scott bought a farm on this site named Cartleyhole, which was a euphemism for the real name, Clartyhole (*clarty* means muddy or sticky in Scots). The name was surely not romantic enough for Scott, who renamed the property and eventually had it entirely rebuilt in the Romantic style, emulating several other Scottish properties. The resulting pseudo-monastic, pseudo-baronial mansion became the repository for the writer's collection of Scottish memorabilia and historic artifacts. The library holds some 9,000 volumes. Scott died here in 1832. Today the house is owned by his descendants. *B6360, tel. 0896/2043. Admission: £2.20 adults, £1.10 children. Open late Mar.–Oct., Mon.–Sat. 10–5, Sun. 2–5.*

⓮ **Galashiels,** a gray and busy Borders town a few miles farther west, is still active with textile mills and knitwear shops. At the **Peter Anderson Woollen Mill** is a museum of the town's history and industry; visitors can go on a mill tour and learn about the manufacture of tartans and tweeds. *Nether Mill, Galashiels. Admission: £1 adults, 50p children. Open year-round, Mon.– Sat. 9–5; June–Sept., also Sun. noon–5. Guided tours Mon.– Thurs. 10:30, 11:30, 1:30, 2:30, Fri. 10:30 and 11:30.*

Also nearby is the **Borders Wool Centre,** complete with live sheep and spinning demonstrations: It is difficult to escape the Borders' primary industry. *Wheatlands Rd., off A72, northwest of Galashiels, tel. 0896/4293. Open Apr.–Oct., Mon.–Fri. 9–5, Sat. 9–4; Nov.–Mar., weekdays 10–4. Open Sun. in Aug.*

From Galashiels you have a choice of southern routes to Selkirk. You can take a small western diversion along the A707 to ⓯ **Bowhill.** Another of the stately homes in the Borders, this 19th-century building houses an outstanding collection of works by Gainsborough, Van Dyck, Canaletto, Reynolds, and Raeburn, as well as porcelain and period furniture. *Off A708, 3 mi west of Selkirk, tel. 0750/20732. Admission to house: £3 adults, £1 children; admission to grounds: £1 adults, children free. House open July, Mon.–Sat. 1–4:30, Sun. 2–6; grounds and playground open May–Aug., Sat.–Thurs. noon–5, Sun. 2–6 (open Fri. in July).*

⓰ **Selkirk** itself is a hilly outpost with a smattering of antiques shops and an assortment of bakers selling the Selkirk Bannock and other cakes—evidence of Scotland's incurable sweet tooth. The local museum, **Halliwell's House,** contains a reconstructed old-style ironmonger's shop. *Off main square, tel. 0750/20096 or 0750/20096. Admission free. Open Apr.–June and Sept.– Oct., Mon.–Sat. 10–12:30 and 1:30–5, Sun. 2–4 (July and Aug., daily 10–6); Nov.–mid-Dec. daily 2–4.*

The main A7 then switchbacks gently southward to **Hawick,** the largest of the Borders towns but not necessarily the most interesting. The town does have a good leisure center, as well as a number of workaday shops on its bustling main street. There are also mill tours: try **Wrights of Trowmill** (tel. 0450/ 72555). Hawick also has an attractive recreational area, **Wilton Lodge Park,** which encompasses the **Hawick Museum,** featuring, inevitably, plenty of material on textile heritage, as well as other aspects of Borders life, notably rugby football. *Wilton Lodge Park, western outskirts of Hawick, tel. 0450/73457. Admission: 70p adults, 35p children. Open Apr.–Sept., Mon.–Sat. 10–noon and 1–5, Sun. 2–5; Oct.–Mar., Mon.–Fri. 1–4, Sun. 2–4.*

From Hawick it's just a short drive back to Jedburgh.

Tour 2: The Galloway Highlands

Numbers in the margin correspond to points of interest on the Dumfries and Galloway map.

Galloway is the name given to the southwest portion of Scotland, west of the main town of Dumfries. This tour takes in a number of the area's diverse scenic options—from its gentle coastline and breezy uplands to places that are gradually disappearing below blankets of conifers. Use caution when negotiating the various side roads off the A75 that are mentioned in this tour: although the main trunk road has been improved in recent years, dawdling visitors are liable to find aggressive trucks tailgating them as these commercial vehicles race for the Irish ferries at Stranraer and Cairnryan. (Anything as environmentally sensible as a direct east–west railway link was closed years ago.) Trucks notwithstanding, Galloway offers some of the most pleasant touring roads in Scotland. The local folk are also quite friendly; the area has thus far been able to avoid being overrun by tourists.

17 The M6 deteriorates into the A74 before reaching **Gretna.** Gretna and **Gretna Green** are, quite simply, an embarrassment to native Scots. What else can you say about a place that advertises "amusing joke weddings," as does one of the visitor centers here? This focus on all things tartan and kitsch provides a rather tawdry introduction to Scotland. The reason for all these strange goings-on at anvils and village blacksmiths is tied to the reputation the community received as a refuge for runaway couples from England, who once came north to take advantage of Scotland's less strict marriage laws. At one time anyone could perform a legal marriage in Scotland. Often the village blacksmith did the honors, presumably because he was conveniently situated near the main road. The runaway weddings stopped in 1940.

The landscape is not very impressive around the flat fields of the **Upper Solway Firth.** You'll find more of interest as you con-
18 tinue west beyond the town of Annan. Inside **Ruthwell Parish Church,** 4 miles west of Annan, is the eighth-century **Ruthwell Cross,** an Anglican Christian sculpture admired for the quality of its carving. Considered an idolatrous monument, it was destroyed by the Scottish authorities in 1640 but was later reassembled. Nearby is the **Savings Bank Museum,** which tells the story of the savings-bank movement, founded by the Reverend Doctor Henry Duncan in 1810. *Ruthwell, 6½ mi west of Annan, tel. 038/787–640. Admission free. Open daily 10–1 and 2–5; closed Sun. and Mon. in winter.*

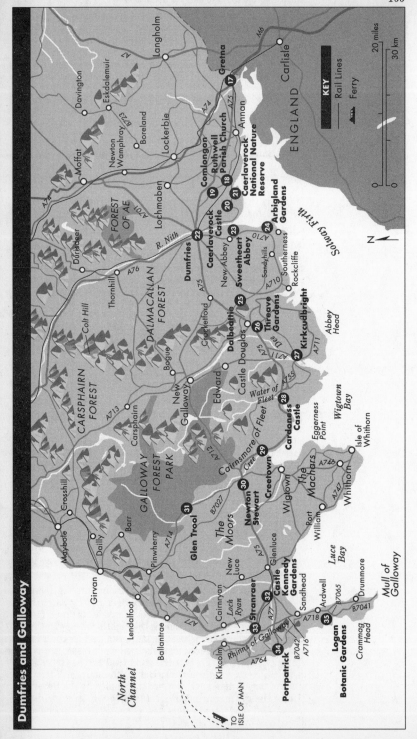

Dumfries and Galloway

KEY

Rail Lines

Ferry

20 miles

30 km

North Channel

Langholm

Davington

Eskdalemuir

Moffat

Boreland

Newton Wamphray

Lockerbie

FOREST OF AE

Durisdeer

Lochmaben

Gretna

Annan

Carlisle

ENGLAND

Solway Firth

M6

17

Comlongon 19

Ruthwell Parish Church 18

Caerlaverock National Nature Reserve 21

20

Arbigland Gardens 24

Thornhill

R. Nith

Caerlaverock Castle 23

Sweetheart Abbey

22

Dumfries

New Abbey

DALMACALLAN FOREST

CARSPHAIRN FOREST

Colt Hill

Bogue

Carsphairn

New Galloway

Cocketford

25

Dalbeattie

Threave Gardens 26

27 Kirkcudbright

Sandyhills

Southerness

Rockcliffe

Abbey Head

Castle Douglas

Edward

Water of Fleet

GALLOWAY FOREST PARK

Cairnsmore of Fleet

28 Cardoness Castle

Eggerness Point

Wigtown Bay

Crosshill

Maybole

Dailly

Barr

Girvan

Pinwherry

Lendalfoot

Ballantrae

Glen Trool 31

The Moors

30 Newton Stewart

29 Creetown

Wigtown

The Machars

Isle of Whithorn

Port William

Whithorn

Cairnryan

Loch Ryan

New Luce

Glenluce

Castle Kennedy Gardens

Sandhead

32 Stranraer

33

Ardwell

35

Luce Bay

Drummore

Mull of Galloway

Crammag Head

Kirkcolm

34 Portpatrick

Rhinns of Galloway

Logan Botanic Gardens

TO ISLE OF MAN

N

Less obscure perhaps is what may be the first Scottish castle
⑲ you'll see, **Comlongon,** on the B724. A more recent mansion
house adjoins this well-preserved 15th-century border keep.
The owner of Comlongon is in step with his medieval dwelling:
He makes armor. Visitors can also enjoy the accommodations of
a bed-and-breakfast at the castle. *B724, midway between
Dumfries and Annan, tel. 038/787–283. Admission: £1 adults,
70p children. Open Mar.–Nov., Mon.–Wed. and Fri.–Sat.
10–4, Sun. noon–4.*

Farther along the B725 is the **Brow Well,** a square, rock-cut pool
in a field by the road. A sickly Robert Burns visited the well in
1796 at the urging of his doctor, an advocate of open-air bath-
ing; Burns died later that month.

⑳ A few minutes away, on a coastal loop of the B725, is **Caerlaverock Castle,** moated and built in a triangular design unique
in Britain. This 13th-century fortress has solid-sandstone ma-
sonry and an imposing double-tower gate house. King Edward
of England besieged the castle in 1300, when his forces occupied much of Scotland as the Wars of Independence com-
menced. The castle suffered many times in Anglo-Scottish
skirmishes. *Off B725, 9 mi south of Dumfries, tel. 031/244–
3101. Admission: £1.20 adults, 60p children. Open Apr.–
Sept., Mon.–Sat. 9:30–6, Sun. 2–6; Oct.–Mar., Mon.–Sat.
9:30–4, Sun. 2–4.*

㉑ Also on the B725 is the **Caerlaverock National Nature Reserve,** a
treat for bird-watchers, who can observe wintering wildfowl
from blinds and a visitor center. *B725, by Caerlaverock Castle,
tel. 038/777–275. Admission free. Open year-round.*

㉒ The nearby town of **Dumfries,** where Robert Burns spent the
last years of his short life, is a no-nonsense, red-sandstone community. The **River Nith** meanders through Dumfries, and the
pedestrian-only town center makes shopping a pleasure (the
A75 now bypasses the town).

Not surprisingly, in view of its close association to the poet,
Dumfries has a **Robert Burns Centre,** housed in a sturdy former
mill overlooking the river. The center has an audiovisual program and an extensive exhibit on the life of the poet. *Mill Rd.,
tel. 0387/64808. Admission free. Open Apr.–Sept., Mon.–Sat.
10–8, Sun. 2–5; Oct.–Mar., Tues.–Sat. 10–1 and 2–5.*

The town also contains Burns's favorite pub (the Globe Inn),
the house he lived in, and his mausoleum.

As you travel westward again, the real Galloway begins. Cross
the River Nith and head out of town by the A710, another coastal loop. Within a few minutes you reach the village of **New Ab-**
㉓ **bey. Sweetheart Abbey,** which provides a mellowed red and
roofless backdrop to the village, was founded in 1273 by
Devorgilla Balliol, in memory of her husband, John. The couple's son, also named John, was the puppet king installed in
Scotland by Edward of England, when the latter claimed sovereignty over Scotland. After John's appointment the Scots gave
him a scathing nickname that would stay with him for the rest
of his life: *Toom Tabard,* meaning "Empty Shirt." *A710 at New
Abbey, tel. 031/244–3101. Admission: £1 adults, 50p children.
Open Apr.–Sept., Mon.–Sat. 9:30–6, Sun. 2–6; Oct.–Mar.,
Mon.–Wed. and Sat. 9:30–4, Thurs. 9:30–noon, Sun. 2–4.*

Continue south through bright-green landscape along the
A710 to the sign for **Arbigland Gardens.** Here pops up another
of Galloway's curious tales: The son of the former gardener of
Arbigland, whose name was John Paul, left Scotland and became the founder of the U.S. Navy. This seafaring son, John
Paul Jones, returned to his native coast in a series of daring
raids in 1778. The gardens tended by Jones's father are typical
of the area: lush and sheltered, with blue water visible through
the protecting trees. You are only moments from the coast. *Off
A710, by Kirkbean, tel. 038/788–283. Admission: £1 adults,
50p children. Open May–Sept., Tues., Thurs., and Sun. 2–6.*

The road to **Southernness** (A710) ends in a welter of caravan
holiday homes in the shadow of one of Scotland's earliest lighthouses, built in 1749 by the port authorities of Dumfries, anxious to make the treacherous River Nith approaches safer.

The road then turns west and becomes faintly Riviera-like. You
can take a brisk walk from **Rockcliffe** to **Sandyhills,** two of the
sleepy coastal communities overlooking the creeping tides and
endless shallows of the **Solway coast.** Eventually the road turns
north to **Dalbeattie.** Like the much larger Aberdeen far to the
northeast, Dalbeattie's buildings were built with local granite
from the town's quarry. Granite has a well-scrubbed gray glit-
ter, but Dalbeattie is not typical of Galloway towns, whose
housefronts are predominantly painted in pastels.

Castle Douglas lies just a few minutes west, away from the
coast. Although it is a pleasant town with a long main street
where the home bakeries vie for business, Castle Douglas's
main attraction is its proximity to **Threave Gardens.** As Scotland's best-known charitable conservation agency, the National Trust for Scotland cares for several garden properties. This
horticultural undertaking demands the employment of many
gardeners—and it is at Threave that the gardeners train, thus
ensuring there is always some fresh development or experimental planting here. This gives lots of vigor and interest to the
sloping parkland around the mansion house of Threave. There
is a good visitor center as well. *South of A75, 1 mi west of Castle
Douglas, tel. 031/244–3101. Admission £2.80 adults, £1.40
children and senior citizens. Gardens open daily 9–sunset;
walled garden and greenhouses open daily 9–5.*

Threave Castle (not to be confused with the mansion house in
Threave Gardens) is a few minutes away by car and is signposted from the main road. To get there you must leave your car
in a farmyard (trying to pretend you don't have the feeling
you're intruding) and walk the rest of the way. Reassured by
the Historic Scotland signs (because Threave is being cared for
by the national government), you make your way down to the
reeds by the river on an occasionally muddy path. At the edge
of the river you can then ring a bell, and, rather romantically, a
boatman will come to ferry you across to the great, gaunt tower
looming from a marshy island in the river. Threave was an early
home of the Black Douglases, the earls of Nithsdale, and lords
of Galloway. The castle was dismantled in the religious wars of
the mid-17th century, though enough of it remains to have
housed prisoners from the Napoleonic Wars of the 19th century. *North of A75, 3 mi west of Castle Douglas, tel. 031/244–
3101. Admission £1 adults, 50p children (inc. ferry). Open
Apr.–Sept., Mon.–Sat. 9:30–6, Sun. 2–6.*

From Threave you can make your way from **Castle Douglas**
southwest to **Kirkcudbright.** (The unclassified road just east of
the A711 is recommended if you want a glimpse of rural Galloway.) The River Dee meets the sea at Kirkcudbright, which is
one of the best looking of Galloway burghs, at least when the
tide is in (as in all Solway estuaries there is a lot of mud about at
low water). Kirkcudbright is an 18th-century town of unpretentious houses, some of them color washed in pastel shades
and roofed with the blue slates of the district. For much of this
century it has been known as an artists' town, and its L-shaped
main street is full of crafts and antiques shops. Conspicuous in
the town center is **Maclellan's Castle,** the shell of a once-elabo-
rate castellated mansion dating from the early 16th century.
*Off High St., tel. 031/244–3101. Admission: £1 adult, 50p chil-
dren. Open Apr.–Sept., Mon.–Sat. 9:30–6, Sun. 2–6; Oct.–
Mar., Sat., 9:30–4, Sun. 2–4.*

The delightfully old-fashioned **Stewartry Museum,** stuffed with
all manner of local paraphernalia, allows you to putter and absorb as much or as little as takes your interest in the mahogany
display cases. *St. Mary St., tel. 0557/31643. Admission: £1
adults, 50p students and senior citizens, children free. Open
Easter–Apr. and Oct., Mon.–Sat. 11–4; May, June, Sept.,
Mon.–Sat. 11–5; July, Aug. Mon.–Sat. 11–7:30, Sun. 2–5;
Nov.–Easter, Sat. 11–4.*

You can twist your way westward by the A755, across the
bridge to reach **Gatehouse of Fleet,** a peaceful, pleasant back-
woods sort of place, with a castle guarding its southern approach from the A75. **Cardoness Castle** is a typical Scottish
tower house, severe and uncompromising. The 15th-century
structure once was the home of the McCullochs of Galloway,
then later the Gordons. *A75, 1 mi southwest of Gatehouse of
Fleet, tel. 031/244–3101. Admission: £1 adult, 50p children.
Open Apr.–Sept., Mon.–Sat. 9:30–6, Sun. 2–6; Oct.–Mar.,
Sat. 9:30–4, Sun. 2–4.*

If you single-mindedly pursue the suggested policy of avoiding
the A75, then your route will loop to the northwest. Take a
right by the Anwoth Hotel in Gatehouse of Fleet, where the
signpost points to Gatehouse Station. This route will provide
you with a taste of the Galloway hinterland. Beyond the wooded
valley where the **Water of Fleet** runs (local rivers are often referred to as "Water of . . ."), dark hills and conifer plantings
lend a brooding, empty air to this lonely stretch. Soon the road
circles left, returning to the low-ground community of
Creetown, noted for its **Gem Rock Museum.** The museum has an
eclectic mineral collection and is the perfect place to pick up a
pair of earrings or another rocky trinket. *A75, tel. 0671–82/
554. Admission: £2 adults, £1 child, £1.50 senior citizens, £5
family ticket. Open Easter–Sept., daily 9:30–6; Nov.–Easter,
daily 9:30–5.*

The solid and bustling little town of **Newton Stewart** makes a
good touring base with the far western region of Galloway (*see*
The Machars in Off the Beaten Track, *below*). One possible excursion to the north from Newton Stewart takes you to the **Galloway Forest Park** (open at all times, admission free). Take the
A714 north from town along the wooded valley of the **River Cree**
(there is a nature reserve, the Wood of Cree) on the far bank.
After about 10 miles turn right at the signpost for **Glen Trool.**
This road leads you toward the hills that have thus far been the

backdrop for the woodlands. Watch for another sign for Glen Trool. Follow this little road through increasingly wild woodland scenery to its terminus at a car park. Only after you have left the car and climbed for a few minutes on to a heathery knoll does the full, rugged panorama become apparent. With high, purple-and-green hilltops shorn rock-bare by glaciers; a dark, winding loch; and thickets of birch trees sounding with birdcalls; the setting almost looks more highland than the real Highlands to the north. Glen Trool is one of Scotland's best-kept secrets. Note **Bruce's Stone,** just above the car park, marking the site where Scotland's champion Robert the Bruce (King Robert I) won his first victory, in 1307, in the Scottish Wars of Independence.

If this excursion has whetted your appetite for the wilder side of Galloway, retrace your route to the A714, then cross over to the B7027 farther westward, taking a road west at **Glassoch Bridge** (on the B7027). Once you escape the thick conifers, this passage leads high into the moorland. If in doubt, follow signs for the moor community of **New Luce.** You can drop down to the green valleys of the Lowlands from there to visit **Castle Kennedy Gardens,** a high point of the area. The original Castle Kennedy is the gaunt shell seen on the grounds. It was burned out in 1716. The present property owners, the earl and countess of Stair, live on the grounds, at **Lochinch Castle,** built in 1864. Pleasure grounds dispersed throughout the property were built by the second earl of Stair in 1733. The earl was a field marshal and used his soldiers to help with the heavy work of constructing banks, ponds, and other major landscape features. When the rhododendrons are in bloom, the effect is kaleidoscopic. *North of A75, 3 mi east of Stranraer, tel. 0776/ 2024. Admission: £1.80 adults, 50p children, £1 senior citizens. Open Apr.–Sept., daily 10–5.*

Time Out   There is a pleasant **tearoom** at the Castle Kennedy Gardens, but if a more substantial meal is required, try the **Eynhallow Hotel** nearby, for its homecooked bar food (tel. 05814/256).

The green and rolling countryside of the western end of Galloway affords dairy herds plenty of pasture. **Stranraer** is the main ferry port (if you happen to make a purchase in one of its shops, you may wind up with some Irish coins in your change). More scenic, perhaps, is the holiday town of **Portpatrick,** a few miles west on the A77, across the Rhinns of Galloway. Once an Irish ferry port, Portpatrick's exposed harbor eventually proved too risky for larger vessels. Today the village is the starting point for Scotland's longest official long-distance footpath, the **Southern Upland Way,** which runs a switchback course for 212 miles to **Cockburnspath,** on the eastern side of the Borders. Just south of Portpatrick are the lichen-yellow ruins of 16th-century **Dunskey Castle,** accessible by a cliff-top path. Within the village is **Little Wheels Museum,** which displays model cars and railways and toys. *Tel. 077/681–536. Admission: £1.20 adults, 80p children, £1 senior citizens, £3.50 family ticket. Open Easter–Oct., Sat.–Thurs. 11–4 (telephone to confirm times).*

Portpatrick is halfway down the **Rhinns of Galloway,** and this area's southern portion has a number of interesting places to visit. Take the B7042/A716 to **Ardwell House Gardens,** a pleasant garden on a domestic scale. *Ardwell, 11 mi southeast of*

*Stranraer. Admission: 70p adults, 35p children. Open Mar.–
Oct., daily 10–6.*

35 More spectacular for garden lovers are the **Logan Botanic Gardens,** an outstation of Edinburgh's **Royal Botanic Garden.** The
Logan Gardens feature plants that enjoy the prevailing mild
climate: especially tree ferns and cabbage palms and other
southern-hemisphere exotica. *Off B7065, 14 mi south of Stranraer. Tel. 077/686–231. Admission: £1.50 adults, 50p children,
£1 senior citizens. Open Mar. 15–Oct., daily 10–6.*

If you wish to continue to the southern tip of the Rhinns, to the
Mull of Galloway, follow the B7065/B7041 until you run out of
land. The cliffs and seascapes here are rugged, and there is a
lighthouse and a bird reserve.

The Borders and the Southwest for Free

Glen Trool (*see* Tour 2)
Scott's View (*see* Tour 1)
View from Smailholm Tower (*see* Tour 1)
Walks on the Southern Upland Way (*see* Tour 2)

What to See and Do with Children

Biggar Puppet Theatre regularly presents performances by
Purves Puppets. The theater also has games and a picnic area.
*B7016, east of Biggar, tel. 0899/20631. Admission: £3.50
adults, £3 children. Open Mon., Tues., and Thurs.–Sat 11–5;
Sun. 2–5.*

Castle Douglas's **Blowplain Open Farm** provides guided tours
showing the area's daily life on a small hill farm. *Balmaclellan,
Castle Douglas, tel. 06442/206. Admission: £1.50 adults, 75p
children. Open Easter–Oct., weekdays and Sun. 2–6.*

Border Collie and Sheepdog Centre (*see* Off the Beaten Track,
below)

Bowhill Adventure Playground, Bowhill (*see* Tour 1). *Off A708, 3
mi west of Selkirk, tel. 0750/20732. Admission to grounds and
playground: £1 adults, children free. Open Apr.–Aug., Sat.–
Thurs.*

Drumlanrig Castle adventure playground (*see* Off the Beaten
Track, below)

Little Wheels Museum, Portpatrick (*see* Tour 2)

Luce Bay Shore Centre, at the village hall in Monreith, is home
to an activity center based on seashore life. *Tel. 09887/527.
Open July–Aug., Sun.–Fri. 10:30–5.*

Palgowan Open Farm, for ardent ranch lovers, has everything
from Highland and Galloway cattle to sheep and sheepdogs to
stone dyking and skin curing. *By Glen Trool, Newton Stewart,
tel. 0671/84–227. Admission: £1.50 adults, £1 children. Open
Easter week, May, June, Sept., and Oct., Tues.–Thurs. from
2PM on; July–Aug., weekdays from 2.*

Teviotdale Leisure Centre, one of the best-equipped centers in
the area, has all manner of recreational facilities, including a
swimming pool, squash courts, bowls, and a sauna. *Mansfield
Rd., Hawick, tel. 0450/74440. Open daily 10–9.*

At the children's nursery in **Thirlestane Castle,** children are allowed to play with Victorian-style toys and masks and to dress up in costumes. The nursery is one of myriad rooms in the 17th-century castle. *Lauder, 28 mi south of Edinburgh, tel. 05782/430. Admission: £3 adult, £2 children, £8 family ticket. Open Easter week, May, June, and Sept., Wed., Thurs., and Sun. 2–5; July–Aug., Sun.–Fri. 2–5 (grounds open noon–5).*

Off the Beaten Track

The **Border Collie and Shepherd Centre,** housed in what was once the smallest school in Scotland (closed since 1937), resembles a sheepdog shrine. The dogs demonstrate their skills, and there is a photography exhibition, a tearoom, and a crafts shop. *Rte. A701, 12 mi north of Moffat, tel. 08997/267. Admission: £1.70 adults, £1 children. Sheepdog-handling demonstrations daily at 11, 2, and 3:30 or by appointment.*

Drumlanrig Castle is an ornate red-sandstone structure built on the site of an earlier Douglas stronghold about 15 miles northwest of Dumfries in Nithsdale. The 17th-century castle contains Louis XIV furniture and a valuable collection of paintings by Leonardo da Vinci, Holbein, Rembrandt, and others. There's also a crafts shop and visitor center on the grounds. *Off A76, tel. 0848/30248. Admission: £3.50 adults, £1.50 children, £2.50 senior citizens; park only £1.50. Castle open May–Aug., Mon.–Wed., Fri., and Sat. 11–5, Sun. 1–5. Grounds open May–Sept.*

Grey Mare's Tail waterfall, on the wild road to Selkirk (A708), makes a dramatic 220-foot plunge as it drops down a cataract from Loch Skene. The short path to the cascade is treacherous in wet weather, but after heavy rain a close-up view is impressive. (Heed the warnings at the information kiosk on the site.) The area around the falls is noted for its wild flowers. *Off A708, 10 mi north of Moffat, tel. 041/552–8391 (the National Trust for Scotland).*

Hermitage Castle is the most complete remaining example of the gaunt and grim medieval border castles. Restored in the early 19th century, it was built in the 14th century (replacing an earlier structure) to guard what was at the time one of the important routes from England into Scotland. The original owner, Lord Soulis, notorious for diabolical excess, was captured by the local populace, who wrapped him in lead and boiled him in a cauldron, or so the tale goes. The castle lies on an unclassified road between the A7 and B6399, about 10 miles south of Hawick. *Liddesdale, tel. 031/244–3101. Admission: £1 adults, 50p children. Open Apr.–Sept., Mon.–Sat. 9:30–6, Sun. 2–6; Oct.–Mar., Sat., 9:30–4, Sun. 2–4.*

Manderston House is a good example of the grand, no-expenses-spared Edwardian country house. The family who built it made their fortune selling herring to Russia. An original 1790s Georgian house on the site was completely rebuilt to the specifications of John Kinross. The finest craftsmen from overseas made the decorative stucco work. The staircase is silver plated (thought to be unique) and was modeled after the Petit Trianon at Versailles. There is also much to see downstairs in the kitchens, and outdoors, among a cluster of other buildings, is the unique marble dairy. *Off A6105, 2 mi east of Duns, tel. 0361/83450. Admission to house and grounds: £3.75 adults, £1 chil-*

dren; admission to grounds only: £2 adults, 50p children. Open mid-May–Sept., Thurs. and Sun. 2–5:30.

The **Museum of Scottish Lead Mining,** which can be reached from the A76 (the main Dumfries–Kilmarnock road) by taking the Mennock Pass through rounded moorland hills, tells the story of one of Scotland's lesser-known industries. There are underground trips for the stout-hearted. The museum is at Wanlockhead, a fairly bleak spot and Scotland's highest-elevated village. *B797, tel. 065974/387. Admission: £2.50 adults, £1 children, £1.80 senior citizens and students. Open Easter–Oct., daily 11–4:30.*

The Machars **The Machars** is the name given to the triangular promontory south of the main east–west route (A75) in western Galloway, roughly 10 miles from the Rhinns of Galloway (*see* Tour 2). This is an area of gently rolling farmlands, yellow gorse hedgerows, rich grazings for dairy cattle, and a number of stony prehistoric sites. Most of the glossy, green expanse is used for dairy farming. Fields are bordered by dry stane dykes (dry walling) of sharp-edge stones; and small hills and hummocks give the area its characteristic frozen-wave look, a reminder of the glacial activity that shaped the landscape.

Places of interest in the Machars include the sleepy hamlet of **Wigtown,** which has a broad main street and colorful housefronts. Down by the muddy shores of Wigtown Bay there's a monument to the Wigtown Martyrs, two women who were tied to a stake and left to drown in the incoming tide during the anti-Covenant witch-hunts of 1685. Much of Galloway's history is linked with Border feuds, but even more with the ferocity of the so-called Killing Times, when the Covenanters were persecuted for their belief that the king should be second to the church, and not vice versa. Wigtown, like several other places in the region, is dominated by a hilltop Covenanters' Monument, a reminder of the old persecutions.

Just a mile south of Wigtown is the **Bladnoch Distillery,** Scotland's southernmost producer of malt whiskey. The local product is smooth; some even say it's sweet. You can try a free taste for yourself at the end of the tour. There's also a shop and visitors center. *A714, tel. 09884/2235 or 2236. Admission free. Open Apr.–Oct., Mon.–Fri. 10–4.*

The Machars are well known for their early Christian sites. The A746 was a pilgrim's way and a royal route. It ends at **Isle of Whithorn** (which is not in fact quite an island), a place that early Scottish kings and barons sought to visit at least once in their lives. The pilgrimage was often prescribed as a penance, but these pleasant shores impose no penance today. The goal was St. Ninian's chapel, the 4th-century cell of Scotland's premier saint. Some pilgrims made for Whithorn village and others for the sandspit "isle." Both places claimed to be the site of the original "Candida Casa" of the saint. As you approach Whithorn's 12th-century priory, observe the royal arms of pre-1707 Scotland (that is, Scotland before the Union with England) carved and painted above the arch of the Pend (covered way). The **Whithorn Dig and Visitor Centre** explains the significance of what is claimed to be the site of the earliest Christian community in Scotland. *45–47 George St., Whithorn, tel. 09885/ 508. Admission: £2.50 adults, £1.25 children and senior citi-*

zens, £6 family ticket. Open Easter–Oct., daily 10:30–5, Sun.
1–5.

Near the visitor center stands the **Whithorn Museum,** which includes a collection of early-Christian crosses and the shell of a
12th-century priory. *Main St., Whithorn, tel. 031/244–3101.
Admission: £1 adults, 50p children. Open Apr.–Sept., Mon.–
Sat. 9:30–6, Sun. 2–6; Oct.–Mar., Sat. 9:30–4, Sun. 2–4.*

Shopping

As with other, more rural areas of Scotland away from the Central Belt, shopping in the Borders and Galloway area centers or
the larger towns; stores in the smaller towns and villages usually fulfill only day-to-day requirements. The Borders in particular has a fairly affluent population, which is reflected in the
variety of upscale shops in Peebles, for example, where there
are more deluxe stores than might be expected. If you want to
spend a morning shopping, Peebles is the place to do it. Below
are a few of the interesting shops to be discovered on your travels.

The Borders   For made-to-measure kilts and suits in Borders tweeds and tartans, your first stop should be **George Wright** (22 Horsemarket,
Kelso, tel. 0573/224542), where they are made on the premises
and can be shipped to your home address. As the center of Scotland's woolen-goods industry, this area also provides the
country's widest choice of ready-made items. Try **Peter Anderson Woollen Mill** in Galashiels (Nether Mill, tel. 0896/2091);
Hawick's cashmere and lambswool specialist, **Tom Scott Knitwear Shop** (Kirkside, Denholm, tel. 045087/531); or the **Scottish
Museum of Woollen Textiles** (Walkerburn, tel. 089–687/619 or
281), where a large mill shop offers a wealth of styles.

Throughout the Borders region look for the specialty sweets indigenous to the area—Jethart Snails, Hawick Balls, Berwick
Cockles, and Soor Plums—which, with tablet (a solid cara-
mellike candy) and fudge, are available from most local confectioners.

Peebles   You can easily spend a day browsing on Peebles High Street
and in the courts and side streets leading off it, where you will
find temptation at every turn. Do not miss **Scott's Hardware
Store** (50 High St.), which modern merchandising methods
have thankfully not yet penetrated. Every kind of tool, imple-
ment, fixture, fitting, and garden requirement (and mouse-
traps) is spread in glorious array over floors and walls—and
even hang from the ceiling. Not far away is **Jumpers** (38 High
St.), which sells its namesakes, as well as cardigans in a variety
of colors and designs in cotton or wool. **Head to Toe** (43 High
St.) stocks natural beauty products of all descriptions; dried
flowers and porcelain display dishes are also available. High
Street is also the place to browse for antiques: both **Cobwebs** (68
High St.) and **Town House Antiques** (25 High St.) have a large
inventory that includes everything from furniture to china to
jewelry. Craftsmen and jewelers are also well represented on
the street: Gold- and silversmith **Keith Walter** (28 High St.)
makes items on the premises and stocks jewelry made by other
local designers. Visitors to **The Country Shop** (56 High St.) will
have a hard time leaving this upscale gift store without purchasing something.

Dumfries and Galloway In the western half of the area covered in this chapter, **Dumfries** is the main shopping center, with all the big-name chain stores. Here there are also specialty shops, such as the **Bryden Gallery** (11 Galloway St.), which offers an assortment of artists' work—mainly paintings but also ceramics and porcelain. You can even commission a painting, perhaps a portrait or a favorite landscape, and it will be ready in two weeks. **Greyfriars Crafts** (56 Buccleuch St.) has mainly Scottish goods, including Edinburgh Crystal, Caithness Glass, and Ettrick Valley textiles. For a souvenir that's easier to pack, try **David Hastings** (Marying, Shieldhill, Amisfield, Dumfries, tel. 0387/710451), which has more than 40,000 old postcards, as well as mounted photographic prints of Scottish life 100 years ago.

If you are visiting Drumlanrig Castle (*see* Off the Beaten Track, *above*), north of Dumfries at **Thornhill**, do not miss the crafts center (tel. 0848/31555) in the stable block, chock full of all types of crafts work, including marionettes and engravings. To the northeast, at **Moffat, The Corner Gallery** (Churchgate) stocks Scottish designer knitwear from the smaller producers; here you are likely to see a more original selection of goods than in the larger knitwear outlets. Farther west, at Castle Douglas, **The Posthorn** (26–30 St. Andrew St., tel. 0556/2531) consists of two shops specializing in gift items, including the figurines made by Border Fine Art; export facilities are provided. **Galloway Gems** (7 Carlingwark St.) not only has gold and silver jewelry, but also stocks mineral specimens and polished stone slices. At **Gatehouse of Fleet,** there is a well-stocked gift and crafts shop (and a tearoom with delicious home-baked goods) at the newly opened **Mill on the Fleet** heritage centre (High St., tel. 0557/814099). Also in the town is **Galloway Lodge Preserves** (24–28 High St.), whose Marmalade, Mustard and Merchandise Shop stocks the complete line of the company's locally made produce.

At **Kirkcudbright,** the **Harbour Cottage Art Gallery** may be just the place to find a painting of the part of Scotland that is dearest to you; prices vary, depending on the artist exhibiting. Pictures of a different sort can be found at **Benny Gillies Books, Maps and Prints** (31 Victoria St., Kirkpatrick Durham), which stocks hand-colored antique maps and prints featuring areas throughout Scotland.

Finally the **Creetown Gem Rock Museum** (Creetown, tel. 0671/82554; *see also* Tour 2 in Exploring the Borders and the Southwest, *above*) sells extraordinary mineral and gemstone crystals in its gift shop—both loose and in settings.

Sports and Fitness

Bicycling Bicycles may be rented from **Hawick Cycle Centre** (45 N. Bridge St., Hawick, tel. 0450/73352), **Glentress Mountain Bike Centre** (Glentress, Peebles, tel. 0721/22934), **On Yer Bike** (Dunsdale Rd., Selkirk, tel. 0750/20168), **Scottish Border Trails** (Bowhill, Selkirk, tel. 0750/22515), and **North Riding Cycles** (4 Blair Terr., Portpatrick, tel. 077/681–568).

Fishing The **Solway Firth** is noted for sea angling, notably at **Isle of Whithorn, Port William, Portpatrick, Stranraer,** and **Loch Ryan.** Game fishing far exceeds the reputation (and the expensive salmon beats) of the River Tweed, sometimes called the

Queen of Scottish Rivers. A comprehensive guide, *Angling in the Scottish Borders*, is the only way to find your way around the many Borders waterways. The *Castabout Anglers Guide to Dumfries and Galloway* covers the southwest. The tourist-information boards for Galloway and the Borders (*see* Important Addresses and Numbers in Essential Information, *above*) carry these and other publications (including a comprehensive information pack). In short, finding suitable water in this area is quite easy.

Golf   There are 23 courses in Galloway and 17 in the Borders. Both tourist boards (*see* Important Address and Numbers in Essential Information, *above*) supply comprehensive leaflets.

Health and   The **Teviotdale Leisure Centre** (Mansfield Rd., Hawick, tel.
Fitness Clubs   0450/ 74440), one of the best-equipped centers in the area, has a swimming pool, squash courts, bowls, a sauna, and locker-room facilities. *Open 10–9.*

Horseback Riding   The Borders and Galloway have a strong tradition of horseback riding, sustained partly through the Common Ridings, a popular annual rite. There are many riding and trekking centers, including **Pony Trekking Centre** (Brighouse Bay Holiday Park, Borgue, Kirkcudbright, tel. 05577/267), **Barend Properties Riding School and Trekking Centre** (Sandyhills, by Dalbeattie, Kirkcudbright, tel. 038778/663), **Westertoun Riding Centre** (Westruther, Gordon, Berwickshire, tel. 05784/270), **Hazeldean Holiday and Riding Centre** (Hassendean Burn, Hawick, tel. 045087/373), and **Bowhill Riding Centre** (Bowhill, Selkirk, tel. 0750/20192).

Water Sports   The **Galloway Sailing Centre** (Loch Ken, tel. 06442/626) rents dinghies, windsurfing equipment, and canoes.

Dining and Lodging

The Borders region is reasonably well served by hotels ranging from the budget to the luxury categories. Being slightly off the beaten tourist track, Dumfries and Galloway offer a good selection of relatively inexpensive options for accommodations and food.

Dining

Highly recommended restaurants are indicated by a star ★.

Category	Cost*
Very Expensive	over £40
Expensive	£30–£40
Moderate	£15–£30
Inexpensive	under £15

per person, including appetizer, main course, dessert, and VAT

Lodging

Highly recommended hotels are indicated by a star ★.

Category	Cost*
Very Expensive	over £120
Expensive	£100–120
Moderate	£80–100
Inexpensive	under £80

All prices are for a standard double room, including breakfast and tax.

Boreland **Nether Boreland.** A member of the Farm Holiday Bureau,
Lodging Nether Boreland offers an insight into Scottish farming, combined with spacious accommodations and fresh local produce at meals. Golf, fishing, and pony trekking are close by. *Boreland, Lockerbie, Dumfriesshire, tel. 05766/248. 3 rooms with bath. No credit cards. Closed Nov.–Feb. Inexpensive.*

Dalbeattie **Auchenskeoch Lodge.** This quaint and informal Victorian
Lodging shooting lodge, now a country-house hotel, has five bedrooms and delicious food (for residents only). Guests are urged to help themselves to each of the delectable puddings on offer. Many of the vegetables and herbs are home grown on the 20 acres of gardens and woodland surrounding the house. The furnishings have a comfortable, faded, chintzy elegance; there is a full-size billiards table in the game room. The sitting room offers crammed bookshelves and an open fire, and a private loch and croquet lawn provide outdoor entertainment. *Auchenskeoch, by Dalbeattie, tel. 038778/277. 5 rooms with bath. MC, V. Closed Nov.–Feb. Inexpensive.*

Galashiels **Woodlands House Hotel.** This wonderful hotel has stunning
Dining and Lodging views over Tweeddale. The restaurant, too, is first-class and specializes in fresh seafood and hearty Scottish cuisine. *Windyknowe Rd., TD1 1 RG, tel. 0896/4722. 9 rooms with bath. Facilities: restaurant, garden, golf, horseback riding. MC, V. Moderate.*

Gatehouse-of-Fleet **Cally Palace.** This hotel was once a private mansion (built in
Dining and Lodging 1759), and many of the public rooms in the Georgian building
★ retain their original grandeur, which includes elaborate plaster ceilings and marble fireplaces. The house is surrounded by 100 acres of gardens, loch, and parkland, and an outdoor heated swimming pool, solarium, and sauna are some of the facilities at visitors' disposal. Scottish produce features in the French-influenced restaurant, and the bedrooms are individually decorated and well equipped. The staff is exceptionally friendly and prepared to spoil you. *Gatehouse-of-Fleet, Galloway, tel. 0557/814341. 55 rooms with bath. Facilities: restaurant, bar, pool, extensive leisure facilities. V. Closed Feb. Moderate.*

Jedburgh **Spinney Guest House.** Made up of unpretentiously converted
Lodging and modernized farm cottages, this is a bed-and-breakfast of-
★ fering the highest standards for the price. *Langlee, TD8 6PB, tel. 0835/63525. 3 rooms, 2 with bath. No credit cards. Closed Nov.–Mar. Inexpensive.*

Kelso **Sunlaws House.** Situated a few miles from Floors Castle, home
Dining and Lodging of the duke of Roxburghe, this magnificent country house is
★ also owned by him and is reputed to have accommodated Prince Charles Edward Stuart in 1745. More than 200 acres of secluded woodlands surround the hotel, and croquet, game shooting, tennis, and fishing are available along private stretches of

the Tweed and Teviot rivers. Public rooms are comfortably furnished with relaxing lighting and plenty of plants. The bedrooms, decorated in keeping with the style of this country-gentleman's retreat, are well equipped; bedrooms are also available in the stable courtyard for avid sports enthusiasts who are likely to want to come and go at odd hours. Fresh local produce cooked in hearty but contemporary style with a Scottish/French flavor satisfies the largest appetites, and packed lunches are prepared on request. *Heiton, by Kelso, Roxburghshire, tel. 05735/331. Restaurant reservations required. Jacket and tie advised. 22 rooms with bath. AE, DC, MC, V. Expensive–Very Expensive.*

Lodging **Ednam House Hotel.** This large, attractive hotel is on the banks of the River Tweed, close to Kelso's grand abbey and the many fine Georgian and early Victorian buildings in the old Market Square. Ninety percent of the guests are return visitors, and the open fire in the hall, sporting paintings, and cozy armchairs give the place a homey feeling. *Bridge St., TD5 7HT, tel. 0573/224168. 32 rooms with bath. Facilities: restaurant, garden, fishing, horseback riding. MC, V. Closed Dec. 24–Jan. 12. Moderate.*

Melrose **Marmion's Brasserie.** This cozy restaurant features outstand-
Dining ing country-style cuisine. It is a great place to stop for lunch
★ after a visit to nearby Abbotsford or Dryburgh Abbey. *Buccleuch St., tel. 089/682–2245. Reservations advised. Dress: casual. No credit cards. Closed Sun. Moderate.*

Dining and Lodging **Burts Hotel.** Built in 1772, this quiet hotel in the center of Melrose retains a considerable amount of its period style, updated with modern conveniences. It has a particularly welcoming bar, with a cheerful open fire and a wide selection of fine malt whiskies, that is ideal for a quiet dram before or after a meal in the elegant dining room, with its choice of Scottish and international cuisines. Most of the hotel was recently refurbished, so the bedrooms and public areas are freshly and attractively decorated in their own individual styles. *Market Sq., Melrose, Roxburghshire, tel. 089/682–2285. Restaurant reservations advised. Dress: neat but casual. 21 rooms with bath. AE, DC, MC, V. Inexpensive.*

Peebles **Peebles Hydro.** This is one of those rare places that not only has
Dining and Lodging something for everyone, but has it in abundance. Archery,
★ snooker, pony trekking, squash, a whirlpool, and a sauna are just a few of the diversions the hotel offers. The elegant Edwardian building, reminiscent of a French château, is set on 30 acres. Bedrooms are comfortably furnished, though inevitably in a hotel of this size, room sizes and decorative standards can vary. In the public areas the high ceilings emanate an airy, spacious ambience. The restaurant features a Scottish menu, with local salmon, lamb, and beef. *Peebles, tel. 0721/20602. Restaurant reservations advised. Dress neat but casual. 137 rooms with bath. AE, DC, MC, V. Moderate–Expensive.*
★ **Cringletie House.** Surrounded by grounds that include an old-fashion walled garden whose produce is used in the hotel, this privately owned property, personally supervised by the owners and their family, is well worth seeking out. There are turrets and crow-step gables in traditional Scottish baronial style, and the spacious first-floor drawing room has an elaborate ceiling and pretty views of the valley. The simple yet comfortably furnished bedrooms are a prelude to the hotel's major achieve-

ment: its food. The restaurant is popular with locals (especially for Sunday lunch) for its straightforward, delicious home cooking, a welcome contrast to the oversauced and overdecorated food served in many country-house hotels. *Eddleston, by Peebles, tel. 07213/233. Restaurant reservations required. Dress: neat but casual. 13 rooms with bath. MC, V. Closed Jan.–Feb. Moderate.*

Park Hotel. This hotel, on the banks of the River Tweed at the northern tip of the Ettrick Forest, offers comfort and tranquility. The restaurant serves superior Scottish cuisine, many of the dishes based on local salmon, trout, and seafood. *Innerleithen Rd., EH45 8BA, tel. 0721/20451. Restaurant reservations advised. Dress: casual. 24 rooms with bath. Facilities: restaurant, golf. AE, DC, MC, V. Moderate.*

Port William
Dining and Lodging

Corsemalzie House. This attractive 19th-century mansion is set on 40 acres of peaceful grounds behind the fishing village of Port William. Sporting pursuits are the hotel's main attraction, with shooting, sea and game fishing, and golf on tap. The restaurant features a "Taste of Scotland" menu, and the public rooms and bedrooms are in keeping with the country-house style of the hotel. *Corsemalzie, Port William, Newton Stewart, Wigtownshire, tel. 098886/254. 15 rooms with bath. AE, MC, V. Closed late-Jan.–Feb. Inexpensive–Moderate.*

Quothquan
Lodging

Shieldhill. This foursquare Norman manor has stood on this spot since 1199 (though it was greatly enlarged in 1560). It is in an ideal location for touring the Borders—just 27 miles from Edinburgh and 31 from Glasgow. The rooms are named after great Scottish battles—Culloden, Glencoe, Bannockburn— and are furnished with great comfort (miles of Laura Ashley fabrics and wallpaper). Shieldhill is one of the few British members of the Romantik Hotels association. *Quothquan, near Biggar, ML12 6NA, tel. 0899/20035. 11 rooms with bath. Facilities: restaurant, garden. AE, DC, MC, V. Expensive–Very Expensive.*

St. Boswells
Dining and Lodging

Dryburgh Abbey Hotel. Right next to the abbey ruins, this civilized hotel is surrounded by beautiful scenery and features a satisfactory restaurant (dinner only). Specialties include traditional Scottish fare. *St. Boswells TD6 0RQ, tel. 0835/22261. Restaurant reservations required. Dress: casual. 29 rooms, 21 with bath. Facilities: restaurant, golf. AE, DC, MC, V. Moderate.*

Selkirk
Dining and Lodging

Philipburn House. An 18th-century house set on 5 acres of gardens, Philipburn is an ideal place for families. The property has deluxe accommodations furnished in traditional style. The house has recently been extended and the bedrooms updated; these rooms and the dining room have a Scandinavian feeling, all pine and floral prints. A bit of advice: The hotel is renowned for its food, so work up a good appetite in the heated swimming pool and do not gorge yourself on the superb home-baked afternoon teas. Venison; Borders lamb; and, of course, salmon and trout from the nearby River Tweed are featured on Philipburn's imaginative menu. *Selkirk, tel. 0750/20747. 16 rooms with bath. AE, DC, MC, V. Moderate.*

Swinton
Dining

Four Seasons Restaurant. This eatery is part of the Wheatsheaf Hotel, a country inn on the main street, which also offers good bar lunches. However, if you are not in a hurry, lunch or dine in this little restaurant for a real taste of the chef's skills. The sheer class of the cuisine, whether the meal is beef, salmon, or venison, has won widespread praise, yet neither the food nor the small but carefully chosen wine list is overpriced. *Wheatsheaf Hotel, Swinton, tel. 089/086–257. Jacket and tie advised. Reservations required. MC, V. Closed Mon. Moderate–Expensive.*

The Arts and Nightlife

The Arts

Some of the Borders area approaches the sphere of Edinburgh and its artistic life. Farther afield, **Gracefield Arts Centre** (Edinburgh Rd., Dumfries, tel. 0387/62084) has public art galleries and studios with a constantly changing exhibition program. **The Dumfries and Galloway Arts Festival** is usually held at the end of May, at several venues throughout the region.

Some of the major towns have movie houses showing films on general release. Note also the **Robert Burns Centre Film Theatre** (Mill Rd., Dumfries, tel. 0387/64808), which features special-interest, foreign, and other films that are not widely released.

Nightlife

Small towns in a rural hinterland generally do not offer a wild, urban-style nightlife, although Hawick has the closest thing: **Humphreys Night Club** (Exchange Building, Towerdykeside, Hawick, tel. 0450/72445). Galashiels has **Digby's Discotheque** (Kingsway Entertainment Centre, Market St., tel. 0896/2767). Overall, there is a wide choice of hotel bars and pubs.

7 Fife and Angus

St. Andrews, Dundee

Introduction

By Gilbert Summers

The regions of Fife and Angus sandwich Scotland's fourth-largest—and often overlooked—city, Dundee. This is typical eastern-seaboard country: open beaches, fishing villages, and breezy cliff-top walkways. Scotland's east coast has only light rainfall throughout the year; northeastern Fife, in particular, may claim the record for the most sunshine and the least rainfall in all Scotland. Though the hills that attract so many visitors to Scotland may seem a long way west when you're touring the East Neuk of Fife (*neuk*, pronounced *nyook*, is Scots for *corner*), the particular charm of Angus is its variety: In addition to its seacoast and pleasant Lowland market centers, there's also a hinterland of lonely rounded hills with long glens running into the typical Grampian Highland scenery beyond.

Fife stretches far up the Forth Valley (which is west and a little north of Edinburgh). In these western parts the region still bears the scars of heavy industry, especially coal mining. These signs are less evident as you move farther east. Northeastern Fife, around the university-and-golf town of St. Andrews, seems to have played no part in the industrial revolution; the residents instead earned a livelihood from the grain fields or from the sea. Fishing has been a major industry, and in the past a string of Fife ports traded across the North Sea. Today the legacy of Dutch-influenced architecture— crow-step gables and distinctive town houses, for example—is still plain to see and gives these East Neuk villages a distinctive charm.

St. Andrews is unlike any other Scottish town. Once Scotland's most powerful ecclesiastical center, seat also of the country's oldest university, and then, much later, the very symbol and spiritual home of golf, the town has a comfortable, well-groomed air, sitting almost smugly apart from the rest of Scotland.

On the surface Dundee is a small workaday city, its heritage bound up with processing jute, making jam, and producing newspapers and comics (it's often referred to as the city of "jute, jam, and journalism"). In the 19th century it was a thriving whaling port. In short, the city has a rich and varied heritage, set in an industrial urban environment. Nevertheless, like Glasgow, Dundee has been dusting itself off and nowadays presents a brighter image to the visitor.

Angus—Dundee's hinterland—provides considerable attractions and diversions, though they're often overlooked by travelers who are driving between Fife or Perth and the Grampian countryside to the north. One of Angus's interesting features, which it shares with the eastern Lowland edge of Perthshire, is its fruit-growing industry. Seen from roadside or railway, what at first sight appear to be sturdy vineyards on field-length wires, turn out to be soft-fruit plants, mainly raspberries. The chief fruit-growing area is Strathmore, the broad vale between the northwesterly Grampian mountains and the small coastal hills of the Sidlaws behind Dundee. Striking out from this valley—the heart of the Angus region—visitors can make a number of day trips to uplands or seacoast.

Essential Information

Important Addresses and Numbers

Tourist Information Information is available from the **St. Andrews and North East Fife Tourist Board** (Information Centre, South St., St. Andrews, tel. 0334/72021), **Dundee Information Centre** (4 City Sq., Dundee, tel. 0382/27723), **Angus Tourist Board** (Information Centre, Market Pl., Arbroath, tel. 0241/72609). Smaller tourist-information centers operate seasonally in the following towns: Anstruther, Brechin, Carnoustie, Crail, Cupar, Forfar, Kirriemuir, and Montrose.

Emergencies For police, fire, or ambulance, dial 999 from any telephone. No coins are needed for emergency calls made from public telephone booths.

Doctors and Dentists Consult your hotel, a tourist-information center, or the yellow pages of the telephone directory for listings of local doctors and dentists.

Late-Night Pharmacies Late-night pharmacies are not found outside the larger cities. In St. Andrews, Dundee, and other larger centers pharmacies use a rotating system for off-hours and Sunday prescription service. Consult the listings displayed on pharmacy doors for the names and addresses of pharmacies that provide service outside regular hours. In an emergency the police can help you contact a pharmacist. Note that in rural areas general practitioners may also dispense medicines.

Arriving and Departing by Plane

Glasgow Airport (tel. 041/887–1111, ext. 4552), 50 miles west of Edinburgh, is now a major point of entry for international flights. Passengers landing in Glasgow have easy access to Edinburgh and Fife and Angus. **Edinburgh Airport** (tel. 031/333–1000), 7 miles west of downtown Edinburgh, has airlinks throughout the United Kingdom, as well as with a number of cities on the Continent.

Arriving and Departing by Car, Train, and Bus

By Car The M90 motorway from Edinburgh takes visitors to within a half hour of St. Andrews and Dundee. Travelers coming from Fife can use Route A914 or A92, then cross the Tay Bridge to reach Dundee, though the quickest way is to use the M90 and the A85. Travel time from Edinburgh to Dundee is about 1 hour, from Edinburgh to St. Andrews 1½ hours.

By Train **Intercity Rail** (tel. 031/556–2451) stops at Leuchars (for St. Andrews), Dundee, and at Arbroath and Montrose, in Angus.

By Bus Two companies, **Lothian Regional Transport** (tel. 031/220–4111) and **Guide Friday** (tel. 031/556–2244), run buses between Edinburgh Airport's main terminal building and Waverley Bridge in downtown Edinburgh, and from there, to various points throughout Fife and Angus. The buses run every 30 minutes during the day (9–5) and less frequently (roughly every 45 minutes) during off-peak hours and on weekends. The trip from the airport takes about 30 minutes (about 45 minutes during rush hour).

Getting Around

By Car   Fife is an easy area to get around and presents no major obstacles to the traveler. Most of the roads are quiet and
uncongested. The most interesting sights are in the east, which
is served by a network of cross-country roads. Angus is likewise an easy region to explore, being serviced by a main fast
road—the A94—which travels through the middle of the
Strathmore valley and then on to Aberdeen; another, gentler
road—the A92—that runs to the east near the coast; and a network of rural roads between the Grampians and Route A94.
Farther inland lies a series of long glens with cul-de-sac roads,
the perfect option for travelers seeking the solitude of high hills
and breezy moorlands.

By Train   The stations listed in Arriving and Departing, above, are the
area's only stations.

By Bus   A local network provides service from St. Andrews and Dundee
to many of the smaller towns throughout Fife and Dundee. The
fare for the Kirkaldy–St. Andrews run is £2.55; Perth–Dundee, £2.50; Perth–Montrose, £5.10. For information about
routes and fares call **Fife Scottish** (tel. 0592/642394) or
Strathtay Scottish (tel. 0382/28054).

Guided Tours

Orientation   The local bus companies listed in Getting Around by Bus,
above, offer a variety of general orientation tours of the main
cities and the region.

Special-Interest   The following operators offer tours tailored to individual requirements: **Highland Highlights** (Easter Colzie, Auchter-
muchty, Fife, tel. 0337/28977), **Links Golf Tours** (13 Argyle St.,
St. Andrews, tel. 0334/78639), and **Xcursions** (52 Portree Ave.,
Dundee, tel. 0382/730008).

Exploring Fife and Angus

Highlights for First-time Visitors

Angus Folk Museum (*see* Tour 2)
Crail Harbour (*see* Tour 1)
Edzell Castle (*see* Tour 2)
Falkland Palace (*see* Tour 1)
Fife Fisheries Museum (*see* Tour 1)
Glamis Castle (*see* Tour 2)
House of Dun (*see* Tour 2)

Tour 1: Around Fife

*Numbers in the margin correspond to points of interest on the
Fife Area and St. Andrews maps.*

❶   This tour starts in **St. Andrews**, Scotland's golf mecca and possibly the most visited town in the country after Edinburgh. The
center of this compact city retains its original medieval street
plan of three roughly parallel streets—North Street, Market
Street, and South Street—leading away from the city's earliest religious site, near the cathedral. The local legend regarding the founding of St. Andrews has it that a certain St.

Regulus, or Rule, acting under divine guidance, carried relics of St. Andrew by sea from Patras in Greece. He was shipwrecked on this Fife headland and founded a church. The holy man's name survives in **St. Rule's Church**, a square tower standing near the **cathedral** and predating it (1126) as the earliest building in St. Andrews. There are steps to the dizzying view from the top. The cathedral seen today is only a ruined, poignant fragment of what was formerly the largest and most magnificent church in Scotland. Work on it began in 1160, and consecration was finally celebrated in 1318, after several setbacks. The cathedral was subsequently damaged by fire and repaired, but finally fell into ruin during the Reformation, in the 16th century. Only ruined gables, parts of the nave south wall, and other fragments survive. The on-site museum helps visitors interpret the remains and gives a sense of what the cathedral must once have been like. *Museum and St. Rule's Tower, tel. 031/244–3101. Admission: £1.20 adults, 60p children and senior citizens. Open April–Sept., Mon.–Sat. 9:30–6, Sun. 2–6; Oct.–Mar., Mon.–Sat. 9:30–4, Sun. 2–4.*

Directly north of the cathedral on the shore stands **St. Andrews Castle**, which was started at the end of the 13th century. Its stature grew with the community's role as a religious center. Although now a ruin, there remains some vivid evidence of its turbulent history, including a rare example of a bottle dungeon, cold and gruesome, in which many prisoners spent their last hours. Even more atmospheric is the castle's mine and countermine, a tunnel dug by besieging forces in the 16th century. The defenders tunneled out to meet them below ground. You can stoop and crawl into this narrow passageway—an eerie experience, despite the addition of electric light. *Tel. 031/244–3101. Admission: £1 adults, 50p children. Open April–Sept., Mon.–Sat. 9:30–6, Sun. 2–6; Oct.–Mar., Mon.–Sat. 9:30–4, Sun. 2–4.*

After visiting the castle, you can walk west along the street called The Scores to reach the **Royal & Ancient Golf Club of St. Andrews** (open to club members only). This is the ruling house of golf worldwide and the spiritual home of all who play or follow the game. Its clubhouse on the dunes—a building of some dignity, more like a town hall than a clubhouse—is adjacent to St. Andrew's famous **Old Course**. The town of St. Andrews prospers on golf, golf schools, and golf equipment (the manufacture of golf balls has been a local industry for more than 100 years), and the Old Course is associated with the greatest players of the game, the most famous of whom is perhaps Tommy Morse. Tommy's father, old Tom, was the greatest golfer in the world—until his son reached the age of 17, won his first professional title, and went round the Old Course in 47. That was when fairways were not mown and greens were cut with a hand-scythe. The next year, 1868, Tommy won the Open Championship and held the title for five years. Then he died, at age 24, unchallenged supremo of golf, the likes of whom the game may never see again. In the churchyard near St. Rule's Tower and on a wall tablet in Holy Trinity church at South and Church streets, you will see memorials to Tommy Morris.

Just opposite the Royal & Ancient Golf Club is **The British Golf Museum,** which explores the centuries-old relationship between St. Andrews and golf and displays a variety of golf memorabilia. *Golf Pl., tel. 0334/78880. Admission: £3 adults, £1*

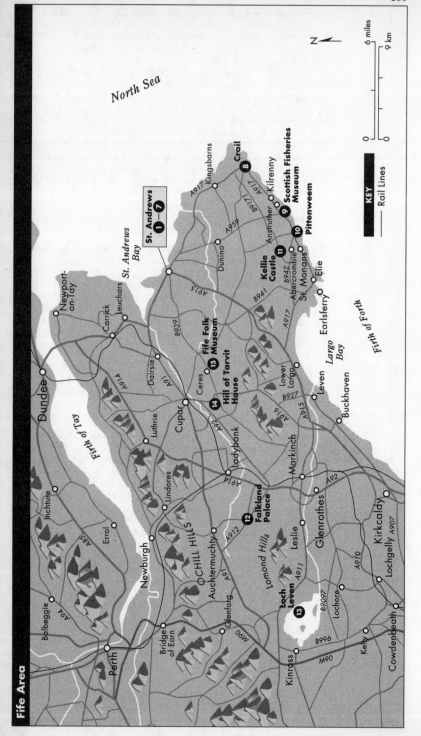

Fife Area

North Sea

St. Andrews **1 – 7**

St. Andrews Bay

Crail **8**

Kilrenny

Scottish Fisheries Museum **9**

Anstruther

Pittenweem **10**

Kellie Castle **11**

St Monans

Abercrombie

Elie

Earlsferry

Firth of Forth

Largo Bay

Lower Largo

Leven

Buckhaven

Fife Folk Museum **15**

Hill of Tarvit House **14**

Ceres

Cupar

Ladybank

Markinch

Glenrothes

Kirkcaldy

Lochgelly

Cowdenbeath

Kelty

Lochore

Kinross

Loch Leven **13**

Falkland Palace **12**

Leslie

Auchtermuchty

Lomond Hills

OCHIL HILLS

Newburgh

Lindores

Luthrie

Dairsie

Carrick

Leuchars

Newport-on-Tay

Dundee

Firth of Tay

Perth

Bridge of Earn

Glenfarg

Errol

Inchture

Balbeggie

Dunino

Kingsbarns

KEY
— Rail Lines

6 miles

9 km

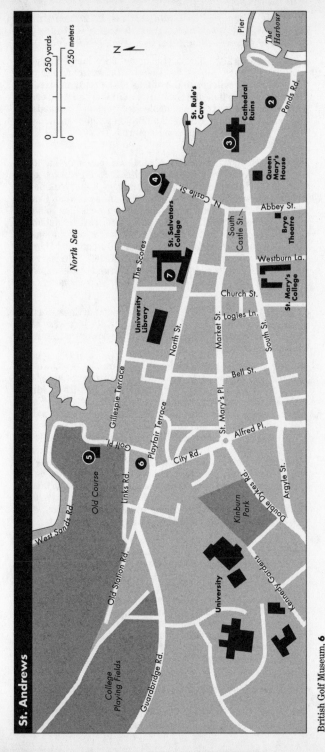

St. Andrews

250 yards
250 meters

N

North Sea

The Harbour

Pier

St. Rule's Cave

Cathedral Ruins 3

Queen Mary's House

Pends Rd.

2

Abbey St.

Brye Theatre

St. Salvators College 7

N. Castle St.

South Castle St.

Westburn La.

St. Mary's College

Church St.

The Scores

University Library

Logies Ln.

Market St.

North St.

South St.

Bell St.

Gillespie Terrace

St. Mary's Pl.

Playfair Terrace

City Rd.

Alfred Pl.

Argyle St.

Golf Pl.

Links Rd.

5

Old Course

West Sands Rd.

Double Dykes Rd.

Kinburn Park

Kennedy Gardens

University

Old Station Rd.

Guardbridge Rd.

College Playing Fields

British Golf Museum, **6**
Cathedral, **3**
Royal & Ancient Golf
Club of St. Andrews, **5**
St. Andrews Castle, **4**
St. Andrews
University, **7**
St. Rule's Church, **2**

children, £2 senior citizens and students, £7.50 family ticket. Open Mar. and Apr., Thurs.–Tues. 10–5; May–Oct., daily 10–5:30; Nov., Thurs.–Mon. 10–4; Dec.–Feb., Thurs.–Mon. 11–3.

7 St. Andrews is also known as the home of Scotland's oldest university. Founded in 1411, **St. Andrew's University** now consists of two fine old colleges in the middle of the town and some attractive modern buildings on the outskirts. A third old college (1512) has become the fashionable girls' school. The handsome university buildings can be explored on guided walks, sometimes led by students in scarlet gowns. *Tel. 0334/76161, ext. 258/488.*

8 Having sampled the religious, academic, and sporting ambience of St. Andrews, leave town by Route A917, which leads to the east and then south past the numerous East Neuk fishing communities along the Fife coast. Stop in the town of **Crail** to see its picturesque Dutch-influenced Town House, or Tolbooth, which contains the the oldest bell in Fife, cast in Holland in 1520. Full details on the heritage and former trading links of this tiny port can be found in the **Crail Museum and Heritage Center.** *62 Marketgate, Crail, tel. 0333/50869. Admission: £1 adults, 50p children. Open Easter week and June–Sept. 10–12:30 and 2:30–5 (confirm with the tourist information center).*

There is a superb photographic vantage point of the waterfront from the seaward edge of the housing estate just west of the harbor—especially if the tide is in and the flowers in the nearby garden are blooming.

9 A few minutes farther along A917 to the southwest is **Anstruther,** which boasts an attractive waterfront (larger than Crail's) with a few shops brightly festooned with children's buckets and spades as a gesture to seaside vacationers. Facing the harbor is the **Scottish Fisheries Museum,** housed in a colorful cluster of buildings, the earliest of which dates from the 16th century. This museum illustrates the difficult life of Scottish fishermen, past and present, through documents, artifacts, paintings, and tableaux. (These displays, complete with the reek of tarred rope and net, have been known to induce nostalgic tears in not a few old deckhands.) There are also floating exhibits at the quayside. *Anstruther harbor, tel. 0333/310628. Admission: £1.80 adults, £1 children. Open Apr.–Oct., daily 10–5:30, Sun. 11–5; Nov.–Mar., daily 10–4:30, Sun. 2–4:30.*

10 About 1½ miles farther down the road is **Pittenweem,** a working harbor with many examples of East Neuk architecture. Look for the crow-step gables (the stepped effect on the ends of the roofs), the white *harling* (Scots for *rough-casting,* the rough mortar finish on walls), and the red pantiles (S-shaped in profile). The "weem" part of the town's name comes from the Gaelic *uaime,* or *cave.* This town's particular cave is at Cove Wynd up a close (alleyway) behind the waterfront and contains the shrine of St. Fillan, a 6th-century hermit who lived there. *Cove Wynd, near harbor, tel. 0333/311495 (St. John's Episcopal Church). Admission: 25p adults, children free. Open Mon., Tues., Thurs.–Sat. 10–5, Sun. noon–5.*

11 For a break from this nautical atmosphere follow B942 inland to **Kellie Castle.** Dating from the 16th and 17th centuries and restored in Victorian times, the castle stands among the grain fields and woodlands of northeastern Fife. The castle is surrounded by four acres of attractive gardens. *B9171 (3 mi north-west of Pittenweem), tel. 033/38–271. Admission: £2.80 adults, £1.40 children for castle and gardens; £1 adults, 50p children for gardens only. Castle open Easter weekend and May–Oct., daily 2–6 (last admission 5:30).*

You could continue along the coast to take in **St. Monans,** with its working harbor and ancient church by the sea, as well as the twin communities of Elie and Earlsferry, whose sheltered waters are appreciated by sailboard enthusiasts. Alternatively, rejoin the A917 and pass through **Lower Largo,** birthplace of Alexander Selkirk, the Scottish sailor who was the prototype for Daniel Defoe's Robinson Crusoe. Follow signs for **Glenrothes,** a modern town with a selection of sporting facilities that is also notable for its public murals and sculptures.

From Glenrothes take the A92 north then the A912 northwest to reach **Falkland,** one of the most attractive communities in all Fife. A royal burgh of twisting streets and crooked stone houses, the town is dominated by **Falkland Palace,** a former hunting lodge of the Stuart monarchs and one of the earliest examples in Britain of the French Renaissance style. Overlooking the main street is the palace's most attractive feature—the south range of walls and chambers, rich with Renaissance buttresses and stone medallions, built for James V in the 1530s by French masons. James V died here in 1542, and the palace was also a favorite resort of his daughter, Mary, Queen of Scots. Behind the palace are gardens that contain a most unusual survivor: a "royal" tennis court (not at all like modern tennis) like the one at Hampton Court near London; the Falkland court was built in 1539 and is still in use. *A912 (11 mi north of Kirkcaldy, tel. 033–757/397. Admission: £3 adults, £1.50 children and senior citizens; gardens only: £2 adults, £1 children and senior citizens. Open Apr.–Sept., Mon.–Sat. 10–6, Sun. 2–6; Oct. and Nov., Mon.–Sat. 10–5, Sun. 2–5.*

The community lies at the foot of the Lomond Hills, which visitors traveling by car can explore via a road that climbs steeply to the west out of Falkland. These windy moorlands—with a hint of Highland air about them—are the place to get out of the car and do some walking; from these hills there are outstanding views over the fairly industrialized Forth Valley. Farther to the west as you follow A911 is Scotland's largest Lowland loch, **Loch Leven,** famed for its fighting trout. The area is also noted for its birdlife, particularly its wintering wildfowl. You can find out more about the ecology of the loch at the **Vane Farm Nature Reserve,** a well-equipped visitor center run by the Royal Society for the Protection of Birds, on the southern shore overlooking the loch. *Vane Farm, Rte. B9097, just off M90 and B996, tel. 0577/62355. Admission: £1.50 adults, 50p children, £1 senior citizens. Open Apr.–Oct., daily 10–5; Nov.–Mar., daily 10–4. Closed Christmas–New Year's Day.*

Strictly speaking, you've now reached the edge of the old county of Kinross, so to continue your Fife tour, circle back to the northeast along A91 through the green and rural dip in the center of Fife called the **Howe of Fife** (*howe* is Scots for *hollow*). Once it was marshy ground; it's now used for the cultivation of barley and soft fruits. Your next destination is **Cupar,** a busy market town with a variety of shops. On rising ground south of town (take Route A916) is the National Trust for Scotland's **Hill of Tarvit House.** A 17th-century mansion, the house was later altered in the high-Edwardian style at the turn of the 20th century by the Scottish architect Sir Robert Lorimer. Inside the house are fine collections of antique furniture, Chinese porcelain, bronzes, tapestries, and Dutch paintings. *A916 (2 mi south of Cupar), tel. 0334/53127. Admission: £2.80 adults, £1.40 children, students, and senior citizens; gardens only £1 adult, 50p children. Open Easter and April, Sat.–Sun. 2–6; May–Oct., daily 2–6 (last admission 5:30).*

Time Out In summer the National Trust operates a **tearoom** inside the Hill of Tarvit House, which is always stocked with tasty home-made Scottish baked goods.

Before making your way back to St. Andrews, you can learn more about the history and culture of rural Fife by visiting the ⑮ **Fife Folk Museum** at Ceres, reached by going south on A916 and east on B939. The life of local rural communities is reflected in artifacts and documents, all housed in suitably authentic buildings that include a former weigh house and adjoining weavers' cottages. *Tel. 033–482/250. Admission: £1.25 adults, £1 senior citizens, 50p children. Open Apr.–Oct., Sat.–Thurs. 2:15–5.*

Tour 2: Dundee and Angus

Numbers in the margin correspond to points of interest on the Angus Area map.

⑯ This tour starts with a walk through **Dundee** and continues with a drive up the coast as far as Montrose. The return loop leads you along peaceful back roads as far as Kirriemuir. Most of the roads in this area are uncluttered, with the exception of the main road from Perth/Dundee to Aberdeen—the A94—on which special care is needed.

Dundee's urban-renewal program—its determination to shake off its grimy industrial past—was motivated in part by the arrival of the **RRS (Royal Research Ship)** *Discovery,* the vessel used by Captain Robert Scott on his polar explorations, which was recently returned and made a permanent exhibit in the port where it was built. Visitors can sample life in the Antarctic aboard the ship. *Victoria Dock (just east of Tay Rd. Bridge), tel. 0382/201175 or 25282. Admission: £2.20 adults, £1.70 children. Open Apr.–May, Sept., weekdays 1–5, weekends 11–5; bank holidays, 11–5; June–Aug., daily 10–5.*

Also in the dock nearby is the frigate *Unicorn,* a 46-gun wooden warship. The *Unicorn* has the distinction of being the oldest British-built warship afloat (the fourth-oldest in the world), having been launched at Chatham, England, in 1824. On-board models and displays offer a glimpse into the history of the Royal Navy. *Victoria Dock (just east of Tay Rd. Bridge), tel. 0382/ 200900. Admission: £2 adults, £1.50 children, students, and senior citizens. Open daily 10–5.*

Dundee's principal museum and art gallery is **McManus Galleries,** which offers displays—many of them new—on a range of subjects, including local history, trade, and industry. *Albert Sq., tel. 0382/23141. Admission free. Open Mon.–Sat. 10–5.*

The **Barrack Street Museum** specializes in natural history, offering exhibitions on the wildlife and geology of Angus and the

Angus Area

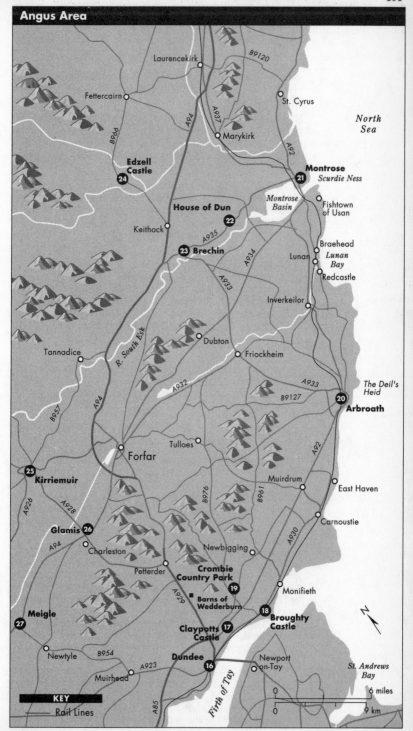

North Sea

Laurencekirk

B9120

Fettercairn

St. Cyrus

A94

A937

Marykirk

Edzell Castle
24

Montrose
21 *Scurdie Ness*

B966

House of Dun
22

Montrose Basin

Fishtown of Usan

Keithock

A935

23 Brechin

Braehead
Lunan *Lunan Bay*
Redcastle

A934

A933

Inverkeilor

Tannadice

Dubton

Friockheim

R. South Esk

A932

A933

The Deil's Heid

B9127

20

B957

A94

Arbroath

A926

25 Kirriemuir

Tulloes

Forfar

A928

Muirdrum

East Haven

A92

Glamis 26

Charleston

Carnoustie

B976

B961

Petterder

Newbigging

A930

A929

Crombie Country Park
19

■ Barns of Wedderburn

Monifieth

Meigle
27

Claypotts Castle 17

18 Broughty Castle

Newtyle

B954

Dundee
16

Muirhead

A923

Newport-on-Tay

St. Andrews Bay

A85

Firth of Tay

N

6 miles

9 km

Highlands. The museum also displays the skeleton of the famous Tay Whale, immortalized by Scotland's worst poet, William MacGonagall, born in Dundee in 1830. His consistently dire poems caused him to be lionized by Edinburgh's legal and student fraternity. The stranding of a whale locally was one of many incidents that moved him to verse. *Barrack St. and Meadowside, tel. 0382/23141, ext. 65152. Admission free. Open Mon.–Sat. 10–5.*

The **University Botanic Gardens** are a well-landscaped collection of native and exotic plants. Also on the premises are tropical and temperate greenhouses and a visitor center. *Riverside Dr., tel. 0382/66939. Admission free. Open Mar.–Oct. daily, 10–4:30; Nov.–Feb. daily, 10–3.*

In the eastern suburbs of Dundee, away from the surviving Victorian architecture of the city center, are two castles of interest. **Claypotts Castle** is a well-preserved 16th-century Z-plan tower house laid out on a Z-plan. *South of A92 (3 mi east of city center), tel. 031/244–3101. Admission £1 adults, 50p children. Open Apr.–Oct. Mon.–Sat., 9:30–6, Sun. 2–6.*

Approximately one mile farther east is **Broughty Castle.** This former fortress guarding the Tay estuary is now a museum with displays on fishing, ferries, and the history of the town's whaling industry. There is also a display of arms and armor. *Broughty Ferry (4 mi. east of city center), tel. 0382/23141 or 76121. Admission free. Open Oct.–June, Mon.–Thurs., Sat. 10–1 and 2–5; July–Sept., Mon.–Thurs., Sat. 10–1 and 2–5, Sun. 2–5.*

Dundee is ringed by country parks that offer ample sports and leisure activities. **Crombie Country Park** features a reservoir with extensive woodlands in 250 acres, as well as wildlife blinds, nature trails, a children's play park, picnic areas, and a display-and-interpretation center staffed by a ranger. *Off Rte. B961, 7 mi from Newbigging. tel. 024–16/360. Admission free. Open daily 10–dusk.*

Leave Dundee by the A92 coast road, which leads to **Arbroath** (15 miles north of Dundee), a holiday resort and fishing town where traditional boat-building can still be seen. Arbroath has several small curers and processors, with shops offering the "Arbroath smokie"—whole haddock gutted and lightly smoked—the town's most famous delicacy.

Arbroath Abbey, founded in 1178, in the center of town, is unmistakable and seems to straddle whole streets, as if the town was simply ignoring the redstone ruin in its midst. Surviving today are remains of the church, as well as one of the most complete examples in existence of an abbot's residence. From here in 1320, a passionate plea was sent by King Robert the Bruce and the Scottish church and nobles to Pope John XXII in far-off Rome. The pope had until then sided with the English kings, who refused, even six years after the Scots victory at Bannockburn, to acknowledge Scottish independence. The Declaration of Arbroath stated firmly, "For as long as but a hundred of us remain alive, never will we on any conditions be brought under English rule. It is in truth not for glory, nor riches, nor honours that we are fighting, but for freedom—for that alone, which no honest man gives up but with life itself." Some historians describe this plea (originally drafted in Latin) as the single most important document in Scottish history. The pope advised English King Edward to make peace, but warfare was to break out along the border from time to time for the next 200 years. *Arbroath town center, tel. 031/244-3101. Admission: £1 adults, 50p children. Open Apr.-Sept., Mon.-Sat. 9:30-6, Sun. 2-6; Mar.-Oct., Mon.-Sat. 9:30-4, Sun. 2-4.*

Also notable in the town is the **Signal Tower Museum.** Arbroath was the shore base for the construction of the Bell Rock lighthouse, on a treacherous, barely exposed offshore rock in the early 19th century. This signal tower was built to facilitate communication between the mainland and the builders working offshore. The museum in the tower now tells the story of the lighthouse, built by Robert Stevenson in 1811. (The name Stevenson is strongly associated with the building of lighthouses throughout Scotland, though the most famous son of that family is remembered for another talent: Robert Louis Stevenson gravely disappointed his family by choosing to become a writer instead of an engineer.) The museum also houses a collection of items related to the history of the town, its folk life, and the local fishing industry. *Ladyloan (west of harbor), tel. 0674/ 73232. Open Nov.-Mar., Mon.-Fri. 2-5, Sat. 10:30-1 and 2-5; Apr.-Oct., Mon.-Sat. 10:30-1 and 2-5, also Sun. 2-5 in Jul. and Aug.*

21 A few minutes' drive to the north, along the coast via the A92, is **Montrose,** a handsome, unpretentious town with a museum and a selection of shops. The town is also noted for its attractive beach. Behind Montrose the River Esk forms a wide estuary known as the Montrose basin. The Scottish Wildlife Trust operates a nature reserve here, with a good number of geese, ducks, and swans.

22 From Montrose head west on the A935. Signs will direct you to the National Trust for Scotland's leading attraction in this area, the **House of Dun**, overlooking the Montrose Basin. This 1730s mansion, built by architect William Adam, is particularly noted for its ornate plasterwork. *A935 (4 mi west of Montrose), tel. 067-481/264. Admission: £3 adults, £1.50 children. Open Easter and May-mid-Oct., daily 11-5:30.*

23 Farther west is **Brechin,** a small market town in Strathmore. Its cathedral was founded in about 1200 and contains an interesting selection of antiquities. Also nearby is the 10th-century **Round Tower,** one of only two on mainland Scotland (they are more frequently found in Ireland). It was originally built for the local Culdee monks.

24 Make your way due north by the B966, north of Edzell (which most Scots now associate with the U.S.-run, obscure military listening post nearby). **Edzell Castle,** an impressive ruin from the 16th century, is nestled among the Grampian foothills. This structure was originally a typical Scottish fortified tower, but was later transformed into a house that gave some degree of domestic comfort as well as protection from the elements. The simple "L" shape of the original building was extended, and a pleasance, or walled garden, was added in 1604. This formal garden, along with unique heraldic and symbolic sculptures, survives today. *Off of B966 (6 mi north of Brechin), tel. 031/ 244-3101. Admission: £1.50 adults, 80p children. Open Apr.-Sept., Mon.-Sat. 9:30-6, Sun. 2-6; Oct.-Mar., Mon.-Wed. and Sat. 9:30-4, Thurs. 9:30-noon, Sun. 2-4.*

You can rejoin the hurly-burly of the A94 for the journey back to Dundee, though the more pleasant route leads southwestward using minor roads (there are several options) along the face of the Grampians, following the fault line that separates highland and lowland at this point. Visitors to the region are struck by the fine ridge-top views that encompass great open spaces; this is relatively rare for Scotland, where so many vistas are framed by crags and thickets.

㉕ At the intersection of Routes B957 and A926 is **Kirriemuir,** heart of Angus's red sandstone countryside and birthplace of the writer and dramatist Sir James Barrie (1860–1937), most well known abroad as the author of *Peter Pan.* Barrie's house, now in the care of the National Trust for Scotland, contains a collection of manuscripts and personal mementos. In the wash house is a Peter Pan display. *9 Brechin Rd., Kirriemuir, tel. 0575/72646 or 72538. Admission: £1.20 adults, 60p children. Open Easter weekend; May–Sept., Mon.–Sat. 11–5:30, Sun. 2–5:30 (last admission 30 min. before closing).*

About 6 miles due south on the A928, across pleasantly rolling countryside, is the village of **Glamis,** site of the **Angus Folk Museum.** This museum village is made up of a row of 19th-century cottages with unusual stone-slab roofs; exhibits focus on the crafts and tools of domestic and agricultural life in the region over the past 200 years. *Off A94 (5 mi southwest of Forfar, tel. 0307/84288. Admission: £1.30 adults, 60p children. Open Easter and May–Sept., daily 11–5 (last tour 4:30).*

Approximately another mile to the southwest is **Glamis Castle,** one of Scotland's best-known castles because of its association with the present Royal Family. This was the childhood home of the current Queen Mother and the birthplace of Princess Margaret. The property of the earls of Strathmore and Kinghorne since 1372, the castle was largely reconstructed in the late-17th century; the original keep, which is much older, is still intact. One of the most famous rooms in the castle is Duncan's Hall, the legendary setting for Shakespeare's *Macbeth.* Guided tours offer visitors a look at fine collections of china, tapestries, and furniture. Other visitor facilities include shops, a produce stall, and tearoom. *A94 (5 mi southwest of Forfar), tel. 030–784/242. Admission: £3.70 adults, £2 children, £2.90 senior citizens and students, £11 family ticket. Open Easter, mid-Apr.–June, and Sept.–mid-Oct., daily noon–5:30; July and Aug., daily 11–5:30. Last admission 4:45.*

㉗ The local museum at **Meigle,** on the A94 in the wide swathe of Strathmore, has a magnificent collection of some 25 sculptured monuments from the Celtic Christian period (8th to 10th centuries), nearly all of which were found in or around a local churchyard. This is one of the most notable collections of medieval work in Western Europe. *A94 in Meigle (12 mi west/southwest of Forfar), tel. 031/244–3101. Admission: £1 adults, 50p children. Open Apr.–Sept., Mon.–Sat. 9:30–6.*

From Meigle you can take Route B954 back to Dundee, just 15 miles.

Fife and Angus for Free

Alexander Selkirk Statue (*see* Tour 1)
Arbroath Cliffs Nature Trail stretches for 3 miles along sand-

stone cliffs that are home to varied birdlife. The trail starts at the north end of the Arbroath Promenade.

Claypotts Castle (*see* Tour 2)

Mills Observatory. This public observatory has an astronomer in residence. Here you'll find telescopes, displays on astronomy and space exploration, a planetarium, and an audiovisual program. Viewing of the skies is subject to weather conditions. *Balgay Hill, Dundee, tel. 0382/67138. Admission free. Open Apr.–Sept., Mon.–Fri. 10–5, Sat. 2–5; Oct.–Mar., Mon.–Fri. 3–10, Sat. 2–5.*

Red Castle, Lunan Bay. This 15th-century sandstone tower house overlooks a sandy beach. *Off A92, 7 mi south of Montrose.*

St. Andrews Cathedral (*see* Tour 1)

White and Brown Caterthun Hill Forts (*see* Tour 2)

What to See and Do with Children

Craigtoun Country Park. Here children can choose from among a miniature railway, a re-created Dutch village, boating, bowling, putting, trampolines, and guided country walks. *Off A915 (2½ mi southwest of St. Andrews), tel. 0334/73666. Admission: £1.50 adults and children over 5, 75p children under 5, senior citizens, and students. Open Easter–early Oct., daily 10:30–6:30 (last admission 5:30).*

Monikie Country Park. This 185-acre park on a reservoir complex includes mixed woodlands and parklands with guided walks. There are children's play areas and picnic areas, as well as opportunities for canoeing, sailing, windsurfing, and rowing. *Off B961 (1 mi north of Newbigging, 10 mi north of Dundee), tel. 082–623/202 (Newbigging). Admission free. Open daily 10–dusk.*

Scottish Deer Centre. Here children can see red deer at close quarters on ranger-guided tours. There are also nature trails, an indoor adventure playground, a shop, and a restaurant. *A91, near Rankelour Farm (3 mi west of Cupar), tel. 033781/391. Admission £3.25 adults, £2 children, £2.50 senior citizens and students, £9 family ticket. Open Apr.–Oct., daily 10–5.*

Sea Life Centre. Sea lions, penguins, and many other forms of marine life are displayed here in settings designed to simulate their natural environment. The exhibits include numerous aquariums and pool gardens. *The Scores, West Sands, St. Andrews, tel. 0334/74786. Admission: £3.85 adults, £2.55 children 4–14, £3.25 senior citizens and students, £11.40 family ticket. Open daily 10–6.*

Off the Beaten Track

Fife Two points of interest are often overlooked by motorists touring rural Fife. Only minutes from the famous Old Course of St. Andrews, on Route A191 at **Leuchars,** is a 12th-century church with some of the finest Norman architectural features to be seen anywhere in Scotland. Note in particular the blind arcading (arch shapes on the wall) and the beautifully decorated chancel and apse.

A few minutes west of St. Andrews on the B939, an unclassified road goes through Strathkinness and about 3 miles later runs by the River Eden. The nearest community is at Dairsie (back on the A91). Stop for a moment at **Dairsie Bridge** over the river. It is 450 years old and has three arches. Above the trees rises the spire of **Dairsie Church,** dating from the 17th century, and the stark ruin of **Dairsie Castle**, often overlooked, stands gloomily over the river nearby. With wild-rose hedges, grazing cattle, and pheasants calling from the woody thickets, this is the very essence of rural, Lowland Fife, yet it's only about 15 minutes from the Old Course.

Angus The **White and Brown Caterthuns** are the remains of Iron Age hill forts that crown two rounded hills to the west and south of Edzell Castle. Lovers of wild places will enjoy the drive to the Caterthuns from Edzell (if in doubt at junctions, turn left), especially the climb up the narrow road (from Balrownie to Pitmudie) that passes between the two hills; along the way there are magnificent views southward to the patterned fields of Strathmore. Marked paths run up to each fort (both are now officially protected sites) from the main road. The White Caterthun, so called because of the pale quartzite rock that was used to build its now-tumbled ramparts, is the better preserved of the two. After you've explored the Caterthuns, drop southward to rejoin main routes running along Strathmore. *Tel. 031/244–3101. Admission free.*

The **Glens of Angus** extend north from various points on Route A94. Known individually as the glens of Isla, Prosen, Clova, and Esk, these long valleys run into the high hills of the Grampians and offer a choice of clearly marked walking routes (the choices in the Glen of Clova are especially appealing). A reasonable place to start is the area around Kirriemuir. From here the B955 penetrates the rounded hills for more than 10 miles, and there are walking trails beyond that point. If you like the breezy upland flavor of grouse-croaking moorlands and deep pine forest, this is the place for you.

Shopping

Shopping in this mainly rural region is inevitably concentrated in the larger towns. St. Andrews, with its university and its world-renowned golfing facilities, attracts enough affluent people to sustain some interesting smaller specialty shops. Dundee, as Scotland's fourth-largest city, is an important retail shopping center for the northern part of Angus, but the choices for shoppers here are similar to those found in most large towns (department stores, such as Marks and Spencer, predominate).

Fife If you're approaching the shopping mecca at St. Andrews from the south and are interested in women's fashion, it's worth stopping in **Cupar** to visit **Margaret Urquhart** (13–17 Lady Wynd, tel. 0334/52205), a boutique that attracts customers from as far away as Edinburgh and Glasgow and stocks a wide range of British and international designer names. Among the worthwhile specialty shops you'll find in **St. Andrews** are **Graeme Renton** (72 South St., tel. 0334/76334), the best place in the region, if not in all Scotland, for Oriental rugs and carpets of all colors, patterns, and sizes—many of them antiques; **Church Square Ceramics and Workshops** (Church Sq., between South St. and Market St., tel. 0334/77744), which offers decorative and domestic stoneware, ceramic, and enameled jewelry, as well as golf clubs—something for everyone there; **Bonkers**

(80 Market St., tel. 0334/73919), with a huge selection of knit-wear, clocks, books, cards, pottery, and gift items; and **St. Andrews Fine Art** (84 Market St., tel. 0334/74080), the place to go for Scottish paintings from 1800 to the present (oils, watercolors, drawings, and prints are available).

In the west of Fife, **Glenrothes, Dunfermline,** and **Kirkaldy** are the main shopping towns for day-to-day needs. The **Balbirnie Craft Centre,** however, in an 18th-century stable mews near Balbirnie House, Glenrothes, is a peaceful setting in which to buy items made by craftspeople who live on the premises: their work includes pottery, woodwork, stained glass, landscape paintings, lingerie, silver, jewelry, and leather goods.

Dundee The modern covered shopping mall in **Dundee**—the Wellgate Shopping Centre, off Panmure Street—is the place to visit if you're looking for the major retail chains. If you search around a little, however, you'll find a scattering of smaller shops that have more character and unusual selections. The **Compleat Cookshop** (27 Wellgate Centre, tel. 0382/21256), for example, stocks an enormous variety of cooking equipment and other kitchenware. A treat for overseas visitors whose own home grocers may only stock tea bags and packaged coffee is **J. Allan Braithwaite** (6 Castle St., tel. 0382/22693), where you can select from over 30 blended teas (including mango and apricot) and 12 freshly roasted coffees (remember that such specialty teas can usually be taken home without import restriction if you purchase them as gifts). There are also several good jewelers in Dundee; try **Rattrays** (32 Nethergate, tel. 0382/27258), which has been in business for over 140 years, or **Matthew M. Henderson** (1 Union St., tel. 0382/21339) for a good selection of Scottish silver and onyx curling stones, which would make an unusual—if weighty—present.

Sports and Fitness

Bicycling The back roads of Fife make pleasant bicycling terrain, as does the long valley of Strathmore (except for the A94), where some roads run deep into the Angus Glens. The following firms rent bicycles: **Bodden's** (218 Blackness Rd., Dundee, tel. 0382/65295), **East Neuk Outdoors** (tel. 0333/311929), **C & M Ritchie** (33 Gray St., Broughty Ferry, Angus, tel. 0382/75516), **Nicholson's Cycle Centre** (2 Forfar Rd., Dundee, tel. 0382/461212), and **Gordon Christie Cycle and Toy Shop** (86 Market St., St. Andrews, Fife, tel. 0334/72122).

Fishing As in most of the rest of Scotland, there is a wide choice of fishing in sea, loch, and river. Leaflets giving detailed information are available at tourist-information centers (*see* Important Addresses and Numbers in Essential Information, *above*).

Golf Every golfer's ambition is to play at St. Andrews, and once you are in Fife the ambition is easily realized. The following four St. Andrews courses are open to visitors (all are part of the St. Andrews Club). For details of availability—there is sometimes a waiting list—call the course number listed below or contact the secretary, Links Management Committee, Golf Place, St. Andrews (tel. 0334/75757).

Old Course (15th century). Tel. 0334/73393. 18 holes, 6,578 yards, SSS 72.

New Course (1894). Tel. 0334/73938. 18 holes, 6,604 yards, SSS 72.

Jubilee Course (1899). Tel. 0334/73938. 18 holes, 6,284 yards, SSS 72.

Eden Course (1913). Tel. 0334/74296. 18 holes, 5,971 yards, SSS 69.

There are more than 40 other courses in the region. Most have refreshment facilities and offer golf to the visitor by the round or the day. Details about locations and opening hours are available from tourist-information centers (*see* Important Addresses and Numbers in Essential Information, *above*). Many of the area's hotels offer golfing packages or will arrange a day's golf.

Health and Fitness Clubs **Arbroath Sports Centre** (Keptie Rd., Arbroath, tel. 0241/72999) offers a swimming pool, squash courts, games hall, and a gymnasium.

Cupar Sports Centre (Main St., Cupar, tel. 0334/54793) has a swimming pool, sports hall, fitness rooms, outdoor pitches, greens, and picnic areas.

Dundee Leisure Centre (Earl Grey Pl., Dundee, tel. 0382/23141, ext. 4187) has four swimming pools, a diving pool, sauna, pool tables, exercise equipment, and table tennis.

Montrose Sports Centre (Marine Ave., Montrose, tel. 0674/76211) is an indoor sports center with a gymnasium.

Dining and Lodging

Dining

In St. Andrews and in some of the West Fife towns, such as Kirkcaldy and Dunfermline, you will find restaurants serving traditional Scottish fare, as well as ethnic food (Italian and Chinese are popular), in addition to numerous small cafés of all kinds. Bar lunches are becoming the rule in large and small hotels throughout the region, and in seaside places the "carry oot" (to go) meal is an old tradition.

Category	Cost*
Very Expensive	over £25
Expensive	£15–£20
Moderate	£10–£15
Inexpensive	under £10

**per person, excluding VAT, tax, service, and drinks*

Lodging

If you're staying in Fife, the obvious base is St. Andrews, where you will find ample accommodations of all kinds, including school-vacation-time accommodations at a university hall of residence (tel. 0334/72281, single with meals from £19.30). Other towns also offer a reasonable selection, and you will find good hotels and guest houses at Dunfermline and Kirkcaldy, and all the royal burghs have hotels or inns in the town or the neighborhood. Along the coastal strip and in the Howe of Fife between Strathmiglo and Cupar there are some superior country-house hotels, many with their own restaurants.

Category	Cost*
Very Expensive	over £120
Expensive	£100–£120
Moderate	£80–£100
Inexpensive	under £80

All prices are for 2 people sharing a double room, including service, breakfast, and VAT.

Highly recommended restaurants and hotels are indicated by a star ★.

Anstruther
Dining
★

The Cellar. Specializing in fish, but offering a selection of Scottish beef and lamb as well, the Cellar is devoted to serving top-quality ingredients cooked simply to preserve all the natural flavor. The crayfish-and-mussel bisque is famous, and the wine list reflects high standards. Entered through a small courtyard, the restaurant is charmingly furnished in an unpretentious, old-fashioned style. It is popular with the locals, and its fame is spreading quickly. Reservations are essential, but you still stand a better chance of getting a table here more quickly than at the Peat Inn (*see* below). *24 East Green St., Anstruther, Fife, tel. 0333/310378. Reservations required. Jacket and tie advised. AE, MC, V. Closed Sun., Mon. lunch in summer, and Mon. in winter. Expensive.*

Ceres
Dining and Lodging
★

The Peat Inn. Sitting squarely at a T-junction of the B940 and B941, 5 miles southwest of St. Andrews in the heart of the Kingdom of Fife, this bed-and-breakfast was once a coaching inn. For many years it has been at the pinnacle of culinary excellence in Scotland, setting standards of which many other restaurants can only dream. Whole lobster with coriander and ginger or pigeon in pastry with wild mushrooms justify the high prices charged for dinner; lunch is slightly cheaper, but for either you may have to book well in advance. More recently, eight comfortable double suites have been added in the separate residence, making the inn into a French-style restaurant with rooms. *Fife KY15 5LH, tel. 0334/84206. 8 rooms with bath. Facilities: restaurant, bar. AE, MC, V. Closed Mon. and Sun. and 2 weeks in Jan. Reservations required in restaurant. Jacket and tie advised. Expensive. Restaurant, Very Expensive.*

Dundee
Dining and Lodging

Angus Thistle Hotel. In the center of Dundee, this hotel offers guests pleasant views extending in all directions, especially from rooms on the higher floors. Some suites have four-poster beds, whirlpool baths, and private sitting rooms. The public sitting rooms are also very comfortable. The decor is modern throughout. The hotel's restaurant serves adequate meals, offering primarily Continental food. *101 Marketgait, Dundee DD1 1QT, tel. 0382/26874. 58 rooms with bath. Facilities: restaurant, bar. AE, DC, MC, V. Moderate.*

Forfar
Dining
★

The Drovers Inn. Set in the heart of the Angus farmlands, the Drovers is a rare find in Scotland, having more of the feeling of an English country pub. Plain but friendly surroundings, decorated with old farm implements and historic photographs, are the setting for simple bar food, homemade pies, and nourishing soups. It's best to make reservations, even for bar meals, because the restaurant is popular with the locals, especially on weekends. *Memus, near Forfar, tel. 0307/86322. Reservations advised. Dress: casual. MC, V. Closed Wed. dinner. Inexpensive.*

Lodging **Royal Hotel.** In the center of Forfar, this former coaching inn has been fully modernized and has a leisure complex with swimming pool, gymnasium, and roof garden. The bedrooms are well equipped, if of somewhat variable standards, and some are rather small. The public rooms have retained their 19th-century charm. This hotel makes an attractive base for exploring or golfing. *Castle St., Forfar, Angus DD8 3AE, tel. 0307/ 62691. 19 rooms with bath. Facilities: 2 restaurants, leisure complex. AE, DC, MC, V. Inexpensive.*

St. Andrews **The Grange Inn.** On a breezy hilltop overlooking St. Andrews,
Dining and Lodging the Grange Inn offers an attractive blend of old-fashioned charm with polished brass, low lights, and open fires and total professionalism in its approach to its menus. This restaurant depends on seasonal local produce—haddock, salmon from the River Tay, venison from Perthsire—and the menu changes weekly. The baked fresh seatrout in filo pastry with a garden sorrel sauce brings out the natural flavors of the fish, while the hot cherry pancake laced with Kirsch is a sophisticated indulgence. *Grange Rd., St. Andrews, Fife KY16 8LJ, tel. 0334/ 72670. 2 rooms with bath. Reservations advised. Dress: smart but casual. AE, DC, MC, V. Closed Mon. except for bar meals. Expensive.*

St. Andrews Golf Hotel. Situated on the cliffs with magnificent views over the golf links and bay, this establishment is only 200 yards from the Old Course. Dating from Victorian times, it has been tastefully modernized over the years. The works of Scottish artists line the walls; the bedrooms are modern and comfortable; and there are elegant public rooms, including an oak-paneled dining room. Dishes such as éclairs filled with a delicate trout mousse or strips of Perthshire venison sautéed with julienne of fresh vegetables and served with smoked oysters, mean that you certainly have a satisfying meal to look forward to after your round of golf. *40 The Scores, St. Andrews, Fife KY16 9AS, tel. 0334/72611. 23 rooms with bath. Facilities: restaurant, bar. AE, DC, MC, V. Expensive.*

Rufflets Country House Hotel. This ivy-bedecked country house just outside St. Andrews is surrounded by 10 acres of formal and informal gardens. All the rooms are attractively decorated and comfortable, with all the amenities one would expect of a top-class hotel, but at a moderate price. Dinner is served in the roomy Garden Restaurant, famous for its use of local produce to create memorable Scottish dishes, such as fillet of Aberdeen Angus beef and Tay salmon. *Strathkiness Low Rd., St. Andrews, Fife KY16 9TX, tel. 0334/72594. 20 rooms with bath. Facilities: restaurant, bar. AE, DC, MC, V. Moderate–Expensive.*

Lathones Manor Hotel. A useful alternative for those whose families are not utterly infatuated with the "Royal and Ancient sport" and who prefer to stay a little way outside St. Andrews. This traditional, whitewashed, and pantiled inn-style hotel is 6 miles southeast of St. Andrews and provides easy access to the East Neuk of Fife and its fishing villages. With old beams, stone walls, and log fires, the hotel offers a warm welcome. *Largoward, Fife KY9 1JE, tel. 0334/84494. 14 rooms with bath. Facilities: restaurant, bar. AE, DC, MC, V. Inexpensive.*

The Arts and Nightlife

The Arts

Theater **Byre Theatre** (Abbey St., St. Andrews, tel. 0334/76288) has a resident repertory company that performs during the summer months.

Dundee Repertory Theatre (Tay Sq., Dundee, tel. 0382/23530). This award-winning complex, which includes an exhibition gallery, is home to a resident theater group, as well as a dance company. Both offer diverse programs.

Whitehall Theatre (Wellfield St., Dundee, tel. 0382/23141) offers a variety of choices, including Scottish shows, light opera, and variety and musical entertainments.

Little Theatre (Victoria Rd., Dundee, tel. 0382/25835) presents a wide variety of performances, especially modern theatrical works by local and visiting groups.

Music **Caird Hall** (City Sq., Dundee, tel. 0382/23141, ext. 4288) is one of Scotland's finest concert halls.

Bonar Hall (Park Pl., Dundee, tel. 0382/29450).

Film **Cannon Film Centre** (Seagate, Dundee, tel. 0382/25247).

Steps Film Theatre (Wellgate Centre, Dundee, tel. 0382/24938).

Nightlife

Discos Dundee has about 10 discos in and around the city, including **Buddies Night Club** (Broughty Ferry, Dundee, tel. 0382/77581), **De Sthils** (S. Ward Rd., Dundee, tel. 0382/200066), **Fat Sam's Disco** (31 S. Ward Rd., Dundee, tel. 0382/26836), **Flicks** (High St., Brechin, tel. 0356/24313), and **The Venue** (Camperdown Leisure Park, Dundee, tel. 0382/400515).

Folk Music The following establishments occasionally offer ceilidhs and/or evening performances of traditional folk music: **Old Manor Hotel** (Lundin Links, Fife, tel. 0333/320911), **Royal Jubilee Arms Hotel** (Dykehead, Cortachy, Angus, tel. 05754/381), **West Port Bar** (Henderson's Wynd, Dundee, tel. 0382/200993) offers folk music on most Mondays—phone to confirm.

The rest of the area is, by comparison, fairly rural and has little to offer in terms of lively entertainment, though some of the hotels have shows in their restaurants and lounges. Consult the local tourist-information centers (*see* Important Addresses and Numbers in Essential Information, *above*) for more details.

8

Aberdeen and the Northeast

Royal Deeside

Introduction

By Gilbert Summers

Early in united Scotland's history—some historians cite the year 1124—Aberdeen, now Scotland's third-largest city (after Glasgow and Edinburgh), became a royal burgh. This meant that the little community near the mouth of the River Dee had a town council and its own guard, as well as full trading rights and permission to hold fairs and markets. While many other royal burghs remained small towns (some even disappeared completely), Aberdeen continued to prosper and grow over the centuries.

Because of its geographic isolation, Aberdeen has, throughout its history, been a fairly autonomous place. Even now, it is still perceived by many inhabitants of the United Kingdom as lying almost out of reach in the north. In reality, this northeastern locale is only 90 minutes flying time from London or—thanks to recent road improvements—a little more than two hours by car from Edinburgh.

Although situated between the River Dee and the River Don, the center of town actually lies closer to the Dee. In fact, its now-deepened estuary forms part of the city's harbor. The community nearer the Don was formerly known as Old Aberdeen or Aulton, and it led a separate civic existence as recently as the 1890s. Old Aberdeen also had its own university.

For centuries the only major town in a rich agricultural hinterland, Aberdeen retains the atmosphere of a large market town. It is a scaled-up provincial community in the best possible sense. Besides working to service an agricultural area, Aberdeen also performs its other role as a port. Like many other east-coast communities, Aberdeen has been trading with Europe since medieval times.

A lucrative export in those early days was stockings, a fact recorded by the Welsh-born traveler Thomas Pennant, whose *Tour in Scotland* (1769) is one of the earliest travel guides ever written on Scotland. Pennant earnestly recorded that 69,333 dozen pairs of stockings were made from wool, much of it imported. Although northeastern Scotland is hardly recognized for its textiles, Aberdeen was, until recently, home to one of Scotland's largest woolen mills, Crombie at Grandholm Works, by the River Don. (This company also once supplied huge orders of "rebel gray" cloth to the Confederate armies in the U.S. Civil War.) A visitor center is still open on the site, telling the mill's story.

In the 18th century, local granite quarrying produced a durable silver stone that would be used to build the Aberdonian structures of the Victorian era. Thus granite was used boldly—in glittering blocks, spires, columns, and parapets—to build Aberdeen. Downtown Aberdeen remains one of the United Kingdom's most distinctive urban environments, although some would say it depends on the weather and the brightness of the day. The mica chips embedded in the rock are a million mirrors in sunshine. In rain and heavy clouds, however, their sparkle is snuffed out.

In the 1850s, the city was famed for its fast clippers, sleek sailing ships that raced to India for cargoes of tea. The story of Aberdeen's maritime heritage is told at length at the city's excellent maritime museum.

The course of Aberdeen's history was unequivocally altered in the late-1960s when oil and gas were discovered in the North Sea. Aberdeen was able to hold onto its special, independent character until the early 1970s. Since then much has changed: new merchandise in shops, new accents, new office blocks, new hotels, new industries, new attitudes. At one point, Aberdeen seemed destined to become a boomtown, surrendering its independence for an obsession with the international price of a barrel of North Sea crude.

Fortunately, some innate local caution has helped the city to retain a sense of perspective and prevented it from selling out entirely. Aberdeen is still worth visiting, except perhaps when a major oil conference or trade fair is being held in its local exhibition center.

Even if Aberdeen vanished from the map of Scotland, however, an extensive portion of the Northeast would still be worth exploring. Aberdeen's hinterland is now called, for administrative purposes, Grampian and encompasses the old counties of Aberdeenshire, Kincardineshire to the south, then Banffshire and Morayshire hanging from the Moray Firth coast to the north.

Grampian's chief scenic attraction lies in the gradual transition from high mountain plateau—by a series of gentle steps through hill, forest, and farmland—to a coastline where the word *unadulterated* truly applies. The Grampian coastline includes some of the United Kingdom's most perfect wild shorelines, both sandy and high cliff. The Grampian Mountains to the west contain some of the highest ground in the United Kingdom, in the area of the Cairngorms. But the Grampian hills have also shaped the character of the folk who live in the Northeast. In earlier times, the massif made communication with the south somewhat difficult. As a result, native Northeasterners still speak the richest Lowland Scottish (*not* Gaelic, which is an entirely different language).

Essential Information

Important Addresses and Numbers

Tourist Information The **City of Aberdeen Tourist Board** (St. Nicholas House, Broad St., Aberdeen, tel. 0224/632727) provides information on rental cars, tour tickets, and Rail Rovers and sells maps, souvenirs, and tour publications. In fact, this tourist information center supplies information on all Scotland's Northeast. The Aberdeen Tourist Board also has a currency exchange.

Aberdeen serves as the headquarters for the various other tourist boards in this region, most of which are seasonal: **Aboyne–Kincardine and Deeside** (information caravan, Ballater Rd. Car Park, tel. 03398/86060), **Alford–Gordon District** (information center, Railway Museum, Station Yard, tel. 09755/62052), **Ballater** (information center, Station Sq., tel. 03397/55306), **Ellon** (information caravan, Market St. Car Park, tel. 0358/20730), **Huntly** (information center, 7a The Square, tel. 0466/792255), and **Inverurie** (information center, Town Hall, Market Place, tel. 0467/20600).

Elgin (Moray District Council, Information Cente
St., tel. 0343/542666 or 0343/543388). For other tour
mation centers located in the Moray District, *see* Tour 4,

Emergencies For fire, police, or ambulance, dial 999 from any telephone. N
coins are needed for emergency calls made from public tele-
phone booths.

Grampian Police (Force Headquarters, Queen Street, Aberdeen, tel. 0224/639111).
Aberdeen Royal Infirmary (Accident and Emergency Department, Foresterhill, Aberdeen, tel. 0224/681818).

Doctors and The **Grampian Health Board** (Primary Care Department,
Dentists Woolmanhill, tel. 0224/681818, ext. 55537) can help you find a
doctor or dentist.

Pharmacies The following Aberdeen pharmacies keep longer hours than
most:

Anderson Pharmacy (4 Union Grove, tel. 0224/587148).
Boots the Chemists Ltd. (Bon Accord Centre, George St., tel.
0224/626080).
Charles Michie (391 Union St., tel. 0224/585312).
Savory & Moore (3 Alford Pl., tel. 0224/646325).

There also is an in-store pharmacist at **Safeway Food Store** (215
King St., tel. 0224/624398).

Notices on pharmacy doors will guide you to the nearest open
pharmacy at any given time. The police can provide assistance
in an emergency.

Arriving and Departing by Plane

Airport and Aberdeen's airport—serving both international and domestic
Airlines flights—is in Dyce, 7 miles west of the city center on the A96
(Inverness). The terminal building is modern (expanded in recent years because of Dyce's prominent role in North Sea oil-
rig communications) and generally uncrowded.

Airlines linking Aberdeen with Europe include **Air U.K.**, with
flights linking Amsterdam (the Netherlands), Paris (France),
and Bergen and Stavanger (Norway); **SAS (Scandinavian Airlines)**, linking Copenhagen (Denmark) and Stavanger; and
Business Air linking Esbjerg (Denmark). An extensive network of domestic flights linking Aberdeen with most major
U.K. airports is operated by **Air U.K., British Airways, Aberdeen Airways, Dan-Air Services, Brymon Airways**, and **Gill Air**.
Consult the individual airlines or your travel agent for arrival
and departure times (airport information desk, tel. 0224/
722331). Also worth noting is the direct Amsterdam–Aberdeen
link enabling transatlantic passengers to visit Scotland's
northeast by first flying from the United States to Amsterdam
and then flying on to Aberdeen with Air U.K.; this can actually
be faster than traveling to Aberdeen from other parts of Scotland or England.

Between the **Grampian Transport**'s number 27 bus operates between the air-
Airport and port terminal and Union Street in the center of Aberdeen.
City Center Buses (exact fare 90p) run every 40 minutes, and the journey
By Bus time is approximately 20 minutes.

By Train For those interested in train service to the airport, Dyce is on
British Rail's Inverness–Aberdeen route. The rail station is a

short taxi ride from the terminal building. Alternatively, **Whytes of Newmachar** runs early morning and late-afternoon bus service, on weekdays only, between the airport and Dyce railway station. Departures from the airport run 7–9 AM and 4–6:30 PM at approximately 30-minute intervals; the bus leaves from the terminal building. The ride by rail into Aberdeen from the airport takes 12 minutes. Trains run approximately every 90 minutes (more frequently at peak times, less frequently in the middle of the day). If you are intending to visit the western part of the area first, it is possible to travel northwest, away from Aberdeen, by rail direct to Elgin via Inverurie, Insch, Huntly, and Keith.

By Rental Car   The following car rental firms have desks at Aberdeen Airport: Avis (tel. 0224/722282, **Budget** (tel. 0224/771777), **Europcar** (tel. 0224/770770), and **Hertz** (tel. 0224/722373). The drive to the center of Aberdeen is very easy via the A96 (which can be busy in the rush hour).

Arriving and Departing by Car, Train, and Bus

By Car   Aberdeen's road links to the southern portion of Scotland have been greatly improved in recent years because of the construction of new divided highways. Soon, it will be possible to travel from Glasgow and Edinburgh to Aberdeen on a continuous stretch of the A94, a fairly scenic route that runs up Strathmore, with a fine hill view to the west. The coastal route, the A92, is a more leisurely alternative, with its interesting coastal resorts and fishing villages. The most scenic route, however, is probably the A93 from Perth, north to Blairgowrie and into Glen Shee. The A93 then goes over the Cairnwell Pass, the highest main road in the United Kingdom. At Braemar the road then swings eastward and down Deeside, offering scenic views most of the way to Aberdeen. (This route is not recommended in the winter months when snow can make driving over high ground difficult.)

By Train   Travelers can reach Aberdeen directly from Edinburgh (2½ hours), Glasgow (3 hours), and Inverness (2½ hours). See Scot-Rail timetable for full details. There are also London–Aberdeen routes that go through Edinburgh and the east-coast main line. Both Motorail and sleeper service are available.

By Bus   Long-distance coach service operates to and from most parts of Scotland, England, and Wales. Main operators include **Scottish Citylink** (Aberdeen bus station, tel. 0224/212307) and **Caledonian Express** (tel. 0738/33481). Your travel agent can supply further details.

Getting Around

Aberdeen is not a large city, and its center is Union Street, the main throughfare running east–west. Anderson Drive is an efficient ring road on the western side of the city; inexperienced drivers should be extra careful on its many traffic circles. In general, road signs are clear and legible, and parking near the center of Aberdeen is no worse than in any other U.K. city.

By Car   Car rental firms in Aberdeen include **British Car Rental** (tel. 0224/685324), **Budget Rent a Car** (tel. 0224/639922), **Europcar** (tel. 0224/631199), **Guy Salmon** (tel. 0224/770955), **Kenning** (tel. 0224/571445), and **Mitchells** (tel. 0224/642642). Street maps are available from the tourist-information center or from newsagents and booksellers.

By Bus **Grampian Transport** operates services throughout the city. There is an inquiry kiosk on St. Nicholas Street, outside Marks and Spencers department store, and timetables are available at the kiosk or from the tourist information center at St. Nicholas House nearby.

By Taxi Taxi stands can be found throughout the center of Aberdeen: along Union Street, at the railway station at Guild Street, and at Regent Quay. Taxis are mostly black, though variations in fawn, maroon, or white exist.

Guided Tours

Orientation City tours are available on most days between June and mid-September. Contact **Grampian Transport** (tel. 0224/637047). **Grampian Coaches** (operated by Grampian Transport), **Bluebird Northern** (operated by Northern Scottish, tel. 0224/591387), and **Swallow McIntyre Coaches** (tel. 0224/493112) all operate tours encompassing the Northeast coastline and countryside. Some of the tours are of general interest, others are based on one of the area's various trails: Malt Whisky, Coastal, Castle, Quality, or Royal.

Personal Guides The **Scottish Tourist Guides Association** (contact Mrs. Annie Lamont, Towie More, Clifton Rd., Turriff, Aberdeenshire, tel. 0888/62200) can supply experienced personal guides, including foreign-language-speaking guides if necessary.

The following firms offer chauffeur-driven limousines to take clients on tailor-made tours: **Glenhire Executive Travel** (tel. 0224/722322), **Guy Salmon Car Rentals** (tel. 0224/770955), and **Scotland Scene Ltd.** (tel. 0343/541468)

Walking Tours The **Scottish Tourist Guides Association** (*see above*) organizes the following walks in the center of Aberdeen during the summer months: "Old Aberdeen," "City Centre Stroll," and "Graveyard Gander." **Hiking and Biking Scotland** (tel. 0467/43441 or in the United States 800/548–6375) organizes walking and cycling tours to various parts of Scotland's Northeast, including Royal Deeside, Castle Country, and the coastline.

Exploring Aberdeen and the Northeast

A major attraction in the Northeast is its wealth of castles. There are so many that one part of the area, Gordon District, has assembled them into a Castle Trail, leading you to fortresses like the ruined medieval Kildrummy Castle, which once controlled the strategic routes through the valley of the River Don. Later work, such as Craigievar, a narrow-turreted castle resembling an illustration from a fairy-tale book, reflects the changing times of the 17th century, when defense became less of a priority. Later still, grand mansions, such as Haddo House, with its symmetrical facade and elegant interiors, surrender any defensive need entirely and instead make statements about their owner's status and power. Nowhere else in Scotland offers such an eclectic selection of castles. The Northeast offers visitors an opportunity to touch the fabric of Scotland's story, with the added advantage that the area is slightly off the beaten path.

As a visitor to Scotland, you can be sure of one thing: No matter where you are, a whiskey distillery can't be far off, an assessment that would undoubtedly hold true in Morayshire. In this part of Scotland the distilling is centered in the valley of the River Spey and its tributaries. Just as the Loire in France has famous vineyards clustered around it, the Spey has famous single-malt distilleries. Instead of Muscadet, Chinon, Vouvray or Pouilly-sur-Loire, there's Glenfiddich, Glen Grant, Balvenie, Tamdhu, or Tamnavulin. As well as being sweeter and less peaty than some of the island malts, eastern or Speyside malts have the further advantage of having generally easier-to-pronounce brand names.

Orientation

Union Street is the center of Aberdeen, and through traffic from the north and northwest is signposted through Aberdeen beyond its east end and to the harbor. Through traffic from the south is signposted around Anderson Drive, from where all the main routes into the Grampian hinterland are also signposted: for example, the Deeside and Donside routes, the main Inverness A96, as well as coastal routes to the north. Outside Aberdeen, the Castle and Whisky trails are generally well marked.

Highlights for First-time Visitors

Craigievar Castle (*see* Tour 3)
Cullen (*see* Tour 4)
Duthie Park (Rose Hill) (*see* What to See and Do with Children)
Elgin Cathedral (*see* Tour 4)
Glen Muick (*see* Tour 3)
Glenfiddich Distillery (*see* Tour 4)
Haddo House (*see* Off the Beaten Track)
Kildrummy Castle and Gardens (*see* Tour 3)
King's College Chapel (*see* Tour 2)
Marischal College (facade) (*see* Tour 1)
Maritime Museum (*see* Tour 1)
Upper Deeside, beyond Braemar (*see* Tour 3)

Tour 1: Aberdeen—The Silver City Center

Numbers in the margin correspond to points of interest on the Royal Deeside and Aberdeen maps.

What Princes Street is to Edinburgh, Union Street is to **①** **Aberdeen**: the central pivot of the city plan and the product of a wave of enthusiasm to rebuild the city in a contemporary style. This tour encompasses some of Aberdeen's best early 19th-century buildings. Some hints of an older Aberdeen have survived and can be noticed while touring. Conversely, this tour will also show you how today's plans are changing the face of Aberdeen, a city of handsome granite buildings that give it a silvery complexion.

Start outside the tourist information center on Broad Street. **②** Immediately opposite is **Marischal College**, founded in 1593 by

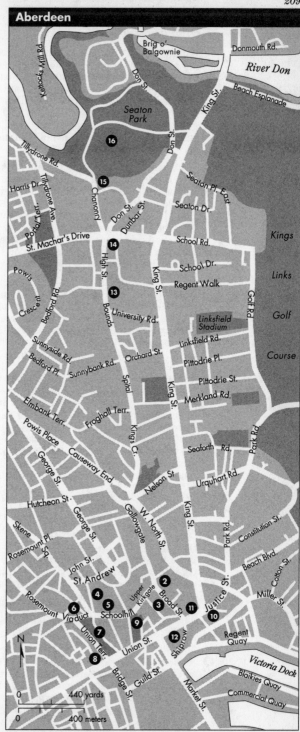

Aberdeen

the earl Marischal as a Protestant alternative to the Catholic King's College in Old Aberdeen (*see* Tour 2: A Short Excursion in Old Aberdeen, *below*), though the two combined to form Aberdeen University in 1860. (The earls Marischal held the hereditary office as keepers of the king's mares.) The original university buildings on this site have undergone extensive renovations. What you see in front of you is a facade built in 1891. The spectacularly ornate work is set off by the gilded flags, and this turn-of-the-century creation is still the second-largest granite building in the world. Only the Escorial in Madrid is larger. *Broad St., tel. 0224/632727. Admission free. Museum open weekdays 10–5, Sun. 2–5.*

To find a survivor from an earlier Aberdeen, go underneath the concrete supports of St. Nicholas House (of which the tourist-information center is a part) to find **Provost Skene's House** (*provost* is Scottish for mayor). Formerly one of a closely packed area of town houses, Provost Skene's House, steeply gabled and rubble-built, survives in part from 1545. It was originally a domestic dwelling house and is now a museum portraying civic life, with restored furnished period rooms and a painted chapel. *Guestrow, off Broad St., tel. 0224/641086. Admission free. Open Mon.–Sat. 10–5.*

The tour then takes on a more contemporary twist, away from the well-wrought granite and the portion of a 16th-century townscape. Provost Skene's House is close to a 1960s shopping development, the St. Nicholas Centre. Go down Upperkirkgate to the lowest point, where you will see shopping malls— the **St. Nicholas Centre** on the left, the fairly new **Bon-Accord Centre** on the right. Until recent years, George Street, at the foot of the hill here, was a bustling shopping street running at right angles. But not even Aberdeen—in its far northern perch—has exempted itself from the British trend toward chain-store anonymity, and it has thus demolished traditional stonework to accommodate the chains. If you do enter the portals of the Bon-Accord Centre, you will eventually emerge at the truncated George Street. Note the spacious John Lewis Store, built in a design closely resembling a double-decker sandwich, with an illuminated filling and the crusts left on.

Although shopping is hard to resist here, try to do so for the moment and continue up Schoolhill, with its range of smaller speciality shops. Opposite is St. Nicholas Kirk, which you can examine on your way back, along Union Street.

On your right, as the slope eases off, is a complex of silver-toned buildings, in front of which stands a statue of General Charles Gordon, the military hero of Khartoum (1885). Interestingly, he is not, however, the Gordon recalled in **Robert Gordon's Institute of Technology** behind the statue. Built in 1731, the structure was originally called Robert Gordon's Hospital and it was used to educate poor boys. It became an independent school later and then an institute of higher education, a kind of technical university.

Adjacent to the school is the **Aberdeen Art Gallery,** which plays an active role in Aberdeen's cultural life and is a popular rendezvous for the locals. It houses a wide-ranging collection— from the 18th century to contemporary work. The sculpture court is certainly worth seeing, with its gallery supported by columns of polished granite, each showing a different shade.

Schoolhill, tel. 0224/646333. Open Mon.–Sat. 10–5, Thurs. 10–8, Sun. 2–5.

By going back outside, you will see a war memorial on the next corner, consisting of a very handsome and dignified granite lion.

Cross the street here to get a better view of the next three buildings, one of the city's prized collections. The library, church, and nearby theater are collectively known by all Aberdonians as Education, Salvation, and Damnation. Silvery and handsome, the Central Library and St. Mark's Church date from the last decade of the 19th century, while **His Majesty's Theatre** (1904–08) has been restored inside to its full Edwardian splendor. If you carry a camera, you can choose an angle that includes the statue of Scotland's first freedom fighter, Sir William Wallace, in the foreground, pointing majestically to Damnation. Wallace has been pointing this way since 1888, and thus his gesture predates the theater. *Rosemount Viaduct in city center, box office tel. 0224/641122.*

Turning left onto Union Terrace, you will see another statue, this one of **Robert Burns** addressing a daisy. Behind Burns are the **Union Terrace Gardens,** faintly echoing Edinburgh's Princes Street Gardens in that they separate the older part of the city to the east, with the 19th-century development of Union Terrace and points westward (as well as Union Street itself). Most of the buildings on Union Terrace around the grand-looking Caledonian Hotel are late-Victorian, when exuberance and confidence in style was at its height. The results are impressive. Note for example, at the corner of Union Street, the wonderfully elaborate **Commercial Union Insurance building** (1885). Its Doric portico (plain-column extension) has been a landmark and meeting place for generations of locals. They call it the "monkey house," though few can tell you why. Perhaps the close columns resemble the bars of a cage.

Turn left onto Union Street (though there is plenty of this main street to explore should you wish to turn right). Note the smug cats seated primly on the parapet of **Union Bridge.** The bridge was built in the early years of the 19th century, as was much of Union Street. The bridge has a gentle rise —or descent, if you are traveling east—and the street is carried on a series of blind arches. The north side of Union Bridge is the most obvious reminder of the grand thoroughfare's artificial levels. Much of the original work remains.

As you make your way through the main-street crowds, you will also pass, on your left, the colonnaded facade of 1829 that screens the churchyard of **St. Nicholas** from the shopping hustle and bustle. Behind the facade is the church itself, already seen from Schoolhill. This is the Mither Kirk, the original burgh church, yet curiously it is not within the bounds of the early settlement that was located to the east, near the end of present-day Union Street. During the 12th century, the port of Aberdeen flourished and room could not be found for the church within the settlement. Its earliest features are the pillars—supporting a tower built much later—and its clerestory windows: Both date from the original 12th-century structure. St. Nicholas was divided into east and west kirks at the Reformation, followed by a substantial amount of renovation from 1741 on. Some early memorials and other works have survived. *Union St. Open weekdays 10–1.*

If you are a keen observer of architecture, you may notice during your walk down Union Street that Aberdeen continued to build commercial buildings in neoclassical style using silvery granite until well into the present century. However, upon arriving at the east end of the street you are not only within a few moments of your starting point at the tourist-information center but also within the original old town. This is the **Castlegate.** The actual castle once stood somewhere behind the Salvation Army Citadel of 1896, an imposing baronial granite tower whose design was inspired by Balmoral Castle. Just beyond King Street is the impressive **Mercat Cross** (built in 1686 and restored in 1820), always the symbolic center of a Scottish medieval burgh. Note that along its parapet, among its 12 panels are the portraits of the Stewart monarchs. Opposite is the handsome tower of the **Tolbooth,** dating from the 17th century. Also in sight here is the stylishly colonnaded facade of the Atheneum, built as a library, but now serving mainly as offices and eating places.

As the final reminder of this older part of Aberdeen, turn away from the Town House and head down to the left to Shiprow, once the main road into town in bygone days. Much has been swept away and redeveloped, but one building has survived since 1593: **Provost Ross's House** now houses **Aberdeen's Maritime Museum,** which tells the story of the city's involvement with the sea, from early inshore fisheries by way of tea clippers to the North Sea oil boom (*see* Aberdeen for Free, *below*).

Below is the harbor, which contains some fine architecture from the 18th and 19th centuries. Explore it only if time permits and you don't mind the background traffic.

Tour 2: A Short Excursion in Old Aberdeen

Formerly an independent burgh near the River Don, Old Aberdeen enters the sea above the River Dee. Although swallowed up by the expanding main city before the end of the 19th century, Old Aberdeen, which lies between **King's College** and **St. Machar's Cathedral,** still retains a certain degree of character and integrity. (Pronounce Machar with a Scottish *ch* and stress the first syllable.) The 18th-century travel writer Thomas Pennant visited Old Aberdeen, and his description compares interestingly with what can be seen today. While Pennant rode there, visitors today may find it more convenient to take a No. 20 bus north from a stop near Marischal College or a No. 1, 2, or 3 up King Street, off the Castlegate.

Visitors should alight in **College Bounds,** with its handsome 18th- and 19th-century houses, cobbled streets, and paved sidewalks not too far removed from Pennant's time. **King's College,** founded in 1494, can be seen, the flying (or crown) spire of its Chapel unmistakable. Built around 1500, the college attracted Pennant's attention, and he relates that the building was "very ruinous within; but there still remains some woodwork of exquisite workmanship." The fact that this structure survived at all was due to the zeal of the principal, who managed to defend his church against the destructive fanaticism that swept through Scotland during the Reformation, when the building was less than a century old. Though the church was already in a state of disuse during Pennant's day, today's visitor will find a renovated structure with the chapel playing an important role in university life. The woodwork referred to by Pennant is a tall oak screen separating nave and choir. Today, the work, along with the ribbed wooden ceiling and stalls, constitutes the finest medieval wood carving to be found anywhere in Scotland.

The **King's College Chapel** comprised one side of what was Old Aberdeen's original quadrangle, refurbished in the last century; 19th-century work currently obscures two towers constructed earlier. A memorial to Bishop Elphinstone, the university's founder, was placed in front of the chapel in 1926. Pennant relates that when this great man died, "supernatural voices were heard at his interment, as if Heaven more peculiarly interested itself in the departure of so great a character." Much of the other work seen from this point, notably Elphinstone Hall, with its piazza, and New King's, with its ornate Gothic style tracery, are 20th-century works. *High St. Visitor Centre (with shop and cafeteria) open Mon.–Sat. 10–5; summer, Mon.–Sat. 10–5, Sun. noon–5.*

Continuing up what is now the High Street of Old Aberdeen, you will see some restored houses built during Pennant's time, though the **Town House,** straight ahead, in its present form postdates the author's visit by nearly 20 years. This Georgian work, plain and handsome, uses parts of an earlier building from 1720. Behind the Town House the modern intrusion of St. Machar's Drive destroys some of the old-town ambience, but the atmosphere is restored by a stroll down the **Chanonry,** past the elegant houses once lived in by the officials connected with the cathedral nearby. Today, they house mainly university staff.

It is said that St. Machar was sent by St. Columba to build a church on a grassy platform near the sea, where a river flowed in the shape of a shepherd's crook. This spot fitted the bill, and the **St. Machar's Cathedral** was built in AD 580. However, nothing remains of the original foundation. When Pennant came here, he noted, "The cathedral is very antient; no more than two very antique spires and isle, which is used as a church, are now remaining. This bishopric was founded in the time of David I, who translated it from Mortlick in Bamffshire, to this place." (Mortlick is Mortlach by Dufftown, covered in Tour 4, *below.*) The original central spire collapsed in 1688. The twin octagonal spires that replaced it date from the first half of the 16th century; they were commissioned by Gavin Dunbar, Bishop Elphinstone's successor. The nave is thought to have been rebuilt in red sandstone in 1370, but the final renovation was completed in granite by the middle of the 15th century. Along with the nave ceiling, the twin spires were finished in time to take a battering in the Reformation.

The Reformers, whom Pennant described as the barons of the Mearns, were turned back in their assault on King's College Chapel, but they did succeed in stripping the lead off the roof of St. Machar's and stealing the bells. Pennant then recounted how they "shipped their sacrilegious booty with an intention of exposing it to sale in Holland; but the vessel had scarcely gone out of port, but it perished in a storm with all its ill-gained lading." The cathedral suffered further mistreatment—including the removal of stone by Oliver Cromwell's English garrison in the 1650s—until a 19th-century restoration program restored the church to its former grandeur. *Chanonry, tel. 0224/485988. Open daily 9–5.*

🔟 Beyond St. Machar's Cathedral lies **Seaton Park,** with its spring daffodils, tall trees, and herbaceous borders boldly colored. Until 1827, the only way out of Aberdeen to the north was over the River Don on the Brig o' Balgownie, a single-arch bridge found at the far end of Seaton Park—a 15-minute walk. It dates from 1314 and is thought to have been built by Richard Cementarius, Aberdeen's first provost. After enjoying the scenery of Seaton Park, which today has restored houses at either end, you can return to the city center.

Tour 3: Royal Deeside and Castle Country

Numbers in the margin correspond to points of interest on the Royal Deeside map.

Although basically a car tour, much of this area is accessible either by public transportation or on tours from Aberdeen. Deeside, the valley running west from Aberdeen down which the River Dee flows, earned its "Royal" appellation when discovered by Queen Victoria. To this day, where royalty goes, lesser aristocracy and fast-buck millionaires from across the globe follow. In fact, it is still the aspiration of many to own a grand shooting estate on Deeside. In a sense, this yearning is understandable, since piney hill slope, purple moor, and blue river intermingle most tastefully here, as you will see from the main road. Royal Deeside's gradual scenic change adds a growing sense of excitement as the road runs deeper and deeper into the Grampians.

There are castles along the Dee and to the north. This tour rises out of the river valley to find them, returning to Aberdeen by a route illustrating this gradual geological change: uplands lapped by a tide of farms.

The first 15 miles toward Banchory by either north or south Deeside roads (leaving the city by the Bridge of Dee) have only 🔟 a subtle scenic flair. Castle hoppers can explore **Drum Castle,** an ancient foursquare tower dating from the 13th century, with later additions. Note the rounded corners of the tower, said to make battering-ram attacks more difficult. Nearby, fragments of the ancient Forest of Drum still stand, dating from the early days when Scotland was covered by great woodlands of oak and pine. *Off the A93, 10 mi west of Aberdeen, tel. 03308/204. Admission: £3 adults, £1.50 children. Open May–Sept., daily 2–6; Oct., weekends 2–5.*

🔟 Perhaps of greater interest is **Crathes Castle,** 3 or 4 miles west on the A93. The Burnett family had been keepers of the Forest of Drum for generations but acquired lands here by marriage and later built a new castle, completed in 1596. Crathes is in the care of the National Trust for Scotland; the trust also looks after the grand gardens, with their calculated symmetry and clipped yew hedges. Be careful not to confuse Crathes Castle, near Aberdeen, with Crathie Kirk, near Balmoral, where folk go to gaze at royalty. *Off the A93, 3½ mi east of Banchory, tel. 033/044–525. Admission: grounds only £1.10 adults, 60p children; castle, garden, and grounds £3.50 adults, £1.80 children*

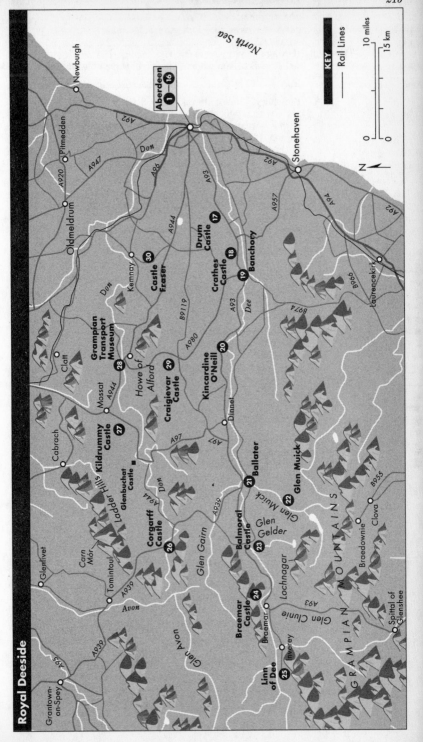

Royal Deeside

Newburgh
Pitmedden
A920
A947
Oldmeldrum
Don
A96
A92
A93
Aberdeen **1 — 16**
North Sea
Stonehaven
A92
A957
A94
A92
Laurencekirk
B9120
B9120
Kennay
Castle Fraser **30**
Drum Castle **17**
Crathes Castle **18**
Banchory **19**
B974
A944
A980
A93
Dee
A92
Clatt
Grampian Transport Museum **28**
Howe of Alford
Craigievar Castle **29**
Kincardine O'Neill **20**
Dinnet
Mossat
A944
Cabrach
Kildrummy Castle **27**
Glenbuchat Castle
Don
A97
A97
Ballater **21**
Glen Muick **22**
Ladder Hills
Corgarff Castle **26**
A944
A939
Glen Gairn
Balmoral Castle **23**
Glen Gelder
Glen Muick
Lochnagar
B955
Clova
Braedownie
Carn Mór
Glenlivet
Tomintoul
A939
Avon
Glen Avon
Braemar Castle **24**
Braemar
Glen Clunie
A93
Grampian Mountains
Spittal of Glenshee
Grantown-on-Spey
A95
A939
A93
Linn of Dee **25**
Inverey
A93

KEY
—— Rail Lines

N

0   10 miles
0   15 km

and senior citizens. Castle open Easter–Oct., daily 11–6. Garden and grounds open all year, 9:30–sunset.

Time Out Having enjoyed your castle visit, sample the excellent National Trust of Scotland's home baking in the castle's **tearoom** (tel. 033/044–525).

---

⑲ Banchory, a few minutes west on the A93, is an immaculate place with a pinkish tinge to its granite. It is usually bustling with ice-cream eating city strollers, out on a day trip from Aberdeen. If you visit in autumn and have time to spare, drive out to the **Brig o'Feuch** ("Bridge of," then pronounce it "Fyooch" with "ch" as in loch). Here, salmon leap in season, and the fall colors and foaming waters make for an attractive scene.

If you are pressed for time, continue west on the A93, through a landscape where the mixed farmlands are confined to the valley floor, sheltered by birch thickets and blankets of dark woods. **⑳** Note, as you pass through, the ruined kirk in **Kincardine O'Neill.** Built in 1233, it was once a shelter for travelers, the last hospice before the Mounth, the name given to the massif that shuts off the south side of the Dee Valley. Beyond Banchory (and the B974), no motor roads run south until you reach Braemar, though the Mounth is crossed by a network of tracks used in former times by Scottish soldiers, invading armies (including the Romans), and cattle drovers.

There are many other intricate features to examine in the area, especially if you have the time. There's the picture-postcard bridge at **Potarch** and the **Braeloine Interpretative Centre** in Glen Tanar beyond Aboyne, which has a display on natural history, a picnic area, and walks. *Glen Tanar, tel. 03398/86072. Open Apr.–Sept., daily 10–5.*

Also notable just south of the A93 is the **Muir of Dinnet,** which has a visitor center and a nature reserve.

Back on the main road, look for a large granite boulder on which is carved, YOU ARE NOW ENTERING THE HIGHLANDS. You may find this piece of information superfluous, given the quality of the scenery. Drive another 5 miles west on the A93 and you will **㉑** reach **Ballater.** This quaint holiday resort, once noted for the curative properties of its local well, has profited from the proximity of the royals, nearby at Balmoral. Visitors are amused by the array of BY ROYAL APPOINTMENT signs proudly hanging from many of its various shops (even monarchs need bakers and butchers). If you get a chance, take time to stroll around this neat community—well laid out in silver-gray masses. Note that the railway station now houses the tourist information center and a display on the former glories of this Great North of Scotland branch line, closed in the 1960s along with so many others in this country.

Ballater makes a good pausing place, and, if you can afford it, Craigendarroch is an excellent base. Nearby, visitors have the opportunity to capture the feel of the eastern Highlands—as long **㉒** as they have their own transport. Start your expedition into **Glen Muick** (pronounced "mick," Gaelic for pig) by crossing the River Dee and turning upriver on the south side, shortly after the road forks into this fine Highland glen. The native red deer are quite common throughout the Scottish Highlands, but Glen Muick is one of the very best places to see them in abundance, with herds grazing the flat valley floor. Beyond the white water and feathery larches of the lower glen, the prospect opens to reveal not only grazing herds, but also fine views of the battlement of cliffs edging the mountain called Lochnagar.

However, there is no public transportation into this cul-de-sac glen, and your tour or local coach service will instead take you west again, on the A93. The enormous car park roughly 7 miles ahead is indicative of the popularity of **Balmoral Castle,** the rebuilt castle modified by Prince Albert in 1855 for his queen. The architectural style, Scots Baronial, is characterized by towers and turrets. Balmoral's visiting hours depend on whether the royals are in residence. In truth, there are more interesting and historic buildings to explore. *On the A93, tel. 03397/ 42334. Admission: £1.75 adults, £1.25 senior citizens, children free. Open May–July, Mon.–Sat. 10–5.*

Continuing west into Highland scenery, you can get further pine-framed glimpses of the "steep frowning glories of dark Lochnagar," as it was described by the poet Byron. About 8 miles farther on the A93 sits **Braemar Castle,** dating from the 17th century, with defensive walls later built in the plan of a pointed star. At Braemar (the braes or slopes of the district of Mar), the standard or rebel flag was first raised at the start of the spectacularly unsuccessful Jacobite rebellion of 1715. Thirty years later, during the last rebellion, Braemar Castle was strengthened and garrisoned by Hanoverian (government) troops. *On the A93, at Braemar, tel. 03397/41219, off-season tel. 03397/41224. Admission: £1.45 adults, 75p children, £1.10 senior citizens. Open May–early Oct., daily 10–6.*

The village of Braemar is associated with the Braemar Highland Gathering held every September. Although it's one of many such events celebrated throughout Scotland, Braemar's gathering is distinguished by the presence of the royal family. Although a popular holiday respite for generations, Braemar is at its most crowded on Games Day, a September event founded to ensure the survival of traditional dances and music. Today's version also includes athletics. Braemar also has a tricky golf course laden with foaming waters. However, erratic duffers take note: The compassionate course managers have installed, near the water, poles with little nets on the end for those occasional shots that may go awry.

Although the main A93 slinks off to the south from Braemar, a little unmarked road will take you farther west into the hilly heartlands. In fact, even if you do not have your own transport, you can still explore the area by catching the post bus that leaves from Braemar Post Office once a day. The road offers you delectable views over the winding river Dee and the blue hills before passing through the tiny hamlet of Inverey and crossing a bridge at the **Linn of Dee.** *Linn* is a Scots word meaning rocky narrows, and the river's rocky gash here is deep and roaring. Park beyond the bridge and walk back to admire the sylvan setting of the river and woodland, replete with bending larch bows and deep, tranquil pools with salmon glinting in them. Also, if you're staying in the area, there are several quite demanding walks, including a through route all the way to Speyside—but only for the fit and well equipped. Some of the routes use old stalkers' tracks (deer stalking is big business locally).

Less-energetic explorers will return to Braemar, retracing the route as far as Balmoral. From Balmoral, there is an interesting way out of Royal Deeside by car. Look for a narrow road going north, signposted B976. Be careful on the first twisting mile through the trees. Soon you will emerge from scattered pines into the open moor in upland Aberdeenshire. Behind is the massif of Lochnagar again, and to the west are snow-tipped domes of the big Cairngorms. Roll down to a bridge and go left on the A939, which comes in from Ballater. Another high moor section follows: As the road leaves the scattered buildings by the bridge, see if you can spot the roadside inscription to the company of soldiers who built the A939 in the 18th century.

The soldiers paved their military highway roughly 12 miles north to **Corgarff Castle,** a lonely tower house with another star-shaped defensive wall—a curious replica of Braemar Castle. To get there, you will find it signposted left at the next junction. Corgarff was built as a hunting seat for the earls of Mar in the 16th century. After an eventful history that included the wife of a later laird being burned alive in a family dispute, the castle ended its career as a garrison for Hanoverian troops. The troops also had the responsibility of trying to prevent illegal whiskey distilling, at one time a popular hobby in these parts. *Off A939, tel. 031/244–3101. Admission: £1.50 adults, 80p children. Open Apr.–Sept., Mon.–Sat. 9:30–6, Sun. 2–6.*

If you return south to the A939/A944 junction and then make a left onto the A944, the excellent castle signposting will tell you that you are on **Gordon District's Castle Trail.** The A944 meanders along the River Don to the village of Strathdon, where a great mound by the roadside—on the left—turns out to be a *motte*, or the base of a wooden castle, built in the late 12th century. Surviving mottes are significant in terms of confirming the history of Scottish castles, but it is difficult for visitors to become enthusiastic about a great grassed-over heap, no matter what its historic content.

From here, a sign points to **Glenbuchat Castle,** a plain Z-plan tower house; about 12 miles to the northeast you will encounter the more interesting **Kildrummy Castle.** Visitors can enjoy three attractions here: the ruins of the castle itself, the gardens behind it, and the country house–style Kildrummy Castle Hotel. Kildrummy is significant because of its age (13th century) and because it has ties to the mainstream medieval traditions of European castle building. It shares features with Harlech and Caernarvon in Wales, as well as with continental sites, such as Château de Coucy near Laon, France. Kildrummy had undergone several expansions at the hands of English King Edward I when, in 1306, back in Scottish hands, the castle was besieged by King Edward I's son. The defenders were betrayed by a certain Osbarn the Smith, who had been promised a large amount of gold by the English besieging forces. They gave it to him after the castle fell, pouring it molten down his throat, or so the ghoulish story goes. Kildrummy's prominence came to an end after the collapse of the 1715 Jacobite uprising. It had been the rebel headquarters and was consequently dismantled. *Tel. 031/ 244–3101. Admission: £1 adults, 50p children and senior citizens. Open Apr.–Sept., Mon.–Sat. 9:30–6, Sun. 2–6; Oct.– Mar., Sat. 9:30–4, Sun. 2–4. Open weekends-only in winter.*

The **garden** behind the castle—with a separate entrance from the main road—is built in what was the original quarry for the castle. This sheltered bowl within the woodlands has a broad range of shrubs and alpine plants and a notable water garden. If the weather is pleasant, it makes for a nice place to pause and plan the next stage of your journey. *A97, off the A944, Aberdeenshire, tel. 09755/71264 or 09755/71277. Admission: £1.50 adults, 20–50p children. Open Apr.–Oct., daily 10–5.*

Time Out The **Mossat Shop,** 4 miles past Kildrummy, at the junction of the A97 and the A944, is another possible pit stop for tea or some light shopping. If you have more time, however, then the **village hall** in the tiny rural community of **Clatt,** 7 miles northeast just off the A97, has a savory reputation for its home baking. Local ladies bake the delicious breads and cakes at this cooperatively run establishment (weekends only). People come from miles around to sample the results. There is also a produce and crafts shop.

If you wish to forego Clatt and its cream cakes, make a right onto the A944 for Alford (pronounced *Ah*-furd) at the A97/A944 junction. Alford, a plain and sturdy settlement in the Howe (Hollow) of Alford, gives those visitors who have grown somewhat weary from castle hopping a break: it has a museum instead. The **Grampian Transport Museum** specializes in roadbased means of locomotion. One of its more unusual exhibits is the *Craigievar Express,* a steam-driven creation invented by the local postman to deliver mail more efficiently. *Alford, tel. 09755/62292. Admission: £2.30 adults, 80p children, £1.50 senior citizens, £5 family ticket. Open Apr.–Oct., daily 10–5.*

Your return to Aberdeen leads you to two of the finest castles on the trail. The first is **Craigievar.** Located about 5 miles to the south on the A980, this historic structure represents one of the finest traditions of local castle building. It also has the advantage of having survived intact, much as the stonemasons left it in 1626, with its pepper-pot turrets and towers, the whole slender shape covered in a pink-cream pastel. It was built in relatively peaceful times by William Forbes, a successful merchant in trade with the Baltic Sea ports (hence he was also known as Danzig Willie). Centuries of care and wise stewardship have ensured that the experience proffered today's visitor is as authentic as possible. *On the A980, tel. 03398/83635. Admission: £3 adults, £1.50 children and senior citizens. Open May–Sept., daily 2–6. Grounds open all year 9:30–sunset.*

Your return to Aberdeen could be by way of **Castle Fraser,** a massive structure—in fact, it is the largest of the castles of Mar. While this building shows a variety of styles reflecting the taste of previous owners from the 15th to the 19th centuries, it's design is typical of the cavalcade of castles that exist here in the Northeast. It has the further advantages of a walled garden, a picnic area, and a tearoom. *3 mi south of Kemnay off the A944, tel. 033/03–463. Admission: £3 adults, £1.50 children and senior citizens. Open May, June, and Sept., daily 2–6; July and Aug., daily 11–6; Oct., weekends 2–5. Gardens and grounds open all year 9:30–sunset.*

From Castle Fraser, your quickest route back to the city is to turn south to join the A944 or north to the A96.

Tour 4: The Northeast

Numbers in the margin correspond to points of interest on the Northeast map.

Tour 3 covered the immediate hinterland of Aberdeen. This tour ranges more widely to sample the seaboard, including some of the best-preserved coastal scenery in Scotland. The tour also meanders inland, to revisit briefly the malt-whiskey theme. Speyside—the valley or strath of the River Spey—is famed for its whiskey distilleries, which it promotes in yet another signposted trail. Whiskey distilling is not an intrinsically spectacular process. It involves pure water, malted grain, and sometimes peat smoke, then a lot of bubbling and fermentation, all of which causes a range of extremely odd smells. The end result is a prestigious product with a fascinating range of flavors that you either enjoy immensely or not at all.

On this tour, instead of assiduously following the whiskey trail, we will dip into it and blend it with some other aspects of the lower end of Speyside—the old county of Moray, now part of Grampian. Whiskey notwithstanding, Moray's scenic qualities, low rainfall, and other reassuring weather statistics are worth remembering when you plan your route.

Because of its convenient transport links to both the coast and the countryside, this tour starts from **Elgin.** As the center of the fertile Laigh (low-lying lands) of Moray, it has been of local importance for centuries. Like Aberdeen, it is self-supporting and previously remote, sheltered by great hills to the south and lying between two major rivers, the Spey and the Findhorn. Beginning in the 13th century, Elgin became an important religious center, a cathedral city with a walled town growing up around the cathedral and adjacent to the original settlement. Left in peace for at least some of its history, Elgin prospered and became, by the early 18th century, a mini-Edinburgh of the north: a place where country gentlemen came to spend the winter. It even echoed Edinburgh in the widescale reconstruction of the early 19th century: Much of the old town was swept away in a wave of rebuilding, giving Elgin the fine neoclassical buildings that survive today.

The old shape of the town survived almost intact until this century, until it succumbed to the modern madness of demolishing great swaths of buildings for the sake of better traffic flow. It suffered from its position on the Aberdeen–Inverness main road. However, the central main street plan and some of the older little streets and wynds (alleyways) remain. Visitors can also recall Elgin's past by observing the arcaded shop fronts, some of which date from the late-17th century. The older shop fronts, which can be found at the east end of town, give the main shopping street a quaint appeal.

At the center of town, the most conspicuous, positively unavoidable building is **St. Giles Church,** which divides High Street. The grand foursquare building built in 1828 exhibits the style known as Greek Revival: Note the columns; the pilasters (half-columns attached to the walls); and the top of the spire, surmounted by a representation of the Lysicrates Monument. Farther east, past the arcaded shops, you can see the **Little Cross** (17th century), which marked the boundary between the town and the cathedral grounds.

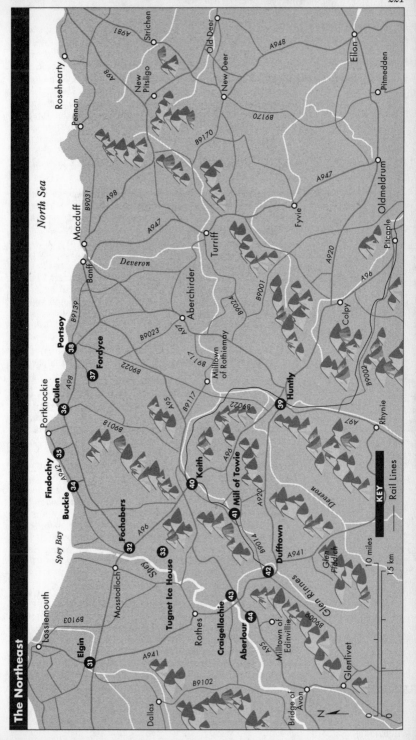

221

The Northeast

North Sea

Lossiemouth
Elgin · 31
B9103
Dallas
A941
B9102
Mosstodloch
Spey
Rothes
Spey Bay
Fochabers · 32
33 · Tugnet Ice House
Craigellachie · 43
Aberlour · 44
A95
Milltown of Edinville
Bridge of Avon
Glenlivet
B9008
Glen Rinnes
Dufftown
42
A941
Glen Fiddich
Mill of Towie · 41
A920
B9014
Keith · 40
A96
B9022
B9117
Buckie · 34
Findochty
35
A942
B9018
Portknockie
Cullen · 36
A98
37 · Fordyce
Fordyce · 38 Portsoy
B9139
Banff
Deveron
Macduff
A98
B9031
A947
B9023
B9022
A97
Aberchirder
Turriff
B9025
B9024
Milltown of Rothiemay
B9117
B9001
Huntly · 39
A96
Deveron
Rhynie
A97
Colpy
B9002
Pennan
Rosehearty
New Pitsligo
A981
Strichen
A98
B9170
Old Deer
New Deer
A948
A947
Fyvie
A920
Pitcaple
Oldmeldrum
A96
B9170
Ellon
Pilmedden

KEY
—— Rail Lines

10 miles
15 km

N

Cooper Park, located a short distance to the southeast across the modern bypass road, is home to a magnificent ruin, the cathedral consecrated in 1224. The cathedral's eventful story included devastation by fire: a 1390 act of retaliation by Alexander Stewart, the Wolf of Badenoch. The illegitimate son-turned-bandit of King David II had sought revenge for his being excommunicated by the bishop of Moray. The cathedral was rebuilt but finally fell into disuse after the Reformation in 1560. By 1567, the highest authority in the land at the time, the regent earl of Moray, had stripped the lead from the roof to pay for his army. Thus ended the career of the religious seat known as the Lamp of the North. Some traces of the cathedral settlement survive, although they have been drastically altered: the gateway Pann's Port and the Bishop's Palace.

32 Take the A96 east to **Fochabers.** Just before reaching it, you will see the works of a major local employer, Baxters of Fochabers, a family-run firm with an international reputation for fine foods. From Tokyo to New York, upmarket stores stock their soups, jams, chutneys, and other gourmet products—all of which are made here, close to the River Spey. Factory tours yield glimpses of impeccably attired staff stirring great vats of boiling marmalade and other concoctions. The **Baxters Visitors Centre** also offers a video presentation, a re-creation of the Baxters' first grocery shop, as well as a real shop and a restaurant offering an assortment of delectables. *1 mi west of Fochabers on the A96, tel. 0343/820–393. Open weekdays 9:30–4:30; Easter and May–Sept., weekdays 9:30–4:30, weekends 11–4:30. Guided tours on weekdays only; no tours during factory holiday weeks in April (1 wk), June (2 wks), and Aug. (1 wk).*

After traversing the Spey bridge and entering Fochabers, visitors will find this community has the symmetrical village green typical of the planned village. The fourth duke of Gordon, the local landowner, decided that the original village site was too close to his castle and consequently moved his tenants to the present site. The village conserves much of the building style of 200 years ago. Perhaps this pleasing, mellow ambience attracts the extraordinary range of antiques dealers in Fochabers, with shops' wares ranging from near-junk to designer pieces. Through one of these shops you can enter the **Fochabers Folk Museum,** which offers an excellent display of rural items in a converted church, ranging from carts and carriages to interesting farm implements. *Tel. 0343/820362. Admission: 60p adults, 30p children, 40p senior citizens, £1.50 family ticket. Open winter, daily 9:30–1 and 2–5; summer, daily 9:30–1 and 2–6.*

If you have your own car, you may care to divert up the road that runs south directly opposite the museum. Leaving the houses behind for well-hedged country lanes, you will discover a Forestry Commission sign to the **Earth Pillars.** These curious eroded sandstone pillars are framed by tall-trunked pines and overlook a wide prospect of the lower Spey Valley. Another option for motorists is to take the B9108 from Fochabers down to the mouth of the River Spey. Here, by a storm beach with a high stone swell of smooth-washed pebbles, the river enters **33** the sea. Nearby is the **Tugnet Ice House,** once the centerpiece of the local salmon fishing industry. Before the days of mechanical refrigeration, the salmon were stored in icy chambers. The ice was gathered in the winter and lasted in its insulated cellars throughout the fishing season. Now a museum housed in the Ice House tells the story. *Spey Bay, 5 mi west of Buckie, tel. 0309/673701. Admission free. Open June–Sept., daily 10–4.*

From Fochabers, take the A98 east for about 3 miles before making a left on the A942, which runs closer to the coast **34** through the fishing port of **Buckie** and its satellite villages. This outpost is gray and workaday, with plenty of Victorian architecture. The **Buckie Maritime Museum** explores the nautical theme that still consumes this port, while the Peter Anson Gallery in the same building shows a selection of watercolor works also related to the development of the fishing industry. *Cluny Pl., tel. 0309/673701. Admission free. Open weekdays 10–8, Sat. 10–12.*

Visitors will find a string of other fishing communities down by the shore, running east. These salty little villages paint a colorful scene with their gable-ended houses and fishing nets set out to dry amid the rocky shoreline.

35 The residents of **Findochty**—located about 2 miles east of Buckie on the A942—are known for their fastidiousness and creativity in painting their fisher-houses, taking the fine art of housepainting to a new level. Some residents even paint the mortar between the stonework a different color. The small town also has a harbor with a faint echo of the Mediterranean about it. Its neighbor along the coast, Portknockie, has a sheltered little harbor of its own. This harbor, however, is noted more for its curious rock formation, the **Bowfiddle Rock**: an eroded stack of stone with a hole in it bearing a fanciful resemblance to its name.

36 You will see some wonderfully painted homes again at **Cullen,** 2 to 3 miles from Portknockie on the A98, in the old fishermen's town below the railway viaduct. But the real attractions of this little resort are its white-sand beach and the fine view west toward the Bowfiddle Rock. A stroll along the beach reveals the shape of the fishing settlement below and planned town above. As did the fourth duke of Gordon in Fochabers, the local landowner in Cullen, this time the earl of Seafield, decided the original village was too close to his property, Cullen House (now private apartments). He knocked down old Cullen and built, starting in 1822, a fine town of wide streets and functional buildings. The handsome railway viaduct is also a legacy of the Ogilvie Earl. Even the might of a railway company had to bow to his refusal to allow anything so vulgar as an iron road through his grounds. The line was pushed to the seaward edge, on expensive arches and embankments, so he could have his privacy. Cullen and its little shops are far enough away from major town superstores to survive on local, intermittent trade; most unusual for a town of its size, Cullen has a full range of speciality shops—ironmongers, butchers, a baker, a haberdasher, and a locally famous ice-cream shop among them.

Time Out | **The Seafield Arms,** built as a coaching inn for the new town, serves a friendly pub lunch.

If Cullen represents a neat and planned town, contrast it with the much more ancient layout of **Portsoy,** about 6 miles east along the coast. But travelers with their own means of transportation can make two intriguing discoveries before they even

reach Portsoy. For the first, follow signs off the main road to
the little holiday village of **Sandend,** about 4 miles east of Cullen, then follow another sign for **Sunnyside Beach.** Simply follow the local authority's signs down a narrow road until you
find yourself in a farmyard. Park and then walk until you come
to grassy cliffs, the site of the ruined Findlater Castle, half-
perched and half-tumbling on to a rocky shoreline. The Ogilvies
lived on this draughty site before building the more palatial
Cullen House mentioned above. If you continue to the west, you
will probably find one of the most perfect beaches in Scotland:
no advertising signs, no ice-cream salesmen, no holiday cottages, and no access roads. Perhaps in the quiet season, no visitors either.

The second discovery lies just off the A98 opposite the Sandend
turning, but this time you make a right, heading south. The
(37) conservation village of **Fordyce** lies among the barley fields of
Banffshire like a small slice of rural England gone far adrift.
You can stroll by the churchyard; picnic on the old bleaching
green (an explanatory notice board tells you all about it); or buy
stamps from the local post office, where the lady behind the
counter still weighs the letters using old-style brass weights.
There is also a restored 19th-century carpenter's workshop to
visit.

Public transportation will take you straight from Cullen to
(38) **Portsoy.** This substantial village boasts the oldest harbor on the
Moray Firth, built in the 17th century. Once a North Sea trading port and later participating in the 19th-century fishing
boom, the community thereafter fell into a decline. But
thoughtful conservation programs have revitalized much of
Portsoy's old fabric. The crafts shop, located in the converted
18th-century warehouse by the waterfront, sells souvenirs
made from the local Portsoy marble that once was exported to
decorate the Palace of Versailles. Portsoy is also one of the
places where the traditional and very economical fare, the fish
supper, can be sampled at its best. Keep in mind that, in Scotland, fish and chips eaten from a paper bag is usually ordered as
a "fish supper" no matter what time of day.

Although there's a lot more of the coast to explore (*see* Off the
Beaten Track, *below*), there are a number of inland routes that
lead to **Keith,** the next main town on the itinerary. You can
drive along an attractive stretch of the River Deveron valley
by taking the B9022 to the B9023 south from Portsoy to
Aberchirder. Once in Aberchirder make a right onto the A97,
and then a right again onto the B9117, where you will discover
the essence of rural Banffshire: woodlands tilting gently to a
quiet river and sturdy farms following the seasons around. The
B9117 winds west through the peaceful, gray-roofed village of
Rothiemay, called **Milltown** on some maps (short for Milltown of
Rothiemay). At this point you have a choice: You can continue
on to Keith to the west or make a short detour to the south
(39) along the B9022 to visit **Huntly.**

An agricultural center for the hinterland, Huntly is laid out on
a typical planned grid. The Gordons, the powerful Northeast
family, had their stronghold, **Huntly Castle,** here. You can find
the castle by driving to the town center and on through the arch
of the Gordon Schools, straight ahead, following the road to the
riverside. The ruin—complete with heraldic carvings and unusual decorative work on the oriel windows (inspired by a

French château)—sits on top of a 12th-century motte. The decoration belongs to the last building phase at the beginning of
the 17th century, although there were several other building
periods between the motted fortress and the ornate palace.

40 To reach **Keith** from Milltown follow the B9117 west to join the
A95 in the valley of the River Isla. A major agricultural center,
similar to Huntly, Keith shows the typical Grampian pattern of
a town planned by the lairds of the late-18th and early 19th centuries.

41 Follow the B9014 south to reach the **Mill of Towie,** a fully restored oatmeal mill, dating from a time when the meal mill
played a vital role in the local economy. Mill tours are available.
*Drummuir, Keith, Banffshire, tel. 054/281–274. Admission:
75p adults, 25p children. Open Easter and May–Oct., daily
10:30–4:30.*

Time Out   The Mill of Towie's former grain store is now a **restaurant** serving morning coffee, lunches, and teas.

42 **Dufftown,** on one of the Spey tributaries, farther south on the
B9014, is a town planned in 1817 by the earl of Fife. One of the
most famous malt whiskies of all, the market leader **Glenfiddich**
is distilled here. The independent company of William Grant
and Sons Limited was the first distillery to realize the tourist
potential of the distilling process. It subsequently built an entertaining visitor center in addition to offering tours. In short,
if you do intend to visit a distillery, it may as well be Glenfiddich, especially because it probably offers the most complete
range of on-site activities, from floor malting to bottling. In
fact, it is the only Speyside distiller that bottles on the premises.

The Glenfiddich guides will take you—step by step—through
the stages of making malted barley into 12-year-old malt whiskey. They point out with pride that the copper stills are exactly
the same size and shape as they were when the plant opened in
1887. The audiovisual show and displays in the visitor center
are also worthwhile, and the traditional stone-walled premises
with the typical pagoda-roofed malting buildings have a pleasant period ambience. Not all visitors have to like whiskey to
come away from the visit feeling that they've learned something about a leading Scottish export that is clearly an important part of the Speyside economy. *North of Dufftown on the
A941, tel. 0340/20373. Admission free. Open weekdays 9:30–
4:30, except Christmas and New Year's; Easter–mid-Oct., Sat.
9:30–4:30, Sun. noon–4:30.*

However, there is much more to Dufftown than Glenfiddich, as
well as six other distilleries. On a mound just above the distillery is a grim, gray, and squat curtain-walled castle, **Balvenie**
(only incidentally giving its name to yet another malt whiskey).
This fortress, dating from the 13th century, once commanded
the glens and passes toward Speyside and Elgin. Back in the
center of Dufftown, the conspicuous battlemented clock tower—the centerpiece of the planned town and a former jail—
houses a local museum open in summer. *Dufftown, A941, tel.
031/244–3101. Admission: £1 adults, 50p children. Open Apr.–
Sept., Mon.–Sat. 9:30–6, Sun. 2–6.*

Down the hill (east), look for a sign to Mortlach Church. Set in a hollow by the Dullan Water, this church is thought to be one of the oldest Christian sites in Scotland, perhaps founded by St. Moluag, a contemporary of St. Columba, as early as AD 566. Note the weathered Pictish cross in the churchyard and the even older stone under cover in the vestibule, with a strange Pictish elephantlike beast carved on it. Though much of the church was rebuilt after 1876, some early work survives, including three lancet (thin, pointed) windows from the 13th century and a leper's squint (a hole extended to the outside of the church so that lepers could hear the service but be kept away from the rest of the congregation).

From Dufftown take the A941 about 4 miles northwest to **Craigellachie,** renowned as an angling resort on the Spey. Like so many Speyside settlements, Craigellachie is sometimes enveloped in the malty reek of the local industry. As you arrive in the village, you will notice the huge cooperage, the place where barrels are made and repaired. The Spey itself is crossed by a handsome suspension bridge, designed by Thomas Telford in 1814 and now bypassed by the modern road. Go left and upstream by the A95 to **Aberlour** (often marked as Charlestown of Aberlour on maps). This is another handsome little burgh, essentially Victorian in style, though actually founded in 1812 by the local landowner. While Glenfarclas, Cragganmore, and Aberlour itself are names of noted local whiskies, for a nonalcoholic change of pace, take a look at the Village Store. After the owners died the shop was locked away intact, complete with stock. Recently, new owners discovered they had bought a time capsule—a range of products dating from the early decades of the present century—as well as all the paraphernalia, books and ledgers, accounts, and notes of a country business.

Time Out Nearby, **The Old Pantry** (tel. 0340/871617) serves everything from a cup of coffee to a four-course spread.

At this point, you are only about 15 miles south of Elgin, the starting point of this tour.

Aberdeen for Free

The **Aberdeen Art Gallery** (*see* Tour 1) hosts a varied entertainment program.

Aberdeen Maritime Museum (*see* What to See and Do with Children)

The Crombie Woollen Mill, where Crombie cloth was made until recently, houses a museum and has an audiovisual program describing the history of the company. *Grandholm Mill, Woodside. Open Mon.–Sat. 9–4:30, Sun. 12–4:30.*

James Dun's House (*see* What to See and Do with Children)

The **Marischal Museum** houses artifacts from around the world and exhibitions on world history from prehistoric times, with a special emphasis on Scotland. *Broad St., tel. 0224/273131.*

Provost Skene's House (*see* Tour 1)

What to See and Do with Children

Amusement Centers

The **Adventure Playground** has a fishing-village theme, including model houses, fishing nets, and a paddling pool. *Beach Esplanade.*

Codona's Amusement Park, like Adventure Playground, is also located on the shore. *Beach Blvd. Open Easter school holidays and June–July, daily; May–Sept., holiday Mon.*

Museums

The **Aberdeen Maritime Museum** is a fascinating place for grade-schoolers, with its ship models, paintings, and equipment associated with the fishing industry, local shipbuilding, and the North Sea oil and gas industries. *Provost Ross's House, Ship Row, tel. 0224/585788. Admission free. Open Mon.–Sat. 10–5.*

James Dun's House is an 18th-century dwelling in which a variety of exhibitions are held, everything from cooking to archaeology. *Schoolhill, tel. 0224/646333. Admission free. Open Mon.–Sat. 10–5.*

The **Rutherford Celebration Centre** has an activities-based heritage museum and learning center called Jonah's Journey, based on life in a 2,000-year-old Israelite village. The center offers costumes, spinning and weaving, mosaic making, puppet plays, and jigsaw puzzles. *Rosemount Pl., tel. 0224/647614. Open weekdays 10–4 (closed Tues. PM in winter season). Admission: £1 adults, 50p children.*

Zoos and Parks

All the city's parks have free entry, including the very popular **Winter Garden** in **Duthie Park.**

At the **Darnaway Farm Visitor Centre,** visitors can discover the varied activities of the Moray Estates and enjoy an exhibition on forestry and farming, with an audiovisual program. Younger family members will enjoy the farm animals, as well as nature trails and woodland walks. The center also has a tearoom. *Off A96, Nairn-Forres, tel. 0309/672213. Admission: £1.50 adults, £1 children. Open May–mid-Sept., daily 10–5.*

Doonies Farm, run by Aberdeen's Department of Leisure and Recreation, is a model farm with Clydesdale horses, ponies, cattle, sheep, and small animals, some of which children may handle. *Off A956 from Aberdeen. Open daily dawn–dusk.*

Duthie Park and Winter Gardens. In addition to being a great place to feed the ducks, Duthie Park has a boating pond and trampolines, carved wooden animals, and playgrounds. In the Winter Gardens children can see fish in ponds, free-flying birds, turtles, and terrapins. *Polmuir Rd., Riverside Dr. Park and gardens open all year, entertainment in summer only. Admission free. Gardens open daily 10–dusk.*

Hazlehead Park and Zoo has a potpourri of domestic animals and birds, a free-flight aviary, and an aquarium house. A maze (very uncommon in Scotland), electric cars, putting, and trampolines are also available during the summer. *Groats Rd., Hazlehead Ave. Admission free. Zoo open all year, daily 10–dusk; maze open July–Sept., daily 10–dusk, also weekends in early summer.*

Storybook Glen displays a fairy-tale theme in a 20-acre parkland/garden setting: the Jolly Miller, Old MacDonald's Farm, and the Old Woman Who Lived in a Shoe are some of the charac-

ters featured in large-scale models. The Andersons run a famous rose-growing company, one of several in the Aberdeen
area. *Off S. Deeside Rd., B9077, about 4 mi from Aberdeen, tel.
0224/732941. Open Mar.–Oct., daily 10–6, Nov.–Feb., weekends 11–4.*

Off the Beaten Track

Because of the geographic shape of the far northeastern corner
of this region, many tours tend to ignore the edge of this fascinating part of Scotland. Here is a selection of some of the places
that do not fit easily into the given tours but nevertheless are
worth searching out.

A unique re-creation by the National Trust for Scotland of a
17th-century garden, **Pitmedden Garden,** is best visited in high
summer, from July onward, when annual bedding plants form
intricate formal patterns of the garden plots. The 100-acre
estate also has a variety of woodland and farmland walks, as
well as the Museum of Farming Life. *Tel. 06513/2352. Admission
£2.40 adults, £1.20 children and senior citizens. Garden open
all year, 9:30–dusk. Museum open May–Sept., daily 10–6.*

Created as the home of the earls and marquesses of Aberdeen,
Haddo House—designed by William Adam—is now cared for
by the National Trust for Scotland. Built in 1723, the elegant
mansion has a light and graceful design, with curving wings on
either side of a harmonious facade. It is promoted within Gordon District's Castle Trail, but its potential as a defensive fortress was minimal. Much of the interior is circa 1880, at a time
when Adam features, such as ornate plasterwork, were revived. The house, which also has a tearoom, is set in sprawling
parkland, popular with the locals for country walks and picnics.
*Off B99, northwest of Ellon. Admission: £3 adults, £1.50 chil-
dren and senior citizens. House open mid-Apr.–May and
Sept., daily 2–6; June–Aug., daily 11–6; Oct., weekends 2–5.*

The Bullers of Buchan, located off the A975 south of Peterhead,
is worth seeing for those explorers who like their sites austere
and elemental. On a stretch of windy cliff and cove coastline—
once used by smugglers—the sea has cut through a cave, col-
lapsing its roof and forming a great rocky cauldron, fearsome in
bad weather. This natural phenomenon has been a tourist spectacle since the English man of letters Dr. Samuel Johnson came
this way in 1773 with his Scottish biographer, James Boswell.
The two men dined at nearby Slains Castle to the south, now in
ruins. A later visitor was Bram Stoker, and the castle's setting
is said to have inspired him to create Dracula, though this may
not actually encourage you to visit. The Bullers of Buchan is an
impressive site, but not for the vertigo prone. Approach the
cliff edge with great care.

A major element in Aden Country Park, the **Northeast Scotland
Agricultural Heritage Centre,** tells the moving story through
videos of life on the land and the hard toil of the farming folk.
Implements, tableaux, models, and displays create a vivid
impression. Aden Country Park is also an important recreational resource for the locals, with countryside trails that meander throughout the park's 230 acres. *Off A92, just west of
Mintlaw, tel. 0771/22857. Heritage Centre open May–Sept.,
daily 11–5; Apr. and Oct., weekends noon–5.*

A huddle of houses tucked below a crescent of grassy cliffs, **Pennan** shot to minor fame as the setting for some of the filming of *Local Hero*, which starred Burt Lancaster. The phone box and the hotel featured in the film are still there. Pennan is set in a remote cliff coastline about as far from the tourist trail as is possible. *Off B9031 between Fraserburgh and Macduff.*

In an area rife with castles, many are distinguished within their own categories: Craigievar for untouched perfection, Corgarff for sheer loneliness, Haddo House for elegance. Perhaps **Fyvie** stands out in its own category: most complex. Five great towers built by five successive powerful families turned a 13th-century foursquare castle into an opulent Edwardian (early 20th century) statement of wealth. Fyvie is also considered to be the jewel in the crown among Northeast castles in the care of the National Trust for Scotland. There is also an array of superb paintings on view, including 12 Raeburns, as well as myriad sumptuous interiors and walks on the castle grounds. Fyvie is praised for its sheer impact, if you like your castles oppressive and gloomy. *Off A947 between Oldmeldrum and Turriff, tel. 065/16–266. Admission: £3 adults, £1.50 children and senior citizens. Open mid-Apr.–May and Sept., daily 2–6; June–Aug., daily 11–6; Oct., weekends 2–5.*

If a whole town could be considered off the beaten track, then **Banff** fits the category. This town is an exception to the Northeast's prevailing granite burghs with its domestic Scottish architecture of the 17th and 18th centuries, especially the former town houses of the local lairds and merchants. *Take A947 from Aberdeen.*

Given the general destruction caused by the 16th-century religious upheaval of the Reformation, abbeys in Scotland tend to be ruinous and deserted sites, but at **Pluscarden Abbey** the way of life of the monks continues. Originally a 13th-century foundation, the religious community abandoned their abbey after the Reformation. The third marquis of Bute bought the remains in 1897 and initiated a repair and restoration program that continues to this day. Monks from an abbey near Gloucester, England, returned here in 1948, and today the abbey is an active religious community. *Off B9010 from Elgin. Admission free. Open daily 5 AM–8:30 PM.*

Califer Braes Viewpoint is the best place to see the shape of Moray or, rather, the Laigh of Moray, the low-lying wooded grounds between the hills and the sea. This vantage point offers inspiring views of the blue Highlands both north across the narrowing Moray Firth and west beyond Inverness. It is well worth the effort to find, so look carefully for signs off the A96, about 6 miles west of Elgin. The signs will lead you to minor circular roads that will take you to the edge of a long rolling ridge overlooking the town of Forres.

An interesting mansion house, **Leith Hall,** contrasts with the fortified appearance of many other Grampian castles. Nevertheless, military history is portrayed within this house, formerly owned by the Leith-Hay family, whose own military careers are illustrated in the mansion's displays. The Leith Hall estate is a typically Scottish arrangement of a grand house, parkland, and associated tenant farms. Visitors will gain valuable insights into the house's former role in the local life of the area. There is a modest selection of walks and trails through an attractive garden. *Off B9002, 7 mi south of Huntly, tel. 04643/216. Admission: £3 adults, £1.50 children and senior citizens. Open May–Sept., daily 2–6; Oct., weekends 2–5. Garden open daily 9:30–sunset.*

Shopping

Aberdeen serves a large and fairly prosperous hinterland. Elgin is a smaller center. The shopping pattern fits accordingly: Aberdeen with the widest choice, Elgin with a few shops of interest. However, because of the fishing and farming prosperity, plus new money from oil and even newer money from people moving from the south, there are a few shopping surprises in some of the smaller towns.

Aberdeen Aberdeen's shopping scene is in the throes of change. For generations, folk from round about would come into Aberdeen for the day—the city is a kind of large-scale market town—and their chief delight would be to stroll the length of Union Street and perhaps take in George Street as well. Now this pattern is changing, thanks mainly to the modern and faceless shopping developments (pleasant enough in an anonymous way), the St. Nicholas and Bon-Accord centers (George St.), which have taken the emphasis away from Union Street.

However, smaller specialty shops are still to be found, particularly in the Chapel Street/Thistle Street area at the west end of Union Street and on the latter's north side, which has a series of interesting little businesses well worth discovering. These include **Nova** (20 Chapel St., tel. 0224/641270), where the locals go for gifts. Nova stocks major U.K. brand names, such as Liberty of London, Dartington Glass, and Crabtree and Evelyn, as well as Scottish Caithness Glass and a wide range of Scottish silver jewelry. **The Farmhouse** (11 Chapel St., tel. 0224/640681) is a delicatessen that includes some Scottish specialties in its offerings. **Colin Wood** (25 Rose St., tel. 0224/643019) is the place to go for antiques and prints. **Harlequin** (65 Thistle St., tel. 0224/635716) stocks a large selection of embroidery and tapestry kits, designer yarns, and colorful expensive knitwear. Antiques collectors will also enjoy a browse in **Elizabeth Watt's** little shop (69 Thistle St., tel. 0224/647232).

Elsewhere in town, **Helen Hunter** (100 Rosemount Pl., tel. 0224/63097) is where discriminating, slightly older women go to be looked after and advised in matters of smart dressing. Visitors looking for bargains can try the **Crombie Woollen Mill** on the edge of town (Grandholm Mills, Woodside, off the A96, tel. 0224/483201); a particularly good value are the men's overcoats bearing the Crombie name (known for high quality).

At the **Aberdeen Family History Shop** (152 King St., tel. 0224/646323) you can browse through a huge range of publications related to local history and genealogical research. If you have roots in northeast Scotland and you want to start filling in some names in the family tree, one of the shop's staff members can show you what to do and how to get started. For the payment of a small membership fee (to the Aberdeen & North East Family History Society), they will undertake some research on your behalf.

Aberdeen shops catering to children include **The Toy Bazaar** (45 Schoolhill, tel. 0224/640021), which stocks a range of toys for children preschool age and up. **Craftplay** (282 Holburn St., tel. 0224/584784) stocks toys and crafts materials. **The Early Learning Centre** (Bon-Accord Centre, George St., tel. 0224/571882) specializes in toys with educational value.

Deeside   Farther afield from Aberdeen, the opportunities for shopping are certainly more scattered. **Banchory** on Royal Deeside has **The Hebridean Workshop** (74 High St., Banchory, tel. 03302/4795), which offers an interesting and authentic range of tapestry kits, some from Victorian designs. Further up the valley, the **McEwan Gallery** (on A939, 1 mi west of Ballater, tel. 03397/55429) displays a good range of fine paintings, watercolors, prints, and books (many with a Scottish theme) in an unusual house built by the Swiss artist Rudolphe Christen in 1902. For a low-cost gift you could always see what is being boiled up at **Dee Valley Confectioners** (Station Sq., tel. 03397/55499), sweets makers in **Ballater** itself.

Also in Ballater (where the royals seem to do much of their Scottish shopping, as evidenced by the many BY APPOINTMENT TO signs), you can buy Scottish designer knitwear at **Goodbrand Knitwear** (1 Braemar Rd., tel. 03397/55947). At either of **Countrywear's** two shops (15 and 35 Bridge St., tel. 03397/55453) you'll find everything you need for Scottish country living, including fishing tackle, shooting accessories, cashmere, tweeds, and that flexible garment popular in Scotland between seasons: the bodywarmer.

Elsewhere in the Northeast   To the north of the region is **Fochabers,** the place for antiques hunters, with nearly a dozen antiques shops. Try **Sylvan Antiques** for pottery and bric-a-brac; **Granny's Kist** for kitchenware and furniture; **Alexander Forsyth** for upscale furniture and furnishing fabrics; and **L'Antiques** for small furniture, pottery, glassware, and jewelry. All the shops are within a few yards of each other on the main street. Another interesting shop is **Balance,** which stocks homeopathic remedies, potpourris, and the like. Finish your visit at **The Gallery,** a good place to sit with a cup of tea and a home-baked snack.

Elgin has, in addition to the usual range of High Street stores, **Gordon and MacPhail** (South St., tel. 0343/45111), an outstanding delicatessen and wine merchant that, in addition to wine, stocks a breathtaking range of otherwise scarce malt whiskies. The range of foods available is also impressive, with the upscale Epicure brand prominent. This is a good place to shop for gifts for those foodies among your friends. **J. D. Yeadon** (32 Commerce St., tel. 0343/542411) is a dependable bookshop. **Johnstons of Elgin** (Newmill, tel. 0343/49319) has a worldwide reputation for its luxury fabrics, including cashmere. The color range is particularly noteworthy because it breaks away from the otherwise slightly predictable pastel blue, pink, yellow, and green of most mill shops.

Sports and Fitness

Bicycling   Northeast Scotland is excellent biking country, with networks of minor roads and farm roads crisscrossing rolling fields. Tourist-information centers can provide lists of suggested cycle tours. Rates for bicycle rentals vary, depending on the type of bike. An average rate for a three-speed bike is £3 a day.

You can rent bicycles at **Aberdeen Cycle Centre** (188 King St., Aberdeen, tel. 0224/644542).

Camping Most of the population centers in the area have campsites. It is possible to camp on private land, but you must obtain the permission of the landowner first. Except for the more remote upland areas, "wild land" camping is better pursued farther west.

Canoeing For information on canoeing in the area, contact **Aberdeen University Canoe Club** (Secretary, AA Office, Butchart Recreation Centre, Aberdeen, tel. 0224/272311), **Inverurie Surf Kayak Club** (R. Flemming, 15 Hartington Rd., Aberdeen, tel. 0224/572809), **Donside Canoe Club,** (contact S. Taylor, Craigmill, Muir of Fowlis, Craigmill, tel. 0336/4369), or **Ellon Centre Canoe Club** (contact P. Thomson, Mill of Fochel Cottage, St. Katherines, tel. 06514/230).

Fishing With major rivers, such as the Dee, Don, Deveron, and Ythan, as well as popular smaller rivers, such as the Ugie, plus loch and estuary fishing, this is one of Scotland's leading game-fishing areas. Details of beats, boats, and permit prices can be obtained from local tourist-information centers. Some local hotels offer fishing packages or, at least, can organize permits. Prices vary widely, depending on the fish and individual river beat.

Golf The Northeast has over 50 golf clubs, some of which have championship courses. All towns and many villages have their nine- and 18-hole municipal links, at which you pay £3–£5 per round. The more prestigious clubs charge up to £20 a day and expect you to book by letter or to bring a letter of recommendation from a member. The following courses in and around Aberdeen are open to visitors.

Balnagask (St. Fitticks Rd.). 18 holes, 5,468 yards, SSS 69.
Hazlehead (tel. 0224/35747). Course 1: 18 holes, 5,673 yards, SSS 70. Course 2: 18 holes, 5,303 yards, SSS 68.
Murcar (Bridge of Don, tel. 0224/704346). 18 holes, 6,226 yards, SSS 70.
Westhills (tel. 0224/740159). 18 holes, 5,866 yards, SSS 68.

Health and Fitness Clubs The major clubs in the area are **Bon-Accord Swimming and Leisure Centre** (Justice Mill Lane, Aberdeen, tel. 0224/587920), **Kincorth Sports Centre** (Corthan Dr., Aberdeen, tel. 0224/879759), **Sheddocksley Sports Centre** (Springhill Rd., Aberdeen, tel. 0224/692534), **Balmedie Leisure Centre** (Eigie Rd., Balmedie, tel. 0358/43725), **Fitness n' Fun** (130 High St., Elgin, tel. 0343/549307), and **Westerdyke Leisure Centre** (4 Elrick Way, Skene, tel. 0224/743098).

Skiing The area's main skiing development is at **Glenshee,** just south of Braemar, though the season can be brief here. Visitors accustomed to long alpine runs and extensive choice will find the runs here short, unlike the lift lines. The **Lecht** lies at even lower altitude, also within easy reach of the area, and is mainly suitable for beginners. The development at **Cairngorm** by Aviemore is also within easy reach (*see* Chapter 10). There is a dry ski slope at **Alford** (tel. 0336/2380).

You've Let Your Imagination Go, Now Get Up And Follow Your Dreams.

For The Vacation You're Dreaming Of, Call American Express Travel Agency At 1-800-YES-AMEX.

American Express will send more than your imagination soaring. We'll fly you, sail you, drive you to any Fodor's destination and beyond. Because American Express believes the best vacations happen from Europe to the Orient, Walt Disney World to Hawaii and everywhere in between.

For dependable service, expert advice, and value wherever your dreams take you, call on American Express. After all, the best traveling companion is a trustworthy friend.

It's easy to recognize
a good place
when you see one.

American Express Cardmembers have been doing it for years.

The secret? Instead of just relying on what they see in the window, they look at the door. If there's an American Express Blue Box on it, they know they've found an establishment that cares about high standards.

Whether it's a place to eat, to sleep, to shop, or simply meet, they know they will be warmly welcomed.

So much so, they're rarely taken in by anything else.

Always a good sign.

Dining and Lodging

Dining

Partly in response to the demands of spendthrift oilmen, the number of restaurants in Aberdeen has grown over the past several years, and the quality of the food has improved. Elsewhere in the region you will never be far from a good pub lunch or a hotel high tea or dinner.

Highly recommended restaurants are indicated by a star ★.

Category	Cost*
Very Expensive	over £40
Expensive	£30–£40
Moderate	£15–£30
Inexpensive	under £15

per person, including appetizer, main course, dessert, and VAT

Lodging

The Northeast has some splendid country hotels with log fires and rich furnishings, where you can also be sure of eating well if you have time for a leisurely meal.

Highly recommended hotels are indicated by a star ★.

Category	Cost*
Very Expensive	over £120
Expensive	£100–£120
Moderate	£80–£100
Inexpensive	under £80

**All prices are for a standard double room, including breakfast and tax.*

Aberdeen

Dining
★

The Silver Darling. Situated right on the quayside, the Silver Darling is one of Aberdeen's most acclaimed restaurants. It specializes, as its name suggests, in fish. The style is Provençal, with an indoor barbecue guaranteeing flavorful grilled fish and shellfish. *Pocra Quay, Footdee, AB2 1DQ, tel. 0224/576229. Reservations advised. Dress: casual but neat. AE, MC, V. Closed weekend lunch. Moderate–Expensive.*

Lodging

Caledonian Thistle Hotel. This is one of the larger hotels in the Granite City. Well situated and offering pleasant views over tidy gardens, the Caledonian is generally considered to be one of the best hotels in the city. Despite its size, the service here is very friendly. *Union Terr., AB9 1HE, tel. 0224/640233, fax 0224/641627. 80 rooms with bath. Facilities: restaurant, wine bar, coffee shop. AE, MC, V. Expensive–Very Expensive.*

★ **Ardoe House Hotel.** A magnificent, Baronial-style country house situated on expansive grounds by the River Dee, the Ardoe House is full of charm and character. This is a stylish place to stay. Although a huge extension has been added, if possible, try for a room in the older, original part of the building. *Banchory Devenick, Aberdeenshire AB1 5YP (a few mi from the city center), tel. 0224/867355, fax 0224/861283. 71 rooms with bath. Facilities: restaurant, 2 bars. AE, DC, MC, V. Expensive.*

Holiday Inn. The main attraction of the Holiday Inn is that it's extremely convenient to the airport. There's virtually no noise problem, however, because of double glazing of the windows throughout the hotel (and because the airport shuts down at night!). Long and low in layout, this hotel has many amenities that help make it a good place for families (for example, the indoor swimming pool is beside the bar, which makes it possible for parents to keep an eye on their children while the adults engage in less strenuous exercise). *Riverview Dr., Farburn, Dyce, AB2 0AZ, tel. 0224/770011, fax 0224/722347. 154 rooms with bath. Facilities: restaurant, bars, pool, gymnasium. AE, DC, MC, V. Moderate–Expensive.*

Auchterless
Dining

Towie Tavern. On the main Aberdeen–Turriff road, the Towie Tavern is a friendly and informal traditional-style eating place. Located in the hinterland of Aberdeenshire, the Towie is a good place to recharge your batteries while on an excursion to Fyvie Castle. The menu emphasizes hearty local fare—check the blackboard carefully for the "Towie Treats," which change daily and often feature excellent fresh seafood specials. The puddings, on the other hand, are not of great interest—most are fairly unimaginative. The good-natured staff and the tavern's cozy atmosphere add to the experience and make it well worth seeking this place out. *Near Turriff, AB5 8EP, tel. 08884/201. Reservations advised. Dress: casual. MC, V. Moderate.*

Banchory
Lodging

Raemoir Hotel. The core of this large mansion dates from the 18th century, though a number of additions have been built over the years. Central heating has been added as well, so there is no need to fear chilly, windy rooms. All the guest rooms are comfortable and well appointed; many are hung with beautiful tapestries. The hotel is set on spacious grounds and overshadowed by the 1,500-foot-high Hill of Fare. Adjoining the hotel's property are 3,500 acres of land on which fishing, stalking, and shooting can be arranged. Guests who don't want to venture too far away from the hotel can make use of the minigolf course and tennis court. *Raemoir, Kincardineshire AB3 4ED, tel. 03302/4884, fax 03302/2171. 28 rooms with bath. Facilities: restaurant, baby-sitting service, golf, tennis, fishing, helipad. AE, DC, MC, V. Expensive.*

Banchory Lodge. With the River Dee running past just a few yards away at the bottom of the garden, the Banchory Lodge is an ideal resting place for anglers. This is a fine example of a Georgian country house; well maintained inside and out, the lodge has retained its period charm. Tranquillity is the keynote here. *Kincardineshire AB3 3HS, tel. 03302/2625. 24 rooms with bath. Facilities: restaurant, fishing. AE, DC, MC, V. Moderate–Expensive.*

Drybridge
Dining
★

The Old Monastery. Standing on a broad, wooded hill slope set back from the coast near Buckie, with westward views as far as the hills of Wester Ross, this was once a Victorian religious establishment. This theme has been preserved and carries through to the restrained decor of the Cloisters Bar and the Chapel Restaurant, with its hand stenciling. The local specialties—the freshest fish from sea and river and Aberdeen Angus beef—make up the major part of the menu, cooked in traditional style with flashes of adventure. Homemade soups and delicious puddings are bonuses, as is the no-smoking dining room. This is quite simply the best for miles around. *Buckie, Banffshire AB5 2JB, tel 0542/32660. Reservations advised. Jacket and tie advised. Closed Sun., Mon., 3 weeks in Jan. and 2 weeks in Nov. AE, DC, MC, V. Expensive.*

Glenlivet **Minmore House.** Former home of George Smith, founder of the
Lodging Glenlivet Distillery, Minmore is now a family-run hotel that retains a strong private-house feel. Faded chintz in the drawing room and a paneled library (which now houses the bar) are complemented by very comfortable bedrooms (one, allegedly, with a ghost) and exceptionally well-cooked food. *Glenlivet, Ballindalloch, Banffshire, tel. 08073/378. 10 rooms with bath. Facilities: walking (on the Speyside Way), bird-watching. MC, V. Inexpensive.*

Old Deer **Saplinbrae House.** The restaurant in this country-house hotel is
Dining very popular with the locals. As elsewhere in this farming region with its bounteous salmon rivers, local produce is the basis of the menu. Game pie, roast duck, and hefty steamed puddings require forward planning to ensure that you have the capacity to stay the course (try a healthy breakfast followed by a day's hill walking before booking a meal here). *Near Mintlaw, Aberdeenshire AB4 8PL, tel. 0771/23515. Reservations advised. Jacket and tie advised. AE, DC, MC, V. Moderate.*

The Arts and Nightlife

The Arts

As you would expect, Aberdeen is the main cultural center of the region. The main Aberdeen newspapers—the *Press and Journal* and the *Evening Express*—and *Aberdeen Leopard* magazine can fill you in with what's going on anywhere in the Northeast. Outside Aberdeen a number of small-town local papers list events under the "What's On" heading. Tourist information centers usually print their own listings of events. Aberdeen's tourist-information center has a monthly "What's On" with a full calendar, as well as contact telephone numbers.

Theater **His Majesty's Theatre** (Rosemount Viaduct, Aberdeen, tel. 0224/641122) is one of the most beautiful theaters in Britain. Live shows are presented throughout the year, many of them in advance of their official opening in London's West End.

Concerts **The Music Hall** (Union St., Aberdeen, tel. 0224/632080) presents seasonal programs of concerts by the Scottish National Orchestra, the Scottish Chamber Orchestra, and other major orchestras and musicians. Its wide-ranging program of events also includes folk concerts, crafts fairs, and exhibitions.

Aberdeen Arts Centre (King St., tel. 0224/635208) is a theater and concert venue where experimental theater, poetry readings, exhibitions by local and Scottish artists, and many other arts-based presentations can be enjoyed.

The **Aberdeen International Youth Festival** in August has worldwide recognition and attracts youth orchestras, choirs, dance, and theater companies from many countries. During the festival, many of the companies that appear also take their productions to other venues in the Northeast. For details, contact AIYF Box Office (Music Hall, Union St., Aberdeen, tel. 0224/641122).

Another arts base in the area is **Haddo House,** 20 miles north of Aberdeen (off B9005 near Methlick, tel. 06515/770), where the Haddo House Hall Arts Trust runs a wide-ranging program of events.

Dance **His Majesty's Theatre** and **Aberdeen Arts Centre** (*see above*) are regular venues for dance companies. Contact the box offices for details of current productions.

Film Major theaters in the area include the **Cannon** (Union St., Aberdeen, tel. 0224/591477), **Capitol** (Union St., Aberdeen, tel. 0224/583141), **Odeon** (Justice Mill La., Aberdeen, tel. 0224/587160), **Moray Playhouse** (High St., Elgin, tel. 0343/542680), **Victoria** (W. High St., Inverurie, tel. 0467/21436), and the **Playhouse** (Queen St., Peterhead, tel. 0779/71052).

Opera Both **His Majesty's Theatre** in Aberdeen and the **Haddo House** (*see above*), near Methlick, present operatic performances at certain times throughout the year; telephone for details or inquire at the tourist-information center in Aberdeen's St. Nicholas House.

Nightlife

In part because of the oil-industry boom, Aberdeen has a fairly lively nightlife scene, though much of it revolves around pubs and hotels. Visitors interested in trying their luck at the gaming tables can place their bets at the **Stakis Regency Casino** (61 Summer St., tel. 0224/645273). Several of the larger hotels in the area run dinner dances in the summer season; check with the local tourist information centers for details.

Discos Two notes of warning about discos in Aberdeen: Most of these establishments do not allow jeans or athletic shoes, and it's advisable to check beforehand that a particular disco is not closed because of a private function.

Buskers (62–64 Shiprow, Aberdeen, tel. 0224/585815)
Cotton Club (491 Union St., Aberdeen, tel. 0224/647544)
Eagles (120 Union St., Aberdeen, tel. 0224/640641)
Hotel Metro (17 Market St., Aberdeen, tel. 0224/583275)
Mr G's (70–78 Chapel St., Aberdeen, tel. 0224/642112)
Ritzy's (Bridge Pl., Aberdeen, tel. 0224/581135)
Roosters (above the Tappit Hen, Back Wynd, Aberdeen, tel. 0224/643241)
The Soda Fountain (492–494 Union St., Aberdeen, tel. 0224/647544)
Zig-Zag (2 Diamond St., Aberdeen, tel. 0224/641580)

Jazz Clubs Jazz artists perform regularly at **Elrondo and Cafe on the Terrace** (Caledonian Hotel, 10 Union Terr., Aberdeen, tel. 0224/640233). There is also jazz on Saturday night at the **Masada Continental Lounge** (Rosemount Viaduct, Aberdeen, tel. 0224/641587).

Rock Club **Aberdeen Rock** (10 Belmont St., Aberdeen, tel. 0224/641931) can give details on rock artists appearing locally.

9 The Central Highlands

Stirling, Loch Lomond and the Trossachs, Perthshire

Introduction

By Gilbert Summers

The Central Highlands consist of what were once the counties of Perthshire and Stirlingshire. Today the county seats of Perth and Stirling, respectively, still play important roles as the primary administrative centers in the region. Both municipalities lie on the edge of a Highland area that offers reliable road and rail connections to the central belt of Scotland. Just how near the area is to the well-populated Midland Valley can be judged by the visitor who looks out from the ramparts of Edinburgh Castle: the Highland hills—which meander around the Trossachs and above Callander—are clearly visible. Similarly, the high-tower blocks of some of Glasgow's peripheral housing developments are noticeable from many of the higher peaks, notably Ben Lomond.

In fact, the Lowland/Highland contrast is quite pronounced in this region. Geologists have designated a prominent boundary between the two distinct landscapes as the Highland Boundary Fault. This geological barrier, however, also marked the differences between Scotland's two languages and cultures, Gaelic and Scots, with the Gaels ensconced within a mountain barrier. In the Central Highlands the fault line runs through Loch Lomond, close to Callander, to the northeast above Perth, and into the old county of Angus.

As early as 1794 the local minister in Callander, on the very edge of the Highlands, wrote: "The Trossachs are often visited by persons of taste, who are desirous of seeing nature in her rudest and unpolished state." What these early visitors came to see was a series of lochs and hills, whose crags and slopes were hung harmoniously with shaggy birch, oak, and pinewoods. The tops of the hills are high but not too wild (real wilderness would have been too much for these fledgling nature lovers). The Romantic poets, especially William Wordsworth, sang the praises of such locales. Though Wordsworth is most closely associated with the Lake District in England, his travels through Scotland and the Trossachs inspired several poems. But it was Sir Walter Scott who definitively put this Highland-edge area on the tourist map by setting his dramatic verse narrative *The Lady of the Lake*, written in 1810, firmly in the physical landscape of the Trossachs. Scott's verse was an immediate and huge success, and visitors flooded in to trace the events of the poem across the region. Today visitors continue to flock here, though few can quote a line of his poem.

If the Trossachs have long attracted those with discriminating tastes, then much of the same sentimental aura has attached itself to Loch Lomond. This is Scotland's largest loch in terms of surface area. By looking at the map, you will see that the loch is narrow to the north and broad in the south. The hard rocks to the north confine it to a long thin ribbon, and the more yielding Lowland structures allow it to spread out and assume a softer, wider form. Thus Lowland fields and lush hedgerows quickly give way to dark woods and crags (all this just a half hour's drive from the center of Glasgow). The song "The Banks of Loch Lomond" said to have been written by a Jacobite prisoner incarcerated in Carlisle, England, seems to capture a particular style of Scottish sentimentality, resulting in the notoriety of the "bonnie, bonnie banks" around the world, wherever exiled Scots are to be found.

Loch Lomond and the Trossachs aren't the only Highland settings to have been immortalized in song and verse. Perth—formerly referred to as "St. John's town" in the ballad "Bonny St.
Johnstoun, stands fair upon Tay"—and other Perthshire locales have likewise been famed in song: "Bonny lassie will ye
go/ to the Birks of Aberfeldy," or "Blair and Atholl's mine lassie, Little Dunkeld is mine/ St. Johnstoun's bower and
Huntingtower/ and all that's mine is thine, lassie." These and
other ditties testify that Perthshire has a strong reputation as
a beautiful place to visit, as well as an equally rich tradition in
sentimental Scottish ballads. (By the way, *birks* is Scots for
birches, which still grow in profusion in Aberfeldy, and *bonny*
was an irresistible word for early Scots balladeers.)

The main towns of Perth and Stirling serve as roadway hubs for
the area, but there are also a number of options in many of the
area's smaller towns. Many of these smaller settlements owe
their very existence and progress to their position close to the
Highland Boundary Fault, which runs close to Callander,
Crieff, Pitlochry, Dunkeld, and Aberfeldy. There is also a
string of smaller villages: Killin, Crianlarich, Lochearnhad,
Kenmore, and Kinlochrannoch, minor route centers tucked
into the hills and covered in the tours described below.

Finally, remember that even though the Central Highlands are
easily accessible, there is still much high, wild country in the
region. Ben Lawers, near Killin, is the ninth-highest peak in
Scotland, and the moor of Rannoch is as bleak and empty a
stretch as can be seen anywhere in the northlands. But if the
glens and lochs prove to be too lonely or intimidating, it's a
short journey to the softer and less harsh Lowlands.

Essential Information

Important Addresses and Numbers

Tourist The **Loch Lomond, Stirling, and Trossachs Tourist Board** (41
Information Dumbarton Rd., Stirling FK8 2QQ, tel. 0786/75019) and the
Perthshire Tourist Board (45 High St., Perth PH1 5TJ, tel.
0738/38353) can provide information on the region. Local tourist-information centers can be found throughout the region and
are open during the peak season (generally Apr.–Oct.) in the
following towns: Aberfeldy, Aberfoyle, Auchterarder, Balloch, Blairgowrie, Callander, Crieff, Dunblane, Dunkeld, Helensburgh, Inveralmond, Killin, Kinross, Milton, Pirnhall,
Pitlochry, Tarbet, Tillicoultry, and Tyndrum. All are clearly
marked with the standard I sign in white on a blue background.

Emergencies For police, fire, or ambulance, dial 999 from any telephone. No
coins are needed for emergency calls from telephone booths.

Doctors and Local practitioners will usually treat visiting patients. Infor-
Dentists mation is available from tourist-information centers, and
names of doctors can also be found in the yellow pages of the
telephone directory. The main hospital emergency rooms in the
region are **Perth Royal Infirmary** (Tullylumb, Perth, tel. 0738/
23311), **Bridge of Earn Hospital** (Bridge of Earn, by Perth, tel.
0738/812331), **Stirling Royal Infirmary** (Livilands Gate, Stirling, tel. 0786/73151), and **Vale of Leven Hospital** (Main St., Alexandria, tel. 0389/54121).

Late-Night Pharmacies Pharmacies are found only in the larger towns and cities. In an emergency, the police will provide assistance in locating a pharmacist. In rural areas, general practitioners may also dispense medicines.

Arriving and Departing by Plane

Airports and Airlines Perth and Stirling can be reached easily from **Glasgow**, **Edinburgh**, and **Prestwick** airports (*see* Chapters 3 and 4) by train, car, or bus.

Arriving and Departing by Car, Train, and Bus

By Car Visitors will find an easy access to the area from the central belt of Scotland via the motorway network. The M9 runs within sight of the walls of Stirling Castle, and Perth can be reached via the M90 over the Forth Bridge.

By Train The Central Highlands are linked to Edinburgh and Glasgow by rail, with through routes to England (some direct-service routes from London take fewer than five hours). A variety of Saver ticket options are available, although in some cases on the Scotrail system, the discount fares must be purchased before your arrival in the United Kingdom.

By Bus There is a good network of buses connecting with the central belt via Edinburgh and Glasgow. Express services also link the larger towns in the Central Highlands with all main towns and cities in England.

Getting Around

By Car There is an adequate network of roads, and the area's proximity to the central belt speeds road communications. The Scottish Tourist Board's touring map is useful.

By Train The **West Highland Line** runs through the western portion of the area. Services also run to Stirling, Dunblane, Perth, and Gleneagles; destinations on the Inverness–Perth line include Dunkeld, Pitlochry, and Blair Athol.

By Bus The following companies offer reliable service on a number of convenient routes.

Caledonian Express (Walnut Grove, Perth, tel. 0738/33481).
Loch Lomond Coaches Ltd. (Argyll Garage, Heather Ave., Alexandria, tel. 041/956–3636 or 041/956–5678).
Midland Bluebird Bus Services (Goosecroft Rd. bus station, Stirling, tel. 0786/73763).
Strathtay Scottish Omnibuses Ltd. (Leonard St., bus station, Perth, tel. 0738/26848).

Guided Tours

Orientation The bus companies listed above in Getting Around by Bus offer a number of general orientation tours. Inquire at the nearest tourist information center, where tour reservations can usually be booked.

Special-Interest There are many taxi and chauffeur companies offering tailor-made tours by the day or week; the nearest tourist-information center is your best source for detailed, up-to-date information. In the eastern portion of the Central Highlands, try **Turpie's**

Tours (21 Arthur St., Blairgowrie, tel. 0250/872116) or **Gordon Muir** (Classic Car Tours, Kinnoull, Rosemount Pl., Perth, tel. 0738/22570). Possibilities in the south and west include **Goosecroft Station Taxis** (Cunningham Rd., Springkerse Industrial Estate, Stirling, tel. 0786/72220–75700), **Ians Taxi and Minibus** (Gargunnock filling station, Gargunnock by Stirling, tel. 0786/86207), and **Dumbarton and Alexandria T.O.A.** (Main St., Alexandria, tel. 0389/57171).

Do not miss the opportunity to take a boat trip on a Scottish loch. The S.S. *Sir Walter Scott* sails on Loch Katrine in the summer season; you can book it through the tourist-information center at Callander. On Loch Lomond there are a number of cruise possibilities: from Tarbet, **Cruise Loch Lomond** (Shore Cottage, Tarbet, tel. 03012/356); from Balloch, the *Lomond Duchess* and *Lomond Maid* (Balloch Marina, Riverside, tel. 0389/51481) and **Sweeney's Cruises** (Riverside, tel. 0389/52376); and from Balmaha, **Macfarlane and Son** operates the **Royal Mail boat** to the islands on the loch and takes passengers (Balmaha Boatyard, tel. 036087/214).

Exploring the Central Highlands

The main towns of Stirling and Perth are located at the junction of many routes, making both places natural starting points for Highland tours. Stirling itself is worth covering in some detail on foot. The successive waves of development of this important town—from castles and Old Town architecture to Victorian developments and urban and industrial sprawl—can be traced quite easily. There are also peripheral points of interest worth visiting, including the **Bannockburn Heritage Centre,** which recounts how Scotland secured its independence for 400 years in one of its few victories over the English. The center commemorates an important date in Scotland's history and provides insight into the psyche of the Scots. The **Wallace Monument** also provides a glimpse of Scotland's past by commemorating Scotland's earliest freedom fighter, William Wallace. The top of the monument offers pretty views of the Highlands.

The Trossachs are a short distance from Stirling, and visitors usually cover them in a loop. Those visiting **Loch Lomond** can get there from either Glasgow or Stirling, and there are two other routes available as well. The main road up the west bank (A82) is not recommended for leisurely touring. Do use this road, however, if your are on your way to Oban, Kintyre, or Argyll. Loch Lomond is best seen from one of two cul-de-sac roads: by way of Drymen at the south end, up to Rowardennan or, if you are pressed for time, west from Aberfoyle to reach Loch Lomond near its north end, at Inversnaid. Visitors should note that in the Trossachs, the road that some maps show going all the way around Loch Katrine is a private road belonging to the Strathclyde Water Board and is open only to walkers and cyclists.

Getting around Perthshire is made interesting by the series of looped tours accessible from the A9, a fast main artery. Exercise caution while driving the A9 itself, however. There have been many auto accidents in this area. The loops provide visitors with vistas of lochs and mountains. Although the entire route can be completed in a single day, travelers with some time on their hands who seek a little spontaneity can take their chances on a variety of accommodations in villages along the way.

Highlights for First-time Visitors

Bannockburn Heritage Centre (*see* Tour 1)
Blair Castle (*see* Tour 3)
Doune Castle (*see* Tour 2)
Dunblane Cathedral (*see* Tour 2)
Loch Lomond Cruises (*see* Special-Interest Tours in Essential Information, *above*)
Pass of Killiecrankie (*see* Tour 3)
Scone Palace (*see* Tour 3)
S.S. *Sir Walter Scott* on Loch Katrine *(see* Tour 2)
Stirling Castle (*see* Tour 1)
The Trossachs (*see* Tour 2)

Tour 1: Around Stirling

Numbers in the margin correspond to points of interest on the Stirling and Central Highlands maps.

❶ In some ways, **Stirling** is like a smaller version of Edinburgh. Its castle, built on a steep-sided plug of rock, dominates the landscape, and its Esplanade offers views of the surrounding valley-plain of the River Forth. To take advantage of its historical heritage (the Stuart monarchs held court here from time to time, as they did in Edinburgh), Stirling maintains a busy tourism calender that includes a summer program of open-air historical tableaux. These reenactments conjure some of the famous events that have unfolded here. Details of this presentation, plus a program of concerts, ceilidhs, piping, country dancing, and similar Scottish entertainment is available from the tourist-information center (*see* Important Addresses and Numbers in Essential Information, *above*) on Dumbarton Road, where this tour begins.

Opposite the tourist center, visitors can see that an impressive proportion of Stirling's town walls remain. Diagonally to the left is **Corn Exchange Road,** with a modern statue of Rob Roy MacGregor, notorious cattle dealer and drover, part-time thief and outlaw, and Jacobite (most of the time). Farther along
❷ Dumbarton Road to the west is the **Smith Art Gallery and Museum,** founded in 1874 with the bequest of a local collector and now a good example of a community art gallery offering a varied exhibit program. *Tel. 0786/71917. Admission free. Open all year.*

❸ Nearby, a gentle but relentless uphill path known as the **Back Walk** leads to the city's most famous and worthwhile sight— **Stirling Castle.** The Back Walk will take you along the outside of the city's walls, past a watchtower and the grimly named Hangman's entry, cut out of the great whinstone boulders that once marked the outer defenses of the town. The walk begins opposite the Dumbarton Road tourist-information center. However, if you take time first to visit the Smith Gallery, a few doors down the road, you can still join Back Walk a little farther up the road.

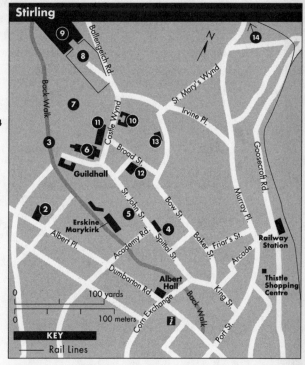

Walk east, keeping to the outside of the walls, until you reach Academy Road and the Old High School, built in 1854 on the site of the former Greyfriars Monastery. At the far end of the street, note two fine examples of Scottish domestic architecture. Now used for private housing, **Darrow House** dates from the 17th century. Look for the characteristically crow-stepped gables, dormer windows, and a projecting turn-pike stair. The adjacent **Spittal House** on the right has been restored to match its handsome partner. Turn left and uphill onto St. John's Street. There is another typical town house farther up the street, on the left, sometimes known as **Bothwell Ha** (Hall), that is said to have been owned by the earl of Bothwell, Mary, Queen of Scots' third husband. Behind it, also on the left, is the former military detention barracks that are awaiting redevelopment, along with the adjacent **Erskine Marykirk**, a neoclassical church built in 1824 that has been nearly destroyed by vandals.

There are a number of points of interest at the top of St. John Street. Most notable among them is the **Church of the Holy Rude,** with part of the nave surviving from the 15th century. A portion of the original medieval timber roof can also be seen. The church has the distinction of being the only church in Scotland still in use that witnessed the coronation of a Scottish monarch: James VI in 1567. Adjacent to the church is the **Guildhall,** built as Cowane's Hospital in 1639 for *decayed breithers* (unsuccessful merchants). The ancient facility is now the setting for summer concerts and ceilidhs. Above the entrance is a small, cheery statue of the founder himself, John Cowane, that is said

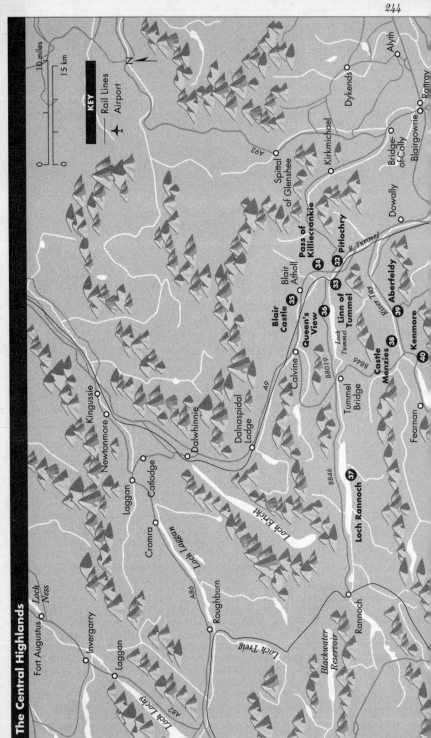

244

The Central Highlands

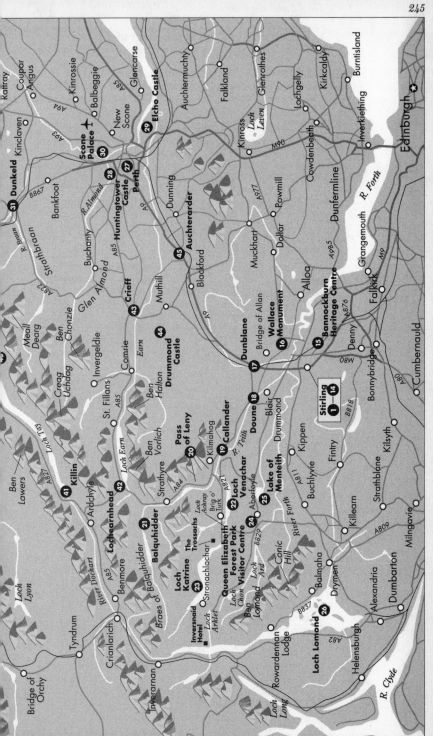

to come alive on Hogmanay Night (December 31) to walk the streets with the locals and join in their New Year's revelry. Outside the hall, you will see cannons, made at the famous Carron Works in Falkirk, then exported to Russia only to be captured in the Crimean War and returned to Scotland. They guard the adjacent bowling green of 1712, said to be the oldest in Scotland. *St. John St., tel. 0786/62373. Admission free. Open weekdays 9–5 (except when functions are being held).*

7 You'll encounter some unusual monuments at this point on the Back Walk. The most notable are the **Star Pyramid** of 1858 and the curious macabre glass-walled **Martyrs Monument**, erected in memory of two Wigtownshire girls who were drowned in 1685 for their Covenanting faith. At this point, you are approaching the castle, which dominates the foreground. Photographers may appreciate the aesthetically pleasing vistas of the fortress available from the high perch within the churchyard called the **Ladies' Rock**, which also has an airy seat on it. The ladies of the court used to watch tournaments on the ground below the castle from this point.

8 From the churchyard, paths and steps lead you to the **Esplanade,** a broad space with a car park and views in all directions except to the west, now filled by the castle's bulk. A trip inside the walls of this once-impregnable castle is still intriguing.

9 **Stirling Castle's** strategic position made it the last prize and the key to the kingdom in the Scots Wars of Independence in the late-13th and early 14th centuries. The Battle of Bannockburn in 1314 was fought within sight of its walls, and the victory by Robert the Bruce (King Robert I) yielded both the castle and freedom from English subjugation for the Scots for almost four centuries.

King Robert's daughter Marjory married Walter, the High Steward of Scotland, and their descendants included the Stewart dynasty of Scottish monarchs (Mary, Queen of Scots, was a Stewart, though she preferred the French spelling, *Stuart*). The Stewarts were mainly responsible for many of the works that survive within the castle walls today. They made Stirling Castle their court and power base, creating fine Renaissance-style buildings that were not completely obliterated, despite subsequent reconstruction for military purposes.

Start your tour of the castle in the **National Trust for Scotland's Visitor Centre,** conspicuous on the Esplanade. After an audio-visual briefing, you will enter the castle from its outer defenses, which consist of a great curtain wall and batteries dating from 1708, built to bulwark earlier defenses by the main gatehouse. From this lower square the most conspicuous feature is the **palace,** built by King James V between 1538 and 1542. This edifice shows the influence of French masons in the decorative figures festooning the ornately worked outer walls. Overlooking the upper courtyard is the **Great Hall,** built by King James IV in 1503. Before the Union of Parliaments in 1707, when the Scottish aristocracy sold out to England, this building had been used as one of the seats of the Scottish Parliament. After 1707 it sank into decline, becoming a riding school, then a barracks. Today, its interiors are gutted, although a slow restoration is under way.

Another building associated with the Stewarts is the **Chapel Royal,** dating from 1594. It was built by King James VI to commemorate the baptism of his son. It also suffered at the hands of the military, and it was a storehouse before being restored. Among the later works of the regiments stationed here, the **King's Old Building** stands out; it is a 19th-century baronial revival on the site of an earlier building. The oldest building on the site is the **Mint, or Coonzie Hoose**, perhaps dating as far back as the 14th century. Below is an arched passageway leading to the westernmost section of the ramparts, the **Nether Bailey.** You'll have the distinct feeling here that you are in the bow of a warship sailing up the *carselands* (valley-plain) of the Forth Valley, which fans out before the great superstructure of the castle.

This is the place, among the gun platforms and the crenellations of the ramparts, to ponder the strategic significance of Stirling. To the south lies the hump of the Touch and the Gargunnock Hills (part of the Campsie Hills), diverting would-be direct routes from Glasgow and the south. The Ochil Hills loom to the northeast, with a long, steep face fading away into the distance, overlooking the Forth Valley. Due east, over the smoke of the once-heavily-industrialized Lowlands around Falkirk, the River Forth winds and widens; it was an insurmountable barrier to early bridge builders. Due west are the flat fields of the upper floodplain of the river. They look tame and traversable now, but in former times these carselands were treacherous marshes. For centuries all roads into the Highlands across the narrow waist of Scotland led to Stirling, formerly the lowest bridging point of the River Forth. If you look carefully northward, you can see Old Stirling Bridge, for centuries the lowest crossing point of the river, further emphasizing Stirling's strategic position. For all these geographic reasons, the castle here was perhaps the single most important fortress in Scotland. *Central Stirling, tel. 031/244–3101. Admission: £2.30 adults, £1.20 children and senior citizens, £6 family ticket. Open Apr.–Sept., daily 9:30–5:15; Oct.–Mar., daily 9:30–4:15.*

Below the castle's Esplanade is the heart of the old town of Stirling, which you passed on the way up. As you walk down from the Esplanade along **Castle Wynd,** the path leads to a series of interesting buildings. Below the Portcullis Hotel (formerly the grammar school, on a site that has had schools built on it since 1500) is one of the most important buildings surviving from the 16th century. This is **Argyll's Ludging** (lodging), now a youth hostel. Step into the courtyard and read the notice board that explains the three phases of its construction, from the 16th century onward. It is older than the name it bears—that of Archibald, ninth earl of Argyll, who bought it in 1666.

Farther down, you will encounter a long and ornate facade, windowless and roofless and constructed in a distinctive Renaissance style. Look for the armorial carved panels, the gargoyles and the turrets flanking a railed-off *pend* (archway). This is **Mar's Wark** (Work or Building), the stark remains of a palace built in 1570 by Lord Erskine, earl of Mar as well as Stirling Castle governor. A later earl of Mar, John, was a political opportunist heavily involved in court matters. His tendency to switch allegiance depending on how the political winds were blowing earned him the nickname Bobbin (that is, *bobbing*) John. After being overlooked for promotion by the House of Hanover in 1714, Bobbin John sided with the Jacobites; unfortunately his leadership of the 1715 Jacobite rebellion was ineffectual, and he was subsequently exiled. Ironically, Mar's Wark was damaged by the siege of Stirling Castle in the 1745 rebellion. Its shell survives, however; some say it is to block the wind that gusts down the length of Broad Street. *At top of Castle Wynd, tel. 031/244–3101. View from outside only.*

When you stand in front of Mar's Wark and look downhill, you are gazing into the heart of the Old Town. The Old Town serves as an ideal setting for the program of historical reenactments and medieval street fairs. One of the Old Town's most notable **⑫** structures is the **Tolbooth** of 1705 (on the right), which has a traditional Scottish steeple and gilded weathercock. For centuries the Burgh Court handed down sentences here; the jail was next door. Opposite is a row of Scottish tenement-style housing, renovated and full of tenants: There is still plenty of life in the Old Town. The tourist board operates an orientation center in one of the buildings during the summer months.

Time Out | **Darnley's Coffee House** faces you at the foot of Dumbarton Road and serves reasonable coffee and fresh carrot cake, among other sweet treats. The building housing Darnley's is from the late-16th century and derives its name from a popular tale that maintains that Lord Darnley used to prefer to stay here rather than at his wife's (Mary, Queen of Scots') residence in the castle.

If you go left from Darnley's Coffee House (instead of right, to the town center), down the hill you will find the 16th-century **⑬** shell of **Cowane's House** (the same Cowane was associated with the Guildhall, visited earlier). Much has been swept away here, but this is one of the oldest through routes in Stirling and formerly the only main road out of town to the north. However, it is probably better to go straight from Darnley's and continue down the hill, diverging as often as your shopping fancy allows you. The Old Town soon gives way to the Victorian developments of Stirling. Still farther down the hill, these developments are, in turn, swept aside by the modern **Thistle Centre,** with all the thin charm of British High Street stores. One of the bastions of the Old Town walls has been preserved, rather eerily, inside the center.

⑭ Farther out is the **Old Stirling Bridge,** by the A9, off the center of town. Dating from the 15th century, the bridge can still be crossed on foot. It was near this site that the Scottish freedom fighter William Wallace and a ragged army of Scots won a major victory in 1297. The English had taken advantage of Scottish power squabbles over succession to occupy Scotland as their own territory. Wallace rose up against their rule, and much blood was shed, but the Scots regained control of many of their castles and towns. After regaining control, Wallace's forces gathered near Stirling.

Galled by the impudence of a bunch of ill-equipped spearmen challenging the glittering, mailed, and mounted knights of England, the English governor in Scotland, the earl of Surrey, ordered his heavy cavalry across a narrow wooden bridge over the River Forth. The Scots, lined up beyond the bridge, moved in to cut down the knights, both on the narrow bridge and in the marshy meadow beyond. Their victory was short-lived, however. The following year, King Edward of England himself led an army that destroyed Wallace's lightly armed troops at Falkirk. The Guardian of Scotland, as Wallace was then called, disappeared, reappearing only briefly before he was betrayed by treachery in 1305. He was put to death in London.

Numbers in the margin correspond to points of interest on the Central Highlands map.

The next year, rising from the uncertainties and timidity of the great lords of Scotland (ever unsure of which way to jump and whether or not to bow to England's demands), Robert the Bruce materialized as the nation's champion, and the last bloody phase of the Wars of Independence began. This tale is recounted at the **Bannockburn Heritage Centre,** hidden among the sprawl of housing and commercial developments on the southern edge of Stirling. This was the site of the famed Battle of Bannockburn in 1314. In Bruce's day, the Forth had a shelved and partly wooded floodplain. He chose the site cunningly, noting the boggy ground on the lower reaches, in which the heavy horses of the English would founder. The atmosphere has been re-created within the center by means of an audiovisual presentation and an arresting mural depicting the battle in detail (look closely for some very unsavory goings-on), as well as models and costumed figures. *Off M80, tel. 0786/ 812664. Admission: £1.40 adults, 70p children. Open Apr.– Oct., daily 10-6.*

Tour 2: The Trossachs and Loch Lomond

Inspired by the views of mountainous terrain seen from the ramparts of Stirling Castle, you can now make your way out to the Highland line. Start by navigating out of Stirling on the A9 past the pencil-thin **Wallace Monument** on the Abbey Craig, from which you can see the Ochil Hills as a rocky moorland beyond. Follow Bridge of Allan signs northward, crossing the River Forth by Robert Stephenson's New Bridge of 1832, next to the historic old one. The Wallace Monument is signposted at the next traffic circle. Up close, this Victorian shrine to William Wallace, built between 1856 and 1869, becomes less slim and soaring, revealing itself to be a substantial square tower with a creepy spiral stairway. The monument is currently closed to visitors, and at press time there were no details as to when it may reopen. Contact the tourist-information center for up-to-date details.

You may wish to detour east for a minute or two on the A91, along the south side of the Abbey Craig, on which the Wallace Monument stands, to visit **Cambuskenneth Abbey** (signposted south off the A91). Noted for their historic significance, the scanty remains of this 13th-century religious seat lie in a sweeping bend of the River Forth, with the dramatic outline of Stirling Castle as a backdrop. Important meetings of the Scottish Parliament were once held here, and King Edward I of England visited in 1304. The abbey was looted and damaged during the Scots Wars of Independence (1307–14). The reconstructed tomb of King James III (who died in 1488) can be seen near the outline of the high altar.

The road west to **Bridge of Allan** lies along the edge of the Ochil Hills and runs past the campus of Stirling University. Bridge of Allan was formerly a spa town and has substantial Victorian properties. Rejoin the A9 for a few moments' journey north to

⑰ **Dunblane.** Its 13th-century cathedral has been restored, and the oldest part of the community—with its twisting streets and mellow town houses—huddles around the square and churchyard where the cathedral stands.

The A9 continues west for a few minutes to another Highland-edge community, **Doune.** This was once a center for pistol making. No Highland chief's attire was complete without a prestigious and ornate pair of pistols. Today, Doune is more widely known as the site of one of the best-preserved medieval castles in Scotland. (It is signposted left as you enter the town from the Dunblane road.) It looks like an early castle is supposed to look: grim windowed, high walled, with echoing stone vaults and numerous drafts. Construction of the fortress began in the early 15th century on a now-peaceful riparian tract. *Off A84, tel. 031/ 244–3101. Admission: £1.20 adults, 60p children and senior citizens. Open Apr.–Sept., Mon.–Sat. 9:30–6, Sun. 2–6; Oct.– Mar., Mon.–Thurs. 10–4, alternate Sat. 10–4, Sun. 2–4.*

The best place to photograph this squat, great-walled fort is from the bridge, a little way upstream, which carries the A9 west from Stirling. The locals will tell you that the earliest bridge built over the River Teith here was constructed by King James V's tailor, Robert Spittal, in 1535. Either very rich or subtly vindictive, he built it to spite the ferryman who refused him passage at this point.

⑲ Rejoin another main road, the A84, which continues to **Callander.** Though still surrounded by a landscape of Lowland farms and woods, the hills begin to fill the skyline, especially Ben Ledi, above Callander; Stuc a' Chroin (pronounced *stook a kroyn*; and Ben Vorlich farther east (to the right). Callander is a traditional Highland-edge resort, with a choice of accommodations, from simple bed-and-breakfasts to lavish, sophisticated hotels (*see* Dining and Lodging, *below*).

In the early 1960s Callander was the setting for a popular television drama about the life of a rural medical practice, called "Doctor Findlay's Casebook." This show about the domestic adventures of two doctors and their housekeeper was set against the townscape and hillsides of the Callander area and helped sustain the resort's popularity. Tales were told in town of landladies pitching tents in the backyard for their children to sleep in so there could be another bedroom free for the tourists. But most of those tales were inspired 30 years ago, and contemporary Callander has moved on. Relicts from the series include words like *Tannochbrae*, the show's thinly veiled mythical town, and *Arden House*, the doctors' residence. There are currently plans to make a new series of "Dr. Findlay's Casebook."

Callander bustles throughout the season—even on Sunday during off-peak times—simply because it is a gateway to Highland scenery within easy reach of Edinburgh and Glasgow. There is plenty of window shopping here, plus nightlife in pubs and hotels. (Avoid main-street accommodations if you want peaceful sleep.) The **Rob Roy and Trossachs Visitor Centre,** housed in the former St. Kessog's Church, provides visitors with their first encounter with the famed Rob Roy MacGregor. As defender of the downtrodden and scourge of the authorities, MacGregor is known as a tartan Robin Hood. An old-style and much revered Highland hero, Rob Roy died peacefully at his home in 1734. You can learn more about his high jinks in a high-tech account—replete with displays and tableaux—in the visitor center. *Ancaster Sq., tel. 0877/30342. Admission: £1.65 adults, £1.25 children. Open Mar.–May and Oct.–Dec., daily 10–5; June and Sept., daily 9:30–6; July–Aug., daily 9 AM–10 PM.*

Callander's other attractions away from the bustle of the main street are mainly rural in nature: a walk signposted from the east end of the main street to the **Brack Linn Falls,** over whose lip Sir Walter Scott once rode a pony to win a bet, or another walk through the woods up to the Callander Crags, with views of the Lowlands as far as the Pentland Hills behind Edinburgh. (This walk is for the fit and well-shod only.)

Time Out   **Pip's Coffee House,** just off the main street in the center, is bright and cheerful and has a little picture gallery.

Callander is the gateway to the Trossachs, but since it is on the main road, the A84, to the west, it also attracts overnight visitors on their way to Oban, Fort William, and beyond. All this traffic enters the proper Highlands just north of Callander, where the thickly clad slopes squeeze both the road and rocky **㉒** river into the narrow **Pass of Leny.** An abandoned railway—now a pleasant walking or bicycling path—also goes through the pass. If time permits, go part of the way along this road out of Callander past **Ben Ledi** and Loch Lubnaig.

Beyond Strathyre and its extensive forestry-commission plantings, within a 20-minute drive of Callander, is a road that will **㉑** take you west to **Balquhidder** (pronounced *bal*-whidd-*er*). In this northern extension of the excursion, the first Highland glen that many visitors will see runs westward. Note its characteristics, seen throughout the north: a flat-bottomed, U-shape profile formed by prehistoric glaciers; extensive forestry plantings replacing much of the natural woodlands above; a sprinkling of farms; and farther up the glen, new hill roads bulldozed into the slopes to provide access for shepherds and foresters. Note also the shut-up look of some of the houses, many of which are second homes for affluent residents of the south. The glen is also where **Lochs Voil and Doune** spread out, adding to the stunning vistas. This area is often known as the Braes (Slopes) of Balquhidder and was once the home of the MacLarens and the MacGregors. Rob Roy MacGregor's grave is signposted beside Balquhidder itself. The site of his house, now a private farm, is beyond the car park at the end of the road.

The glen has no through road, although in earlier times local residents were familiar with hill passes to the north and south. There still exists, for example, a right-of-way from the churchyard where Rob Roy is buried, via the plantings in Kirkton Glen and then on to open windy grasslands and a blue *lochan* (little lake). This path eventually drops into the next valley, Glen Dochart, and rejoins the A84.

Retrace the A84 to within a mile of Callander. Here is a sign for the Trossachs, at the little community of **Kilmahog,** where you will find two rival mill shops locked in a competition to attract the most tour buses. Note that the Kilmahog Woollen Mill has preserved its water wheel.

The A821 runs west along with the first and gentlest of the **㉒** Trossachs lochs: **Loch Venachar.** The sturdy gray-stone build-

ings with a small dam at the Callander end control the water
fed into the River Teith (and, hence, into the Forth) to compensate for the Victorian tinkerings with the water supply. Within
a few minutes the A821 becomes muffled in woodlands and
twists gradually down to **Brig o' Turk.** (*Turk* here is Gaelic for
tuirc, meaning wild boar, a species that sadly has been extinct
in this region since about the 16th century.)

Time Out **Dundarroch and the Byre** (tel. 08776/200) is a well-run pub and
restaurant just beyond Brig o' Turk, with dark beams and
loosely defined Victorian decor, as well as attentive, friendly
service. It's a lunchtime haven, particularly on a wet day in the
woodlands. A number of signposted walks also start from here.

West of Brig o' Turk stretches **Loch Achray**, dutifully fulfilling
expectations of what a verdant Trossachs loch should be: small,
green, reedy meadows backed by dark plantations, rhododendron thickets, and lumpy, thickly covered hills. Note the car
park on the left, where walkers begin their ascent of the steep,
heathery **Ben An.** To enjoy the best Trossachs' views, you will
need a couple of hours and your wind. If you don't have much
time, continue driving to the end of Loch Achray, following the
road (turn right) into a narrow pass. This is the heart of the
Trossachs. During the time of Sir Walter Scott, the path was
narrow and almost hidden by the overhanging crags and mossy
oaks and birches. Today it leads to a slightly anticlimactic car
park with a shop, a café, and a visitor center. Not readily visible from the park, the 90-year-old steamer, the S.S. *Sir Walter*
❷❸ *Scott*, embarks on cruises of **Loch Katrine** every summer. To
see the finest of the Trossachs lochs or to locate some of the
landmarks cited in Scott's *Lady of the Lake*, you must—even
for just a few minutes—go westward on foot. The road beyond
the car park is open only to Strathclyde Water Board vehicles
and is well paved and level.

After going back through the pass on the main A821, turn right
and head south, to higher moorland blanketed with conifer
plantations (some of which have near-mature timber planted
about 60 years ago by the forestry commission). The conifers
hem in the views of Ben Ledi and Ben Venue, which can be seen
over the spiky green waves of trees as the road snakes around
heathery knolls and hummocks. There is another viewpoint at
the highest point here, indicated by a small car park on the
right. Aside from this main road loop, the Trossachs region is
threaded by trails, mainly for walkers and cyclists. However,
there is a forest road signposted nearby that takes the adventurous driver down to the shores of little **Loch Drunkie**, which
can be seen to the east, above more dark pine thickets.

Soon the road swoops off the Highland edge and leads downhill.
❷❹ Near the start of the descent, the **Queen Elizabeth Forest Park
Visitor Centre** can be seen on the left. The center features displays on the life of the forest, a summer-only café, some fine
views over the Lowlands to the south, and a network of foot-
paths. *Off A821. Open mid-Mar.–mid.-Oct., daily 10–6.*

At the foot of the hill is **Aberfoyle,** where in the old station yard
you will find the **Scottish Wool Centre,** with live sheep (including native Scottish breeds), a children's play area, and a shop.

The Trossachs end here. The route back east to Stirling gradu-
❷❺ ally leaves the hills behind and is noted mainly for the **Lake of**

Menteith, a few minutes east of Aberfoyle. Mary, Queen of Scots, was stowed away at the lake for her own safety as a child in 1547. On a wooded islet the ruined **Inchmahome Priory** associated with the queen can be reached by boat from the Port of Menteith. The unusual usage of *lake* in a Scottish context was a non-native-speaking mapmaker's misunderstanding: *Laigh* (pronounced with the *gh* as a hard Scots *ch*) is a Scottish word, meaning low-lying area, that now has become anglicized.

Instead of returning to Stirling (barely half an hour), those visitors who want to cover **Loch Lomond** in one day have a couple of options. To reach Loch Lomond quickly from Aberfoyle, you can choose to see either the southern, wider end of the loch—studded with islands—near the Highland line, or the more enclosed northern portion. The distances to Balmaha, toward the south end, and to Inversnaid farther north, are about the same: approximately 14 miles, though there is an optional extension of about 7 miles to Rowardennan north of Balmaha. These distances will be easier to follow by consulting your map. Both routes are recommended and are briefly described here. Which one you choose depends on your taste. The **Aberfoyle–Inversnaid** trip is bereft of tea shops. In fact, during the off-season, the route has, in certain places, a wild and windswept air when it extends beyond the shelter of trees. The **Aberfoyle–Balmaha** section (via Drymen) offers a wider choice of pubs and hotels—and even a good-quality dress shop in Drymen.

For the Aberfoyle–Inversnaid trip, take the B829 (signposted Inversnaid and Stronachlachar), which runs west from Aberfoyle and offers outstanding views of **Ben Lomond**, especially in the vicinity of **Loch Ard**. The next loch, where the road narrows and bends, is **Loch Chon,** dark and forbidding. Its ominous reputation is further enhanced by the local legend, the presence of a dog-headed monster prone to swallowing passersby. Beyond Loch Chon, the road climbs gently from the plantings to open moor with a breathtaking vista over **Loch Arklet** to the **Arrochar Alps,** the name given to the high hills west of Loch Lomond. Hidden from site in a deep trench, Loch Arklet is dammed to feed Loch Katrine.

Go left at a road junction (a right will take you to Stronachlachar) and take the open road along Loch Arklet. These deserted green hills were once the rallying grounds of the Clan Gregor. Near the dam on Loch Arklet, on your right, **Garrison Cottage**'s name recalls the days when the government had to billet troops here to keep the MacGregors in order. The remains of the garrison building are built into a sheepfold.

From Loch Arklet, the road zigzags down to **Inversnaid,** where you will see a hotel, a house, and a car park, with Loch Lomond stretching out of sight above and below. The long-distance walkers' route, the **West Highland Way,** running 95 miles from Glasgow to Fort William, follows the bank here. Take a brief stroll up the path, particularly if you are visiting during the spring, when the oak-tree canopy is filled with bird song. You may get an inkling why Scots get so romantic about their bonny, bonny banks.

The only return to Aberfoyle is by retracing the same route—except that you may wish to go down to **Stronachlachar** on Loch Katrine. This is where the steamer calls; the town is no more than a pier with neatly clipped hedges and a cluster of houses belonging to Strathclyde Water Board workers. Loch Katrine's water is taken by aqueduct and tunnel to Glasgow—a Victorian feat of engineering that has ensured the purity of the supply to Scotland's largest city for more than a hundred years.

The second way of getting to Loch Lomond from Aberfoyle involves a faster trip on the main road to **Drymen,** a respectable and cozy town in the Lowland fields, with shops and pubs catering to the well-to-do Scots who have moved here from Glasgow.

Time Out There is a lot to choose from in Drymen, but try **the Clachan Inn** (tel. 0360/60824), which offers real ale and appetizing bar meals and makes children welcome.

The B837 from Drymen, signposted Rowardennan and Balmaha, heads northwest, and in a few minutes Loch Lomond comes into view. At the little settlement of **Balmaha,** the versatile recreational role filled by Loch Lomond becomes clearer: Cruising craft are at the ready, hikers appear out of woodlands on the West Highland Way, and day-trippers stroll at the loch's edge. The heavily wooded offshore islands look alluringly near. One of the best ways to explore them is to take a cruise with the boat-hire company **MacFarlane and Son** (Boatyard, Balmaha, Loch Lomond G63 0JG, tel. 036087/214). The island of **Inchcailloch** (*Inch-* is really *Innis,* Gaelic for *island*), just offshore, can be explored in an hour or two. There are pleasant pathways through oak woods planted there—as in many other parts of the Loch Lomond area—in the 18th century, when the bark was used in the tanning industry.

Behind Balmaha is **Conic Hill,** a wavy ridge of bald heathery domes above the pine trees, and you can note from your map how Inchcailloch and the other islands line up with it. This geographic line is indicative of the Highland Boundary Fault, which runs through the loch and the hill.

If you want to take in even more of Loch Lomond, the cul-de-sac road continues northwest to **Rowardennan,** with the loch seldom more than a field's length away. Where the drivable road ends, in a car park crunchy with pinecones, you can have fun comparing and contrasting the fashionable visitors from downtown Glasgow who sometimes make their way here, with the walkers following the long-distance footpath or staggering off Ben Lomond. It is a fine place to observe the Scots at play. Then return to Drymen for a fast and easy journey back to Stirling.

Tour 3: Around Perthshire

❷ Some say **Perth** took its name from a Roman camp, Bertha, on the shores of the Tay. Whatever the truth, this strategic site has been occupied continuously for centuries. Today's Perth has been built and rebuilt over its historic past. No traces remain of the monasteries that existed here before the Reformation and contributed to Perth's importance after it became Royal Burgh, in 1210. The town is a focal point in Scottish history, and several critical events took place here, including the assassination of King James I in 1437 and John Knox's preaching in St. John's Kirk in 1559. Knox's sermon undoubtedly stirred his congregation: Afterward, they went rampaging through the town, igniting the Reformation in Scotland. Later, the

17th-century religious wars in Scotland saw the town occupied first by the marquis of Montrose, then later by Oliver Cromwell's forces. Perth was also occupied by the Jacobites in the 1715 and 1745 rebellions.

Perth has swept much of its tumultuous history under a grid of bustling shopping streets. The town serves a wide rural hinterland and has a well-to-do air, making it one of the most interesting shopping towns aside from Edinburgh and Glasgow. Typical of this upscale ambience is **Cairncross the Goldsmith's,** with its display of Scottish pearls. Scotland's native pearl fishery is long established. In fact, the Scottish regalia (crown jewels) in Edinburgh Castle contain pearls from Scotland's deep and pure waters.

Perth, however, has more than upscale goldsmiths and antiques shops to offer. Unlike Stirling, its attractions—with the exception of the shops—are more scattered and take more time to reach on foot. Some, in fact, are far enough away to necessitate the use of a car, bus, or taxi. The following places are near the town center: **St. John's Kirk** (St. John St., tel. 0738/26159 or 23358) dating from the 15th century, escaped the worst excesses of the mob and is now restored; **Perth Art Gallery and Museum** (George St., tel. 0738/32488), which has a wide-ranging collection of local history and archaeology, plus a rotating exhibit program; and the nearby **Fair Maid's House** (North Port, tel. 0738/25976), which features an art gallery and crafts shop. The Fair Maid is a reference to Sir Walter Scott's novel *The Fair Maid of Perth*, which contains a description of an extraordinary event that took place on the level grounds known as inches, by the River Tay, in 1396: To settle a point of honor, 30 champions from the two clans of Chattan and Kay fought to the death on the North Inch in a specially constructed enclosure, with King Robert III and his court looking on. Clan Chattan won, and only one Kay escaped, after climbing out of the battlefield and swimming across the river.

The North Inch of Perth is also where **Balhousie Castle** and the **Regimental Museum of the Black Watch** can be found. Some will tell you the Black Watch was a Scottish regiment whose name is a reference to the color of their tartan. An equally plausible explanation, however, is that the regiment was established to keep an undercover watch on possibly rebellious Jacobite activities. The *Black* is the Gaelic word *dubh*, meaning hidden or covert, used in the same way as the English word, *blackmail*. The Gaelic phrase *sgian dubh* is often translated to mean *black knife*, but could also mean *the hidden knife. Facing North Inch Park (entrance from Hay St.), tel. 0738/21281, ext. 8530. Admission free. Open weekdays 10–4:30 (3:30 in winter). Closed Dec. 23–Jan 3.*

On a more peaceful note, visitors who visit in May or June can catch the glorious blue of the Himalayan poppies at the **Branklyn Garden,** signposted on the outskirts of Perth, across the river on the Dundee side. *Dundee Rd. (A85), tel. 0738/ 25535. Admission: £1.50 adults, 80p children. Open Mar.– Oct., daily 9:30–sunset.*

Off the A9, west of town, you can visit **Caithness Glass,** where from the viewing gallery you can watch glassworkers creating smoky-smooth bowls, vases, and other glassware. There are also a small museum, restaurant, and shop. *Inveralmond,*

*Perth, tel. 0738/37373. Admission free. Factory open weekdays
9–4:30. Shop open Easter–Oct., Mon.–Sat. 9–5, Sun. 11–5;
Oct.–Easter, Mon.–Sat. 9–5, Sun. 1–5.*

A modest selection of castles is also within easy reach.
28 Huntingtower Castle, a curious double tower dating from the
15th century, is associated with a political attempt to wrest
power from the young James VI in 1582. Some early painted
ceilings survive, the vaguest hint of the sumptuous decor once
found in many such ancient castles that are now reduced to bare
and drafty rooms. *Off A85, tel. 031/244–3101. Admission: £1
adults, 50p children. Open Apr.–Sept., Mon.–Sat. 9:30–6,
Sun. 2–6; Oct.–Mar., Mon.–Wed. and Sat. 9:30–4, Thurs. 9–1,
Sun. 2–4.*

29 Much the same description applies to **Elcho Castle,** a fortified
mansion on the east side of Perth. Some fabric and plasterwork
still cling to the cold stone in this abandoned 15th-century seat
of the earls of Wemyss. The effect is slightly eerie: Instead of a
long-dead shell, there are hints of a building barely alive. *On
River Tay, tel. 031/244–3101. Admission: £1.20 adults, 60p
children. Open Apr.–Sept., Mon.–Sat. 9:30–6, Sun. 2–6.*

30 Scone Palace is another story altogether: More cheerful and vi-
brant, the palace is the present home of the earl of Mansfield
and is open to visitors. Although it incorporates various earlier
works, the palace today consists mainly of a 19th-century
theme, featuring mock castellations that were fashionable at
the time. There is plenty to see for the visitor with an interest
in the acquisitions of an old Scottish family: magnificent porcelain, furniture, ivory, clocks, and 16th-century needlework.
Visitor facilities also include a coffee shop, restaurant, gift
shop, and play area, as well as extensive grounds that include a
pinetum. The palace has its own chapel nearby, on the site of a
long-gone abbey. The chapel stands by Moot Hill, the ancient
meeting and crowning place of the Scottish kings. *Braemar
Rd., tel. 0738/52300. Admission: £3.70 adults, £2 children, £3
senior citizens, £11 family ticket. Open Easter–Oct., Mon–
Sat. 9:30–5, Sun. 1:30–5 (July–Aug., Sun 10–5).*

To take in the rest of Perthshire, go north on the A9 into the
31 Highlands at **Dunkeld,** where the hills and woodlands con-
verge. Exit from the A9 and cross Thomas Telford's handsome
river bridge of 1809 to enter the city. Note the antiques shop on
the right, facing the river across the bridge; it is well worth a
browse. In Dunkeld you will find that the National Trust for
Scotland not only cares for grand mansions and wildlands but
also actively restores smaller properties. The work it completed under its "Little Houses" scheme can be seen in the
square off the main street, just opposite the fish-and-chips
shop. All the houses in the square were rebuilt after the 1689
Battle of Killiecrankie (*see below*), when, after its victory, the
Jacobite army marched south and was defeated here, though at
great cost to the town. Nearby, **Dunkeld Cathedral,** dating as
far back as the 14th century, has a choir that has been reroofed
and now serves as the parish church. *High St., tel. 031/244–
3101. Admission free. Open Apr.–Sept., Mon.–Sat. 9:30–6,
Sun. 2–6; Oct.–March, Mon.–Sat. 9:30–4, Sun. 2–4.*

32 The A9 continues north to **Pitlochry,** perhaps the typical cen-
tral-Highland resort. Always full of leisurely hustle and bustle, Pitlochry has wall-to-wall souvenir and gift shops, large

hotels recalling even more laid-back days, and a mountainous golf course. One popular attraction is the **Pitlochry Dam and Fish Ladder.** Just behind the main street is an exhibition on the hydroelectric projects found in the Highlands. So that generating needs do not clash with sports interests, most Scottish dams have salmon passes or ladders of some kind, enabling the fish to swim upstream to their spawning grounds. In Pitlochry the fish pass goes into a pipe with a glass panel in it so that they can observe the visitors.

For those with a whiskey-tasting bent, Pitlochry also is home to **Edradour Distillery,** which claims to be the smallest single-malt distillery in Scotland (but then, so do others). *2½ mi east of Pitlochry, tel. 0796/2095. Admission free. Open for tours and tastings Mar.–Oct., daily 9:30–5; shop also open Nov.–Feb., daily 10–4.*

In summer **Pitlochry Festival Theatre** is a must if you are making Pitlochry your base. It runs a casual program and encourages visitors not to dress up. The theater restaurant is a good place to pause and plan your next excursion.

③③ The **Linn of Tummel,** a series of marked walks along the river and through tall, mature woodlands, is a little way north of the town. Above the Linn, the new A9 is raised on stilts and gives an exciting view of the valley. Visitors can pick up a walks booklet at the **Killiecrankie Visitor Centre,** a short distance farther on. To reach the Linn and Killiecrankie from Pitlochry, stay on the old A9, heading north. From the old A9, note the B8019 road heading west. (The tour returns to this point later.) The **③④** **Pass of Killiecrankie,** set among the oak woods and rocky river, was a key strategic point in the Central Highlands: A famous battle was won there in the Jacobite rebellion of 1689. The National Trust for Scotland's visitor center explains the significance of this, the first attempt to restore the Stuart monarchy. The battle was noted for the death of the Jacobite leader, James Graham of Claverhouse, also known as Bonnie Dundee, hit by a stray bullet; the rebellion fizzled out after that. *Off A9, tel. 0796/3233. Admission free. Open Apr., May, Sept., Oct., daily 10–5, June–Aug., daily 9:30–6.*

The river also had a role in the tale of another small riparian site, **Soldier's Leap,** where an English soldier, hotly pursued by a Highland clansman, decided he would rather jump to a certain death into a formidable gorge on the river than be skewered on a Jacobite broadsword. There are also plenty of interesting walks for those less enamored of historical details. You can walk among tall oaks and pines down to the Linn of Tummel, a sylvan spot that attracts plenty of interest.

Only a few minutes farther north from the Pass of Killiecrankie **③⑤** sits **Blair Castle.** Take the A9 to Blair Atholl, where the castle is clearly signposted. Because of its historic contents and its war-torn past, this is one of Scotland's most highly rated castle visits. White painted and turreted, Blair Castle has been home to successive dukes of Atholl and their family, the Murrays, for a long time, playing an important part in Scotland's story. It was Lord George Murray, by far the most talented commander in the Jacobite forces, who rallied to the aid of Prince Charles Edward Stuart in 1745. Indeed, if Lord George's advice had been taken, the last Jacobite battle, on Culloden Moor, would never have been fought on such unfavorable ground.

Not that the family was unanimously Jacobite, as Lord George Murray in the same campaign unsuccessfully besieged Blair Castle itself (at that point garrisoned by governmental troops). One of the many historical details in the interior is a preserved piece of flooring with marks of the red-hot shot fired through the roof. It was the last occasion in Scottish history that a castle was besieged. The castle holds not only military artifacts—the duke is allowed to keep a private army, the Atholl Highlanders—but also a fine collection of furniture and paintings. Outside, extensive parklands are backed by high rounded hills. As at Killiecrankie, tall, old trees can be found that were planted in the 18th century at the behest of the fourth duke, who was an enthusiastic planter. Today the castle is home to the 10th duke and his family. *Tel. 0796/481207. Admission: £4 adults, £2.50 children and senior citizens. Open Apr.–late Oct., daily 10–6; Sun. in Apr., May, and Oct. 2–6.*

From Blair the main A9 heads north over the watershed by way of the Pass of Drumochter to Speyside. To stay in Perthshire, return south to the B8019, noted earlier, below Killiecrankie. It leads to the best of Perthshire's lochs and hills. The introduction to this natural scenery begins at the **Queen's View,** after you drive on the B8019 for a few minutes. Here in 1866 Queen Victoria paused to admire the open vista with Loch Tummel spread before the shapely peak of Schiehallion (pronounced *shee*-haal-*ee-on*). Close by is the **Tummel Forest Centre,** with a forestry-commission presentation on the life of the forest. *Off A809, tel. 0796/3123. Admission free. Open all times.*

The B8019 turns into the B846 at Tummel Bridge and continues to Loch Rannoch. Take this section if you have plenty of time and are following this tour over two days. **Loch Rannoch,** with its shoreline birch trees and dark pines behind, is the quintessential Highland loch. Continuing westward the road ends at Rannoch, where you meet the West Highland railroad line on its way across Rannoch Moor to Fort William. This section of railway was opened in 1894, but not until the engineers had solved the problem of taking the route across the boggy wastes of the moor. They came up with the idea of floating the track bed on rafts of brushwood in an effort to stabilize the ground. Fans of Robert Louis Stevenson, especially of *Kidnapped*, will not want to miss the last, lonely section of road. Stevenson describes the setting:

The mist rose and died away, and showed us that country lying as waste as the sea; only the moorfowl and the peewees crying upon it, and far over to the east a herd of deer, moving like dots. Much of it was red with heather; much of the rest broken up with bogs and hags and peaty pools. . . .

Apart from the blocks of alien conifer plantings in certain places, little here has changed.

It is possible to loop around by the south side of Loch Rannoch to the **Black Wood of Rannoch,** a surviving fragment of the ancient woodlands that once clothed much of the Highlands. The open woods with red-limbed pines and a well-lighted understory of juniper and heather contrast with the sterile darkness of more modern plantings. Farther east, a lonely road climbs out of the main glen and over a shoulder of Schiehallion. If you have somehow not seen any of Scotland's native red deer, you can encounter them at close quarters at the **Glengoulandie Deer**

Park shortly after you join the B846, turning south at the Tummel Bridge. *A830, tel. 039783/250. Admission: £1 adults, 50p children. Open Apr., May, Sept.–mid-Oct., daily 10–1 and 2–5:30; June–Aug., daily 9:30–6:30.*

As you drop into the little **Strath of Appin**, among the green hills of Perthshire, several choices will open up for you (*see* Off the Beaten Track, *below*, for Glen Lyon and the Ben Lawers Visitor Centre). If you stay on the B846, now heading east, you will pass **Castle Menzies**. This Z-plan 16th-century fortified tower/house is now the setting for the **Clan Menzies' Museum**. *Tel. 0887/20982. Admission: £1.50 adults, 75p children. Open Apr.–mid-Oct., Mon.–Sat 10:30–5, Sun. 2–5.*

39 A little farther on, travelers will reach **Aberfeldy** by way of General Wade's Aberfeldy Bridge of 1733. This is the most impressive of the English military road builder's spans, a five-arch, hump-back bridge designed by William Adam. Note that the inscription engraved on the parapet describes General Wade as the "Commander-in-Chief of the Forces in Scotland." Aberfeldy itself is a sleepy town that is popular as a tourist base. You may want to take a break here to work out your schedule. Remember, if you have to return to Perth, the A9 is only about a 10-mile (16-km) drive east on the A827.

Time Out Wholesome cooking is available at **Country Fare** (tel. 0887/20729), located on the main street. The small eatery has home-baked goods and sustaining soups, and everything inside is clean and sparkling.

40 The next loop returns west to **Kenmore**, at the eastern end of Loch Tay. **Taymouth Castle** nearby has a famous parkland golf course. However, before continuing west, you should explore an interesting route running southeast from Kenmore. An unclassified road hairpins spectacularly out of the valley, giving superb views over the Ben Lawers mountain range to the north of Loch Tay and back to Schiehallion. After taking that slight detour, take the north-bank road by Loch Tay, the A827. At Fearnan you can divert a few minutes northward to Fortingall to view the **Fortingall yew**, near the Fortingall Hotel, in the churchyard. Wearily resting its great limbs on the ground, this tree is thought to be more than 3,000 years old. Legend has it that Pontius Pilate was born beside it, while his father served as a Roman legionnaire in Scotland.

The A827 offers fine views west along Loch Tay toward Ben More and Stobinian. Keep in mind that the sign to Ben Lawers **41** Visitor Centre (*see* Off the Beaten Track, *below*) leads to **Killin**, a village with an almost-alpine flavor. Known for its modest but surprisingly diverse selection of crafts and woolen wares, Killin is also noted for its scenery. The **Falls of Dochart**, whitewater rapids overlooked by a pine-clad islet, are located at the west end of the village. Across the River Dochart and near the golf course sit the ruins of **Finlarig Castle**, built by Black Duncan of the Cowl, a notorious Campbell laird. The castle's beheading pit is certainly its most hair-raising surviving feature. The castle may be visited at any time.

Time Out **Shutters Restaurant** (Main St., Killin, tel. 05672/314) serves reasonably priced meals all day. Also of interest is the display of old photographs.

Southwest of Killin the A827 joins the main A85, going west. By turning south over the watershed, you will see fine views of the hill ridges behind Killin. The road leads into Glen Ogle, "amid the wildest and finest scenery we had yet seen . . . putting one in mind of prints of the Khyber Pass," as Queen Victoria recorded in her diary when she passed this way in 1842.

42 The glen drops into the settlement of **Lochearnhead.** Make a left at the intersection, and you will see the **Lochearnhead Watersports Centre** by the shore of Loch Earn; the center offers instruction and equipment rentals for water-sports enthusiasts, from novices to experts. **Loch Earn** is the last of the lochs on this Perthshire loop. Still on the A85 going east you will have good views of the long, gray screes of Ben Vorlich southward across the loch.

You will then drive by the village of **St. Fillans,** through lush Perthshire estates and farmlands, and on to **Comrie** and the **Museum of Scottish Tartans.** The museum has an important collection of tartans and Highland dress, with some old tartan fabric, as well as prints and manuscripts related to and recording the manufacture of tartans years ago. Comprehensive displays on manufacturing and natural dyeing processes make this a fascinating stop for anyone who is keen to sort out historical accuracy from the often-preferred tartan mythology. *Drummond St., Comrie, tel. 0764/70779. (Telephone for details of opening times and admission charges.)*

The countryside east of Comrie looks more lush and is reminiscent of the Lowlands; the higher hills can be seen to the north. **43** **Crieff,** the hilly town you will encounter next, offers walks with Highland views from **Knock Hill** above the town, as well as tours of the **Glenturret Distillery,** signposted on the west side of the town. Crieff's small-town ambience and its location in a side valley make it appealing. *Tel. 0764/2424. Open Mar.–Dec.*

Crieff's next cluster of visitor attractions lies south of the town, on the A822 by the River Earn. **Stuart Strathearn,** a glassmaker, offers self-guided factory tours to watch glassworkers transform molten blobs into sophisticated crystal ware. There is also a bargain seconds shop stocked with etched and polished crystal products. *Muthill Rd., tel. 0764/4004. Admission free. Open June–Sept., daily 9–7; Oct.–May, daily 9–5.*

Across the road is a paperweight manufacturer, part of a complex called the **Crieff Visitors Centre.** Adjacent to the complex are a pottery and restaurant. *A822, south of Crieff, tel. 0764/4014. Admission free. Open daily 9–6.*

Perth is less than half an hour away via the A85, but an equally interesting return can be made by diverting through Auchterarder. **44** On the way, the A822 passes **Drummond Castle,** with its unusual formal Italian garden. *Off Crieff/Muthill Rd., tel. 076481/257. Admission to garden: £2 adults, £1 children and senior citizens. Gardens open May–Sept., daily 2–6.*

Other minor points of interest within easy reach of this road include **Innerpeffray Library** (B8062, tel. 0764/2819), the oldest (1691) library in Scotland; **Muthill Church,** with its 12th-century tower (A822 at Muthill, tel. 031/244–3101); and a number of Roman architectural remains, mostly faint and overgrown. The best-preserved remnants can be found near **Braco,** to the south, just off the A9, where substantial ditches and turf ramparts remain from a major Roman fort dating to around 150 BC.

45 The A822 leads to **Auchterarder,** famous for the **Gleneagles Hotel** and its recreational facilities (*see* Dining and Lodging, *below*). A number of antiques shops have also made a name for themselves at Auchterarder. The nearby **Glenruthven Weaving Mill** has been converted into a heritage center with a Scottish theme. The steam engine that once powered the mill can also be viewed. From Auchterarder, the fast-moving A9 stretches northeast to Perth.

Central Highlands for Free

Bells Cherrybank Gardens (Cherrybank, off Glasgow Rd., Perth, tel. 0738/27330) has 18 acres of landscaped gardens and the Bells national heather collection. *Admission free. Open May–mid-Oct., daily 9–5.*
Bracklinn Falls (*see* Tour 2)
Factory tours at Crieff Visitor Centre (*see* Tour 3)
Falls of Leny in Pass of Leny above Callander (*see* Tour 2)
The **Pitlochry Power Station Fish Ladder and Dam** (tel. 08824/251) is an ideal place to see salmon swimming upstream, viewed through windows in the fish ladder.
The **Trossachs** (*see* Tour 2)
Views from Stirling Castle ramparts (*see* Tour 1)
Walks at Pass of Killiecrankie (*see* Tour 3)
Walks from Rowardennan at Loch Lomond (*see* Tour 2)

What to See and Do with Children

Other than the sports-and-leisure facilities listed under Sports and Fitness, *below*, attractions for children are limited. There are several bicycle routes suitable for older children, however. Pony trekking is an option throughout the area (check with your local tourist information center for details).

Most children will enjoy the **Rob Roy and Trossachs Visitor Centre** (*see* Tour 2), and older children will find the glassblowing at **Stuart Strathearn's** in Crieff of interest (*see* Tour 3).

Near Perth, **Fairways Heavy Horse Centre** (Walnut Grove, by Perth, tel. 0738/32561) offers Clydesdale horses for day rides.

The **Vane Farm Nature Centre** (near Loch Leven, Kinross, tel. 0577/62355) is operated under the auspices of the Royal Society for the Protection of Birds and is a visitor center with a screened viewing area, nature trail, shop, and picnic area.

Off the Beaten Track

If Stirling is your base and you feel like taking a brisk evening walk and have your own transport, seek out the little road that starts by the campus of Stirling University and climbs toward Sheriffmuir. On the way it passes close to the hill called **Dumyat,** on the breezy moors of the Ochils. A short walk is rewarded by superb views across the midland valley of Scotland, to Stirling and far beyond. The road is signposted Sheriffmuir from the old A9.

The ospreys that frequent Speyside's Loch Garten in summer get so much attention from conservation societies that they sometimes overshadow **Loch of the Lowes,** a Scottish Wildlife Trust reserve behind Dunkeld. Here the domestic routines of the osprey, one of Scotland's conservation success stories, can be observed in relative comfort. The reserve is off the A923 northeast of Dunkeld. *Tel. 03502/337. Visitor center open Apr.–Sept. Observation blind open at all times.*

The **Queen's View** is the spot from which Victoria first viewed Loch Lomond in 1879. It is a much more impressive approach to the loch than that from Balloch. This is an ideal evening drive if you are based in Glasgow. The view is signed from the A809 Drymen road, north of Glasgow.

Duncryne Hill has possibly the most outstanding Loch Lomond view from the south end. It takes only a few minutes' clambering up a bracken-covered hill to get there. You may be rewarded by a spectacular sunset. You can't miss this unmistakable dumpling-shaped hill, behind Gartocharn on the Balloch–Drymen road, the A811.

Glen Lyon is worth exploring if you are in the Killin area. Lyon is one of central Scotland's most attractive glens. All the elements of Scottish glens can be found here: a rushing river, forests, high hills on both sides, prehistoric sites complete with legendary tales, and the typical *big hoose* hidden on private grounds. There is even a dam at the head of the loch, as a reminder that little of Scotland's scenic beauty is unadulterated. You can reach the glen either by way of Fortingall (*see* Tour 3) or by a high road from Loch Tay (*see* Ben Lawers, *below*).

The botanically rich **Ben Lawers** (3,984 feet, which for Scotland is a very large mountain) has a visitor center that is proficient in informing visitors about the former life of the mountain pastures and the range of plants found on the hill. However, many conservationists think the center, operated by the National Trust for Scotland, was built in the wrong place: on the open green slopes of Ben Lawers.

Shopping

The Central Highlands presents an interesting assortment of shopping choices, ranging from the larger population centers of Perth and Stirling, where High Street stores compete with long-established local firms, to the smaller towns and villages, where the selection is more limited but the relaxed pace makes for a pleasant shopping environment.

Starting in the east, **Perth** proffers an unusual buy: Scottish freshwater pearls from the River Tay, in delicate settings that take their theme from Scottish flowers. The Romans coveted these pearls. If you do, too, then you can make your choice at **Cairncross Jewellers and Goldsmiths** (18 St. John St.), where you can also admire a display of some of the more unusual shapes and colors of pearls found. Antique Scottish jewelry and silver can be found at **Timothy Hardie** (25 St. John St.), and **Whispers of the Past** (George St.) has a collection of linens and jewelry. A comprehensive selection of sheepskins, leather jackets, and hand-knit Aran sweaters are on sale at **L & C Proudfoot** (104 South St.). Perth is an especially popular hunting ground for china and glass: **Watson of Perth** (163–167 High

St.) has sold exquisite bone china and cut crystal since 1900 and can pack your purchase safely for shipment overseas. Just outside Perth, at **Caithness Glass** (Inveralmond, off the A9 at the northern town boundary), you can see glassware being made and then buy the product in the factory shop.

Crieff is another center for china and glassware. The **Crieff Visitors Centre** (Muthill Rd.) offers factory tours that give visitors the opportunity to see the manufacturing process of the famous Thistle hand-painted pottery, intricate millefiori glass, and lamp-work Perthshire paperweights. Those visitors already bogged down with too heavy a suitcase will be happy to learn that small paperweights—as well as the larger ones—are on sale at the factory shop, together with a variety of pottery. Nearby, at **Stuart Strathearn's** premises, Stuart crystal is produced and engraved; factory tours and a factory shop are also available here. If you want something to put in your new set of crystal glasses, visit **Glenturret Distillery,** also in Crieff, which offers a guided tour and a free sampling of its product, Glenturret Pure Single Highland Malt.

You may wish to compare this malt with that produced at **Blair Athol Distillery** (Pitlochry, tel. 0796/2234), which offers free tours, tastings, and a well-stocked shop. There is also a coffee shop in a converted whiskey warehouse.

To find the **Highland Horn and Deerskin Centre** (City Hall, Atholl St.), travel to **Dunkeld.** Here stag antlers and cow horns are turned into horn-handled walking sticks, cutlery, and tableware. Deerskin is made into shoes, handbags, wallets, and purses. The center offers a worldwide postal service and a tax-free shop.

Moving to the south, shoppers should allow plenty of time to browse among the antiques shops of **Auchterarder,** a mecca for those visiting nearby **Gleneagles.** In **Stirling, Murray Place** and the **Thistle Centre** provide all the standard High Street names. Lovers of antiquarian books should trek to the older part of town, where, at 55 King Street, the **Corn Exchange Bookshop** will keep them happy for an hour or two with its extensive number of titles, including books on every aspect of Scotland. Not far away, on Friars Street, is **Stewart Campbell Antiques and Pine Studio,** for furniture, paintings, silver, jewelry, and china. On the same street, at No. 11, is **William Hamilton Jewelers,** which stocks Scottish silver jewelry, and at Nos. 6–8 is **R. R. Henderson Ltd.,** a kilt maker established in 1923 (knitwear and tweeds can be sent worldwide). Farther along, at Nos. 29–31, is **John M. Hay,** where you can buy a set of bagpipes or a record or cassette of Scottish music (it also offers an overseas-shipment service). Finally, do not miss the **Medieval fairs** held on Broad Street from time to time in the summer season.

East of Stirling is **Mill Trail** country, along the foot of the Ochil Hills. A leaflet from a tourist-information center will lead you to the delights of a real mill shop and low mill prices—even on cashmere—at **Tillicoultry, Alva,** and **Alloa.**

Northwest of Stirling are the bustling shops of **Callander.** A vast selection of woolens is on display at **Kilmahog Woollen Mill** and **Trossachs Woollen Mill** (to the north of town at the Trossachs turning) and at the **Callander Woollen Mill** on Main Street. All the stores offer overseas mailing and tax-free shopping. **Presentations** (86 Main St.) stocks Scottish gifts and crafts and specializes in producing clan crests and badges that can be mailed anywhere in the world. Also uniquely Scottish is the stoneware of **Mounter Pottery** (Ancaster Square La.), which you can see being made.

If you are traveling west to Loch Lomond, visit **Mr. Macpherson,** who has a weaving shed at **Tarbet** (Inverhoulin, tel. 03012/269), where you can see tartans weaved in a traditional hand-loom manner. Also in Tarbet, housed in a converted church at Station Road, is **The Black Sheep,** which specializes in crafts and offers a good cup of coffee and a meal. South of Loch Lomond are some of the larger shopping centers: **Alexandria, Dumbarton,** and **Helensburgh.** Try **R & A Urie** (45 W. Clyde St., Helensburgh) for fine china and crystal (it has an export service) and nearby **MacGillivrays** (89 W. Clyde St.) for Scottish gifts. Scottish silver jewelry, including the Charles Rennie Mackintosh Collection, is featured at **Hudsons Jewellers** (101 Main St., Alexandria). This part of the Central Highlands also offers an exceptional selection of paintings by contemporary Scottish artists: try **Helensburgh Fine Arts** (78 W. Clyde St., Helensburgh) or **The Rowan Gallery** (36 Main St., Drymen).

Sports and Fitness

Bicycling — **Loch Tay Mountain Bike Hire** (Pedlars, Main St., Killin, tel. 05672/201).

New Heights Mountain Bike Hire (26 Barnton St., Stirling, tel. 0786/50809).

Trossachs Cycle Hire (Trossachs Holiday Park, Aberfoyle, tel. 08772/614).

Wheels (Manse Lane, Callander, tel. 0877/31100).

Fishing — There are several fishing options in the area, including course and game fishing, loch and river fishing, and sea angling. Tourist-information centers produce annually updated leaflets.

Golf — **Blairgowrie** (Rosemount, tel. 0250/2622), 18 holes, 6,581 yards, par 72.

Callander (Aveland Rd., tel. 0877/30090), 18 holes, 5,292 yards, par 66.

Hiking — Tourist-information centers carry information on a variety of local routes. The publications *Walk Loch Lomond and the Trossachs* or *Walk Perthshire* are invaluable for hikers and trekkers and are available at bookshops or tourist-information centers.

Horseback Riding — Approved by the British Horse Society, **Balnakilly Riding Centre** (Balnakilly, Kirkmichael, Perthshire, tel. 0250/881305) accepts beginners and experienced riders alike and is located on the Highland estate.

Water Sports — **Lochearnhead Water Sports Centre** (Loch Earn, tel. 05673/330) has sailboats, canoes, and sailboards for wind surfing.

Loch Tay Boating Centre (Carlin and Brett, Pier Rd., Kenmore, tel. 08873/291) has cabin cruisers, water skis, jet skis, canoes, and sailboards.

519 M.P.H.

190 M.P.H.

75 M.P.H.

0 M.P.H.

WE LET YOU SEE EUROPE AT YOUR OWN PACE.

Regardless of your personal speed limits, Rail Europe offers
everything to get you over, around and through anywhere you
want in Europe. For more information, call
your travel agent or **1-800-4-EURAIL.** *Rail Europe*

MCI brings Europe and America closer together.

Call the U.S. for less with MCI CALL USA®.

It's easy and affordable to call home when you use MCI CALL USA!

- Less expensive than calling through hotel operators
- Available from over 65 countries and locations worldwide
- You're connected to English-speaking MCI® Operators
- Even call 800 numbers in the U.S.

Call the U.S. for less from these European locations.

Dial the toll-free access number for the country you're calling from. Give the U.S. MCI Operator the number you're calling and the method of payment: MCI Card, U.S. local phone company card, Telecom Canada Card or collect. Your call will be completed!

Austria	022-903-012	Hungary	00*800-01411	Poland	0*-01-04-800-222
Belgium	078-11-00-12	Ireland	1800-551-001	Portugal	05-017-1234
Czechoslovakia	00-42-000112	Italy	172-1022	San Marino	172-1022
Denmark	8001-0022	Liechtenstein	155-0222	Spain	900-99-0014
Finland	9800-102-80	Luxembourg	0800-0112	Sweden	020-795-922
France	19*-00-19	Monaco	19*-00-19	Switzerland	155-0222
Germany	0130-0012	Netherlands	06*-022-91-22	United Kingdom	0800-89-0222
Greece	00-800-1211	Norway	050-12912	Vatican City	172-1022

* Wait for 2nd dial tone. Collect calls not accepted on MCI CALL USA calls to 800 numbers

Call 1-800-444-4444 in the U.S. to apply for your MCI Card® now!

Dining and Lodging

Dining

The restaurants of this region have been continually improving over the past several years. Regional country delicacies, such as loch trout, river salmon, mutton, and venison, are now found regularly on modest menus; this was extremely rare just 20 years ago. The urban areas south and southwest of Stirling, in contrast, lack refinement in matters of eating and drinking. There you will find simple low-built pubs, often crowded and noisy but serving substantial food at lunchtime (eaten balanced on your knee, perhaps, or at a shared table). Three heavy courses at one of these pubs will cost you about £10.

Highly recommended restaurants are indicated by a star ★.

Category	Cost*
Very Expensive	over £40
Expensive	£30–£40
Moderate	£15–£30
Inexpensive	under £15

*per person, including appetizer, main course, dessert, and VAT

Lodging

In Stirling and Callander, as well as in the small towns and villages throughout the region, you will find a selection of tourist accommodations out of all proportion to the size of the communities. (The industrial towns are the exceptions.) Standards of inexpensive and moderate-price establishments have improved in recent years and are still improving. The grand hotels, though few, were brought into existence by the rich carriage trade of the 19th century, when travel in Scotland was the fashion, and the level of service at these places has, by and large, not slipped. You will also find many country hotels, however, that match the grand hotels in comfort.

Highly recommended hotels are indicated by a star ★.

Category	Cost*
Very Expensive	over £120
Expensive	£100–£120
Moderate	£80–£100
Inexpensive	under £80

*All prices are for a standard double room, including breakfast and tax.

Auchterarder **Gleneagles Hotel.** One of Britain's most famous hotels,
Lodging Gleneagles is the very image of modern grandeur. Like a vast, secret palace, it stands hidden in breathtaking countryside amid three world-famous golf courses. Recreation facilities are

seemingly endless, and there are also five restaurants: **Conservatory** for intimate haute cuisine; the **Strathearn** for table d'hôte; and three other, more informal restaurants. All this plus a shopping arcade, Chamneys Health Spa, Gleaneagles Mark Phillips Equestrian Centre, and Gleneagles Jackie Stewart Shooting School make a stay here a luxurious and unforgettable experience. *PH3 1NF, tel. 0764/62231. Reservations advised. Jacket and tie required in formal areas of the hotel after 7 PM; otherwise dress casual. 236 rooms with bath. Facilities: tennis, swimming pool, saunas, golf. AE, DC, MC, V. Very Expensive.*

★ **Auchterarder House.** This wood-paneled, richly furnished, Victorian country mansion is secluded and superbly atmospheric. Once owned by the steam locomotive magnate James Reid, the Auchterarder House still shows all the ebullience of the Victorian railway age. The staff is particularly friendly, and guests will enjoy the personal attention in this family home. Many of the bedrooms have their original furniture, and all share views of private parkland and the Perthshire countryside. All meals are served at a time suitable to the guest, and breakfast at noon is not unheard of. The plush, exuberantly styled dining room, filled with glittering glassware, is an appropriate setting for the hotel's creative use of locally produced foods: Typical dishes include lamb with a Dubonnet-and-red-wine sauce and poached langoustines with rhubarb. *B8062, Perthshire PH3 1DZ, tel. 0764/63646. Restaurant reservations required. Jacket and tie required. 15 rooms with bath. Facilities: golf, swimming pool, tennis, squash, croquet. AE, DC, MC, V. Expensive.*

Balloch
Lodging
★
Cameron House. This luxury hotel offers a mix of top-quality hotel and country-club facilities (including swimming pools, a gymnasium, and squash courts) on the shores of Loch Lomond. Award-winning chef Jef Bland (formerly of the Caledonian Hotel in Edinburgh) oversees Scottish-French cuisine of the highest order, served in rich Victorian surroundings. Bedrooms are decorated in modern pastel shades with high-quality reproductions of antique furniture. *Loch Lomond, Alexandria, Dumbartonshire G83 8QZ, tel. 0389/55565. Reservations required. Dress: casual but neat. 68 rooms with bath. Facilities: lounge, bar, health club, 2 pools. AE, DC, MC, V. Expensive–Very Expensive.*

Brig o' Turk
Dining and Lodging
Dundarroch and The Byre. This Victorian, antiques-furnished country house, set on 14 acres of grounds, offers first-class guest-house accommodations, and the adjoining **Byre Restaurant** serves savory Scottish meals in a Victorian setting. *Trossachs, Perthshire FK17 8HT, tel. 08776/200. Reservations advised. Dress: casual but neat. 3 rooms with bath. AE, MC, V. Closed Feb. Inexpensive.*

Callander
Dining and Lodging
★
Roman Camp. This former hunting lodge, dating from 1625, has 20 acres of gardens with river frontage, yet is within easy walking distance of Callander's town center. Private fishing on the River Teith is another attraction, as are the sitting rooms and the library, which, with their numerous antiques, are more reminiscent of a stately family home than a hotel. The restaurant has high standards, with a good reputation for its salmon, trout, and other seafood cooked in an imaginative, modern French style. *Perthshire FK17 8BG, tel. 0877/30003. Reservations advised. Dress: casual but neat. 14 rooms with bath. AE, DC, MC, V. Moderate–Expensive.*

Glenfarg
Lodging

Bein Inn. Once a drovers' inn on the old road from Perth to Edinburgh, the surroundings are of leafy seclusion, bird song, and a rippling river just across the road. This inn is for those who are willing to venture 2 miles (3km) from the main road, the M90. Family run, the retreat retains the feel of an inn, with a friendly bar and a traditionally furnished lounge and dining room (with a Taste of Scotland menu). All the bedrooms are spacious, with modern furnishings. *Perthshire PH2 9PY, tel. 0577/830216. Reservations advised. Dress: casual. 14 rooms, 12 with bath. MC, V. Restaurant reservations advised. Inexpensive.*

Kinclaven
Dining and Lodging

Ballathie House. This country-house hotel beside the River Tay was recently refurbished and now offers individually decorated bedrooms and comfortable, relaxed public rooms. Considering the region, it's not surprising that the restaurant menu emphasizes salmon, game, and fresh fruit. *Near Stanley, Perthshire PH1 4QN, tel. 0250/883268. Reservations advised. Dress: Casual. 22 rooms, 19 with bath. AE, DC, MC, V. Closed Feb. Moderate–Expensive.*

Scone
Dining and Lodging

Murrayshall. Another Victorian mansion, this one is set on 300 acres of parkland where golf is the special feature. A challenging 18-hole course lies within the park, and golfers can enjoy quick, light meals in the clubhouse. Bedrooms and public rooms are well equipped, with high-quality furnishings. Quality can also be found in the restaurant, where dishes are superbly prepared in a Scottish or modern French style and the local ingredients—salmon, game, seafood, and fruit—abound. *Perthshire PH2 7PH, tel. 0738/51171. Resevations required. Dress: casual but neat. 19 rooms with bath. AE, DC, MC, V. Expensive–Very Expensive.*

Stirling
Dining

Heritage. This elegant 18th-century establishment is run by a French family. The decor is all fanlights and candles; the menu features French and Scottish classics. *16 Allan Park, tel. 0786/73660. Reservations advised. Dress: casual. MC, V. Closed Christmas, Jan. 1. Moderate.*

Cross Keys Inn. A quaint, stone-walled dining room adds atmosphere to this restaurant's varied traditional Scottish menu. *Main St., Kippen (A811, west of Stirling), tel. 078687/293. Reservations advised. Dress: casual. MC, V. Inexpensive.*

No. 39. Only 200 yards from the castle, this highly recommended restaurant has a menu for varied tastes and budgets. *39 Broad St., tel. 0786/73929. Reservations advised. Dress: casual. MC, V. Inexpensive–Moderate.*

Lodging

Stirling Highland Hotel. This recently opened hotel occupies a handsome building that was once the Old High School. Many original architectural features, retained during the conversion, add to the historic atmosphere. The decor is old-fashioned in style, with solid wood furnishings in tartan or florals and other low-key, neutral color schemes. *Spittal St., FK8 1DU, tel. 0786/75444. 76 rooms with bath, 4 suites. Facilities: 2 restaurants, piano bar, sports and leisure club. AE, DC, MC, V. Very Expensive.*

Terraces Hotel. This is a centrally located hotel, useful for exploring Stirling; since there is plenty of parking space, it makes a good base for touring the region, too. It's a Georgian town house that has been comfortably converted, and the service is attentive. *4 Melsille Terr., FK8 2ND, tel. 0786/72268. 18 rooms* *with bath or shower. Facilities: restaurant. AE, DC, MC, V. Moderate.*

West Plean. This handsome house is part of a working farm. It also has a walled garden and woodland walks. Well-cooked food and spacious rooms make certain that your stay is enjoyable. *Denny Rd., FK7 8HA, tel. 0786/812208. 3 rooms. No credit cards. Inexpensive.*

The Arts and Nightlife

The Arts

Outside the main cities, opportunities for cultural activities are limited, except when communities hold arts festivals—a growing phenomenon in Scotland—or if the community is on the itinerary of one of Scotland's major artistic companies; for example, the Scottish Opera. The following venues have a rotating program of cultural events, but check with local tourist-information centers for schedules of other events at such places as **Alloa Town Hall,** the **Guildhall, Stirling** and **Denny Civic Theatre,** and **Dumbarton.**

Theater The **Macrobert Arts Centre** (Stirling University, tel. 0786/61081) has a theater, art gallery, and studio with a program that ranges from films to pantomime. The **Perth Repertory Theatre** (High St., Perth, tel. 0738/21031) is a Victorian theater offering a variety of plays and musicals.

Pitlochry Festival Theatre (Pitlochry, tel. 0796/2680) presents six plays each season and features concerts on most Sundays. The theater is open from May to October.

Nightlife

The nightlife in the area tends toward ceilidhs and Scottish concerts. Folk evenings in a number of hotels are also popular. Consult local tourist-information centers for entertainment options. In general, local pubs are friendly and down-to-earth, with patrons who don't mind talking to visitors about what to see and do.

Nightclubs **Electric Whispers Nightclub** (40 Canal St., Perth, tel. 0738/30503).

Scorpios (35 James Sq., Crieff, tel. 0764/4772).

Yorkys Nightclub (15 York Pl., Perth, tel. 0738/26467).

10 Argyll and the Isles

Introduction

By Gilbert
Summers

This popular and alluring region in western Scotland, divided
in two by the long peninsula of Kintyre, is characterized by a
splintered, complex seaboard. Kintyre also separates the islands of the Firth of Clyde (including Arran), from the islands
of the Inner Hebrides, the largest of which are Mull, Islay, and
Jura. You could spend all your time touring these larger islands, but keep in mind that there are plenty of small islands
that can also be explored—Bute in the Clyde estuary or the
captivating gem of Colonsay between Islay and Mull.

Those visiting the mainland cannot avoid the touring center of
Oban, an important ferry port with a main road leading south
into Kintyre. The west is an aesthetic delight, though it's regularly drenched by rain. The same soggy saga also holds true in
the Great Glen area, but an occasionally wet foray is the price
visitors pay for the glittering freshness of oakwoods and bracken-covered hillsides and for the bright interplay of sea loch and
rugged green peninsula.

Essential Information

Important Addresses and Numbers

Tourist
Information
Local tourist-information centers include **Dunoon and Cowal**
Tourist Board (7 Alexandra Parade, Dunoon, Argyll, tel. 0369/
3785), **Isle of Arran Tourist Board** (Tourist Information Centre,
The Pier, Brodick, Arran, tel. 0770/2140), **Isle of Bute Tourist**
Board (Tourist Information Centre, The Pier Rothesay, Bute,
tel. 0700/502151), **Mid-Argyll, Kintyre, and Islay Tourist Board**
(The Pier, Campbeltown, tel. 0586/52056), and **Oban, Mull,**
and District Tourist Board (Argyll Sq., Oban, tel. 0631/63122).
There are also seasonal information centers at Bowmore (Is-
lay), Craignure (Mull), Inveraray, Lochgilphead, Lochranza
(Arran), Tarbert, and Tobermory (Mull).

Emergencies
For police, fire, or ambulance, dial 999 from any telephone. No
coins are needed for emergency calls from public telephone
booths.

Doctors and
Dentists
Local general practitioners will usually treat visiting patients
by appointment or immediately in case of emergency. Information is available from your hotel, the local tourist-information
center, and the police, or look under "Doctors" or "Dentists" in
the Yellow Pages telephone directory. There is an emergency
room at **West Highland Hospital** (Glencruitten Rd., Oban, tel.
0631/63727).

Late-Night
Pharmacies
Pharmacies are not found in rural areas. In an emergency the
police will provide assistance in locating a pharmacist. In rural
areas general practitioners may also dispense medicines.

Arriving and Departing by Plane

Airports and
Airlines
Although the nearest full-service airport for the entire area is
in Glasgow (*see* Chapter 4), there are two airports within Argyll and the Isles. Both **Campbeltown** (on the mainland Kintyre
peninsula) and the island of Islay are served daily by **Loganair**
(tel. 041/889–3181) from Glasgow.

Arriving and Departing by Car, Train, and Bus

By Car The A85 reaches Oban, the main ferry terminal for Mull, and the A83 rounds Loch Fyne and heads down Kintyre to reach Kennacraig, the main ferry terminal for Islay. Farther down the A83 is Tayinloan, the ferry departure point for Ghigha. Brodick (Arran) is reached from Ardrossan on the Clyde coast (A8/A78 from Glasgow), and Rothesay (Bute) from Wemyss Bay (same roads from Glasgow).

By Train Oban (tel. 0631/63083) and Ardrossan (tel. 041/204–2844) are the main rail stations. All trains connect with ferries.

By Bus Daily bus service from Glasgow Buchanan Street Station to Mid-Argyll and Kintyre is available through **Scottish Citylink** (tel. 041/332–9191) and **Caledonian Express** (tel. 041/332–4100).

Getting Around

By Car and Ferry Negotiating this area can be quite easy, except in peak season, when the roads around Oban can be congested. There are some single-lane roads, especially on the east side of the Kintyre peninsula and on the islands. Car-ferry services to and from the main islands are operated by **Caledonian MacBrayne** (CalMac, main office is at the Ferry Terminal, Gourock, tel. 0475/33755). Other relevant mainland offices for this area include Oban (tel. 0631/62285), Ardrossan (tel. 0294/63470), Wemyss Bay (0475/520521), and Kennacraig (tel. 088073/253). **Western Ferries** (tel. 041/332–9766) operates the Islay–Jura ferry service.

By Train Aside from the main line to Oban, with stations at Dalmally, Loch Awe, Falls of Cruachan, Taynuilt, and Connel Ferry, there is no train service. You can travel from the pier head at **Craignure** on **Mull** to **Torosay** by narrow-gauge railway, a distance of about one mile.

By Bus The following companies operate in the area: **Arran Coaches** (Arran, tel. 0770/2121), **B. Mundell Ltd.** (Islay, tel. 049/684–273), **Bowman's Coaches** (Mull, tel. 06802/313), **C. MacLean** (Jura, tel. 049/682–221), **Cowal Motor Service** (Dunoon, tel. 0369/2088), **Midland Bluebird** (Oban and Lorne, tel. 0631/62856), and **West Coast Motor Service** (Mid-Argyll and Kintyre, tel. 0586/552319).

Guided Tours

Orientation The bus companies listed above offer orientation tours.

Special-Interest Bowman's Tours (*see above*) offers trips to Mull and Iona. **Gordon Grant Marine** (Staffa Ferries, Isle of Iona, tel. 06817/338) offers a "Three Isle" excursion to Mull, Iona, and Staffa. Other boat cruises are available on **Loch Etive Cruises** (from Taynuilt near Oban, tel. 08662/430, or call the tourist-information center at Oban) and **Sea Life Cruises** on the MV *Kittiwake* (from Dervaig on Mull, tel. 06884/223). Cruises to the islands and along the Argyll coast are offered on the MV *Falls of Lora* (tel. in winter, 041/339–0297; in summer, 0631/71–634) and can be tailored to your interests (bird-watching, diving, or sea angling, for example). **MacDougall's Tours** (Oban, tel. 0631/62133) runs a half-day sailing-and-touring expedition to Tobermory, Mull.

Exploring Argyll and the Isles

Orientation

On mainland-based tours Loch Fyne tends to get in the way. It is a long haul around the end of this fjordlike sea loch to reach Inveraray, a popular destination. If you enjoy islands, then the ferry services provided by Caledonian MacBrayne (*see* Getting Around by Car, *above*) make all kinds of linked tours possible. From Ardrossan, southwest of Glasgow, you can reach the island of Arran, then exit westward to Kintyre by a short ferry crossing. You can continue to the islands of Islay and Jura. From there a ferry can take you northeast to Oban. (All the ferries transport cars and pedestrians. Travelers can purchase *CalMac Hopscotch* tickets, which will reduce the cost of these island-hopping excursions.) The tours described below begin on the mainland but also highlight the main islands.

Highlights for First-time Visitors

Auchindrain Museum (*see* Tour 1)
Brodick Castle and Country Park (*see* Tour 2)
Crarae Gardens (*see* Tour 1)
Cruachan Dam Visitor Centre (*see* Tour 1)
Inveraray (*see* Tour 1)
Iona (*see* Tour 4)
Islay Woollen Mill (*see* Tour 3)
Kilchurn Castle (*see* Tour 1)
Kildalton Cross (*see* Tour 3)
Torosay Castle (*see* Tour 4)

Tour 1: Around Argyll

Numbers in the margin correspond to points of interest on the Argyll and the Isles map.

Just as it is impossible to avoid Fort William when touring the north, it is almost impossible to avoid **Oban** when touring this part of Scotland. Unlike Fort William, however, Oban has a legitimate waterfront and several ferry excursions from which to choose. It also has a more pleasant environment, though it does get busy during the peak season. Oban is a traditional Scottish resort where you can find ceilidhs and tartan kitsch, as well as late-night revelry in pubs and hotel bars. There is an inescapable sense, however, that just over the horizon, on the islands or down Kintyre, loom more peaceful and authentic environs. In short, Oban should be the starting point for your west-coast Scotland swing.

Take the main A85 east out of town. After about 2 miles a sign points north (left) to **Dunstaffnage Castle**, once an important stronghold of the MacDougalls. There are outstanding views from the ramparts across the **Sound of Mull** and the **Firth of Lorne**, a nautical crossroads of sorts once watched over by Dunstaffnage Castle and commanded by the galleys (in Gaelic, *birlinn*) of the Lords of the Isles. You should also be able to see the **Connel Bridge**, 2 miles farther east. This elegant structure once carried a branch railway along the coast but has since surrendered to the all-conquering automobile. When you reach the bridge, look below the narrows in the shadow of the girders to see if the Falls of Lora are running. Upstream is fjordlike **Loch Etive** (with cruises from Oban). The water leaving this deep, narrow loch foams and fights with the sea tides, creating turbulence and curious cascades.

2 Continue 6 miles on the A85 to Taynuilt. The **Bonawe Iron Furnace** is signposted to the left. No industrial activity takes place there now, but once the peaceful wooded slopes overlooked the smoky glow of furnaces burning local timber to make charcoal. The furnaces played a central role in the iron-smelting industry, which flourished here between 1753 and 1876. Today, Historic Scotland cares for the well-preserved buildings. *Bonawe, 12 mi east of Oban, off A85, tel. 031/244–3101. Admission: £1.50 adults, 80p children. Open Apr.–Oct., Mon.–Sat. 9:30–6, Sun. 2–6.*

Ardanaiseig House (*see* Dining and Lodging, *below*) sits nearby, down the B845 side road on the right. A sumptuous country-house hotel, Ardanaiseig has pleasant gardens planted with primroses and rhododendrons. There are also interesting views from the grounds, of Ben Cruachan with its high dam (*see below*). Continue through the narrow Pass of Brander to the **3** **Cruachan Dam Power Station Visitor Centre.** (The frequent railway-signal posts on the track above are actually avalanche warnings. If stones move the wires by the track, the signals fly to danger.) **Ben Cruachan** is the mountain that gave you the view from Dunstaffnage Castle; now you have no view at all, since you are almost underneath it. If you want to go underneath the mountain, stop at the visitor center for instructions. Actually a horseshoe-shape series of peaks, Ben Cruachan has a dam built within its confines. Water flows down from the dam to Loch Awe, the loch on your right, turning turbines along the way. All this becomes clear both at the visitor center and on a trip taken by minibus a half mile down a tunnel into a huge cavern or turbine hall. Nothing should stop you from taking this trip, underneath several cubic miles of mountain. *Off A85, 18 mi east of Oban, tel. 086/62–673. Admission: £1.50 adults, 50p children over 8 (under 8 free). Open Apr.–Oct., daily 9–4:30.*

By continuing east, you will reach Lochawe Station, where cruises (try the *Lady Rowena*) run from the pier. As an alternative you can visit **Kilchurn Castle,** a ruined fortress at the eastern end of Loch Awe. Park and cross the railway line, then walk across the grassy flats, where you will see more fine panoramas (complete with explanatory information boards) from airy vantage points amid the towers. Kilchurn Castle was built by Sir Colin Campbell of Glenorchy in the 15th century and was rebuilt in the 17th century. The Campbells had their original power base in this area. As the earls of Breadlabane they once owned vast tracts of the country stretching east. Nearby Glen Orchy, which can be found by referring to the castle panorama boards, was just one glen cleared of its inhabitants by the Campbells in the 19th century. *Northern tip of Loch Awe, 21 mi east of Oban, tel. 031/244–3101.*

There is a superb view from the **Duncan Ban Macintyre Monument** near Dalmally (*see* Off the Beaten Track, *below*). After the monument turn right on the A819, signposted Inveraray

(possibly the most misspelled place in the Highlands). **Loch Awe** is the longest loch in Scotland; the road soon leaves its pleasant banks, turning south to join the A83. This road is usually busy carrying traffic from Glasgow and Loch Lomond by way of the high pass of the **Rest and Be Thankful.** (Though not covered in this tour, many visitors come up Loch Lomond and head west by the A83. The Rest and Be Thankful is perhaps its most scenic point, an aptly named, almost Alpine pass among high green slopes and gray rocks.)

Time Out The simple decor—wood-top tables and fittings—lets you concentrate on the seafood at the **Loch Fyne Oyster Bar** (A83, on the approach to Loch Fyne). Local oysters and crisp white wine certainly are a far cry from roadside hamburgers and french fries.

Strone House Gardens, around the head of Loch Fyne (go left at the junction), is home to Scotland's tallest tree, a grand fir standing 200 feet high. *A83, 12 mi east of Inveraray, tel. 049/ 96–284. Admission: £1 adults, children free. Open Apr.–Oct., daily 9–9.*

If neither the oysters nor the tall trees have diverted you, make a right at the A819/A83 junction for **Inveraray.** Note on the approaches to this little town the ornate 18th-century bridgework that carries the road along the lochside. This is the first sign that Inveraray is not just a higgledy-piggledy assembly of houses. In fact much of Inveraray was designed as a planned town for the third duke of Argyll. The present Campbell duke's seat is **Inveraray Castle,** a grayish-green, turreted stone castle that can be seen through the trees on the right. Like Inveraray, the castle was built around 1743. Plenty of this powerful family's history can be seen on a tour. *½ mi north of Inveraray, tel. 0499/2203. Admission: £3 adults, £1.50 children, £2 senior citizens, £7.50 family ticket. Open Apr.–June, Mon.–Thurs., Sat. 10–12:30 and 2–5:30, Sun. 1–5:30; July and Aug., Mon.–Sat. 10–5:30, Sun. 1–5:30; Sept.–mid-Oct., Mon.–Thurs., and Sat., 10–12:30 and 2–5:30, Sun. 1–5:30.*

The **Combined Operations Museum** sits nearby, a reminder that this sleepy place among the hills was an important wartime training area. *Cherry Park, tel. 0499/2203. Admission: 90p adults, 50p children. Open mid-May–June and Sept., Mon.– Thurs., Sat. 10–1 and 2–6, Sun. 1–6; July and Aug., Mon.– Sat. 10–1 and 2–6, Sun. 1–6.*

Other attractions include the **Inveraray Jail,** one of the latest generation of visitor centers. The old town jail and courtroom now house realistic courtroom scenes, period cells, and all the other paraphernalia that enable the visitor to glimpse life behind bars in Victorian times. The Inveraray Bell Tower has also made its mark with visitors: The 126-foot granite tower houses Scotland's finest peal. *Center of Inveraray, tel. 0499/2381. Admission: £3.25 adults, £1.60 children, £1.75 senior citizens, £8.90 family ticket. Open daily 9:30–6 (last admission 5 PM).*

Continue along the loch southward beyond Inveraray to reach the **Auchindrain Museum.** Formally a communal tenancy farm, this 18th-century cooperative venture has been restored. The old thatched buildings provide information about early farming life in the Highlands. There is also an interpretation center and shop. *A83, 5½ mi south of Inveraray, tel. 049/95–235. Admis-*

sion: £2.20 adults, £1.40 children, £1.70 senior citizens, £6.80 family ticket. Open Apr., May, Sept., weekdays and Sun. 10–5; June–Aug., daily 10–5.

❼ Your next stop may be **Crarae Gardens,** farther south, which are occasionally likened to a wild valley in the Himalayas. There are paths through the plantings to suit trekkers of every fitness level. Magnolias and azaleas give the area a moist and lush atmosphere, undoubtedly aided by the local rainfall. *A83, 10 mi southwest of Inveraray, tel. 0546/86614 or 0546/86607. Admission: £2.50 adults, 70p children, £6.50 family ticket. Open daily 9–6; Visitor Centre open Apr.–Oct.*

❽ **Lochgilphead**, the area's main town, is at its aesthetic best when the tide is in: **Loch Gilp,** really a bite out of Loch Fyne, reveals acres of mud at low tide. Lochgilphead is really a little route center as the main road from Oban to the north joins here. Where you go from here will depend on how much time you have. If, for example, you're spending only a day in the area, then follow the suggestion for a short looping tour, given here. If you have more time, you can go down Kintyre to take in the little island of Ghigha (*see* Off the Beaten Track, *below*) or cross to Islay and Jura from Kennacraig, a short drive to the south.

The area to the south of Lochgilphead is known as **Knapdale,** an expanse of rolling hills sandwiched by parallel valleys that contain dense woodlands (*see* Castle Sween in Off the Beaten Track, *below*). Go south on the A83, then right on the B8024, signposted Kilberry. The road crosses some moorlands with views east to the hills of Cowal before dropping to Loch Caolisport. Here Knapdale scenery consists typically of gnarled and wind-twisted woodlands by the pebbly shore. The awe-inspiring spectacle of glittering sea and constantly changing island views from ashore compensate for the infrequent points of interest. Kilberry has ancient carved crosses signposted off the road, but you can see equally good examples later.

Time Out   Just when you least expect it, in the hinterland of rural Knapdale—you come upon an award-winning pub. **The Kilberry Inn** (B8024) serves savory food in an informal and friendly setting.

This loop then continues past Loch Stornoway, offering slightly disorienting views of the Arran Hills to the east: You have changed direction in your circle back toward the main road, which soon reaches Tarbert. The **Kennacraig** ferry terminal is nearby, and the **Putechan Lodge Hotel** (*see* Dining and Lodging, *below*), is about 20 miles farther south on Campbeltown Road. (Also *see* Mull of Kintyre in Off the Beaten Track, *below*.)

Return to Lochgilphead and take the A816 Oban road north. To **❾** discover the gentle delights of the **Crinan Canal,** turn left within 2 miles. This waterway was opened in 1801 to enable fishing vessels to avoid the long haul around the south-stretching peninsula Kintyre, thus allowing them to reach the Hebridean fishing grounds more easily. Shortly you will find yourself at the western end of the canal, where it drops to the sea in a series of lochs. This area can be a busy spot, with yachting enthusiasts strolling around and frequenting the coffee shop beside the Crinan Hotel.

To capture a glimpse of early Scottish history, return to the
⑩ main road (A816), turn north, and look for a sign to **Dunadd** (4
miles north of Lochgilphead). If you follow the track to a rocky
hump that rises out of the levels that lie around Crinan, you will
find—by clambering up the rock—a basin, a footprint, and an
outline of a boar carved on the smooth upper face of the knoll.
This breezy refuge was once the capital of the early kingdom of
Dalriada, founded by the first wave of Scots who migrated
from Ireland. *West of A816, 4 mi northwest of Lochgilphead,
tel. 031/244–3101. Admission free.*

Dunadd is only one of a number of early sites to be noted here.
For a short stretch almost every field has its set of standing
stones, stone circles, or cairns. The medieval grave slabs at
Kilmartin churchyard to the north are worth at least a few minutes of inspection.

⑪ A little farther north sits **Carnasserie Castle,** a tower house
with the peculiar distinction of having belonged to the writer of
the first book printed in Gaelic. The writer was John Carswell,
bishop of the Isles, who translated a text by the dour Scottish
reformer John Knox into Gaelic and published it in 1567. *Off
A816, 9 mi north of Lochgilphead, tel. 031/244–3101. Admission free.*

Time Out   The **Cuilfail Hotel** at Kilmelford (A816), formerly a coaching
inn, offers pleasant bar meals.

Before you reach Oban, one more side road may divert you. The
⑫ B844 leads to the island of **Seil** via the Bridge over the Atlantic.
This crossing is less spectacular than it sounds. The island is so
close to the mainland that a single-span bridge, built in 1791,
carries the road across. The small road crosses the island from
the bridge and ends at what was once a cluster of workers' cottages and is now a not-consistently-high-quality crafts village.
⑬ From Seil, visitors are ferried to neighboring **Easdale Island**
and its folk museum. Once Easdale and Seil were known as the
slate islands: extensive quarrying for roofing materials was un-
dertaken on both isles. *Admission to folk museum: £1 adults,
50p children. Open Apr.–Oct., Mon.–Sat. 10:30–5:30, Sun.
10:30–4:30.*

Tour 2: Arran

Many Scots, especially from Glasgow and the west, are well dis-
posed toward **Arran,** which reminds them of unhurried childhood holidays. In fact its cafés and boarding houses exude a
1950s mood, suggesting that this small isle has been caught in a
time warp. Only a few decades ago the Clyde estuary was the
coastal playground for the majority of the populace living in
Glasgow and the Clydeside conurbation. Their annual holiday
comprised a trip by steamer to any one of a number of Clyde
coast resorts, known as going *doon the watter* (down the water,
the estuary of the Clyde). Today the masses go to Spain. But,
like other parts of the Clyde, the island of Arran has for a long
time been associated with the healthy outdoor life.

While you are strolling on the deck of the ferry from Ardrossan
on the way to Arran, note the number of fellow travelers wearing walking boots, ready for the delights of **Goat Fell,** an im-

pressive peak (2,868 feet) that gives the island one of the most distinctive profiles of any in Scotland.

14 The ferry arrives in **Brodick** in less than an hour from Ardrossan, with the cone of Goat Fell and its satellites serving as an eye-catching northwestern backdrop. As you will have seen while crossing, the southern half of the island is less mountainous: The Highland Boundary Fault crosses just to the north of Brodick Bay.

Brodick, the largest township on the island, is really just a village, with a frontage spaciously set back from a promenade and beach. Head south (left) from the pier by the A841, a road that encircles the island and makes it difficult to get lost. A sign to Corriegills moments later indicates the first of many short walks, which you may take if you have time. A walk to Corriegills offers fine views over Brodick Bay.

Beyond dense conifer woods the A841 drops suddenly into **Lamlash,** with views offshore to steep-flanked Holy Island. This entire area has a breezy seaside holiday atmosphere. The only sobering note is the plaque on the three-boulder roadside monument, which recalls the Arran Clearances: a reminder that even this island, so close to the Lowlands, was subject to immigration and upheaval.

To reach the highest point accessible by car on the island, go through the village and turn right beside the bridge. This is known as **The Ross road.** It climbs steeply up a thickly planted valley, yielding fine views of Lamlash Bay.

The narrow road ends east of Sliddery with a return to the A841. Make a left by the church to reach nearby **Lagg.** This little community in a hollow beneath the sheltering trees sits peacefully by the banks of the Kilmory Water.

Time Out The **Lagg Hotel** (tel. 077087/255), an inn since 1791, is a warm place offering appetizing buffet lunches.

To work up a hardy appetite, you can either walk to **Kilmory Church** (which has the oldest occupied manse in Scotland) or follow a Historic Scotland sign, beyond the main road bridge over the river, to a chambered cairn, just a few minutes away. Were it not fenced off with an explanatory notice, you might think this ancient monument could pass for a random arrangement of boulders. The walk is worthwhile for its sea breezes and the bluebells encountered along the way.

Continue east on the A841 along the bottom end of the island past white-painted farmhouses and cottages. There are views across gently tilting fields to the steep hump of **Ailsa Craig,** offshore in the Firth of Clyde. Cheese connoisseurs will be pleased to know the creamery at Torrylinn makes Arran Cheddar from local milk. Beyond Kildonan the road twists north; the trees extend to the sea edge, where gannets seem to dive through the branches. The route soon reaches **Whiting Bay,** a string of hotels and well-kept property along the seafront. From there return to Brodick; on the way back you will enjoy scenic mountain views over the conifer spikes.

15 Brodick is the site of the **Isle of Arran Heritage Museum,** which documents the life of the island from ancient times to the present century. A number of buildings, including a cottage and *smiddy* (blacksmith's), are furnished in period and provide displays on prehistoric life, geology, farming, fishing, and many other aspects of the island's heritage. *Rosaburn, Brodick, tel. 0770/2636. Admission: £1 adults, 50p children, 75p senior citizens. Open Apr.–Oct., Mon.–Sat. 10–5.*

Just beyond the museum is the junction where String Road cuts across the island. Drive up String Road a short way to find a signpost to the right, for Glen Rosa. The road soon becomes undrivable, but visitors can walk through a long glen that offers a glimpse of the wild ridges that call so many outdoor enthusiasts to the island.

16 To find the island's most important draw for those other than the outdoor enthusiasts, return to the A841. **Brodick Castle and Country Park** is on the north side of Brodick Bay, its red sandstone cosseted by trees and parkland. Now under the auspices of the National Trust for Scotland, this former seat of the dukes of Hamilton has a number of rooms open to the public. Though the furniture, paintings, silver, and sporting trophies are opulent in their own right, the real attraction is the brilliantly colored rhododendrons, particularly in late spring and early summer. Though there are many unusual species, you will find the ordinarily deciduous yellow variety unmatched for its scent: your initial encounter with them is comparable to hitting a wall of perfume. The park, with a walled garden and an array of other shrubs, is graced by trees with massive trunks. *1½ mi north of Brodick pier, tel. 0770/2202. Admission to castle, gardens, and park: £3 adults, £1.50 children and senior citizens; admission to gardens and park: £1.50 adults, £1 children. Castle open Apr.–Sept., daily 1–5; Oct., Mon., Wed., and Sat. 1–5. Park and gardens open daily 10–sunset.*

Time Out The tearoom is an important feature of **Brodick Castle,** offering those visitors who have walked its many acres plunging their noses into every blossom a chance to quench their thirst. The menu includes an assortment of sandwiches and cakes.

Northward from Brodick the road is built along a raised beach platform, quite common in Scotland and caused by the lifting of the land after its burden of ice melted at the end of the Ice Age. Large, round boulders rest on softer sandstones in certain places on the shore. These stones, called *erratics*, were once carried by glaciers off the granite mountains that loom in the distance to your left as you approach **Corrie.** This brief string of settlements offers pottery and crafts items, another common feature on the island.

Farther on, at **Sannox,** a locale consisting of another cluster of houses, there is a sandy bay of ground granite, washed down from the mountainous interior. There are also outstanding views of the rugged hills of the interior, particularly the steep pyramid of **Cir Mhor.** The road then climbs away from the coast, although there is a good coastal walk from North Sannox. Look for red deer grazing above on the slopes of the green glen where the road runs.

17 The road rejoins the coast at **Lochranza.** This attractively situated settlement is yet one more community that focuses on crafts. The sheltered bay of Loch Ranza, spilling in shallows up the flat-bottomed glacial glen, is set off by a picturesque ruin. Situated on a low sand spit, **Lochranza Castle** is said to have been the landing place of Robert the Bruce, who returned from Rathlin Island in 1307 to start the campaign that won Scotland's independence. *Tel. 031/244–3101. Admission free. Open Apr.–Sept., Mon.–Sat. 9:30–6, Sun. 2–6; Oct.–Mar., Mon.–Sat. 9:30–4, Sun. 2–4.*

Make a right before the castle, to the north shore, then go left to the road end and park. A 10-minute welly walk over the raised, sheep-cropped beach brings you to **Hutton's Unconformity.** At the point where a tiny burn flows off the rounded hills above and crosses the brackeny flats between slope and rocky tide line, look for a change in rock color and angle. The geologist James Hutton noticed this aberration in 1787. A young red Devonian sandstone, roughly 400,000,000 years old, lies over a grayish-green, Cambrian schist 200,000,000 years its senior. This observation helped Hutton work out his theories about the age of the Earth. The rock differences are quite marked, more so at low tide.

Beyond Lochranza the raised beach backed by a cliff continues to make a scenic platform for the road. There are fine views across the sound to the long rolling horizon of Kintyre. At **⑱ Catacol,** immediately after the hotel, sit the **Twelve Apostles:** a row of fishermen's houses identical except for differences in the window shapes (so they can be recognized from offshore). Farther south you can see the stranded former sea caves by Dougarie Lodge and the notched hills up Glen Iorsa, on the left.

Near the scattered homesteads of **Machrie**—which has a popular beach—look for a Historic Scotland sign to the **Machrie ⑲ Moor Stone Circles.** The sign says the site is 1 mile farther, but it's a little farther than that. A well-surfaced track will take you to a grassy moor by a ruined farm, where you will be able to see small rounded granite-boulder circles and much taller, eerie, red-sandstone monoliths. The Machrie area is littered with these sites: chambered cairns, hut circles, and standing stones. Walking options are further enhanced at nearby **Tormore**, where a coastal trek leads to the **King's Cave.** A disheartened Robert the Bruce was inspired by the patience and determination of a web-spinning spider there, it is said, though the same claim is also made for arachnid-infested caves elsewhere in Scotland.

Continuing to **Blackwaterfoot,** you can return to Brodick by the String Road, unless you want to drive the only part of the island not otherwise covered in the tour, the main road south as far as the Ross road. If you decide to take Ross road, there are good views of Campbeltown Loch and the end of the Kintyre peninsula. Otherwise, to return to Brodick, turn left by the Kinloch Hotel, up the hill. There are more fine views of the granite complexities of Arran's hills: gray notched ridges beyond brown moor and, beyond the watershed, a vista of Brodick Bay. From this high point you roll down to Brodick, your starting point.

Tour 3: Islay and Jura

Islay   **Islay** has a personality distinct from that of the rest of the Hebrides. The western half, in particular, has large farms rather than crofts. A number of distilleries—the source of the island's delectable malt whiskies—provide jobs for the locals. Islay is also rated highly for its wildlife, especially its birds, including the rare chough—a crow with red legs and beak—and, in winter, its barnacle geese.

Islay's whiskey makers and bird-watchers have not always had a harmonious relationship. A local and national furor developed over distillers' proposals to strip peat from a part of the island that the geese use as a roost site. Conservation squabbles about forestry speculation and "second homes" aside, Islay seems less of a southerners' playground than some of the other islands.

20 The town of **Bowmore** is compact and about the same size (population 1,000) as the ferry port of Port Ellen, but is perhaps slightly better suited as a base for touring. Bowmore, which gives its name to the whiskey made in the distillery (founded 1779) by the shore, is a tidy town. Its grid pattern was laid out in 1768 by the local land owner Daniel Campbell of Shawfield. Bowmore's Main Street stretches from pierhead to the dominating parish church of 1767, built in an unusual circular design (so the devil could not find a corner to hide in). The town has a modest selection of accommodations and restaurants despite its small size.

Time Out Rub elbows with the locals at the **Harbour Inn** (Main St., tel. 049681/330), with its cheerfully noisy and cramped public bar frequented by off-duty distillery workers who are happy to exchange island gossip.

Many of Islay's best beaches—as well as wildlife and historical preserves—lie in its western half, contrasting with the southeast area, which is mainly an extension of Jura's inhospitable quartzite hills. Take the A846 north out of Bowmore (signposted Bridgend) to the A847 in order to skirt the sand flats at the head of Loch Indaal. Follow the loch shores all the way to Bruichladdich, which, like Bowmore, is the name of a malt whiskey, as well as a village with a distillery. You will **21** reach **Port Charlotte** a few minutes later. Above the road on the right, in a converted kirk, is the **Museum of Islay Life,** a haphazard but authentic and informative display of times past. *Tel. 049/685–358. Nominal charge. Open daily in high season (call for specific times); in winter open Sun. 2–5.*

For further exploration continue on the A847 into the wilder landscape of the **Rhinns of Islay.** At the southern end are the scattered cottages of **Portnahaven** and its **Port Wemyss** twin. You can return to Port Charlotte by the bleak unclassified road that loops westward and passes by the recumbent stone circle at Coultoon and the chapel at Kilchiaran before returning to Port Charlotte.

To get a glimpse of Islay's peerless western seascapes, make a left onto the B8018, north of Bruichladdich. After 2 miles turn left again onto a little road that meanders past Loch Gorm and ends close to **Machir Bay** and its superb (and probably deserted) sandy beach. Soon after you turn around to go back, make a right, which will lead you to the derelict kirk of **Kilchoman.** In the kirkyard are some interesting grave slabs and an excellent introduction to the island's wealth of stone carvings: two crosses of late-medieval date from the Iona school of carving. (There was another Scottish "school" in Kintyre.) From Kilchoman turn right and then left to circle

Loch Gorm, pausing as the road all but touches the coast at Saligo. It's worth a stroll beyond the former wartime camp to enjoy the view of some fine seascapes, especially if the wester-lies are piling up high breakers on the rock ridges.

On the return journey east there is a standing stone north of Ballinaby. Also for the keen-eyed, the sketchy remains of a Bronze Age settlement can be seen shortly afterward. To com-plete this exploration of the ancient history of Islay, turn right at the B8018, then left on the B8017. Take a left at Aoradh Farm on to a minor road that runs north along the west side of Loch Gruinart. The road soon brings you to **Kilnave** (Cill Naoimh on local maps). Kilnave's ruined chapel is associated with a dark tale in which a group of wounded Maclean clansmen were defeated in a nearby battle with the MacDonalds in 1598. The Macleans sought sanctuary in the chapel; their pursuers set its roof aflame, and the clansmen perished within. In the graveyard is a weathered, eighth-century carved cross.

Visitors are inevitably drawn to viewing the long reaches of **Loch Gruinart.** Dunes flank its sea outlet, and pale beaches rise out of the falling tides. For the best view return to the B8017, cross the flats at the head of the loch, and then go left and up its eastern shore. Park before a gate, where the road deteriorates. Those who appreciate wide skies, crashing waves, and lonely coast will continue on, possibly around the headland held to-gether with marram grass. From the far dunes there are views of Colonsay and Oronsay across Hebridean waters, on which plumes and fans of white spray rise from hidden reefs. The pri-ory on the island of Oronsay is barely distinguishable, as is its famous carved cross.

Another feature of the Gruinart landscape is unavoidable: The multitude of seals provide an unexpectedly noisy background. From your open-ended exploration of the long horizontals of Gruinart Bay, return to Bowmore by the B8017/A847/A846.

To discover what the south of the island has to offer, take the long straight of the A846 that passes the island airport just in-land from the endless sandy curve of Laggan Bay. Before you reach Port Ellen, go straight ahead to a minor road to Imeraval, then make a right at a junction and then a left. This takes you to the southern peninsula of **The Oa,** a region of caves rich in tales of smuggling. Visitors to The Oa usually go as far as the Mull of Oa, the tip, where there is a monument recalling the 650 men who lost their lives when the troopships *Tuscania* and *Otranto* went down nearby in 1918. Retracing your route east to Port Ellen, note the signpost to Kintra (before Imeraval); from there you can continue to the sands of Laggan Bay.

Port Ellen is a sturdy community, founded in the 1820s, with much of its architecture still dating from the 19th century. It has a harbor, a few shops, and some inns, but not enough com-mercial development to mortgage its personality. The A846 continues eastward, passing more names known to the malt-whiskey connoisseur: the whiskey of the **Laphroaig distillery—** which offers tours—is perhaps one of the most distinctive of the local whiskies, with a tangy, peaty, seaweed/iodine flavor. *1½ mi along road to Ardbeg from Port Ellen, tel. 0496/2418 or 0496/2393. Tours Mar.–Oct. 10:30 and 2; Nov.–Feb. by ap-pointment. Phone in advance to arrange a tour.*

After Ardbeg the A846 becomes narrower and passes through a pleasantly rolling, partly wooded landscape. The reason for taking this route east is not to take a scenic tour of distillery premises, but to see the finest carved cross anywhere in Scotland: the eighth-century **Kildalton Cross.** Carved from a single slab of epidiorite rock, this ringed cross is encrusted on both sides with elaborate designs in the style of the Iona school. Interesting early grave slabs from the 12th and 13th centuries can also be seen in the yard around the chapel, which stands down a lonely side road, signposted from Ardbeg. From Kildalton retrace your route to Bowmore.

From Bowmore take the A846 north (following signs for Port Askaig) through Bridgend. Hardly a mile beyond, you will see a sign for the **Islay Woollen Mill.** Set in a wooded hollow by the river, the mill has a shop selling high-quality products that are woven on site. There is also a riveting selection of working machinery to inspect.

Back on the main road again, you will find yourself traveling into a corridor of greenery and farmland. Bands of limestone run through this pleasant landscape and contribute to the intermittent richness of crops and vegetation. The Paps of Jura can be seen, gray and ridged on the skyline as if they were an extension of Islay.

If time permits, before reaching Port Askaig (a fairly frequent ferry service runs from here to Jura), you may wish to explore a side road to the left a mile beyond Ballygrant. To get to **Loch Finlaggan,** make a left and then drive through a gate. There is not, at first sight, a great deal to see. But the little island on the loch, with its scanty and overgrown traces of early buildings, was the council seat of the Lords of the Isles. This former western power base of the Clan Donald threatened the sovereignty of the Stuart monarchs of Scotland in its heyday: a reminder of how independent the Highlands were in those times. A cottage interpretative center has recently opened nearby; check with the tourist-information center for opening times.

Return to the main road (A846) and continue driving northeast. Note that just beyond Keills is another side road that will take you for a pleasant ride along the coast until you come to a turning space and car park at the **Bunnahabhain Distillery,** which sits on an attractive shore site (tel. 049/684–646, visits by appointment). There are impressive views of Jura on the way. Then retrace the route to the main road, going left then steeply downhill to the tiny ferry community by the pier.

Jura Although it is possible to meet an Islay native in a local pub, such an event is statistically less likely on **Jura,** with its one road, one distillery, one hotel, and six sporting estates. In fact visitors have a better chance of bumping into one of the island's 5,000 red deer, which outnumber the human population by at least 20 to 1. The island has a much more rugged look than Islay, with its profiles of the Paps of Jura, a hill range at its most impressive when basking in the rays of a west-coast sunset.

Having crossed the Sound of Islay by ferry from Port Askaig (it takes just a few minutes), explorers will find it easy to choose which road to take: Jura has only one. Apart from the initial stretch it is all single-lane. The A846 starts off below one of the many raised beaches then climbs across poor moorland, providing scenic views across the Sound of Jura. Look for the standing stone, right, then note the ruined **Claig Castle** on an island just offshore. The Lords of the Isles built it to control the sound. Beyond the farm buildings of Ardfin, you reach **Jura House** in the woodlands, with its sheltered garden walks and fine views. *Tel. 049/682–315. Admission to gardens: £1.50 adults, children free. Open daily 9–5.*

㉗ Beyond the Jura House the road turns northward for **Craighouse,** across open moorland with scattered forestry blocks and the faint evidence, in the shape of parallel ridges, of the original inhabitants' lazy beds or strip cultivation. The original settlements were cleared with the other parts of the Highlands when the island became more of a sheep pasture and deer forest. The road soon drops down to the community of **Craighouse,** home to the island's only distillery.

Time Out The **Jura Hotel** (tel. 049/682–243), in spite of its monopoly, genuinely welcomes its guests and can be relied on for high-quality accommodations and food.

㉘ The aptly named **Small Isles Bay** has a superb strip of beach to the north of Craighouse. As the road climbs away from the bay, the little cottage above the burn is a reminder of the history of this island: The cottage is the only survivor of a village with a population of 56 that was destroyed in 1841. Ironically, a sheep **fank** (fold) farther up the burn shows what happened to the stones of the demolished cottages. Although the landscapes of Jura seem devoid of life, they are in fact populated with many ghosts, most of which are overlooked by the casual visitor.

Beyond the River Corran the road climbs, offering austere views of the Paps, with their long quartzite screes and of the fine, though usually deserted, anchorage in the scoop of Lowlandman's Bay. The next section of road is more hemmed in and runs to **Lagg,** formerly a ferry-crossing point on the old cattle-driving road between here and Feolin. Beyond Lagg, the sea views are blocked by conifer plantings. Views of fjordlike **Loch Tarbet,** westward to the left, are at their best beside the forestry plantation a little farther on. At this point the road leads through a stretch of rough, uninhabited landscape. A gate and cattle grid by **Ardlussa** to the north mark the start of a Site of Special Scientific Interest in a shady oakwood. The coast here is rocky and unspoiled. Choose your own picnic site, but be sure to park sensibly. Yellow flag (a Scottish iris), bracken, strands of crisp seaweed on the salty grass, and background bird song from the mossy woods make this an idyllic stretch when the sun shines. Try not to be too loud: you don't want to distract the area's resident otter population.

The last house you will see is at **Lealt,** where you cross the river. Only a little way beyond this point the tarmac ends, rather abruptly, with a turning space paved into the hill. Ordinary cars should not attempt to go any farther on the remainder of this trail, though jeeps, rovers, and other high-clearance vehicles can make it through. The track beyond the surfaced road continues for another 5 miles to **Kinuachdrach,** a settlement that once served as a crossing point to Scarba and the mainland. The coastal footpath to Corryvreckan lies beyond, over the bare moors. This area has two enticements: The first, for fans of George Orwell, is the house of **Barnhill,** where the author wrote *1984;* the second, for wilderness enthusiasts, is the whirlpool of the **Corryvreckan** and the unspoiled coastal scenery.

To return to the ferry that will take you to Islay, you have no choice but to retrace your route. If time permits, however, the tearoom at Craighouse is worth a visit.

Tour 4: The Isle of Mull

It's possible to spend a long weekend on Mull and not meet a single resident who was born north of Manchester, England. Though Mull certainly has an indigenous population, the island is often referred to as the Officers' Mess because of its popularity with retired military men. It has a thriving tourist industry, with several thousand visitors making their way across the Ross of Mull to Iona, cradle of Scottish Christianity and ancient burial site of the kings of Scotland.

㉙ Most visitors arrive at **Craignure** by way of Oban, but you should seriously consider the short ferry crossing from Lochaline on the mainland to **Fishnish,** a little west of Craignure. This summer-only service is first-come, first-served.

㉚ Either ferry will leave you close to Mull's two best-known castles, **Torosay** and **Duart. Torosay Castle** is probably more fun. It also has the novelty of a steam-and-diesel service on a narrowgauge railway, which takes 20 minutes to run from the pier at Craignure to Torosay's grounds. Scottish baronial in style, Torosay has a friendly air. Visitors have the run of much of the house, which is full of intrigue and humor by way of idiosyncratic information boards and informal family albums. The main feature of the castle's gardens—a gentle blend of formal and informal—is its Italian statue walk. *A849, 1½ mi southeast of Craignure, tel. 06802/421. Admission to castle and gardens: £3.50 adults, £1.50 children, £2.75 students and senior citizens; admission to gardens: £1.50 adults, £1 children, senior citizens, and students. Castle open mid-Apr.–mid-Oct., daily 10:30–5:30; gardens open summer, daily 9–7; winter, daily sunrise–sunset.*

㉛ The energetic can walk along the shore from Torosay to **Duart Castle;** if you're driving use the A849. This ancient Maclean seat was ruined by the Campbells in 1691 but bought and restored by Sir Fitzroy Maclean in 1911. *Off A849, tel. 068/02–309. Admission: £2.50 adults, £1.50 children. Open May–Sept., daily 10:30–6.*

Beyond Duart Castle the double-lane road narrows as it continues southwest, touched by sea inlets at Lochs Don and Spelve. Gray and green are the most prevalent colors of the interior, with vivid grass and high rock faces in Glen More. These stepped rock faces, the by-product of ancient lava flows, reach their ㉜ highest point in **Ben More,** the only island *munro* outside Skye. (A munro is a Scottish mountain over 3,000 feet high.) Its high, bald slopes are prominent by the time you reach the road junction at the head of Loch Scridain. Stay on the A849 for a pleasant drive the length of the **Ross of Mull,** a wide promontory with scattered settlements. Good views abound on the right, of the dramatic cliff ramparts of Ardmeanach, the stubbier promontory to the north. The National Trust for Scotland cares for ㉝ the rugged stretch of coast known as the **Burg,** which is home to a 40,000,000-year-old fossil tree (at the end of a long walk from the B8035, signposted left off the A849).

The well-used A849 continues through the village of **Bunessan** and eventually ends in a long car-park opposite the houses of **Fionnphort.** The vast parking space is made necessary by the popularity of the nearby island of **Iona,** on which visitors do not need cars. Ferry service is frequent in summer months.

The fiery and argumentative Irish monk Columba chose Iona for the site of a monastery in AD 563 because it was the first place he landed from which he could not see Ireland. Christianity had been brought to Scotland (Galloway) by Saint Ninian in 397, but until Saint Columba's church was founded, the word had not spread widely among the ancient northerners, called Picts. Iona was the burial place of the kings of Scotland until the 11th century. It survived repeated Norse sackings and finally fell into disuse around the time of the Reformation. Restoration work began at the turn of this century, and later, in 1938, the **Iona Community** was founded. Today the restored buildings serve as a spiritual center under the jurisdiction of the Church of Scotland. The ambience of the complex is a curious amalgam of the ancient and the earnest. But beyond the restored cloisters the most mystifying aspect of all is the island's ability to absorb visitors and still feel peaceful—a phenomenon often remarked upon by visitors. Most folk only make the short walk from the ferry pier by way of the nunnery to the abbey. *Tel. 06817/404. Abbey gift and bookshop open Mon.–Sat. 10–5, Sun. noon–5; abbey coffee house open Mar.–Oct., Mon.–Sat. 11–4:30, Sun. noon–4.*

On your return to Mull retrace your route eastward and look for a sign on the right to Carsaig as you approach the head of Loch Scridain. This route takes you to the remote south coast. From the pierhead at the tiny settlement a rough path meanders west below lava cliffs to the impressive **Carsaig Arches.** Taking on the arches is a separate excursion reserved for the agile.

After your foray to the arches take the B8035 at Loch Scridain. The road rises away from the loch to the conifer plantations and green slopes of **Gleann Seilisdeir.** Tiroran House (*see* Dining and Lodging, *below*), a cossetting country house and perhaps the best hotel on Mull, is signposted left, which is also the way to the Burg. The main road through the glen breaches the stepped cliffs and drops to the shore, offering inspiring views of the island of Ulva guarding Loch na Keil. This stretch of the B8035, with splinters of rock from the heights strewn over it in places, feels remote. The high ledges eventually give way (not literally) to vistas of the screes of Ben More.

Continue to skirt the coast by way of the B8073, and you will enjoy a succession of fine coastal views with Ulva in the foreground. After crossing the headland that leads to Calgary Bay, plant lovers may wish to visit the **House of Treshnish,** with its exotic shrubs, though the paths were greatly overgrown on a recent visit. *B8073, 14 mi from Tobermory. Small admission charge. Open Apr.–Oct., daily 8 AM–9PM.*

Beyond Calgary Bay the landscape is gentler, as the road leads to the village of **Dervaig.** Just before Dervaig the **Old Byre** is signposted.

Time Out The wholesome catering at the restaurant at the **Old Byre** heritage center (signposted just before Dervaig) certainly will be appreciated by weary travelers, particularly those who have driven all the way from the Ross of Mull. Thick and hearty homemade soups and real oatcakes head the menu.

In Dervaig the Mull Little Theatre (*see* The Arts and Nightlife, *below*) offers a varied program and claims the record as the smallest professional theater in the United Kingdom. After the small town the road leads through woodlands to **Tobermory.** Founded as a fishing station, this community gradually declined, hastened by the arrival of the railroad station at Oban, which took away fishing traffic. However, the brightly painted crescent of 18th-century buildings gives Tobermory a Mediterranean look.

Time Out   The chintz-clad **Tobermory Hotel** (tel. 0688/2091), located on the waterfront, can be relied upon for lunch or a snack and dependable accommodations.

To return to the ferry, make your way southward on the A848, which yields pleasant, though unspectacular, views across to Morven on the mainland. On the coast just beyond **Aros,** look back and across the river flats for a view of the ruined 13th-century **Aros Castle.** Continue through Salen to either Fishnish for Morven or Craignure for Oban.

Argyll and the Isles for Free

Crinan Canal (*see* Tour 1)
Dunadd Fort (*see* Tour 1)
Kilchurn Castle (*see* Tour 1)
Kildalton Cross (*see* Tour 3)
Loch Gruinart (*see* Tour 3)
Machrie Moor standing stones (*see* Tour 2)
Whiskey distillery tours on Islay (*see* Tour 3)

What to See and Do with Children

The Argyll Wildlife Park has 60 acres with extensive collections of wildfowl and other Scottish wildlife. *Dalchenna, Inveraray on A83, tel. 0499/2284. Admission: £2.95 adults, £1.25 children, £2.75 senior citizens. Open daily 9:30–6. (Tearoom open Apr.–Oct.)*

Auchindrain Old Farming Township (*see* Tour 1)

Cruachan Dam Power Visitor Centre and Tour (*see* Tour 1)

Ganavan Sands Leisure Centre (tel. 0631/66479) has sandy beaches, indoor game rooms, an outdoor play area, a boating pool, and donkey rides. To get there, follow the road from the center of Oban, where the promenade starts.

Inveraray Jail (*see* Tour 1)

Lady Rowena Steam Launch runs an Edwardian peat-fired steamboat that cruises Loch Awe from BR station pier at Lochawe on A85. *Tel. 08382/440–449. Reservations can be made on the spot or in advance.*

Mull and West Highland Narrow Gauge Railway (*see* Tour 4)

The Sea Life Centre displays native marine life in a spacious aquarium. One of the most entertaining places in Argyll, the center also has a shop and a café. *On the A828, Barcaldine, 11 mi north of Oban, tel. 0631/72386. Admission: £3.75 adults, £2.75 children, £3.25 senior citizens. Open Mar.–June and Sept.–Nov., daily 9–6; July and Aug., daily 9–7; Dec.–Feb., weekends 9–6. Call to check opening hours in winter season.*

A World in Miniature has an exhibit on a ½ scale, with miniature rooms and furniture. *North pier, Oban, tel. 085/26–272 or 0631/66300. Admission: £1.50 adults, £1 children. Open Easter–mid-Oct., Mon.–Sat. 10–5, Sun. noon–5.*

Off the Beaten Track

Castle Sween, the oldest stone castle on the Scottish mainland (12th century), sits in a rocky sea-edge setting 15 miles southwest of Lochgilphead. The castle is reached by an unclassified road from Crinan yielding outstanding views of the Paps of Jura across the sound. There are also some attractive white sand beaches here.

Duncan Ban Macintyre Monument (Monument Hill) was erected in honor of the Gaelic poet Duncan Ban Macintyre (1724–1812), sometimes referred to as the Robert Burns of the Highlands. The monument is situated not far from the village of Dalmally, just east of the top end of Loch Awe in Argyll. From there, follow an old road running southwest toward the banks of Loch Awe. At the road's highest point, often called Monument Hill, the round, granite monument can be seen. The view from here is one of the finest in Argyll, taking in Ben Cruachan and the other peaks nearby, as well as Loch Awe and its scattering of islands.

Island of Ghigha is a delectable Hebridean island, barely 5 miles long, sheltered in a frost-free, sea-warmed climate between Kintyre and Islay. The isle is noted for the **Achamore House Gardens.** It is possible to take the ferry (a 20-minute trip), walk to the gardens, and return to the mainland, all on a short day-trip, but there are good accommodations on the island. *Tel. 058/35–254 or 058/35–267. Admission to gardens: £2 adults, £1 children. Open daily 10–dusk.*

Famous in song, the **Mull of Kintyre** is, in reality, a road to the lighthouse at the tip of Kintyre beyond Campbeltown. The narrow road crosses moors and sheep pastures. There is a parking place before the road suddenly dips to reach the lighthouse tower, placed well down the steep slope that tilts into the sea. There is one caveat, however. Do not go down the hill. The best sunset views are from the adjacent moors. From this point you can see Ireland quite plainly.

Shopping

It must be said that in this predominantly rural area, shopping is not a highlight for visitors, although the day-to-day needs of the local population are well cared for. Nonetheless, there are several interesting crafts outlets; the islands, in particular, offer many opportunities to sample and purchase fine island whiskies. Starting in **Oban,** the **Oban Glassworks** (part of Caithness Glass, Lochavullin Estate, tel. 0631/63386) offers factory tours and a well-stocked factory shop.

Also worth a visit is the **Highbank Porcelain Pottery** (Highbank Industrial Estate, Lochgilphead, tel. 0546/602044), where visitors can watch slip casting, hand painting, and firing. Highbank also has a shop that sells pottery animals (including reasonably priced seconds).

Another attractive memento of your visit to the area may be a photographic print, framed or unframed, from the **Scotland in Colour Photo-Gallery** (1 Crombie St., Oban, tel. 0631/65493).

East of Oban, in **Taynuilt,** stop at **Inverawe Fisheries and Smokery** (tel. 08662/446, open daily 9–5): The smoked salmon and other fish produced and served on the premises are impractical to take home (at least abroad), but they make a delicious picnic.

Also recommended are the products of **Loch Fyne Oysters** (Clachan Farm, on the A83, tel. 04996/264). You can sample them in the oyster bar, which serves all types of seafood and game products, before buying them in the adjacent Seafood Shop.

Farther down the A83, at **Inveraray,** is a fine selection of shops, including **Cottage Antiques** (The Post Office, tel. 0499/2407). You can buy Scottish crafts at the shop within **Inveraray Jail** (*see* Tour 1 in Exploring Argyll and the Isles, *above*). **Campbeltown** is the center for local shopping requirements on the Kintyre peninsula. Here you will also find **Oystercatcher Crafts and Gallery** (10 Hall St., tel. 0586/553070), with original paintings, woodcarvings, and knitwear.

A few miles north, at **Carradale,** is **Wallis Hunter Design** (The Steading, tel. 05833/683), which makes gold and silver jewelry, and at **Tarbert** shoppers will discover **Earra Gael Craft Shop** (The Weighbridge, tel. 0880/820428), with locally produced crafts and knitwear. You can find an original gift at **Clachan,** south of Tarbert on the A83, where **Fiadh Mor Wood & Antler** (Battery Point, tel. 08804/226) specializes in wood-turning and products made from antlers and cattle horns. Walking sticks, carvings, and cutlery are also sold. Clachan is also the home of **Ronachan Silks** (Ronachan Farmhouse, tel. 08804/242), which produces distinctive jewel-color scarves, cushion covers, and clothing.

On **Islay** you'll be spoiled by the sheer number of distilleries from which to choose. Most of them welcome visitors by appointment: **Bruichladdich** (Port Charlotte, tel. 049/685–221), **Caol Ila** (Port Askaig, tel. 049/684–207), **Bunnahabhain** (Port Askaig, tel. 049/684–646), **Isle of Jura** (Craighouse, Jura, tel. 049/682–240), **Laphroaig** (Port Ellen, tel. 0496/2418), **Bowmore** (School St., Bowmore, tel. 049/681–441), and **Lagavoulin** (Port Ellen, tel. 0496/2250). Their delicious products, characterized by a peaty taste, can be purchased at off-license shops on the island, at local pubs, or at those distilleries that have shops. **The Islay Woollen Mill** (Bridgend, tel. 049681/563) is also worth a visit, not only for its shop, but for its mill tour. Beside the usual tweed lengths, the mill has a distinctive range of hats, caps, and clothing made from its own cloth.

Arran's shops are particularly well stocked with island-produced goods: **Arran Aromatics** (The Pier, Brodick, tel. 0770/2426), makes soaps, creams, and other beauty products from natural ingredients, and **Arran Provisions** (The Old Mill, Lamlash, tel. 0770/6606) is famous for its mustards, preserves, and marmalades. **Crafts of Arran** (Whiting Bay, tel. 0770/7251) prides itself on stocking craftwork produced in Arran. **Corriecraft and Antiques** (Corrie, tel. 0770/81–661) also stocks craftwork (though it may come from different parts of Scotland), together with a carefully chosen mix of small antiques and curios. At **Machrie** (near the stone circles at Machrie Moor) shoppers frequent the **Old Byre Showroom** (Auchencar Farm, tel. 0770/84–227), which sells sheepskin goods, locally hand-knit jumpers, leather goods, and tweeds.

Mull and **Iona** have one or two surprises, the biggest being the excellent antiquarian and secondhand bookshop on the tiny island of Iona (The Old Printing Press Building, St. Columba Hotel, Iona, tel. 068/17–304). The shop at the Abbey is also worth a visit, for its selection of Celtic-inspired gift items. Near **Dervaig**, on Mull, do not miss the **Old Byre Heritage Centre's craft shop** (nor the restaurant with delicious home baking). The shop's inventory is definitely more extensive than most and includes locally made, as well as other Scottish-produced items.

Sports and Fitness

Bicycling Take your waterproofs! Bicycles can be rented from **Argyll Hotel** (Argyll St., Dunoon, tel. 0369/2059), **Brown's Shop** (Main St., Tobermory, Isle of Mull, tel. 0688/2020), and **Oban Cycle Hire** (D. Grahams, 9–15 Combie Street, Oban, tel. 0631/62069). Arran is a popular island for cycling, with a large number of bicycle-rental shops, including **Brodick Cycles** (Roselynn, Brodick, tel. 0770/2460) and **Mr. Bilsland** (The Gift Shop, Brodick, Isle of Arran, tel. 0770/2272). Other cycle shops in the area covered by this chapter include **Islay Leisure** (Bowmore Post Office, Bowmore, tel. 049/681–366) and **Tarbert Leisure Sports Ltd.** (The Columba Hotel, Tarbert, Argyll).

Fishing Local tourist-information centers (*see* Important Addresses and Numbers in Essential Information, *above*) can provide you with information. Local fishing literature identifies at least 50 fishing sites on lochs and rivers for game fishing and at least 20 coastal settlements suited for sea angling.

Golf The area has about two dozen golf courses; notably scenic examples are the outstanding courses on Bute, as well as the fine coastal links, of which Machrihanish near Campbeltown is the most famous (tel. 058/681–213; 18 holes, 6,228 yards, SSS 70). The local tourist-information centers can provide detailed leaflets.

Pony Trekking Explorers will find riding outlets on the mainland and on the islands: **Achnalarig Farm and Stables** (Glen Cruitten, Oban, Argyll, tel. 0631/62745), **Ballivicar Pony Trekking** (Ballivicar Farm, Port Ellen, Islay, tel. 0496/2251), **Castle Riding Centre and Argyll Trail Riding** (Brenfield, Ardrishaig, Argyll, tel. 0546/603274), **Coilessan Trekking and Riding Centre** (Ardgartan, by Arrochar, Argyll, tel. 03012/523), **Isle of Arran Riding Holidays** (Woodside, Balmichael, Isle of Arran, tel. 0770/86230), **Lettershuna Riding Centre** (Appin, Argyll, tel. 0631/73227), and **Rothesay Riding Centre** (Canada Hill, Rothesay, Isle of Bute, tel. 0700/504971).

Water Sports The assortment of sea, island, and sea-loch make this a popular area for a variety of water sports. Local operators include **Creran Moorings** (Barcaldine, near Oban, tel. 0631/72265),

Linnhe Marine Watersports Centre (Lettershuna, Appin, Argyll, tel. 0631/73227), and **Oban Marine Jet Hire** (Ganavan Sands Leisure Centre, Oban, tel. 0631/64176).

Dining and Lodging

Dining

This part of Scotland is not usually considered a great gastronomic center. You can expect meals to be plain and simple, but the servings are generous. Still, the food ingredients used in dishes are of good quality and are locally produced. Fish, fresh from the sparkling lochs and sea, could hardly be better. The region has only a few fine restaurants of distinction. In the rural districts, your best bet is to choose a hotel or guest house that can provide a decent evening meal as well as breakfast.

Highly recommended restaurants are indicated by a star ★.

Category	Cost*
Very Expensive	over £40
Expensive	£30–£40
Moderate	£15–£30
Inexpensive	under £15

*per person, including first course, main course, dessert, and VAT; excluding drinks

Lodging

Accommodations in Argyll and the Isles range from château-like hotels to modest inns. The traditional provincial hotels and small coastal resorts have been modernized and equipped with all the necessary comforts, yet they retain the charm that comes with older buildings and their sense of personalized service. Away from these areas, however, your options are more restricted, and your best overnight option, with some exceptions, is usually a modest guest house offering bed, breakfast, and an evening meal.

Highly recommended hotels are indicated by a star ★.

Category	Cost*
Very Expensive	over £120
Expensive	£100–£120
Moderate	£80–£100
Inexpensive	under £80

*All prices are for two people sharing a double room, including service, breakfast, and VAT.

Brodick
Dining and Lodging
★ **Auchrannie Country House Hotel.** Undoubtedly, the jewel in the crown of Arran's hotel base is in Brodick. Determined to leave behind the relatively unsophisticated and safe chips-and-crusted-ketchup school of cookery still found in a few establish-

ments, the Auchrannie offers not just interesting cuisine but sophisticated leisure facilities. Island residents have finally realized that the *doon the watter* Glasgow Fair crowds are gone forever and that higher standards are needed to attract a new clientele. Recently refurbished using distinctive colors and fabrics, the bedrooms are spacious and comfortable, and the public areas have plenty of choice, including a delightful dining room housed in a conservatory projecting into the garden. The cuisine can vary, but, at its best, the Taste of Scotland menu is inventive in incorporating local produce, particularly seafood (try the marinaded scallops) into its dishes. *Auchrannie Rd., Isle of Arran, tel. 0770/2234. 28 rooms with bath. Facilities: 2 restaurants, fitness center, pool, beauty salon, boutique. MC, V. Inexpensive–Moderate.*

Campbeltown
Dining and Lodging
★

Putechan Lodge. A relaxing atmosphere, good food, and thoroughly comfortable surroundings make this one of the most pleasant hotels in Scotland. The sitting room used to be the private sitting room of the owners and still feels like it, with beautiful antique furniture. The bar area has a practical and handsome stone-flag floor and a log fire, and the bedrooms—within earshot of the sea—are also furnished with handsome oak antiques. The dining room, off the bar, is intimate without being cramped, and the menu features local produce, competently and unpretentiously prepared. *Bellochantuy, by Campbeltown, Argyll, tel. 05832/323. 12 rooms, 10 with bath. DC, MC, V. Restaurant: Moderate–Expensive; hotel: Inexpensive.*

Dervaig
Dining and Lodging

Druimard Country House and Theatre Restaurant. An attractive Victorian house on the outskirts of the village, the Druimard has loch and glen views over the River Bellart. The restaurant is elegantly furnished and offers an original menu with several vegetarian options. Smoked venison with mango coulis or spiced mushrooms with almond topping are popular dishes, and the vegetables are carefully prepared. Bed-and-breakfast accommodations are also available. *Dervaig, Isle of Mull, Argyll, tel. 06884/345. MC, V. Reservations advised. 6 rooms, 4 with bath. Closed Nov.–Feb. Restaurant: Moderate; hotel: Inexpensive.*

Kentallen
Dining and Lodging
★

Holly Tree. Railway buffs will enjoy this converted Edwardian railway station, complete with some of its original fixtures and fittings, which have been carefully extended over the onetime platform to create a spacious restaurant with superb views of Loch Linnhe. Seals can be seen from your dinner table, as can memorable sunsets over the Ardgour mountains. The hotel's elegant bedrooms are furnished with comfort and modern restraint. The food is generally of a high standard, though appetizers and puddings may hit the mark more often than the main courses. *Kentallen, Appin, Argyll, tel. 063174/292. Reservations required. Jacket and tie advised. 12 rooms with bath. MC, V. Inexpensive–Moderate.*

Kilchrenan
Dining and Lodging
★

Ardanaiseig House. Set on the shores of Loch Awe and framed by rhododendron blossoms in May and June (the gardens are famous), this excellent, privately run hotel reflects the interior-design expertise of June Brown, one of the proprietors. All the bedrooms, which vary in size, have been decorated individually in traditional style, and the public rooms, with an abundance of chintz and polished wood, are just as comfortable. The food more than matches the decor, featuring five imaginative courses prepared with local ingredients; home-smoked scallops, fresh fruit from the garden, pickled salmon, and wood pigeon are featured. *Kilchrenan, near Taynuilt, Argyll, tel. 08663/333. 14 rooms with bath. AE, DC, MC, V. Closed Nov.–mid-Apr. Expensive–Very Expensive.*

Knipoch
Dining and Lodging

The Knipoch Hotel. With a history dating to the 16th century, this sprawling Georgian-style house on the banks of Loch Feochan has been extensively modernized in recent years. Although the hotel offers views of the countryside, the food will undoubtedly command your attention first. The owners smoke their own fish, which they catch themselves, and specialize in preparing pickles and marinades. The menu reflects the quality of local Scottish produce and, though limited in choice, is complemented by an eclectic wine list. *Near Oban, Argyll, tel. 08526/251. 17 rooms with bath. AE, DC, MC, V. Closed mid-Nov.–mid-Feb. Expensive–Very Expensive.*

Lochaline
Dining and Lodging

Sruthan House. Convenient for the "back door" ferry to Mull, this period guest house spread over 2 acres of grounds is noted for its excellent cooking. When the tables are free, the dining room is open to nonguests. The tab for dinner and accommodation is reasonable and a good value. Dinner can be as large as five courses, and the homemade soups, moist salmon steaks, and churned-on-the-premises ice creams are unforgettable. Locally grown vegetables are also featured on the menu. Antiques and velvet furnishings add to the period atmosphere of the house. *Lochaline, Morvern, tel. 0967/421632. Dinner reservations required. 3 rooms (no private facilities). No credit cards. Inexpensive.*

Oban
Lodging

Columba Hotel. Situated between the quayside and the town, this lovely hotel offers modern elegant public areas and attractive bedrooms. There are two bars, one with a cheerful nautical theme, and a cozy coffee shop open from 10 AM to 6 PM. *North Pier, Corran Esplanade, PA34 5QD, tel. 0631/62183. 49 rooms with bath. Facilities: in-house movies. AE, DC, MC, V. Moderate.*

Port Askaig
Dining and Lodging

Port Askaig Hotel. This modernized drovers inn by the roadside overlooks the Sound of Islay and the island of Jura. The hotel, whose grounds extend to the shore, is conveniently located near the ferry terminal. Accommodations are comfortable without being luxurious, and the food is well prepared, using home-grown produce, but is not very imaginative. *Port Askaig, Isle of Islay, Argyll, tel. 049/684–245. 9 rooms, 4 with bath. No credit cards. Inexpensive.*

Strachur
Dining and Lodging

Creggans Inn. This traditional inn overlooking Loch Fyne dates to the 17th century. Visitors can enjoy an appetizing lunch in the bar or a more formal dinner in the inn's attractive dining room, replete with views of the water. Once again, local produce and seafood, including Loch Fyne oysters, are featured on the menu. Accommodations are available, although the bedrooms, brightly decorated, are somewhat small. The staff is friendly and hospitable. *Strachur, Argyll, tel. 0369/86–279. Dinner reservations advised. Jacket and tie required in dining room. 21 rooms, 17 with bath. AE, DC, MC, V. Restaurant: Expensive; hotel: Moderate–Expensive.*

Tiroran
Dining and Lodging
★

Tiroran House. This secluded country-house hotel overlooks Loch Scridain and is surrounded by more than 50 acres of grounds and woodlands. Tiroran has the atmosphere of a privately run sporting lodge: Everyone eats at the same time under candlelight, with a fixed main course of lamb, beef, venison, or salmon and perhaps a choice of appetizer and traditional British puddings. The bedrooms are individually decorated, and the public rooms, including the conservatory dining room, are furnished in accordance with the price level. Sportsmen should note that the packed lunches have won awards for their excellence. *Tiroran, Isle of Mull, Argyll, tel. 06815/232. 9 rooms with bath. No credit cards. Closed Nov.–Apr. Expensive–Very Expensive.*

Tobermory **Tobermory Hotel.** This 18th-century building by the quay on
Lodging the northeastern tip of the island of Mull commands superb views. The ambience is crisp and bright; fresh flowers dot every windowsill, and the rooms are spacious and sunny (weather permitting, of course). *Tobermory, Isle of Mull, Argyll PA75 6NT, tel. 0688/2091. 15 rooms, 5 with bath or shower. AE, DC, MC, V. Inexpensive.*

The Arts and Nightlife

The Arts

This predominantly rural area with a small population relies on touring companies and small local exhibitions and events, to a great extent, for its cultural fulfillment. Tourist-information centers (*see* Important Addresses and Numbers in Essential Information, *above*) can supply an up-to-date events list.

Theater **Mull Little Theatre** (Dervaig, Isle of Mull, tel. 06884/267) is Britain's smallest playhouse (43 seats) and presents a number of productions throughout the season. The theater also has a restaurant (*see* Druimard Country House in Dining and Lodging, *above*).

Film The **Highland Discovery Centre** (George St., Oban, tel. 0631/62444) shows feature films and also has a theater for plays.

Nightlife

Cabaret The **Highland Discovery Centre** (*see above*) features a summer cabaret, *This Is Scotland*.

Bars and Lounges **McTavish's Kitchen** (George St., Oban, tel. 0631/63064) is a long-established institution in Oban offering meals accompanied by a Scottish show of the heavily tartan variety.

11 Around the Great Glen

Loch Ness, Speyside

Introduction

*By Gilbert
Summers*

The ancient rift valley of the Great Glen is a dramatic feature on the map of Scotland, giving the impression that the top half of the country has slid southwest. Geologists confirm that this actually occurred, having matched granite from Strontian in Morvern, west of Fort William, with the same rocks found at Foyers, on the east side of Loch Ness, some 65 miles away. The Great Glen, with its sense of openness, lacks the grandeur of Glen Coe or the Torridons, but the highest mountain in the United Kingdom, Ben Nevis (4,406 feet), looms over its southern portals, and spectacular scenery lies within a short distance of the main glen. Inverness lies at the top end and Fort William at the bottom end of this east–west passage. Because they are easily accessible by road and rail, both locales are established stops on the "milk-run" for visitors with limited time. This is, for many reasons, a pity. Lacking the inherent charm or historic ambience of such towns as St. Andrews, Stirling, or Elgin, Fort William and Inverness may not impress you at first sight. Neither town is especially quaint, and both serve as entrances to rural hinterlands: Fort William to the Great Glen, and Inverness to the Western or Northern Highlands. As a result, the two towns always appear packed with holiday visitors who are unnecessarily laying in supplies for their trips to the farthest reaches of Scotland. (There are, of course, plenty of shops north and west of the Great Glen.)

Though it's the capital of the Highlands, Inverness has the flavor of a Lowland town, its winds blowing in a sea-salt air from the Moray Firth. Inverness is also home to one of the world's most famous monster myths: In 1933, during a quiet news week for the local paper, the editor decided to run a story about a strange sighting of something splashing about in Loch Ness. More than 60 years later the story lives on, and the dubious Loch Ness phenomenon continues to keep cameras trained on the deep waters, which have an ominous tendency to create mirages in still conditions. The loch also has the distinction of being Scotland's largest body of water.

Fort William, without a monster on its doorstep, makes do with Ben Nevis and the Road to the Isles, a title sometimes applied to the breathtakingly scenic route to Mallaig, which is best seen by rail. On the way, road and rail routes pass Loch Morar, the country's deepest body of water, which laid claim to its own monster, Morag. Morag threatened Loch Ness's publicity for a while, but she has kept a low profile in recent years.

Away from the Great Glen to the north lie the heartlands of Scotland, a bare backbone of remote mountains. The great hills that loom to the south can be seen clearly on either side of Spey Valley, the name chosen by tourism authorities to describe Strathspey, the broad valley of the River Spey. The area is also commonly known as Speyside. The Spey Valley/Speyside/Strathspey area has scenic qualities and points of interest rivaling anything in the Great Glen. If you're touring in the area, take note of the A86 (Spean Bridge–Kingussie) road, which links the southwest, or Fort William, end of the Great Glen with the top end of Speyside.

Essential Information

Important Addresses and Numbers

Tourist Information
The principal centers in the area are the **Aviemore Tourist Information Centre** (Grampian Rd., tel. 0479/810363), the **Fort William Tourist Information Centre** (Cameron Centre, Cameron Sq., tel. 0397/703781), and the **Inverness Tourist Information Centre** (23 Church St., tel. 0463/234353).

Emergencies
For police, fire, or ambulance, dial 999 from any telephone. No coins are needed for emergency calls from phone booths.

Hospitals
Emergency rooms are located at the following hospitals: **Belford Hospital** (Belford Rd., Fort William, tel. 0397/702481), **Raigmore Hospital** (Perth Rd., Inverness, tel. 0463/234151) and **Town and County Hospital** (Cawdor Rd., Nairn, tel. 0667/52101).

Late-Night Pharmacies
Pharmacies are not common away from the larger towns. In an emergency, the police will assist you in locating a pharmacist. In Inverness, **Kinmylies Pharmacy** (1 Charleston Court, Kinmylies, tel. 0463/221094) is open weekdays until 6 PM and Saturday until 5:30. The pharmacy at the co-op superstore **Milton of Inshes** (Perth Rd., outside Inverness, tel. 0463/242525), is open Monday to Wednesday 9 to 8, Thursday and Friday 9 to 9, and Saturday 9 to 6. In Fort William, **Boots the Chemist** (High St., tel. 0397/702038) is open Monday to Saturday 8:45 to 5:30. A rotation system provides limited Sunday service—consult the list on any pharmacy door.

Arriving and Departing by Plane

Airports and Airlines
Inverness Airport (Dalcross, tel. 0463/232471) has direct flights from London operated by **Dan Air** (tel. 041/8809–1246 or 041/8809–1247). Alternatively, Fort William has bus and train connections with Glasgow, so **Glasgow Airport** can be an appropriate access point. *See* Chapter 4, Glasgow, for further information.

Arriving and Departing by Car, Train, and Bus

By Car
As in all areas of rural Scotland, a car is a great asset for exploring the Great Glen and Speyside, especially since the best of the area is away from the main roads. The fast A9 brings you to Inverness in roughly three hours from Glasgow or Edinburgh, even if you take your time.

By Train
The area is surprisingly well served by train. There are sleeper connections from London to Inverness and Fort William, as well as reliable links from Glasgow and Edinburgh. For information call **ScotRail** (Fort William, tel. 0397/703791; Inverness, tel. 0463/238924) or contact any main-line station in Scotland.

By Bus
There is a long-distance **Citylink** service from Fort William to Glasgow (Glasgow coach station, tel. 041/332–9191). Inverness is also well served from the central belt of Scotland (tel. 0463/237575).

Getting Around

By Car You can use the main A9 Perth–Inverness road (via Aviemore) to explore this area or use one of the many other smaller roads (some of them old military roads) to explore the much quieter east side of Loch Ness. The same applies to Speyside, where a variety of options open up away from the A9, especially through the pinewoods by Coylumbridge and Feshiebridge, east of the main road. Mallaig, west of Fort William, also has improving road connections, but rail still remains the most enjoyable way to experience the rugged hills and loch scenery between these two places. In Morvern, the area across Loch Linnhe southwest of Fort William, you may encounter single-lane roads, which require slower speeds and concentration. Never hold up a vehicle trying to pass. Pull into the next passing place and signal the driver through.

By Train Though the Great Glen has no rail connection (in Victorian times Fort William and Inverness had different lines built by companies that could not agree), this area has the **West Highland line,** which links Fort William to Mallaig, a small fishing and ferry port on the west coast.

By Bus There is limited service available in the Great Glen area and some local service running from Fort William (Highland Scottish Omnibuses Ltd., tel. 0397/702373). A number of post-bus services will help get you to the more remote corners of the area. The timetable is available from the **Head Post Office** (Edinburgh, tel. 031/550–8232) or the **District Head Post Office** (14–16 Queen's Gate, Inverness, tel. 0463/234111, ext. 248).

Guided Tours

Orientation From Fort William, **Highland Scottish Omnibuses Ltd.** (Travel Centre, Fort William, tel. 0397/702373) operates coach tours in the summer season. **ScotRail** runs a not-to-be-missed steam-hauled service to Mallaig in the summer season (other non-steam connections run to Mallaig). Contact **ScotRail** (tel. 0397/703791) for further details; advance booking is recommended. **Caledonian MacBrayne** runs scheduled service and cruises to Skye, the Small Isles, and Mull from Mallaig (tel. 0687/2403). **Arisaig Marine** (tel. 068/75224) operates highly recommended Hebridean day cruises on the MV (motor vessel) *Shearwater* to the Small Isles and Skye. **Scott II Cruises** (tel. 0463/233140) runs daily boat trips on Loch Ness and the Caledonian Canal.

From Inverness, **Highland Scottish Omnibuses Ltd.** (Inverness bus station, tel. 0463/237575) offers coach tours during the summer season, as do **Macdonald's Tours** (tel. 0463/240673), and **Spa Coaches** (tel. 0997/421311).

Special-Interest From Fort William, **Mr. James Gordon** (64 Castle Dr., Lochside, Fort William, tel. 0397/704817) offers a choice of chauffeur-driven limousine, minibus, or coach for tours tailored to suit the client.

From Inverness, **Highland Insight Tours and Travel** (tel. 0463/83403), offers personalized touring holidays and full-day or half-day tours that cater to any interest, with **James Johnson Chauffeur Drive** (tel. 0463/790179) offering a similar service. **Linnmhor Limousines** (Linnmhor, Strathpeffer, tel. 0997/421528), has chauffeur-driven Rolls Royce limousines for daily hire. **Jacobite Cruises Ltd.** (Tomnahurich Bridge, Glenurquhart Rd., Inverness, tel. 0463/233999 or 0463/241730) runs morning, afternoon, and evening cruises to Loch Ness; an afternoon excursion to Urquhart Castle; and boat and coach excursions to the Monster Exhibition. **Macaulay Charters** (12 Pict Ave., Inverness, tel. 0463/ 225398) provides trips by boat to Nairn and the surrounding coastline, offering visitors the chance to see dolphins in their breeding area.

Exploring the Great Glen

Orientation

Think of this area as two parallel glens, with appendages both north and south. Of the two tours decribed below, the first takes in some of the byways of both the Great Glen and Speyside, demonstrating that the best sights are hidden from the main road. However, the tour initially highlights some of the attractions within easy reach of Inverness along the inner Moray Firth. The second tour, originating in Fort William, takes in the special qualities of birch-knoll and blue island West Highland views. The tours also point out the romantic and historic associations of this area, where the rash adventurer Prince Charles Edward Stewart both arrived for and departed after the final Jacobite rebellion of 1745–46.

Highlights for First-time Visitors

Arisaig to the Small Isles by boat (*see* Guided Tours)
Cawdor Castle (*see* Tour 1)
Culloden Moor (*see* Tour 1)
Fort George (*see* Tour 1)
Fort William to Mallaig by steam-powered train
(*see* Guided Tours)
Glen Nevis (*see* Off the Beaten Track)
Loch an Eilean (*see* Tour 1)
View down Loch Shiel, including Glenfinnan Monument
(*see* Tour 2)

Tour 1: Speyside and Loch Ness

Numbers in the margin correspond to points of interest on the Great Glen Area map.

① **Inverness** seems designed for the tourist, with its banks, souvenirs, high-quality woolens, and well-equipped tourist information center. Compared with other Scottish towns, however, Inverness has less to offer visitors with a keen interest in Scottish history. Relatively little evidence remains of the town's rich and stormy past. Some say this is because of its strategic position as a gateway to the Highlands. Frequently throughout its history Inverness was burned and ravaged by one or another of the restive Highland clans competing for dominance in the region. Thus a decorative wall panel here and a fragment of tower there are all that remain amid the solid 19th-century downtown developments and modern shopping facilities.

Above the river is the **castle** (the local Sheriff Court), which is Victorian, although the site itself is ancient. The fort that formerly stood here was blown up by the Jacobites in the 1745

campaign. Because Jacobite tales are interwoven with landmarks throughout this entire area, you may enjoy your touring
a little more if you first learn something about this thorny but
colorful period of Scottish history. One of the best places to do
this is at **Culloden,** just 5 miles east of Inverness on the B9006.

❷ At **Culloden Moor** on a sleety April day in 1746, 5,000 Jacobites
under Prince Charles Edward Stuart faced 9,000 well-armed
British army troops at the command of the prince's distant
cousin, General Cumberland. The latter became known in Scotland after the war as Butcher Cumberland because of the atroc-
ities committed by his men after the battle ended. The story of
the encounter, of how the ill-advised, poorly organized, and
exhausted rebel army was swept aside by superior British
firepower, is illustrated in the visitor center by a moving
audiovisual presentation.

The National Trust for Scotland has restored the moorland to
re-create some of the windswept gloom from the site of the last
major battle on mainland soil (there is also a tearoom and a shop
for those who want to reminisce indoors). For a proper perspective of the battle, it is important to remember that this was not
a Scots-versus-English confrontation. Lowland Scottish regiments sided with the Hanoverian government as did the Campbell militia. Many other Highland clans were slow or unwilling
to rally around the prince's mad jaunt. However, none of this
mattered to the government of the day: After the battle legisla-
tion was passed banning tartan, kilts, and other symbols of the
Gael. The Highlands were seen as potential hotbeds of rebellion, and the clan system was therefore dismantled forever.
*B9006, tel. 0463/790607. Admission to visitor center £1.50
adults, 80p children, senior citizens, and students. Site open
all year. Visitor center open Apr.–May and mid-Sept.–Oct.,
daily 9:30–5:30; June–mid-Sept., daily 9–6:30; Nov.–Mar.,
daily 10–4 (may be closed early in year).*

Not far from Culloden, on a narrow road southeast of the bat-
❸ tlefield, are the **Clava Cairns,** dating from the Bronze Age.
These stones and monuments constitute a large ring with passage graves in a cluster among the trees. On-site information
placards explain the graves' signficance: They gave their name
to a distinctive type of early site found in this area. As is the
case with most of Scotland's ancient sites, however, these
mounds of broken stone require an imaginative mind to revive
their past.

To get to the next chapter of the Highlands' history, drive
northeast from Culloden. Use either the B9039 or B9006 to get
❹ to **Fort George,** a fortress that was started in 1748 and completed some 20 years later. As a direct result of the battle at
Culloden, the nervous government in London ordered the construction of a large fort on this promontory reaching into the
Moray Firth. It survives today as perhaps the best-preserved
18th-century military fortification in Europe. Because it is low
lying, its immense scale can be seen only from within. The huge
walls, as broad and high as harbor quays, are large enough to
contain a complete military town. A walk along the wall-tops
affords fine views of the Highland hills in the distance and of the
firth immediately below. The army still uses the barracks, and
if you happen to meet any of the fort's current military residents, you will find them unfailingly polite. Nobody has

The Great Glen Area

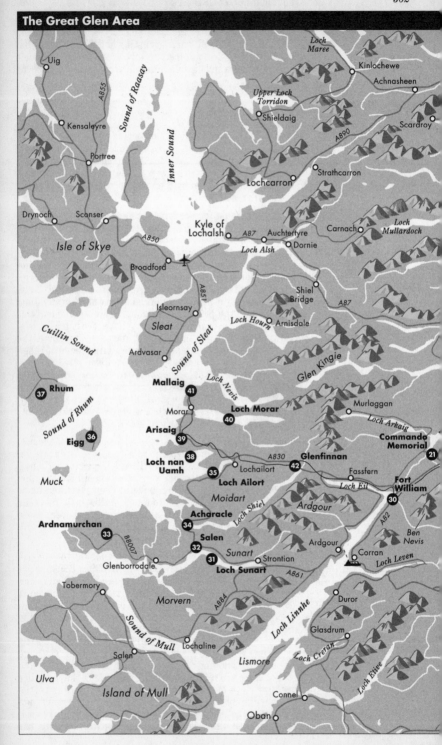

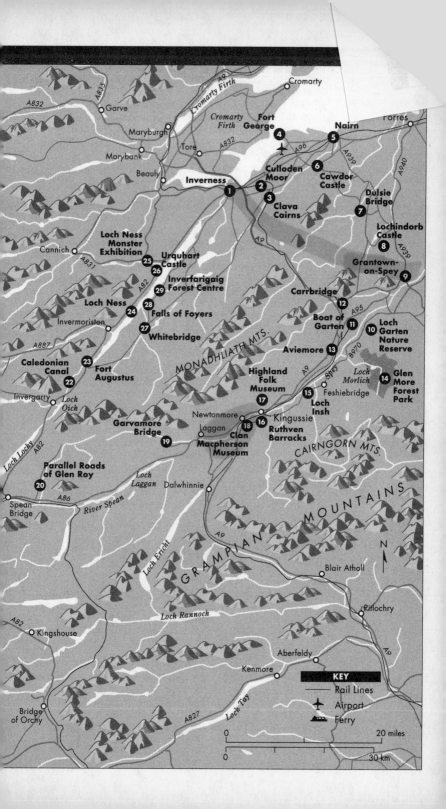

sighted a Jacobite here for more than 200 years. A visitor center and a number of tableaux at the fort portray the 18th-century Scottish soldier's way of life, as does the **Regimental Museum of the Queen's Own Highlanders.** *B9039, off A96 west of Nairn, tel. 031/244-3101. Admission to fort: £2 adults, £1 children, £5 family ticket; free admission to museum. Fort open Apr.–Sept., Mon.–Sat. 9:30–6, Sun. 2–6; Oct.–Mar., Mon.–Sat. 9:30–4, Sun. 2–4. Museum open Apr.–Sept., Mon.–Sat. 10–6, Sun. 2–6.*

❺ To the east is **Nairn,** which has the air of a Lowland town yet looks, administratively speaking, to Inverness as part of the Highlands. A former fishertown, Nairn does in fact have something of a split personality. King James VI once boasted that there was a town in his kingdom so large that the residents at either end of town spoke different languages. He was referring to the fact that Nairn's fisherfolk spoke Lowland Scots by the sea, while the uptown farmers and crofters spoke Gaelic. The fishing boats have since moved to larger ports, but the town's historic flavor has been preserved in the **Nairn Fishertown Museum,** a hall crammed with artifacts, photographs, and model boats. This is an informal museum in the best sense, where the volunteer staff are full of information and eager to talk. *Laing Hall, King St., tel. 0667/53331: Admission: 50p adults, 30p children. Open June–Sept., Mon.–Sat. 2:30–4:30, also Mon., Wed., and Fri. evenings 6:20–8:20.*

❻ Next head southwest to **Cawdor Castle.** Shakespeare's Macbeth was Thane of Cawdor, but the sense of history that exists within these turreted walls is more than fictional. Cawdor is a lived-in castle, not an abandoned, decadent structure to be preserved in conservation body aspic. The earliest part of the castle is the 14th-century central tower; the rooms contain family portraits, tapestries, fine furniture, and paraphernalia reflecting 600 years of history. Outside the castle walls there are sheltered gardens and walks. Visitors will be surprised to see the preserved trunk of a hawthorn tree in the dungeon. Legend has it that one of the early thanes of Cawdor, who was searching for a site on which to build a new castle, was instructed in a dream to load a donkey with gold and follow it until it rested. The beast chose to sleep under a hawthorn, and the castle was built around it. *B9090, 5 mi southwest of Nairn, tel. 06677/615. Admission: £3.50 adults, £1.90 children, £2.80 senior citizens, £10 family ticket; Garden and grounds only: £1.80. Open May–Sept., daily 10–5:30.*

If Cawdor has inspired you to seek the wild Highlands, make your way to the southeastern portion of the region, using either the unclassified roads southeast of Cawdor or heading northeast along the B9101 to pick up the A939 south. If you use the unclassified roads, you will find yourself in a classic Highland "edge" landscape, where the open moor contrasts with the improved upland pasture and thickets of birch and fir. (Clunas may be the first road sign you see, but reaching Dulsie is your first objective.) As you take to the higher ground, look for the longest views back over the Firth—you should still just barely be able to see Fort George in the distance. Follow what was the former military road built in the 1750s to service the garrison. Look for the point where the road crosses the River Findhorn
❼ by a narrow span, the **Dulsie Bridge.** Just beyond the bridge, on the right, is a parking place and kissing gate. If you park and go

through the gate, a walk of a few yards brings you to a viewpoint over the birch-scattered rocky confines of the river. An information placard explains how the sturdy bridge withstood the Moray floods of 1829.

Shortly after Dulsie Bridge, turn right off the unclassified road onto the B9007. Shakespeare's Thane of Cawdor met the three prophesying witches on a bare moor very much like this one. Rolling folds of marbled purple and brown are broken here and there by a roofless cottage. You can either switch to the A938 and Carrbridge on Speyside heading south (*see below*), or if you have more time, you can take a short diversion to the east for a
⑧ view of the lonely ruin of **Lochindorb Castle.** What appears to be a walled enclosure fills and surrounds an entire island on Lochindorb loch. This 13th-century stronghold was the former power base of the Wolf of Badenoch (the marauding earl of Buchan who damaged Elgin Cathedral). The castle was eventually dismantled by a 15th-century Thane of Cawdor, on the order of the king. (Lochindorb's iron *yett* [gate] is now on view at Cawdor.)

After you have viewed Lochindorb, drive farther south along
⑨ the A939 to **Grantown-on-Spey.** This sturdy settlement amid the tall pines of the River Spey gives visitors access to many points of interest, including a heavily stocked heather nursery at **Skye of Curr** nearby. The A95, which runs southwest along the river, is an attractive road, but you may wish to follow the more tranquil B970 via **Nethy Bridge.** Then look for signs to the
⑩ **Loch Garten Nature Reserve,** administered by the Royal Society for the Protection of Birds (RSPB). This sanctuary achieved fame when the osprey, a bird that was facing extinction in the early part of this century, returned to breed here. Instead of cordoning off the nest site, the RSPB encouraged visitors by constructing a blind from which to watch the birds. Now thousands of bird lovers visit annually to get a glimpse of the domestic arrangements of this fish-eating bird, which has since bred in many other parts of the Highlands. *Off B970, 8 mi northeast of Aviemore, tel. 0479/82409 or 031/557–3136. Admission: £1.50 adults, 50p children, £1 senior citizens. Osprey observation post open Apr.–Aug. 10–6:30; other areas of reserve open daily year-round.*

⑪ Near Loch Garten is **Boat of Garten,** a peaceful village where the scent of pine trees is interrupted by an equally evocative smell. This is the terminus of the **Speyside Railway,** and the acrid scent of smoke and steam hang faintly in the air near the authentically preserved station next to the **Boat Hotel.** The 5-mile train trip to Aviemore not only offers a chance to wallow in nostalgia, but also yields superb views southward to the high and often white domes of the Cairngorms.

Time Out At the **Boat Hotel,** in Boat of Garten, you can have a friendly pub lunch while you wait for the train. The malt-whiskey selection behind the bar may be of interest as well.

⑫ In **Carrbridge,** just about 5 miles northwest of Boat of Garten (use A95 and then B9153), you'll find the **Landmark Visitor Centre,** an early pioneer in the move toward more sophisticated visitor attractions. It has an audiovisual presentation on the history of the Scottish Highlands, a permanent exhibition, a display on forestry, plus a bookshop and restaurant. Outdoors

are nature trails and a viewing platform, as well as plenty of diversions for children, such as a woodland maze and an adventure playground. *Old A9, 6 mi north of Aviemore, tel. 047–984/
613. Admission: £3.95 adults, £2.60 children. Open Apr.–
June, Sept., and Oct., daily 9:30–6; July and Aug., daily
9:30–8; Nov.–Mar., daily 9:30–5.*

No matter which side of the Spey you choose to travel (the quiet
B970 on the southeast side is recommended), signs will point
you to **Aviemore.** Once a quiet junction on the Highland Railway, Aviemore now possesses all the brashness and concrete
boxiness of a year-round holiday resort. A resort environment
certainly translates into a lot of things to do, however, and here
you can swim, curl, skate, see a movie, dance, and shop. Signs
will direct you to other sights, such as the **Cairngorm Whisky
Centre** (tel. 0479/810574) and the **Rothiemurchus Estate Visitor
Centre** (tel. 0479/810786).

The Aviemore area is a versatile walking base, but walkers
must be properly dressed for high-level excursions onto the
near-Arctic plateau. Visitors interested in skiing and rugged
hiking can follow the B970 from Aviemore past Loch Morlich in
the **Glen More Forest Park** to the high car parks on the exposed
shoulders of the **Cairngorm Mountains.** The chair lifts take you
even higher, during and after the ski season, for extensive
views of the broad valley of the Spey. But be warned: It can get
very cold at over 3,000 feet, and weather conditions can change
rapidly even in the middle of summer. *Off B9152, tel. 05404/223
or 047986/271. Open all year.*

While you are on the high slopes, you may sight the reindeer
herd that was introduced here in the 1950s. In fact, by inquir-
ing at the **Cairngorm Reindeer Centre,** by Loch Morlich, you can
go along with the keeper on his daily check. *Loch Morlich, Glen
More Forest Park, tel. 0479/861228. Admission: £2.50 adults,
£1.50 children. Departures daily at 11 AM (subject to weather
conditions).*

The place that best sums up Speyside's piny ambience is probably **Loch an Eilean,** a mile or so south of Aviemore, signposted
off the B970 (parallel with the main A9). A converted cottage
on the **Rothiemurchus Estate** houses a visitor center (the area is
a National Nature Reserve). Visitors should exercise care upon
entering the cottage: It has an extremely low door and a very
hard lintel! All around the loch you can still see some stands of
old Scots pines; look for the characteristic red limbs high up.
These are the descendants of the Caledonian Forest that once
covered much of Scotland and now survives only in remnants.
Dependent on these mature trees are such Speyside species as
crested tits and crossbills, the latter a slightly exotic-looking
bird. Crossbill males are brick-red and look something like
small parrots; you may need binoculars and a bird book to identify them. *Rothiemurchus Estate Visitor Centre, tel. 0479/
810858. Free admission. Open all year, daily 9–5.*

If you take the time to stroll to the loch, at least as far as the
island (*eilean* is Gaelic for island), you will see a ruin, amid the
trees, of what was once a 15th-century stronghold of the Mack-
intoshes. The well-shod will want to walk around the loch and
may even make their way toward the high hills, sensed through
a cool wind rather than seen, at this point. The characteristically open woodland has tall pines, an understory of blue-green

juniper, and carpets of what the Scots call *blaeberries* (bilberries or myrtles). This is Speyside at its uncluttered best.

⓯ About a mile west of **Feshiebridge** is **Loch Insh.** Other lochs in the vicinity, notably Loch an Eilean and Loch Garten, are what geologists call kettle holes—round depressions that remained after huge blocks of ice melted at the end of the Ice Age. Loch Insh is thought to be the remains of a much larger loch, which, until recent geological times, filled the valley's floor. Loch Insh is known for its recreational diversions; it has sailboats and canoes and is a popular water-sports center. Beyond the loch the valley floor broadens into marshland, the haunt of watery tribes of birds and hence bird-watchers. Look for ospreys here.

Gaunt against the rounded **Monadhliath Mountains** (*monadhliath* is Gaelic for gray moors) to the north is what appears, at first glance, to be a ruined castle on a mound. The re**⓰** mains are not of a castle, however, but of **Ruthven Barracks,** roofless and redolent with tales of the '45 (as the last Jacobite rebellion is often called). The defeated Jacobite forces rallied here after Culloden, but then abandoned and blew up the government outpost they had earlier captured. *B970, ½ mi south of Kingussie, tel. 031/244–3101. Admission free.*

The barracks lie within a few minutes of the village of **Kingussie** (pronounced Kin-*yoo*-see) and can be seen clearly from the main A9. The village is of interest primarily because of the **⓱** **Highland Folk Museum.** The interior exhibits are housed in what was an 18th-century shooting lodge, its paneled and varnished ambience still apparent. Displays include 18th-century furniture, clothing, and implements, and, outside, various types of Highland buildings have been reconstructed. In summer, local weavers and other artisans demonstrate Highland crafts. The village also has a pottery manufacturing fine china. Visitors can wander around the grounds freely or see the highlights of the museum on a guided tour. *A9 at Kingussie, tel. 0540/661307. Admission: £2 adults, £1 children and senior citizens. Open Apr.–Oct., Mon.–Sat. 10–6, Sun. 2–6; Nov.–Mar., Mon.–Fri. 10–3.*

Down the road from Kingussie is neighborly **Newtonmore,** **⓲** home of the **Clan Macpherson Museum.** One of many clan museums scattered throughout the old homelands, the Macpherson Museum displays a number of interesting artifacts associated with the '45 rebellion, as well as of clan chiefs of the even more distant past. *A9/A86, Newtonmore, tel. 0540/673332. Admission free. Open May–Sept., Mon.–Sat. 10–5:30, Sun. 2:30–5:30.*

Newtonmore also claims to have invented the sport of pony trekking. The sturdy highland ponies that trek around the Highlands were bred for carrying deer off the hill after a successful kill in the stalking season. It was inevitable that an enterprising Scot would come up with the idea of using the beasts to carry visitors when there were no dead deer to haul.

At Newtonmore you will leave the great artery of the A9 behind. It veers off to the southeast for the Pass of Drumochter at this point. This tour continues westward on the A86 around the edge of the Monadhliath range, which separates Speyside from the Great Glen. The Monadhliath are less often explored by hill walkers than the Cairngorms, which form Speyside's southern side. At **Laggan,** where the main road crosses the young River

Spey, an unclassified road runs west up the glen to **Garvamore**. If you are staying in the area and you are not pressed for time, it's worth making this detour to view the **Garvamore Bridge** (about 6 miles from the junction, at the south side of the Corrieyarick Pass). This dual-arched bridge was built in 1735 by English General Wade, who had been charged with the task of improving Scotland's roads by a British government concerned that its troops would not be able to travel the Highlands quickly enough to quell an uprising. There are many traces in Scotland of Wade's work: military roads built from as early as the 1720s by Wade and his assistant Caulfield.

If you opt not to take the Garvamore Bridge detour, you may continue south on the A86, which hugs the western shore of **Loch Laggan.** This was the route chosen by later road builders to avoid the high Corrieyarick Pass. Still quite narrow in a few places, this stretch of the A86 is a road to be enjoyed, offering superb views of the mountainous heartlands to the north, where high shoulders loom, and to the south, over the silvery spine of hills known as the **Grey Corries** and culminating with **Ben Nevis.** Note that the West Highland train line from Glasgow joins the road, having rolled off the high moors of Rannoch and snaked around the hills that block its direct approach to Fort William.

Road and rail run on to **Roybridge,** where you'll find the first of the Great Glen cul-de-sac diversions. The so-called **Parallel Roads of Glen Roy** are three curious terraces, parallel and level, cut across the hillsides on both sides of the glen. Their levelness lends a clue to their origins as former shorelines of lochs dammed by ice that melted in stages at the end of the last Ice Age. *Unclassified road off A86 at Roybridge.*

Turn right and north at the junction with the main Great Glen road, the A82, to reach **Spean Bridge.** Uphill and beyond this little village, easily visible from the road, is the arresting and dignified **Commando Memorial.** The rugged glens and hills of this area were a training ground for elite forces during World War II. Today, three battle-equipped figures on a high stone plinth overlook the panorama, while the veterans and younger generations who visit follow their gaze. Few visitors, however, make the additional short detour westward down the B8004, where, on the left, there is a gate. Look carefully for a rough track emerging on the right from a pine plantation. It continues beyond the gate, rolling gently downhill to the wooded valley of the **River Spean.**

Although it looks like a farm-access track, it is, in reality, a remnant of war—the often overlooked remains of the military road through the Great Glen on its way to Fort William. Over the Spean—keen students of the '45 rebellion will seek this out—are the ruins of the bridge on which the first shots were fired in the rebellion, when a party of Jacobites ambushed governmental troops.

Those who want to explore farther can go through the **Dark Mile,** a narrow pass dripping with lichen-covered pines that leads to **Loch Arkaig.** Here, visitors will find themselves in another atmospheric cul-de-sac, the romance of the road enhanced by tales of a hidden hoard of Jacobite gold still lying somewhere on the hillside near Muirlaggan, where the public road ends.

Time Out If you're passing Invergarry (just east of Loch Lochy) around lunchtime, you may stop at the rambling **Glengarry Castle Hotel,** an interesting building with a pleasingly old-fashion ambience, for a soup-and-sandwich meal. More substantial fare is also available. The ruined **Glengarry Castle,** a seat of the MacDonnell Clan, can be seen on the grounds. The hotel entrance is south of the A82/A87 road junction.

22 Traveling north up the Great Glen by the A82 takes you parallel to Loch Lochy (on the eastern shore) and over the **Caledonian Canal** at Laggan Locks. From this beautiful spot, which offers stunning vistas of lochs, mountains, and glens in all directions, you can look back on the impressive profile of Ben Nevis. The canal, which links the lochs of the Great Glen—Loch Lochy, Loch Oich, and Loch Ness—owes its origins to a combination of military as well as political pressures that emerged at the time of the Napoleonic Wars with France. First of all, the British needed a better and faster way to get naval vessels from one side of Scotland to the other. Second, the government in London also realized that if it didn't do something to improve the economy of the Highlands, the number of recruits available for service in the British armed forces would continue to dwindle as more and more Highlanders left Scotland for better opportunities in the New World.

The great Scottish engineer Thomas Telford surveyed the route in 1803. The canal, which took 19 years to complete, has 29 locks and 42 gates. Telford took advantage of the three lochs that lie in the Great Glen (which have a combined length of 45 miles), and only 22 miles of canal were constructed to connect the lochs and complete the waterway from coast to coast. As it turned out, a strategic use was out of the question for the canal: It was too small for naval vessels. Today it is used by fishing boats and recreational craft.

23 The best place to see the locks in action is at **Fort Augustus,** at the southern tip of Loch Ness. (Fort Augustus itself was captured by the Jacobite clans during the 1745 rebellion. Later the fort was rebuilt as a Benedictine abbey and boys' school.) The canal activity at a series of locks that rise from Loch Ness takes place in the village center.

24 From the B862 just east of Fort Augustus you'll get your first good long view of the formidable and famous **Loch Ness,** which has a greater volume of water than any other Scottish loch and a maximum depth of more than 800 feet. Early travelers who passed this way included English lexicographer Dr. Samuel Johnson and his guide and biographer James Boswell, who were on their way to the Hebrides in 1783. They remarked at the time about the condition of the population and the squalor of their homes. Another early travel writer, Thomas Pennant, noted that the loch kept the locality frost-free in winter. Even General Wade came here, his troops blasting and digging a road up much of the eastern shore. None of these observant early travelers ever made mention of a monster. Clearly, they had not read the local guidebooks.

25 If you're in search of the beast, it's best to continue northward along the coast on the A82. At **Drumnadrochit** you will find the **Official Loch Ness Monster Exhibition,** which presents the facts and the fakes, the photographs, the unexplained sonar contacts, and the sincere testimony of eyewitnesses. It's then up to you to make up your own mind. *A831, tel. 04562/573 and 04562/218. Admission: £3.50 adults, £2 children, £2.50 senior citizens and students, £9.50 family ticket. Open July–mid-Sept., daily 9 AM–9:30 PM. Off-season opening times vary; please phone to check.*

26 **Urquhart Castle,** near Drumnadrochit, is another favorite monster-watching spot. This plundered fortress stands on a promontory overlooking the loch, as it has since the Middle Ages. Because of its central and strategic position in the Great Glen line of communication, the castle has a complex history involving military offense and defense, as well as its own destruction and renovation. The castle was begun in the 13th century and was destroyed before the end of the 17th century to prevent its use by the Jacobites. The ruins of what was one of the largest castles in Scotland were plundered for building material. Today swarms of bus tourers pass through after investigating the Loch Ness phenomenon. *West shore of Loch Ness, 2 mi southeast of Drumnadrochit, tel. 031/244–3101. Admission: £1.50 adults, 80p children, £4 family ticket. Open Apr.–Sept., Mon.–Sat. 9:30–6, Sun. 2–6; Oct.–Mar., Mon.–Sat. 9:30–4, Sun. 2–4.*

The west-bank road, the A82, offers intermittent views of the loch, often glittering hypnotically in the sun. You can be caught up in the fast-moving traffic on this busy road and can find yourself in Inverness before you know it. Or you can choose a more leisurely alternative—combining monster watching with peaceful road touring—by taking the B862 from Fort Augustus and following the east-bank route to Inverness.

The B862 runs around the end of Loch Ness then climbs into moorland and forestry plantation. Fine views of Fort Augustus can be seen by climbing a few yards up and to the right, on to the moor; here you'll be able to see above the conifer spikes. The half-hidden track beside the road is a remnant of the military road built by General Wade. Loch Ness quickly drops out of sight, but is soon replaced by the peaceful, reedy **Loch Tarff.** The road then climbs to a breezy viewpoint, at more than 1,200 feet. The Monadhliath range rises in moorland waves to the right (east), and far beyond the trough where Loch Ness lies, to the northwest, the hills spread across the spine of Scotland. Straight ahead is the quiet green of **Stratherrick.**

Just ahead, the road runs along the line of the former military route and shows appropriate military precision nearly all **27** the way to **Whitebridge,** where a handsome single-arch Wade bridge (look for it on your right) has been restored. Just before the bridge is the **Whitebridge Hotel,** a former Kingshouse, one of a chain of inns built by authorities in the 18th century to service the military roads. The Kingshouse name is still used by a few of Scotland's hotels. Beyond Whitebridge the small banks on either side of the road are thought to have survived from the military's original work in 1726; thus you find yourself traveling one of the earliest roads in the Highlands. Take the B852, left at the junction beyond Whitebridge, to regain the shores of Loch Ness by some fine woodlands.

Just before you reach the level of the loch at **Foyers,** a sign out-**28** side the general store will direct you to the **Falls of Foyers.** Steep, pine-cone-strewn paths lead to a viewpoint where a thin waterfall streams into a dark pot and then down a ravine. The original volume of the falls was much reduced shortly before the turn of the century when the power generated here was harnessed for the first commercial application of hydroelectricity (1896), in an aluminum-smelting plant on a site by the loch.

The B852 meanders pleasantly from Foyers, offering some views of the loch on the way to **Inverfarigaig.** Just before the main road bridge is the **Inverfarigaig Forest Centre,** on the right. The center has several displays on forestry activities, and a number of trails lead from the center into the woodlands. Half hidden by the trees immediately below today's bridge is its crumbling predecessor, a Wade bridge. The original road north from Whitebridge dates from around 1726. The high-level direct route proved too difficult to negotiate in winter, however, so Wade's men then built a new road in 1732 along the loch side, which provided more shelter. Now widened, Wade's road runs close by the loch. Along the road are safe stopping places, should something unexpected rear up from the water. Urquhart Castle and the main road traffic whizzing by can be plainly seen on the far bank. **Dores** is the last settlement at the head of the loch before the road gently climbs into Lowland fields and returns to Inverness.

Tour 2: Toward the Small Isles

Fort William probably has enough points of interest for visitors—a museum, exhibits, and shopping—to compensate for its less-than-picturesque milieu. The town's primary purpose is to serve the west Highland hinterland; its role as a tourist stop is secondary. This is a relatively wet part of Scotland, and visitors staying in the vicinity are strongly recommended to take the opportunity to go west if the weather looks settled. The main town can always be explored if it rains. Go west on a sunny day when the silver sands at Loch Morar are gleaming and the Small Isles—Rhum, Eigg, Canna, and Muck—are as blue as the sea and sky together. Use Mallaig as an alternative gateway to Skye, or take a day cruise (*see* Off the Beaten Track, *below*) from Arisaig to the Small Isles for just a glimpse of traffic-free island life.

Begin your visit to Fort William by stopping by the helpful tourist-information center in **Cameron Square.** Just a few doors down is the **West Highland Museum** , which explores the theme of Prince Charles Edward Stuart and the 1745 rebellion. Included in the museum's folk exhibits is a section on tartans. *Cameron Square, tel. 0397/702169. Admission: 70p adults, 20p children, 40p senior citizens. Open July and Aug., Mon.–Sat. 9:30–6, Sun. 2–5; Sept.–June, Mon.–Sat. 10–5.*

High-quality crafts can be found at the **Scottish Crafts and Ben Nevis Exhibition.** The information offered about Britain's highest mountain is very much a sideshow to the main business of displaying a substantial selection of artifacts produced in the Highlands, from handmade haggis to kilt socks. In fact, the best reason for dallying in Fort William may be to shop. *Main St., tel. 0397/704406. Open Easter–June, daily 9–5:30; July and Aug., daily 9 AM–10 PM; Sept.–Nov., daily 9–5:30.*

The sound of a steam-train whistle may remind you that this is the terminus of ScotRail's spectacularly successful Fort William–Mallaig steam-hauled line. British Rail dispensed with steam traction more than 20 years ago and ironically has had to hire locomotives from various steam-preservation societies to run its extra trains. However, not all the services to Mallaig are run by steam. If you visit Fort William by car, leave the car behind to take this trip. *Tel. 0397/703791.*

If you're not reliant on public transportation, you can make an interesting West Highlands circuit by traveling down the Great Glen and along the side of **Loch Linnhe** to take the **Corran Ferry** across the narrows to the mountainous area called **Ardgour.** (From the map you will see you can avoid the ferry by driving around the head of Loch Eil, the continuation of Loch Linnhe. Aside from fine views of Fort William straggling up the shoulders of Ben Nevis, this route has no particular points of interest, hence the recommendation to take the ferry.) This West Highlands loop through Ardgour, Sunart, and Moidart is not packed with specific places of interest, but visitors can approach the loop in a leisurely and unstructured manner and enjoy the opportunity to view new vistas at every bend. Take note of the subtle light of the far west and the depth of the colors on the leaves, hills, and sea lochs. All that sparkle comes from the large volume of rain that falls here, so make sure you listen to a weather forecast before setting out.

A reliable two-lane road runs along the Ardgour side of Loch Linnhe before turning into Glen Sanda, crossing the watershed, and running down to the long shores of **Loch Sunart.** This is a typical West Highlands sea loch: Orange wrack marks the tide lines, and herons stand muffled and miserable, wondering if it is worth risking a free meal at the local fish farm. As for the fish farms themselves, visitors will become accustomed to their floats and cages turning up in the foreground of every sea-loch view. The farms were originally hailed as the savior of the Highland economy because of the number of jobs they created, but questions are now being raised about their environmental effects, and the market for their product is being threatened by Scandinavian imports.

The village of **Strontian,** which straggles up the glen at right angles to the road, derived its name from the element strontium, discovered here in 1790 among the now-spent lead mines at the head of the glen. Mining is no longer a source of employment here; some of the residents do forestry work, others make their living from various crafts. One of these artisans, guitar maker Aidan Edwards, works from a house overlooking the loch (signposted from the main road, the A861). Edwards also makes bowed psalteries—stringed instruments resembling zithers—which you may select as a conversation piece for your living room.

The next stretch of A861 to the west passes through mixed woodland, where the Atlantic mildness and moistness become apparent. At **Salen** you have a choice. The B8007 runs on, blind-bending partly through thickets of rhododendrons to **Ardnamurchan,** the most western point of mainland Scotland and a must-see for those who love unspoiled coastal scenery. Here you'll find crofting communities and holiday homes. Otherwise, swing right and to the north from Salen along the B8044 and head for **Acharacle** (Scots "ch"—ach-*ar*-ra-kle). You'll pass through deep-green plantations and moorland lily ponds to reach this strung-out settlement backed by the hills of Moidart and **Loch Shiel.** The south end of Loch Shiel is shallow and reedy. The north end is more dramatic and sits deep within the rugged hills. A few minutes beyond Acharacle—where the main road turns sharply right—take the narrow road to the left, overhung in places by mossy trees, to emerge at **Castle Tioram.** This ruined keep dominates a bracken-green islet, barely anchored to the mainland by a sand spit. The castle was once the home of the chief of the MacDonalds of Clan Ranald, but the last chief burned the castle to prevent its falling into the hands of his enemies, the Campbells, during the 1715 Jacobite rebellion. Conservation agencies do not yet require an admission charge to this fragment of Highlands history guarding the south channel of Loch Moidart. *Reached by an unclassified road north of A861. Always accessible.*

The upper sandy reaches of **Loch Moidart** are reached by returning to the main road, climbing a high moorland pass and then dropping down to a two-lane road again. On the next ascent from the shores of Loch Moidart you'll be rewarded with
㉟ stunning sea views. The coast is reached by the mouth of **Loch Ailort** (pronounced *eye*-ort), and there are plenty of places to pull off among the boulders and birch scrub and sort out the view of the islands. Off-shore in the distance you'll be able to
㊱ spot **Eigg,** a low island marked by the dramatic black peak of An
㊲ Sgurr. Beyond Eigg is the larger **Rhum,** with its range of hills, the Norse-named Rhum Coullin, looming cloud-capped over the island.

Loch Ailort itself is another picturesque inlet, now cluttered with the garish floats of fish cages. You meet the bustle of the main road again at its head, at the junction with the A830, the main road from Fort William to Mallaig. Turn left here to reach Mallaig. This road is sometimes called the Road to the Isles, a name borrowed from an old cattle-driving trail that once ran through the hills to the north until the railways put an end to the trade. The railway survives here, a fact that may be brought to your attention by the quantity of photographic equipment that sprouts from every hummock or lay-by that overlooks the track. All the way to Mallaig, rail enthusiasts spring from the heather wherever road and rail meet, in search of the next steam-powered train.

The breathtaking seaward views continue to distract you from the road (hence the recommendation to take the train) as you
㊳ travel by **Loch nan Uamh** (from the Gaelic meaning cave, and pronounced *oo*-am). This loch is associated with Prince Charles Edward Stuart's nine-month stay on the mainland, during which he gathered a small army, marched as far south as Derby in England, alarmed the king, retreated to unavoidable defeat at Culloden in the spring, and then spent a few months as a fugitive in the Highlands. A cairn by the shore marks the spot where the prince was picked up by a French ship. Prince Charles never returned to Scotland, and many say it would have been better if he had not arrived in the first place, because the backlash by the Hanoverian governors that his adventure provoked was particularly severe.

㊴ **Arisaig,** signposted off the A830, offers many options for dining and lodging (*see* Dining and Lodging, *below*). Beyond this point the road cuts across a headland to reach a stretch of coastline where the silver sands around Loch Morar are made glittering by the presence of mica in the local rock; clear water, blue sky, and white sand lend a tropical flavor to the beaches—when the sun shines. Sapphire seas and tiny bays backed by sandy wildflower meadows, called *machair*, conjure images of the Hebrides, Scotland's scatter of islands in the western seas. The nearest of these isles should be in plain view: not only Muck, Eigg, and Rhum, but also the magical Cuillin Hills of Skye, a little to the north. If viewed under clear skies, these postcard-perfect images may tempt you to find the nearest ferry for the passage across the sound. If you reach Morar under a steady drizzle and lowering gray skies, however, you may be quite content to scurry eastward again.

40 A small, unclassified side road off to the right leads to an even smaller road that will bring you to **Loch Morar,** the deepest of all the Scottish lochs (over 1,000 feet); the next deepest point is miles out into the Atlantic, beyond the Continental Shelf. Apart from this short public road, the area around the loch is all but roadless; the area to the immediate north and west, beyond Loch Nevis, one of the most remote in Scotland, is often referred to as the Rough Bounds of Knoydart.

41 After the approach along the coast, the town of **Mallaig** itself is anticlimactic. It has a few shops, and there is some bustle by the quayside when fishing boats unload or the Skye ferry departs. Mallaig is also the starting point for day cruises up the Sound of Sleat, which separates Skye from the mainland and offers views into rugged Knoydart and its sea lochs (*see* Off the Beaten Track, *below*).

42 You can get back to Fort William by retracing your route along the A830 to the **Lochailort** junction. From here, the road eastward to Fort William has many points of interest. **Glenfinnan,** perhaps the most visitor-oriented stop on the way, has the most to offer visitors interested in Scottish history. Here the National Trust for Scotland has capitalized on the romance surrounding the story of the Jacobites and their intention of returning a Stuart monarch and the Catholic religion to a country that had become staunchly Protestant. In Glenfinnan in 1745 the sometimes-reluctant clans joined forces and rallied to Prince Charles Edward Stuart's cause. The raising of the prince's standard is commemorated by the Glenfinnan Monument (an unusual tower on the banks of Loch Shiel), and the story of his campaign is told in the nearby visitor center. Note that the figure at the top of the monument is of a Highlander, not the prince. *A830, tel. 039783/250. Admission: £1 adults, 50p children. Open Apr.–May and early Sept.–late Oct., daily 10– 5:30; June–early Sept., daily 9:30–6:30.*

The view down Loch Shiel from this point, with the monument in the foreground and the silver-gray hills tilting steeply into the water, is, along with Eilean Donan Castle in Wester Ross, one of the two most-photographed views in Scotland. Equally impressive (for visitors who have tired of the Jacobite "Will He No Come Back Again" sentiment) is the curving railway viaduct that stretches across the green slopes behind. The **Glenfinnan Viaduct,** 21 spans and 1,248 feet long, was in its time the wonder of the Highlands. The railway's contractor, Robert MacAlpine, known as Concrete Bob by the locals, pioneered the use of mass concrete for viaducts and bridges when his company built the Mallaig extension, which was opened in 1901.

Between Glenfinnan and Fort William the road drops to the level of Loch Eil, affording views to the east that include a hint of

Ben Nevis's rugged buttresses. Note also, amid the industrial developments of Fort William's satellite settlements, the main road crossing the Caledonian Canal at an impressive flight of locks known as Neptune's Staircase.

The Great Glen for Free

Castle Tioram (*see* Tour 2)
Clava Cairns (*see* Tour 1)
At the **Farigaig Forest Centre,** visitors can take forest walks and visit the Forestry Commission Interpretative Centre, which disseminates information about wildlife conservation. *Off of B862, Inverfarigaig, 17 mi southwest of Inverness, tel. 0320/6322. Open Easter–mid-Oct., daily 9:30–7.*
Inverness Museum and Art Gallery is devoted to the history of the Highlands. Exhibits include fine collections of silver and bagpipes. *Castle Wynd, Inverness, tel. 0463/233813. Open Mon.–Sat. 9–5; July and Aug., also Sun. 2–5.*
Loch an Eilean (*see* Tour 1)
Rothiemurchus Estate Visitor Centre (*see* Tour 1)

What to See and Do with Children

Aigas Dam Fish Lift has a viewing chamber, from which migrating salmon can be seen swimming up the River Beauly. *Near Beauly. Open June–Oct., weekdays at 3, weekends at 10:15 and 3.*

Darnaway Farm Visitor Centre, of the Moray Estates, has farm animals, a woodland walk, and a place where children can watch the cattle being milked. *Off A96, 3 mi west of Forres, tel. 0309/672213. Admission: £1.50 adults, £1 children. Open May–mid-Sept., daily 10–5.*

Fort George (*see* Tour 1)

Landmark Visitor Centre, in Carrbridge, is one of the best visitor centers in Scotland. Its attractions include a dramatic exhibition on Highland history, a nature center, an adventure playground, a tree-top trail, and a 65-foot viewing tower. *Old A9, Carrbridge, 6 mi north of Aviemore, tel. 047/984–613. Admission: £3.95 adults, £2.60 children. Open Apr.–June and Sept.–Oct., daily 9:30–6; July–Aug., daily 9:30–8; Nov.– Mar., daily 9:30–5.*

The **Official Loch Ness Monster Exhibition** offers an (arguably) balanced view of the question of Nessie's existence. *A82, Drumnadrochit, tel. 04562/573 and 04562/218. Admission: £3.50 adults, £2 children, £2.50 senior citizens and students, £9.50 family ticket. Open July–mid-Sept., daily 9 AM–9:30 PM; off-season opening times vary (phone to check).*

Off the Beaten Track

The **Strontian to Polloch** route is a cul-de-sac road that runs up from Strontian and over a high shoulder toward Glen Shiel and offers outstanding hill views. **Ariundle Oak Wood,** in Strontian Glen, is a national nature reserve that evokes the original woodlands that once covered great tracts of the West Highlands. Gnarled, mossy oaks occupied the lower and more sheltered slopes of these mild moist glens, with pine and birch above. Humanity has greatly altered the landscape, but the original woodlands remain in some places.

Just a few minutes southeast from Fort William (signposted at the traffic circle just north of the town center), the magnificent **Glen Nevis** has an almost alpine flavor. Many visitors to Fort William miss it, although plenty of walking and climbing enthusiasts know its secrets and the routes to the high hills that soar, gray flanked, on every side. Go all the way to the end to capture the glen's full effects.

Remote **Lochs Nevis and Hourn** are long, fjordlike sea lochs that can be seen from the Sound of Sleat between the mainland and Skye. Visitors can also reach the lochs by sea from Mallaig. Check the range of rail/cruise options promoted from Fort William by contacting the **Transport Centre** (tel. 3927/2305) at the Fort William Station or by calling **Bruce Watt Sea Cruises** (Western Isles Guest House, Mallaig, tel. 0687/2320).

Anyone with a day to spend in Fort William can visit at least a couple of the **Small Isles: Rhum, Eigg, Muck, and Canna.** Caledonian MacBrayne ferries (*see* Getting Around, *above*) connect from Mallaig, but a better option is to contact **Murdo Grant** (Arisaig Marine, Arisaig, Inverness-shire, tel. 06875/224), which runs a service from the harbor at Arisaig. The MV *Shearwater*, a former naval inshore minesweeper, delivers supplies and mail as well as visitors to the diminutive island communities. What sets Grant's operation apart from the tourism-oriented excursions is that it offers visitors a glimpse of island life from a working vessel going about its summer routine.

Two outstanding mountain landscapes, those of **Glens Affric and Cannich,** located toward the northern end and to the west of the Great Glen, can be viewed in one easy day from Inverness. For visitors who have limited time but wish to see the Scottish heartland, these two glens offer a cross section of landscape. Accessible by way of Beauly and Strathglass (A831), Glen Cannich is constricted by crags and birch-clad slopes before opening into a broad valley with a hydroelectric dam at its far end. Glen Affric is, if anything, even more aesthetically appealing, with oak woodlands and hayfields in the lower reaches and wild lochs (also dammed) and pine forests, similar to the Trossachs, but on a grander scale.

Just a few minutes west of Invergarry and the A82, the main A87 climbs away from Loch Garry then heads into a moorland badly scarred by conifer planting. Just before you reach the moorland, note the outstanding westward view up the long cul-de-sac road that heads through **Glen Garry,** by Loch Quoich and ends up at the headwaters of Loch Hourne, deep in the hills. This is a sight to photograph from the main road, only a short diversion from the Great Glen.

If you're touring the West Highlands, you can take the backdoor ferry route to the **island of Mull** (*see* Chapter 9) from the area called Morvern, southwest of Fort William. This route affords views of moorland and woodland scenery and has little traffic. (No need to book car space on this ferry—just turn up.)

Shopping

Aviemore   In Aviemore **Jigsaw Designs** (1 Grampian Rd.) manufactures unusual and distinctive three-dimensional jigsaw puzzles and models, as well as mobiles and wood-painted pictures. The **Cairngorm Whisky Centre** (tel. 0479/810574) at Rothiemurchus has one of the largest selections of malt whiskies in the world, more than 500. There is a tasting room to help you make your choice.

Fort William   The majority of the shops here are located along High Street, which in summer attracts ever-present, bustling crowds intent on stocking up for excursions to the west. **Nevis Bank Woollen Mill**, at the north end of town, is a major supplier of tartans, woolens, and tweeds and has a restaurant. On High Street try **J & K Ness** at **The Granite House** for Scottish jewelry (including some by local designer Pat Cheney), china and crystal giftware, wildlife sculptures, and other collectibles. Opposite J & K Ness, at 49 High Street, is the **Nevis Bakery,** which sells plain and chocolate-chip shortbread and can supply packed lunches if visitors find the weather too pleasant to eat indoors. (The same proprietors also run the **Harvester Restaurant,** farther along High Street.)

Grantown on Spey and Environs   **Speyside Heather Centre,** at Skye of Curr (tel. 047985/359), not only has 200 varieties of heather for sale (some in sterile planting media), but also has a crafts shop and floral-art sundries. **The Kist** (74 High St., Grantown on Spey), is a well-stocked high-quality gift shop specializing in local and Scottish crafts.

Inverness   Although Inverness has the usual High Street chain stores and department stores—including **Arnott's** and **Marks and Spencer**—the most interesting goods are to be found in the various specialty outlets in and around town.

For antiques and antiquarian books try **Highland Antiques** (15 Tomnahurich St.) or the **Inverness Secondhand Bookshop** (10 Bank St.), which also specializes in antique prints. **The Riverside Gallery** (11 Bank St.) sells paintings and prints of Scottish natural history and sporting themes. For contemporary art there's the **Highland Printmakers Workshop and Gallery** (20 Bank St.). **Duncan Chisholm and Sons** (47–51 Castle St.) manufactures Highlands dress, tartans, and Scottish crafts, and the **Scottish Sweater Store** (Drummond St.) stocks the famous Pringle and Lyle & Scott brand names. Visitors can view Scottish textiles being manufactured at **James Pringle Ltd.** (Holm Woollen Mills, Dores Rd.), which offers factory tours, as well as a shop stocked with a vast selection of cashmere; lambswool; and Shetland knitwear, tartans, and tweeds. If you fancy trying your hand at a tartan or tweed, try **Jean Dodgson Woolly Shop** (Gorthleck). It sells needlework cushion kits in addition to designer knitwear and handmade horn buttons.

In a different vein entirely is **Highland Aromatics** (Drumchardine, Kirkhill), where, in a converted church, sweet-smelling soaps with the scents of the Highlands are manufactured. Equally appealing but probably more difficult to take home are the harps and *clarsachs* built by Tim Hobrough at the **Harpmaker's Workshop** (Mid St., Beauly). **Highland Wineries** (Moniack Castle, Kirkhill), purveyor of authentic Scottish wines, conducts tours and offers take-home bottles of birchbark wine.

Nairn and Environs In Nairn do not miss **Nairn Antiques** (St. Ninian Pl., near the traffic circle) for a wide inventory of antique jewelry, glassware, furniture, pottery, and prints. At Gollanfield, midway between Nairn and Inverness, **Culloden Pottery** offers you the chance to throw your own pot (which is then fired, glazed, and mailed to your home) or to choose from an original and extensive selection of hand-thrown domestic stoneware. There is also a gift-and-crafts shop and a restaurant that prides itself on serving only fresh—never frozen—food; there are fine views from the restaurant as well. East of Nairn is the **Brodie Country Fare,** guaranteed to affect your wallet in a pleasant way; unusual knitwear, gifts, toys, and a restaurant beckon from beyond the fare's foodstore and delicatessen. The fare is well worth a visit, which could be combined with a trip to nearby Brodie Castle.

Sports and Fitness

Beaches The most extensive beaches are at **Nairn,** with miles of clean, golden sand. The best known are at **Morar,** home of the famous white-and-silver sands.

Bicycling Bicycles can be rented from **Lee's Cycle Hire** (Fort William, tel. 0397/704204), **Lochaber Mountain Bike Hire** (Fort William, tel. 0397/703035), **Nevis Outdoor Hire Centre** (Glen Nevis, tel. 0397/703601), and **Off Beat Bikes** (Fort William, tel. 0397/702663).

Fishing The Great Glen offers many rivers and lochs where you can fly-fish for salmon and trout. Tourist-information centers (*see* Important Addresses and Numbers in Essential Information, *above*) can provide information on locations, permits, and fishing rights (which differ from those in England and Wales). The fishing seasons are as follows: salmon, depending on the area, early February through September or early October; brown trout, March 15 to September 30; sea trout, May through September or early October; rainbow trout, no statutory-close season. Sea angling from shore or boat is also possible; information is available from tourist-information centers.

Golf As is the case with most of Scotland, there is a broad selection of courses, especially toward the eastern end of this area. Nairn, with two courses, is highly regarded among Scottish players. The following courses are 18 holes unless otherwise specified: **Inverness Golf Club** (tel. 0463/239882), **Nairn Dunbar Golf Club** (tel. 0667/52741), **Nairn Golf Club** (tel. 0667/52787), **Torvean Golf Course** (Inverness, tel. 0463/237543).

Skiing **Aviemore** is perhaps the most advanced ski resort in the area, though the word "resort" is only loosely applicable to skiing in Scotland. **Nevis Range on Aonach Mor** (tel. 0397/705825 or 0397/705826; ski hotline, tel. 0898/654660), near Fort William, offers some long runs.

Walking The Great Glen area is renowned for its hill-walking opportunities, but walkers should be fit and properly outfitted. Tourist-information centers (*see* Important Addresses and Numbers in Essential Information, *above*) can offer guidance on low-level routes, and several excellent hill-walking guides available locally can and should be consulted for high-level routes. Remember that on **Ben Nevis,** a popular route even for inexperienced hill-walkers, it can snow on the summit plateau at any time of the year. Ben Nevis is a large and dangerous hill.

Dining and Lodging

Dining

Highly recommended restaurants are indicated by a star ★.

Category	Cost*
Very Expensive	over £40
Expensive	£30–£40
Moderate	£15–£30
Inexpensive	under £15

per person, including first course, main course, dessert, and VAT; excluding drinks

Lodging

Highly recommended hotels are indicated by a star ★.

Category	Cost*
Very Expensive	over £120
Expensive	£100–£120
Moderate	£80–£100
Inexpensive	under £80

All prices are for two people sharing a double room, including service, breakfast, and VAT.

Arisaig
Dining and Lodging

Arisaig House. This secluded and grand Victorian mansion offers tranquility and some marvelous scenery, including views of the Inner Hebrides. The bedrooms are plush and restful, with soft-pastel colors, original moldings, and antique furniture. The cuisine at the restaurant is quietly celebrated, with an emphasis on fresh local produce. *Beasdale (6 mi south of Mallaig on A830), Arisaig PH39 4NR, tel. 06875/622. 15 rooms, 13 with bath. Facilities: croquet, sailing, fishing, island trips, library, billiards. AE, MC, V. Closed Nov.–Easter. Expensive–Very Expensive.*

Arisaig Hotel. An old coaching inn close to the water, with magnificent views of the Small Isles, this hotel offers a slightly more modest environment than Arisaig House. The inn has retained its provinciality with simple decor and home cooking. High-quality local ingredients are used here to good advantage; locally smoked fish and king prawns are specialties, as are proper "puddings," such as fruit crumbles and upside-down cakes. *PH39 4NH, tel. 06875/210. Dress: casual. 15 rooms, 6 with bath. No credit cards. Inexpensive.*

Old Library Lodge and Restaurant. This guest house with a restaurant gives visitors another reason to believe that the village of Arisaig is unusually well endowed with good places to eat at all price levels. Situated on the waterfront, it offers traditional Scottish cooking, served in a beamed, pine-furnished dining room. The bedrooms are very comfortable. *PH39 4NH, tel.*

06875/651. Dress: casual. 7 rooms with bath. No credit cards. Closed Nov.–Mar. Inexpensive.

Aviemore
Dining

The Winking Owl. Cozy green-and-red tartan carpets increase the appeal of this "après-ski" resort restaurant. The cuisine includes English and Scottish dishes. *Grampian Rd., tel. 0479/810646. Reservations advised. Dress: informal. AE, MC, V. Closed Sun. and mid-Nov.–mid-Dec. Inexpensive–Moderate.*

Dalcross
Lodging

Easter Dalziel Farm. This working 210-acre livestock and arable farm offers plenty of interest for guests staying one night or longer. The Victorian farmhouse, with log fire, home baking, and pretty gardens, is a welcome change from an impersonal hotel. *Dalcross, Inverness, tel. 0667/62213. 3 rooms. No credit cards. Closed Dec.–Feb. Inexpensive.*

Drumnadrochit
Dining and Lodging

Polmaily House. This country house is located on the northern edge of Loch Ness amid lovely parkland. A home away from home, Polmaily is slightly faded and worn, but perhaps all the more relaxing because of its mellow ambience. Books, log fires, and a helpful staff contribute to an atmosphere that is warmer and more personal than that found at grander, more expensive hotels. The restaurant is noted for its international cuisine, which takes advantage of fresh Highland produce. Imaginatively prepared specialties include wild salmon with sorrel cream, smoked-cheese soufflé, and peppered venison. Homemade ice cream is a Polmaily favorite. The fact that the menu is somewhat limited is more of a reassurance than a drawback. *Milton, near A82, 12 mi southwest of Inverness, IV3 6XT, tel. 04562/343. Reservations advised. Dress: casual. 9 rooms, 7 with bath. Facilities: outdoor pool, tennis. MC, V. Closed mid-Oct.–Mar. No lunch for nonguests. Moderate.*

Lodging

Borlum Farmhouse. Spectacular views over Loch Ness are the outstanding feature of this farm guest house on a working farm. The rooms are freshly decorated and the food is well cooked. *Drumnadrochit, Inverness IV3 6XN, tel. 04562/358. 6 rooms, 3 with bath. Facilities: riding center. No credit cards. Closed Dec.–Feb. Inexpensive.*

Fort William
Dining and Lodging
★

Inverlochy Castle. A red-granite Victorian castle, Inverlochy stands in 50 acres of woodland in the shadow of Ben Nevis, with striking Highland landscape on every side. Queen Victoria stayed here and wrote, "I never saw a lovelier or more romantic spot." Dating from 1863, the hotel retains the splendor of its period, with a fine frescoed ceiling, crystal chandeliers, and a handsome staircase in the Great Hall; paintings and hunting trophies everywhere; and plush, comfortable bedrooms. The restaurant is exceptional. Many of the specialties are made from local produce, as are roast saddle of roe deer and wood-pigeon consommé. Orange soufflé is the final touch. For those in search of some pampering, this is the place to stay—Inverlochy Castle spares no expense to ensure the comfort of its guests. *Torlundy (3 mi northeast of Fort William on A82), Inverness-shire PH33 6BN, tel. 0397/702177. 16 rooms with bath. MC, V. Closed mid-Nov.–mid-Mar. Very Expensive.*

The Factor's House. Next to the gates of Inverlochy Castle sits a guest house and restaurant with a reputation for preparing a good meal for your money. The restaurant aims to present traditional Scottish cooking at its best, offering such favorites as trout in oatmeal, venison pie, and Atholl brose, all of which is prepared in a straightforward, appetizing manner. There are only seven bedrooms, with several comfortable sitting rooms. A stay here is a pleasant, friendly experience. *Torlundy, near Fort William, PH33 6SN, tel. 0397/705767. Reservations advised. Dress: casual. 7 rooms with bath. AE, DC, MC, V. Closed mid-Dec.–mid-Jan. No lunch. Moderate.*

Inverness
Dining and Lodging

Dickens. This friendly restaurant offers international fare. *77–79 Church St., tel. 0463/713111. Reservations advised. Dress: casual. AE, DC, MC, V. Inexpensive.*

Bunchrew House. This turreted mansion set on the banks of the Beauly Firth abounds with handsome wood paneling. The dining room is particularly attractive, with fine antique furniture, and the lounge and comfortable bedrooms are decorated with velvet and chintz. The grounds are extensive and are delightful for a predinner stroll, and the views of the Firth are superb. *Bunchrew, Inverness-shire IV3 6TA, tel. 0463/234917. 11 rooms with bath. AE, MC, V. Expensive.*

Culloden House. This imposing Georgian mansion was Bonnie Prince Charlie's headquarters during the Battle of Culloden. Handsome public rooms with beautifully crafted plasterwork provide the ambience in a restaurant renowned for its fine cuisine (though occasionally the chef's wilder flights of fancy do not come off). The menu includes many adventurous entrées, a number of which feature the use of fruit to cut the richness of game, salmon, duck, or beef. Try the wild salmon in lobster sauce or venison in Madeira. Culloden House has been awarded five crowns (the highest accolade for accommodations) by the Sottish Tourist Board. *Culloden, 6 mi east of Inverness by A9 and B9006, IV1 2NZ, tel. 0463/790461. 20 rooms with bath. AE, DC, MC, V. Expensive.*

★ **Dunain Park Hotel.** Guests receive individual attention in a private-house atmosphere in this 18th-century mansion 2½ miles southwest of Inverness on the A82. A log fire awaits you in the living room, where you can sip a drink and browse through books and magazines. Antiques and traditional decor make the bedrooms equally cozy and attractive. You can enjoy Scottish and French dishes in the restaurant, where candlelight is reflected in bone china and crystal. Saddle of venison in port sauce and boned quail stuffed with pistachios are two of the specialties. *Dunain IV3 6JN, tel. 0463/230512. Reservations advised. Jacket and tie required. 14 rooms, 12 with bath. Facilities: indoor heated pool, sauna. AE, DC, MC, V. Closed 1st week of Feb. and 1st week of Nov. Restaurant: Moderate. Hotel: Moderate–Expensive.*

Ballifeary House Hotel. A Victorian property that was recently redecorated and is well maintained. Offering high standards of comfort and service, the Ballifeary is within easy reach of downtown Inverness. *10 Ballifeary Rd., IV3 5PJ, tel. 0463/235572. 8 rooms with bath. No smoking in hotel. No credit cards. Closed Nov.–Feb. Inexpensive.*

Daviot Mains Farm. A 19th-century farmhouse, 5 miles south of Inverness on the A9, provides the perfect setting for home comforts and traditional Scottish cooking; lucky guests may find wild salmon on the menu. *Daviot Mains, tel. 0463/772215. 3 rooms (no private baths). No credit cards. Inexpensive.*

Lodging

Atholdene House. This family-run, 19th-century stone villa offers a friendly welcome and modernized accommodations. The bus and railway stations are a short walk away. *20 Southside*

Rd., IV2 3BG, tel. 0463/233565. 9 rooms, 7 with bath. No credit cards. Inexpensive.

Kingussie
Dining and Lodging

The Cross. Meals are superb, and the wine list is even more extensive than Osprey's (*see below*). It is difficult to get a room here, but you may be lucky. *Kingussie, Inverness-shire PH21 1EN, tel. 0540/661762. 3 rooms with shower. Closed May, Dec., and Sun.–Mon. No lunch for nonguests. MC, V. Expensive.*

Osprey Hotel. This friendly hotel in the village of Kingussie has no special frills, just good basic home comforts and cooking and an impressive wine list. It is ideally located for skiing and hill walking. *Kingussie, Inverness-shire PH21 1HX, tel. 0540/661510. 8 rooms, 4 with bath. MC, V. Inexpensive–Moderate.*

Whitebridge
Dining and Lodging
★

Knockie Lodge. Set on rising ground not far from Loch Ness, this former shooting lodge has superb views and is especially popular with fishermen and other outdoor-sports enthusiasts. Decorated with traditional and antique furniture, this hotel provides very peaceful surroundings, though with easy access to Inverness. The restaurant offers enticing fixed menus with a choice of desserts. The chef uses top-quality produce and prepares everything with great care. Bar lunches are also wholesome. The dining room is quite small, so advance reservations are needed if you are not a guest of the hotel. *Whitebridge IV1 2UP, tel. 04563/276. Reservations required. 10 rooms with bath. AE, MC, V. Closed late-Oct.–Apr. Moderate.*

The Arts and Nightlife

Do not visit this area expecting to have a big-city choice of late-night activities. With the exception of Inverness, evening entertainment revolves around pubs and hotels, with the ceilidh, or Scottish evening, the most popular form of entertainment offered to visitors.

The Arts

Theater **Eden Court Theatre** (Bishops Rd., Inverness, tel. 0463/239841) offers not only drama, but also a program of music, film, and light entertainment.

Nightlife

Bars and Lounges **Inverness** has an array of bars and lounges. Among the most popular are **Gunsmith's** (Union St.), a traditional pub offering bar meals, and **Hayden's** (37 Queensgate, open 9–12 on Sundays, later on weekdays), which serves everything from breakfast to late-night cocktails. **Fort William** offers a similarly wide range, and the pubs of **Aviemore** offer an après-ski ambience.

Cabaret **Scottish Showtime** (Cummings Hotel, Church St., Inverness, tel. 0463/233246 or 0463/232531) and **McTavish's Kitchens** (High St., Fort William, tel. 0397/702406) are the two most popular choices in the region. They both offer Scottish cabaret of the tartan-clad dancer and bagpipe/accordian variety.

Discos There are a number of places to go dancing, particularly in Inverness, some in local hotels. To obtain a complete list, it is best to consult the local tourist-information center (*see* Important Addresses and Numbers in Essential Information, *above*).

Jazz Details of concerts held by the **Inverness Jazz Platform** are available from the group's secretary (tel. 0463/790137).

12 Northern Highlands

*Sutherland and Wester Ross,
Isle of Skye,
the Outer Hebrides*

Introduction

By Gilbert Summers

The old counties of Ross and Cromarty (sometimes called Easter and Wester Ross), Sutherland, and Caithness constitute the most northerly mainland portion of Scotland. The population is sparse; mountains and moorland limit the choice of touring routes; and distances are less important than whether the winding, hilly roads you travel are two lanes or one. Tourism authorities have billed this area as one of unspoiled wilderness, but there is some question as to whether any part of Scotland—tree shorn and overgrazed over the centuries—can truly be described as unspoiled. However, the question of the area's accessibility is more relevant. Although it appears a long way from London on the map, Inverness has an airport with direct links to the south, and you can reach such destinations as the fishing town of Ullapool in about an hour by car from Inverness. In fact, much of the western seaboard is perfectly accessible, so do not be misled by an excess of literature that talks about "remote mountain fastness."

The area undoubtedly contains some of Scotland's most fascinating scenery. Much of Sutherland and Wester Ross, for example, is comprised of a rocky platform of Lewisian gneiss, certainly the oldest rocks in Britain, scoured and hollowed by glacial action into numerous lochs. On top of this rolling wet moorland landscape sit strangely shaped sandstone or quartzite mountains, eroded and pinnacled.

Many of the place names in this region reflect its early settlement links with Scandinavia. Sutherland, the most northern portion of mainland Scotland, was once the "southern land" of the Vikings. Scotland's most northern point, Cape Wrath, got its name from the Viking word *hvarth*, meaning a "turning point," and Laxford, Suilven, and dozens of other names in the area have Norse rather than Gaelic derivations.

As for the islands of Skye and the Outer Hebrides, they are the stronghold of the Gaelic language, especially the Outer Hebrides (which are now often referred to as the Western Isles). Skye, famous for the misty mountains called the Coullins, offers scenic excitement, and the Outer Hebrides perhaps less so, though some of Scotland's finest beaches are found there.

Finally, do not assume that the farther north on the mainland you go, the more "Scottish" the communities become. On the contrary, the northwest has seen a major influx in recent years of southerners seeking to escape the rat race. With their purchasing power, these new settlers from the more affluent regions of England have been driving up the prices of homes in the region, making it harder for young natives to find affordable housing.

Essential Information

Important Addresses and Numbers

Tourist Information | **Caithness Tourist Board** (Whitechapel Rd., off High St., Wick, tel. 0955/2596), **Western Isles (Outer Hebrides) Tourist Board** (Information Centre, 4 S. Beach St., Stornoway, tel. 0851/703088), **Isle of Skye and South West Ross Tourist Board** (Tourist Information Centre, Portree, Isle of Skye, tel. 0478/2137),

Ross and Cromarty Tourist Board (Tourist Information Centre, North Kessock, tel. 046/373–505), Sutherland Tourist Board (The Square, Dornoch, tel. 0862/810400). Seasonal tourist information centers can be found at Bettyhill, Bonar Bridge, Broadford (Skye), Castlebay (Outer Hebrides), Durness, Gairloch, Glen Shiel, Helmsdale, John o' Groats, Kyle of Lochalsh, Lochboisdale (Outer Hebrides), Lochcarron, Lochinver, Lochmaddy (Outer Hebrides), Strathpeffer, Tarbert (Outer Hebrides), Thurso, and Ullapool.

Emergencies For police, fire, or ambulance, dial 999 from any telephone. No coins are needed for emergency calls from public telephone booths.

Late-Night Pharmacies These are not found in rural areas. In an emergency the police will provide assistance in locating a pharmacist. In rural areas general practitioners may also dispense medicines.

Arriving and Departing by Plane

Airports and Airlines The main airports for the Northern Highlands are Inverness and Wick (both on the mainland). There is direct air service from London to Inverness. Contact Dan Air (tel. 0667/62666). Loganair (tel. 041/889–3181) and British Airways (tel. 041/332–9666) offer flights to Wick from the south, departing via Edinburgh, Aberdeen, or Glasgow. There are island flight connections to the Outer Hebrides via Glasgow or Inverness. For Stornoway, the largest town in Lewis (Outer Hebrides) contact British Airways. For the Hebridean islands of Barra and Benbecula contact Loganair.

Arriving and Departing by Car, Train, and Bus

By Car The fastest route to this area is the A9 to the gateway town of Inverness. The ferry service Caledonian MacBrayne links the Outer Hebrides: Ferries run from Ullapool to Stornoway (tel. 0854/612358), from Oban to Castlebay and Lochboisdale (tel. 0631/62285), and from Uig on the island of Skye to Tarbert and Lochmaddy (tel. 047/042–219). Causeways link North Uist, Benbecula, and South Uist.

By Train Main railway stations in the area include Oban (for Barra and the Uists) and Kyle of Lochalsh (for Skye) on the west coast or Inverness (for points north to Thurso and Wick). There is direct service from London to Inverness and connecting service from Edinburgh and Glasgow.

By Bus Caledonian Express (tel. 0738/33481) runs buses to Inverness and beyond to Ullapool. Scottish Citylink (tel. 041/332–9191) connects with Ullapool and Dingwall. There are also coach connections between the ferry ports of Tarbert and Stornoway.

Getting Around

You can use a seven- or 13-day Scottish Travelpass in the Highlands and Islands area. The pass, which will save you money on ScotRail, CalMac ferries, and Orkney ferries, as well as on some bus lines, is available at main-line British Rail stations in London, the Scottish Tourist Board (19 Cockspur St., London), and British Travel (4–12 Regent St., London, tel. 071/730–3400). The pass is also widely available in Scotland at most large British Rail stations, at bus stations, at the CalMac Ferries at the Ferry Terminal, and at Gourock and the larger tourist-information centers in the Highlands of Scotland, including Aviemore, Inverness, Fort William, Oban, Thurso, Wick, John o' Groats, Dornoch, Lochinver, Durness, Arran (Brodick), and Bute (Rothesay).

By Car   Besides the ferry services listed above, it is also important to note that in this sparsely populated area, distances between gas stations can be considerable. Although getting around is easy, even on single-lane roads, the choice of routes is more restricted by the rugged terrain.

By Train   Stations on the northern lines (Inverness to Thurso/Wick and Inverness to Kyle of Lochalsh) include Muir of Ord, Dingwall; on the Thurso/Wick line, Alness, Invergordon, Fearn, Tain, Ardgay, Culrain, Invershin, Lairg, Rogart, Golspie, Brora, Helmsdale, Kildonan, Kinbrace, Forsinard, Altnabreac, Scotscalder, and Georgemas Junction; and on the Kyle line, Garve, Lochluichart, Achanalt, Achnasheen, Achnashellach, Strathcarron, Attadale, Strome Ferry, Duncraig, Plockton, and Duirinish.

By Bus   **Highland Scottish** provides bus service in the Highlands area (mainland and Skye, tel. 0463/233371). On the Outer Hebrides a number of small operators and post buses—which also deliver mail—run regular routes to most towns and villages. However the post-bus service becomes increasingly important in remote areas. It supplements the regular bus service, which runs only a few times per week because of the small population on the islands. A full timetable of services for the Northern Highlands (and the rest of Scotland) is available from the **District Head Post Office** (14–16 Queensgate, Inverness, tel. 0463/234111, ext. 248) or from the **District Head Post Office** (2–4 Waterloo Pl., Edinburgh, tel. 031/550–8232).

By Air   **Loganair** (tel. 041/889–3181) operates flights (from Glasgow) between the islands of Barra, Benbecula, and Stornoway in the Outer Hebrides.

Guided Tours

Orientation   The bus companies named above also operate orientation tours in summer, as does **Spa Coach Tours** (Strathpeffer, tel. 0997/421311), which covers a large portion of the Northern Highlands and Skye.

Special-Interest   **Caledonian Wildlife** (30 Culduthel Rd., Inverness, tel. 0463/233130), offers birdlife and wildlife tours of the north. **North-West Frontiers** (19 West Terr., Ullapool, Wester Ross, tel. 0854/612571) offers walking itineraries in some of Scotland's most vivid scenery, in Skye, Wester Ross, and Sutherland. A number of small firms run boat cruises along the spectacular west-coast seaboard; one such firm is **Lochinver Wildlife Cruises** (WC Watson, 171 Stoer, tel. 05714/446), which operates a passenger boat from Culag pier for two-hour cruises to the seal colonies and bird islands. On Skye there is also a broad selection of mountain guides. A list can be obtained from Skye's tourist-information center (*see* Important Addresses and Numbers, *above*).

Exploring the Northern Highlands

Orientation

From Inverness, gateway to the Northern Highlands, roads fan out like the spokes of a wheel to join the coastal route around the rim of mainland Scotland. Most visitors tour from east to west, saving the best scenery for last. The tour described below takes the visitor quickly to the west. The main points of interest in the east are mentioned in the Off the Beaten Track section that follows the tour.

An important caveat for visitors driving in this area: There are still some single-lane roads in this part of Scotland. These twisting, winding thoroughfares demand a degree of driving dexterity. Local rules of the road require that when two cars meet, whichever driver reaches a passing place first must stop in it or opposite it and allow the oncoming car to continue. Small cars tend to yield to large commercial vehicles. Never park in passing places and never forget that these sections of the road allow traffic behind you to pass. Don't hold up a vehicle trying to pass you. Feelings run high about this in the northwest every year. The good news is that you can drive for long distances west or north—practically all the way from Inverness to the Butt of Lewis (the northernmost tip of the main island of the Outer Hebrides)—and never encounter a single-lane road.

Highlights for First-time Visitors

Corrieshalloch Gorge (*see* Tour 1)
Glenbrittle (*see* Tour 2)
Glen Torridon (*see* Tour 1)
Inverewe Gardens (*see* Tour 1)
Quiraing (*see* Tour 2)
View of the Cuillins from Elgol (*see* Tour 2)
View of Slioch from Loch Maree (*see* Tour 1)
View of Suilven from Lochinver (*see* Tour 1)

Tour 1: The Northern Landscapes— Wester Ross and Sutherland

Numbers in the margin correspond to points of interest on the Northern Highlands and Skye map.

It takes roughly one hour to travel from Inverness to Ullapool: You need to know this if you are planning to catch a ferry to Stornoway on the isle of Lewis, part of the Outer Hebrides. If you prefer to be more leisurely, however, loiter along the way in the former Victorian spa town of **Strathpeffer**—where you can even taste the waters. Not far from Strathpeffer are the tumbling **Falls of Rogie,** where an alarmingly sagging suspension bridge leaves visitors with a fine view of the splashing waters below and an uneasy stomach.

If you really want to give yourelf a touch of vertigo, however, the **Corrieshalloch Gorge** should be next on your sightseeing agenda. You can reach the gorge by following the A835 (to Ullapool) west of **Garve,** the bare backbone of Scotland. As the

The Northern Highlands and Skye

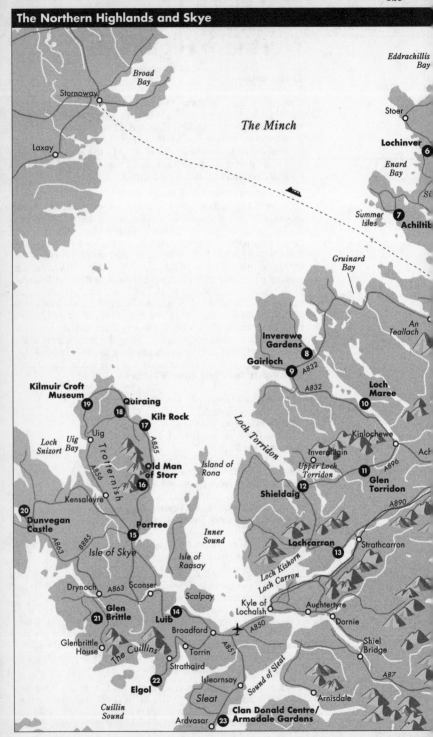

The Minch

Broad Bay

Stornoway

Laxay

Eddrachillis Bay

Stoer

Lochinver 6

Enard Bay

Si

Summer Isles

7 **Achiltib**

Gruinard Bay

An Teallach

Inverewe Gardens 8

Gairloch 9 A832

A832

Loch Maree 10

Kilmuir Croft Museum 19

Quiraing 18

Kilt Rock 17

Uig

A855

Kinlochewe

Inveralligin

Upper Loch Torridon

Ach

A896

Old Man of Storr 16

Island of Rona

11 **Glen Torridon**

12 **Shieldaig**

Loch Snizort

Uig Bay

Trotternish

A856

Kensaleyre

Loch Torridon

A890

Dunvegan Castle 20

A863

B885

Portree 15

Inner Sound

Isle of Raasay

Lochcarron 13 Strathcarron

Isle of Skye

Drynoch A863 Sconser

Scalpay

Loch Kishorn Loch Carron

Auchtertyre

Glen Brittle 21

Luib 14

Kyle of Lochalsh

A850 Dornie

Glenbrittle House

The Cuillins

Broadford

A851

Shiel Bridge

Torrin

Strathaird

Isleornsay

Sound of Sleat

A87

Elgol 22

Arnisdale

Cuillin Sound

Sleat

Ardvasar

23 **Clan Donald Centre/ Armadale Gardens**

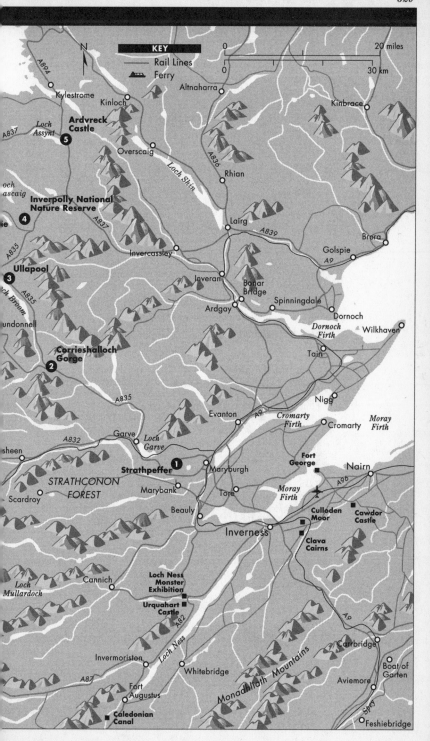

N

0   20 miles
0   30 km

Kylestrome
Kinloch
Altnaharra
Kinbrace

A894
A837

Ardvreck Castle
Loch Assynt
5
Overscaig

Loch Shin
A836
Rhian

och ascaig

Inverpolly National Nature Reserve
4
A837
Lairg
A839
Brora
Golspie
A9

ie

A835

Ullapool
3

Invercassley
Inveran
Bonar Bridge
Spinningdale
Dornoch

ch Broom

undonnell
Ardgay
Dornoch Firth
Wilkhaven

Corrieshalloch Gorge
2
Tain

A835
Nigg

sheen
Evanton
A9
Cromarty Firth
Cromarty
Moray Firth

A832
Garve
Loch Garve

Strathpeffer
1
Maryburgh
Fort George
Nairn

STRATHCONON FOREST
Marybank
Moray Firth
A96

Scardroy
Tore
Culloden Moor
Cawdor Castle

Beauly

Loch Mullardoch
Inverness
Clava Cairns

Cannich
Loch Ness Monster Exhibition

Urquhart Castle
A82

A9

Invermoriston
Whitebridge
Monadhliath Mountains
Carrbridge

A87
Boat of Garten

Fort Augustus
Aviemore

Caledonian Canal
Spey
Feshiebridge

road begins to drop down from the bleak lands of the interior, look for Braemore junction and continue on the A835. Shortly after, as you draw closer to the woods, you'll see the Corrieshalloch Gorge car park on the left. A burn draining the high moors plunges 150 feet into a 200-foot-deep, thickly wooded gorge. There is a suspension-bridge viewpoint and certainly an atmosphere of romantic grandeur, like an old Scottish print come to life.

❸ The road then rolls down to **Ullapool** by the shores of salty **Loch Broom.** This community was founded in 1788 as a fishing station, to exploit the local herring stocks. In recent years the fishing activity here has included "klondyking," the direct purchase of fish from local boats by large, Eastern European factory ships. From time to time Ullapool certainly has a cosmopolitan air and comes alive when the Lewis ferry docks and departs. There is a local potter and a modest selection of shops selling books, souvenirs, waterproof jackets and trousers, insect repellent, and other northwest touring aids.

Time Out   Several years ago, the **Ceilidh Place** (W. Argyle St., tel. 0854/ 612103) spotted a gap in the market for an enlightened, trendy eatery. Since then, this warm, friendly coffeehouse and restaurant has filled that niche in its own nonconformist way. The prices are sensible, and musicians perform here from time to time.

If you travel northward, you will find yourself on a two-lane road, the A835/A837, which takes you past the strange landscape of **Wester Ross.** Look westward for the little mountain **Stac Polly**—which resembles a ruined fortress—and the humps of **Suilven.** At **Knockan,** about 15 miles north of Ullapool, a nature trail along a cliff illuminates some of the interesting local geology, as well as the area's flora and fauna. If this jaunt sounds too energetic, a more restful alternative may be to **❹** enjoy the good views of the mountains from the **Inverpolly National Nature Reserve.**

❺ Following the signs for Lochinver along Loch Assynt will bring you to the ruins of **Ardvreck Castle,** on the edge of Loch Assynt. This was a **MacLeod** clan stronghold, built in the 15th century. It was also the place of capture of the **marquis of Montrose.** He was defeated in battle near Carbisdale (to the east) in 1650, in the struggle for the restoration of the monarchy, which so convulsed both Scotland and England in the 17th century.

❻ From Ardvreck Castle it's only a 20-minute drive on a two-lane road to **Lochinver,** a charming community with a few choices of accommodations and places to eat. Behind the town the mountain Suilven rises, pillar shaped. This unusual edifice is best seen from across the water, however: Take the cul-de-sac, **Baddidarach Road,** for the finest photo opportunity.

A single-lane unclassified road winds south from Lochinver, offering outstanding sea views within the first 5 miles. Do not fall victim to the breathtaking landscape, however: The road has several blind bends that demand special care. You will then find yourself near what is perhaps Scotland's most remote bookshop. The road will swing left and inland immediately after **Loch Kirkaig;** nearby is a car park beside the River Kirkaig, and a short stroll away is **Achins Bookshop** (look for signs by the river bridge).

This wild though harmonious landscape of bracken and birch tree, heather and humped hill horizons, prevails until you see ❼ signs for **Achiltibuie:** You'll then encounter a strung-out line of crofts, many now owned by incomers. Offshore are the **Summer Isles,** romantic enough as a notion, but in reality bleak and austere. You must make up your own mind about these landscapes—they will either appeal to you because of their elemental qualities (moorland, mountain, wind, and wide skies) or they will make you turn southward to softer scenery. Remember, it isn't far to Perthshire or Argyll. In Achiltibuie there's a smokehouse, offering succulent smoked cuts of venison and other delicacies, and the Hydroponicum, which certainly looks out of place but is effective in producing giant strawberries.

Return to Ullapool, then retrace your route as far as the Braemore Road junction, noted earlier, which juts above the Corrieshalloch Gorge. Take the A832 for **Gairloch.** Soon you will be traversing wild country once more. The toothed ramparts of the mountain **An Teallach** (pronounced *tyel*-lach, with Scots *ch*, of course) can be seen on the horizon ahead. The moorland route you travel is known chillingly as **Destitution Road.** It was commissioned in 1851 to give the local folk (long vanished from the area) some way of earning a living following the failure of the potato crop; it is said the workers were paid only in food.

The road descends to the woodlands of **Dundonnell** and to Loch Broom (*see* Dundonnell Hotel in Dining and Lodging, *below*). The coastal scenery hereabouts improves with views of **Gruinard Bay** and its white beaches, but the highlight for most ❽ travelers is the **Inverewe Gardens,** another half hour to the south. The reputation of the gardens at Inverewe, in spite of their comparatively remote location, has grown steadily through the years. The main attraction lies in the contrast between the bleak coastal headlands and thin-soiled moors and the lush plantings of the garden behind the dense shelter-belts. These are proof of the efficiency of the warm North Atlantic Drift, part of the Gulf Stream, which takes the edge off winter frosts. Inverewe is sometimes described as subtropical, an inaccuracy that irritates the head gardener. Do not expect coconuts and palm trees here. Inverewe is home to a spectacular variety of temperate species, many from the southern hemisphere. It is run as a series of separate gardens that blend together, with each member of the gardening team responsible for his or her own section. There is a new setting to explore around every corner. If you're inspired to emulate some of the gardens' horticultural successes, you'll find seeds in the shop, replete with an ample gardening inventory. *A832, 6 mi northeast of Gairloch, tel. 044586/200. Admission: £2.80 adults, £1.40 children. Gardens open all year, daily 9:30–sunset. Visitor center open Apr.–mid-May and Sept.–mid-Oct., Mon.–Sat. 10–5, Sun. 12–5; mid-May–Aug., Mon.–Sat. 9:30–6, Sun. noon–6.*

Time Out The National Trust for Scotland, which now looks after the gardens, also runs an adequate **tearoom** (tel. 044586/200) with a selection of cakes and biscuits.

❾ **Gairloch,** the region's main center, lies to the south of the gardens and has some choice of shops and accommodations. The **Myrtle Bank Hotel** (tel. 0445/2004), for instance, serves cream-scone teas as well as bar meals. Also in the village is the **Gairloch Heritage Museum,** with exhibitions covering the area from prehistoric times to the present. Gairloch has one further advantage: Lying just a short way from the mountains of the interior, this small oasis often escapes the rainclouds that sometimes cling to the high summits. Guests can enjoy a game of golf here and perhaps stay dry, even when the nearby Torridon hills are deluged.

From Gairloch the road goes inland to one of Scotland's most scenic lochs, **Loch Maree.** Look for the sign, soon after the road reaches the loch side, for **Victoria Falls,** an attractive waterfall named after the queen who visited them. The harmonious environs of the loch, with its tall Scots pines and the mountain Slioch looming as a backdrop, witnessed the destruction of much of its tree cover in the 18th century. Iron ore was shipped in and smelted using local oak to feed the furnaces. Oak now grows here only on the northern limits of the range.

The Nature Conservancy Council has an information center and nature trails by the loch side. Red-deer sightings are virtually guaranteed; locals say the best place to spot another local denizen, the pine marten, is around the trash containers in the parking turnoffs.

The tall pines of Loch Maree prepare the visitor for the contrasting scenic spectacle of **Glen Torridon,** which you can reach by turning right at Kinlochewe. Some say that Glen Torridon has the finest mountain scenery in Scotland. It consists mainly of the long gray quartzite flanks of **Ben Eighe** (pronounced to rhyme with *say*), which make up Scotland's oldest national nature reserve, and **Liathach** (pronounced *leea*-gach with the Scots *ch*), with its distinct ridge profile that looks like the keel of an upturned boat. At the far end of the glen the National Trust for Scotland operates a visitor center that explains the ecology and geology of the area.

If time permits, you can explore the small communities that are accessible via roads along Loch Torridon. For a real end-of-the-road feeling, follow the road west along the north shore of **Loch Torridon,** from the A896 to **Diabaig.** Here you will find superb views of the **Applecross Mountains** across the loch, and the road finally drops steeply down to **Lower Diabaig,** which consists of a pier and a few cottages. You can walk back along the rugged northern coast of **Upper Loch Torridon** toward **Inveralligin,** but ask a local about the path before walking it (it's a bit hard to find).

Not too far from the southern coast of Upper Loch Torridon is **Shieldaig,** a village that sits in an attractive crescent over a loch of its own, **Loch Shieldaig.** For an atmospheric evening foray, walk north toward Loch Torridon at the northern end of the village, by the church. The path is fairly well made, though hiking shoes are recommended. You will find exquisite views and tiny rocky beaches.

You can then continue south by the A896, passing **Rassal Ash Wood** on your left. The lushness of the fenced-in area within this small nature reserve is a reminder of what Scotland might have been had sheep and deer not been kept here in such high numbers. The combined nibbling of these animals ensures that Scotland's natural tree cover does not regenerate without human intervention.

The road continues past **Kishorn,** a daunting oil-platform construction yard taking advantage of the deep water nearby. (It was originally to have been built nearer the **Kyle of Lochalsh** railhead, where it would have looked more appropriate, but one of Scotland's conservation agencies, which owned land nearby, ironically intervened.) The road soon takes you to **Lochcarron,** a village strung along the shore. The community has an ample number of bed-and-breakfast accommodations. Return toward Inverness by the A890, a single-lane road in some stretches, with plenty of open vistas across the deserted heart of northern Scotland.

Tour 2: Skye, the Misty Island

Skye ranks near the top of most visitors' priority lists: The romance of Bonnie Prince Charlie, the misty **Cuillin Mountains,** and the ease of the five-minute crossing from the mainland all contribute to its popularity. The following tour takes you around the island in two or three days. Orientation is easy: Follow the only roads around the loops on the northern part of the island. There are some stretches of single-lane road, but none is a problem.

After making the crossing from Kyle of Lochalsh, follow the A850 along the coast. At **Luib,** note the **Old Skye Crofter's House,** with its traditional thatch and 19th-century furnishings. The hills ahead have a reddish hue—they comprise the **Red Cuillin,** the gentler companions of the Black Cuillins, which swing spectacularly into view on the approaches to **Sligachan,** which consists of a hotel and a bridge.

Turning away from the hills, the road goes north through tranquil scenery to **Portree,** the population center of the island. Not overburdened by historical features, Portree is a pleasant center clustered around a small and sheltered bay (*see* Cuillin Hills Hotel in Dining and Lodging, *below*).

To see the northern peninsula of **Trotternish,** head out on the A855, noting the cliffs rising to your left. The cliffs are actually the edge of an ancient lava-flow that runs for miles as your rugged companion, set back from the road. In some places the hardened lava has created spectacular features. Soon you will see one of them on the horizon: a curious pinnacle called the **Old Man of Storr.** Continue past neat white crofts and forestry plantings until you reach **Kilt Rock.** Everyone on the Skye-tour circuit stops here to peep gingerly over a cliff from a safe platform to look at the curious geology of the cliff edge. Here, bands of two different types of rock give a folded, pleated effect just like the material of a kilt.

Even more spectacular is the **Quiraing,** 5 miles farther. For a closer view of the strange pinnacles and rock forms, make a left onto a small road at **Brogaig** by **Staffin Bay.** There is a car park near the point where this road breaches the ever-present cliff line, though you will have to be physically fit to walk back toward the Quiraing itself, where the rock formations and cliffs are most dramatic. Once, stolen cattle were hidden deep within the Quiraing's rocky jaws.

Return to the main A855, continuing around the top end of Trotternish, to the **Kilmuir Croft Museum,** where you can see the old farming ways brought to life. Included in the displays and exhibits are documents and photographs, reconstructed interiors, and implements. Flora Macdonald, helpmate of Prince Charles Edward Stuart, is buried nearby.

The west coast of Trotternish is pleasant, but this is probably all you could easily manage in one day. You may want to return to Portree before making a separate expedition to **Dunvegan Castle.** In a commanding position above a sea loch, Dunvegan has been the seat of the chiefs of Clan Macleod for more than 700 years. Though greatly changed over the centuries, the gloomy ambience is certainly atmospheric, and there is plenty of family history on display, notably the fascinating "Fairy Flag"—a silk banner, thought to be originally from Rhodes or Syria and believed to have magically saved the clan from danger. The banner's powers are said to suffice for only one more use. *Tel. 047–022/206. Admission: £3.50 adults, £1.90 children, £3 students and senior citizens. Open mid-Mar.–Nov., Mon.–Sat. 10–5:30, Sun. 1–5.*

There are two other excursions to consider, both taking in spectacular mountain scenery. The first is to **Glen Brittle,** off the A863 on the west side of the island. This jaunt provides some fine views of the Cuillin ridges—not a place for the ordinary walker (there are many dangerous ridges and steep faces). The second suggestion follows a small road, a cul-de-sac resembling Glen Brittle, which leads you to one of the finest views in Scotland. At **Broadford,** take the A881 for Elgol. This road passes through **Strath Suardal** and little **Loch Cill Chriosd (Kilchrist)** by a ruined church. If there are cattle wading in the loch and the light is soft—typical of Skye—then this place takes on the air of a romantic Victorian oil painting. Mindful of the marble quarry at **Torrin** and the breathtaking views of the mountain **Blaven,** simply follow the road to **Elgol.** This is just a gathering of crofts along the suddenly descending road, which ends at a pier. You can admire the heart-stopping profile of the Cuillin peaks from the shore or, at a point about halfway down the hill, find the path that goes toward them across the rough grasslands. Either way, you may want to stop for a cup of tea at the local tea shop, which sits by the road.

To leave the island you can take the alternative ferry running from **Armadale** to **Mallaig.** If you go this way, you can take in the popular **Clan Donald Centre and Armadale Gardens** on the A851. The center tells the story of the Macdonalds and their proud title: the Lords of the Isles. In the 15th century they were powerful enough to threaten the authority of the Stuart monarchs of Scotland. There is also a major exhibition in a restored part of the castle, as well as extensive gardens and nature trails. *A851 at Armadale, ½ mi north of Armadale Pier, tel. 04714/305 or 04714/277. Admission to center: £3 adults, £2 children and senior citizens, £8 family ticket. Center open Apr.–Oct., daily 9–5:30. Gardens open at all times.*

Tour 3: The Outer Hebrides (Western Isles)

Numbers in the margin correspond to the points of interest on the Outer Hebrides map.

The Outer Hebrides—in common parlance also known as the Western Isles—stretch about 130 miles from end to end and lie about 50 miles from the Scottish mainland. This splintered archipelago extends from the pugnacious Butt of Lewis in the north to the 600-foot Barra Head on Berneray in the south, whose lighthouse has the greatest arc of visibility in the world. The **Isle of Lewis and Harris** is the northernmost and largest of the group. The islands' only major town, **Stornoway,** is situated on a big land-locked harbor on the east coast of Lewis. **Harris** has the highest mountain in the islands (Chisham, at 2,600 feet) and was the home of the world-famous Harris tweed (the local weaving industry is now centered in Stornoway). Together, Lewis and Harris comprise about two-thirds of the Outer Hebrides.

Just south of the Sound of Harris is **North Uist,** rich in monoliths and chambered cairns and other reminders of a prehistoric past. Though it is one of the smaller islands in the chain, **Benbecula,** sandwiched between North and South Uist and sometimes referred to as the Hill of the Fords, is in fact less bare and neglected looking than its bigger neighbors to the north. **South Uist,** once a refuge of the old Catholic faith, is dotted with ruined forts and chapels; in summer its wild gardens burst with riots of Alpine and rock plants. **Eriskay** and a scattering of islets almost block the 6-mile strait between South Uist and **Barra,** the southernmost major formation in the Outer Hebrides, an isle you can walk across in an hour.

Lewis and Harris The port capital for the Outer Hebrides is **Stornoway** on Lewis, which can be reached by car ferry from Ullapool on the mainland. This is probably the most convenient starting point for a driving tour of the islands if you're approaching the Western Isles from the Northern Highlands. In Stornoway itself are two museums that vividly illustrate Lewis's past. The **An Lanntair Gallery** offers a varied program of contemporary and traditional exhibitions that change monthly, as well as frequent musical and theatrical events emphasizing traditional Gaelic culture. *Town Hall, S. Beach St., Stornoway, tel. 0851/703307. Admission free. Open Mon.–Sat. 10–5:30.*

Displays at the **Museum nan Eilean (Museum of the Isles)** focus on key aspects of the island's history, as well as the daily life and work of its people. There are exhibits on archaeology, agriculture, fishing, and the sea. *Francis St. Contact the tourist information center for details of opening times.*

The best road to use to explore the territory north of Stornoway is the A857, which runs first across the island to the northwest and then to the northeast all the way to Port of Ness (about 30 miles). At the northernmost point of the island—just a few minutes northwest of **Port of Ness** along the B8014—stands the **Butt of Lewis lighthouse,** designed by David and Thomas Stevenson (of the prominent engineering family, whose best-known member was, ironically, the novelist Robert Louis Stevenson). The lighthouse was first lit in 1862. The adjacent cliffs provide a good vantage point for viewing seabirds, whales, and porpoises.

Time Out The **Harbour View Tearoom** in Port of Ness is the perfect place to recharge your batteries before heading back south. Delicate fish pâtés, a choice of real (not bagged) teas, and scrumptious cakes are served in a cozy room in what used to be a boatbuilder's house. Accommodations are also available here.

Go back south on the A857 and pick up the A858 at Barvas. From there it's about a 10-minute drive to the small community

The Outer Hebrides

ATLANTIC OCEAN

Isle of Lewis and Harris

Butt of Lewis Lighthouse
25
Butt of Lewis

Port of Ness

A857

Arnol Black House
26
Barvas

Tolsta

Shawbost

27

Arnol

Shawbost School Museum

B895

Tiumpan Head

East Loch Roag

Loch Roag

28
Dun Carloway

Callanish

Stornoway

24
Stornoway

Valtos

29
Callanish Standing Stones

Eye Peninsula

Brenish

MORSGAIL FOREST

Lewis

A859

Seaforth Island

TO ULLAPOOL

Amhuinnsuidhe

FOREST OF HARRIS

Amhuinnsuidhe Castle
32

The Minch

Traig Luskentyre
33

Tarbert

31
Rhenigidale

Harris

Luskentyre

30
Tarbert

Loch Seaforth

A859

South Harris

North Uist

34
St. Clement's Church

Rodel

Sound of Harris

Newtonferry
35

Balranald Nature Reserve
38

Trinity Temple
36

Bayhead

A865

37

Lochmaddy

Barpa Langass Chambered Cairn

Clachan-a-Luib

A867

Uig

Trotternish

Benbecula

A865

39
Our Lady of the Isles

Loch Druidibeg National Nature Reserve
40

Sandwick

Isle of Skye

Ormaclete Castle

A865

Howmore

Flora Macdonald's Birthplace
41

42

Sea of Hebrides

South Uist

Lochboisdale

Barra

Eoligarry

Cille Bharra
44

Kisimul Castle
43

Castlebay

N

Berneray

Barra Head

KEY

⛴ Ferry

0 ____ 10 miles
0 ____ 15 km

TO OBAN

26 of **Arnol.** Look for signs off the A858 for the **Arnol Black House,** a well-preserved example of an increasingly rare type of traditional Hebridean home. Once in common use throughout the islands (as recently as 50 years ago), these dwellings were built without mortar and thatched on a timber framework without eaves. Other characteristic features include an open central peat hearth and the absence of a chimney—hence the sooty atmosphere and the designation "black." On display inside are many of the house's original furnishings. *Off A858, Arnol, tel. 031/244–3101. Admission: £1 adults, 50p children. Open Apr.– Sept., Mon.–Sat. 9:30–6; Oct.–Mar., Mon.–Sat. 9:30–4.*

Continue south on A858 another 5 miles or so to reach **Shaw-**
27 **bost,** home of the **Shawbost School Museum.** This museum came to life as a result of the so-called Highland Village Competition in 1970, during which school pupils gathered artifacts and contributed to displays aimed at illustrating a past way of life in Lewis. Though it has, sadly, become a bit dog-eared and dusty, the museum does provide a glimpse at the old life and customs of the island. *A858, tel. 0851/71213. Admission: voluntary donation. Open Apr.–Nov., Mon.–Sat. 10–6.*

28 Approximately 8 miles farther south on A858, at **Dun Carloway,** you can see one of the best preserved Iron Age brochs in Scotland. The mysterious circular defensive towers of the Dun Carloway broch, built about 2,000 years ago possibly as protection against sea-borne raiders, provide fine views of a typical Lewis landscape. Parts of the storied walls still stand as high as 30 feet. *A858, tel. 031/244–3101. Admission free. Open 24 hrs.*

Follow A858 about 10 miles to the southeast, along the inlet called East Loch Roag, to reach **Callanish.** A few miles west of
29 the village (along B8012) are the **Callanish Standing Stones,** a setting of megaliths rated second only to Stonehenge in England. Probably positioned in several stages between 3,000 and 1,500 BC, this grouping is made up of an avenue of 19 monoliths extending northward from a circle of 13 stones, with other rows leading south, east, and west. It's believed they may have been used for astronomical observations. The site is accessible at any time.

Time Out The **Callanish Tearoom** specializes in hearty soups and home baking. This place may save your life if you've just wandered around the stones during a day of driving rain.

30 To reach **Tarbert,** the main port of Harris, head back east toward Stornoway on the A858 and pick up the A859 south (a distance of some 50 miles). If you want to break up the ride south, you could make a slight detour about two-thirds of the way
31 down A859 to explore the area around **Rhenigidale.** Considered to be the most isolated inhabited village in Harris, Rhenigidale was for a long time accessible only by sea or via a rough hill path. A newly completed road, which offers fine views high above Loch Seaforth, has now linked the village with the rest of Scotland.

Time Out Probably the best refreshment stop in this area is the **Rose Villa Tearoom** in Tarbert (tel. 0859–2060) a small outpost that serves wholesome and tasty snacks and light meals.

About 10 miles northwest of Tarbert on the B887 stands **32** **Amhuinnsuidhe Castle,** a turreted structure built in the 1860s by the earls of Dunmore (who owned Harris) as a base for fishing and hunting in the North Harris deer forest. (The name is almost impossible to pronounce—try *avun-shooee*). The castle overlooks the sea and is close to the Amhuinnsuidhe River, where salmon can be seen leaping the nearby falls. These falls, which are on the castle grounds, can be seen only from the road.

33 Sitting roughly 5 miles southwest of Tarbert, **Traigh Luskentyre** is a spectacular example of Harris's tidy selection of beaches—2 miles of yellow sands adjacent to **Traigh Seilebost,** where there are superb views northward to the hills of the Forest of Harris.

At the southernmost point of the island, about a 20-mile drive **34** from Tarbert, is the community of **Rodel.** Here you'll find **St. Clement's,** a cruciform church standing on a prominent site right on route A859. It was built around 1500 and contains the magnificently sculptured tomb of the church's builder, Alasdair Crotach, eighth chief of Dunvegan Castle.

North Uist   At **Newtonferry (Port nan Long),** the port of entry for ferries **35** coming from Harris (via Berneray), stand the remains of what was reputed to be the last inhabited broch in North Uist, **Dun an Sticar.** This defensive tower, approached by a causeway over the loch, was occupied by Hugh MacDonald, a descendant of MacDonald of Sleat, until 1602.

Eight miles southwest of Lochmaddy, off the A865, are the **36** ruins of **Trinity Temple (Teampull na Trionaid),** a medieval college and monastery said to have been founded by Beathag, daughter of Somerled, progenitor of the Clan Donald, in the 13th century. *Admission free.*

Sitting very close to the A867 on the stretch between Loch- **37** maddy and Clachan is the **Barpa Langass Chambered Cairn.** Dating from the third millennium BC, this is the only chambered cairn in the Western Isles known to have retained its inner chamber fully intact.

On the western side of North Uist, about 3 miles northwest of **38** Bayhead, which you can reach via A865, is the **Balranald Nature Reserve,** administered by the Balranald branch of the Royal Society for the Protection of Birds. Large numbers of waders and seabirds, including red-necked phalarope, can be seen here in a varied habitat of loch, marsh, machair (grasslands just behind the beach), and sandy and rocky shore. The reserve can be viewed anytime, but visitors are asked to keep to the paths during breeding season (March to July) so as not to disturb the birds. *Reception cottage at Goular, tel. 031/556–5624 or 031/ 557–3136. Admission free. Open daily Apr.–Sept.*

South Uist   You can travel the length of South Uist along route A865, making short treks off this main road on your way to Lochboisdale on the southeastern coast of the island; at Lochboisdale you can get ferries to Barra, the southernmost principal island of the Outer Hebrides, or to Oban on the mainland. About 5 miles south of the causeway from Benbecula, atop Reuval Hill, stands the 125-foot-high statue of the Madonna and Child **39** known as **Our Lady of the Isles.** The work of sculptor Hew Lorimer, the statue was erected in 1957 by the local Catholic community. A few miles farther south, to the west of A865, you will come to the **Loch Druidibeg National Nature Reserve** (tel. 08705/206). One of only two remaining British native—nonmigrating—populations of greylag geese make their home here in a fresh and brackish loch environment. (Stop at the warden's office for full information about access.)

A few miles south of Howmore, just west of A865, stand the ruins of **Ormaclete Castle,** which was built in 1708 for the chief of the Clan Ranald, but was accidentally destroyed by fire in 1715 on the eve of the Battle of Sheriffmuir, during which the chief was killed. At Gearraidh Bhailteas (just west of A865 near Milton), you can see the ruins of **Flora Macdonald's birthplace.** South Uist's most famous daughter, Flora helped the Young Pretender Prince Charles Edward Stuart avoid capture and was feted as a heroine afterward.

Barra Barra is an island with a rocky east coast and a west coast of sandy beaches. **Kisimul Castle,** the largest ancient monument in the Western Isles, is situated on an islet in Castlebay, Barra's principal harbor. Kisimul was the stronghold of the Macneils of Barra, noted for their lawlessness and piracy. The main tower dates from about AD 1120. A restoration that was completed in 1970 was started by the 45th clan chief, an American architect. *Tel. 08714/336. Admission: £2.50 (includes short boat ride to the castle). Open May–Sept., Wed. and Sat. afternoons.*

Craigston Museum, in a thatched cottage at Baile ne Creige (Craigston), displays artifacts of local crofting life. (It's open only during the main summer season.) At Eolaigearraidh (Eoligarry), the departure point for the passenger ferry to South Uist, you can view **Cille Bharra,** the ruins of the church dedicated to the saint who gave his name to the island. Also nearby is the restored **chapel of St. Mary** and part of a medieval monastery and cemetery.

Barra's airport is on a simple stretch of sand known as **Traigh Moor** (the Cockle Strand)—which is washed twice daily by the tides. The departure and arrival times for the daily flights to and from Glasgow, Benbecula, and Stornoway are scheduled to coincide with low tide.

What to See and Do with Children

Northern **Baile an Or.** On the site of an 1869 gold rush (*baile an or* means
Highlands *gold town*), panning is still possible, using pans supplied by Strathullie Local and Scottish Crafts. *Helmsdale, tel. 04312/343.*

Timespan. The dramatic story of the Highlands is told through life-size displays, sound effects, and an audiovisual program. Exhibits here contain artifacts preserved by the local heritage society. This living statement of Highland life is well worth seeing. *Helmsdale, Sutherland, tel. 04312/327.*

Off the Beaten Track

It can be argued that all of the Northern Highlands are off the beaten track. Below are some examples of the peerless views and open countryside for which the area is renowned.

Applecross. The tame way to reach this little community facing Skye is by a coastal road from near Shieldaig; the exciting way is by a series of hairpin turns up the steep wall at the head of a corrie (a glacier-cut mountain valley), approached from the A896 a few miles farther south. There are spectacular views of Skye from the bare plateau on top, and you can boast afterward that you have been on what is probably Scotland's highest motorable road. The town of Applecross itself is pleasant but not riveting.

Cape Wrath. Those that tour far to the north will want to go all the way to the northwest tip of Scotland. You can't drive the entire way in your own car; a ferry carries you across the Kyle of Durness, a sea inlet, then a minibus takes you to the lighthouse. The highest mainland cliffs in Scotland lie between the Kyle and Cape Wrath. These are the 800-foot **Cleit Dubh** (the name means "black cleft" in Gaelic and comes from the Old Norse *klettr*, or crag).

Drumbeg loop from Lochinver. Bold souls spending time at Lochinver may enjoy the interesting single-lane B869 Drumbeg loop to the north of Lochinver—it has several challenging hairpin turns and offers breathtaking views. (The junction is just north of the River Inver bridge on the outskirts of the village, signed Stoer and Clashnessie.) Just beyond the scattered community of Stoer, a road leads west to **Stoer Point Lighthouse.** Energetic walkers can hike across the short turf and heather along the cliff top for fine views east toward the profiles of the northwest mountains. There is also a red-sandstone sea-stack to view: the **Old Man of Stoer.** This makes a pleasant excursion on a long summer evening. If you stay on the Drumbeg section, there is a particularly tricky hairpin turn in a steep dip that may force you to take your eyes off the fine view of Quinag, yet another of Sutherland's shapely mountains.

Eas Coul Aulin waterfall. This is the longest waterfall in the United Kingdom. Located east of the Kylesku Bridge on the A894, these falls have a 685-foot drop. A rugged walk that leads to the falls is popular with hikers; in summer, cruises offer a less taxing way to view the falls. *At the head of Loch Glencoul, 3 mi west of A894; contact the tourist information center in Ullapool or Lochinver for more information.*

Shopping

As in Argyll and the Western Isles, shopping in the Northern Highlands tends to be more interesting for the variety of crafts available rather than for the number and types of shops. After all, the population of the area is scattered, and if the locals have any special needs, they can travel to the larger population centers, as well as to Inverness. Perhaps the best-known purveyor of crafts in the northeastern corner of the area is **Caithness Glass** (Harrowhill, tel. 0955/2286) at **Wick** (now with branches at Oban and Perth). Producing a distinctive style of glassware and paperweights familiar to those traveling around Scotland (most of the better gift shops stock Caithness Glass), the factory offers tours of the glassblowing workshops and a shop stocking the full product range.

There are two other interesting craft outlets farther south: At **Golspie** the **Orcadian Stone Company** (Main St., Golspie, tel.

04083/633483) makes stone products (including items made from local Caithness slate and modern versions of the carpet bowls, beloved of the Victorians and of today's interior designers), jewelry, and prepared mineral specimens. There is also a geological exhibition on site.

The former **town jail of Dornoch** (Castle St., Dornoch, tel. 086/2810555) is now a textile-and-crafts center where tartans are woven. There's also an exhibition of prison life in past times just to remind you of the building's origins.

On the north coast at **Durness** is **Balnakeil Craft Village,** where a dozen or so independently owned and operated crafts businesses receive visitors during the summer season. Among the more unusual crafts practiced here are enameling, bookbinding, marquetry, and batik, together with pottery and hand-weaving.

At **Lochinver,** on the west coast, **Highland Stoneware** (Baddidarroch, Lochinver, tel. 05714/376) manufactures tableware and decorative items with handpainted designs of Highland wild flowers, animals, and landscapes. There is a showroom where you can browse and purchase wares.

At **Inverkirkaig,** just south of Lochinver, do not miss **Achins Bookshop** (Inverkirkaig, tel. 05714/262): Anyone with enough courage to run a bookshop with an ample inventory this far from a main population center deserves all the customers he or she can get. The range of stock—especially Scottish books on natural history, hill walking, fishing, and crafts—is worth a browse. Also available is a well-chosen variety of craftware: knitwear, tweeds, and pottery.

There are also several well-stocked gift shops south of Lochinver, at **Ullapool.** At **Lochcarron,** the premises of **Lochcarron Weavers** (North Strone, Lochcarron, tel. 05202/212) are open to the public: Weavers can be seen at work, producing pure-wool worsted tartans that can be bought on site or at the firm's other outlets in the area.

East of Lochcarron, at **Achnasheen,** is the **Highland Line Craft Centre** (center of Achnasheen, tel. 044/588227), where silver and gold jewelry is made, and you can watch the silversmiths; products are available in the shop on the premises.

Skye Shopping is limited on Skye, although there are quite a few gift outlets—as well as more crafts businesses—that cater to visitors. Among those worth a visit: **Ragamuffin** (Armadale Pier, tel. 04714/217), which specializes in designer knitwear and clothing, and **Skye Batiks** (Armadale, tel. 04714/396), where designs are influenced by Celtic motifs, and wall hangings and cotton, silk, and linen clothing are for sale at reasonable prices. **Harlequin Knitwear** (Duisdale, Sleat, tel. 04713/321) is where you will find colorful wool sweaters designed by local designers. **Skye Silver** (The Old School, Colbost, tel. 047081/263) makes gold and silver jewelry with a Celtic theme. **Craft Encounters** (Broadford, tel. 0471/822201) stocks an array of Scottish crafts, including marquetry and jewelry. For wood-fired stoneware, try **Edinbane Pottery** (Edinbane, tel. 047/082234). There are also several art galleries and studios of interest on Skye, among them **Skye Original Prints** (Portree, tel. 0478/2388) and **The Smithy Gallery** (Glenelg, tel. 059982/371).

Outer Hebrides At the **Callanish Stones Tea Room,** Beatrice Schulz sells craft items, knitwear, clothing made from locally woven tweed, and tweed lengths in a kaleidoscopic range of colors. At **Stornoway Pottery** (confusingly not at Stornoway, but at **Borve,** on the road to Ness, tel. 0851/85345), you can buy squat pottery glazed in a wash of red and blue. Harris tweed is available at many outlets on the islands, including some of the weavers' homes. Try **Norman MacDonald** (35 Arnol, Isle of Lewis, tel. 0851/71531) or **Alistair Campbell** (4 Plocrabol, Isle of Harris, tel. 0859/81217). On South Uist, **Hebridean Jewelry** (Garrieganichy, Lochdar, tel. 0870/4288) makes decorative jewelry and framed pictures; the owners also run a crafts shop.

Sports and Fitness

Bicycling Bicycles may be rented from **Richards Garage** (Francis St., Wick, tel. 0955/4123), **The Bike Shop** (35 High St., Thurso, tel. 0847/66124 or 0047/64223), **Island Cycles** (Struan Rd., Portree, tel. 047072/284), **Alex Dan Cycle Centre** (67 Kenneth St., Stornoway, tel. 0851/704025), **Sportsworld** (1–3 Francis St., Stornoway, tel. 0851/705464), and **Hebridean Pedal Highway** (The Cycle Shop, Old Plock Rd., Kyle of Lochalsh, tel. 0599/4842).

Fishing The possibilities for fishing are endless here, as a glance at the loch-littered map of Sutherland suggests. As in other parts of Scotland, post offices, local shops, and hotels usually sell permits to fish in these waters, and tourist-information centers carry lists of the best locales for fishing.

Golf There are only about 15 courses in the area—a low number compared with other regions of Scotland—with almost no courses on the west coast, though **Gairloch Golf Club** has its enthusiasts. *60 mi west of Dingwall, tel. 0445/2407. 9 holes, 1,942 yds., SSS 71.*

The best-known club in the area is **Royal Dornoch.** Were it not for its northern location, the club would undoubtedly be a candidate for the Open Championship. *40 mi north of Inverness, tel. 0862/810219. 18 holes, 6,533 yds., SSS 72.*

Pony Trekking Pony trekking was invented to give the sturdy highland ponies a job to do when they weren't carrying dead deer off the hills during the "stalking" (deer-hunting) season. Treks last from two hours to a whole day, and ponies can be found to suit all ages and levels of experience.

Contact one of the following centers for information about specific opportunities and costs: **The Black Isle Riding Centre** (tel. 046373/707), **Uig Pony Trekking** (Skye, tel. 047/042205), **East Sutherland Riding Stables** (tel. 0408/633045), and **Latheron Pony Centre** (tel. 05934/224).

Water Sports **Raasay Outdoor Centre** (Raasay House, Isle of Raasay, near Kyle, Wester Ross, tel. 047/862266) offers a variety of courses in canoeing, sailing, windsurfing, and navigation skills.

Dining and Lodging

Dining

In an area with such a low population, the choice of restaurants is inevitably restricted. The places selected below can be relied upon for both accommodations and acceptable standards in the dining room.

Highly recommended restaurants are indicated by a star ★.

Category	Cost*
Very Expensive	over £40
Expensive	£30–£40
Moderate	£15–£30
Inexpensive	under £15

per person, including first course, main course, dessert, and VAT; excluding drinks

Lodging

This region of Scotland has some good modern hotels and some charming inns but not many establishments in the more expensive categories. Travelers often find that the most enjoyable accommodations are low-cost guest houses (often family run), offering bed and breakfast. Dining rooms of country-house lodgings frequently reach the standard of top-quality restaurants.

Highly recommended hotels are indicated by a star ★.

Category	Cost*
Very Expensive	over £120
Expensive	£100–£120
Moderate	£80–£100
Inexpensive	under £80

All prices are for a standard double room, including breakfast and tax.

Dundonnell **Dundonnell Hotel.** Set on the roadside by Little Loch Broom, just south of Ullapool, this hotel has been a family-run enterprise since 1962 and has cultivated a solid reputation for hospitality and cuisine. The bedrooms, decorated in a fresh, modern style, are well equipped, and many have stunning views over pristine hills and lochs, as do the public rooms. The "Taste of Scotland" menu features homemade soups, seafood, salmon, and desserts worth leaving room for. *Dundonnell, near Garve, Ross-shire, tel. 085483/204. Reservations advised. Dress: casual. 24 rooms with bath. Facilities: restaurant, bar. MC, V. Inexpensive.*

Harris **Ardvourlie Castle.** A Victorian hunting lodge recently restored
★   to its original grandeur, Ardvourlie is set in splendid isolation amid the dramatic mountain scenery of Harris, an ideal habitat

for hill walking. The bathrooms are magnificent, with mahogany paneling and Victorian-style fixtures, and the decor of the bedrooms and public rooms is bold, idiosyncratic, and entirely in keeping with the High Victorian atmosphere of the castle. The country-house hospitality is perpetuated by the well-stocked library and roaring fires. The cooking is along traditional lines and is of a high standard, favoring fresh local produce and, often, wild game. The portions are generous. *Isle of Harris, tel. 0859/2307. Reservations advised. Dress: casual. 4 rooms, 3 with private bath. No credit cards. Inexpensive.*

Scourie **Eddrachilles Hotel.** This old, established traditional inn has one of the best views of any hotel in Scotland—across the islands of Eddrachillis Bay (which can be explored by boat from the hotel). The hotel sits on 320 acres of private moorland and is near the Handa Island bird sanctuary, just to the north. Inside, the hotel has been carefully renovated in recent years; the outside is well preserved as well. The bedrooms are modern and comfortable, and each is outfitted with tea- and coffee-making facilities. The chef uses local produce to prepare meals cooked in straightforward Scottish style, with the emphasis on fish and game. *Badcall Bay, Scourie, tel. 0971/502080. Reservations advised. Dress: casual. 11 rooms with bath or shower. Facilities: restaurant, bar. No credit cards. Closed Nov.–Feb. Inexpensive.*

Skye **Kinloch Lodge.** This hotel offers elegant comfort on the edge of the world. Run by Lord and Lady MacDonald with flair and considerable professionalism, Kinloch Lodge is a supremely comfortable country house, with warm, restful lounges, snug bedrooms, and a handsome dining room that serves imaginative cuisine. *Sleat IV43 8QY, tel. 04713/333. Reservations advised. Dress: casual but neat. 10 rooms with bath. Facilities: restaurant, shooting, fishing. MC, V. Closed Dec.–mid-Mar. Very Expensive.*

Cuillin Hills Hotel. Situated on lovely grounds just outside Portree, this gabled hotel is within easy walking distance of the town center. Many of the rooms have outstanding views over Portree Bay toward the Cuillin Hills. Bedrooms are reasonably spacious and well equipped, decorated in a pleasant, fairly neutral style—no wildly patterned fabrics or ornate furniture, just fresh, clean, and inoffensive ensembles. The public rooms offer a choice of sitting areas and a friendly bar. The meals, especially seafood dishes, are prepared in straightforward fashion, with few gimmicks and a lot of flavor. *Portree, Isle of Skye, tel. 0478/2003. Reservations advised. Dress: casual. 26 rooms with bath. Facilities: restaurant, bar. MC, V. Moderate.*

Ullapool **Altnaharrie Inn.** Be prepared for a real treat. Follow the A9/
★ A832 to the A835 for 60 miles from Inverness, to Ullapool, where a private launch takes you to Dundonnell, some 5 miles south, on the banks of Loch Broom. A set menu of local specialties is skillfully prepared, including scallops in white-burgundy-and-bitter-cress sauce and medallions of roe deer with leek, grape juniper, and dill sauce, with wild-raspberry ice cream and a selection of cheeses to finish. As the name implies, this is also an inn—eight rooms are available, but you must book far in advance. *Ullapool, Highland IV26 2SS, tel. 0854/83230. Reservations required. Jacket and tie required. 8 rooms with bath. Facilities: restaurant, 2 lounges. No credit cards. Lunch for guests only. Closed Nov.–Easter. Expensive.*

Ceilidh Place. Famous for its unique style of hotel keeping, the Ceilidh Place refuses to be pigeonholed. This hostelry is extremely comfortable; guests can while away the hours on deep luxurious sofas in the first-floor sitting room—which overlooks the bay—or borrow one of the many books scattered throughout the inn to read back in the room or over breakfast. About as far away in style as you can get from a major chain hotel, the Ceilidh Place must be taken strictly on its own terms—relax and fit in and you will thoroughly enjoy a stay here. The inn's restaurant specializes in seafood and vegetarian cooking, and ceilidhs and other musical events are held here frequently. *W. Argyle St., Ullapool IV26 2TY, tel. 0854/612103. Reservations essential. Dress: casual. 24 rooms (8 with bath). Facilities: restaurants. AE, DC, MC, V. Inexpensive–Moderate.*

The Arts and Nightlife

The Arts The **Lyth Arts Centre,** between Wick and John o' Groats on the A9, presents local and touring exhibitions of contemporary fine art in an old country school. *4 mi off A9, tel. 0955–84/270. Admission: 80p adults, children free. Open: June 26–Sept. 6, daily 10–6.*

The **Ceilidh Place** in Ullapool (*see* Dining and Lodging, *above*) frequently offers ceilidhs and entertainment featuring typical Northern Highland music. **An Lanntair,** in the Stornoway town hall (Isle of Lewis and Harris), also conducts an eclectic program of monthly exhibitions and evening events. Various Scottish ballet- and opera-touring companies perform in local halls. Consult tourist-information centers' event lists for details.

Nightlife The nightlife here is confined mainly to hotels and pubs. Ceilidhs, dances, and concerts are performed on a sporadic basis and advertised locally.

13 The Northern Isles

Orkney and Shetland

Introduction

By Gilbert
Summers

Both Orkney and Shetland possess a Scandinavian heritage that gives them an ambience unlike that of any other region of Scotland. For mainland Scots, visiting this archipelago is a little like traveling abroad without having to worry about a different language or currency. Both of these isles are bound by the sea, and both are essentially bleak and austere, with awesome seascapes and genuinely warm, friendly people. Neither island has yet been overrun by tourists. Orkney is the greener of the two island groupings, which number 200 islets between them.

There are more prehistoric sites in Orkney than anywhere else in the United Kingdom, although Shetland has a few historic sites of great interest. Orkney's wealth of sites include stone circles, burial chambers, ancient settlements, and fortifications that emphasize several centuries of continuous settlement. Most of the sites are open to view, offering an insight into the life of bygone eras. At Maes Howe, for example, visitors will discover that graffiti is not solely a problem borne by today's troubled youths: The Vikings left their marks here in the 8th century.

The differences between Orkney and Shetland can be summed up with the description that an Orcadian is a farmer with a boat, while a Shetlander is a fisherman with a croft (small farm). Shetland, rich in ocean views and sparse landscapes, is endowed with a more remote atmosphere than its neighbor Orkney. However, don't let Shetland's bleak countryside fool you; this island is far from being a backwater island. Oil money from the mineral resources around its shores and the fact that it has been a crossroads in the northern seas for centuries have helped make it a cosmopolitan place.

Essential Information

Important Addresses and Numbers

Tourist
Information

The two main sources of tourist information in the area are the **Orkney Tourist Board** (Broad St., Kirkwall, Orkney, tel. 0856/872856) and the **Shetland Tourist Organization** (Information Centre, Market Cross, Lerwick, Shetland, tel. 0595/3434).

Emergencies

For police, fire, or ambulance, dial 999 from any telephone. No coins are needed for emergency calls from public telephone booths.

Doctors and
Dentists

Most general practitioners will see visitor patients by appointment or immediately in case of emergency. Your hotel or local tourist-information center can advise you accordingly. You can also consult the Yellow Pages of the telephone directory, under "Doctor" or "Dentist." Hospitals with emergency rooms are **Gilbert Bain Hospital** (South Rd., Lerwick, Shetland, tel. 0595/5678) and **Balfour Hospital** (New Staffa Rd., Kirkwall, Orkney, tel. 0856/872763).

Late-Night
Pharmacies

There are no late-night pharmacies on the islands. In case of emergency, police can provide assistance in locating pharmacists. Doctors in rural areas also dispense medication.

Arriving and Departing by Plane

Airports and Airlines British Airways (Aberdeen Airport, tel. 0224/722331, ext. 5122) provides regular service to **Sumburgh Airport,** in Shetland, 25 miles from Lerwick. You can also reach Shetland from Inverness via **Kirkwall** in Orkney (Inverness, tel. 0463/239871). **Loganair** (tel. 041/889–3181 or 0595/84–246) flies directly from Edinburgh to **Tingwall Airport,** 5 miles from Lerwick. British Airways also flies from Aberdeen to Kirkwall (tel. 0224/722331, ext. 5122). Loganair flies to Edinburgh, Inverness, Wick, and from there to Kirkwall.

Arriving and Departing by Car, Train, and Bus

By Car To get to Lerwick, Shetland, take the ferry from the port in Aberdeen. To reach Stromness, Orkney, take the ferry from the port in Scrabster. Contact **P & O Ferries** (Orkney and Shetland Services, Jamieson's Quay, Aberdeen, tel. 0224/572615 for Shetland; tel. 0856/850655 for Orkney) for reservations.

By Train There are no trains on Orkney or Shetland, although Aberdeen (for the Shetland ferry) is well served by train (for information contact the Aberdeen Travel Centre, tel. 0224/594222), and Thurso is the terminus of the far-north line. From Thurso a bus connects to Scrabster for Orkney. Contact the Inverness Travel Centre (tel. 0463/238924) for information on Inverness and Thurso-to-Scrabster service.

By Bus Aberdeen and Thurso have reliable bus links: **Scottish City Link** (Guild St., Aberdeen, tel. 0224/212307) and **Caledonian Express** (Friarton Rd., Perth, tel. 0738/33481).

Getting Around

By Car Because of the oil wealth, the roads on Shetland are in very good shape. Both Orkney and Shetland are part of a network of islands with interconnecting ferries that are heavily subsidized. In fact, it's a good idea to book ferry tickets in advance. For information, contact the Shetland Tourist Organization (*see* Important Addresses and Numbers, *above*) or tel. 0957/82259–82268 if you are visiting during peak season. Shetland visitors who want to get to Orkney can do so by way of ferry from Scalloway on Shetland to Kirkwall, Orkney's largest town.

Orkney also has causeways connecting some of the islands, but using these roads will, in some cases, take you on fairly roundabout routes, thus making for a longer journey than you might have if you took a ferry.

Although Shetland has a number of car-rental firms, you have the option of taking your car from Aberdeen by sea. The general rule of thumb is that for any visit under five days it is better to rent a car in Shetland. Most of the rental companies are based in Lerwick; they include **Star Rent-a-Car** (22 Commercial St., Lerwick). On Orkney try **J & W Tait** (Sparrowhawk Rd., Hatston Industrial Estate, Kirkwall, tel. 0856/872490) or **James D. Peace & Co.** (Junction Rd., Kirkwall, tel. 0856/872866).

By Train There are no trains on Shetland or Orkney.

By Bus The main bus service on Orkney is operated by **James D. Peace & Co.** (tel. 0856/872866) and on Shetland by **J. Leask** (tel. 0595/3162).

By Air Note that because of the isolation of Orkney and Shetland there is a network of inter-island flights. Tourist-information centers (*see* Important Addresses and Numbers, *above*) will provide details, or call Loganair (*see* Arriving and Departing by Plane, *above*).

Guided Tours

Orientation In addition to the bus companies mentioned above, well-run personally guided tours are offered in Orkney by **Go-Orkney** (tel. 0856/874260). Other companies that schedule general orientation tours include **Causeway Coaches** (tel. 0856/83444), **Rosie Coaches** (tel. 0856/75227), **David Lea** (tel. 0856/874260), and **Shalder Coaches** (tel. 0856/850809). The tour companies that service Shetland are **Bolts Car and Minibus Hire** (tel. 0595/2855) and **Shalder Coaches** (tel. 059588/217).

Special-Interest All the above companies offer special-interest tours to specific places of interest on the islands, and most can also tailor tours to your interests. Guided walks are available on Orkney: Contact **Wildabout** (tel. 0856/75307) for details of early morning, late evening, and all-day walks with an environmental theme.

Exploring the Northern Isles

Highlights for First-time Visitors

Eshaness Cliffs (*see* Tour 1)
Hermaness and Muckle Flugga, island of Unst (*see* Tour 1)
Italian Chapel (*see* Tour 2)
Jarlshof (*see* Tour 1)
Maes Howe (*see* Tour 2)
Mousa Broch (*see* Tour 1)
Ring of Brogar (*see* Tour 2)
St. Magnus Cathedral, Kirkwall (*see* Tour 2)
Shetland Croft Museum (*see* Tour 1)
Skara Brae (*see* Tour 2)

Tour 1: Around Shetland

Numbers in the margin correspond to points of interest on the Shetland Islands map.

All the indentations of the Shetland coastline add up to an incredible 900 miles, yet there isn't a point on the island farther than 3 miles from the sea. Settlements away from Lerwick, the primary town, are small and scattered. By asking for directions, you may find yourself having tea with a resident.

Visitors would be remiss if they failed to explore some of Lerwick's nearby diversions, before venturing beyond it. **Fort Charlotte** is a 17th-century Cromwellian stronghold, built to protect the Sound of Bressay. *Tel. 031/224–3101. Admission*

Shetland Islands

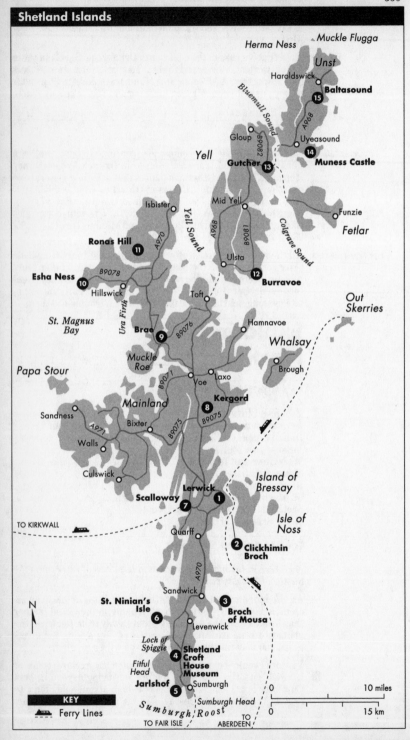

Muckle Flugga

Herma Ness

Unst

Haroldswick

Baltasound ⑮

Bluemull Sound

A968

Uyeasound

Gloup

B9082

Muness Castle ⑭

Gutcher ⑬

Yell

Isbister

Yell Sound

Mid Yell

A968

Funzie

Colgrave Sound

Fetlar

Ronas Hill ⑪

A970

Ulsta

B9081

Esha Ness ⑩

B9078

Hillswick

Ura Firth

Toft

Out Skerries

Burravoe ⑫

St. Magnus Bay

Brae ⑨

B9076

Hamnavoe

Whalsay

Papa Stour

Muckle Roe

Brough

B9071

Voe

Laxo

Kergord ⑧

Sandness

A971

Bixter

B9075

B9075

Walls

Mainland

Culswick

Island of Bressay

Lerwick ①

Scalloway ⑦

Isle of Noss

TO KIRKWALL

Quarff

② **Clickhimin Broch**

A970

Sandwick

③ **Broch of Mousa**

St. Ninian's Isle ⑥

Levenwick

Loch of Spiggie

④ **Shetland Croft House Museum**

Fitful Head

Jarlshof ⑤

Sumburgh

Sumburgh Head

Sumburgh Roost

0 — 10 miles

0 — 15 km

N

KEY
🛳 Ferry Lines

TO FAIR ISLE

TO ABERDEEN

free. Open Apr.–Sept., Mon.–Sat. 9:30–6, Sun. 2–6; Oct.–Mar., Mon.–Sat, 9:30–4, Sun. 2–4.

The **Shetland Museum** in Lerwick gives an interesting account of the development of the town and includes displays on archaeology, art and textiles, shipping, and folk life. *Lower Hillhead, tel. 0595/5057. Admission free. Open Mon., Wed., Fri. 10–7, Tues., Thurs., Sat. 10–5.*

② **Clickhimin Broch,** on the site of what was originally an Iron-Age fortification, can be your introduction to the mysterious Pictish monuments, whose meaning is still largely obscure. *1 mi south of Lerwick, tel. 031/244–3101. Admission free. Open Apr.–Sept., Mon.–Sat. 9:30–6, Sun. 2–6; Oct.–Mar., Mon.–Sat. 9:30–4, Sun. 2–4.*

From the broch go south on the A970, and you will find vivid views of the cliffs at the south end of the island of Bressay, **③** which shelters Lerwick harbor. The **Broch of Mousa,** the most complete of all the broch towers remaining in Scotland, can be reached by boat from Sandwick, just off the main road. *Mousa, tel. 031/244–3101. Admission free. Open Apr.–Sept., Mon.–Sat. 9:30–6, Sun. 2–6; Oct.–Mar., Mon.–Sat. 9:30–4, Sun. 2–4. Boat for hire May–Sept. afternoons, Sat., Sun. mornings, some evenings.*

④ Continue south on A970 until you see a sign for the **Shetland Croft House Museum.** This traditionally constructed 19th-century thatched house contains a broad range of artifacts that depict the former way of life of the rural Shetlander, which the museum attendant will be delighted to discuss with you. *Voe, Dunrossness, unclassified road east of A970, tel. 0595/5057. Admission: 50p adults, 20p children. Open May–Sept., Tues.–Sun. 10–1 and 2–5.*

The A970 then continues south to **Sumburgh.** Be sure to look for **⑤** puffins by the lighthouse, but the big attraction is **Jarlshof,** a complex site that includes the extensive remains of Norse buildings, as well as wheel houses and earth houses representing thousands of years of continuous settlement. The site includes a 17th-century laird's (landowner's) house on top of a medieval farmstead. *Sumburgh Head, tel. 031/244–3101. Admission £1.50 adults, 80p children. Open Apr.–Sept., Mon.–Sat. 9:30–6, Sun. 2–6. Closed Oct.–Mar.*

Retrace your route to **Skelberry,** making a left on the B9122, for a respite on white beaches that includes inspiring views of the island of **Foula.** The most dazzling beach of all can be found at **⑥** **St. Ninian's Isle,** actually a tombolo, a term for a spit of sand that moors an island to the mainland. It was here in the 1950s, in the nave of a ruined pre-Norse church, that archaeologists uncovered the St. Ninian treasure, a collection of 28 silver objects from the 8th century. This Celtic silver is now in the royal Museum of Scotland in Edinburgh (*see* Chapter 3), though good replicas are on view in the Shetland Museum in Lerwick (*see above*).

Time Out   Back in Lerwick, try the breaded haddock as a bar meal at the **Kvelsdro House Hotel** (tel. 0595/2195), located near the harbor.

West of Lerwick, on the western coast of Mainland Island, is **⑦** **Scalloway.** Look for the panorama board just off the main road

(A970), which overlooks the settlement and its castle. **Scalloway Castle** was built in 1600 by Earl Patrick, who coerced the locals to build it for him. He was executed in 1615 for his cruelty and misdeeds, and the castle was never used again. *6 mi west of Lerwick, tel. 031/244–3101. Admission free. Open Apr.–Sept., Mon.–Sat. 9:30–6, Sun. 2–6; Oct.–Mar., Mon.–Sat. 9:30–4, Sun. 2–4.*

8 Take the B9075 east off the A970, at the head of a narrow sea inlet. This leads into the unexpectedly green valley of **Kergord**, noted for its trees, which would be unremarkable farther south but here are a novelty.

9 Rejoin the A970 by making a left off the B9075 at Laxo, then drive through Voe to **Brae**, home of the Busta House Hotel, probably the best hotel on the island. Beyond Brae the main road meanders past **Mavis Grind**, a strip of land so narrow you can throw a stone—if you are strong—from the Atlantic, in one inlet, to the North Sea, in another.

Time Out Follow the A970 left for Hillswick to reach the **St. Magnus Bay Hotel** (tel. 080623/372), which serves fresh fish in a wood-panel bar and dining room.

10 To take in some extraordinary views of cliff scenery around **Esha Ness**, return to the A970 and drive a few miles to the northeast, then turn left onto the B9078. On the way, look for the sandstone stacks in the bay that resemble a Viking galley under sail. After viewing the cliffs at Esha Ness, return to join the A970 at Hillswick and follow an ancillary road from the head of Ura Firth. This road provides vistas of rounded, bare **11** **Ronas Hill**, the highest hill in Shetland. Though only 1,468 feet high, it is noted for its arctic-alpine flora growing at low levels. To visit Yell and Unst, the two main northern islands, go south as far as Brae and take the B9076.

12 After crossing over to Ulsta on **Yell** from the Shetland port of Toft, take the B9081 east to **Burravoe**. There's not a lot to say about the blanket bog that covers two-thirds of Yell, but the **Old Haa** (hall) of Burravoe, the oldest building on Yell, is architecturally interesting and has a museum upstairs. One of the displays tells the story of the wrecking of the German sailship, the *Bohus*, in 1924. A copy of the ship's figurehead is displayed outside the Old Haa itself; the original is at the shipwreck site overlooking Otters Wick, along the coast on the B9081. *Tel. 095782/339 or 0957/2127. Admission free. Open Apr.–Sept., Tues., Wed., and Thurs.–Sun. 10–4.*

Time Out The **Old Haa,** formerly a merchant's house, also serves light meals and acts as a kind of unofficial information point. The staff, like all native Shetland folk, are friendly and offer advice to sightseers.

13 Rejoin the main A968 at Mid Yell to reach **Gutcher,** the ferry pier. If time permits, turn left on the B9082 for a pleasant drive to **Gloup,** a cluster of houses at the end of the road. Behind a croft, in a field overlooking a long voe (sea inlet) is the **Gloup Fisherman's Memorial,** which recalls an 1881 tragedy involving all hands of ten six-oared local fishing boats.

Across the water, on the other side of the Bluemull Sound, lies **Unst,** the northernmost inhabited island in Scotland. Because of its strategic location—it protrudes well into the northern seas—Unst is inhabited by the military. Follow the A968 until

⑭ you reach the right turn on the B9084 for **Muness Castle.** Scotland's northernmost castle, it was built just before the end of the 16th century. Those visiting the castle will be pleasantly surprised to find some photogenic Shetland ponies in the field nearby. *Southeast corner of Unst, tel. 031/244–3101. Admission free. Ask for the key-keeper. Open Apr.–Sept., Mon.–Sat. 9:30–6, Sun. 2–6; Oct.–Mar., Mon.–Sat. 9:30–4, Sun. 2–4.*

⑮ Return to the A968 to reach **Baltasound,** which was a fishing station in the early days of the Scottish herring industry. In the early decades of this century vast herring shoals would appear off Shetland in spring and gradually move down the coast as the year progressed. In pursuit were not only the fishing boats, but also the shore-based herring lassies, who gutted and packed the fish barrels of brine.

Just to the north is the **Keen of Hamar** national nature reserve. Farther north is **Haroldswick,** with its post office and heritage center. Scotland's most northerly house is in **Skaw,** on the B9086. If you take the B9086 at Haroldswick you will go around the head of **Burra Firth** (a sea inlet) and eventually reach a car park. From there a path goes north across moorland and up a gentle hill. Bleak and open, this is bird-watchers' territory and is replete with diving skuas, single-minded sky pirates that attack anything that strays near their nest sites. Gannets, puffins, and other seabirds nest in spectacular profusion by the cliffs on the left as you look out to sea. Visitors should make sure they keep to the path; this is a national nature reserve. At the top of the hills, amid the windy grasslands, you can see **Muckle Flugga** to the north, a series of tilting offshore rocks with a lighthouse on the largest rock. This is the northernmost point in Scotland; the sea rolls out on three sides, no land lies beyond.

Tour 2: Around Orkney

Numbers in the margin correspond to points of interest on the Orkney Islands map.

Orkney has the greatest concentration of prehistoric sites in Scotland. Visitors seeking to get to Orkney from the mainland can take a ferry from Scrabster—located roughly 2 miles

⑯ northwest of Thurso off the A836—to **Stromness** on Orkney Island. You will find two points of interest in Stromness as soon as you arrive. The **Pier Arts Centre** is a former Stromness merchant's house (circa 1800) and has adjoining buildings that now serve as a gallery with a permanent collection of 20th-century paintings and sculptures. *Victoria St., tel. 0856/850–209. Admission free. Open Tues.–Sat. 10:30–12:30 and 1:30–5; also Sun. in July and Aug. 2–5.*

Nearby, the **Stromness Museum** has a varied collection of natural-history material on view, inlcuding preserved birds and Orkney shells. The museum also displays exhibits on fishing, shipping, whaling, and the Hudson Bay Company, as well as ship models and a feature on the German fleet that was scuttled on Scapa Flow. *Stromness, tel. 0856/850025. Admission: £1 adults, 50p children. Open Mon.–Sat. 10:30–12:30 and 1:30–5.*

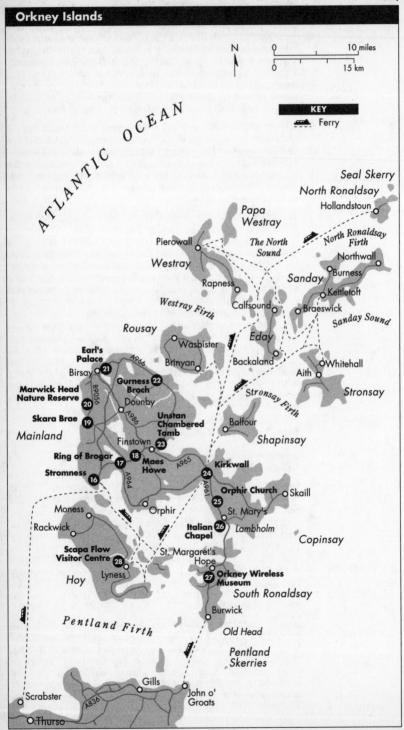

Located just off the A965, 5 miles northeast of Stromness, the
Ring of Brogar is a magnificent stone circle of 36 stones (originally 60) surrounded by a deep ditch. When the mist descends
over the stones—a frequent occurrence—their looming shapes
seem to come alive. Though their original use is uncertain, it is
not hard to imagine strange rituals taking place here in the
misty past. Nearby are other early sites, notably the **Comet
Stone.** *Between Loch of Harray and Loch of Stenness, 5 mi
northeast of Stromness, tel. 031/244–3101. Admission free.
Open at all times.*

One mile farther on the A965 brings visitors to another ancient
site, the huge burial mound of **Maes Howe** (circa 2,500 BC),
which measures 115 feet in diameter and contains an enormous
burial chamber. It was raided by Vikings in the 12th century,
and Norse crusaders sheltered here, leaving a rich collection of
runic inscriptions. *Off A965, 9 mi west of Kirkwall, tel. 031/
244–3101. Admission: £1.50 adults, 80p children, £4 family
ticket. Open Apr.–Sept., Mon.–Sat. 9:30–6, Sun. 2–6; Oct.–
Mar., Mon.–Sat. 9:30–4, Sun. 2–4.*

To reach the neolithic village of **Skara Brae,** take the A965 west
to the B9056. There you will find houses joined by covered pas-
sages and stone beds, fireplaces, and cupboards that have survived since the village was occupied, from 3,000 BC to 2,700 BC.
The site was preserved in sand until it was uncovered in 1850.
*19 mi northwest of Kirkwall, tel. 031/244–3101. Admission:
£1.70 adults, 90p children, £4.50 family ticket. Open Apr.–
Sept., Mon.–Sat. 9:30–6, Sun. 2–6; Oct.–Mar., Mon.–Sat.
9:30–4, Sun. 2–4.*

To the north of Skara Brae, up the B9056, sits the **Marwick
Head Nature Reserve,** with its spectacular seabird cliffs, tended
by Scotland's Royal Society for the Protection of Birds. The
Kitchener Memorial, which recalls the sinking of the cruiser
HMS *Hampshire* with Lord Kitchener aboard in 1916, can also
be seen in the reserve, on a cliff-top site. *Access to reserve
along path north from Marwick Bay, tel. 0856/850176. Admission free. Open at all times.*

Just beyond Marwick at Birsay (11 miles north of Stromness) is
Earl's Palace, the impressive remains of a 16th-century palace
built by the earls of Orkney. *Birsay, tel. 031/244–3101. Admission free. Open at all times.*

Nearby is the **Brough of Birsay,** the remains of a Romanesque
church and a Norse settlement on an island accessible only at
low tide. *Birsay, 11 mi north of Stromness, tel. 031/244–3101.
Admission: £1 adults, 50p children. Open Apr.–Sept., Mon.–
Sat. 9:30–6, Sun. 2–6; Oct.–Mar., Mon., Tues. noon–4, Wed.–
Sat. 9:30–4, Sun. 2–4.*

An Iron-Age tower standing more than 10 feet high, the
Gurness Broch is located off the A966, about 8 miles from
Birsay, along Orkney's northern coast. The broch is surrounded by stone huts. *Off A966 at Aikerness, 4 mi northwest
of Kirkwall, tel. 031/244–3101. Admission: £1.20 adults, 60p
children. Open Apr.–Sept., Mon.–Sat. 9:30–6, Sun. 2–6.*

To reach the **Unstan Chambered Tomb** from the Gurness Broch,
simply follow the A966 south for about 10 miles to Finstown.
This cairn containing a chambered tomb is midway between
Stromness and Kirkwall: roughly 3.5 miles from each village.

Pottery that has been found within the tomb is now known as
Unstan ware. *Tel. 031/244–3101. Admission free. Open Apr.–
Sept., Mon.–Sat. 9:30–6, Sun. 2–6; Oct.–Mar., Mon.–Sat.
9:30–4, Sun. 2–4.*

㉔ Take the A965 east, straight into **Kirkwall,** to reach **Earl
Patrick's Palace,** built in 1607 and perhaps the best surviving
example of Renaissance architecture in Scotland. The **Bishop's
Palace** nearby dates from the 13th century, though its round
tower was added in the 16th century. *Kirkwall. Admission to
both: £1 adults, 50p children. Both open Apr.–Sept., Mon.–
Sat. 9:30–6, Sun. 2–6.*

Founded by Jarl Rognvald in 1137 and dedicated to his uncle St.
Magnus, **St. Magnus Cathedral** in Kirkwall was built between
1137 and 1200; however, additional work was carried out during
the following 300 years. The cathedral is still in use and contains some of the best examples of Norman architecture in
Scotland. The ornamentation on some of the tombstones is particularly striking. *Open May–Aug., Mon.–Sat. 9–5; open Sun.
for services only.*

A fine example of an Orkney merchant-laird's mansion, the
Tankerness House, in Kirkwall, with its courtyards and gardens, dates from 1574. Now it's a museum documenting Orkney
life over the past 5,000 years. *Broad St., tel. 0856/873191. Admission: £1 adults, children free. Open May–Sept., Mon.–Sat.
10:30–12:30 and 1:30–5, Sun. 2–5; Oct.–Apr., Mon.–Sat.
10:30–12:30 and 1:30–5.*

㉕ The remains of the 12th-century **Orphir Church,** Scotland's
only circular medieval church (12th century), lie near the A964,
8 miles southwest of Kirkwall. *Off A964, 8 mi southwest of
Kirkwall, tel. 031/244–3101. Admission free. Open at all
times.*

Travelers can reach **South Ronaldsay** via the A961 causeway
heading south. The island's first distinctive point is the **Italian
㉖ Chapel,** located below the small village of St. Mary's. It was
here, in Lambholm, in 1943, that Italian prisoners of war, using
a Nissen hut, created a beautiful chapel from scrap metal and
concrete. *Lambholm. Admission free. Open at all times.*

㉗ The **Orkney Wireless Museum,** located about 10 miles south on
the A961 at St. Margaret's Hope, is a museum of wartime communications at Scapa Flow. Thousands of service men and
women were stationed here and used the equipment displayed
here to protect the Home Fleet. The museum also contains
many handsome 1930s wireless radios. *St. Margaret's Hope, 11
mi south of Kirkwall, tel. 0856/874272. Admission: £1 adults,
50p children. Open Apr.–Sept., daily 10–7.*

㉘ The **Scapa Flow Visitor Centre** has a growing collection of material portraying the strategic role of the sheltered anchorage of
Scapa Flow (said to be Britain's best diving site) in two world
wars. *Lyness. Admission free. Open daily during May–Sept.*

Off the Beaten Track

Tended by the Royal Society for the Protection of Birds, the
North Hoy Nature Reserve, home to vast numbers of land birds
and seabirds, is comprised of high ground and moor. Huge
cliffs nearby include the Old Man of Hoy, a 450-foot sea stack.

Visitors can visit the reserve any time by boat from Stromness. *Tel. 085679/298. Admission free. Open at all times.*

The **Knap of Howar** is one of the oldest inhabited sites in Europe. Its two 5,000-year-old dwellings—which have yielded some unusual artifacts, such as whalebone mallets, a spatula, and stone grinders—can be found on the west side of Papa Westray, on the island of Westray. *West of Holland House, tel. 031/244-2903. Admission free.*

Shopping

Neither Orkney nor Shetland is visited expressly for shopping. However, both have attracted high-quality crafts workers, and, in the United Kingdom, Shetland is almost synonymous with distinctive knitwear. The following is a selection of island shopping.

On Shetland, **Hjaltasteyn** hand-crafted gems and jewelry (available at a roadside stand on the A971) and **Shetland Silvercraft** (on the A971 and in Lerwick) are close to each other on the West Mainland. In Scalloway the **Shetland Woollen Company** is one of many operators with a selection of Shetland knitwear. Other names for knitwear and woolen goods in Lerwick include **Anderson & Co.** (The Shetland Warehouse, Commercial St.) and **Millers** (108–110 Commercial St., Lerwick). In Sandwick you'll find **Lawrence J. Smith.** In Lerwick **J. G. Rae Limited** (92 Commercial St.) stocks Shetland Silvercraft and gold and silver jewelry with Norse and Celtic motifs.

On Orkney, Kirkwall is the main shopping hub. Do not miss **Ola Gorrie at the Longship** (11 Broad St.). The shop designs gold and silver jewelry with Celtic and Norse themes, including a delightful representation of a dragon, originally drawn on the wall of the burial chamber at Maes Howe. Also in Kirkwall, located at 10 Albert Street, is **Ortak Jewelry,** which stocks a potpourri of gifts. At **Judith Glue** (25 Broad St.) visitors can purchase designer knitwear with traditional patterns, as well as watercolors, prints, and Orkney-made crafts. At **Fursbreck Pottery** on Harray offers an unusual range of ceramics. **Joker Jewelry,** at the East School in Holm, makes eye-catching and whimsical clocks, brooches, and other jewelry using animal motifs (especially puffins).

Sports and Fitness

Bicycling The islands do not have much traffic, but the ever-present wind is a factor to be considered when making cycling plans. Bicycles can be rented on Shetland from **Shetland Cycle Hire** (contact the tourist information center for information) and on Orkney from **Wishart's Shop** (Pier Head, Stromness).

Diving Orkney, especially the former wartime anchorage of Scapa Flow, claims to have the best dive sites in Britain. Part of the attraction is the remains of the German navy, scuttled here in 1919. Consult the Orkney Tourist Board (*see* Important Addresses and Numbers in Essential Information, *above*) for information on the many boat rental firms offering diving charters. Shetland also has exceptional underwater visibility, perfect for viewing the treasure wrecks and abundant marine life. The Shetland Tourist Organization (*see* Important Addresses and Numbers in Essential Information, *above*), as well as the **Skolla Diving Centre** (Gulberwick, tel. 0595/4175), can provide the necessary information.

Fishing   Sea angling is such a popular sport in Orkney that the local tourist board advises fishermen to book early. There are at least seven companies offering sea-angling boat rentals, with fishing rods available in most cases. Loch angling in Orkney is also popular; Loch of Harray and Loch of Stenness are the best-known spots. Contact the Orkney Tourist Board (*see* Important Addresses and Numbers in Essential Information, *above*) for information. Shetland, also renowned for sea angling, holds several competitions throughout the year. Contact the **Shetland Association of Sea Anglers** via the tourist-information center (*see* Important Addresses and Numbers in Essential Information, *above*) for further information.

Pony Trekking   Ponies can be rented on Orkney at **Cruesday Trekking Centre** (Cruesday, Frotoft, Rousay, tel. 0856/82236), **Garson Farm** (off Cairston Rd., Stromness, tel. 0856/850304). **Broothom Ponies** (Braeside, Dunrossness, tel. 0950/60556) and **Westside Riding and Trekking Centre** (Brindister, Bridge of Walls, tel. 059571/427) rent ponies on Shetland.

Water Sports   There are good anchorages among Orkney's many islands. Sailboat-rental companies include **Login's Lugger** (South End, Stromness, tel. 0856/850258), **Orkneyinga Charters** (Walliwall Cottage, St. Ola, tel. 0856/875489), and **Scapa Flow Yacht Charters** (Stromness, tel. 0856/850587). There are also sailboats available from Shetland. Details may be obtained from the **Lerwick Boating Club,** which can be contacted through the Shetland Tourist Information Center (*see* Important Addresses and Numbers in Essential Information, *above*).

Dining and Lodging

Dining

Category	Cost*
Very Expensive	over £25
Expensive	£15–£20
Moderate	£10–£15
Inexpensive	under £10

*per person, including appetizer, main course, dessert, and VAT.

Lodging

Category	Cost*
Very Expensive	over £120
Expensive	£100–£120

Moderate	£80–£100
Inexpensive	under £80

All prices are for two people sharing a double room, including service, breakfast, and VAT.

Highly recommended hotels and restaurants are indicated by a star ★.

Orkney
Dining and Lodging
★

The Creel Restaurant. This award-winning seafront restaurant with a cottage-style interior serves local seafood (including lobster) as its specialty, prepared personally by the owner/chef. The Creel also has some modest accommodations: three rooms are offered in an inexpensive bed-and-breakfast style. *Front Rd., St. Margaret's Hope, tel. 0856/83311. Reservations required. Dress: casual but neat. 3 rooms with bath. MC, V. Closed Jan. Restaurant, Moderate; hotel, Inexpensive.*

Foveran Hotel. Surrounded by 35 acres of grounds and overlooking Scapa Flow, this warm hotel has an attractive Scandinavian-style dining room and an open fire in its sitting room. The menu features Taste of Scotland, and the homemade soups, pâtés, and seafood have helped secure the restaurant's reputation as a very dependable place to eat. *St. Ola, Orkney KW15 1SF, tel. 0856/872389. 8 rooms with bath. Facilities: restaurant, 2 lounges. V. Restaurant, Moderate; hotel, Inexpensive.*

Kirkwall Hotel. This property, a 19th-century building with modern additions overlooking Kirkwall Bay, is the largest of the moderately priced hotels in Kirkwall. The decor is acceptable, and the restaurant specializes in local seafood and Orkney meat. *Harbour St., Kirkwall, tel. 0856/872232. 44 rooms, most with bath. AE, DC, MC, V. Inexpensive.*

Shetland
Dining and Lodging
★

Busta House. Probably the best hotel in Shetland, the Busta House dates in part from the 16th century and is surrounded by terraced grounds. Bedrooms are well furnished in traditional style, and the 16th-century Long Room is a delightful place to sample the hotel's selection of malt whiskies while sitting beside a peat fire. The dining room features a Taste of Scotland menu, with Shetland salmon and lamb usually available. *Brae, Shetland ZE2 9QN, tel. 080/622–506. Jacket and tie advised in restaurant. Facilities: restaurant, bar, cabin cruiser. 20 rooms with bath. AE, DC, MC, V. Restaurant, Very Expensive; hotel, Moderate.*

Shetland Hotel. Modern and well appointed (a result of the oil boom in the area and the needs of high-flying oil executives), with a swimming pool, sauna, and solarium, this hotel is located directly opposite the ferry terminal in Lerwick. Its decor is modern and inoffensive. The food is less than subtle, with large portions, and some dishes are overdone. One entrée consists of a folded fillet of beef with Stilton cheese inside, coated in oatmeal and served with a rich red-currant sauce: enough of a meal to sink the Shetland ferry! *Holmsgarth Rd., Lerwick ZE1 0RB, tel. 0595/5515. 66 rooms with bath. Facilities: 2 restaurants, 2 bars, heated pool. AE, DC, MC, V. Inexpensive–Moderate.*

Irvings' Guest House. Mr. and Mrs. Irving, at Barns on the island of Unst, run a comfortable and relaxed guest house. Travelers staying in this modern dwelling become members of the family. The sunset views from the kitchen rival those anywhere in the United Kingdom. *Barns, Newgord, Westing, Uyea-*

sound, Unst, tel. 095785/249. 2 twin rooms share 1 bath. No credit cards. Inexpensive.

The Arts and Nightlife

The Arts

Shetland has quite a strong cultural identity, thanks to its Scandinavian heritage. There are books of local dialect verse, a whole folklore contained in knitting patterns, and a strong tradition of fiddle-playing, among other artistic features. In the depth of the long winter, at the end of January, the Shetlanders celebrate their Viking culture with the **Up-Helly-Aa festival,** which involves much merry-making, dressing up, and the burning of a replica of a Viking longship. The end of January, however, is hardly a peak time for visitors.

Orkney's cultural highlight is the **St. Magnus Festival,** a festival of music based in Kirkwall and usually held the third week in June (tel. 0856/872669 for details). Orkney also has an annual folk festival at the end of May. The Orkney Tourist Board (*see* Important Addresses and Numbers in Essential Information, *above*) carries a full events list. **The Pier Arts Centre** (Victoria St., tel. 0856/850209) focuses on artistic life in Stromness, with an eclectic display of paintings and sculptures and changing exhibitions.

Nightlife

No one goes to Orkney or Shetland for the nightlife, although bars and lounges with live entertainment are common in Lerwick on Shetland, thanks to the fluctuating population of oil workers and boat crews. The same rule applies in Kirkwall. Tourist-information centers (*see* Important Addresses and Numbers in Essential Information, *above*) will provide information on local concerts and summer programs for visitors.

Index

Personal Itinerary

Departure *Date*

Time

Transportation

Arrival *Date* *Time*

Departure *Date* *Time*

Transportation

Accommodations

Arrival *Date* *Time*

Departure *Date* *Time*

Transportation

Accommodations

Arrival *Date* *Time*

Departure *Date* *Time*

Transportation

Accommodations

Fodor's Travel Guides

U.S. Guides

Alaska

Arizona

Boston

California

Cape Cod, Martha's Vineyard, Nantucket

The Carolinas & the Georgia Coast

Chicago

Disney World & the Orlando Area

Florida

Hawaii

Las Vegas, Reno, Tahoe

Los Angeles

Maine, Vermont, New Hampshire

Maui

Miami & the Keys

New England

New Orleans

New York City

Pacific North Coast

Philadelphia & the Pennsylvania Dutch Country

San Diego

San Francisco

Santa Fe, Taos, Albuquerque

Seattle & Vancouver

The South

The U.S. & British Virgin Islands

The Upper Great Lakes Region

USA

Vacations in New York State

Vacations on the Jersey Shore

Virginia & Maryland

Waikiki

Washington, D.C.

Foreign Guides

Acapulco, Ixtapa, Zihuatanejo

Australia & New Zealand

Austria

The Bahamas

Baja & Mexico's Pacific Coast Resorts

Barbados

Berlin

Bermuda

Brazil

Budapest

Budget Europe

Canada

Cancun, Cozumel, Yucatan Penisula

Caribbean

Central America

China

Costa Rica, Belize, Guatemala

Czechoslovakia

Eastern Europe

Egypt

Euro Disney

Europe

Europe's Great Cities

France

Germany

Great Britain

Greece

The Himalayan Countries

Hong Kong

India

Ireland

Israel

Italy

Italy's Great Cities

Japan

Kenya & Tanzania

Korea

London

Madrid & Barcelona

Mexico

Montreal & Quebec City

Morocco

The Netherlands Belgium & Luxembourg

New Zealand

Norway

Nova Scotia, Prince Edward Island & New Brunswick

Paris

Portugal

Rome

Russia & the Baltic Countries

Scandinavia

Scotland

Singapore

South America

Southeast Asia

South Pacific

Spain

Sweden

Switzerland

Thailand

Tokyo

Toronto

Turkey

Vienna & the Danube Valley

Yugoslavia

Fodor's Travel Guides

Special Series

Fodor's Affordables

Affordable Europe

Affordable France

Affordable Germany

Affordable Great Britain

Affordable Italy

Fodor's Bed & Breakfast and Country Inns Guides

California

Mid-Atlantic Region

New England

The Pacific Northwest

The South

The West Coast

The Upper Great Lakes Region

Canada's Great Country Inns

Cottages, B&Bs and Country Inns of England and Wales

The Berkeley Guides

On the Loose in California

On the Loose in Eastern Europe

On the Loose in Mexico

On the Loose in the Pacific Northwest & Alaska

Fodor's Exploring Guides

Exploring California

Exploring Florida

Exploring France

Exploring Germany

Exploring Paris

Exploring Rome

Exploring Spain

Exploring Thailand

Fodor's Flashmaps

New York

Washington, D.C.

Fodor's Pocket Guides

Pocket Bahamas

Pocket Jamaica

Pocket London

Pocket New York City

Pocket Paris

Pocket Puerto Rico

Pocket San Francisco

Pocket Washington, D.C.

Fodor's Sports

Cycling

Hiking

Running

Sailing

The Insider's Guide to the Best Canadian Skiing

Fodor's Three-In-Ones (guidebook, language cassette, and phrase book)

France

Germany

Italy

Mexico

Spain

Fodor's Special-Interest Guides

Cruises and Ports of Call

Disney World & the Orlando Area

Euro Disney

Healthy Escapes

London Companion

Skiing in the USA & Canada

Sunday in New York

Fodor's Touring Guides

Touring Europe

Touring USA: Eastern Edition

Touring USA: Western Edition

Fodor's Vacation Planners

Great American Vacations

National Parks of the West

The Wall Street Journal Guides to Business Travel

Europe

International Cities

Pacific Rim

USA & Canada

WHEREVER YOU TRAVEL, *H*ELP IS NEVER FAR AWAY.

From planning your trip to replacing
lost Cards, American Express® Travel Service
Offices* are always there to help.

SCOTLAND

4/5 Union Terrace, Aberdeen
224-642-961

Premier Travel
2C Boswell Park, Ayr
292-282-822

D.P. & L. Travel, Ltd.
11 Albert Square, Dundee
382-272-32

139 Princes Street, Edinburgh
31-225-5234

115 Hope Street, Glasgow
41-221-4366

Alba Travel
43 Church St., Inverness
463-239-188

D.P. & L. Travel, Ltd.
8 Mercat Wynd, Market St., St. Andrews
334-74404